THE BEST
AMERICAN
MAGAZINE
WRITING

2023

THE BEST AMERICAN MAGAZINE WRITING

2023

**Edited by
Sidney Holt for the
American Society
of Magazine
Editors**

Columbia University Press   New York

Columbia University Press
Publishers Since 1893
New York   Chichester, West Sussex
cup.columbia.edu

Library of Congress Cataloging-in-Publication Data
ISSN 1541-0978
ISBN 978-0-231-20892-5 (hardcover)
ISBN 978-0-231-20893-2 (pbk.)
ISBN 978-0-231-55769-6 (e-book)

Printed in the United States of America

Cover design: Julia Kushnirsky
Cover image: Shutterstock

Contents

Natasha Pearlman

Introduction

In 2007, I was a fledgling newspaper feature writer in London. And as so many twenty-five-year-olds are, I was as wildly, naively hopeful as I was ambitious. I worked fourteen-hour days. I never said no to an assignment. It wasn't unusual for me to go thirteen days without a break. Whatever it took to "make it," I did it. I devoured every feature story in every rival publication to make sure I wasn't being beaten at the game I was mainly playing against myself. I dreamt big. And as is so often the case for young professionals around the world, I dreamt of New York City.

It was everything to me. The busyness. The life spilling out of bars and restaurants and shops and parks onto the teeming streets. The people literally stacked on top of one another, squeezing themselves into the smallest of living spaces in pursuit of the limitless expansion of their opportunities. The city seemed to burst with possibilities. And as impossible as it quite literally was to move here (work visas are no small feat to come by for us foreigners), it was the place deep down I wanted to belong in. Whenever I came to visit, which wasn't often because of that fledgling British journalist's salary, I ate up every second—on the go, exploring, partying, never stopping.

Until one day in May 2007, I did.

Memory is an extraordinary, unpredictable thing. It can blur when you need to forget, discard details it deems irrelevant with no identifiable pattern, yet can also transport you back to a specific moment in time with absolute, unnerving clarity.

There's so much about that May day I remember and so much I don't. I know I was in a clothes shop in Manhattan, but I couldn't tell you which one or in what part of town. Was it hot? Maybe. Was I alone? I have no idea.

But what I do remember is the pile of magazines on a table for customers to browse through. I remember picking up a copy of the *New Yorker*—because here I was in *New York*—and flipping through idly until I saw a story that stopped me in my tracks. One that I had to read from start to finish standing in the middle of a clothes shop, not looking at any clothes, no matter the strange looks I got (because, well, we all know how long a good *New Yorker* article can take to read). One that even sixteen years later I can still recall words and scenes from.

I'd love to tell you it was a groundbreaking investigation that had brought down a government. It wasn't. It was a story about American commuters: "There and Back Again: The Soul of the Commuter," by Nick Paumgarten. On the surface it was, well, deeply niche—a long and winding written journey, inspired by the equally long and winding seven-hour daily commute of an employer at Cisco Systems, recently honored by his employers for his unmatched dedication. But that belied the truth of it. The piece, in which Paumgarten observed in glorious detail the minutiae of his subjects' travels (sometimes more than six hours a day), also documented humanity in its purest form. The loves and losses and dreams that lead people to make what might seem like truly unfathomable choices—in this instance, belief-beggaring, labor-intensive, multi-hour, cross-state traverses.

Paumgarten's prose made the everyday, the mundanity of something so many of us undertake, extraordinary. It brought to life the question, which was posed directly to his subjects and more figuratively to his readers: How far, literally, would you travel to make your dreams come true? How far would *I* go? And through answering this question the piece became not just a story I read but in a strange way a part of my own history.

Despite the immense volume of writing I have consumed in the course of my nearly two decades as a journalist, it was to that piece and the extraordinary sacrifices and dreams of those commuters I kept returning. It tugged at me for more than a decade as I at times tried to make my move to the city of my dreams, failed, met my partner, got married, tried and failed again, had children, gave up fully, and then when I least expected it, made it happen, becoming one of those commuters in my own roundabout, cross-Atlantic way: "There and Back Again."

That's the thing about great magazine journalism. No matter the size and scope of an article, no matter whether its goal is to expose deep wrongdoing, hold perpetrators to account, upend a patriarchal system, or simply tell a beautiful and unexpected story, tell it well and it can change people's worlds. It can make indelible memories, imprint itself into the fabric of your being, shape you, become you—or your fighting purpose.

But how do you define this kind of writing? Can it be taught as a formula? *Start with an anecdote, add in a news hook, plug in interviews and secondaries, conclude.* That's too simple. For me, as an editor, it's about having purpose. An ambition to tell a story that makes you gasp or laugh or that shakes you to your core. It doesn't *have* to be told with words you need to look up in a dictionary, although those pieces can be as thrilling as those told more sparsely. What it should be is a story told with imagination.

I think about this part of magazine writing often. Magazine journalists are the closest to novelists—in often the lengths of the stories they are telling, and the exposition. But unlike our great fiction authors who are free to create expansive imaginary worlds, magazine writers are grounded in the hard reality of facts. And yet, they are free to tell those facts with the creativity of an unexpected literary structure, through the eyes of an unexpected witness, via years of detailed investigations and research, or through bringing their own story and experiences to bear within it too. There's no formula save originality. Like New York, magazine journalism is bursting with limitless possibilities—no sentence, no story the same.

And in this extraordinary collection of articles, you will find true stories that read like novels, such is the originality of the approach. The story of an international crime syndicate that robs the author's family in *The Believer* for "Aristocrat Inc.," by Natalie So, is enthralling, interweaving and piecing together both a personal history and the jaw-dropping audacity of opportunists who were eventually outrun by the development of the technology they were thieving.

And "Acid Church," by Courtney Desiree Morris, from *Stranger's Guide*, is a deeply powerful personal journey through grief, queer love, and psychedelics that jumps off the page so vividly it is almost like watching the story on a big screen:

> My heart is beating in time with the song, and before I know it, I am rocking and bouncing on the balls of my feet and singing, "Oh I, I want to be with you everywhere." I spin and see Alix dancing alongside me out of the corner of my eye. People flock to the dance floor, and soon, I am enveloped in a crush of vibrating flesh. The molly is pulsing through me in waves, and I can feel the heat of the high spreading from my scalp down my back through my arms and into my feet. I realize the feeling is joy.

I could equally get lost in Jazmine Hughes's sentences in all the pieces she writes, but particularly her National Magazine Award–winning profile of the actor Viola Davis, "Viola Davis, Inside Out," for the *New York Times Magazine*:

> To watch Davis act is to witness a deep-sea plunge into a feeling: even when her characters are opaque, you can sense her under the surface, empathetic and searching. . . . Davis grew up to be the sort of actor whose range feels best measured by her steady command of pressure: maintaining it, raising it, letting it go. She sets the tone of every scene, the eyes of her castmates flicking toward her as soon as she appears, as if reacting to her is a crucial part of the job. She often plays characters who cry only in the moments she's inhabiting, weeping as if it were a rare, almost undignified departure from their norm.

Magazine writers are also unique in the journalism world because they are boundlessly free. Not for us the restriction of a limited news story word count or the adherence to a daily news agenda where the relevance window can be a matter of a few hours in our new world of the endless, pauseless scroll. Magazine writers can take a statistic, an event, a person, something historic and forgotten, a society-altering ruling, and create stories that are so powerful they *become* the agenda. Take, for example, Jia Tolentino's breathtaking triptych on the overturning of *Roe v. Wade*. It is the commentary I, like so many others in the United States, devoured both before and in the ruling's aftermath. Her writing for the *New Yorker* in "A Post-*Roe* Threat," "The Post-*Roe* Era," and "Is Abortion Sacred?" is at once excoriating (of all sides), brave, and deeply personal. They became, too, the foundational pieces many of us all turned to when asked to explain the depths of our emotions in the fallout. *Jia said it best. Read this. Oh god, THIS.* Just some of the messages that flew around my own chat groups. One passage in particular, from "Is Abortion Sacred?" will stay with me forever:

> Even within the course of the same pregnancy, a person and the fetus she carries can shift between the roles of lover and beloved, host and parasite, vessel and divinity, victim and murderer; each body is capable of extinguishing the other, although one cannot survive alone. There is no human relationship more complex, more morally unstable than this . . .
>
> The idea that a fetus is not just a full human but a superior and kinglike one—a being whose survival is so paramount that another person can be *legally compelled* to accept harm, ruin, or death to insure it—is a recent invention.

It was without doubt a year that demanded a vital examination of the standards women are held to versus those of men. And two further pieces in this book that deserve a call out are Samantha Michaels's piece from *Mother Jones,* "She Never Hurt Her Kids. So Why Is a Mother Serving More Time Than the Man Who Abused

Her Daughter?" and "The Landlord and the Tenant," by Raquel Rutledge of the *Milwaukee Journal Sentinel* and Ken Armstrong of *ProPublica*. Both extensively reported and uniquely heartbreaking, they tell the stories of women failed not just by circumstance but also society.

I, too, found myself in the unique position this last year of being able to report on a decades-long failure that most profoundly impacts women—the lack of paid family or medical leave in America. I tried to approach it anew, reporting on both the urgent need to pass the country's first paid family leave policy and also following eight women through the first twenty-eight days of their postpartum period to show the impact of having no paid time to care for your newborn or yourself. You can find my reported piece "The Time to Pass Paid Leave Is Now" alongside two of the stories from the women I followed. And you can find our interactive "28 Days" piece on Glamour.com (where you can hear directly from the women during one of the most vulnerable times in their lives). I hope the pieces speak for themselves.

Interestingly, in the course of reporting and writing these pieces, I had to confront a tenet of journalism that for more than a decade I thought needed to define me: impartiality. It had been drilled into me in my newspaper reporting days. Report the facts, not the feelings. But then here I was, working on a story that I cared about, perhaps more than I had ever cared about a story in my life. It felt discombobulating.

Then, in the course of working on this introduction, a colleague directed to me to a note she had found in *Glamour* archives from *Glamour's* longtime and legendary editor in chief, Ruth Whitney, who helmed the magazine from 1967 to 1999. In 1991, after the second Women of the Year awards (which now, in their thirty-fourth year, have come to define the publication), she had written herself a personal memo: "My own epiphany: This ceremony brought it home to me that I really belong in the part of the journalism world that allows me to be an advocate for women. Spare me the 'impartial news' end of the business."

This approach could well sum up Caitlin Dickerson's peerless, years-long investigation for *The Atlantic*, "We Need to Take Away Children," an examination of the Trump-era border policies that ripped apart families and separated children from their parents— sometimes for years. Meticulously reported and rightly deserving of the 2023 Pulitzer Prize for Explanatory Reporting, it is both devastatingly dispassionate in the assessment of the mountains of evidence she uncovered and unshakably emotional, too. You feel Dickerson's disgust at the officials who perpetrated the separations and the deliberate obfuscations and prolongation:

> Trump-administration officials insisted for a whole year that family separations weren't happening. Finally, in the spring of 2018, they announced the implementation of a separation policy with great fanfare—as if one had not already been under way for months. Then they declared that separating families was not the goal of the policy, but an unfortunate result of prosecuting parents who crossed the border illegally with their children. Yet a mountain of evidence shows that this is explicitly false: separating children was not just a side effect but the intent. Instead of working to reunify families after parents were prosecuted, officials worked to keep them apart for longer.

While this year was undoubtedly marked by an extraordinary set of hard-hitting investigations and discoveries—many more of which you will also find in this book—there is also joy and wonder and, yes, great magazine writing to be found in the niche. Who knew that in 2023 we would all lose our collective minds to *New York* magazine's deliciously biting treatise on celebrity offspring, "The Year of the Nepo Baby," with an introduction by Nate Jones? It didn't just capture a moment and a conversation, it *created* it. It *was* the moment. It was everything we were talking about, even the so-called Nepo Babies themselves.

And Allison P. Davis's "Tinder Hearted," also for *New York*, became in its writing not just a piece about a dating app or even a piece about how an app reshaped dating for a generation; it captured a cultural shift in our lives that might even come to be defined by the article itself.

As an editor who has worked on so-called popular publications for large portions of my career, it delights me that this tome of the year's great magazine writing is also celebrating those articles so skillfully written that they take on a life of their own: viral hits, for want of a better word. That elusive goal chased by every publication and writer—because who doesn't want the world to read their work? But too often these pop-culture hits aren't lauded enough. It's an art and a skill to create a story that jumps right into cultural zeitgeist and then rewrites what that culture is.

This all raises the question, once again, of what the definition of great magazine writing is. How do you pull together a category that is so vast in its span and its execution? You can't. But perhaps that's really the heart of it. Great magazine journalism defies definition, much like it defies boundaries. It is limitless in its possibilities. It can take you on the most unexpected journey of your life. It can break your heart, and it can make you laugh until your sides split. It can be dispassionate, or it can be impassioned. It can be devastating. It can be meticulous. It can be beautiful. It can spur you into action. It can reshape the way you think of your world. Or the whole world.

But what does unite the best of writing, what it must have, is ambition. And you will find it on every page, and in every piece, of this book. Read, and learn.

Sidney Holt

Acknowledgments

And they say magazines are dead. Here, in the 2023 edition of *The Best American Magazine Writing*, you will find abundant evidence that despite the unarguable decline of print and the equally incontestable rise of digital media, magazine storytelling is not only thriving but increasingly coming to define the way writers, editors, and readers share news and information in the twenty-first century. Whether the medium is a traditional magazine or the newest website, a newspaper or a podcast, the way news is reported and stories are told is now shaped by the model pioneered by American magazines in the nineteenth and twentieth centuries.

In her introduction to this anthology, *Glamour*'s Natasha Pearlman explains what makes magazine storytelling unique—and uniquely exciting. If you haven't read it already, I urge to stop now and turn back to Pearlman's piece. Nothing I can say—nothing, really, anybody can say—can better Pearlman's description of the power of magazine journalism.

Nothing, that is, except the stories included in this volume.

The twenty-two articles in this year's edition of *The Best American Magazine Writing* range from opinion pieces and "as told to" vignettes to celebrity profiles and deeply reported feature stories. Each is an example of the best journalism published in print or online last year, and each was a National Magazine Award finalist or winner. Several of the stories included here also received other awards, most notably "We Need to Take Away Children," by Caitlin Dickerson of *The Atlantic*, which won the Pulitzer Prize for Explanatory Reporting.

The American Society of Magazine Editors was founded in 1963 with the express purpose of establishing the program that became the National Magazine Awards. From the beginning—the first award was presented to *Look* magazine in 1966 "for its skillful editing, imagination and editorial integrity, all of which were reflected particularly in its treatment of the racial issue during 1965"—the awards have been sponsored by ASME in association with the Columbia University Graduate School of Journalism.

The National Magazine Awards are now presented in seventeen categories, ranging from Reporting and Feature Writing to Video and Podcasting. Several of the publications nominated this year for the most prestigious award—the National Magazine Award for General Excellence, which is presented in four separate categories based on content and audience—are represented in the 2023 edition of *The Best American Magazine Writing*. They include *The Atlantic*, ESPN Digital, *New York*, the *New York Times Magazine*, *Stat*, *Mother Jones*, and *Stranger's Guide*. Another General Excellence finalist represented here—the *Paris Review*—won the ASME Award for Fiction, which is judged and presented alongside the National Magazine Awards.

A complete list of the National Magazine Awards 2023 finalists and winners is posted at https://www.asme.media/. When you look at the list, you will note that the National Magazine Awards are platform agnostic; in other words, print stories and publications are judged alongside work published digitally. Indeed, several of the stories included in this book first appeared online. If you like one of those stories, you may want to look for it online as well—many include multimedia elements impossible to put into print.

Nearly 250 media organizations entered the National Magazine Awards in 2023, submitting close to 1,100 entries, of which more than half were originally published online (that includes, of course, podcasts and videos). Some 300 editors, writers, art directors, and photo editors participated in the judging of National Magazine Awards and the ASME Award for Fiction, as well as the ASME Awards for Design, Photography, and Illustration and the ASME NEXT Awards for Journalists Under 30, which are judged at the same time.

The judging was conducted both in person—at Columbia University on New York's Morningside Heights—and on Zoom, but the presentation of the awards was very and exclusively live. More than 350 editors and publishers gathered at a music venue, also in New York, called Terminal 5 in early April 2023 to honor the ninety-five National Magazine Award finalists and winners.

Fifty-seven media organizations were nominated for National Magazine Awards in 2023, led by *New York* with ten, the *New Yorker* with seven, the *New York Times Magazine* with six, and *The Atlantic* with five. Each of those publications also won awards—*New York* for Single-Topic Issue and Lifestyle Journalism; the *New Yorker* for Columns and Essays; the *New York Times Magazine* for Reporting and Profile Writing; and *The Atlantic* for General Excellence.

The 2023 winners also included *Cook's Illustrated, Grist,* and the Marshall Project, all in General Excellence; Gimlet Media for Spotify in Podcasting; *Glamour* in Public Interest; *GQ* in Design; *Mother Jones* in Video; the *New York Review of Books* in Reviews and Criticism; *ProPublica* and the *Milwaukee Journal Sentinel* in Feature Writing; *Romper* in Service Journalism; and *Smithsonian* in Photography.

Long before the judges ever see a single entry—they first receive virtual bundles of entries several weeks before they meet at Columbia—hundreds of magazine journalists are already at work on the National Magazine Awards, preparing submissions and writing the statements that accompany each entry. It is they—the editors who choose to enter the awards and the staff members who organize the submissions—who are largely responsible for the success of the National Magazine Awards.

The journalists and educators who lead the judging are charged with guiding their fellow judges toward the selection of finalists and winners that exemplify contemporary standards of editorial excellence. The judging this year was led by a distinguished group of editorial leaders, which included:

- Sudip Bose, editor, *American Scholar*
- Joe Brown, editor, *one5c*
- Maile Carpenter, editorial director, Warner Bros. Discovery Partnership Magazines, Hearst Magazines
- Ben Goldberger, executive editor, *Time*
- D. D. Guttenplan, editor, *The Nation*
- Clara Jeffery, editor in chief, *Mother Jones*
- Radhika Jones, editor in chief, *Vanity Fair*
- Lauren Kern, editor in chief, Apple News
- Lindsey B. King, editor, *5280*
- Amanda Kludt, group publisher, Lifestyle, Vox Media
- Cindi Leive, cofounder and chief executive officer, *The Meteor*
- Stephanie Mehta, chief executive officer and chief content officer, Mansueto Ventures
- Mary Melton, editorial director, Godfrey Dadich Partners
- Janice Min, chief executive officer, *The Ankler*
- Puja Patel, editor in chief, *Pitchfork*
- Kyle Pope, editor and publisher, *Columbia Journalism Review*
- Paul Reyes, editor, *Virginia Quarterly Review*
- Debra Adams Simmons, executive editor, history and culture, *National Geographic*
- Bill Strickland, editorial director, Enthusiast and Consumer Group, Hearst Magazines
- Duy Linh Tu, professor, Columbia University Graduate School of Journalism
- Julia Turner, deputy managing editor, *Los Angeles Times*
- Liz Vaccariello, editorial director, Dotdash Meredith
- Geoff Van Dyke, editorial director, *5280*
- Charles Whitaker, dean, Medill School of Journalism, Northwestern University

The results of the judging are sanctioned by the National Magazine Awards Board. The members of the 2023 board were:

- Dan Goodgame, editor in chief, *Texas Monthly*
- Anna Holmes, executive vice president, Higher Ground Productions
- Mark Jannot, story editor, *New York Times Magazine*
- Clara Jeffery, editor in chief, *Mother Jones*
- Radhika Jones, editor in chief, *Vanity Fair*
- Lucy Kaylin, vice president, print content, Hearst Magazines
- Cindi Leive, cofounder and chief executive officer, *The Meteor*
- Janice Min, chief executive officer, *The Ankler*
- Alison Overholt, adjunct professor, Columbia University Graduate School of Journalism, and founder, Good People LLC
- Liz Vaccariello, editorial director, Dotdash Meredith
- Charles Whitaker, dean, Medill School of Journalism, Northwestern University
- Abi Wright, executive director, professional prizes, Columbia University Graduate School of Journalism
- Sidney Holt, executive director, American Society of Magazine Editors, ex officio

Inclusion in a mere list does little to reward the journalists who, without any recompense save the pleasure of reading the best magazine stories published in the previous year, devote so many hours to the judging. That said, a complete list of the National Magazine Awards 2023 judges is posted at https://nationalmagazineawards .org.

The ASME board of directors is responsible for overseeing the administration, judging, and presentation of the National Magazine Awards. The members of the 2022–2023 board—all of whom are journalism educators or the leaders of well-known media organizations—are listed at https://www.asme.media/. Clara Jeffery, the editor in chief of *Mother Jones*, deserves special recognition, however, for the success of the 2023 awards, her last as president of ASME.

As director of operations at ASME, Nina Fortuna is responsible for the day-to-day management of the National Magazine Awards. Her patience and efficiency are now close to legendary. ASME's literary agent, David McCormick, and the editors of *The Best American Magazine Writing* at Columbia University Press, Philip Leventhal and Michael Haskell, also deserve more thanks than I can express for their contributions to the success of this series. I also want to repeat my appreciation for the work of Natasha Pearlman, the executive editor of *Glamour*, who wrote the introduction to this year's edition of *BAMW*.

On behalf of ASME, I want to thank the leadership of the Columbia University Graduate School of Journalism—especially Jelani Cobb, the dean and Ira A. Lipman Professor of Journalism, and Abi Wright, the executive director of professional prizes, who also serves as a National Magazine Awards judge—for their continuing support of the National Magazine Awards. Finally, I want to thank the writers who let ASME use their work in this anthology. At the risk of committing an act of self-plagiarism, all I can say is that without them, there would be no *The Best American Magazine Writing*—in fact, there would be no magazines, period.

THE BEST AMERICAN MAGAZINE WRITING

2023

New York Times Magazine

"The Battle for Baby L." begins with a night raid in a mountain village in central Afghanistan and ends in the United States as two families struggle over the future of a little girl orphaned on that far-away battlefield. The judges who chose "The Battle for Baby L." as the winner of the National Magazine Award for Reporting—one of the most prestigious of the seventeen National Magazine Awards presented this year by the American Society of Magazine Editors and the Columbia Journalism School—described this piece as "a parable of America's tortured relationship with Afghanistan." A contributing writer at the New York Times Magazine, Ali is at work on a book about Islamophobia. The Times Magazine also won the Reporting award last year for "The Collapse," by Matthieu Aikins, about the fall of Kabul in 2021.

Rozina Ali

The Battle for Baby L.

The Night Raid

Around ten p.m. on the night of September 5, 2019, a counterterrorism team of United States Army Rangers and partner forces
descended onto a small village in the mountains of central
Afghanistan, on a mission to capture or kill foreign fighters associated with al-Qaeda. The soldiers approached a row of three mud
houses near a line of trees, beyond which lay farmland. Gunfire
erupted. Shouting, booms, more shots. A man and a woman
emerged from one of the houses; the woman was carrying a baby.
The man was wearing a suicide vest, and he set it off. Bits of him
flew into the air. Through their night vision goggles, the rangers
saw the woman, wounded but moving. She tugged at something—a bomb?—and a ranger shot her dead.

The Afghan and American soldiers stood amid the remains of
the house, debating what to do with the infant. Her head was
bleeding and her left leg was oddly bent, but she was alive. The
Americans carried her away to a medical unit at the international
military base in the province.

Word spread about the baby girl who was found in battle,
hardly two months old, with big, bright eyes. The Americans
called her by a name that started with L. (I am using only the initial to protect the identity of the child.) On September 25, L.
arrived at the Craig Joint Theater Hospital at Bagram Air Base,
outside Kabul, to be treated for fractures to her skull and femur

and for second-degree burns on her face and neck. A child on the base was rare, and the Americans, entranced, passed her around so much that she barely seemed to touch her crib.

Joshua Mast, a marine captain and judge advocate general who was in Afghanistan as part of an interagency effort to evaluate civilian casualties, took a particular interest in her. Mast had left his wife, Stephanie, and their children back home in Palmyra, VA. The couple met at Liberty University, a Christian college in Lynchburg, VA, founded by the evangelical pastor and activist Jerry Falwell "to influence the moral and ethical course of America." On his Facebook page, Mast described himself as "a Christian man, a husband, a father, an American and a Marine."

At the medical unit, Mast, wearing a camouflage uniform and a wide smile, cradled L. in his arms. His lawyer would later tell a U.S. court that he "saw the writing on the wall"—that L., as an abandoned girl in Afghanistan, would be trafficked or trained as a child soldier. That October, Mast appealed to the White House for help in adopting the baby; using his connections, he reached Vice President Mike Pence's office. He made inquiries about securing immigration parole for L., which would allow her to enter the United States. And he reached out to an American lawyer named Kimberley Motley for advice. Motley opened a practice in Kabul in 2009 and had gained recognition for her work representing Afghan women and children. She had been contacted by another American who wanted to adopt L. and was already in conversations with U.S. military officers at Bagram about the baby's health and legal status.

At the base, L. was in the custody of the U.S. Department of Defense and almost certainly would be handed over to the Afghan authorities and then, some of the Americans feared, to an orphanage. An informal group of American service members at Bagram was concerned about her immediate medical needs and her fate: they wanted to find a legal avenue to have her evacuated to a health-care facility in the United States, and they asked Motley for guidance. But the legal avenue was unclear. State Department representatives, Afghan officials, and the International Committee of the Red Cross, which conducts family tracing in conflict zones, met to discuss the situation. Mast, who was present alongside other American military officers, asked about adoption. The Afghan officials explained that under their rules, they would have to look for the baby's family first. "The Afghan government assumes responsibility for the welfare of the child within the Afghan guardianship system," the State Department later confirmed in an email to the office of a U.S. senator who was asking about adoption for two of his constituents, a military couple who had taken an interest in L.

Mast, however, decided to continue his efforts. Armed with preliminary intelligence about the September operation, he and his wife petitioned the family court in Fluvanna County, VA, where they lived, with an unusual argument: L.'s parents were foreign fighters, which meant that L. wasn't Afghan at all; Afghan law simply did not apply to her. With the help of Mast's brother, Richard, an attorney with Liberty Counsel, a conservative Christian legal-aid group affiliated with Liberty University, they made their appeal: the Masts wanted custody of the baby.

Another matter fell to Richard E. Moore, a State Circuit Court judge, who came under fire earlier that year for ruling that city officials had no authority to remove Confederate statues from public grounds. On November 10, 2019, Moore approved an interlocutory adoption order for the Masts, the first step toward permanent adoption. That same day, the Commonwealth of Virginia issued a certificate of foreign birth for L. Her adoptive parents were listed as Joshua and Stephanie Mast.

One Baby, Two Countries

Over the next three years, the case of Baby L. would expand into a legal battle over her adoption, allegations of a transnational child-abduction scheme in federal court, and investigations by state and federal agencies. The U.S. government has stated that the adoption should not have happened.

For five months, I have been investigating how an American Christian man was able to take custody of a Muslim child from a country that does not allow adoptions to non-Muslims. To piece together what went wrong, I have interviewed dozens of Afghan and U.S. officials, lawyers and experts; pored over hundreds of pages of legal records and internal emails; and gathered reporting from the village where the baby was made an orphan. But what I found is that the system didn't break down. Almost everyone, technically, did their job—members of the broad evangelical Christian network who aided Mast, the Afghan officials who followed government protocol, the State Department officials at Bagram who tried to stop attempts to evacuate the baby to the United States, and the American government agencies that would see only the court order listing Mast as the child's father and allow him to take her.

Two central questions seemed to drive how people considered the fate of this baby: One, who were her parents—Afghan or foreign insurgents? Two, should the United States have the authority to determine the future of a child half a world away? This fundamental issue of sovereignty is one that has troubled the United States for two decades of its occupation of the country—and it was made all the more complicated against the fall of Kabul.

Afghanistan is not a signatory to the Hague Convention, which sets standards on international adoption, but the former Afghan government had its own guardianship system that placed a child with relatives or relied on a court to decide who her new family would be. Despite American interest, only thirty-four Afghan children have been adopted in the United States since 2001.

Mast did not wait for that process to unfold. In November 2019, he and his brother convinced the family court in Virginia that this child in Afghanistan was stateless and had no family. Moreover, the court noted when granting the Masts custody, the Afghan government intended to waive its authority in the matter; a written copy of the waiver would come "in a matter of days."

The brothers appeared to understand that they were engaged in an extraordinary legal project, with equally extraordinary moral repercussions. According to text exchanges I obtained through Freedom of Information Act requests, Richard Mast, Judge Moore, and Allyson Tysinger, a senior officer at the Virginia attorney general's office, had discussed some knotty legal issues around the case in early November. The family court had granted the Masts custody of the child, and two days later, Moore, in Circuit Court, ordered a certificate of foreign birth to be issued. It would establish a legal identity for Baby L. But Tysinger, who appeared to have a friendly relationship with Richard, was concerned: Virginia couldn't issue the certificate listing the Masts as the baby's parents without a court order that approved them for adoption, not just custody. On November 9, she spoke with Moore, who had questions about his authority to issue such an order in this case. He was reassured. On November 10, Moore and Richard discussed the matter over the phone, Richard drafted the order, and Moore signed it the same day. In a letter, Richard told the attorney general's office that Baby L.'s case presented "exceptional circumstances" and that "these facts will probably never occur again in any of our lifetimes." (Joshua Mast, Stephanie Mast, and Richard Mast did not respond to multiple requests for comment.)

What helped the Masts succeed was a set of assumptions that for many have become accepted truths: that those we kill abroad in the dead of night are terrorists, that Islam is inherently dangerous, that the courts are inherently just, that prosperity confers morality. In all the time that politicians, religious leaders, lawyers, and federal and local government officials sought to help the Masts obtain custody of this baby, no one took seriously the possibility that she might have a family and that they might care for her, too. Despite the rumors that spread through Bagram that fall, L. was not without a past or loved ones. She had relatives, and one day, they were located.

This is the story of a baby girl who was rescued by Americans in a battlefield they helped create. Ultimately, this is a story about the fictions we tell ourselves about the twenty years we spent in Afghanistan. "It's the complete collapse of rule of law that allowed this abduction to happen," Sehla Ashai, one of the lawyers who would go on to represent the baby's relatives, told me. "And it didn't happen in Afghanistan—it happened in America."

The Baby's Afghan Family

In recent years, the welfare of orphans in Afghanistan had fallen to the Ministry of Labor and Social Affairs, which in late 2019 was led by a former provincial governor named Syed Anwar Sadat. He faced a delicate situation: A man from the village where the raid took place had approached the local authorities about a missing baby. The Americans, meanwhile, were caring for the infant at Bagram, and they were saying that her parents were foreign insurgent fighters. Some wanted to send her to the United States for medical care, even adopt her. Now the case had reached the ears of Sadat's boss, President Ashraf Ghani, who was trying to navigate not only peace talks between American forces and the Taliban about the future of the country but also the disputed outcome of a very close reelection victory.

Ghani was open to the possibility of sending the baby to the United States to be adopted if an Afghan court would allow it, Sadat told me, but first he wanted the ministry to look for her family. There appeared to be some urgency: The State Department had encouraged the Afghan authorities to speed up their investigation. One State Department official with direct knowledge of the matter told me that the agency grew alarmed when it learned there had been requests to the presidential palace for a waiver. Additionally, they were concerned about the baby's welfare; she had been at Bagram for months now, and the base was ill-equipped to care for an injured infant over the long term.

An investigation by the Afghan authorities and the Red Cross led to two direct relatives: the baby's maternal and paternal uncles. Each was Afghan, and each wanted to care for the baby. It also emerged that the baby had siblings who survived the attack and remained in the village. The State Department reviewed the investigation's findings and on January 5, 2020, sent a message to the Ministry of Labor and Social Affairs: "We stand ready to transfer custody of the infant." According to Sadat, an Afghan court decided that L. would be placed in the care of her paternal uncle. The transfer date was set for February 11.

Mast, who was back in the United States, heard that a potential uncle had come forward but didn't believe he was L.'s real relative. The uncle was Afghan; how could he be the brother of a foreign fighter? Richard Mast told Allyson Tysinger, at the Virginia attorney general's office, that this was "demonic activity from principalities over Afghanistan." Together, the brothers continued their appeals to American allies for help in bringing L. to the United States, including Jerry Falwell Jr., then the president of Liberty University, and Dr. Russell Moore, then the president of the Ethics and Religious Liberty Commission at the Southern Baptist Convention. Mast met with Senator Ted Cruz's staff on Capitol Hill and sent out packets of information about L., including her patient records and photos. In one appeal to policy makers, Mast noted that attributes of the girl's "physical appearance are consistent" with the "ethnic Chinese foreign fighters" he said had been targeted in the coalition raid in September. Falwell told me that he does not remember the case well, but he said that in one email chain he was on, the Masts asked Cruz's staff if the senator would make public remarks about Joshua Mast's good deed. (Cruz did not respond to requests for comment.)

The Mast brothers also appealed to Jenna Ellis, a senior legal adviser for the Trump administration. Ellis elevated the situation to Mick Mulvaney, President Donald Trump's acting chief of staff, and wrote to Richard, "I'm praying for your success." In his emails to Mulvaney, Mast requested that the president order the baby to be "evacuated immediately to the United States." (Mulvaney and Ellis did not respond to requests for comment.) Mast worried about her injuries. He sent around a patient summary of L. from Bagram that recommended checkups for, in part, "delayed-onset seizures." But according to incomplete medical records from Bagram that I obtained, L. didn't appear to be at great risk. She was sleeping well and playing on her stomach. She would need long-term health-care maintenance to "ensure childhood development," the reports noted, but she appeared to be "happy and in stable condition."

On February 3, Richard Mast sent a stern letter to U.S. Central Command from Liberty Counsel. His client, he wrote, "categorically forbids" the removal of the child from the medical facility at Bagram and placement into Afghan care. He added a warning: "You may be held personally liable for any harm that comes to an infant female with medical needs in a country known for child abuse, neglect and sexual trafficking of children." The February 11 transfer day came and went. The baby remained at Bagram. Richard Mast had been updating Tysinger on developments, and he shared that Garrett Exner, a military legislative assistant from Cruz's office, was helping and had "been outstanding." He also told Tysinger he had spoken about the case with Ken Cuccinelli, a former Virginia attorney general who was by then at the Department of Homeland Security. "Cuccinelli is standing by," Richard texted Tysinger.

A new date was set for the transfer—February 27—as the Masts continued to make their case. Just hours before L. was to be removed from Bagram, Richard Mast argued before Norman Moon, a federal judge in the Western District of Virginia, that the Department of Defense and the State Department were handing L. over to someone who had not been properly vetted, who might potentially be a terrorist. He added that his brother was invested in the best interest of the child and was ready to care for her. The matter would be resolved quickly, Richard argued in the hearings, if the State Department "would just get out of the way." One Justice Department lawyer responded that the custody order Mast had obtained was "deeply flawed and incorrect"—contrary to the court's understanding, President Ghani never waived custody of the child.

Moon decided against the Masts. A private litigant couldn't "determine the foreign policy of the United States," he said. Joshua might have been unhappy with the results of the Afghan government's investigation, Moon said, but he had no legal basis for bringing Baby L. to the United States. The transfer would proceed.

On February 27, 2020, a small contingent of Afghan officials arrived at Bagram. The commander of the hospital seemed reluctant to hand over the baby, one of them told me. As the group walked to the car, they were met by a line of about a dozen U.S.

military personnel, standing in salute. A few, the official recalled, had tears in their eyes.

Later that day, the baby landed in southern Afghanistan on a Red Cross plane. Her uncle, a white beard framing his narrow face, was waiting at the airport. As the passengers disembarked, he saw a small bundle of pink and started to cry. Boxes of baby supplies accompanied her from Bagram, bearing the name L. He didn't know who that was. He called her by the name her parents had given her: R.

"He Wants to Take Care of Her"

R. was with her family now, but her uncle was an elderly man. He had to consider how best to care for her. His son, who lived in a city with good hospitals, had just married. It wasn't uncommon for families to collectively assume responsibility for a child, and after observing the baby in their care for several days, R.'s uncle decided that the young couple—John and Jane Doe, as they were later named in the federal suit they filed against Mast—would serve as her parents.

John Doe, a twenty-three-year-old with a trimmed beard and soft eyes, worked at a medical office and ran a tutoring center for schoolchildren. Jane Doe, who was born shortly before the United States invaded in 2001, was finishing high school at the top of her class. She was nineteen, her cheeks still round with baby fat, but she had raised her five brothers and three sisters alongside her mother. From the first night R. arrived at her home, Jane told me, she fell in love with the baby. Soon, bottles and diapers appeared next to Jane's notebooks and English-language awards. She began to plan where R. would go to school when she was older.

An ocean away, Joshua Mast was making his own plans. Shortly after R. left Bagram, he reached out again to Kimberley Motley, the American lawyer with a practice in Kabul. Motley had been involved in the case in various ways. A different American who initially wanted to adopt R. told me that he paid her more than $10,000 before it became clear that the Afghan government was not going to give her up. (Through her lawyer, Motley disputed the amount, saying it was less.) To U.S. military and State Department officials at Bagram, Motley described herself as an unofficial guardian ad litem for the baby, someone typically appointed by a court to represent her best interest. "This was uncharted territory within Afghanistan," Motley told me in August, adding that she was happy to "essentially volunteer" as the child's advocate. "I was trying to do the right thing," she said. (Motley's own lawyer later emphasized that Mast himself was never a client.)

Mast sent Motley a copy of the certificate of foreign birth he acquired in Virginia, as well as an identity card he secured from the Department of Defense, both of which would clear hurdles to bringing R. to the United States. "He wanted to adopt her," Motley recalled to me, and he wanted her help in tracking down the baby. That he had the certificate and identity card for the child surprised her. "I've never seen anything like it," she said. (The Department of Defense did not answer queries, citing ongoing litigation.)

Nonetheless, the fact that R.'s relatives had been found in Afghanistan gave her pause: She, too, had heard that the baby's parents were foreign insurgents. Despite her skepticism about the legal basis of his adoption effort—which, in her view at that time, probably should have come to an end once the baby was reunited with her Afghan family—Motley said she would find her and report back. "You know, *I'm* concerned about where she is going," she told me.

Using her network in Afghanistan, Motley tracked down R.'s uncle and explained that she was an American lawyer who knew about the baby girl who lost her parents. The uncle connected her to John Doe, and on March 6, 2020, the two started texting. "I think she has medical problems," Motley wrote, "and I know someone who wants to help her." The couple had heard stories of Americans offering money to families of civilians who were killed during conflict, and John Doe told me they thought she wanted to do the same. He said a local Red Cross representative had vouched for Motley, and they began to trust her.

Months passed. R. started to crawl and then, steadily, to walk. Her legs learned to pedal a tricycle. Her tongue began to sound words, her first attempts at her native Pashto. Jane Doe liked to tease her new family. "Who is crazy?" she would ask R., who would point to John Doe. More than anyone, R. clung to Jane. She would place Jane's shoes in front of her door and forbid anyone else to use them. Motley asked for photos of R., which Jane sent, including one of the baby playing in a tub of water in her underwear.

As Motley came to know the Does, it became clear to her that they loved R. Motley told Mast, she said, that whatever he thought he was doing about adoption, Jane was not going to give up the baby. According to her, Mast told her he was focused on getting R. medical care. Motley decided to continue connecting him with the Does. I asked Motley if, in all her conversations with the Does, she ever mentioned that the Masts had a custody order and a certificate of foreign birth for R. from an American court. She said she had not. She had considered the documents briefly when Mast first contacted her and then, she told me, didn't think about them again as she focused on the baby's health concerns. What did she tell the Does about who Mast was and what he wanted? "I said he wants to take care of her," she told me. "I don't think 'adopt' was really used that much—but that's because it was more a semantic thing."

When Motley told the Does that R. needed advanced treatment and that an American family was ready to help, they were baffled. How could parents allow their child to be sent so far without them? The skin on R.'s forehead would redden at times, and her eyes would swell, itchy and watery; the local doctors they visited were unsure of the cause but seemed largely unconcerned.

While the Does and Motley were discussing medical matters, the Masts were taking the final steps to secure their legal right to the baby in Fluvanna County, VA. R. had been living with the Does for ten months, but on December 3, 2020, Judge Moore determined that she remained "orphaned, undocumented, stateless." The waiver from President Ghani never came, but Moore granted the American couple permanent adoption. The Masts, he wrote, "are suitable parents and will provide the child with a loving and stable home."

In Virginia, final adoption orders are binding after six months and can be challenged only by someone with an "actual relationship of parental responsibility." Motley told me that Mast updated her when he obtained permanent adoption, but she did not inform the Does. In her view, the adoption was moot. "It's one thing to have an order on paper, but how do you enforce it?" she told me. The baby was in Afghanistan; the Masts were in the United States. (Through her lawyer, Motley later denied knowing about the final adoption order before mid-2021.)

About half a year later, in the summer of 2021, Motley introduced the Does to Mast over the phone. An Afghan man who went by the name Ahmad Osmani was also present to interpret for him. The Does remember Osmani saying he lived outside Afghanistan and was married to a Turkish woman. Mast explained to the Does that he met R. when he was a volunteer at Bagram and that he wanted to help her.

"Why?" John Doe asked. For humanity, he remembered Mast saying.

Mast and Osmani began contacting John Doe frequently, encouraging him to come to the United States with the baby. According to the couple, Osmani said they could all stay with the Masts. The Does were facing financial troubles, and Osmani persuaded them to accept assistance; in late July, they received $1,000 by wire transfer. Jane Doe, though, was growing suspicious of Mast's eagerness to help an Afghan family he'd never met. She suggested that John ask Osmani about the American privately. According to the couple, Osmani reassured them that he had worked for Mast for years, that Mast was a good person. "We didn't trust Joshua," John told me. "We trusted Ahmad because we knew him; he's Afghan."

Still, Mast and Motley's warnings about the baby's injuries had started to worry the Does. They admitted that the doctors they visited did not know what to make of the redness on her face.

They had not scanned her brain for any lasting damage from her head wound. Had the doctors missed something?

The Does considered taking her to India or Pakistan, somewhere closer to Afghanistan with medical specialists. There was another consideration: by late summer 2021, Jane was eight months pregnant, and the Does hoped to return home quickly after whatever treatment R. might need. But when they suggested their idea to Mast, they recalled, he said that those countries did not have the necessary medical equipment. The Does, he said, had to bring the baby to the United States.

The Fall of Afghanistan

In August 2021, the war's front lines, which had been relegated to the hinterlands for much of the last two decades, were suddenly in major cities, and at the Does' doorstep. At night, they heard the pop-pop of gunfire as the police battled Taliban fighters. By morning, only the Taliban roamed the streets. On August 15, the Taliban took control of Kabul, and with it the entire country.

The Does watched videos of Afghans rushing to the airport. Everyone was trying to flee. Mast and Osmani called and texted, imploring them to leave. It was their last chance to get on a plane, the Does remembered the men saying. Mast, meanwhile, left an excited message at the Virginia attorney general's office, explaining that a group of former marines, "sponsored by a very wealthy American" he did not name, had volunteered to help get the baby out. They would pay Afghan guards at the airport. "They're Christians," Mast said of the former marines in the voice message I obtained. Pray for their safety, he implored.

On August 22, Jane Doe quickly packed up their home and handed the keys to her mother. They would be back in two months, after R.'s treatment, she promised. They hired a taxi, John Doe in the front, Jane and R. in the back. For eight hours, they passed fields, hills, and dirt roads where Taliban checkpoints waved them through toward Kabul. According to the Does, Osmani told them to delete their text conversations with him and Mast. But Jane, noting that the Taliban wasn't inspecting phones, told her husband not to.

When they reached Kabul, Osmani and Mast directed them where to go over WhatsApp. It turned out that Osmani's three younger siblings, two boys and a girl, would be joining them. At the airport, desperate Afghans were shot at the gates and small children fainted from dehydration, but their group was picked up in a car and taken to an entrance. Behind the gates, an American military officer called out their name. He recognized them by Jane's pregnant belly, he explained, and escorted them to the military plane.

The Does, R., and Osmani's siblings landed in Qatar early the next morning. Mast sent Jane a message to show to an American soldier at the airport who could direct them. "I am a Judge Advocate with MARSOC," the message read, adding that he was helping to escort this group of passengers. Osmani also sent a photo: Mast was standing on the steps of a red-brick house, surrounded by three blond sons, a baby in his arms. What confused Jane was what he was wearing: a camouflage uniform. Mast was in the American military. Jane was frightened. Why had he not told them he was in the military? Was he hiding something? John was equally perplexed, but he assuaged her fears. Osmani said Mast could be trusted.

They were flown to Ramstein Air Base in Germany, where they expected to meet Mast. To their surprise and confusion, his wife, Stephanie, was also waiting for them. The Does had hardly eaten since Kabul, and Jane's back ached from the hours on the plane. Now they sat around a table. The Masts wanted to take the baby to the United States with them, Jane recalled Joshua saying. If R. went with them, her medical treatment and school would be free. Jane translated for her husband. "We don't need money," John said, angry.

Jane started crying, and Stephanie tried to comfort her. You will forget your last life when you come to the United States, Jane remembered her whispering in her ear. "No, I don't want to forget," she replied. John tore off the bracelet that Afghan arrivals were required to wear on the base. They would return to Afghanistan, he said. Mast hurriedly called Osmani. According to John, Osmani told him that Jane had mistranslated—the Masts were only trying to help them because Jane was pregnant; they weren't trying to take R. Mast added his own plea, invoking Abraham, Isaac, and Joseph. I swear by them I will not harm you, the couple recall him saying.

The Masts flew back to the United States alone. Though Joshua had calmed the couple's fears, Jane recalled an odd remark that Osmani's sister made to her. While Jane was playing with R., the teenage girl asked why she was getting close to the baby when they would be separated soon. Jane was surprised. "Why will she be separated from me?" Jane said. "She's my daughter." The girl didn't respond.

The Does pushed their anxiety aside and continued their journey to Dulles International Airport outside Washington. They arrived on August 29 along with hundreds of other evacuated Afghans. Mast met them there with another woman, who led Osmani's three siblings away. He escorted the couple through passport control, then to a resting area. It was past midnight, but Mast handed John Doe a black bag he was carrying and went into a room, where he appeared to be meeting with some officers. Mast emerged more than thirty minutes later. His face, Jane remembered, was red with anger, his lips pressed together. Mast didn't explain. He went home, leaving the black bag in John's hands.

The Does and R. settled into beds at an airport hangar. It was their first night in America, and something gnawed at them. At passport control, an officer took their fingerprints and asked for R.'s identification. The Does explained that they didn't have any, but then Mast, to their surprise, presented a passport. The officer handed it back to John, who kept it. Outside, "Islamic Republic of Afghanistan" was printed in gold. Inside was a familiar picture. It was one Jane had sent to Motley, of R. playing in the tub. The same wet hair was plastered to her forehead, except instead of a naked torso, someone had photoshopped a burgundy and teal top. The name read L. Mast.

"This Is Not Your Child"

After the U.S.-backed Afghan government collapsed in 2021, more than 64,000 Afghans arrived in the United States in August and September alone, settling into eight military bases around the country. During his presidency, Trump had slashed the number of refugees allowed to enter the United States, and the Biden administration, which carried out the U.S. withdrawal from Afghanistan, struggled to handle the sudden influx. Community and religious groups raced to fill the gaps.

Following Mast's direction, the Does requested to be sent to Fort Pickett, 45,000 wooded acres in southeastern Virginia. The base had a close relationship with the surrounding community, including Liberty University, Mast's alma mater, which was sending student volunteers to help with the Afghan arrivals. The Masts visited them their first night. The next day, John held R.'s hand as the family strolled the wide roads of the base. Pink bangles decorated her wrist.

Three days after they arrived, on the afternoon of September 3, Jane lay on one of the twin beds in their room while John dozed on the other. They had eaten lunch, showered, and prayed. Now Jane was trying to put R. to sleep. The toddler's brown hair had lightened over time and was speckled with gold. The redness on her forehead that worried the Does was starting to fade. She still had the same wide eyes, and they stared up at Jane, refusing to close. With one hand, R. clutched a pink stuffed pig; with the other, she played with Jane's dangling braid.

A knock sounded at the door. Two men in uniform told them to collect their items—they were being moved to a new apartment. The couple stuffed their belongings in their bags, Jane gathered R. in her arms and they walked out. On the street, a black van waited for them. Sitting inside next to an infant car seat was an American woman: an official from the State Department named Rhonda Slusher.

They drove around the base and stopped in front of a low building. Slusher insisted on holding R., Jane said, because she was pregnant. The Does couldn't see any other Afghans or security guards, and they approached the building warily. They were led to a room with a desk and some chairs. A tall blond woman greeted them—another government official. An interpreter was also present. Neither of the Does remember what the official's name was or what department she represented, but what she said next pierced their memory: This is not your child, she told them, gesturing to R.

John explained that R. was his cousin, and now his daughter. "I raised her for two years," he said. But the official repeated the same thing: they were not the biological parents of the child, and therefore they could not keep her.

John was confused and started to panic. He tried calling Mast, the only American he knew, but there was no answer. And then, suddenly, Mast entered the room. John rushed to him. "What is this lady telling me?" he asked in English, desperate. Mast, the Does recalled, said he came because he had received an email: he had to take the child from the base, or she would be sent to an orphanage. Don't worry, the Does recalled Mast saying. We are family. He would sort everything out.

Jane ran to Slusher, the State Department official, who was still holding R. "Please, give my daughter," Jane pleaded. According to the Does, Slusher refused. R. was wailing now, and Slusher led her out of the room, the pink pig still in her hand.

Jane screamed and fell to the ground. John grabbed Mast's arm. "You told me you are my brother," he said. "Why are you doing this to me?" John Doe told me that Mast stepped hard on his foot and shoved him away. Then he left the room.

The Web of Bureaucracy

Operation Allies Welcome, the operation led by the Department of Homeland Security that oversaw the Afghan evacuees' arrival in the United States, was strict about people and information getting in or out. But several people who were employed at Fort Pickett in September 2021 told me they were not surprised that Mast entered the base multiple times, even though he didn't work there. It was not difficult to get through checkpoints to the area where the Afghans resided, they said, if you had friends in the military, especially if you were wearing a military uniform. Security would tighten in later months.

Slusher did not respond to requests for comment. In an email statement in October, a State Department spokesman said that its employees at Fort Pickett "had no awareness of the U.S. Embassy's previous involvement in reuniting the child with her next of kin in Afghanistan." A Department of Homeland Security spokesman said the department "has and will continue to cooperate as appropriate with federal investigations into this matter." The interpreter who was in the room was too frightened to talk, someone close to her told me.

For days afterward, the Does sent Mast desperate messages. They texted Osmani. "Let go of whatever happened," Osmani advised them in voice messages I obtained. When they reached Mast, he tried to placate the Does. He told them everything would be OK and offered to bring them food and baby supplies. "No sir we do not want anything," the Does wrote back. They only wanted to see R.

Mast made excuses for why he could not put the baby on the phone—he was asleep, his phone wasn't charged—but he continued to dangle the possibility that they would see her soon. He was making plans for John to get a scholarship at Liberty University, he told them, and his community was gathering furniture for their new home. He texted Jane to explain the tradition of a baby shower. "We will have one for you after you are out of the camps," he promised. "We love you guys," he said in a voice message, one week after he took the child.

Jane tried to appeal to his fatherhood. "You have four sons if any of them separate from you how will you feel."

"I know exactly how it feels," Mast wrote back, explaining that he had lost R. before, too. "That is why I have compassion on you."

The Does had no idea that back in Palmyra, Joshua and Stephanie threw a "little welcome-home party" for R. In one photo I obtained, she is in Joshua's arms, in front of a large chocolate cake. Stephanie hugs them, surrounded by their sons.

Jane stopped eating and drinking. When she slept, she placed R.'s clothes on top of her, as if to embrace the child again. Most nights, though, she sat at the stairwell at the end of their hallway. Twice, she told me, she considered throwing herself down the stairs. The Does pleaded with one agency after another for help. They approached one person at the base who worked for the State Department. She grew teary when she heard their story, they recalled, but after she looked into the matter, she said she could do nothing.

One day, as Jane cleaned their room, she came across the black bag that Mast had inadvertently left with John at Dulles. Inside were pages of text she couldn't comprehend. At their next medical appointment, the Does showed one of the documents to the staff there. It was a copy of the adoption order, and an interpreter explained to the couple what it meant. It was the first time John and Jane understood that Mast had become R.'s father under U.S. law, almost a year after he had done so. The staff alerted the authorities on base, who took photos of the papers.

In late September, Mast finally returned to Fort Pickett. He brought only his brother, Richard. The Masts sat across from Jane and John. I spoke to an Afghan friend the couple met at the base, who was in the room when the Masts came in. He told me that Joshua explained he was going to get R. medical treatment because the Does didn't have the means to do so. "You're not treating her," Jane said. "You're keeping her." The couple's friend turned to Richard. "If you just have her for treatment, then give us a promise that you'll release the child." Before Richard could respond, the friend recalled, Joshua Mast told him not to say, "Yes."

Jane went into labor a few days later. She gave birth to a healthy baby girl, and almost immediately after, she texted Mast, telling him the news and pleading with him to bring R., even if only to visit. Mast wrote back: "We are very excited for you both! Having a baby is one of the best experiences in life."

Not long after, Jane received her first and only message from Stephanie Mast. "Motherhood brings a lot of change and can be challenging at times," she wrote. "I would love to be your friend and support you." Jane didn't respond.

On October 25, the Does approached Martha Jenkins, a lawyer working with the United States Conference of Catholic Bishops at Fort Pickett who was helping to run information sessions for those arriving from Afghanistan. Jenkins's supervisor was also present and went to higher-ups at the conference, as well as to the Marine Corps and government agencies. The issue "kept getting kicked down the road," Jenkins told me. "Everyone had sympathy but no direction, nothing to be done." After a few days, Jenkins told me, she and the supervisor heard back from someone who looked into the matter: "The Masts really covered their bases."

They encouraged the Does to reach out to Motley, the American lawyer in Afghanistan, whom the couple had not spoken to since August. Perhaps she had not known what Mast would do, Jenkins reasoned. "The person who is introduced to us by you, by the name of Joshua Mast" took R. "from us by force," the Does wrote in a WhatsApp message. "You are the one who knows about our story and we kindly requesting you to help us please." Motley did not respond. Motley told me that Mast informed her R. was with him and that she didn't ask for more details. She texted the Does months later; she didn't do so immediately because, she explained, she was receiving hundreds of requests for help from Afghans in the wake of the U.S. withdrawal.

Jenkins and her supervisor were growing concerned about Jane's deteriorating mental health. In one of their meetings, Jane cried uncontrollably, and the interpreter in the room held her. They took Jane to the behavioral health clinic, where a health officer heard what happened and, alarmed that Mast had taken the child, immediately contacted Department of Homeland Security law-enforcement officers on base. The interpreter who was present for the subsequent conversation told me that both officers appeared to be upset by what they heard.

One person at Fort Pickett, who has long worked with refugees and who asked to remain anonymous because they did not have permission to speak, told me that they heard of the "baby case" at the time but that it was one fire among many in the context of the rushed resettlement operation itself. "None of us that were there, including military and government actors and international NGOs, had a blueprint for what we were doing," they said. Still, one thing remained a mystery to them: "How did this man think he had the right to adopt this baby?"

By November, the Does' story had reached almost every agency at Fort Pickett. On November 6, staff members gathered to discuss the situation. One person who was at the meeting told me that Chris Cronen, the federal coordinator for the Department of Homeland Security on the base, was shocked. "His eyebrows were all the way up to his hairline," this person recalled. An immigration officer in the room who had some understanding of Afghan law explained that the adoption should never have happened. The group agreed to notify the FBI.

In their first two months in America, the Does had lost R. and become entangled in a web of a foreign government's bureaucracy. They presented documents and pictures of the child. They shared their story again and again. But no one could bring R. back. The response they received was always the same: legal papers stated the baby belonged to an American family. The couple, who had just arrived in a new country without family or jobs or money, would have to take the fight to court.

What Really Happened That Night?

The central argument in Mast's claim to the baby comes down to whether her parents were Afghan villagers or foreign fighters. Who, exactly, did the army rangers kill the night of September 5, 2019? This summer, I decided to find out.

From a satellite view, R.'s village, along a river in central Afghanistan, emerges from lush green and blue, beyond which the land is brown and flat until it fades into the mountains. Reaching it from the district capital requires a day of driving on unpaved, craggy road. By 2019, the Ghani government had lost effective control over the area to the Taliban, al-Qaeda, and insurgent groups. Around the country, the United States was redoubling counterterrorism efforts in a last bid to force the Taliban into a negotiating position for a political settlement.

That summer, a group of foreigners moved into the village, women living among them. Locals noticed that they all kept to themselves and didn't speak their language, Pashto. The military operation in September lasted more than four hours. After the forces left, when dawn broke, a few men from the village rushed to one of the houses, now only half standing. They knew it well. It belonged to a man who worked in the fields nearby, who was born in that house and raised his eleven children there. The villagers shouted his name. Near the door, they saw two partly charred bodies. But they recognized them, a man and a woman.

Suddenly, they heard muffled yells and started digging. For hours, the men pulled out bodies, one by one, trying to ascertain who was alive, who was dead. In the final tally, five children were killed, two boys and three girls. The youngest was a girl of eleven. The eldest boy was fifteen. "He still didn't have any facial hair," one of the men told me over the phone.

When Trump loosened the rules of engagement in the Afghanistan war in 2017, it lowered the bar for intelligence that would justify airstrikes and night raids. Across the country, civilian deaths started ticking up. The United Nations Assistance Mission in Afghanistan, which monitors human rights abuses, found that in the first half of 2019, Afghan and international forces were responsible for more civilian deaths than the Taliban and insurgent groups, "a trend that UNAMA had not documented before 2019." Ground operations were one of the leading causes.

Hours after the September 5 operation, U.S. forces produced an initial summary report, assessing the targets and casualties. Not long after, according to a former ranger I spoke with who had been stationed at Bagram and was familiar with the contents of the report, the military conducted an investigation to gather more information about what took place on the ground. He recalled that the investigation revealed that the Americans shot at the mother—the woman with the baby—because she appeared to be detonating a device, but it turned out she was unarmed. A representative for U.S. Special Operations Command told me that two civilian casualties were officially registered from that night: a baby, injured, and an Afghan woman, who died from her wounds.

According to the former ranger, as well as a legal adviser I spoke with who worked with the ranger regiment in Afghanistan, Mast would have most likely seen the initial assessment of the operation, which was more widely shared, as was typical, but not the subsequent reports alleging a civilian casualty. "The joke is that the first report is always wrong," the former ranger said. Still, he and another ranger I spoke with said they did not think the woman killed was Afghan, because the targeted compounds were assessed to be teeming with foreign fighters. They pointed out that she may have been registered as a civilian because she was not actively engaged in hostilities. But no one I spoke with could provide me with proof of her identity.

In a report about the September operation that I obtained, Afghanistan's former National Directorate of Security noted that casualties included "foreign national and domestic Taliban." Unlike the United States, the Afghan agency appeared to believe that not everyone who died that night was a foreigner. It was also unclear if the Afghans killed were, in fact, Taliban. A former NDS official told me that the agency helped gather intelligence for months before the raid. But the sources were not from the district, and they did not return after the operation to confirm the identities of the dead.

R.'s other uncle, her mother's brother, lived near his sister and watched her children grow. They were Afghan, like him, and, like him, they spoke Pashto. He was one of the men who pulled bodies from the rubble, bodies of his nephews and nieces. They had accounted for everyone, he told me over the phone, except the baby. They searched into the late afternoon hours but couldn't find her. Days later, they heard that the baby was with the Americans. That's when the uncle approached the local authorities.

Najibullah Akhlaqi, the former director of child protection at the Ministry of Labor and Social Affairs, which oversaw the locating and vetting of R.'s family members, told me that the ministry's starting point was that R.'s family were foreigners, because that's what the Americans told them. By the end of its inquiry, that suspicion vanished. I asked three other former Afghan government officials familiar with the case if they had any reason to believe R.'s parents were not Afghan. They all told me no.

R. had siblings who survived the attack that night. I briefly spoke with one of them, her nine-year-old brother. He seemed withdrawn and spoke haltingly. He and several of his siblings had been sleeping when they heard a loud boom, the boy recalled to me over the phone. His parents were in the other room with the baby. "It was a lot of bombs," he told me. There was other noise too: the sound of gunfire, his parents yelling from behind the wall to sit down.

In court filings, Mast said that R.'s "likely biological father detonated a suicide vest." But the man in the suicide vest might have been someone else. R's maternal uncle told me that her father was wearing only clothes when they found him and that his body was largely intact. Mast also said in the filings that R.'s mother had sustained "multiple gunshot wounds" while "reportedly resisting." Or was she trying to protect her family from gunmen as her children cowered in the next room?

Implicit in the Masts' court filings is that the Does' claim over R. is a conspiracy by two different families—the supposed maternal and paternal uncles, living in two different provinces—to dupe the Red Cross and the American and Afghan governments. This perplexed the former Afghan officials I spoke with. One, who helped investigate the case and agreed to speak with me on the condition of anonymity, told me that the family had no incentive to claim the baby as theirs, especially when Afghans struggle to feed their own children. "It was not about money or privilege," she said.

"They were feeling attached to her, because they lost their whole family."

I later showed John Doe the photos of the village I had gathered. It had been a long time since he had seen the province where he was born. He left as a child, he told me, but he remembered the foreign armies who descended with their tanks and planes that seemed, to him, to shoot everything, cows, sheep, trees. "Every family has a story of someone killed," he said. Doe's father left, but his uncle remained. They visited him in later years. At mealtime, his uncle would sit on his haunches and eat quickly, then rush back out to the fields.

Mast, Motley, and other Americans at Bagram said they were convinced R. would suffer a terrible fate if she stayed in Afghanistan. Yet all the photos and videos I saw of her showed a happy, healthy child. She giggled in her polka-dot *shalwar kameez*; her eyes grew in wonder when someone asked her a question. She was hugged and coddled by those around her.

But the Masts did articulate one of the major threats to R.'s life if she stayed in Afghanistan as the war dragged on, a threat that, as John Doe pointed out, came to even the happiest of families. In court, Richard Mast said, "She's going to die because the U.S. is going to kill whoever she's with."

A Legal Battle Begins

The Does waited for weeks at Fort Pickett, hoping Mast would change his mind and bring R. back. But the base was only a temporary option; they had to resettle somewhere. Their Afghan friend had family in Texas, and the Does decided to follow him there.

The couple had started talking to the FBI. Aware of the agency's tense history with Muslims, a volunteer at a resettlement organization recommended that the couple speak to agents with lawyers present. A chain of contacts led them to Sehla Ashai, an immigration attorney based in Dallas. They also connected with an experienced adoption lawyer in Virginia, Elizabeth Vaughan, who was initially skeptical. There are statutory safeguards for international adoptions, Vaughan told me, because it is "fraught with ethical problems." Then she saw the court order.

In December 2020, as Mast sought a final adoption order, the Virginia court appointed a guardian ad litem, someone who would represent R.'s best interests during the proceedings to determine if the Masts should be her permanent guardians. I spoke with the person who served in this role, John David Gibson, a lawyer who has known Judge Moore for years. The case was unusual, he told me. "I didn't know how it would fit into Virginia law," he said. Gibson explained that he supported the Masts' adoption based on the limited information he had: the baby's birth parents died in a violent confrontation overseas, there were no other known relatives, and the child had severe injuries. "There was no family to care for her," he told me. Fluvanna County's Department of Social Services had visited the Masts at their two-story home and determined them to be fit parents. This was strange, because R. was not with them at the time—she was not even in the United States. When I pressed Gibson, he repeated that he had little information. "If I knew the child's parents were living or relatives were interested, I would have brought the issue to the court," he said.

Last December, Vaughan, the adoption lawyer in Virginia, filed a petition on behalf of the Does to vacate the Masts' adoption order. Ashai, the immigration attorney in Dallas, contacted the State Department, the Department of Health and Human Services, and the Justice Department. She was met with little interest. As the Does and their lawyers started putting together their case, they discovered something else: Osmani, Mast's interpreter, seemed to have misled them about his life. He was not Muslim, and his wife was not Turkish after all—she was an American named Natalie Gandy, whom Osmani met in Turkey. The couple live in Tennessee with Osmani's three siblings and two children of their own. When I called Osmani in August and introduced myself, he hung up the phone. I tried again. "I don't want to talk about anything," he told me, and hung up again. I contacted his lawyer, Tyler Brooks, who also serves as special counsel to the Thomas More Society, a conservative legal group that has pursued cases against abortion providers and filed legal challenges to the 2020 presidential election. After an initial message, Brooks stopped responding to queries.

This summer, I visited the Does in their home in Texas. They live in a small apartment compound off a highway. Debris floated in a swimming pool surrounded by broken chairs. John Doe found work at a milk factory, where he hauls crates onto trucks, sometimes late into the night. In the apartment, a crib stood in the living room, next to a small kitchen, where Jane Doe was baking bread. Their nine-month-old baby crawled from one person to the next, her hair bouncing. John tickled her and put her on his shoulders.

The hearings in the case to vacate the adoption order began in December, in a small courthouse amid the lush green hills of Virginia, before the same judge who approved the adoption, Richard Moore. Despite the challenge to their adoption, the Masts decided to share their story with others. In February, they traveled to Fredericksburg, Ohio, to tell a congregation of 300 people at the Mennonite Christian Assembly how they saved a child from Afghanistan. "Stories of rescue and redemption are always inspiring and encouraging," John Risner, the assembly's pastor, told me.

Several months after the hearings began, Joshua Mast suddenly sought a protective order to limit the Does' access to information about the American couple. According to Ashai, the Does' attorney in Texas, Mast claimed that John Doe had terrorist ties and that insurgent groups might retaliate against the Masts. This was a reversal from the Masts' overtures to the government about the Afghan couple last year. In emails Richard Mast sent to U.S. Citizenship and Immigration Services and the State Department during the evacuations, he explained that the Does "are helping US DoD at great risk to themselves." They would be killed by the Taliban if they didn't leave Afghanistan, he added.

"Before, we were his family members," and John "was his brother," Jane told me. "Now we're terrorists."

Every few months, the Does travel to the Virginia courthouse, where Mast sits in his military dress uniform with his wife. R. is never there. In early August, I contacted Judge Moore's office and was informed that "direct and/or ex parte communication with the judge about cases is prohibited." About a week later, the case number disappeared from the Virginia court database.

In the Does' Texas apartment, Jane cooked as we spoke, plate upon plate of Afghan stuffed bread. She told me that John's testimony in court took three days because the attorneys representing the Masts—Richard Mast and a Virginia lawyer named Hannon Wright—questioned everything he said, including how he knew where his relatives lived. When they asked John if he ever saw foreign fighters in Afghanistan, he said, in earnest, Yes, the Americans.

I asked the couple how they felt about R. probably being raised Christian. They fell silent. Then Doe spoke. Do they know what she wants to drink and eat? The things she likes? "How do they understand?" he asked. "How can she understand them?"

They reach for her the only way they are able, swiping through the photos on their phones. In one, R. sits between Jane's parents, a large chocolate cake before them. In another, Jane and R. beam in matching outfits. It wasn't just her absence but the reason for the absence that consumed them. "She's living with a person who kidnapped her," Jane said.

"We Don't Know If She Remembers Us"

According to Islamic legal tradition, an adopted child's lineage and history must be preserved, in part to protect the child's rights. American law, on the other hand, tends to sever a child's relationship to the biological family and past life, to help them assimilate. After adoption, the child assumes a new name, culture, religion. R. Doe becomes L. Mast.

The Islamic and American adoption systems, though, are not entirely at odds with each other. Both try, in their own way, to give the child dignity. One Department of Health and Human Services official with knowledge of U.S. and Islamic family law, who asked to remain anonymous because they did not have direct knowledge of the case or permission to speak about it, told me that they didn't see a competition between them in this case. "If the accusation is true that this soldier absconded with the child," they said, "no legal authority, Virginia or Islamic, would permit such a thing." (The department did not respond to multiple requests for comment about this case.)

Late last year, the FBI started interviews and took possession of the contents of the bag that Mast had left with John Doe; it appeared that some of the documents may have been classified. The Does had earlier turned over the passport for R. that Mast presented at Dulles to the Department of Homeland Security.

To Ashai, the Afghan passport suggests the Masts' willingness to deceive. "If Mast is saying the baby is stateless, and then getting a passport for her, he knows she's not stateless," she told me. An investigator from the Naval Criminal Investigative Service has been looking into whether Mast, who has been promoted from captain to major in the last three years, mishandled classified information. The Does' team of lawyers has grown to more than fifteen, all working pro bono.

On September 2, the Does filed a lawsuit in a federal court against Joshua, Stephanie, and Richard Mast; Osmani, the interpreter; and Motley, the lawyer. It accuses them variously of conspiracy, fraud, and false imprisonment of a child. A victory in the federal case could win the Does compensatory and punitive damages, but it still would not return R. As part of their filed response, the Masts called the allegations in the complaint "outrageous," adding that they "have acted admirably." They hired a different attorney for the case. "Joshua and Stephanie Mast have done nothing but ensure she receives the medical care she requires, at great personal expense and sacrifice, and provide her a loving home," their lawyer wrote. In his response, Richard wrote that "the Does have no legal authority to assert claims on behalf" of R. Motley and Osmani have also filed motions to dismiss the complaint, partially on grounds that they have no connection to Virginia. They all deny all charges against them.

In August, before the federal lawsuit was filed, I asked Motley how she felt about introducing the Masts and the Does, after learning how Mast had taken the child. Motley told me that if R. stayed in Afghanistan, she would have little prospect for a formal education or a good life. "If I didn't introduce them," she said, "I don't think she would be here right now."

Though the Masts have since moved to North Carolina, to a town near the coast, the case over who should have legal custody of R. continues in Fluvanna County, VA. The Masts and the Does have not spoken. The legal argument that the Does' lawyers are making is that Judge Moore did not have the authority to issue the adoption order and that Joshua Mast presented fraudulent information to the court to obtain it. But they face a significant hurdle. By law, the Does first have to prove that they have enough of a relationship to R. to even challenge the adoption. "When the legislature made that law, they didn't have in mind what happens when someone internationally abducts a child," Vaughan, the Virginia adoption lawyer, told me. The Does have offered testimony and presented documents from the Afghan government, the Red Cross, and Bagram. After I tracked down Sadat, the former head of the Ministry of Labor and Social Affairs, for this article, the Does' lawyers asked him to testify to the authenticity of the Afghan government documents. The Does have never seen records of the court proceedings that granted the Masts custody.

The Virginia case will probably be decided this month, before Judge Moore's scheduled retirement. Any decision will most likely be appealed by the losing party. The court appointed a new guardian ad litem for these proceedings, even though the questions at hand are about whether Mast adopted the child through fraud and whether the court had authority to grant that adoption, not who should have the child.

At least one U.S. Army ranger who participated in the 2019 raid has testified about his recollection of that night on Mast's behalf. However, the U.S. government officially entered the proceedings and submitted a Statement of Interest, in late August, outlining its position on the case; that statement remains under seal.

At every step of his journey, Mast portrayed R.'s parents and John Doe's family as a dangerous people, driven by religious ideology, who traffic young children and transform them into terrorists, who seek to gain what they want by murdering and lying. But from the Does' perspective, Mast is an officer of a military that has killed their countrymen, women, children, with impunity over the last twenty years, who was driven by his own moral compass and abducted their daughter, removing her from a loving family and forcing a religion upon her that is not her own.

R. is three years old now. It has been over a year since Jane and John Doe have seen her. In the bedroom of their apartment, a table displays both girls' toys. It reminded me of a shrine. Bright plastic cups, unused, bore the girls' names. A toy piano was carefully set near a stuffed teddy bear. Jane pulled out two identical white dresses with pearls and tulle, unworn. "We don't know if she remembers us or forgot us," Jane told me. There is no one to speak to R. in Pashto, no one to teach her Muslim prayers. Does she still like to eat rice and tomatoes? Is she still frightened by the sounds of an airplane flying above?

In Texas, a couple collect dresses and carefully set them aside, waiting for the child who will wear them. In North Carolina, white faces smile at a little girl, coaxing her to sound out foreign words. Seven thousand miles away, in a small mountain village at the edge of a dirt path, are seven graves. They are marked by stones and curved tree branches, a piece of white cloth tied to each. In two of these graves lie a mother and a father who once had a baby girl.

Mother Jones

FINALIST—REPORTING

"This story," said the judges who nominated it for the National Magazine Award for Reporting, "uncovers the tragedy of laws that penalize women—particularly low-income women and women of color—for crimes committed by their boyfriends or husbands." As part of her reporting, Samantha Michaels conducted twenty-five hours of interviews in twenty-minute increments during strictly limited prison visits and reviewed data on 1.5 million cases. Michaels was also nominated for a National Magazine Award in 2021 for "Whose Streets?," about gun violence in Oakland, California. Mother Jones won the National Magazine Award for Video this year for Failure to Protect, a film by Mark Helenowski, which was based on the reporting for "She Never Hurt Her Kids. So Why Is a Mother Serving More Time Than the Man Who Abused Her Daughter?" and is now on YouTube.

Samantha Michaels

She Never Hurt Her Kids. So Why Is a Mother Serving More Time Than the Man Who Abused Her Daughter?

A week before Christmas last year, Kerry King helped three of her children build gingerbread houses in a prison visitation room in Oklahoma. King wanted to make the holiday special for the kids, even under the circumstances. But as the Black thirty-five-year-old spread frosting on a graham cracker while dressed in her orange jumpsuit, her hair braided for the occasion, the mood still felt bittersweet. Since she was incarcerated six years earlier, her kids could only visit once a month, and soon it would be time to say goodbye.

"Do you love me?" Lilah, ten, the most outgoing of King's children, asked her mother as the visit was ending.

"Of course I do," King answered.

Lilah thought a moment, her brown eyes serious, and then said something that caught King off guard. "Do you still love *him*?" she asked. "Because if you still love him, I'll never forgive you."

King's heart dropped. Her ex-boyfriend had abused them both, years ago. He was the reason King was in prison now. But her daughter had never said anything like that to her before. And there wasn't enough time to have the long conversation they both craved.

Back in her cell, King agonized over whether a letter to Lilah would suffice. She had been mothering her children over letters and phone calls for too long. *No matter what,* King wanted to tell her daughter, *I love you more than I could have loved anyone else, any man. And you should never, ever have to even consider whether I do.*

"I am not guilty," King had said to me over the phone, months before the Christmas visit. "I just wanna go home. I wanna see my kids so bad. It kind of eats you up."

•   •   •

King has spent countless nights tossing and turning in her cell, replaying the night that pulled her away from her family. (The following descriptions are confirmed in court records and testimony.)

In January 2015, in the small yellow house she shared in Tulsa with her boyfriend and a roommate, King had been bathing Lilah, then four, when she saw bruises on the girl's legs and arms. Purdy "was mean," Lilah said, sitting in the soapy water. John Purdy was King's boyfriend at the time; he'd recently lost his telemarketing job and sometimes watched Lilah while King worked at a gas station. He'd been physically abusing King for more than a year, often high on heroin, which he'd recently forced her to try. But she had never seen him harm her children. When she asked about the bruises, he claimed Lilah had slipped on the ice.

Two days later, King woke up in the middle of the night and noticed Purdy was not in bed. She was groggy—he had ordered her to shoot up again—but saw a light on in Lilah's bedroom. When she entered the room, Purdy was holding Lilah's shoulders, with his fingers wrapped around her little neck. He said they were having a pillow fight, but Lilah whimpered beneath his grasp. "I thought he was hurting her," King later told detectives. So she tried to free her daughter the only way she knew how, by clenching her fist and punching Purdy in the face. *What makes you think you can hit me?* she remembers him telling her, turning toward her. He slammed her head against a wall, insisting Lilah needed to be spanked.

King agreed to hold Lilah down like Purdy demanded, hoping that if she complied it would be over faster. But when she saw how hard his blows were, she threw her body over her daughter's, receiving Purdy's belt lashes on her own back. Purdy pulled King off Lilah, and King tried to run out of the house to get help from the neighbors or the police—but he blocked her at the door. *You ain't going nowhere*, she recalls him saying. "I was scared. I didn't know what to do," she later told me, adding that it felt like she "had been in chains." Purdy dragged King to the master bedroom by her hair and threatened to kill her if she didn't stay there. He reentered Lilah's room and locked the door, leaving King outside, listening to her daughter's cries.

Purdy held King's phone in his pocket, making it hard for her to call for help. She begged him to come out of Lilah's room and then asked him to take a shower with her, anything to distract him. Around six a.m., he directed her to lie down in bed. Still high, King reluctantly fell asleep. When she woke up, he wouldn't let her or her daughter leave the house.

It wasn't until later that day, when a contractor came to work in the yard, that King's housemate snuck out and asked the man to call 911. The police found Lilah in a locked room, sobbing. Bruises covered her forehead, cheeks, ears, and neck, and belt lashes cut into her back. Chunks of her curly brown hair were missing.

The police arrested Purdy. King, who had bruises on her own body, helped investigators take her daughter to a hospital. Then she returned home, exhausted. But her nightmare was far from over.

Less than a week later, King was sitting inside in her pajamas when a police car pulled up to her house around eleven a.m. Two white officers asked her to come with them for an interview. "I didn't want him to hurt my baby," she told them. "I was trying to prevent this."

But the officers didn't buy it. They wanted to know why King waited so long without seeking help for her daughter. Why had she held Lilah down for the beating? Why didn't she call 911?

They arrested King and put her in jail, where she would stay for more than a year awaiting trial. They accused her of child neglect and permitting child abuse. By the time it was all over, though she had never laid a hand on Lilah, she would be sentenced to thirty years in prison—twelve more years than Purdy, the man who had assaulted both her and her daughter.

·　　·　　·

In a parallel universe, you could imagine the police leaving King in the care of a women's shelter. But the detectives did not view her as a victim. That's because of Oklahoma's "failure to protect" law, which requires parents to shield their kids from physical harm if they're aware or "reasonably" should have known that another adult was abusing or might abuse the child. Because of this law and how it's interpreted, King was blamed for what happened to Lilah.

The law is "inherently problematic," says Megan Lambert, the legal director of the ACLU of Oklahoma, who studies these cases. "A lot of times, motherhood is used as the grounds that they 'should have known,' simply because they are the child's mother." And mothers in violent relationships are especially vulnerable to prosecution: if they were abused by their partners, juries often believe they should have realized their children might be in harm's way too. "Folks who are charged often haven't actually engaged in any harmful behavior," says Lambert. "They were put in impossible situations and were not able to act fast enough."

Most states have similar laws, opening the door to anywhere from a few years to decades behind bars as a punishment. But Oklahoma, which incarcerates more women for all crimes than almost any other state, has one of the harshest penalties: moms can be sent to prison for life for their supposed failure to protect, with no exception for women who were abused themselves. The ACLU estimates that Oklahomans convicted of the offense receive an average sentence of about a decade behind bars.

These types of laws aren't talked about very much, but they are used to punish parents nearly every week. Last year, I found local news reports of fifty-three people across twenty-nine states who were, within the span of just three months, arrested, prosecuted, or convicted for similar crimes. Many more cases go under the radar. There are no national data sets to show how many parents have been convicted of failure to protect—in part because their convictions are often labeled as "child abuse" or "child neglect," making them difficult to track down. But if Oklahoma is any indication, an enormous number of families have been ripped apart. When my colleague Ryan Little and I conducted a groundbreaking review of the state's court records, we identified hundreds of people who were charged under the law since 2009, when a new version of the statute went into effect.

While the language of these laws refers to parents, prosecutors overwhelmingly target mothers, not fathers. Since 2009, at least 90 percent of the people incarcerated for the offense in Oklahoma were women. Attorneys in multiple states who specialize in this area of law tell me they have never seen a man prosecuted for failing to stop someone else's violence against a child; *Mother Jones* found relatively few examples. "It's sexism," says Lambert. "It's the assumption that women are responsible for all the goings-on in the home." In Oklahoma, the vast majority of women convicted for failure to protect had no prior felony record.

Women of color are disproportionately prosecuted. Black people make up 8 percent of Oklahoma's total population but 19 percent of those found guilty under the statute since 2009. These types of laws are "really enforced in a racist and classist way," says Stacey Wright, a women's rights activist who has also studied these cases.

Not only are the laws used to prosecute women who, like King, are themselves victims of abuse, but there's no proof these laws are successful in protecting kids. Separated from their mothers, children affected by failure-to-protect convictions sometimes end up in foster care or with abusive guardians, according to several attorneys who are familiar with the statutes.

These laws also create an impossible dynamic that makes survivors *less* likely to report what's happening to police. When someone calls 911 after being abused by a partner, some cops open a child welfare investigation if there are kids in the family. So if a mother calls 911, she risks losing her kids; if she doesn't, she risks being prosecuted for failure to protect. As one legal expert suggests, there's no way to win. "It creates another barrier for domestic violence victims to seek help, because now they are also threatened with criminalization and incarceration, which also means losing their children," says Lambert.

In essence, the criminal justice system makes these mothers ultra-culpable, blaming them for things that are largely outside their control. Mothers are punished not only for their partners' violence but for the violence that has been inflicted upon them—for the sexism that leads to domestic abuse, for the poverty that makes it hard to escape, for the racist policing systems that don't protect them, for the circumstances that leave them with few options. As an untold number of women sit in prisons for these supposed crimes, their kids in someone else's care, maybe the real question we should be asking ourselves is: Who is failing to protect whom?

•   •   •

At the police station, the detectives reprimanded King. During the videotaped interrogation, a female officer brought up the moment when Purdy locked the door to Lilah's room. "You should have went and got help," another female officer told her.

"You guys don't understand," King said, her voice quivering. "I was so scared myself." She ran her fingers through her hair, near the scar on the back of her head where another man—her ex-husband and the father of her three older kids—once hit her with the butt of a gun. She had another scar from him over her eyebrow. And another near her wrist, where Purdy had cut her. "I didn't know what to do," she told the detectives. "I wanted to get in there and grab her away from him and hold my baby."

"The problem is, you already held her once . . . while he whipped the shit out of her," the first officer said calmly. "You should have ran for help."

"That's why you're going to jail today," the second officer said. "Because of the things you didn't do. Your job as the mom is to protect your child."

"And you failed," both detectives said in unison.

They handcuffed her and prepared to lead her away. "I love my kids," King said, crying. "I'm not a bad mom. I'm not."

• • •

The officers did not seem to care about the abuse King had endured, abuse that began when she was just a child. She grew up in Stillwater, Oklahoma, the daughter of a Black mother who worked as a social worker and at the financial aid office of a junior college, and a white father who was a math instructor at Northeastern State University. King didn't meet her father until she was four.

When King was about six, her mother, Lela Owens, grew suspicious after King accidentally peed in the driveway one afternoon while playing basketball. Owens took the girl to a therapist, who surmised she had been sexually abused multiple times. King remembers being molested by a preteen in a park when she was about four.

As a kid, King liked animals and dreamed of becoming a veterinarian or a doctor; she wanted to take care of others. But by high school, King had lost much of that self-esteem and began hanging out with boys who used her for sex. "I wanted somebody to love me so bad, I didn't care how they treated me," she recalls. When she was sixteen, she met Ali Jordan Lalehparvaran, whom she would later marry. He was a couple of years older and seemed so sophisticated and kind. He would take her out for dinner or to the candy store for fudge. He bought her a diamond necklace. She'd never been treated that way by a boy before.

Months after they got together, Lalehparvaran learned that King had slept with other people before meeting him, and something seemed to snap. According to court records, one weekend they went boating and he smacked her on the head with an oar so hard she needed stitches. Another time, he broke her arm. But "I felt like I deserved it," she says. "Like there must be something wrong with me . . . I had been very promiscuous and felt like I couldn't do any better."

At twenty, she got pregnant with their first child, Persia. She was thrilled—she and Lalehparvaran had been trying to conceive for a while. "I always wanted a family," she tells me. She loved the feeling of the baby moving inside her. "It's just the most beautiful thing ever," she recalls. She imagined putting her child in colorful dresses and fixing her hair. "I was really excited about it. I could see myself being able to take care of a girl." She hoped that having a daughter would calm Lalehparvaran down.

They married and had two more kids, William and Lilah, and the violence escalated. While she was pregnant with Lilah, Lalehparvaran pushed King up against a wall and broke her clavicle. She left him and went to stay with her friends. But because Lalehparvaran had paid her bills, a relative told her to go back to her husband, and she did. Another night, Lalehparvaran, who was drunk, smacked a gun into King's head and shot up their home with an AK-47. As the bullets flew, King told the kids to lie on the ground, covering them with her body. "I was in survival mode. I wasn't thinking of anything except, I have to protect my kids," she recalls. Lalehparvaran was sentenced to seven years in prison; they divorced in 2013.

Afterward, King struggled. She had a job at a pharmacy that paid ten dollars an hour, but she had just $800 in her bank account, not enough to cover the mortgage and keep the power and heat on. She tried to help her young children, who were missing their father. She showed them how to bake banana bread and solve math equations. She regularly drove them an hour away to visit their dad's mom. On birthdays she organized parties and baked special cakes. "She was a good mother," says Kathleen Araujo, Lalehparvaran's aunt, who still spends time with the children. "If she loved you, she would do anything for you," adds Melissa Williams, Lalehparvaran's mother.

"I think a good mother is someone who can nurture them, loves them, and points them in the right direction," King tells me. "Somebody that they can talk to, that they can rely on, that will always be there."

She was twenty-six when she met John Purdy. Then nineteen, Purdy was handsome and athletic, with big brown eyes and chiseled, tattooed arms. And he made her laugh, a relief after such a volatile marriage. She sympathized with the challenges he'd over-come: As a boy, he'd been abused too.

In 2013, King got pregnant with their child, Trinity. "I was excited but kind of scared, because I wasn't sure how he felt about it," she says. Soon, court records show, the relationship took a turn. Purdy falsely accused her of getting pregnant by someone else. He started controlling her—dictating everything from her hairstyle to when and how she could use her phone.

Violence followed, she would later testify: One time he sliced through her calf with a kitchen knife and left a two-inch cut. Sometimes he backhanded her or choked her. He did heroin in the house and demanded she join, even holding her arm down while his friend injected her. She imagined kicking him out but worried he would retaliate. "I was really scared, more than anything. I felt kind of trapped," she says. In fact, experts say that leaving an abuser can be dangerous for women, and that many mothers with kids struggle to get away.

Purdy sometimes apologized, vowing to be better. "I believed him when he said he was never gonna do it again," King later told investigators.

But he did.

.   .   .

After Purdy was arrested, Lilah went from the hospital to foster care and then to her paternal grandmother's house, where she would stay as the investigation continued. King was devastated: "I was just in shock, just completely distraught, like I just didn't know what to do," she recalls of the separation from her kids. (Lilah's older siblings, who had been living with King's mom near Chicago, were allowed to stay there.) "It's like my greatest fear came true."

In jail, King was put on suicide watch, and she shivered and sweat as she withdrew from heroin. Her housemate bailed her out a few weeks later, but a court soon terminated King's parental rights to Trinity, who was just one year old. Purdy also lost parental rights, but Trinity was adopted by his friend, a man who has prevented King from talking with the girl. It was "like my world was crushed,"

King says. Unable to pay for a lawyer, King lost track of her court schedule and missed a hearing. As a result, she landed back in jail.

If she had any hope of getting her children back, King had to think carefully about her legal options. Her mom urged her not to plead guilty and instead to go to trial. It's something she's regretted ever since. "I gave her the most awful advice ever," Owens tells me now. "I knew she wasn't really guilty of anything, except being used and abused. . . . [But] I should have told her to take the plea bargain." At trial, "she went through hell, and nobody cared."

• • •

Failure-to-protect laws sprang from changes to child abuse protocols in the 1960s, as doctors became obligated to report signs of mistreatment. The idea was to compel parents who witnessed violence to take action. But the provisions didn't become commonplace until after a high-profile child abuse case in the late eighties led to a media frenzy and one of New York's first televised trials.

In 1987, according to court records, six-year-old Lisa Steinberg died in New York City after Joel Steinberg, an attorney who had illegally adopted her, beat her unconscious. His girlfriend, Hedda Nussbaum, a former Random House editor who helped care for Lisa, remained with the dying girl for about twelve hours without calling the police; Steinberg meanwhile freebased crack cocaine in their Greenwich Village apartment. Nussbaum, also high, said she believed Steinberg had supernatural healing powers. Only when Lisa stopped breathing did Nussbaum finally urge Steinberg to dial 911.

Prosecutors initially charged them both but dropped the charges against Nussbaum when the abuse she'd endured became evident, both by her deeply misshapen face and by X-rays and exams that revealed her to be anemic and malnourished, with broken bones and chronic infections. Doctors and other witnesses testified that years of beatings from Steinberg had left Nussbaum traumatized and physically incapable of wounding Lisa, or of intervening to protect the girl.

After watching Nussbaum testify, the evidence of her abuse clearly on display, the public became deeply divided. Some saw her as a victim, but others viewed her as a co-conspirator. A *People* magazine cover showed an image of young Lisa and the question "How could any mother, no matter how battered, fail to help her dying child?" Nussbaum's critics wondered why she had covered up Steinberg's violence and why she hadn't cried when the police arrived at their brownstone for Lisa. In court, she even testified that she "loved Joel more than ever" while Lisa lay dying.

"Why was Hedda Nussbaum given a walk?" *Washington Post* columnist Richard Cohen wrote. She was "a mother who did nothing as her daughter was brutalized—who put up with the most incredible indignities herself and who, even as Lisa was taken to the hospital in a terminal coma, attempted to provide Steinberg with an alibi."

The public backlash against Nussbaum likely helped spur lawmakers and prosecutors to ramp up passing and enforcing failure-to-protect laws, says Karla Fischer, an attorney and expert witness in Illinois who has assisted the defense of women in dozens of these cases around the country. Fischer believes prosecutors are especially hard on these mothers because of political pressure, perceived or real.

Oklahoma approved its first failure-to-protect law in 2000. It's one of several states, including Texas, West Virginia, and South Carolina, that allow maximum sentences of life in prison for the offense. But these prosecutions are not just a red-state phenomenon. They're "a problem nationally," says Colby Lenz of the nonprofit Survived & Punished, who points to California and Illinois as two Democratic-leaning states where parents are often imprisoned for similar crimes. I found recent cases across the country, from Massachusetts to Michigan to North Dakota to New York.

Today, at least twenty-nine states have laws that explicitly criminalize parents for failure to protect against abuse. In many places that don't, prosecutors take similar actions under more general laws—like charging a woman with murder even if her boyfriend killed the child and then using legal theories about failure to protect to convict her. Some prosecutors are now extending similar logic to fetuses, charging women who self-abort. "There seems to be a strange obsession with our lawmakers when it comes to asserting control over women's lives," says Wright, the women's rights activist.

And it is almost always women who are held responsible. Alexandra Chambers, an adjunct professor at Vanderbilt who is tracking these cases in Tennessee, sees a religious underpinning of these prosecutions—springing from the Christian myth of Eve, who was blamed for the fall of Eden, and sexist traditions that dictate women be the "moral center" who rein in men's worst impulses. "Women are judged by what their partner does in a way that men aren't," she says. "And it can be seen as a moral failing that she didn't have the moderating influence" to stop the abuse.

"It becomes insurmountable, the number of things [women] have to do in order to be in compliance with what we think is a good mother," Colleen McCarty, an attorney who worked on commutations in these cases, told *Tulsa People* in 2019. Clorinda Archuleta, an Oklahoma mother who's serving a life sentence for neglect and permitting abuse while her boyfriend serves twenty-five years for the same charges, believes she was punished so harshly because she didn't appear sorry enough; according to a local news organization, the prosecutor described her emotional demeanor as "flat."

Juries are also much more likely to deem Black women as bad mothers, reflecting a structurally racist legal system. Black women face higher incarceration rates than white, Hispanic, and Asian women, and they're more likely to experience domestic violence and poverty. Black parents also face stricter scrutiny from the child welfare system, which investigates more than half of all Black kids nationally, according to a 2017 study in the *American Journal of Public Health*. "Black families get scrutiny that white families don't get," says Cindene Pezzell, the legal director of the National Clearinghouse for the Defense of Battered Women.

On top of all this, failure-to-protect laws ignore how often abuse of a child overlaps with abuse of a parent. One 2006 study sponsored by the Justice Department found that kids are more likely to face mistreatment by either parent if the mother is being beaten by her partner. A survey of 6,000 American families found that half of men who frequently assaulted their wives also frequently harmed their children. So it's not surprising that so many mothers locked in prison for failure to protect are also victims themselves: in

Oklahoma, roughly half of the women convicted under the law between 2009 and 2018 were experiencing intimate partner violence, according to an ACLU analysis of thirteen of the state's counties. "The law should treat someone who's a co-victim as a co-victim, as someone who is in need of support and resources, and not as a co-defendant, as someone who is in need of prosecution and incarceration," says the ACLU's Lambert.

•   •   •

Only a handful of states make exceptions for domestic violence survivors. "We weren't thinking about domestic violence," former Oklahoma state representative Jari Askins, who wrote the state's failure-to-protect law, told *BuzzFeed News* in 2014. Askins argued that women in abusive relationships could tell the court about that history to receive leniency. In reality, such history is often used against them, as prosecutors convince juries that suffering through years of abuse without leaving is a sign of bad parenting.

"It's hard for people who are on the outside looking in to understand how someone could harm their kids or submit to an abuser's demand to do that, but survivors know what the consequence of each choice is," says Pezzell. A mother, for instance, might follow orders to hold her daughter down or even hit her child because she believes that obeying his commands will keep him from going harder against the kid. And for these women, dialing 911 can be dangerous. "If the police don't believe her and send her home, then she feels he's gonna kill [her]. And if she's dead, he has unfettered access to the child," says Fischer, the attorney in Illinois. "Battered women are forced into a position where they think differently about what's safe and what's not."

King says society has unrealistic expectations. "They think we're supposed to be like he-man women, like super strong and able to beat men down whenever they come at us," she says. "It doesn't make any sense to me, how you could expect us to be able to take down a man." (When survivors do kill their abusers, they frequently end up in prison.)

Courts often don't consider the catch-22 that such moms find themselves in. In 2015, a man in Frederick, Oklahoma, fractured a toddler's skull, and the boy later died. The jurors convicted the man and recommended a seventeen-year prison sentence. Another jury recommended that his girlfriend, who was the boy's mother and had been asleep during the injury, go to prison for life. "A lot of the disproportionate treatment is rooted to our psyche in this state: We tend to get madder at the woman who we felt like didn't protect the kid than we do the man who abused the kid," says Tim Laughlin, executive director of the Oklahoma Indigent Defense System, which defended the mother in Frederick. "It seems to be part of our collective consciousness," he adds. In Oklahoma, at least fifteen women accused of failure to protect received longer sentences than their male partners who were accused of abuse. On average, these women got twenty years of prison or probation, while the men got less than eight.

·   ·   ·

Kerry King awoke before dawn on the first day of her trial, on Halloween in 2016. "Inside I was like an earthquake" of nerves, she recalls. A guard handed her a plum-colored dress that her attorney had sent for her to wear to court. Nobody had asked for her size, and it was far too small, the fabric clinging tightly to her hips and thighs. "I felt immodest, like I was stuffed into it," she says. "Like, how would that look to the jury? I was so upset about that dress."

When she arrived at the Tulsa County courthouse in the plum dress, King faced prosecutor Sarah McAmis, who was seeking a decades-long sentence. McAmis had told *Tulsa World* that it disturbed her when mothers entered romantic relationships with men they didn't know well and then chose not to intervene against abuse after warning signs. "If you bring a child into this world," she said, "you must do everything necessary to protect the child." She said she believed child murder victims "are watching from heaven and . . . know we are able to get justice for them." And previously she had employed an extreme tactic to win in another trial, punching and kicking a doll in front of the jury to demonstrate the injuries to a child, even though there was no evidence the child had been kicked in real life.

Her boss, Tulsa district attorney Steve Kunzweiler, told the *New Yorker* in 2018 that a prosecutor's job was to "teach people the morals they either never learned or they somehow forgot." His approach to criminal defendants, he added, was similar to the way he disciplined his daughters: "There are times when your kids need a lecture, times when they need a grounding, and times when they need a spanking."

McAmis began her opening statement to the three men and nine women of the jury, all but one of whom appeared white, by painting King as complicit: "When [Purdy] came back with the belt, this defendant held her daughter down." McAmis soon called Kristi Simpson, a child welfare investigator, to the stand, and asked whether King should have done more after discovering the bruises on Lilah in the bathtub. King had stayed home from work afterward to watch her, but "it was not enough," Simpson replied. At the hospital after the final attack, Lilah could not stay calm while she received a CT scan or an MRI. "We were trying to explain it to her," Simpson recalled of the procedure. "And she was crying and saying, 'Please don't. I'll be good. I'll be good. I'm sorry.'"

"Myself and the medical professionals, we teared up," Simpson added. "We had not seen anything like this."

At a table beside her attorney, King cringed. The prosecutor's questions, she recalled, felt "like a battering ram." McAmis emphasized to the jury that King did not call 911 to save Lilah. And it was true, she never did. But King *had* tried to get help.

As King would later share in court, she had asked Purdy to shower with her when he emerged from Lilah's room around four a.m. After the shower, Purdy briefly left King's phone within her reach. When he walked away, she texted, "Help me," to her mom, then deleted the message from the phone so he wouldn't see it.

Moments later, the phone rang. When Purdy answered, Owens, King's mother, who'd been roused from a deep sleep by the text, was on the other side, asking for answers. Purdy hung up and then pushed King up against the linen cabinet. *What did you say to your mom?* he asked before hitting her in the face. Purdy demanded that she call Owens back to say they were all just fine. So she picked up the phone and dialed.

Everything is just fine, she told her mother, trying to hide her terror as he sat on the couch opposite her, holding Lilah's mouth closed so she wouldn't cry out.

• • •

On the fourth day of the trial, King took the stand, hoping to finally share her side of the story. But during the cross-examination, McAmis "got under Kerry's skin," her attorney Brian Boeheim says. "And that nice, sweet girl that was testifying got angry and got snippy with the prosecutor. That was it for the jury. They saw her as someone who could be aggressive and could allow somebody to do this to a child."

Testifying can be an agonizing experience for survivors of domestic violence, forcing them to recall painful moments in vivid detail. Prosecutors sometimes use the same intimidation tactics that abusers employ, retraumatizing them. McAmis suggested that King was dishonest because a few parts of her testimony did not perfectly match statements she'd made immediately after the assault; decades of research show that some survivors can recall certain moments of abuse in great detail but, because of the fear response in their brains, may have only fragmented memories of other moments.

Throughout her questioning, McAmis often framed the abuse King had endured as evidence that she'd been a bad mother to her children. "Were they having fun after they saw you get pistol-whipped and the blood gushing from your head?" the prosecutor asked her, referring to the night when Lalehparvaran shot up their home while the kids were inside. And when King brought up the ways she had also been a victim, McAmis suggested she was unsympathetic to her daughter's injuries. "Are you telling this jury you have had a more traumatic experience than what Lilah experienced that night?" McAmis asked, referring to Purdy's beating. "Surely you are not minimizing what your daughter went through?" she added later. (McAmis did not respond to requests for comment.)

McAmis's approach, says the ACLU's Lambert, is "heartbreakingly indicative of the attitude behind failure to protect. Prosecutors are using this tool for the noble purpose of protecting children from child abuse, but with the horrific method of criminalizing and vilifying the nonabusive parent who is often the victim of that same abuse."

Before King left the stand, she kept looking over at the judge, wondering, *Are you for real gonna let her say these things to me?*

"This is exactly what survivors fear will happen when they tell someone they are abused," Lambert adds. "To not be believed, and even worse to be blamed."

During closing statements, McAmis focused on how Purdy repeatedly called King from jail and King kept talking to him.

"Those jail phone calls, they're disgusting," McAmis told the jurors. Then she mockingly offered her interpretation of King during the calls: " 'Bummer for you, Lilah. Mommy is still in love. You're on your own, kid.' " On the phone with Purdy, King said she loved him and even wanted to have another child with him.

That "sunk the ship," Boeheim, her attorney, recalls. "You could just see the jury fold up."

Boeheim had tried to tell the jury that during the calls, Purdy incessantly begged King to say she loved him and threatened to hurt her if she didn't. At one point he said he'd take the baby away if King didn't stay in a relationship with him. According to a court document, he said he'd shoot bullets at her kids, kidnap her, tie her up, and rape her:

Tell me you love me. When I get out of here I'm going to drop kick you. I'm going to kick your teeth in. I'm just kidding, baby. I'm just kidding. Tell me you love me. You want to marry me. Come on, just go run down to the courthouse and you can marry me. You can marry me. Come on, we're soulmates. Tell me you love me. I've got to hear you love me. I'll carve your face. I'll carve my initials in your face. Come on, you know I'm just joking, baby.

King talked with Purdy initially because she "wanted to understand why he did what he did," she tells me. She doesn't know why she kept talking with him after that. But experts say it's not uncommon for survivors to continue engaging with their abusers, and that it can be difficult to cut ties. "I really thought I loved him," she says.

During his closing statement, Boeheim tried one last time to convince the jury that his client did not deserve punishment because she had not been the true perpetrator. "*He's* the monster. *He's* the predator," he said of Purdy.

But he may have been fighting an uphill battle. In Oklahoma, "juries are extremely punitive toward women who have children being hurt in their home," McCarty, the attorney who has worked on commutations, tells me. "It's a cultural more, especially in the South or the Midwest, that our job as women is to take care of our children."

The jury deliberated for less than an hour. King's muscles tensed as the foreman read the verdict—guilty on both counts—and recommended thirty years in prison for each. King dropped her head and started to cry.

"It was a travesty," Boeheim says.

"I was flabbergasted," says Araujo, King's ex-husband's aunt, who attended the trial.

"It was like my life was over. Like I'm not gonna see my kids grow up," King recalls.

Only later did the jury learn that Purdy took a plea for eighteen years in prison—twelve years less than one of King's sentences. "I was sick to my stomach," juror Misty Reed, now thirty-seven and with children of her own, recounts. "If I would have known that the boyfriend had gotten way less years, it would have definitely changed my mind" about the proposed sentence for King, she says. "And I guarantee it would have changed many others on the jury as well." (Other jurors did not respond to my calls or declined to comment.)

With the trial over, King braced herself for the sentencing hearing. "All I ask is that you don't make this the end of my life with my children," she wrote to the court. The judge took some mercy and allowed her sentences to run concurrently. It was positive news, but little consolation: by the time she gets out of prison, she will be about sixty years old, and her children will be grown.

But for now they were still young and needed a permanent home. King had lost parental rights to her youngest daughter, Trinity, who was adopted by Purdy's friend. What about the other three? The state of Oklahoma sent her daughter Lilah to live with Lilah's father and King's ex-husband, Lalehparvaran, despite knowing about his violent criminal record and history of substance abuse. Lilah's older siblings, Persia and William, then nine and seven, soon went to live with him too.

That state officials would condemn King as a bad mother for the way she had dealt with her ex-husband's violence and then send her young children to live with him while locking her away in prison, felt like the epitome of a double standard. "My heart sank," King says. "I lost all faith in justice. I lost everything. What was I ever thinking in trusting a system that was not for me? I didn't realize the depth of how much it wasn't for me."

$$\bullet \qquad \bullet \qquad \bullet$$

King entered Mabel Bassett Correctional Center in McLoud, Oklahoma's biggest prison for women, in May 2017. They handed her an orange jumpsuit that was too small and a prisoner ID number and told her to memorize it. She would have one locker for her belongings: a bottle of shampoo, a tiny toothbrush with toothpaste, a bar of soap, two pairs of socks, two bras. Within a week, she watched someone get beaten with a shower rod.

In Oklahoma and around the country, the vast majority of incarcerated women are mothers: national data are scant, but studies have found that upward of 90 percent of them experienced physical or sexual violence before landing behind bars.

In 2018, King learned that she wasn't the only person at Mabel Bassett serving time for failure to protect. Attorneys and advocates from the nonprofit Oklahomans for Criminal Justice Reform, frustrated by lawmakers' lack of action to reduce mass incarceration, had begun a commutation campaign to help incarcerated people petition the state for shorter sentences. Lambert, the ACLU lawyer, joined the effort and introduced King to several other women in the prison who had been convicted under the same law. All were women of color. "It made me see how messed up this state was," King tells me. "There are so many of us in here that really should not be in here."

In November 2019, one of them received good news. Tondalo Hall, now thirty-eight, had already served half of her thirty-year sentence for enabling child abuse. Her ex-boyfriend Robert Braxton broke several bones in two of her children's legs; he served only two years in jail before he was released on probation. Oklahoma governor Kevin Stitt, a Republican, agreed to shorten Hall's sentence as part of a mass commutation of more than 500 incarcerated people around the state—the biggest commutation in U.S. history.

When Hall learned that she would be freed, she could hardly believe it. It had been more than a decade since she'd spent much time with her kids; two of her children were younger than two when she was first incarcerated. When she walked out of the prison gates later that week, she started crying as she hugged her family, rocking back and forth with her son Robert, now a teenager. From inside the prison, inmates cheered Hall's reunion loud enough for her to hear them. "I love all them ladies," Hall said to TV cameras as she looked back toward them. "I'm coming back to help a lot of them."

But since Hall's release, Oklahoma's pardon and parole board has rejected all the other mothers with similar cases who applied for a commutation. Other potential avenues for relief have also closed. In 2019, advocates pressured Oklahoma lawmakers to amend the failure-to-protect law to make it more lenient for survivors of domestic violence. Yet lawmakers balked after prosecutors claimed they needed the law's life sentence provision to properly prosecute child abuse and to use as leverage to convince mothers to testify against their abusers. Around the same time, a committee charged by the legislature to reexamine the maximum punishments for a wide array of crimes recommended that people convicted of permitting child abuse be limited to forty years. But that change has not yet been approved, and even if it were, it would not be retroactive, doing little for women like King.

In states like California, Illinois, and Tennessee, activists are trying to help incarcerated women in similar situations, but their cause hasn't gotten much traction. "These are hard fights," Lenz of Survived & Punished says of the moms pushing for mercy around the country. "There's a fear for politicians of looking like they are excusing child abuse."

Oklahoma continues to pursue failure-to-protect cases at a swift pace. In November, a Cleveland County jury convicted thirty-year-old Rebecca Hogue of first-degree murder after her boyfriend beat her two-year-old son to death while she was away at work. Her boyfriend later died by suicide in the Wichita Mountains Wildlife Refuge, where investigators found the words "Rebecca is Innocent" carved into a tree next to his body. The judge did not allow a photograph of the carving to be shown to the jury, deeming it "hearsay" on behalf of the boyfriend. The jury recommended that Hogue go to prison for life with the possibility of parole.

•   •   •

During King's first year in prison, her children were not allowed to visit her. She was furious that Lalehparvaran had received custody of them. She didn't think he would physically abuse them—he never had—but she worried he wouldn't properly care for them. When they lived together, it had always been on her to hold the family together, to make sure the kids had warm coats and gloves for the winter.

When mothers are convicted of child abuse crimes, some children are sent to foster care and others to live with relatives, but it's not unheard of for them to go to a partner or ex who was previously abusive or to the ex's family, according to attorneys who monitor these cases. After a mother named Ashley Garrison went to prison in Oklahoma about a decade ago for child neglect, her abusive ex-husband got full custody of the kids and prohibited Garrison from contacting them, according to *Tulsa People*. Garrison, in handcuffs, gave birth to another child the day she was sentenced, but the baby soon went up for adoption and her parental rights were terminated. She attempted suicide in one of the prison showers.

Fortunately, Lalehparvaran seemed to have turned over a new leaf. "After prison, he's changed; he's a hard worker," said Williams, his mother. Lacking a driver's license, he rode a bicycle to the classes he needed to get certified for his HVAC job. He made sure the kids did their homework and the chores. "I think they like living with their dad. They feel safe," Owens, King's mother, told me. The kids said the same thing.

But even when there's a decent guardian to step forward, losing a parent to prison can have ripple effects. According to a study by the federal government, kids with incarcerated mothers or fathers are more likely to struggle with mental health conditions like anxiety and depression, and they face a higher likelihood of medical problems as adults, from asthma and migraines to substance abuse. Teenagers with incarcerated mothers are significantly more likely than other teenagers to drop out of school and be arrested themselves.

King tried to stay in touch with her kids however she could. She called them several times a week and wrote them letters. When Persia eventually started her period, King drew diagrams to show her how to use pads. She knitted them socks and blankets with yarn she'd bought at the commissary.

But Trinity's adoptive guardian, Purdy's friend, doesn't answer when King calls. King heard that Trinity likes unicorns, so she sent her a unicorn stuffed animal. No reply. She hasn't been able to learn much else about her daughter.

About a year into her stay at Mabel Bassett, King's older kids were finally approved for visitation rights, and they've been going to meet her about once a month ever since. After Christmas, King looked forward to seeing them in January, when she hoped she and Lilah might continue their conversation. But then King and Lalehparvaran had a disagreement over the phone, and he refused to bring them. She was devastated, she tells me. After all these years, she still had so little control in their relationship and much of the rest of her life.

The day after their missed visit, I met the kids at their house in Stillwater, the same city where King grew up. That evening, they planned to celebrate Lilah's eleventh birthday. In the afternoon, they sat side by side on the couch as they flipped through an album with old family photos, giggling about how they looked as babies.

But Lilah's cheerful demeanor faded a few hours later, when, in the privacy of her bedroom, she began to talk with me about her mother's incarceration. It still confused her. "Like, I kind of know why she's in jail, but I know she's not supposed to be there," Lilah said, beginning to cry.

"I just really miss her. I just want to talk to her," she said, imagining what it might be like to see her mom every day, not just once a month. "You can't really make memories on a phone."

She composed herself and went back downstairs, where she ate dinner with her family and joined a game of hide-and-seek with her siblings. Then they all gathered around the table for cake. Lilah blew out the candles and smiled as they sang to her. Her brother, William, snuck a taste of the white icing speckled with rainbow sprinkles

Dozens of miles away, King sat in prison, missing it all. In May, her ex-husband, Lalehparvaran, was arrested and charged with burglary and reckless handling of a firearm. The kids went to stay with another relative.

Lately King wonders whether someone might take mercy and grant her a commutation, let her "get out of here, be there for them, and be the mom that I always knew that I was." Reed, the juror who spoke with me, recently got in touch with King and apologized for recommending such a long sentence.

During one of our many conversations, I ask King what she wishes people would understand about her case. "I was just as much of a victim as my daughter was, and they should not just look at that one day," she says. "They should look at every day and see all that I went through, and how I had gotten to the point of that day."

The Believer

"The Silicon Valley of the nineties was in many ways an expression of the quintessential American story," writes Natalie So in "Aristocrat Inc.," "but an unexpected one: one that involved organized crime, narcotics trafficking, confidential informants, and Asian gangs. It is also part of my family history." The National Magazine Awards judges described So's reporting as "deep and nuanced" and the portrait of her mother, who owned the small computer-chip company that is central to the story, as "particularly original, defying stereotypes about the model minority." A writer and researcher in San Francisco, So has worked on the development of several television series. An eleven-time National Magazine Award finalist, The Believer shut down in early 2022 but was quickly revived. "Aristocrat Inc." appeared in the first issue of the magazine after its return.

Natalie So

Aristocrat Inc.

On a Wednesday morning during an unbearable late-summer heat wave, I sat in the back seat of my mother's car, my three-month-old baby beside me, as we cruised along the 85, which runs from San Jose up to Mountain View. My mother was at the wheel, and we were on our way to pick up an assortment of Taiwanese snacks—taro cakes, red bean rice cakes, green mango sorbet, and shao bing—from an outpost of a Taiwanese specialty store called Combo Market. Outside, on the freeway, the tall, yellowed grasses and perennially faded shrubbery looked prehistoric, as if they had been there for decades unmoved.

We decided to take a short detour before picking up the food. My mother made her way toward the 237 and then exited onto Lawrence Expressway in Sunnyvale. "Mumu Hotspot," she murmured to herself, as we passed a new hot pot restaurant. We pulled into the parking lot of a nondescript one-story complex: a group of bitonal buildings, cream on top and taupe on the bottom. Each office was marked by a sign whose formatting must have been mandated by the property managers, because the company names were in all-caps, uniformly rendered in a bland and unstylish serif font. I looked around to see what types of businesses were here now: LE BREAD XPRESS, KINGDOM BRICK SUPPLY, BIO-CERYX TECHNOLOGIES INC. One would not have guessed we were in Silicon Valley.

There was only one office that appeared empty, with a company placard that was blank. The door to that office was emblazoned with the numbers 1233 in white. When I peered in, I saw no one, no furniture, nothing. It was a small room that might have been a reception area once, with brown carpet that appeared at least a decade old. There were two closed doors adjacent to each other, one of which had a sign that read EMPLOYEES ONLY. An ominous white camera blinked on the floor in the far corner, likely a deterrent for grifters and interlopers.

2.

Eight years ago, I began researching a story that took place at this very office in August of 1995. It was a story I'd heard many times as a child, though in far vaguer terms than are delineated here. The story went like this:

On a Friday morning, a Hong Kong woman named Grace arrived at work. Grace was tall and extremely thin, with a jutting chin and frizzy, permed, shoulder-length black hair. It was around nine a.m., and two of her coworkers, a husband-and-wife couple named Irene and Paul, were outside the office waiting to be let in.

After Grace unlocked the office for the two of them, she realized she'd left something in the car. Upon approaching the office door a second time, she noticed two men in suits coming out the door of the neighboring company, Freshers Soft Frozen Lemonade, a wholesale distributor for ballparks and stadiums. They were also Asian but darker-skinned than she was. As they approached her, one of them said, "We're here to see Steven." Grace told them that Steven no longer worked at the company. "Then can we see your boss?" they asked. They were insinuating that they were familiar with the company by giving Grace a name, but Grace was suspicious. Clients never showed up this early. "Could you come back later?" she asked.

Instead of answering, the men moved closer to her—so close, in fact, that Grace noticed a large, distinctive mole on one man's chin, as she would later testify. They pushed her into the reception area of the office. The mole-marked man opened his suit jacket, pointed to what appeared to be a gun in the inner lining, and said to her, "You know what I want."

And she did—Grace had heard of things like this happening recently. People had been kidnapped. A man had been killed. Just a few days ago her coworkers had joked about getting robbed. These events were occurring with such frequency that at times they seemed banal, but even then, she had never imagined it would happen at her own workplace. Grace's boss had recently installed a new alarm system and distributed panic buttons to all her employees, but the men had cornered her so quickly that she'd had no time to act. "Don't do anything stupid," the men said. "This robbery is going to be covered by your insurance, anyway." Now Grace, Paul, Irene, and another coworker named Anna—who had arrived at the office shortly after the men confronted Grace—all lay face-down on the floor. Soon they would have their wrists and ankles bound with zip ties.

Except for Anna, because she was the only person besides their boss who knew where all the inventory was kept. This was a precaution taken in the event of a worst-case scenario—the kind of scenario that was happening now. One man pushed her into the back room, a warehouse-like space where all supplies and inventory were kept. Anna was a petite Taiwanese woman who spoke broken English. Later, she would recall that she was scared, but on instinct did not think these men were evil. They did not shout or scream or even raise their voices. Instead, they spoke in calm, measured tones. They were peculiar, she thought: more like businessmen than criminals.

Anna pulled out box after box as the man watched (the other stayed with the rest of the employees). These robbers knew exactly what they were looking for because they had been scouting this office for days. They'd even made an appointment with the wholesale lemonade purveyor next door under the guise that they were interested in purchasing lemonade, so they could keep an eye on this very place. They knew a shipment had come in just a few days ago, and if they could find what they were looking for, they'd be making off with hundreds of thousands of dollars' worth of goods. After all, pound for pound, the loot they were after was more valuable than either heroin or cocaine.

The man who was watching Anna seemed frustrated, and he made a phone call. Anna heard him listing the items in the stockroom, a litany of model names. Not wanting to linger too long, the men grabbed several boxes and then left through the back loading dock, where a getaway car was waiting.

What in Silicon Valley at the time was so valuable, so hotly desired, that even gangs accustomed to trafficking drugs had started to take notice? What was at once easily transported, concealed, disposed of, and virtually untraceable? There was only one thing, which the Santa Clara deputy DA would later call "the dope of the nineties": computer chips.

Not until twenty years later would I learn just how frequently these robberies were taking place. Even though millions of dollars' worth of computer chips were stolen, this era of Silicon Valley would largely be forgotten. Computer hardware would eventually give way to the dot-com bubble, after which social media, the cloud, big data, and, later, Bitcoin, NFTs, and other increasingly intangible technologies would come to the fore. But for a time, the boom of personal computing transformed Silicon Valley into the Wild West, a new frontier that drew every kind of speculator, immigrant, entrepreneur, and bandit, all lured by the possibilities of riches, success, and the promise of a new life. The Silicon Valley of the nineties was in many ways an expression of the quintessential American story, but an unexpected one: one that involved organized crime, narcotics trafficking, confidential informants, and Asian gangs. It is also part of my family history. Grace, as it turns out, is my aunt. And the company being robbed? It was my mother's.

3.

In 1989, Jim McMahon was a thirty-five-year-old mustachioed street cop working the Police Personnel Unit at the San Jose Police

Department. He was also the only officer who brought his own laptop to work. The Toshiba T1000 in his possession consisted of a rectangular screen no taller than six inches and a plastic keyboard with cream and gray keys. When closed, the laptop could fit into a briefcase. The IBM Selectric typewriters that the police department used were slow and clunky. With the Toshiba, he could make corrections without white-out.

A captain named Ken Hawks took notice. One day, he called McMahon into his office. "We notice you carry a computer," he said. In Hawks's view, McMahon was tech savvy in a way the rest of the police department was not. If he owned a portable computer, how could he not be? Hawks's assumption was right in some sense. The son of an engineer employed by Lockheed, McMahon had grown up in nearby Cupertino, a few miles from Apple's headquarters. As a young boy, he had taken a keen interest in electronics. Shortly after he joined the police force at the age of twenty-one, he bought his first computer, a Radio Shack TRS-80 Model 1. He was what people now call an "early adopter." He had even taught himself to program and tinker with computer parts.

Hawks needed someone to run the High-Tech Crimes Detail, a one-man department that had never been particularly effective. Then, that one man transferred to a different division, looking for a retirement opportunity. This unit was not one McMahon had ever intended to work in. Among police cadres, it did not have the same cachet as, say, the Homicide Squad, the department McMahon had initially set his heart on. To his knowledge, there were no serial killers to catch or whodunnit mysteries to solve when dealing with high-tech crimes.

But unbeknownst to him, here in the heart of Silicon Valley in the late 1980s, computer-related crime was on the rise. Criminals were beginning to use computers for embezzlement and fraud, and pedophiles and pornographers had begun to digitize their operations as well. A July 1989 memo published by the U.S. Department of Justice about computer crime investigations noted, "Police say they arrive at the scene of these criminal networks and discover computers in operation."

Captain Hawks gave McMahon no choice. If someone was going to investigate computer-related crimes, it should be the guy carrying the laptop—the guy, in McMahon's words, who "could speak 'tron." McMahon was given his pick of a partner and two desks in the fraud unit, where he began fielding calls.

At the time that McMahon was conscripted to join the High-Tech Crimes Detail, the police department's understanding of computers was so poor that its officers often could not identify when a technology-related crime was being committed. Shortly after McMahon was transferred, he got a call from a patrol officer who had pulled over a man at a traffic stop. When asked what he was carrying in his car, the man said "paperweights." McMahon asked what was written on them. "'Hewlett-Packard' or something. It's 'twenty megabyte,'" said the officer. When McMahon arrived on the scene, he turned to the patrol officer and told him they weren't paperweights—they were hard drives.

Soon the number of calls to McMahon increased. An average day might consist of breaking into a suspect's encrypted computer or driving to the airport to help customs officials identify technological cargo coming in. There were thefts—many of them. People broke in to electronics stores; stockroom employees swiped extra disks and resold them. At one point, several hundred laser-jet printers went missing from Hewlett-Packard—millions of dollars' worth. McMahon later discovered that they were being packed into eighteen-wheelers by a prison gang, driven down to Los Angeles, and resold for fifty cents on the dollar. The high-tech crimes evidence room at San Jose police headquarters was beginning to fill up, littered with piles of stolen computers, hard drives, SIMM strips, and microprocessor chips.

Through the crimes that were being reported, McMahon started to learn what was valuable—what thieves wanted to steal and what they could resell, which at that point was almost any piece of computer hardware. In the early nineties, computer hardware was the bread and butter of Silicon Valley, and global demand for it was starting to surge. In 1989, around 21 million personal computers were sold worldwide. Over the course of the nineties, that number would more than quadruple. By 1998, worldwide sales would reach 93 million.

In November 1993, McMahon received a call from the FBI. Four years after being assigned to the High-Tech Crimes Detail by Captain Hawks, McMahon had developed a reputation among law enforcement for his technological know-how. Most police departments did not yet have high-tech crime units, nor did the FBI. There had been a big robbery up in Tualatin, Oregon, on Halloween night, and the FBI wanted McMahon to investigate.

The site of the robbery was the manufacturing facility of OKI Semiconductor, a subsidiary of Japan's Oki Electric Industry Co. Five robbers in matching blue coveralls, masks, and balaclavas, armed with revolvers and automatic rifles, had entered the premises and attacked a security guard. They tied, gagged, and blindfolded twelve employees, and according to McMahon, they also pistol-whipped a few of them. After they took what they had come for, they fled in a van.

Upon arrival, McMahon noted how organized the robbery was. It looked as though it had been carefully orchestrated and executed, like a paramilitary operation. The thieves were, in his words, "pretty slick." Not only did they already know where the goods were located on site, but they were also familiar with the cargo, transport, and storage systems that OKI used. They didn't pilfer blindly, like men who had decided to rob the factory on a whim, but rather, they took specific items, a strategy that could have been deployed only with foresight and technical knowledge. An abandoned van found near the crime scene had been sprayed down with WD-40, precluding the collection of fingerprints or DNA. These robbers were not amateurs, McMahon deduced.

As was the case in the theft in Sunnyvale, the robbers had come for one thing only: computer chips. At the time of the robbery, law enforcement guessed that approximately $2 million worth of goods had been stolen. Later, they would discover that this number was closer to $9 million. (In 1993, this amount of money could have bought eighteen houses in Palo Alto. Now maybe just one.)

In many ways, computer chips made for the perfect plunder. They had an insanely high dollar-per-pound ratio, and were in heavy demand everywhere. The path from manufacturer to consumer was long and convoluted, often crossing an expansive gray market, with opportunities for interception all along the way. Criminal punishment for selling stolen property was far less severe than for drug dealing, thereby making computer parts a less risky enterprise. And, as Jim McMahon discovered when he joined the High-Tech Crimes Detail, police officers often lacked the technological fluency to recognize computer chips to begin with.

It wasn't the first time that McMahon had been called to investigate a computer chip robbery. By then, chip theft had become fairly common. But the kinds of theft McMahon was accustomed to seeing were either one-off burglaries or cases of missing inventory—the accumulation of many small petty thefts, likely by employees. This chip heist was different, in both scale and level of organization.

Of course, the sheer value of the stolen property was staggering. At the time, the OKI robbery was the largest theft of its kind. But it also marked the beginning of a trend in the world of technology-related crimes. Soon reports of chip heists like the one at OKI would make their way to McMahon's desk with increasing frequency, heists that were planned and executed swiftly and intelligently—almost always by gangs of Asian men.

4.

My mother heard about the OKI robbery shortly after it happened. In 1993, she was thirty years old. She ran a small company called Aristocrat Inc. that bought and sold computer chips, routing surpluses from suppliers to companies that needed them. She was married and living in Cupertino, just a few streets away from where McMahon grew up. In June of that year, she had given birth to a second daughter. I was two at the time. From the outside, there was nothing extraordinary about her: she was just an Asian immigrant working in the technology sector in the Bay Area.

Working in the computer industry had been a matter of time, place, and opportunity for my mother. Unlike her husband, my father, who was an engineer working on inkjet printers at Hewlett-Packard, she was not among the class of highly educated immigrants that accounted for nearly one-third of the Bay Area's scientific and engineering workforce in 1990. Those immigrants, like my father, had come to the States in the eighties for grad school, after which they were routed directly into tech companies in Silicon Valley. This was a fairly common if not archetypal route to ensuring a steady and often sizable income, which could then fulfill the promise of upward socioeconomic mobility.

My mother, on the other hand, was not an engineer and in many ways was the antithesis of the stereotypical straight-A-earning Asian student. She had scored abysmally on the SATs and majored in studio art at Cal State, Long Beach. She was vocationally unequipped in a way that made any version of the immigrant success story seem completely out of reach for her. But by 1993, her knowledge of computer chips had swelled to an encyclopedic level. She knew the exact makes and models of the new chips on the market and how much they were worth. She knew where to buy them and where to sell them. And most important, she knew how to make a profit off them. My parents always joked that my father was book-smart, but my mother was street-smart. While my father ruled by logic and reason, my mother led with intuition and honed instincts.

My mother is a petite woman at five feet, three inches tall. A friend who recently met her described her as "smiley and effervescent." For my entire life, she's maintained the exact same haircut, one that is somewhat universal among Asian moms: a chin-length bob with the ends curled in, always parted on the left side. Her hair—which is jet-black like mine, thick, with very few grays even now, at fifty-nine—frames full, youthful cheeks and dark, almond-shaped eyes, whose lids are tattooed with permanent eyeliner (for the sake of convenience, she has said). Her demure appearance belies the fact that she possesses the kind of boldness, persuasiveness, and doggedness that make her a force to be reckoned with, both as a mother and as a person of the world.

As a child, I was embarrassed by those traits. At airplane ticket counters and in restaurants, she could talk her way from clerk to manager, never afraid to ask for the impossible. In foreign countries she approached strangers for directions without pause and could curry the goodwill of a bus driver with whom she did not share a language, solely through gestures and charm. Once, when I was stuck in Florence, Italy, during a terrible snowstorm, all the taxis had stopped running, and I was left without a ride to the airport. I phoned my mother. Hours later, she called back: a middle-aged Italian housewife was on her way to pick me up in a minivan. In a culture that portrayed Asian American women as docile, passive, and shy, my mother was an anomaly. She had the daring of a free climber and the savviness of a salesperson. Who's to say if this was constitutional or the developed character of an immigrant trying to survive?

Born in Taipei, Taiwan, in the sixties, my mother moved to Orange County in Los Angeles with her family when she was sixteen. In 1971, the United Nations had voted to admit the People's Republic of China, thereby ousting Taiwan from its cohort. This worried my grandparents, who feared that China might try to take over Taiwan. Around the same time, her brother, Richard, had been expelled from several Taiwanese schools for bad behavior; immigrating to America was a last-ditch effort to reform him. Richard was my mother's Irish twin, born 356 days before her. My mother attributes her fearlessness to him; as an uber-athletic, ultra-mischievous child, he would coerce my mother into scrambling over fences and sneaking into neighbors' yards to steal their fruit.

When my mother arrived in America, she spoke little English. There were no ESL courses at her school, so instead she was held back a grade and put in a class with the delinquent kids, the ones who, according to her, showed up to class barefoot, blasting music from their portable stereos. After school, she washed dishes and chopped raw meat at her uncle's Chinese restaurant in exchange for her family's room and board. "You are the girl. You have to stay in the kitchen," she remembers being told. "I was very isolated. It was a very lonely time." In Taiwan she had wanted to be a journalist, but in America that dream was no longer tenable. Instead, while she was in college at Cal State, Long Beach, she heard about a part-time job as a receptionist at a company called Delta Lu Electronics in Cerritos. My mom didn't care what the job was. She needed the money, so she applied.

In 1984, the year my mother started at Delta Lu, the PC industry was on the rise. The year commenced with Apple's launch of the Macintosh computer during a Ridley Scott–directed Super Bowl commercial wherein a Princess Di doppelgänger in running shorts throws a sledgehammer at Big Brother to free a mass of blue-gray-garbed drones from technocratic dominance. This was Apple's proclamation that the Mac would save everyone from the dystopia rendered in George Orwell's *1984*—the irony of which should not escape anybody. That same year, CD-ROMs were the new hot technology, Dell and Cisco were just getting started, and Bill Gates appeared on the cover of *Time* magazine with a floppy disk balanced on his index finger. In Southern California, an enterprising immigrant named Don Lu, eager to ride this wave of technological innovation, began importing memory chips, keyboards, graphics cards, monitors, and motherboards from Japan and Taiwan. Companies and individuals were building their own PCs and needed the parts. As his company grew, he needed a receptionist. So he hired my mother for five dollars an hour.

Delta Lu Electronics was what we might now call a start-up, and because of its fledgling nature, my mother's job description continually shifted and expanded. She was shuffled between departments, through accounting and returns, learning the ropes of the entire business as she went. After about a year she was promoted to a sales position in a new company called Byte Resources, and unsurprisingly, she became very good at her job: she was keenly attuned to people's needs and deft at negotiations. While the average salesperson might turn away a customer when they didn't have a part on hand, my mother never did. Instead, she'd say, "Let me see what I can do for you," and would call around to suppliers until she found exactly what the customer needed. Then she'd smartly quote a higher price and make a sale. She wasn't the type of person who needed permission, and in her eyes, anything was possible with a little extra effort.

My parents got married in August of 1987 after meeting at a party in Long Beach. My mother was twenty-four, my father twenty-seven. After a year and a half at Byte Resources, my mother quit her job to move with her new husband to the Bay Area, where he was starting in the Optoelectronics Division at Hewlett-Packard in San Jose. After growing up in Hong Kong and attending university in England, he'd arrived in California to get a PhD in electrical engineering at Caltech. Now he was working on semiconductors in Silicon Valley. In the middle-class suburbs where I grew up, many Asian parents, mostly Taiwanese, Chinese, and Indian, did the same. They worked at companies like IBM, Intel, and AMD and sent their kids to the best public schools in Cupertino and San Jose.

My parents moved into a seven-hundred-square-foot apartment on Homestead Road in Cupertino, a large boulevard dotted with strip malls and unremarkable one-story houses. While my father was at work, my mother, jobless, passed each day in a state of ennui, waking up at two in the afternoon only to lie in bed and page through whatever newspapers were lying around. She felt lost and directionless, like she was in a foreign country. The feelings were familiar—she had felt the same way when she first moved to the United States. "It was so boring," she told me. She had no friends and nothing to do. But not long after the move, the phone began to ring. Her former colleagues at Byte Resources were calling. Her customers were asking for her, they said. They urged her to start her own company. My mother considered the suggestion—it was not a bad idea.

Gigabyte was the name my mother chose for her company, which she started in December 1987 with two accountant friends. She was in charge of sales and purchasing while the other two processed orders via fax machine and managed the books. The PC business was booming now, and the company did well. But after a year, unable to resolve an argument about salaries and commissions, the three decided to part ways. My mother, not one to back down, was confident she could survive without their help. "I'm not a quitter," she said. "It never came to my mind that I should quit." In fact, the more challenges that arose, the more she felt compelled to persevere. Undeterred, she decided to start over again, by herself. This time, the company was called Aristocrat Inc. My dad picked the name. When asked over thirty years later how he chose it, he said: "Don't remember, but probably from some English classic like *Monte Cristo*."

5.

When Aristocrat Inc. was robbed, I was four years old and just starting preschool. I have very few recollections of that time, except of things that were told to me later. Even so, the robbery remained a strange, vague aberration in my memory that did not square with my otherwise undramatic, comfortable, and privileged childhood. It was an incident that was referenced and alluded to by my family every so often but rarely discussed in detail. When I began working in Silicon Valley myself, after college, at the age of twenty-one— the same age as my mother when she started at Delta Lu—the memory of the robbery came to the fore, contrasting sharply with the shiny, manicured world I had plunged into.

By the fall of 2012, nearly all traces of the Silicon Valley my mom knew had vanished. After moving back to the Bay from the East Coast, I began working for a start-up that bought and sold personal data, a concept I didn't fully understand when I signed my contract but then later discovered was actually quite morally dubious. The tech industry I found myself in trafficked increasingly in the intangible. Earlier that year, Facebook had gone public; WordPress started accepting Bitcoin in November; and I took my first Lyft ride. Hired as a marketing and PR associate, I scrambled to make Twitter, Facebook, and LinkedIn pages for the company to help fluff up the brand's online presence. Around that time, social media had begun to mean something.

The company I worked for tried hard to be a semaphore for a cool new start-up, and as such, the work environment read like a parody. The founders—two brothers from rural Illinois—were avid Burners who participated in a ceremonial, psychedelics-fueled gathering every New Year's Day to set their "intentions" for the year and were buying up millions of dollars worth of land in New Zealand. On Monday mornings, the company-wide meeting began with a "minute of mindfulness," which was often followed by a startling if well-intentioned rap by the younger brother, which he called his "flowetry." It was cute but also not. In the morning before work, I'd take a train down the peninsula to swim laps at a company-subsidized gym, after which I'd walk across the street and eat breakfast in the office kitchen. Occasionally I'd take a nap or do yoga in the Zen Room—activities that were encouraged by the company's "happiness engineer." The entire experience felt at once frictionless and empty, like bad contemporary art. It was a world apart from the Silicon Valley I had heard about from my mother.

The Silicon Valley in which my mother got her start was volatile, high-stakes, and frenzied. For her, there was no goal of an IPO, no fantasies about artificial intelligence or life extension—there was only survival. Hardware reigned supreme, and the technological infrastructure that today supports our one-click consumption was still in its infancy. (Amazon got its start in 1994. Craigslist surfaced on the internet in 1995. Larry and Sergey conceived of a student project in 1996 that would eventually culminate in a start-up called Google in 1998.) Companies like Aristocrat Inc. would eventually disappear as the internet became a more robust marketplace, diminishing the necessity for a gray market and making fluid direct-to-consumer sales. But when my mother started her business, the marketplace was decentralized, and demand often outpaced supply. Frequent shortages meant that companies could not find the parts they were looking for through regular distribution channels, so they searched for components like motherboards, memory chips, and hard drives on the gray market. As a result, hundreds of small companies formed, acting as brokers or speculators. Aristocrat Inc. was one of those companies.

As a twenty-six-year-old in 1989, starting a business out of her own apartment, my mother got hold of as many computer industry trade publications as she could find (like *PC Magazine* and *Byte* magazine) and flipped through their back pages, which were full of ads selling and soliciting computer chips. She would jot down the names of companies and phone numbers as she went along. Then she would call potential sources and clients, big and small, introduce herself, and ask to speak to the purchasing department. She was plucky and audacious, with nothing to lose. "I'm just very bold. I'll call anybody. If I get rejected, that's fine," she said. Once, she called Dell Computer Corporation, hoping she could reel them in as a client. Later on, she told me, she realized it was not conventional for a young woman like herself to call the sales department of a large, established company. But at the time she did not know that, and if she had—well, I'm guessing she would not have cared.

Aristocrat Inc. grew quickly. The margins of buying and selling computer chips were slim, the turnaround fast, and the volume high. The chip industry, my mother said, felt like the stock market, with boom-and-bust cycles that led to occasional chip shortages, called "chip famines." She and her employees were like frantic floor brokers in the pit of the stock exchange. The work was high pressure. The days were long and grueling. Silicon Valley is known for its white-collar labor, but this was not that. My mom was a businesswoman, but much of the daily work of Aristocrat Inc. was nonstop manual labor: moving inventory, packing, and shipping. She says she was lifting boxes until the day before she gave birth—both times. Sometimes she would have a glass of milk in the morning and then nothing else to eat for the rest of the day.

A normal day in the Aristocrat Inc. office began with phone calls to larger brokers and companies with excess inventory to ask for pricing on specific chips. My mother would call around until she found the best selling price. If chips were scarce, she would order them from foreign sources in Taiwan and Japan—she is fluent in Japanese, Mandarin, Taiwanese, and Cantonese, so she had a lot of suppliers in Asia. Based on the selling prices of the day, she would quote a price to her customers. She had customers all over the world, and notably in South America, where, she said, "people were buying and selling like crazy." The continent was several years behind in computer technology, which intensified the demand in countries like Colombia, Venezuela, and Brazil. In the afternoon, customers would call and tell her what they needed, after which my mother would call around again to purchase the merchandise. This was a time-sensitive game, with prices rising and dropping quickly. Once, she lost one hundred thousand dollars before the merchandise she had ordered even arrived—the price of the chips dropped drastically while they were still in the air.

My mother recalls that around 1994, chips started becoming very expensive. In July 1993, on the island of Shikoku, in Japan, an explosion destroyed a factory that produced more than half the world's supply of epoxy resin, a key material in the manufacturing of silicon chips. This disruption in the supply chain led to a chip famine, which resulted in a price hike. The market became increasingly tumultuous. There were stories of Intel employees selling contraband parts in the parking lot. People were scraping the 25 MHz markings off memory chips and reinscribing them with 33 MHz labels—they could make two hundred dollars more per chip if the memory capacity appeared to be larger.

Then, in 1995, Microsoft released a new operating system. For computer technology, this was a seminal year. *Fast Company* called it "the year that everything changed." Windows 95 was an even bigger event than a new iPhone release today or, for those who came of age in the aughts, as I did, a Harry Potter book launch. The *New York Times* reported on the news under the headline MIDNIGHT SALES FRENZY USHERS IN WINDOWS 95, and the writer called it "a computer-age milestone." According to one tech writer, "Windows 95 was the most important operating system of all time . . . the first commercial operating system aimed [at] regular people, not just professionals or hobbyists." Many people were bringing computers (and the internet) into their homes for the first time. With Windows 95, the computer became user-friendly, no longer solely the domain of specialists and nerdy technologists. My mother recalls that because of this launch, the demand for chips—both CPUs and microprocessors—was skyrocketing, not just in the United States, but around the world.

"It was a risky business," my mother told me. The risk grew in tandem with the demand, and there were opportunities for huge losses in almost every part of the business. From the moment she purchased chips from manufacturers in Asia, she had to take exceptional precautions. If chips were being shipped from Taiwan, for instance, she would have to hire an expert to inspect the cargo to make sure none of it was counterfeit or stolen, then pay someone else to pack the shipment in an extra layer of wooden crates so that no one could open it in transit. Once the chips landed stateside, they were delivered by truck to the Sunnyvale office, but only if the truck was not hijacked first, which occasionally happened. And then, after the chips were repacked and shipped, robbers might target the UPS or FedEx trucks.

Once, a client ordered around $180,000 worth of merchandise. The next morning, when the shipment arrived, the client found only sheafs of newspaper and pages ripped out of a telephone book. Sometimes my mother's own employees stole from her: drivers she hired would come back from suppliers short on merchandise. Though they had insurance against these mishaps, the insurance company eventually dropped Aristocrat Inc. because the risk was too steep, and they had to find a new one. This was an industry-wide problem: by 1994, Chubb, which insured almost one-third of the tech companies in Silicon Valley, had reportedly lost $15 million from high-tech computer theft.

The stories my mother heard only grew increasingly more harrowing: Gangs tortured executives until they handed over their merchandise. A computer company employee was shot and killed in his car. A friend who worked for a module assembly manufacturer was kidnapped at gunpoint. My mother, wary and vigilant, said she purposely drove a clunky old car because she did not want to attract attention. Even so, gangs took notice of Aristocrat Inc.

6.

Forty miles north of Sunnyvale, Special Agent Carol Lee was following these stories too, from her desk at San Francisco's FBI headquarters. Lee was in her midthirties, with straight black hair and a broad, tanned face. She was finally starting to piece things together and make progress on a case that had dogged her for years.

In the early nineties, the FBI had learned of a Vietnamese-Chinese heroin organization that was closely aligned with Vietnamese street gangs throughout the United States. Their connections were wide-ranging, and they were loosely affiliated with the Triads (including Frank Ma, one of the last Chinese "godfathers" in New York), as well as with several other high-echelon Asian crime bosses in various American cities. But this heroin organization operated differently from the Asian gangs of previous generations.

First, they relied on two key pieces of technology: the cellular phone and the pager. They were financially and technologically savvy, and instead of being tied to one specific location, they operated a national network, with cells and confederates in various cities. Lee's boss at the time, Kingman Wong, who supervised the Asian Organized Crime and Drug Squad at the San Francisco bureau, noted one other factor that made this group distinctive: though most Asian gangs comprised only one ethnicity, this group was "somewhat of a United Nations," with several Asian ethnicities (Vietnamese, Cambodian, Laotian, Korean, Japanese, Chinese) in the mix. Such intermingling was rare. "When they see they have the same goal, they're willing to break down national barriers," he said.

Lee had spent some time deciphering this gang. To take down the entire organization, she knew she would have to go straight for the top bosses, the masterminds from whom all directives flowed. It was easy to nab the henchmen who did the dirty work—the drug handling, the physical exchange of goods for money—but they were also easily replaced. In essence, you had to lop the head off the monster. As such, buy-bust scenarios, in which law enforcement descends upon the seller as soon as the goods have been exchanged, would be futile. Lee knew that isolated transactions like those revealed almost nothing about the supply chain. And they provided little evidence for a case against the gang's upper management.

Lee's team had narrowed in on one person, a Vietnamese Chinese man in his midtwenties. He went by at least a dozen different nicknames, but his legal name was John That Luong. He was short and had a Korean girlfriend. Since 1990, Luong had been suspected of drug smuggling and distribution, supported by a coterie of Vietnamese Chinese gang members in Boston, Philadelphia, San Francisco, Denver, and Los Angeles. The FBI had reason to believe he played a critical role in trafficking heroin between the East and West Coasts. There was also evidence that he had been involved in alien smuggling, illegal firearms sales, credit card fraud, money laundering, and counterfeit currency production. After nine months of gathering evidence against Luong and his associates for their heroin-trafficking enterprise, Lee could tell that Luong was a cautious operator. He did not trust many people, and he employed aggressive countersurveillance techniques. Every month he switched cell phones and pagers. When he encountered law enforcement, he gave aliases and fake identification. He also used cloned phones, co-opting an unsuspecting stranger's number to make and receive calls. One FBI affidavit noted that Luong frequented mostly Vietnamese and Chinese businesses, making it "extremely difficult for law enforcement to surveil him without detection," because he blended in so well.

After years of traditional investigation—including seven different confidential informants—yielded little about his inner circle, Lee's team submitted an application to intercept all of Luong's wireless and electronic communications. In August 1995, just days before the Aristocrat Inc. robbery, a judge authorized the wiretap.

As Lee began listening to Luong's phone calls, she noticed something unusual. Often, Luong did not sound like he was talking about drugs. Luong and his associates frequently used coded language and nicknames, but Lee, who had spent years tracking Korean meth dealers in Hawaii, could easily recognize a language pattern that insinuated drugs. She also had a general idea of how much dealers paid for heroin and how much they sold it for, but the financial discussions she overheard did not seem to correlate. Luong and his men talked about "big jobs" and staffing those jobs. They talked about scouting job sites, which they often called "fishponds" or "stores." They referred to goods as "food," using different types of seafood (lobster and shrimp) to denote specific items. They talked about "tools" that were needed for the jobs, as well as U-Haul trucks, warehouses, and security. Testifying in court later, Lee's colleague Nelson Low, a special agent on the Asian Organized Crime and Drug Squad, said, "We [started] picking up some sense that maybe these guys were involved in some robberies and things of that sort."

A few weeks earlier, on July 10, a man named Tony Bao Quoc Ly, who had been jailed in San Francisco for a probation violation, told an investigating officer that he wanted to exchange information for his freedom. He said he was part of a group that was intending to rob a computer warehouse in Minneapolis of its entire stock of computer chips, worth around $1 million. The robbery, he said, was going to happen soon.

To prove he was serious, he provided these details: During the last week of June, he had flown to Minneapolis, cased a computer warehouse, picked out weapons—an assortment of Berettas, revolvers, and semiautomatics—and rented a safe house in Champlin, a suburb twenty miles north of Minneapolis. His co-participants were Vietnamese men from the Bay Area, Sacramento, and Los Angeles—most were between the ages of eighteen and twenty-one. They would travel to Minneapolis together to rob the warehouse. Ly had been assigned to drive one of the vans. After the robbery, he would take the chips to the safe house, where they would be stored before being shipped to buyers. The group would then drive to Chicago and fly back to the West Coast.

On the night of July 12, at around nine p.m., four armed men confronted two employees as they were leaving the warehouse of a computer company called NEI Electronics in Blaine, Minnesota. The men tried to coerce the employees to reopen the business, but the employees said they could not—they didn't have the alarm code. The men forced the two employees—a woman and a man—into their van. During the ride, they tried to persuade the male employee to cooperate with them in committing a robbery later, but he refused. Eventually, they dropped the two employees off at a mall and attempted to make an escape.

But their escape was short-lived. The intel from Ly had been relayed to the San Francisco FBI, who then passed it on to the Minneapolis FBI. Tipped off by the Minneapolis FBI, officers from the Blaine Police Department had in fact been surveilling NEI Electronics since the early evening. The police followed the vans and eventually arrested the men. Inside the vans they found bolt cutters, numerous cell phones and paging devices, maps of the Twin Cities, a gun, several rolls of duct tape, plastic wrist cuffs, opaque surgical gloves, an address for a house in Champlin, and the address of NEI Electronics.

The robbers were held at Anoka County Jail, where they made several calls. An FBI agent in Minnesota would later tell the San Francisco FBI that the individuals were involved with a man in California called Ah Sing—his name was mentioned frequently during the phone calls. Ah Sing, it turned out, was one of Luong's many nicknames, which also included Thang, Johnny, Tony, Duong, and John Dao. A court indictment would list ten in total.

Soon, Agent Lee realized that when Luong talked about going to "look at fishponds," or when he said, "The store is wide open. The food is good. Lobster and shrimp only," he was describing computer chip companies and the parts they had on hand. Guns were called "legs" or "tools." The "front line" were the crew members performing the robbery.

In reality, Luong and his associates were not just heroin dealers. They were also businessmen who had identified a lucrative opportunity amid a fast-growing industry. They had diversified their revenue streams, and by selling stolen computer chips, they could finance their heroin operation. The intercepted conversations Lee heard were slowly starting to reveal the full scope of Luong's criminal activities. On August 6, the Asian Organized

Crime and Drug Squad intercepted conversations between John That Luong and a man named Charlie about a robbery they were planning in Sunnyvale.

The FBI was beginning to make sense of things. The Luong investigation would be called Operation Bytes Dust.

7.

After the botched NEI robbery in July of 1995, Luong's gang was strapped for money. The men who were arrested had called for help from jail, and Luong paid sixty-four thousand dollars to cover their legal fees. Wiretaps around this time revealed tension among the group's top-tier leaders regarding their financial troubles. Luong and his associates started talking about the possibility of creating an emergency fund from a portion of their profits in case things went south again. To mitigate their monetary woes, they decided they should rob more computer companies. In early August 1995, John Cheng Jung Chu, a man who the FBI would later discover served as a sales broker and scout for Luong, gave the name and address of Aristocrat Inc. to two of Luong's associates as a potential robbery target. Two weeks later, on August 18, they robbed my mother's company.

My mother was running late to work that day. Her parents were visiting at the time, and when the two men arrived for the computer chips, she was still at home, entertaining. Later that morning, she received a panicked call from one of her employees, Irene, who told her what had happened. My mother told Irene to stop kidding around—it was not funny. But Irene was not joking.

On September 3, 1995, the Stockton police arrested a man named Chhayarith Reth. He was also known as Charlie—presumably the Charlie that the FBI had overheard speaking to Luong just days before the Aristocrat Inc. robbery. Reth had a distinctive mole on his chin, just like the man who had first approached Grace on that Friday morning. Aristocrat Inc. employees had picked his face out of a photo lineup.

Like Tony Bao Quoc Ly, Reth told the police that he had information to give, for a price. A true negotiator, he wanted to be released from jail, and he demanded plane tickets to Cambodia for himself and his fiancée. He also asked that he not receive a sentence greater than five years for any criminal charges. The police said they could not promise him anything. But on the advice of his lawyer, Reth decided to talk anyway.

In front of an audience of police officers from San Jose and Stockton, Reth painted a portrait of an organization that was run like a business, with a hierarchical structure that delineated responsibilities for each individual involved. There was a direct chain of command and an established process for conducting robberies that allowed the group to do so with tactical precision.

At the top of the group, Reth said, were four bosses [the court files offer varying accounts of how many bosses there were: some documents claim there were three; others suggest four or five], whom he called "the main men." They had started the operation with the help of a Chinese store owner in the Bay Area. Three lived in or near Sacramento, and the fourth lived in Los Angeles. One, he said, was a gambler, and another, named Mady, had two wives. The main men essentially performed the duties of CEO, CFO, and COO, devising strategies, issuing directives, and handling financial affairs. They commissioned armed robberies and paid attorneys' fees and bail for their crew members—a kind of workers' compensation that they had the foresight to set aside as an operating expense. Though they were rarely present for the robberies themselves, they coordinated over the phone, occasionally meeting for dinner at a Chinese restaurant to discuss their plans. Reth said he worked mostly for one boss, a man whose name was transcribed on the police report that day as Donovan Wong—likely a mondegreen for John That Luong.

Reth himself was a "crew leader" (also called "crew chief"), one level below the bosses. Crew chiefs conducted surveys of potential targets, recruited crew members, and obtained rental vehicles, weapons, safe houses, and motel rooms for participants. They also supervised the robberies. Reth said that he was one of the most trusted among the multiple crew leaders, with more responsibilities, privileges, and knowledge than the others. Each crew leader had a preference for the ethnicity of the crew they used. Dung employed mostly Vietnamese men; Mark liked Chinese and Italians; Peter used Cambodian and Chinese men; and Vanthieng worked exclusively with Cambodians.

Below the crew chiefs were the "crew," the soldiers who participated in the armed robberies. The bosses sometimes referred to them as "the little ones," as many were in their late teens and early twenties, just barely out of high school. They performed the dirty work, holding employees hostage and transporting the stolen merchandise—this was the role Tony Bao Quoc Ly would have played in the NEI Electronics robbery. The crew was composed of "freelancers," commissioned on a job-by-job basis. For one robbery, Reth said, each crew member was paid two thousand dollars. According to Ly, the bosses received 40 percent of the robbery proceeds and the crews received 60 percent.

To find robbery targets, the bosses worked with "sales brokers," who had "the inside information." Reth called these men "connections." They were the liaisons to the computer industry, and they often ran legitimate businesses of their own. John Cheng Jung Chu, who told the bosses about Aristocrat Inc., was one of these brokers. Because of their established connections, they were also able to assist in the sale of stolen merchandise (for which they received a 10 percent commission). Unsurprisingly, most of the robbery targets they identified were owned by Asian Americans—these were the people they networked with the most. By providing a "shopping list" to the bosses—a list of the parts most desired by buyers—they could ensure successful sales. In some ways, these brokers' jobs were not so different from my mother's.

Once a robbery target was identified, crew chiefs and members would scout the site, often multiple times, up to a month before the robbery. During these visits, they would learn as much as they could about the security systems and identify the best time of day to conduct the robbery. Sometimes, in order to get a better look at an office, they would create a ruse and go into a company asking to use the bathroom or for a job application. Once, during a reconnaissance, they noticed that the employees were wearing headphone-like contraptions, whose communication capabilities, they feared, could thwart a robbery. It was too risky. They decided not to proceed.

The FBI would later learn that the group referred to itself as the Company—an apt moniker—and had more than four hundred members spread throughout the United States. The bosses formed a kind of family business. One of the bosses, Huy Chi Luong, a.k.a. Jimmy, was John That Luong's cousin, and another boss, Mady Chan, was Huy Chi Luong's brother-in-law. It was possible there were even more bosses than Reth mentioned. The FBI believed there was an older man in the shadows who oversaw them all. The bosses called him Dai Lo, or "Big Brother"—his real name was Son Quoc Luu and he lived in Stockton. Assistant U.S. attorney Elizabeth Lee, who would eventually prosecute the criminal case against the group, would call the Company "a powerful alliance of criminal associates . . . [that] knew no limits. The Company was designed to make money for its leaders—and it did."

Back at the San Joaquin County Jail, a detective asked Reth for information about several computer companies that had been robbed: Centon Electronics, Micro Distribution Center, International Memory Source, ASA Computers, CMC, Valtrix, PC Team, MA Labs. He knew them all. Not only that, but also his knowledge of the robberies was detailed, though he claimed not to have participated in any of them. The Centon robbery, he said, was committed in eight minutes, with twenty people involved. During a one-month surveillance, the robbers had made videotapes of the business and learned its security schedule. A twenty-one-year-old, he said, had rented a U-Haul for the job. At ASA Computers, the crew took mostly hard drives. International Memory Source was a small take. Valtrix was hit twice in two months. When MA Labs was robbed, the owner, terrified, had jumped out the window.

8.

With Reth's arrest, and Lee's team still on the wiretap, the Company was becoming more vulnerable. The bosses spoke about Reth's arrest over the phone as Lee and her team listened in. On one call, Luong spoke about the Aristocrat Inc. robbery, later translated as: "That case, there is no evidence. The only unfortunate thing is the mole on the face." Luong worried that if their group did not bail out Reth soon, he could decide to cooperate with law enforcement and disclose a lot of valuable information. They were unaware that he had already done so.

The Company's financial troubles intensified, with lawyer and bail fees starting to pile up. Wiretaps revealed that during the fall of 1995, the main men appeared to be fighting over a large sum of money, somewhere between $480,000 and $750,000. "There were a lot of money problems at that time. . . . It caused a lot . . . of friction amongst the leaders," Agent Nelson Low later testified in court. As a result of that friction, two of the bosses pulled out of the operation for the time being. Another sensed that something was going awry—he thought he was being followed, so he told the group he was going to lie low for a while.

But their troubles were only beginning. The cell phone, the very technology that had allowed the Company to operate so efficiently and expansively, would ultimately be their downfall. They did not know that the FBI had begun to preempt their robberies via wiretap. Less than two weeks after Reth was arrested, another four crew members were arrested after a failed robbery at a computer store called Qualstar in Reseda, California. In early February of 1996, the FBI intercepted conversations between Luong and his associates in which they spoke about planning some robberies before the Chinese New Year. Exactly a week before the holiday, eleven men attempted to rob PKI Computers in Torrance, California. Luong had spent the week prior to the robbery in Los Angeles, tailing the owners of various computer chip companies. On February 12, when the robbers arrived at the PKI warehouse, they were met by police and arrested.

Meanwhile, on the East Coast, the FBI continued to employ undercover agents in heroin deals with Luong's affiliates. On March 4, a courier flew into Newark, New Jersey, from Phoenix, Arizona. He was picked up by a man named Bing Yi Chen, who often worked with Luong. Chen drove the courier to a Burger King, where the courier sold seventy thousand dollars' worth of heroin to an undercover agent in the bathroom.

The bosses were becoming desperate. "If I could only complete one good job, we could get a lot of the guys that are in jail out quickly," said Luong over the wiretap. Luong and his cousin Jimmy were both running low on money, so they asked Mady Chan for "seed money" to finance the next robbery. In March, they began scouting warehouses for a series of robberies they were planning in Los Angeles.

On a Friday evening in March, just as the workweek was winding down, an employee of ACE Micro in San Diego was leaving his office when he was ambushed by five armed Asian men, some of them wearing ski masks. They forced the employee back into the office and then bound him with cable ties. They took seventy thousand dollars' worth of computer chips and parts with them. Afterward, Luong received a call from a man who said that it had been "taken care of." Luong instructed the man to transport the goods to his house in Sacramento. But first they would meet at the Walmart near Elk Grove Boulevard.

When Luong arrived at Walmart the next morning around seven a.m., he saw police searching a U-Haul vehicle and questioning two Asian males, who were then arrested. When the police searched the truck, they found computer chips and five thousand dollars in cash.

The next day, Lee's team overheard Luong talking to Jimmy, wondering how the men had gotten arrested. They couldn't think of a good reason and speculated that the men had hit a parked car. They did not know that the FBI could hear everything they were saying and that Lee's team was closing in.

9.

On the morning of April 11, 1996, Luong took his girlfriend, Gina, out for a driving lesson. She had an appointment for a driving test later that week. A little while later, they pulled up to Connie's Drive-In, a small roadside restaurant owned by his brother Paul and sister-in-law Winnie that served sandwiches, burgers, and hot dogs. According to Luong's lawyer, Luong and Gina had a shift at the restaurant that morning, but when they noticed several police cars, they drove away and went to their friend Tuan Phan's home, in the suburbs of Sacramento. An hour later, around eleven a.m., as Luong was sitting on the backyard patio talking to Gina, he suddenly stood up, took a step, and chucked his cell phone over a brick wall that bordered the yard. FBI special agent William Beck had just rounded the corner of the house. Luong was arrested that day, along with hundreds of his associates across the country.

Luong was only twenty-four years old when he was arrested—my mother's age when she started Gigabyte. He was five feet, six inches tall and weighed 165 pounds, with a stocky build and black hair. For at least three years, if not more, he had run what amounted to a successful though illegal business that spanned the country, without any college education. He had not been in America for even a decade when he was arrested.

Born in Saigon City, Vietnam, Luong was the third youngest of eight children in a lower-middle-class, ethnically Chinese family. His parents had spent their lives continually fleeing from communism, first from China, and then from Vietnam in 1986. Before they immigrated to the States, they spent eight months in refugee camps.

When they arrived in San Francisco, Luong's uncle picked up the family and drove them to Sacramento, where the family lived with Luong's grandfather for some time. Luong was fourteen years old, two years younger than my mother was when she immigrated to the States. The entire family took up menial jobs to survive. Luong's older sisters worked in doughnut shops and grocery stores or as chambermaids in hotels. His older brothers worked at restaurants, just as my mother had. In high school, Luong did well in his math, science, and physics classes, but poorly in English and social studies. This is an oft-forgotten but typical backstory for many Asian American immigrants—the antithesis of the well-to-do Asian, the one who fulfills the model-minority myth.

In 1990, Luong was involved in a car chase, and a warrant was put out for his arrest. He fled to New York City, where he lived under an alias for a few years, before returning to Sacramento with Gina to live with his mother. Later, Luong would be linked to the *Pai Sheng*, a ship that smuggled more than two hundred Chinese aliens onto a pier near the Golden Gate Bridge in 1993. He was paid $650,000 for his help. According to his lawyer, when Luong returned to the Bay Area from New York, he enrolled in a continuing education class and began working at Connie's Drive-In, earning $5.50 an hour. He and Gina had a daughter in 1995.

I learned of Luong's origin story from a single document submitted by his lawyer that still resides in the court files of this case. It was a plea for leniency, given his background. His history was not unfamiliar to me—the escape from communism, the limbo of resettlement, the construction of a new life from nothing at all. But even though Luong and my mother both arrived in this country as immigrants, with little grasp of the language, his circumstances were encumbered by the cruelties of far more recent traumas, which perhaps accounts for the different trajectory of his life. In the end, they both became entrepreneurs, seizing opportunities in an industry in which they were underdogs. Where business was booming, both did whatever they needed to do to survive.

10.

In 2012, as memories of the Aristocrat Inc. robbery surfaced as a reaction to the strange workplace in which I found myself, I began to search for a chapter of Silicon Valley history that seemed to have been lost, written over, and completely forgotten. Google searches turned up a smattering of mostly local news articles about the thefts from the early to mid-nineties, but the information available online was scant, and everyone to whom I told my mom's story— mostly friends in their twenties and thirties—was shocked to hear it. For them, as it did for me, it created a sense of fracture and cognitive dissonance in their understanding of Silicon Valley.

How was it that I had grown up here, with immigrant parents who worked in technology (and with classmates who were mostly the children of Southeast and East Asian immigrants who also worked in technology) but still perceived Silicon Valley to consist of the Steve Jobs and Mark Zuckerbergs and Elon Musks of the world? Who writes the Silicon Valley story? And who is excluded from it? Maybe I had been too naive, glomming on to the narratives that were presented to me and consequently lionizing only the achievements of these lauded white men. Or was it merely that Asian Americans had been left out of the history and hidden away, as they have been since they first arrived stateside?

When I realized that the Silicon Valley I had landed in was focused only on the future, making obsolescent anything and anyone it did not mythologize, I became obsessed with unearthing the past: the Silicon Valley that my mom—and thousands of other immigrants like her—had been a part of. I called my mom frequently with dozens of questions. I talked to my aunt Grace and my mom's employee Anna and the couple of FBI agents who spoke to me very reluctantly. I visited courthouses in San Francisco and San Jose, where I sat in small, windowless rooms paging through thousands of pages of undigitized court files, trying to take photos of important transcripts underneath a desk, where the court clerk could not see me. After several hours, I'd go for a quick lunch, slurp down a bowl of phở, then return and try to get through as many files as I could. It struck me that all the details of these robberies and investigations had been preserved and stowed away in their analog form behind closed doors, in a manner that made them nearly impossible to access. They'd been relegated to a dusty corner, familiar only to those who knew they were there.

I never did interview John That Luong, even though I wanted to. I felt an urgency to bring this story to the fore and a sadness that so many details were lost to the private memories of individuals I could not find, but I was wary, too, of reviving a past that had once been dangerous for my family. I didn't want John That Luong to remember my mom. It's a stereotypically Asian way to be, not wanting to draw too much attention to ourselves. But that, too, is how we let ourselves be forgotten.

11.

For my mother, who is a deeply religious woman, the robbery played out as a series of "small miracles." She counts herself lucky that she was late to work that day. She had heard that company owners often suffered the brunt of the raid. Their families might be held hostage, or they themselves might be tortured. An industry acquaintance, Paul Heng, CEO of the chip manufacturer Unigen, was the target of a kidnapping attempt in 1995, in which armed robbers ambushed his car as he was nearing his house. As he frantically reversed his car, the robbers shot at him. One bullet went through the car radiator.

All in all, the value of the goods stolen from Aristocrat Inc. amounted to around sixty-one thousand dollars, and the majority was returned merchandise, later reimbursed by the company's insurance. But still, the robbery shattered an illusion of invincibility that my mother had previously possessed. The business of computer chips had always been financially risky, and though she had heard the litany of stories about robberies and kidnappings, the danger had still seemed abstract and distant. When Aristocrat Inc. was robbed, the precarious nature of the industry suddenly became tangible. A robbery was not only possible—it had, in fact, happened. Fearing for our family's safety, my mother would move us into the foothills of the Santa Cruz Mountains a year later. She bought the house with the money she had made at Aristocrat Inc.

The robbery was, in a way, a wake-up call that forced her to consider her own mortality. "I was dragged into the business, and the business was booming. I just couldn't stop. There was no time to think. It was the robbery that made me stop and think," she told me. The momentum of the early Silicon Valley computer craze had swept her up, and she had profited from it, but at what cost? After the robbery, she thought about what she would do if she had only one month to live, and she began to realize that running the business was not it. Doing so had caused her a great deal of stress. After dropping me off at school in the morning, she would arrive at the office around nine a.m. In the evening, after bringing me home, she would drive back to the office without eating dinner, and she would often work until ten p.m. or midnight. When my sister started day care, she'd often be the last child to be picked up. After the UPS shipping deadline of six p.m., my mom would speed over to get her, but never fast enough to avoid the ire of the day care lady. "I realized there was something more important to me than the company," she said. "If I were more ambitious, I could have made it bigger. But I'm content with what I have."

Shortly after the robbery, my mother began thinking about dissolving Aristocrat Inc. But the business was still doing well. Then, as luck would have it, in 1996, an acquaintance offered to buy the company from her. She sold Aristocrat Inc. that year. She would work part-time as a consultant for two more years before leaving the industry entirely in 1998. It was good timing, she later told me: right before the dot-com boom rendered companies like Aristocrat Inc. irrelevant. "It was the beginning of a different era," she said.

Both my parents were an integral part of the immigrant labor force in the technology industry, but they worked in entirely different parts of Silicon Valley—my father in the more genteel, privileged, and intellectual sector that is typically conjured when thinking about the technology industry; my mother in a rougher, more brutal, and less visible line of work. Luong, on the other hand, did not formally operate in any sector at all but rather in the merciless, dark underbelly of Silicon Valley that is little known to this day. This stratification of Asian Americans along class and ethnic lines continues to abide in the Bay Area and in the United States, where they are the most economically divided of any racial group.

Even knowing this, I was surprised—though I shouldn't have been—to hear that the underbelly Luong was a part of still exists. In 2011, fifteen robbers stole more than $37 million worth of computer chips from Unigen, the largest chip robbery in the history of the business, and a sum almost twice as large as the biggest bank heist in American history. It was the same company whose owner, Paul Heng, had been ambushed in his car in 1995. When I started reporting this story, my mother urged me to speak to him, and he told me that the very first time he had a gun put to his head was in 1988, even before he started Unigen, when the electronics broker he was working for was robbed. Since Unigen's founding, in 1991, Heng's company has been robbed more than six times, most recently in July of 2019. Still, he said, the 1995 incident (the same year that Aristocrat Inc. was robbed) was the most terrifying. When I asked him if he was ever deterred by the robberies, he said no. "Either you go small and quit, or you grow bigger," he said.

12.

On April 9, 1996, a federal grand jury issued a six-count indictment charging John That Luong with racketeering, RICO conspiracy, conspiracy to interfere with commerce by threats or violence, and conspiracy to distribute heroin. (RICO, or the Racketeer Influenced and Corrupt Organizations Act, was originally created to go after mobs and has since become the prosecution of choice against any form of organized crime.) The court trials were long and drawn out, and Luong did not receive his sentence until 2010: life in prison plus eighty years. For the alien smuggling case, he was sentenced to forty-five months in prison in 1998. He faced a separate indictment for laundering money and stolen cars.

My mother, for her part, does not know John That Luong's name. Nor is she familiar with the intricacies of the Company or of the FBI operation that led to his capture. Luong was just one leader among several gangs that stole and trafficked computer chips, and my mom was but one small-business owner among hundreds whose companies were robbed. He was no El Chapo, and she was no Sheryl Sandberg. But it was in part because she was also an Asian immigrant that Aristocrat Inc. became one of Luong's targets.

Kingman Wong, the FBI agent who supervised Operation Bytes Dust, told me that Asian criminals targeted Asian-run companies because they saw the commonality as an advantage. They were more likely to share a language, and the gangs often knew people who worked at these companies—it made their jobs easier. At one point during our conversations, my mother offhandedly told me that the son of a Chinese nanny that babysat me back in 1992 had been part of the gang that robbed a company called Wintec Industries in 1998, during which one of the employees was shot and killed. What I infer from this is that when immigrants prey on their own, they assume the consequences will be less dire or even nonexistent. Though Luong ultimately received a severe punishment for his crimes, most of the reporting about these computer chip robberies has been buried. If these crimes had been perpetrated against white people, would they have been covered and remembered differently?

13.

The neighborhood my parents live in now is quiet and bosky, with multistory houses shielded by tall deciduous trees that turn red and gold in the fall. Their house is on a cul-de-sac at the end of a windy, hilly road. A majority of their neighbors have been there as long as, if not longer than they have. Many of them are part of the old guard of tech, like the man two doors down who was a marketing manager at Apple in the early eighties; he later started the ad agency that created an early iteration of the eBay logo. When my parents moved to this house, so that Luong's people would not be able to find them, their address was unsearchable on Google Maps. The trick was that you had to use MapQuest—that was the only way to route yourself to their house.

The day we drove to the old headquarters of Aristocrat Inc. in Sunnyvale was the first time my mom had been back to her old office in two decades—and mine too. When my mom described her working days to me before, I'd had a hard time picturing the place where the robbery had gone down, but upon pulling into the parking lot, I suddenly remembered I'd been here before. In my mind's eye I could see the room where all the office workers sat, desks parallel to one another. That room opened up into an expansive, high-ceilinged warehouse, with cold concrete floors and tall metal shelves filled with boxes. I remember how delighted I was when I got to visit my mother at her workplace, mystified by the abundance of packing peanuts and the seemingly endless rolls of pink bubble wrap, which I'd pull out and pop one by one. In that office, I had perceived a magical, grown-up world full of office accoutrements like staplers and mini-receipt-printers and large plastic calculators whose buttons clacked when you pressed them.

At the time I had seen only the surface of things. I was too young to understand the kinds of rigors and tribulations my mom was facing. Back then and for a long time thereafter, she'd just been my mom, who'd worked for a while, and then stopped, and that was it. But part of becoming an adult is beginning to see your parents as distinct and separate humans, and as this story unraveled, my mom slowly began to appear differently to me. I'd always admired her, but now I felt a kind of awe.

My mother seemed indifferent to the sight of her old office; if she felt otherwise, she did not show it. Maybe she'd never had a sentimental attachment, or else it had waned, and now the place just represented a bounded time in her life that had come and gone. She stayed in the car with my baby—her grandson—as I stepped out and looked around. A couple of bespectacled workers in their late twenties or early thirties, both women, walked by me, plastic bags in hand—they must have gotten burritos or Nepalese momos from the food trucks nearby. The entire complex looked like a relic of the nineties, much of its facade and coloring unchanged. "It looks about the same," said my mom.

The Atlantic

In this 12,000-word essay that, in the words of the National Magazine Awards judges, "never falters," Clint Smith visits Germany to explore what he terms "questions of public memory—specifically how people, communities, and nations should account for the crimes of their past." His goal: to understand what the United States can learn from Germany's memorialization of the Holocaust as this nation reckons with the legacy of slavery. A staff writer at The Atlantic, Smith is the author of a new collection of poetry, Above Ground, and the New York Times best-seller How the Word Is Passed: A Reckoning with the History of Slavery Across America. The Atlantic was nominated for five National Magazine Awards this year, accomplishing the rare feat of winning the award for General Excellence two years in a row.

Clint Smith

Monuments to
the Unthinkable

The first memorials to the Holocaust were the bodies in concentration camps.

In January 1945, Soviet forces liberated Auschwitz, in southern Poland. As the German forces retreated, officers at Buchenwald, a camp in central Germany, crammed 4,480 prisoners into some forty railcars in an effort to hide them from the Allies. They sent the train south to yet another camp: Dachau. Only a fifth of the prisoners survived the three-week journey.

When Dachau was liberated in April and American forces came upon the railcars near the camp, they found corpses packed on top of one another. Soldiers turned their heads and covered their noses as the sight and smell of the bodies washed over them. They vomited; they cried.

Dachau was about ten miles northwest of Munich and was the first concentration camp built by the Nazi regime. It had operated as a training center for SS guards and served as the prototype for other camps. Its prisoners were subjected to hard labor, corporal punishment, and torturous medical experiments. They were given barely any food. They died from disease and malnutrition, or they were executed. In Dachau's twelve years of existence, approximately 41,500 people had been killed there and in its subcamps. Many were burned in the crematorium or buried, but thousands of corpses remained aboveground.

The American soldiers wondered how this could have happened. How thousands of people could have been held captive, tortured, and killed at the camp while just outside its walls was a small town where people were going about their lives as if impervious to the depravity taking place inside. Buying groceries, playing soccer with their children, drinking coffee with their neighbors. German people, the Americans reasoned, should have to see what had been done in their name.

And so the soldiers brought a group of about thirty local officials to the camp. When they arrived on that spring day, they saw piles of bodies, mountains of rotting flesh. They also saw thousands of emaciated survivors emerging from the barracks— "walking skeletons," as many soldiers described them, barely holding on to life. Later, American soldiers ordered farmers and local residents who were members of the Nazi party to bury some 5,000 corpses. This is how they were made to bear witness. This is how they were made to remember.

The mass burial was one of the first acts of constructing public memory in a country that has been navigating questions of how to properly remember the Holocaust ever since.

Today, Dachau is a memorial to the evil that once transpired there. Before the pandemic, almost 900,000 people visited every year from all over the world, including many German students. Visitors see the crematorium where bodies were burned, where the smell of smoldering flesh filled the air, where smoke rose through the chimney and lost itself in the sky. They are made to confront what happened, and they realize that it happened not so long ago.

Questions of public memory—specifically how people, communities, and nations should account for the crimes of their past— are deeply interesting to me. Last year I wrote a book, *How the Word Is Passed*, about how different historical sites across the United States reckon with or fail to reckon with their relationship to slavery. As I traveled across the country visiting these places, I found lapses and distortions that would have been shocking if they weren't so depressingly familiar: a cemetery where the Confederate dead are revered as heroes; a maximum-security prison built on top of a former plantation, where prisoners were once tasked with building the deathbed upon which executions would take place; a former plantation where Black employees were once made to dress as enslaved people and give tours to white visitors.

During my travels I often thought of Germany, which is frequently held up as an exemplar of responsible public memory. From afar, it seemed that the Germans were doing a much better job than we were at confronting the past. But the more I invoked Germany, the less comfortable I felt drawing comparisons between America and a place I barely knew. So over the past year I made two trips to Germany, traveling to Berlin and to Dachau, visiting sites that only eight decades ago were instrumental to an industrialized slaughter of human beings unlike any the world had ever seen. I learned that the way the country remembers this genocide is the subject of ongoing debate—a debate that is highly relevant to fights about public memory taking place in the United States.

In recent years, Americans have seen a shift in our understanding of the country's history; many now acknowledge the shameful episodes of our past alongside all that there is to be proud of. But reactionary forces today are working with ever-greater fervor to prevent such an honest accounting from taking place. State legislatures across the country are attempting to prevent schools from teaching the very history that explains why our country looks the way it does. School boards are banning books that provide historical perspectives students might not otherwise encounter.

Many of these efforts are carried out in the name of "protecting" children, of preventing white people from feeling a sense of guilt. But America will never be the country it wants to be until it properly remembers what it did (and does) to Black people. This is why I went looking for lessons in Germany. Sometimes, I found, these lessons are elusive. Sometimes they're not.

I saw that Germany's effort to memorialize its past is not a project with a specific end point. Some people I spoke with believe the country has done enough; others believe it never can. Comparisons to the United States are helpful but also limited.

Soon, those who survived the Holocaust will no longer be with us. How will their stories be told once they are gone? Germans are still trying to figure out how to tell the story of what their country did and simultaneously trying to figure out who should tell it.

•　　　•　　　•

On a cool October morning, I walked with Frédéric Brenner to Gleis 17, or track 17, of Berlin's Grunewald station, the primary train platform from which Jews in Berlin were sent to the camps in Eastern Europe.

Brenner, a photographer known for his portraits of Jewish communities, has spent more than forty years traveling the world to document the Jewish diaspora and a few years ago settled in Berlin with his wife, Hetty Berg, a Dutch woman who now serves as the director of the city's Jewish museum.

Originally, Brenner told me, he had not wanted to come to Germany at all. Many of his relatives had been killed by the Nazis. Brenner grew up in France in the years after the Holocaust. "I was raised that we don't go to Germany, we don't buy German, and we don't speak German," he said.

Yet he was also intrigued by the idea of returning to a country his family had been forced to flee, of not allowing that trauma to exert control over him. It had not been easy. "My father will not come and see me here," he said. His father's father had been one of six siblings, and only three survived the Holocaust. Brenner placed his hands in his pockets and shook his head, almost in disbelief at himself. "I never thought I would come back." In a 2021 exhibition and accompanying book called *Zerheilt: Healed to Pieces*, Brenner used Berlin as a setting to explore Jewish life.

The houses in Grunewald, the neighborhood where we were walking, were large and elegant, with enormous windows that invited in the sun. "These are the homes the Jews were taken from," Brenner told me. Men, women, and children had been forced to march down these streets to the train platform and sent to their death. Most of them were made to pay for their own "tickets."

As we approached the station, we saw a concrete wall etched with silhouettes—a monument to the people who had been deported, designed by the Polish artist Karol Broniatowski and unveiled in 1991.

I walked past the monument and up onto the Gleis 17 platform. I looked down. Lining the tracks were steel plates. Each one had the date of a train's departure, the number of Jewish people on board, and the camp they were sent to. I walked up to the edge of one section and read the date: 1.3.1943.

Next to the date I saw "36 JUDEN," meaning that thirty-six Jews had been deported on that day. Next to the number, the steel plate read "Berlin—Auschwitz." I tried to imagine those people—maybe eight or nine families—handing over their tickets, being shuffled into the cars, and listening as the heavy doors shut behind them.

I looked down again and used my foot to sweep aside a leaf; I realized that I hadn't seen the full number. It wasn't 36 Jews. It was 1,736 Jews.

I stood there and looked at the numbers carved into the plates on either side of me. 1758 JUDEN were deported the next day. 1000 JUDEN had been deported just a few days prior.

I tried to do the math in my head as my feet followed the chronology beneath them. But there were 186 steel plates, and as the numbers reflecting each day's human cargo rose and fell—ranging from a few dozen to a few hundred to more than 1,000—it became impossible.

The platform stretched off into the distance in both directions. I craned my neck over the edge and looked down at the train tracks, their weathered steel stained with spots of brown rust. To the right, the tracks were visible until the rail line curved and disappeared into the forest. To the left, the tracks were partially buried beneath a cluster of trees whose thin trunks arched upward into an orange-and-yellow canopy. The trees' presence was intentional. The trunks growing between the tracks were there to say: No more trains will ever pass here.

This memorial, designed by the architects Nikolaus Hirsch, Wolfgang Lorch, and Andrea Wandel, opened to the public on January 27, 1998: Holocaust Remembrance Day.

I asked Brenner what he felt when standing on this platform and seeing these dates, these numbers, these words. He paused and looked around at the trees above us, his eyes moving slowly back and forth, as if he were searching for the answer in the leaves. "I cannot process it. My mind cannot process it. And obviously"—he wiped at his eyes—"my body *can* process it."

Unfortunately, Brenner said, his experience at Holocaust-memorial sites wasn't always like this. He asked me if I had been to Auschwitz, in Poland. I hadn't. "Don't go there," he said, shaking his head. "People are all with their phones. It should be prevented. And they go"—he raised his hand a few feet from his face and looked at his palm, emulating someone taking a selfie—" 'Me in front of the crematorium.' 'Me in front of the ramp.' I mean, it's so obscene."

I walked to the end of the platform to read the final plate. The last train on record left Berlin on March 27, 1945. Eighteen Jewish passengers were sent to Theresienstadt, a concentration camp in what is now the Czech Republic. Auschwitz had already been liberated by the Soviets by then; a week later, Ohrdruf, a subcamp of Buchenwald, became the first camp liberated by U.S. soldiers. The Germans were in retreat. Dachau would be liberated within weeks. The war in Europe was nearly over. Those eighteen people had been so close to avoiding deportation. I wondered whether they had survived.

After Brenner left, I sat down on the platform and let my legs dangle over its edge. Small blue wildflowers sprouted from the cracks in the wooden railroad ties below. From 1941 to 1945, 50,000 people were sent on these tracks to death camps and ghettos farther east. I closed my eyes and pictured soldiers yelling. Children crying. Bodies tussling. Suitcases rattling. I wondered how much the deportees knew about where they were headed when they got on those trains. I wondered how many days they spent inside those railcars. I wondered if they were able to sleep. I thought of my own children. What would I have told them about where we were going? How would I have assuaged their fear? How would I have assuaged my own?

•   •   •

The first time I saw a Stolperstein, I almost walked past without noticing. I was heading back to my hotel after getting some tea at a café, and there they were, two of them. Small, golden cubes laid into a cobblestone sidewalk. They sat adjacent to each other outside what looked like an office building, or maybe a bank. I stepped closer to read what was written on each of them:

HIER WOHNTE
HELMUT HIMPEL
JG. 1907
IM WIDERSTAND
VERHAFTET 17.9.42
HINGERICHTET 13.5.1943
BERLIN-PLÖTZENSEE

HIER WOHNTE
MARIA TERWIEL
JG. 1910
IM WIDERSTAND
VERHAFTET 17.9.42
HINGERICHTET 5.8.1943
BERLIN-PLÖTZENSEE

Hier wohnte . . . Here lived . . .

The English translation for *Stolperstein* is "stumbling stone." Each ten-by-ten-centimeter concrete block is covered in a brass plate, with engravings that memorialize someone who was a victim of the Nazis between 1933 and 1945. The name, birth date, and fate of each person are inscribed, and the stones are typically placed in front of their final residence. Most of the Stolpersteine commemorate the lives of Jewish people, but some are dedicated to Sinti and Roma, disabled people, gay people, and other victims of the Holocaust.

In 1996, the German artist Gunter Demnig, whose father fought for Nazi Germany in the war, began illegally placing these stones into the sidewalk of a neighborhood in Berlin. Initially, Demnig's installations received little attention. But after a few months, when authorities discovered the small memorials, they deemed them an obstacle to construction work and attempted to get them removed. The workers tasked with pulling them out refused.

In 2000, Demnig's Stolperstein installations began to be officially sanctioned by local governments. Today, more than 90,000 stumbling stones have been set into the streets and sidewalks of thirty European countries. Together, they make up the largest decentralized memorial in the world.

Demnig, now seventy-five, spends much of his time on the road, personally installing most of the stones. Since 2005, the sculptor Michael Friedrichs-Friedländer has made the stones. Mass-manufacturing them would feel akin to the mechanized way that the Nazis killed so many millions of people, Demnig and Friedrichs-Friedländer say, so each one is engraved by hand.

I felt drawn to the Stolpersteine, compelled by the work Demnig was trying to do with them and overwhelmed by how much they captured in such a small space.

The next day I met Barbara Steiner in the city's Charlottenburg-Wilmersdorf district. The neighborhood's narrow streets were lined with five- and six-story buildings whose balconies stretched out over the cobblestone sidewalks. People bundled in coats whizzed past us on bicycles.

Steiner, a convert to Judaism, is a historian and therapist. She has short, jet-black hair. She wore a sky-blue coat and small gold earrings that gleamed when they caught the sun.

"I have a twelve-year-old daughter," Steiner told me as we walked toward a Stolperstein a few meters away, "and whenever we walk in the streets, we stop." She looked down at the engraved brass in front of us. "She really wants to read every stone."

"They mean more than those huge things," Steiner said, stretching her arms wide above her head. "I think the huge monuments are always about performing memory, when this is really connected to a person." Steiner likes that you see the names of specific people. She likes that the stones are installed directly in front of the place these individuals once called home. "You can start to think, *How would it have looked for them to live here?*"

Stolpersteine are largely local initiatives, laid because a family or residents of an apartment complex or neighborhood got together and decided they wanted to commemorate the people who had once lived there. Steiner said that students at her daughter's school had begun researching the building across the street from the school and discovered that a number of Jewish families had lived there. Then they applied to have Stolpersteine installed.

Demnig has said that this is the most meaningful aspect of the project for him. He believes that for children and adults alike, six million is too abstract a number, and individual stories are more powerful tools than statistics for coming to terms with this history. "Sometimes you need just one fate," he has said, to start thinking about how someone's life relates to your own: maybe they lived on your street or were the same age you are now when they were murdered. "Those are the moments I know they will go home as different people." Each stone creates its own unofficial ambassadors of memory.

Steiner and I walked a bit farther down the street. She stopped in front of a beige building with a large white archway above a brown door. "I lived here," she said. I looked at the door, then looked down. Five stumbling stones lay together among the cobblestones, their brass faces shimmering. Steiner translated them into English for me:

Max Zuttermann. Born 1868.
Deported October 18, 1941.
Murdered January 15, 1942.

Gertrud Zuttermann. Born 1876.
Deported October 18, 1941.
Murdered December 20, 1941.

Fritz Hirschfeldt. Born 1902.
Deported October 18, 1941.
Murdered May 8, 1942.

Else Noah. Born 1873.
Deported July 17, 1942.
Murdered March 14, 1944.

> Frieda Loewy. Born 1889.
> humiliated/disenfranchised.
> Died by suicide June 2, 1942.

I did the math to estimate how old they might have been when they died: Max Zuttermann, 74. Gertrud Zuttermann, 65. Fritz Hirschfeldt, 40. Else Noah, 71. Frieda Loewy, 53.

I glanced at Steiner; she was still looking down at the stones, her hands in her coat pockets, her legs crossed at her ankles.

I thought about what it must be like to live in a home where you walk past these stones and these names every day. I imagined what it might be like if we had something commensurate in the United States. If, in front of homes, restaurants, office buildings, churches, and schools there were stones to mark where and when enslaved people had been held, sold, killed. I shared this thought with Steiner. "The streets would be packed," she said.

She was right. I imagined New Orleans, my hometown, once the busiest slave market in the country, and how entire streets would be covered in brass stones—whole neighborhoods paved with reminders of what had happened. New Orleans is, today, at a very different place in its reckoning with the past; it has only recently been focused on removing its homages to enslavers. Over the past few years, the statues of Confederate leaders I grew up seeing have been removed from their pedestals, and streets named after slaveholders have been renamed for local Black artists and intellectuals. My own middle school has a new name as well. As I looked at the stumbling stones beneath me in Berlin, I wondered if there might be a future for them on the streets I rode my bike on growing up.

I asked Steiner how it felt to have these stones here, in front of what was once her home. "My daughter now reads these names and asks herself, *Could this be me?*" she said. "But what I like is to stand here and think about them, how they might have lived here."

As I looked at the house, I began to imagine who these people could have been. Perhaps Max and Gertrud were married; I pictured them making Shabbat dinner for their adult children on Friday evenings. Perhaps Fritz helped them with their groceries as they made their way up the stairs. Maybe they spoke about what the Zuttermanns planned on cooking, whether they would see one another at synagogue on Saturday. Perhaps Max and Gertrud invited Fritz to join them for their meal. Perhaps they invited Else and Frieda too. Maybe they all sat around the table. Perhaps they laughed. Perhaps they sang. Perhaps they played a game of cards to end the evening. Perhaps, as wax began to collect at the bottom of the small plates that held the candles, they discussed the new laws that were restricting their lives, the rumors of war. Perhaps they asked one another whether they still had time to leave. (I later learned that Max and Gertrud were in fact married, and that Fritz was their subtenant. The Zuttermanns' two adult daughters, I found, had been able to escape Germany.)

My eyes moved from the building we stood in front of to the buildings adjacent to it. When German Jews were led to the trains for deportation, the block would have been lined with other Germans who watched from their windows, their storefronts, the sidewalk. Maybe some cheered. Most probably said nothing.

Steiner saw me looking at these other buildings and must have realized what I was thinking about. "There's the relational aspect," she said. "It was their neighbors that had been murdered. It was their neighbors that had been deported. It was their neighbors that had been thrown out to Auschwitz. It was their neighbors who lost their lives. And we need to understand this. It was not an abstract group."

·   ·   ·

So many of Germany's monuments, I was learning, were not built until long after the war. The first Stolperstein was laid in 1996. The Gleis 17 memorial opened in 1998. The Jewish Museum Berlin opened in 2001. The Memorial to the Murdered Jews of Europe, in Berlin, opened in 2005.

When Steiner was a child, the country's major sites of memory about the Holocaust were the concentration camps. Her parents had taken her to Dachau when she was very young. She was left haunted and terrified by the experience.

I asked if she had taken her daughter to any camps. She shook her head and told me she thought that, at twelve, she was still too young. They had considered going to Auschwitz in the summer, but Steiner had changed her mind, ultimately deciding it wasn't yet time. Her daughter had read about the Holocaust, and it seemed to have overwhelmed her. She struggled to sleep. "She was worried that if she fell asleep, she might not wake up," Steiner told me.

Anti-Semitism and racism have been on the rise in Germany in recent years as the right-wing populist party Alternative für Deutschland (AfD) has gained political power; the German government recently reported a 29 percent increase in anti-Semitic crimes. Steiner shared a story about how, on one recent Holocaust Memorial Day, two boys at her daughter's school had pretended to "hunt" her daughter as they chased her through the hallways.

"She was . . . hunted by them?" I asked, wanting to make sure I had heard correctly.

"Yes, she was hunted by them." Then, in a singsongy voice meant to emulate the melody of a nursery rhyme, she said what the boys had said to her daughter: "My grandfather was Adolf Hitler and he killed your grandfather."

I put my hands in my pockets and took a deep breath.

"This is everyday Jewish life for children," she said. "If you raise a Jewish child, how can you avoid this topic?"

Steiner's question echoed the question that Black parents in the U.S. wrestle with every day. How can we protect our children from the stories of violence that they might find deeply upsetting while also giving them the history to understand who they are in relation to the world that surrounds them? My son is five years old; my daughter is three. I think about what it means to strike that balance all the time.

I mentioned this to Steiner, and she nodded then looked back down at the stones in front of us. "I wonder what it's like, because when you're Black in America, at least there are more of you who could connect and support each other. There are so few Jews."

This point—this difference—had become clear to me in my first few days in Germany. In the United States there are 41 million Black people; we make up 12.5 percent of the population. In

Germany, there are approximately 120,000 Jewish people, out of a population of more than 80 million. They represent less than a quarter of 1 percent of the population. More Jewish people live in Boston than in all of Germany. (Today, many Jews in Germany are immigrants from the former Soviet Union and their descendants.) Lots of Germans do not personally know a Jewish person.

This is part of the reason, Steiner believes, that Germany is able to make Holocaust remembrance a prominent part of national life; Jewish people are a historical abstraction more than they are actual people. In the United States, there are still millions of Black people. You cannot simply build some monuments, lay down some wreaths each year, and apologize for what happened without seeing the manifestation of those past actions in the inequality between Black and white people all around you.

Steiner also believes that the small number of Jewish people who do reside in Germany exist in the collective imagination less as people and more as empty canvases upon which Germans can paint their repentance. As the scholar James E. Young, the author of *The Texture of Memory: Holocaust Memorials and Meaning*, writes, "The initial impulse to memorialize events like the Holocaust may actually spring from an opposite and equal desire to forget them." The American Jewish writer Dara Horn puts it more bluntly in her book *People Love Dead Jews*, writing that in our contemporary world, most people "only encountered dead Jews: people whose sole attribute was that they had been murdered, and whose murders served a clear purpose, which was *to teach us something*. Jews were people who, for moral and educational purposes, were supposed to be dead."

Steiner and I continued walking. Before, I had seen stumbling stones only intermittently; now I saw them in front of almost every building. Three here. Six there. Eight here. Twelve there. When we encountered a group of a dozen or more stones, we would stop, look down, and read the names as we had done in front of her old home. I saw dates of birth that read *1938, 1940, 1941*. These were children—a five-year-old, a four-year-old, a two-year-old.

A blackbird landed near the brass plates, jabbing its beak into the spaces between the cobblestones with quick, jerking movements. A little girl walked by and pointed in its direction, turning and saying something to her mother as she held her hand.

．　　．　　．

The Memorial to the Murdered Jews of Europe, recognized as the official Holocaust memorial of Germany, sits in the center of downtown Berlin, just south of the famous Brandenburg Gate and a block away from the site of the bunker where Hitler died by suicide. Designed by the American Jewish architect Peter Eisenman and spanning 200,000 square feet, it consists of rows of 2,711 concrete blocks that range in height from eight inches to more than fifteen feet tall. The space resembles a graveyard, a vast cascade of stone markers with no names or engravings on their facade. The ground beneath them dips and rises like waves.

The memorial is significant not only for its size and location—the equivalent, in the United States, would be the placement of thousands of stone blocks in Lower Manhattan to honor those subjected to chattel slavery or on Constitution Avenue in Washington, DC, to remember the victims of Indigenous genocide—but also because it was constructed with the political support and full financial backing of the German government.

Steiner told me that, in her opinion, the stumbling stones are a much better means of memorialization than something like the Memorial to the Murdered Jews of Europe. "This has more to do with the German society and the expectation of having something big," she said, stretching her hands out again. "We did a big Holocaust, we have a big monument."

Steiner said that whenever she went down to the memorial, she saw people smoking while standing on top of the columns, or jumping back and forth from one to another. "It's lost its purpose and meaning," she said. "Maybe it never got it."

When I visited the memorial, the sky was overcast, its long sweep of endless gray matching the color of the stone columns beneath it. A group of young people took selfies in front of the columns, some throwing up peace signs or puckering their lips as they sat cross-legged on top of a stone. Two women stood in between the shadows, their faces covered in tears, and held each other's hands. A class of students looked up at their teacher as he explained what lay behind him, their eyes moving from him to the columns to one another with a silent solemnity. Three small children played hide-and-seek among the columns, shrieking in delight when they discovered one another. The memorial had become a part of the city's landscape; different people engaged with the space in different ways.

I wondered, as I toured the monument, how much of the motivation to create memorials to the Holocaust reflected a desire for Germany to—internally—reckon with its heinous state-sanctioned crimes and how much of it stemmed from a hope that putting memorials up would demonstrate to the rest of the world that Germany had accounted for its past? Put more directly, were monuments like this one for Germans to collectively remember what had been done? Were they a performance of contrition for the rest of the world? Were they both?

James E. Young writes that "memory is never shaped in a vacuum" and that the reasons for the existence of Holocaust museums and monuments in Germany and across the world "are as various as the sites themselves." Some, he argues, were built in response to efforts of Jewish communities to remember, and others were built because of "a government's need to explain a nation's past to itself." The aim of some is to educate the next generation and forge a sense of collective experience, while others are born of guilt. "Still others are intended to attract tourists." The messy truth is that all of these ostensibly disparate motives can find a home in the same project.

●　　　●　　　●

At the edge of the Memorial to the Murdered Jews of Europe, I met up with Deidre Berger, the chair of the executive board of the Jewish Digital Cultural Recovery Project Foundation and the former director of the American Jewish Committee's Berlin office. She was bundled in an all-black ensemble—jacket, shoes, scarf, and gloves—that matched her short black hair. Berger is American and Jewish. She has lived in Berlin since 1998.

We discussed the differences in the ways the Holocaust is memorialized in the United States versus in Germany, which she called "enormous." In the United States, she said, the push for Holocaust remembrance has come largely from Holocaust survivors themselves, as well as their descendants.

In Germany, after the war hardly any Jews were left—only 37,000 in the entire country in 1950—and the push to create a national Holocaust memorial came largely from non-Jewish communities, many years later.

The idea "came from within German society," Berger said, but there had been, in previous decades, "perhaps some gentle pushing from other countries that felt that it was important for Germany to have a visible symbol of marking the Holocaust." Notably, the German word for guilt, *schuld*, is the same as the word for debt.

It wasn't always obvious that Germany would build memorials to the Nazis' victims; for decades there was mostly silence. In her book *Learning from the Germans*, the philosopher Susan Neiman writes that families in Germany simply did not discuss the war in the years immediately following it. "Neither side could bear to talk about it," she writes, "one side afraid of facing its own guilt, the other afraid of succumbing to pain and rage."

When twenty-two of the Third Reich's leaders stood trial in Nuremberg, from November 1945 to October 1946, the four major Allied powers vowed to publicize the proceedings. Officials in the American zone put up billboards and posters with photographs depicting Nazi crimes, had films made that documented the gruesomeness of the concentration camps, and ensured that German newspapers and radio stations reported on the trial. The Allies hoped that the public nature of the trials and the extensive documentation presented would help educate Germans about the true scope and horror of what the Nazis had done. According to the military historian Tyler Bamford, in the final month of the tribunal, 71 percent of Germans surveyed by American authorities said that they had learned something new from it.

But awareness did not necessarily translate into reckoning. For some, even those who had supported Hitler, Nuremberg provided the opportunity to wash their hands of culpability and pin responsibility only on the Nazi leaders on trial. When confronted with the Nazis' atrocities, many Germans repeated the phrase *"Wir konnten nichts tun"*—"We could do nothing." In the years after the trial, former Nazi officials rejoined mainstream society, and many took on positions similar to those they'd held before the war.

Neiman writes that in those postwar years, many Germans saw themselves not as perpetrators but as victims—as people who had experienced enormous suffering that wasn't being acknowledged by the rest of the world. Husbands, sons, and brothers had died in battle; women and children had spent long, freezing nights in cellars as bombs dropped overhead; civilians survived on scraps of potato peels. Not only were they being asked to accept having lost the war, but they were being told, amid all their hardship, that they were responsible for evil. The German psychoanalysts Alexander and Margarete Mitscherlich write in their book, *The Inability to Mourn*, that the nation experienced a sort of paralysis, in which people couldn't countenance their soldiers moving so quickly from heroes to victims to perpetrators. If they couldn't even mourn their sons and brothers because the world was telling them they were monsters, how could they bring themselves to mourn the people those soldiers had killed?

"There wasn't really a confrontation until the sixties, when the young generation started asking their parents what they did during the war," Berger told me. They wanted to know what had happened in their community—and their country—and why there was so much silence. Germans, Berger said, many of them the children of those who had witnessed or participated in the Holocaust, began tracing Jewish histories, inviting Jewish families who had fled to come back to visit their towns.

As Berger and I spoke, I wondered about the people leading the various museums, memorials, and other cultural institutions that had resulted from this push in the decades since the sixties. How many of them were Jewish? Did it matter?

I had heard that Germans would sometimes create events, commissions, and institutions centered on commemorating Jewish life without meaningfully consulting any Jewish people. Berger closed her eyes and nodded when I mentioned this and said that it had been a major issue for years. She told me about how, in 2009 and 2015, the German Parliament had created independent commissions on fighting anti-Semitism. The 2009 commission included only a single Jewish person. The 2015 commission, at first, had no Jewish members at all. Berger found this unacceptable, so she approached officials in the Interior Ministry. She was appalled by the response she got. "They said, 'Well, Jews are not impartial enough because they're part of the story.'" (Two Jewish members were eventually added to the eight-person committee, bringing its total to ten.) She tucked her lips inside her mouth as if she was preventing herself from saying something she would regret.

I was struck by how much this idea echoed what Black scholars in the United States have navigated for generations. The preeminent early-twentieth-century Black American scholar W. E. B. Du Bois faced questions from white scholars and funders who doubted his ability to do his work objectively and with the appropriate level of scientific rigor because they thought he was too invested in the issues he was studying. He was often encouraged to partner with white scholars, who could balance out his ostensible biases.

When I asked Berger what she thought of the Stolpersteine, she told me she feels ambivalent. On the one hand, she said, the project has brought communities together to research their history. But on the other hand, she finds the idea that people are stepping on the names of Jewish people deeply unsettling. "Every time, I cringe," she said. "They should be plaques on the wall. And why aren't they? Because most of the owners of buildings wouldn't accept, even to this day, a plaque saying, 'Here is where a Jewish family lived.'"

Berger is not alone in this sentiment. In Munich, Charlotte Knobloch, a Holocaust survivor who is the former president of the Central Council of Jews in Germany, persuaded the city to ban Stolpersteine in 2004. The city eventually created plaques at eye level. "It is my firm belief that we need to do everything we can in order to make sure that remembrance preserves the dignity of the victims," Knobloch has said. "People murdered in the Holocaust deserve better than a plaque in the dust, street dirt, and even worse filth."

Berger also believes that sometimes the laying of the stones can serve as a sort of penance: after a Stolperstein has been placed, people wipe their hands and believe that they have done all there is to do.

Even though Berger and the American Jewish Committee had, for years, been some of the most prominent advocates for the memorial where we now stood, she also has mixed feelings about how the space turned out. "It's overwhelming. And the symbolism isn't entirely clear to me. I mean, we don't need to have a cemetery," she said, looking around at the stones. "The whole country is a cemetery."

But Berger says she is grateful—and relieved—that the space exists.

Eisenman, the architect who designed the memorial, was cognizant of how difficult—perhaps impossible—it would be to create a Holocaust memorial commensurate with the history it carries. "The enormity and horror of the Holocaust are such that any attempt to represent it by traditional means is inevitably inadequate," he wrote in 2005.

Criticism of the monument has come in many forms. In 2017, a leader of the far-right AfD party said that the monument was a "symbol of national shame"; he didn't think that shame was a good thing. On the other end of the ideological spectrum, some critics have charged that the memorial isn't inclusive enough. Demnig, the originator of the Stolperstein project, supports the memorial as a whole, but has been critical of its exclusive focus on Jewish victims. "There were other drafts that would have included all groups of victims that, in my opinion, would have been more effective," he said in 2013.

The *New Yorker* writer Richard Brody visited the monument in 2012 and took issue with the very framing of the memorial: "The title doesn't say 'Holocaust' or 'Shoah'; in other words, it doesn't say anything about who did the murdering or why—there's nothing along the lines of 'by Germany under Hitler's regime,' and the vagueness is disturbing," he wrote. "The passive voice of the title—'murdered Jews'—elides the question that wafts through the exhibit like an odor: murdered by whom?"

I understand some of these criticisms, and still, I couldn't help but appreciate the scale and scope of the space. I couldn't help but admire how centrally located it was in the city. There was no missing it. There was no avoiding it. No other nation on Earth has done anything quite like it. Not the United States for its genocide of Indigenous peoples or centuries of enslavement; not France or Britain for their histories of colonial violence; not Japan for its imperial projects across eastern Asia.

Walking through the monument's columns amid the cacophony of the city all around me felt haunting, but appropriately so. It is a space meant to haunt, meant to overwhelm. But beneath the stones, in the memorial's underground museum, there was only silence.

I stepped into one of the subterranean exhibits. The room was dark but for illuminated glass panels underfoot. Other visitors moved through the space like shadows, each of us silent, looking down at the glowing glass beneath us. Below each pane were letters, diary entries, and accounts written by people who had been murdered in the Holocaust. I leaned in closer to the panel I was looking at.

There was a note written by a twelve-year-old girl named Judith Wishnyatskaya, included as a postscript to a letter her mother had written to her father on July 31, 1942:

> Dear father! I am saying goodbye to you before I die. We would so love to live, but they won't let us and we will die. I am so scared of this death, because the small children are thrown alive into the pit. Goodbye forever. I kiss you tenderly.
> Yours J.

Judith and her mother were killed shortly afterward. Their letter was found by a Soviet soldier near the eastern Polish town of Baranowicze (in what is now Belarus).

Each panel told the story of another victim, the floor glowing with accounts of murder and terror, a fluorescent extension of the work the stumbling stones were doing throughout the city. There was something about the physical act of looking down, of having your body pause and hover over the names, that made the experience feel somehow intimate.

After reading all of the panels, I took a seat on a bench toward the back of the room. In front of me and to my left and right and then behind me, I saw numbers with the names of different European countries alongside them. I quickly realized that these numbers reflected estimates of how many Jews from each nation had been killed in the Holocaust.

Belgium 25,000–25,700
Hungary 270,000–300,000
Greece 58,900–59,200
Latvia 65,000–70,000
Italy 7,600–8,500
Lithuania 140,000–150,000
Germany 160,000–165,000
Poland 2,900,000–3,100,000

I stopped at this last number and caught my breath. I hadn't known that half of the 6 million Jews killed in the Holocaust were Polish. (Ninety percent of Jews in Nazi-occupied Poland were murdered, I would later learn.) By the end of the war, only 380,000 Polish Jews survived.

In school, I read more books about the Holocaust than perhaps any other atrocity in human history, including those that took place on American soil. I have watched countless films and documentaries on World War II and the Holocaust. But it wasn't until this moment, surrounded by these numbers that stretched around the room and the stories that glowed underfoot, that I began to fully feel the scale of this atrocity.

Approximately two-thirds of all the Jews in Europe were killed in the span of just a few years, a level of slaughter that is overwhelming to consider. Something about being there—in Berlin, in this museum, in this room—made it all feel so much more real.

. . .

The next day I met Lea Rosh at a small café in the Güntzelkiez neighborhood of Berlin. Rosh, who is not Jewish, is a former television journalist and was among the first women to manage a public broadcasting service in Germany. Along with the historian Eberhard Jäckel (who was not Jewish either), she spent nearly twenty years pushing for Germany to build a memorial to the Holocaust. Their unrelenting advocacy is widely understood as one of the primary reasons the Memorial to the Murdered Jews of Europe exists at all.

Rosh was eighty-five years old when we met. She is not quite fluent in English, and I don't speak German, so we each spoke slowly, attempting not to miss each other's words. She was accompanied by a man named Olaf, and we discussed her work to bring the memorial to fruition in between bites of cake and fruit.

Rosh said that in the mid-1980s she and Jäckel had begun collaborating on a four-part television documentary about the Holocaust. Jäckel, one of Germany's leading historians of Nazism, told her that Germany needed to build a monument to the Jews killed in the Holocaust. Not just the German Jews but the Jews from all across Europe. "The German victims were 2 percent of the whole," she told me. Her conversations with Jäckel, and the experience of working on the series, were transformative for Rosh.

In 1989, Rosh and Jäckel published a formal call to organize German citizens to help erect a memorial. "I was sure we'd have it in three years because it's so clear to do it," she said as she set her fork down. "It was not clear for this country."

So this became her mission, to make the moral imperative for building a memorial undeniably, inescapably clear. She began a public crusade to pressure the German government, she told me, speaking about the need for a memorial on her television show, and her group took out ads in newspapers and met with political and civic leaders. She said that every Saturday for about eight years, she stood on the street with other advocates, collecting signatures in support of a museum. "If it's raining? Okay. It snowed? Okay. Sunshine? Okay. We stood there."

Rosh said that young people were the most supportive of her efforts. I asked her why that was. Then Olaf raised his eyebrows and said, "The old ones were soldiers in the war."

"People did not want to show we were guilty," Rosh said. "But the Holocaust memorial shows . . ." Olaf completed her thought: "Yes, we were guilty."

Despite the resistance, Rosh and others pressed ahead. Then, in 1999, a decade after she began advocating for it and more than five decades after the event itself, the German Parliament approved the construction of a national Holocaust memorial. It would take another six years to build.

Her work, however, has not been without controversy. Barbara Steiner had told me about how, when Rosh gave a speech at the memorial's opening, she held up a tooth—"a tooth that she found on the ground of a concentration camp." Rosh announced that she planned to have the tooth embedded in the memorial. "Everybody was shocked," Steiner told me. "You don't take something of a murdered person with you." Steiner shook her head, exasperated. (The tooth was not ultimately added to the memorial.)

As I walked through the streets of Berlin, past the Memorial to the Murdered Jews of Europe, past the Jewish Museum, past Gleis 17, past Hitler's bunker, and past the Stolpersteine that are scattered across the streets of the city like stars, I had the feeling of being confronted with the past at every moment. I wondered if I would feel different if I encountered these every day. Would the gleam of the stumbling stones eventually dim and fade into the rest of the pavement? Would the Memorial to the Murdered Jews of Europe become a silhouette in the corner of my eye as I sped by in a taxi?

"I think there's a real risk of all these manifestations becoming either senseless or unreadable, or just part of the city landscape at some point," the German historian Daniel Schönpflug told me. "It creates the feeling that we're doing so well at this, we're world champion of Holocaust memory, and this gives us also legitimacy," he said. "This memory loses its pain, once it's put into an almost positive, proud context."

Was Rosh happy with how the memorial and the museum had turned out? I asked. Did she think that it did justice to the victims?

"It's 6 million murdered people. You cannot be happy," she said, her voice becoming low. "You can [only] be satisfied that it was possible to build them a memorial."

I asked Rosh if she thinks that Germany has done enough to account for its past or if she thinks there is still more to do. She paused and looked up, her eyes searching the ceiling. "Difficult to say, because our memorial is a big memorial. It's the biggest. There's no example in the world for such a thing," she said. She told me that memorials and monuments had been constructed to essentially every group of victims and that Germany had come a long way since she first began her advocacy, almost thirty-five years ago.

"I think you cannot do more. What else?"

· · ·

The memory of Jewish life in Berlin is not singularly tied to the spectacle of mass death. There is a museum that attempts to ensure that German Jews are remembered as a people with a rich culture and not only remembered for what was done to them. At a café in Berlin's Schöneberg neighborhood, I met with Cilly Kugelmann, who was a cofounder and, until her retirement in 2020, the program director of the Jewish Museum Berlin.

Kugelmann compared that institution to the Smithsonian's National Museum of African American History and Culture in the sense that both attempt to tell the story of an oppressed group, without the entirety of their cultural identities being linked to that oppression. Jewish history, Kugelmann said, does not begin and end with the Holocaust.

I was curious what she made of the other memorials and museums across Berlin. "Well, I think one has to ask yourself, what would Germany be without these memorials? You can criticize every single memorial. It's an aesthetic expression and it never comes close to what really happened, so it's always ambiguous. But on the other hand, what would we say if it wouldn't be there at all? It's a dilemma. It's an unsolvable dilemma."

Both of Kugelmann's parents were Jews from Poland. They were married before the war and had two children. In 1943 they were all sent to Auschwitz. Her parents survived, but their first set of children—siblings Kugelmann never knew—were killed.

Her parents didn't talk much, or really at all, about their time in the concentration camps. But Kugelmann told me that once, she was watching a film about the liberation of the camps, and as the camera was scanning across survivors, she saw her father's face.

After the war ended and her parents were liberated, they moved to Frankfurt am Main, where they started a new family. As a child, Kugelmann was aware that she had a pair of siblings who "were no longer there," but she did not have a full sense of what that meant. Had they died? Were they living somewhere else? Would she ever meet them? Her mother wore a silver medallion around her neck with photos of the two children, but she never spoke of them.

It was only many years later that Kugelmann was able to put the pieces together. From the work of the Polish Auschwitz survivor Tadeusz Borowski and others, she learned about the ghetto from which her family had been deported. She learned that all the infants and smaller children from this ghetto, including her siblings, would have been killed immediately upon their arrival at Auschwitz. Even when she discovered this information, she never brought it up with her parents.

I asked Kugelmann why not. Kugelmann placed her tea down and traced her fingers along the edge of the saucer. "You have a sense of what you can ask a parent and what you can't ask a parent. If I try to explain it to people, I refer to rape. The most humiliating thing that can happen. And the question is: Would you be able to question your mother about details of the rape? Of course you would not."

"And for you that feels analogous?" I asked.

"Yes, absolutely."

•   •   •

The House of the Wannsee Conference is a villa about half an hour from the center of Berlin, on a narrow, one-way street just off Wannsee Lake.

Everything about the villa is idyllic. Behind the mansion, a small band of brown ducks dipped their heads into the lake and then returned to the surface, their wet feathers gleaming under the mid-day sun. Sailboats swept across the water while gentle waves lapped against a stone wall on the shore. Wind chimes on a nearby tree sang a chorus in the light breeze.

This was where, on January 20, 1942, the leaders of the Nazi regime discussed and drafted their ideas about how to implement "the final solution of the Jewish question."

Exactly fifty years later, the villa was reopened as a museum. But unlike most of the other sites I visited in Berlin, it was not created to remember the victims of the Holocaust so much as the perpetrators.

Because it's outside the city center, the museum is not the sort of place people just happen to stumble upon. If you end up there, you intended to. As I walked through one of the museum's long hallways, I saw a row of fifteen yellowed pages in a glass case: a copy of the Wannsee Conference's minutes, which in thinly veiled language laid out the plan for the mass murder of European Jews.

As the legal scholar James Q. Whitman has documented, when Nazi officials first formulated their Nuremberg race laws, in 1934, they drew inspiration from the U.S., modeling them in part on the Jim Crow laws. The Nazis looked to America's history of oppression in other ways, too. As Susan Neiman writes, "Hitler took American westward expansion, with its destruction of Native peoples, as the template for the eastward expansion he said was needed to provide Germans with *Lebensraum*—room to live."

Toward the top of the Wannsee meeting notes, the leaders outlined how, in the preceding years, the policy had been to facilitate the emigration of Jews from Germany. After emigration was deemed infeasible because of the war, the Nazis changed course and began forcibly expelling Jews from Germany, to the east. "This operation should be regarded only as a provisional option," they wrote, "but it is already supplying practical experience of great significance in view of the coming final solution of the Jewish question."

"The Jewish question" needed to be resolved not only in Germany but throughout all of Europe. The "evacuated" Jews, the Nazis decided, should be put to work, "during which a large proportion will no doubt drop out through natural reduction."

Upstairs, I met with Deborah Hartmann, the museum's director. She sat across from me in her office, her brown hair falling over one shoulder. Behind her, through floor-to-ceiling windows that opened onto a veranda, the lake glimmered. Born in Austria, Hartmann had worked earlier in her career as a guide at the Jewish Museum Vienna and then at Yad Vashem, Israel's national Holocaust memorial. After nearly fifteen years there, she'd applied for the opening at Wannsee.

Walking around the museum, I had felt the presence of the men who had choreographed a genocide, and sometimes wondered whether lifting up the names and ideas of people who had engaged in mass murder could have unintended consequences. Might someone come to a museum like this and be inspired by what they saw? Was there a risk in providing these men with a posthumous platform? I asked Hartmann why she felt it was so important to have a museum that included the thoughts and stories of the perpetrators.

"We cannot only focus on the Jewish perspective and on the perspective of those who perished. We have to learn something about anti-Semitism, about the views of national socialism," she said. "Also, about the bystanders. . . . This could be the neighbor who was not a member of the Nazi Party but was just hanging around, had a nice view out of the window seeing the neighbors being deported." A bird flew by the window, rested on the veranda, looked around, then took off again over the lake. "We need to focus on all of them to be able to understand the picture of what was going on."

Part of what Hartmann wants visitors to understand is that the people who committed these atrocities were, in many ways, just like anyone else. It can be easy, she said, to turn them into two-dimensional caricatures of evil—and in some ways they were. But they also had wives, children, parents, friends. As Hartmann put it, "People who participated in the mass shootings in the morning wrote nice letters to their families back home in the afternoon."

The museum has hosted visitors from all over the world, some of whom are descendants of the perpetrators. Just a few months earlier, Hartmann told me, she'd been flipping through the museum's guest book and saw that one of the visitors who'd left a note was the granddaughter of Martin Luther, one of the fifteen Nazi officials present at the Wannsee Conference. It was Luther's copy of the minutes that American troops discovered in 1945. "She wrote down in the guest book, 'I'm very much ashamed of what my grandfather was doing.'"

I was floored by this revelation. I tried to imagine what it must have been like for this woman to walk through the hallways of the place where her own grandfather had helped orchestrate the slaughter of millions of people. What emotions could she possibly have felt? Beyond the shame she said she experienced, I wonder, too, if there was a sense of culpability. Certainly, she is not responsible for what her grandfather did. But what must it feel like to be part of such a lineage? How does one extract oneself from that legacy?

Hartmann has a master's degree in political science; she titled her thesis "Europe and the Shoah: Universal Remembrance and Particular Memories." But her proximity to this subject matter is not just academic. Hartmann is Jewish, and her great-grandparents were murdered in the Holocaust. When she first started working at the museum, she didn't like to be alone in the building.

The previous director of the museum was not Jewish, and Hartmann wonders whether it would have been possible twenty years ago for a Jewish person to be the head of such a museum in Germany—or whether they would have even wanted to. Now, though, she said that Jewish people are much more a part of the public conversation about the institutions of memory that depict their experience. They are stepping into leadership positions that they previously would not have been considered for.

Hartmann makes a point of emphasizing that she doesn't think non-Jews should be prevented from leading these museums. On the contrary, she believes that Jews and non-Jews should always be working in collaboration. Still, she can't help but think about those who, for generations, were kept from being part of the project of Holocaust memorialization because they were deemed too close to the subject matter.

Hartmann told me about a Jewish historian named Joseph Wulf, a survivor of Auschwitz who wrote books on Nazi Germany and the Holocaust. For years, beginning in 1965, Wulf advocated for the West German government to make the Wannsee house into a Holocaust research center, but his proposal was ignored. On October 10, 1974, Wulf died by suicide after jumping from the window of his Berlin apartment. In a letter to his son a few months before his death he wrote, "I have published 18 books about the Third Reich and they have had no effect. You can document everything to death for the Germans. . . . Yet the mass murderers walk around free, live in their little houses, and grow flowers."

"He was never accepted by German historians, because they had the feeling that he cannot be objective as a Jewish survivor," Hartmann said, echoing a point that Deidre Berger had made. Hartmann always found the idea that Jewish scholars couldn't be "objective" because of their "proximity" to the Holocaust ironic, given that many non-Jewish scholars who ended up writing the history of the Holocaust had their own proximity to the event. "On the German side, those historians? We know who they were," she said. "The Hitler Youth."

•   •   •

In central Berlin stands another museum dedicated to telling the story of the Holocaust's perpetrators. At the Topography of Terror museum, people can learn about the history of the Nazi regime, the way Hitler and his followers gained power, and the way they exerted that power to devastating effect. It is located on the former grounds of the headquarters of the Gestapo, the high command and security service of the SS, and the Reich Security Main Office.

I met Jennifer Neal, a journalist and an author, on the museum's steps. Neal is Black and originally from Chicago. She has lived in Berlin since 2016.

Neal told me that, in some ways, Germany has done an admirable job of reckoning with its history. For example, the government has paid reparations through a program called Wiedergutmachung, which translates roughly to "making good again." In 1952, West Germany agreed to pay Israel 3 billion German marks over time, which played a crucial role in ensuring the young nation's economic stability. It also provided funds for individual payments, which continue to this day. As of 2020, Germany had paid out more than $90 billion. (The process of applying for individual reparations, however, was difficult and traumatic for many survivors, Neiman writes in *Learning from the Germans*. Those who survived Auschwitz, for example, had to outline how and when they'd arrived at the camp; obtain two sworn statements from witnesses who could confirm that they'd really been there; submit the number that had been tattooed on their skin; provide evidence of any injuries they'd suffered at the camp; and also prove that they had a low income.)

Neal said that Germans haven't always been as willing to account for the country's other crimes. From 1904 to 1908, the German military committed genocide against Indigenous communities in present-day Namibia, which at the time was a colony known as German South West Africa. An estimated 80,000 people were exterminated through forced labor, starvation, and disease in concentration camps there. Eighty percent of the Herero people and 50 percent of the Nama people are thought to have been killed.

The Namibian genocide is considered the first genocide of the twentieth century. Many historians contend that the racialized hierarchy used to justify killing Namibians and conducting phrenological studies on them—noting the shape and size of their skulls—was a direct prelude to the Holocaust. Dr. Eugen Fischer, who conducted eugenics experiments on living Namibian people, went on to teach his racial theories to doctors in the Nazi regime. One of the students influenced by Fischer's work was Josef Mengele, who led heinous experiments on prisoners at Auschwitz.

The Namibian government spent years demanding that Germany both apologize and pay reparations for what happened, and after years of resistance to the idea, in May 2021 the German government officially recognized the killings as genocide and issued an apology. Germany offered to fund $1.3 billion worth of projects in Namibia over thirty years, an amount many Namibians felt was far too low. Herero Paramount Chief Vekuii Rukoro said the deal was "an insult" because it did not include the payment of individual reparations.

Neal told me that watching the conversation in the United States about whether Confederate statues should come down seems especially ludicrous from her vantage point in Europe. She's flummoxed by the notion that taking down the statues would somehow be "erasing history."

"What Germany does well in regards to the Holocaust is show that when you honor the victims instead of the perpetrators, you're still remembering history," she said. "But you're making it clear who the aggressors were, who the victims were, and who we honored. I think this is important in terms of how the country heals." She shook her head. "That is why I think the United States is very far from healing."

. . .

In early October of this year, I visited Dachau. To enter the concentration camp—now a memorial site—visitors must walk across a small concrete bridge and through the gates of the Jourhaus, a cream-colored building topped with a watchtower that juts up from the roof like a steeple. Inscribed on the black iron gates is the phrase *Arbeit Macht Frei*, "Work Sets You Free." The slogan, Nazi propaganda meant to present the camps as innocuous places of "work" or "reeducation," appeared at the gates of concentration camps across Europe.

Gravel crunched beneath the feet of visitors walking between exhibitions; the sea of small gray pebbles was interrupted only by the brown and yellow leaves that had been scattered by the wind.

Dachau's history, in part, reflects the different ways that East and West Germany remembered the Holocaust in the postwar years. Former concentration camps in Soviet-controlled territory in the east—such as Buchenwald, Ravensbrück, and Sachsenhausen—were turned into memorials soon after the war, with restoration funds coming from both the state and individual donations. Dachau, located in the Allied-controlled western territory, did not receive any public funding until 1965, when a group of former prisoners persuaded the state of Bavaria to help finance a memorial there. Not until after the reunification of East and West Germany in 1990 did any memorial sites at West German camps receive federal funding.

When Dachau was built, in 1933, it was designed to hold 6,000 prisoners. But by April 29, 1945, when American forces liberated the camp, it held about 32,000. Barracks built to house 200 people held as many as 2,000. The originals were demolished in the 1960s, but as I walked through the reconstructed barracks I tried to imagine so many people living in them at once: the women pushed against one another between the splintered, wooden bed frames. The diseases that swept over men's bodies and turned them into silence. My breathing quickened. My stomach churned.

Visiting the memorial site, I was struck by how close it was to the homes, restaurants, and cafés around it. This was not a concentration camp in the middle of nowhere. *Surely*, I thought, *those who lived nearby during the war knew what was happening there.*

George Tievsky, an American medic who helped liberate Dachau, had a similar reaction. "I could smell the stench from the camp," he said of walking through the town on a Sunday in May 1945.

And I said to myself how can this be? How can this be? How could this exist here? These people. This town. Beside this death camp? These people knew what was in the camp. They heard the trains coming with people, and the trains go out empty. They smelled the smell of death. They saw the smoke from the chimneys . . . and yet when I asked them . . . did you know about this? . . . They all denied it. They all denied knowledge of it. There was no guilt. There was no remorse.

I wondered if this was before or after the American soldiers brought Germans to see the camp, before they entered the gates and saw the emaciated bodies, smelled the rotting flesh. Before local Germans were made to bury the bodies. Did they still deny it then?

At the far end of the camp stands "Barrack X," a crematorium that served as both an SS killing facility and a place to dispose of the dead. To walk through the building is to walk in the shadow of mechanized slaughter.

I have stood in many places that carry a history of death— plantations, execution chambers—but I have never felt my chest get tight the way it did when I stood inside the building's gas chamber. The ceiling was so low, you could reach up and touch it with your hands. It had more than a dozen holes designed to release poison gas.

There were four other visitors in the chamber with me. Our hands were in our pockets; we were silent. Occasionally, we would catch eyes, affirming, if only for a moment, that we each understood the solemnity of the space we were in.

I imagined the people who once stood in rooms like this one in death camps across Europe, the moment they realized what the holes in the ceiling were for. It is a fear I cannot fathom. It is a type of torture I cannot fully grasp.

Historians do not believe that the gas chamber in Dachau, which was fully operational, was ever used for mass killings, though it is unclear why not (one witness account claims that some people were killed by poison gas there in 1944). Still, the building was a site of murders by other means—primarily shootings and hangings.

In the room at the center of the building were four red-brick ovens, each equipped with a slab used to insert bodies into the furnace. Wooden beams crisscrossed the ceiling; a panel explained that most of the hangings done in the camp were done from these beams. After having been suffocated, the bodies were cut down and placed directly into the ovens.

Outside, I looked at the building's chimney and imagined the sight of smoke rising from it—smoke filled with stories, smoke filled with families, smoke filled with futures that had been erased.

I turned to my right and walked down a path that led me through a canopy of trees. I arrived at a square patch of land with a stone cross at its center. Fosse Commune Grab Vieler Tausend Unbekannter. "Grave of Many Thousands Unknown." This was a grave where the ashes of bodies burned in the crematorium had been buried. This was an effort to remember.

I left the camp and stepped out onto the street. A woman was pushing a baby in a stroller, a man rode his bicycle and rang its bell as he passed neighbors on the street, two friends held hands as they laughed and chatted underneath the afternoon sun.

In 1949, W. E. B. Du Bois visited Warsaw, where he witnessed firsthand the aftermath of Nazi destruction. "I have seen something of human upheaval in this world," he said. "The scream and shots of a race riot in Atlanta; the marching of the Ku Klux Klan; the threat of courts and police; the neglect and destruction of human habitation; but nothing in my wildest imagination was equal to what I saw in Warsaw."

Du Bois said that the experience "helped me to emerge from a certain social provincialism into a broader conception of what the fight against race segregation, religious discrimination, and the oppression by wealth had to become if civilization was going to triumph and broaden in the world."

As Du Bois stood amid the rubble of what was once the Warsaw Ghetto, he looked around. "There was complete and total waste, and a monument," he said. He was referring to the Monument to the Ghetto Heroes, which commemorates those who fought in the Warsaw Ghetto uprising in 1943. It was the largest uprising of Jewish people during World War II; approximately 7,000 Jews were killed. That monument helped him see the Jews not simply as victims but as people who rebelled, much like Black people in the United States had rebelled against slavery and Jim Crow.

After spending time in Germany, I, too, gained a sense of clarity about the interconnectedness of racial oppression and state violence. I left with a clearer understanding of the implications of how those periods of history are remembered or not.

I was reminded, too, that many of Germany's most powerful memorials did not begin as state-sanctioned projects but emerged—and are still emerging—from ordinary people outside the government who pushed the country to be honest about its past. Sometimes that means putting down Stolpersteine. Sometimes that means standing on the street for years collecting signatures for the massive memorial to murdered Jews that you believe the country needs. Americans do not have to and should not wait for the government to find its conscience. Ordinary people are the conscience.

Some in the United States have undertaken efforts reminiscent of those in Germany. In Connecticut, a group of educators started the Witness Stones Project, modeled after the Stolpersteine in Germany. The group works with schoolchildren in five Northeast states to help them more intimately understand the history of slavery in their town. In Camden, New Jersey, a local historical society has erected markers in places where enslaved people were sold, echoing the memorials to deported Jews at train stations in Germany. In Montgomery, Alabama, the civil-rights attorney Bryan Stevenson, who often cites Germany in his work, has built the National Memorial for Peace and Justice, which commemorates the history of slavery and the oppression of Black Americans. The space has a similar physical and emotional texture to the Memorial to the Murdered Jews of Europe.

None of these projects, whether in the United States or Germany, can ever be commensurate with the history they are tasked with remembering. It is impossible for any memorial to slavery to capture its full horror or for any memorial to the Holocaust to express the full humanity of the victims. No stone in the ground can make up for a life. No museum can bring back millions of people. It cannot be done, and yet we must try to honor those lives and to account for this history as best we can. It is the very act of attempting to remember that becomes the most powerful memorial of all.

ProPublica and Milwaukee Journal Sentinel

"With 'The Landlord and Tenant,'" said the judges who chose this piece as the winner of the National Magazine Award for Feature Writing, "Raquel Rutledge and Ken Armstrong not only tell the story of two tragically intertwined lives but also probe some of the most troubling realities of American life, including the cruelties inflicted on the working poor and a justice system that is often anything but." Now the investigations editor at the nonprofit start-up The Examination, Rutledge won the Pulitzer Prize for Local Reporting in 2010. A reporter at ProPublica since 2017, Armstrong won the Pulitzer Prize for Investigative Reporting in 2012 and Explanatory Reporting in 2016; his work was also nominated for the National Magazine Award for Feature Writing in 2016 and 2022. ProPublica has won seven National Magazine Awards in the last four years.

Raquel Rutledge and
Ken Armstrong

The Landlord
and the Tenant

1. April 11, 2013, 5:19 p.m. 7750 West Hicks Street, West Allis, Wisconsin

In West Allis, a Milwaukee suburb once dominated by a factory that long ago manufactured steam engines, ore crushers, and kilns, a man living on West Hicks Street opens his back door to let the dog out and sees smoke.

It's coming from the house next door, from the roof. He calls 911. "Seven, seven, five, zero," he says. "The house is on fire." He doesn't see flames. But the smoke keeps pouring. Sunset is more than two hours away, but the smoke gets so thick it darkens the sky. It's cold and wet. In the mud, in the side yard of the smoking house, there are two toy trucks and a stuffed animal.

Engine 1 and Engine 2 arrive within seconds of each other, then Engine 3.

There are two stories to the house. The top story is covered in stucco, the bottom in brick veneer. Angelica Belen lives in the house with her four children, the oldest five, the youngest a toddler. In between are twin boys, four years old, one with cerebral palsy, the other with autism and epilepsy. Belen is twenty-four. She's a renter. The landlord, when she moved in, was Todd Brunner. Known around Milwaukee as the foreclosure king, Brunner collects properties others have lost to banks. He's a familiar figure to building-code inspectors for his long list of violations.

Neighbors gather, drawn by the smoke and sirens. A battalion chief, the commander on scene, sees people watching from a nearby porch. He yells to them, asking if anyone is inside the smoking house. Their car is gone, no one is home, a man answers. The chief returns to his command car, gets on the radio and gives the all clear. The house is vacant, he says.

When firefighters go in, the smoke layer is so thick they can hardly make out anything. On the ground floor, in the kitchen, they see the fire. Flames roll across the ceiling, burning a hole two feet wide.

Embers from a bedroom above fall into the kitchen sink.

2. August 26, 1977. Milwaukee, Wisconsin

Todd Brunner is only twenty when, in the summer of 1977, he buys an old duplex on Milwaukee's south side. He purchases the house with Glen Guldan, a friend from high school. A bank gives them a $24,000 loan.

For Brunner and Guldan, the house is an investment. The two young landlords are from the suburb of New Berlin, where the residents, to quote one magazine, are "remnants of Milwaukee's white flight in the 1960s and '70s or descendants of local farming families."

At New Berlin Eisenhower High School, Brunner had been a football star, defensive tackle on a team that went undefeated his junior year, giving up fewer than one hundred yards a game. Pat Raebel, nose tackle, played right next to Brunner. He remembers Brunner's dad, proud of his son, coming to every game. (Brunner's dad died a few years later in his forties.) Brunner was popular, teammates recall. A nice guy. Into fast cars. His junior year, he was on prom court. Brunner's senior year, students elect him a class officer. He leads the team in tackles. He's all-conference. He's honorable mention all-state. He's the defensive line's biggest player. One newspaper story pegs him at 6'6", 245.

Brunner gets a scholarship to play football at Northern Illinois University. But the university has no record of him ever attending.

Before Brunner and Guldan turn twenty-one, they go in on another nearby duplex. Then they keep going. Together they will buy more than a dozen properties, collecting more than $100,000 a year in rent.

3. December 16, 1985, 8:45 p.m. Milwaukee

In an apartment on Milwaukee's south side, two girls, both toddlers, sit in their cribs, crying. One is naked, the other in a dirty diaper. They've been crying for much of the night.

Police arrive to find the door open and no adult anywhere. The house is filthy, the smell of urine and feces in the children's bedroom so overpowering an officer holds his breath. Neighbors tell police the children's mother, twenty-year-old Dawn Sosa, left the day before and hasn't returned. She often leaves her kids alone, the neighbors say. In the cupboards and refrigerator, police find little other than juice, cake, and canned corn.

Nobody can say where Sosa went. Her husband, the children's father, moved out earlier in the year.

Two days later, Sosa returns from a bar. She had gone to watch her boyfriend play in a band and didn't come home because "it was too dark, too cold, and too late," she tells police. A friend was supposed to be watching the girls, she says.

Sosa is arrested and charged with child neglect. But ultimately, she gets to keep her kids. In 1987, she has a third daughter. Then, on May 20, 1988, at Sinai Samaritan Medical Center, Sosa gives birth to a fourth, a girl with both Puerto Rican and Menominee Indian ancestry.

Sosa names her Angelica.

4. January 16, 1992. Milwaukee

Police detectives get called on a winter afternoon to investigate the death of a child who has been beaten and starved.

The child's name is Marisol. She is Dawn Sosa's daughter and Angelica's younger sister. Marisol was seventeen months old.

An autopsy reveals four broken ribs, a broken leg, a bruised jaw, and bleeding in the brain. Marisol weighs 9.8 pounds. Asked if he's ever seen a baby this malnourished, the pathologist says, "I have not."

Prosecutors charge Sosa and her boyfriend, Ramon Velez. The story is all over the news. Velez tells police he hit Marisol two or three times a day. His reason, a police report says, was "Marisol had a mouth on her and would cry a lot."

Angelica, now three years old, is the middle child of Sosa's seven daughters. After Angelica came Rosalie, then Marisol. Those three sisters had the same father, a man their mom had left for Velez.

Sosa's oldest daughter, eight, testifies at Velez's trial. She says her mom slapped Marisol when she wouldn't walk right. She says Velez took Marisol by the neck and slammed her against a wall. "Almost every day," she says. Velez also brutalized Angelica and Rosalie, she says. When they sucked their thumb, "he would take a bottle of hot sauce and put it in their mouth."

Velez is convicted of reckless homicide and gets fifteen years.

Sosa pleads guilty to child neglect, resulting in death. When her sentencing comes, new horrors emerge, as details of her own childhood come before the court.

When Sosa was little, her mother hit her and her sisters with extension cords or whatever was handy. "The girls were locked in their room for days at a time," a social worker's report says. Food was slipped through the door. The girls peed in their boots. Sosa went into foster care then, as an adult, had relationships with men who beat her. It is not uncommon, the social worker writes, for childhood abuse victims to partner with abusers, "and thus the cycle continues."

The social worker advises against incarcerating Sosa, writing, "Up to this point, her life has been nothing but a prison."

The prosecutor is Mark Williams, an assistant district attorney in his late thirties who handles only homicides. "To find justice for the families of homicide victims is the purest kind of law you can practice," Williams will say. In Sosa's case, Williams tells the judge:

There's "got to be incarceration." How a mother could do this to her child, "I don't understand it," he says.

The judge tells Sosa: "You came from a terrible background. I feel for you." Then he says: "Your mother was mentally ill. Are you mentally ill? I don't think so. You are weak."

The judge sentences Sosa to eight years.

After Marisol's death, a psychologist evaluates Angelica. Angelica tells him that her mom and Velez both hit her with shoes and sticks. Angelica is "affiliative and dependent," traumatized and anxious, the psychologist writes. "She chose to stand very close to examiner during much of the formal psychometrics."

Like her mother before her, Angelica enters foster care. She and Rosalie stay together while the other sisters go elsewhere. At Sosa's sentencing, a lawyer sounds a note of optimism about the girls' future, now in the hands of the state. She says foster parents can undo any damage done and ensure "we don't end up" in another courtroom in years to come, dealing with another generation of child abuse or neglect.

5. May 11, 1992. Milwaukee

In Milwaukee County Circuit Court, Glen Guldan files a breach-of-contract lawsuit against Todd Brunner, and, in the spring of 1992, Guldan prevails. A judge orders Brunner to pay about $11,000. The two men's friendship, and business partnership, is through.

Brunner is thirty-five, married, with two kids, the youngest, a son, about to turn two.

The men's parting is remembered differently, depending on who's remembering.

Rebecca Harms, who was Guldan's wife, says when the partnership unraveled, Brunner would call their home at two a.m., screaming and threatening to kill Guldan. "We got an alarm system installed in our house, we changed our phone number, and my husband got a gun from a friend," Harms says.

By this time, Guldan is fighting mouth cancer. Brunner makes an awful time even worse, Harms says. Guldan would go on to have twenty surgeries before dying at forty-four.

"Absolutely never happened," Brunner will write later of threatening Guldan. They'd been best friends, according to Brunner. Once, while making a wine rack for Guldan, Brunner cut off four fingers; doctors reattached two, he says. They were both type A personalities, with strong opinions, and when Guldan wanted to build a budget movie theater in a Milwaukee suburb, "I strongly disagreed so we went our own ways," Brunner writes.

On the same day that the judgment is entered in favor of Guldan, Brunner declares bankruptcy in federal court in Milwaukee, using Chapter 13, a way to preserve property while slow-paying creditors. Bankruptcy can be seen as failure. Or it can be seen as a fresh start. Brunner sees it as part of being a self-made man. He will say, in years to come, "Every self-made man has filed bankruptcy at least three times in his life."

6. August 13, 1993. Milwaukee

As young children, Angelica and Rosalie move through foster homes. In one, they go to church. Angelica absorbs the stories. She finds solace in scripture's description of a loving Father. She finds comfort in prayer. But not just the typical childlike petitions said before bed. For Angelica, faith becomes a lifeline.

In August of 1993, when Angelica is five and Rosalie four, the girls are placed with two women, a mother and daughter. The girls call them Mom and Grandma. Mom works in a factory, second shift. Grandma is often gone.

And for Angelica and Rosalie, there is freedom—safety, even—in being left alone. Angelica walks to kindergarten then walks home to find Rosalie in the basement or their bedroom, playing by herself. They make peanut butter and jelly sandwiches. They drink Kool-Aid. In the summers, they get up when they want and leave the house when they want. They can play outside, do whatever.

This lasts for three years, and for Angelica, these will be the best three years of her childhood.

"I did not feel neglected, or scared, or any of that," she will write. "It was just that we had no adult supervision."

7. September 1996. Waukesha, Wisconsin

Rosalie and Angelica walk into a beautiful house in Waukesha, a suburb west of Milwaukee. They're seven and eight. Their new foster parents tell the girls they can pick bedrooms. Each has a large bed with a floral print comforter, perfume on the dressers, and closets full of clothes and shoes. The rooms feel fit for princesses.

It is an inviting house, at first. And it's a door to a different world—seats at *The Nutcracker*, insistence on proper enunciation. The girls stay up late, memorizing vocabulary. Angelica reads books usually assigned in middle school or high school. She's reading Dickens and Twain.

But years later, when interviewed separately, Rosalie and Angelica will both describe another side to this home. If the girls don't finish the milk in their cereal, the foster mom forces them to drink glass after glass until they are sick, they both say. When the girls complain of "starving" after a day of errands, the foster mom force-feeds them pancakes, saying, "You don't know what starving is." Sometimes, the foster parents pull the girls' hair. Sometimes they force the girls to kneel, for hours, on gravel or stand on one leg, with arms out to the side, hangers on their wrists. If their arms drop and the hangers fall, they are further punished.

One night, Rosalie watches as the foster dad slams Angelica's head against a wall, both sisters will later recall.

In Milwaukee County there is a Children's Court file, with three manila folders, in which the girls' whereabouts and well-being were charted. In these records, there's no mention of abuse. Social workers often employ boilerplate language. "Angelica is a very energetic 8-year-old child who loves attention. She is extremely friendly and charming." And the next year: "Angelica is a very energetic

9-year-old child who loves attention. She is extremely friendly and charming."

Eventually, social workers note behavioral issues. Angelica "is angry, lashing out, tantruming and refusing to get dressed," a report says. Sometimes she kicks Rosalie. To Rosalie, Angelica was like a cornered dog. "She was fight and I was flight," Rosalie says years later. A caseworker writes that the foster parents have warned Angelica they won't keep her if she doesn't improve: "Angelica understands this and is really trying to be better."

On January 16, 1998, an emergency order is issued to remove the girls from this home. The court record doesn't explain why. All it offers is one sentence with a misspelled word: "Pre-adoptive placement has disrutived." Years later, an aunt will write to a judge: "I knew things were not right in that home. I told the social workers and eventually they found out that Angelica and her sister suffered horrible abuse in that home."

(A *Journal Sentinel* reporter recently interviewed this foster dad. He denied they abused the girls. Sometimes if the girls were lying or acting up, they'd have them kneel and face a wall for ten or fifteen minutes, he said. The agency took Angelica and Rosalie, concluding the placement wasn't a good fit, he said.)

When Angelica is ten, she returns to the foster home of the two women she used to call Mom and Grandma. But things are not as before. They don't want Angelica but must take her to keep Rosalie, they tell her. "I was told on a daily basis that I was unwanted, worthless, and stupid," Angelica will later write.

This family adopts the girls when Angelica is eleven. The two women's home will provide Angelica a "safe, stable and nurturing environment," a caseworker writes. This is where the family court file ends.

Rosalie and Angelica both say later that the two women tormented Angelica; they isolated her, and the woman they called Mom punched and kicked her. She takes Angelica to psychiatrists, who prescribe a litany of powerful antipsychotics and other medications including lithium, Depakote, Zyprexa, Neurontin, Lamictal, and Wellbutrin.

8. February 23, 2002, 1:48 a.m. Pewaukee, Wisconsin

A police sergeant in Pewaukee, a Milwaukee suburb that boasts of country living with a big lake for boating and fishing, gets dispatched to the parking lot of a McDonald's. It's close to two in the morning. The sergeant sees a car, a maroon Cadillac Escalade— it's new, it's a 2002—parked near the drive-through, headlights burning, engine running, with a vanity license plate, "LANDLD."

The driver is asleep.

The sergeant wakes him up and smells alcohol. The driver is Todd Brunner. The sergeant asks Brunner to recite the alphabet. Brunner stops after "E," saying he can go no further because his throat is dry. He blows a .14, well above the legal limit. A subsequent blood test comes back even higher.

Brunner is charged with driving drunk, something he's been convicted of twice before. His first two convictions were in 1989 and 1993. In between those convictions he was charged with driving on a suspended or revoked license (third offense) and driving without a valid license (second offense).

Brunner pleads guilty, and prosecutors recommend a jail sentence of 120 days.

Brunner's lawyer writes the judge, saying Brunner "is basically a hardworking man who was in the wrong place at the wrong time." Of Brunner's prior convictions, the lawyer writes, "Drank a bit too much in an isolated incident, made a bad decision to drive and got caught."

In the fall of 2003, the judge sentences Brunner to thirty-five days.

After Brunner serves seventeen days, his wife writes the judge, asking that Brunner be allowed to serve his remaining time at home on electronic monitoring. She says he hurt his back and can't sleep on the jail bunk and that without sleep he can't run his business and that if he can't run his business all his employees will lose their livelihoods.

In the court file for this case, a handwritten note in the margins of her letter says "denied without medical verification," after which medical verification was provided, with a doctor writing the judge about Brunner's aching back.

The jail no longer has records showing when Brunner was actually released. Brunner will later write that the jail was overcrowded and he was too big for the jail's beds. The best he can remember, "I was released for good behavior."

9. June 17, 2003. West Allis

The house at 7750 West Hicks Street in West Allis, built in 1893, uses balloon framing, with long, wooden studs stretching from basement to roof. That style of construction saved money and time but introduced danger. If a fire broke out, those unbroken studs could become a highway for flames.

Todd Brunner buys this home, with three upstairs bedrooms and a steep, gable roof, in the spring of 2003. The purchase price is $50,507. He later bundles it with ten other properties to get a $1.1 million loan from Tri City National Bank.

For Brunner, the West Allis house becomes part of a growing enterprise. In Milwaukee alone, he buys at least sixty-five properties from 2002 to 2005, many on the city's economically distressed north side. He scoops up a Cape Cod on North Thirty-Eighth, a duplex on North Fifty-Eighth, a ranch on North Seventy-Second. At sheriff's sales, where foreclosed properties go up for auction, he's such a fixture he has his own desk.

Brunner's name is all over property records. It's all over court records, too. He constantly sues, and he is constantly being sued. Court records turn up disputes with contractors, creditors, debtors, tenants, banks, utilities, code enforcers, and tax collectors. He feuds with neighbors and with business associates and with business associates who once were neighbors.

In court, he wins some, he loses some. He'll later say a lot of this litigation stems from tenants who don't pay their rent or from properties he buys in poor condition, not up to code. "I was proud of the work we did on these properties," he'll write. With a crew that grew as big as thirty, "we usually completely rehabbed them turning them from the worst to the best properties in the area."

Brunner lives in Pewaukee, in a sprawling, serpentine house on two acres near the lake. In 2004, a neighbor accuses Brunner of harassment. Home surveillance video captured Brunner, in a Cadillac Escalade, pulling up to the neighbor's home and yelling: "Cocksucker. Fucking piece of shit. Fuck. Come out here. I will kick your fucking ass." At a court hearing, the neighbor testifies that Brunner has also pulled up on other occasions and revved his engine: "He sits out in front of the house, honking, roaring."

A judge orders Brunner to stay away from the neighbor. Months later, according to a police report, the neighbor hears a vehicle outside his house, idling. He sees Brunner on an ATV. "Take a picture, motherfucker," Brunner says, before driving off. Charged with violating the anti-harassment order, Brunner ends up being convicted of disorderly conduct and pays a $181 fine.

Years later, Brunner goes at it with a different neighbor. He pulls up to the neighbor's house and yells at the family to "get off his land," according to a police report. He says, "You want a piece of me?" A deputy writes in his report, "It should be noted, Todd is a very large man approximately 400 pounds." Brunner subsequently appears in the neighbor's driveway with a tape measure. "For some reason," a deputy writes, "Brunner believes the asphalted driveway . . . is now his property."

10. June 7, 2007. Milwaukee

Doctors tell Angelica Belen that her first child will be a boy. So the arrival of a girl, when Belen is nineteen, leaves her with no name prepared. A day later she's doing the word search puzzle and spies, between the circled words, four letters, N-A-Y-A.

Naya will be her name, Angelica says. No, make it Nayeli, the father says. Because it means "I love you" in the language of the Zapotecs, an indigenous population from southern Mexico.

As Naya grows, her mother sees that she is smart, charismatic, funny, kind, "a bit sassy, and very easily distracted." Naya walks early, talks early, reads early. When she's two, she trick-or-treats as a Spanish dancer in a red dress. She loves cute shoes, big bows in her hair, and lip gloss. And she loves ballet. She idolizes Misty

Copeland, a Black ballerina. Her favorite singers are Rihanna and Beyonce. They are brown like her, and true to the title of Beyonce's smash album, they are "fierce." That word is Naya's "every aspiration," Belen later writes. Naya will say, "Mom, I just need to be fierce, I am fierce, I need to look fierce."

In 2008, when Belen is twenty, she has twin boys, born premature.

Adrian, three pounds, twelve ounces at birth, has epilepsy and autism. He gets medication for seizures, and as he grows, he is quiet, gentle, and sweet. He loves wearing his Batman costume. His favorite song is "Bohemian Rhapsody." He keeps pennies in his pocket and helps his mom around the house, putting dishes in the sink. His mom will give him rubber bands and paper clips, and he will make an airplane. On a trip to Famous Footwear, he goes to a bin and starts sorting, white socks here, black socks there.

Alexis, or Alex for short, is even smaller at birth: three pounds, seven ounces. He has cerebral palsy. He gets physical therapy and speech therapy. When he crawls at fifteen months, his mom claps; when he pulls himself up at nineteen months, she cheers; when he walks at twenty-two months, she cries. His mom calls Alex her "little spitfire." If there's trouble to be had—say, smearing grape jelly and mustard everywhere—Alex is the one to start it, while Adrian tags along. Alex's favorite movie is *The Avengers*. He likes to sit in his mom's lap, and if she cries, he strokes her face.

Naya is close to her brothers. She goes along on their visits to therapists and doctors. Belen teaches Naya to protect her brothers. After Belen burns cookies and a smoke alarm goes off, she instructs Naya on fire safety, saying, try to find a safe way out, and if you can't, put a towel under the door to block the smoke and throw toys out a window and scream, so someone can hear.

11. August 15, 2010. West Allis

In the summer of 2010, Todd Brunner sells the house on West Hicks Street in West Allis. Only it's not really a sale, because no money is exchanged. As Brunner will later admit in court papers, he's trying to shield this house—and many others—from creditors.

Brunner creates three shell companies, in which he hides real estate, cars, and boats. He doesn't exactly cover his tracks; they're organized under the name of his son, Shawn. Shawn is in college. He's twenty. He's on Facebook posting "eat pray blowjob" and "getting white boy wasted tomorrow?!?"

When Shawn was seventeen, he was charged with a felony for throwing fireworks at a passing train, causing temporary hearing loss for an engineer leaning out a window. He pleaded guilty to a misdemeanor and paid a $325 fine. When Shawn turned eighteen, his dad, as a birthday present, gave him $100,000 to invest in real estate.

12. June 5, 2011. Milwaukee

Todd Brunner files for bankruptcy, again, declaring, in court records, that he owes more than $18 million to creditors listed across sixty-plus pages.

He owes taxes to twenty-nine municipalities, from Brookfield to West Allis. At least nine banks hold mortgages. He owes First Business Bank $2.2 million for a construction loan for a failed venture to build an assisted-living center for seniors. He has unpaid court fines and condominium dues; outstanding debts to suppliers and lawyers; and credit card balances ranging from $350 to $92,000.

He lists 218 properties he owns in Wisconsin. They include many rentals, with paying tenants, but even so, Brunner lists, as his monthly income, "$0.00."

The bankruptcy records include Brunner's personal possessions, revealing an attraction for what he later calls "some cool toys." He owns a 1918 Rauch & Lang electric car; a 1937 Ford Coupe; a 1959 Jaguar; a 1984 Rolls Royce; and a 2006 Bentley worth $70,000. He also owns a Harley-Davidson motorcycle, an ATV, and at least eight trucks.

Brunner's flashy collection doesn't sit well with some creditors. "A guy doesn't usually come out here in a Bentley to tell you he can't pay you 1,900 bucks," the president of a window-and-door dealer tells the *Journal Sentinel*. Brunner's boats include a thirty-foot catamaran that, he writes, reaches 134 mph and consumes 136 gallons of fuel an hour, wide-open throttle. He also owns a thirty-seven-foot cigarette boat, worth $80,000, named *El Diablo*.

Kerry Kneser, a former football teammate of Brunner's, remembers working at a bank in Pewaukee and seeing Brunner pull up, in a Bentley, and park in a no-parking zone. "At that point he had an attitude, I can do whatever I want."

Dennis Witthun Jr., a former business partner of Brunner's, says Brunner wore a gold necklace with diamond-encrusted propellers. Brunner, Witthun says, "was a good actor." Witthun says he once went with Brunner to meet with bank officials to seek relief with a big loan. In the meeting, Brunner cried with "actual tears," Witthun says. Then outside the bank Brunner stopped crying and said to Witthun, "How was that?"

("Never happened / A total lie," Brunner later writes to a reporter when asked about this.)

One week after Brunner files for bankruptcy, a sheriff's deputy finds two of Brunner's employees on railroad property, according to police records. The two say they were digging a channel under the tracks to run electricity from one of Brunner's rental properties to his boat lifts on Pewaukee Lake.

Brunner tells deputies he did indeed order this work. He says he doesn't have a permit "but would pull one with the City of Pewaukee during the week," according to a deputy's report. A couple of trains get delayed while the track is inspected for possible damage to the railroad bed. The railroad fills the hole—three feet long, one foot wide—and Brunner's employees get charged with and convicted of trespassing.

(Brunner himself wasn't charged, based on what these records show. Asked recently about this incident, Brunner wrote: "I never said I would get a permit because I didn't think I needed one. We were just driving a 1' pipe underneath the railroad tracks, that never hurt anything and we were only copying what other neighbors had done years earlier. I paid for the tickets my people got.")

13. June 14, 2011. 7750 West Hicks Street, West Allis

The West Allis code inspector who shows up at 7750 West Hicks Street doesn't go inside. On this spring day in 2011, he inspects only the house's exterior, checking for violations.

Milwaukee, six miles east, has a program at this time requiring interior inspections of rental units in particularly distressed neighborhoods. Its program recognizes that if a renter notifies the city of some problem—say, failing pipes or faulty wiring—an upset landlord could respond by filing to evict. Milwaukee strives to catch dangerous conditions without exposing renters to retaliation.

West Allis has no such program. Its inspector sees what he can from the outside, and at 7750 West Hicks, he sees five violations, including weeds, a boarded-up window, scattered junk, and wood in need of paint.

The remaining violation falls under the city's electrical code. But the inspector's written notes offer only six words of description: "two outlets east side of house."

On June 14, the inspector sends a "notice," directing the landlord, Todd Brunner, to fix the violations by June 30.

On July 20, the inspector returns and sees the same violations. He sends an "order," demanding Brunner fix them by August 20.

On August 22, the inspector sees that three violations remain, including the problem outlets. He sends a "second order," demanding Brunner fix them by September 22.

14. August 31, 2011. Milwaukee

Angelica Belen didn't plan for another child, but her IUD fails. She's twenty-three when her fourth child is born, and her fourth child, like her second and third, is born premature. Born at twenty-eight weeks, he has a breathing disorder; he needs a nebulizer three times a day, an inhaler twice a day. She carries him constantly, afraid he'll have an asthma attack.

When Belen first met the boy's father, he seemed caring and helpful. He went to the kids' doctor's appointments and sat and played with them. "More than anything else that's what drew me into him," she'll write years later. But a few months after their child's birth, he hits Belen in the face, bloodying her nose, then grabs and shakes her head, according to a criminal complaint. He gets convicted of disorderly conduct and is ordered to stay away from Belen.

For Belen, this is history repeating. The twins' father had also been a good father at first. Then, she says, he became violent and lapsed into drugs, and she knew she had to leave him.

In the spring of 2012, Belen gets evicted from her home in Oak Creek, south of Milwaukee. It's her second eviction, the kind of history that will make it hard to find a new place. The man who served the eviction papers sees three children outside, unattended, near a busy intersection, two in diapers so soiled they hang to the knees.

Belen gets a job at a thrift shop but loses it for missing too many days taking care of her kids.

She enrolls Naya in Saint Lucas, a Lutheran school in Milwaukee, even though it will require her to drive Naya back and forth every day. On days when Belen's minivan breaks down, she takes her by city bus. A fellow mom writes of seeing Belen arrive one winter day, "her baby strapped to her chest and one boy in each hand," out of breath, having walked a half-mile from the bus stop through snow. Robert Gurgel, the parish pastor, notices Belen in the pews at church. "I thought who is this woman with these well-groomed, well-mannered children," Gurgel will later say. "I wondered what her story was."

Belen makes beautiful dresses for Naya, and she makes it to school events, like Pastries with Parents, and she volunteers to help clean the school on weekends.

15. January 3, 2012. Milwaukee

The way Todd Brunner divulges information in his latest bankruptcy declaration, dribbling it out, angers creditors and the U.S. trustee, who monitors cases and enforces bankruptcy laws. Asked in a hearing where he got the information needed to fill out the voluminous bankruptcy forms, Brunner says, "Out of my head." As creditors and the trustee keep digging, he keeps revealing more assets, including a backhoe, a forklift, boat propellers, five guns, and four pieces of real estate in Bend, Oregon.

In January 2012, the trustee asks that Brunner's request for bankruptcy protection be denied. "A core purpose of the Bankruptcy Code is to provide a fresh start for honest debtors," the trustee's motion says. "It is not a safe haven for fraud or deception."

Brunner accused a former secretary of throwing all his records in a snowbank. ("Not truthful," the trustee's motion says.) Brunner transferred properties into shell companies when in financial trouble—a "badge of fraud," the motion says. He then moved many of them back, including the house in West Allis. He didn't disclose his income to the bankruptcy court; he hasn't filed federal tax returns for two years running; and he declared assorted assets only after creditors asked about them, the motion says. The trustee likens Brunner's actions to "a game of 'cat and mouse.'"

In April 2012, the bankruptcy judge tosses Brunner's bankruptcy request out of court. Brunner, the judge says, blamed his poor record-keeping on a former record-keeper, his property transfers on bad advice from a former lawyer, and his poor property management on a property-management company. "You have a propensity to blame others," the judge tells Brunner. "And you seem to be portraying yourself as an innocent victim, and I'm not persuaded by that at all."

Instead of getting protection from creditors, Brunner's now in trouble with law enforcement. In June, an assistant U.S. attorney emails federal and local authorities about what she calls Brunner's "multi-faceted fraud activity." At least three Milwaukee police detectives work with federal agents; their emails back and forth reveal an investigation that keeps expanding. Subpoenas go out to banks, title insurers, property managers. Investigators collect rent ledgers, loan applications, balance sheets. They interview Brunner's business partners, tenants, and at least two of his former lawyers.

Banks swoop in to collect. In October 2012, Brunner, questioned under oath by one bank's lawyer, says, "This is just a witch hunt." He says, "I wasn't meaning to defraud anybody." He says, "If you think I got a big bag of money somewhere, you're wrong." Some questions, he just won't answer. He refers to getting a high-interest loan but treats the loan's source as a secret.

"I borrowed it from an attorney. He makes loans."

"And who is that attorney?"

"He doesn't want his name out there."

"So you're willing not to answer this question under oath to protect the attorney?"

"I'm done with this right now. What else do you want?"

Two days later, the FBI raids Brunner's home, seizing computers and paperwork. Separately, the FBI finds, in a warehouse, expensive engines, superchargers, and gauges that had been stripped from *El Diablo*, Brunner's cigarette boat.

16. March 9, 2012. Brookfield, Wisconsin

A fire starts in the garage of a rental house on Ridgeview Drive in the Milwaukee suburb of Brookfield, and the fire spreads to the house, but thanks to a barking dog, the two people sleeping inside on this Friday morning are alerted to the blaze and able to get out.

Crews from fire departments around Milwaukee respond to the fire, which causes about $150,000 worth of damage. Firefighters fill out a form for the fire, and in the section titled "Ignition," in the subsection for "Heat source," the author types, "Electrical arcing."

The rental home's owner is Todd Brunner.

In nearby Milwaukee, firefighters are accustomed to getting called to Brunner's rental properties.

In December of 2009, they get called to a house of Brunner's on North Forty-First Street. The incident report says "bad outlet." Firefighters shut off power to the outlet and advise the tenant to call an electrician.

In May of 2010, firefighters get called to a house of Brunner's on North Twenty-Eighth Street. The incident report says the woman living there "witnessed sparks coming from electric outlet." Firefighters shut off power to the kitchen, the room with the sparking outlet, and advise her to call an electrician.

In July of 2012, firefighters go to a house of Brunner's on North Sixty-Fifth Street. The incident report says "OUTLET SPARK-ING." Firefighters shut down the circuit and advise: "contact landlord."

17. July 18, 2012. 7750 West Hicks Street, West Allis

Knowing nothing about the house's landlord, Todd Brunner, Angelica Belen signs a lease and moves with her four kids into 7750 West Hicks Street in West Allis. For weeks, Belen's family had been sleeping in her minivan or at a relative's house or in a shelter. Now, with the help of government assistance for her children with disabilities, she can rent this house—a big house—for $825 a month. "This place looked like a dream come true," she'll write later.

In the kitchen, one light flickers. A friend tightens the bulb, but still, Belen needs to flip the switch several times to turn the light on. The light above the kitchen sink is worse. The first time she turns it on, two bulbs blow. She replaces them and tries again, but those bulbs blow as well, leading her to give up. She tells the property manager about the problems with the lighting, but nobody comes to fix whatever is wrong, Belen will say later. Belen considers calling the city but chooses not to, fearing her landlord will kick her out.

Thelma Nash, who rented the house before Belen, says the wiring throughout was "a mess." "The lights were going on and off all the time," Nash says. "I thought there were ghosts in there." She complained to property managers but got no response, she says. She never saw an electrician make repairs.

A month or so after moving out, Nash meets Belen while returning to pick up mail. Nash asks if the electrical wiring has been fixed, and when Belen says no, Nash tells her, "Baby, they shouldn't have let you move in."

There is so much about the house Belen doesn't know. She doesn't know about the code inspector who has flagged two exterior outlets. She doesn't know what the wiring looks like in the basement, because she doesn't go down there. Basements give her the creeps; plus, a property manager told her the floor had been torn up. And she doesn't know the house's history.

In the summer of 1978, decades before Brunner became owner, the house caught fire. As smoke poured from the eaves and windows, firefighters found, in an upstairs bedroom, a teenager. She wasn't breathing. She had no pulse. Firefighters carried her outside and resuscitated her.

The fire department classified the fire's cause as electrical. A TV overheated, the battalion chief wrote. A captain, in a report now preserved on microfilm, requested an electrical inspection of the house by the city's Fire Prevention Bureau. He wrote, "Various electrical code violations were noted in the building while overhauling—especially the basement."

18. December 31, 2012. West Allis

On the final day of 2012, a year and a half after the code inspector first flagged the problem outlets, the city's file on the house on West Hicks Street is closed.

After Todd Brunner failed to respond to the "notice," then the "order," then the "second order," the city filed a citation against Brunner, hoping that would get his attention. Brunner failed to appear in municipal court, resulting in a $5,000 default judgment, after which Brunner's attorney got the case reopened and then resolved with payment of a $50 fine.

But what happened at the house is unclear. The inspector's notes—handwritten and at times barely legible—indicate the issue with the outlets was corrected in March 2012. But just as his initial notes didn't specify the problem, his subsequent notes don't describe the fix.

Nash, the home's renter in early 2012, says she doesn't remember anyone coming to the house to do repairs. There is no record on file of anyone getting an electrical permit. Electrical permits trigger an inspection by city engineers who can ensure work was done—and done properly.

19. February 26, 2013. West Allis

A social worker is on her way to Angelica Belen's house when she notices that Belen is driving right in front of her in a minivan. The social worker sees Belen arrive at her home and get out with only her daughter.

Belen, the worker discovers, has left her three boys in the home, alone. The twins are crying; the toddler is in a high chair. Confronted, Belen makes up a story, then admits the truth: She'd left them for about an hour while picking up Naya from school.

The social worker is with the Bureau of Milwaukee Child Welfare, an agency that helps families in crisis. Child welfare officials have received at least a half-dozen complaints about Belen, all of which they've found to be unsubstantiated or not credible enough to investigate. But there are real problems. Social workers report that Belen has been missing therapy appointments for her children. Their medication isn't being routinely refilled. Her home is often filthy, with dirty diapers and garbage strewn about.

The bureau is doing unannounced visits. Social workers have been meeting with Belen about once a week to work on family safety. They tell her: under no circumstances should she leave her kids alone.

Two weeks later, Belen drives to a store in West Allis and goes inside with Naya to buy art supplies. Outside, in the parking lot, a man discovers the twin boys walking around. One nearly gets hit by a car. Someone else discovers Belen's youngest child inside the minivan, alone and crying. The police are called, and caseworkers notified, and Belen says this is how she was raised, that as a child she'd been left in the car with no harm done.

In a follow-up, a West Allis police detective goes to Belen's home on March 18 and does a walk-through. The children seem OK, the detective reports. There's clutter, the kitchen is dirty, food seems limited, but the detective doesn't see anything dangerous. The detective returns the next day and reports that conditions have "improved greatly." The kitchen's clean, floors vacuumed, refrigerator restocked.

For the two instances of leaving three of her kids alone, Belen gets charged with six misdemeanor counts of child neglect.

While those charges are pending, child welfare officials decide to let Belen's children remain in the home.

On April 9, a social worker visits Belen and sees no cause for concern. The home is fine. The children appear happy. Belen has a new job, as a hostess at a Chinese restaurant, and says she'll be putting her kids in day care.

20. April 11, 2013, 3:49 p.m. 7750 West Hicks Street, West Allis

Angelica Belen wakes up around six a.m.

Then she wakes up Naya, Adrian and Alex.

She makes oatmeal for breakfast, then gets everyone ready, faces washed, teeth brushed. Naya wants to wear her blue tights, but Belen can't find them, so Naya wears pants instead.

Around seven-thirty they pile into the minivan, all four of them. (Belen's youngest child is with his dad today.) Belen drives east into Milwaukee, to Naya's school, Saint Lucas Lutheran. The trip's just six miles, but with city traffic it can take twenty minutes. It's cold and wet. Naya doesn't want to get out of the van. But there's a place to pull up, close to the school's doors. Belen drives up and Naya goes in.

Then it's six miles back.

Belen and her twin boys get home after eight. They watch a movie, *Lilo & Stitch*, for "the thousandth time," as Belen puts it.

Around noon, a social worker comes by to check on the family. The kids are watching another movie, *Stardust*. The social worker stays at the house for thirty, maybe forty minutes.

After she leaves, Belen makes lunch. Macaroni and cheese. She makes two boxes because they always eat more than one.

The boys watch *Lilo & Stitch* again while Belen changes clothes, preparing for work later today. This will be just her third shift at Lychee Garden, a restaurant she'd been going to since she was a child. She's scheduled for four to seven.

Belen changes the boys' diapers. She changes Adrian's shirt, because he got macaroni and cheese on it. Around two-thirty she puts them in the van, and it's back to school, to pick up Naya, then back home again, pulling in sometime after three.

When she worked two nights ago, Belen found neighbors, neighbors she barely knew, to watch her kids. Going forward she'll have subsidized day care; her boss has already signed the form, verifying her employment. She'll be dropping those papers off tomorrow at the county office.

But for today, she's been unable to find anyone to babysit. At 3:47 she tries one more time, she calls one of her sisters, but the sister can't.

Belen gives her kids hugs and kisses, tells them she loves them and promises to bring home almond cookies from the restaurant.

Play with your toys, she tells them. When I get home, we'll have spaghetti for dinner.

She puts Naya, Adrian, and Alex in the boys' bedroom, the one just above the kitchen. She closes the door.

And locks it.

At 3:49, she drives away.

21. April 11, 2013, 10:48 a.m. Milwaukee Municipal Court

The same day, at 10:48 a.m., as Angelica Belen's twins are watching *Lilo & Stitch*, or perhaps by now they're watching *Stardust*, Todd Brunner is supposed to be in Milwaukee Municipal Court.

The court's docket has two cases in which Brunner has been charged with fourteen counts of violating building-maintenance codes. One count is for not fixing a rental home's porch steps. Another is for not fixing a foundation to keep out rodents.

His arraignment is this morning. But Brunner fails to show.

The judge finds Brunner guilty of all fourteen counts and fines him $14,050. If Brunner fails to pay, he could be jailed for 171 days.

That sounds serious. But the threat is hollow.

The year before, city inspectors ordered Brunner to fix defective electrical wiring at one rental, defective electrical fixtures at another, and a defective electrical outlet at a third. When Brunner failed to show he had fixed anything, the city charged him, adding three code violations to a long and growing list.

In 2013, Brunner will be called to court to face 134 code violations. He won't contest any and will be found guilty of all. He'll be fined more than $100,000 and threatened with more than three years in jail. (Nine years later, he will have paid less than half and served not one day.)

On this very day, the city has at least eleven warrants out for Brunner's arrest, for failure to pay his fines. Not one warrant will ever be executed. In this, Brunner is the beneficiary of a practice meant to help the poor. Municipal court, not wishing to jail low-income people who can't afford to pay fines and traffic tickets, generally allows people with warrants to have at least four contacts with police before being arrested.

At 1:18 p.m., two and a half hours after Brunner fails to appear in court, a deed is recorded at the Milwaukee County Assessor's Office showing Brunner no longer owns the house at 7750 West Hicks Street in West Allis. That's the house where, at about this time, Belen is cleaning up after lunch, or perhaps getting ready for work.

Brunner, the foreclosure king, lost the home six weeks ago in foreclosure to Tri City National Bank.

In online records, the new deed will take a while to show up. So this evening, when a member of the West Allis Fire Department searches for the home's owner, Brunner's name will still appear. The firefighter will call Brunner, get no answer, then leave a message and get no response.

22. April 11, 2013, 7:20 p.m. 7750 West Hicks Street, West Allis

Angelica Belen clocks out at the restaurant at 7:06 p.m., then drives home. Nearing her house, she sees fire trucks. A block from her street, she sees a police officer. He tells her a house is on fire. Which one, she asks. He doesn't know the address, but with each detail he offers, the north side of the street, the far side of the alley, realization, then panic, set in.

She jumps out of her car, leaving it where it is, the door open, and runs toward her house, in ballet flats, splashing through puddles, praying, please, God, not this, not my kids. People try to stop her, but she runs past. In her yard she finds a firefighter and asks, frantically, about her kids.

There's nobody in there, the firefighter tells her.

While Belen was at work, firefighters from West Allis and nearby cities had chased the fire through the home. Discovering a locked door on the second floor, they'd used a Halligan tool to force it open. But they couldn't search the room; the smoke was thick, the floor unstable.

Belen tells firefighters that she believes her children are inside. She says her sister was with them and may be inside, too.

A firefighter climbs a ladder up the side of the house and goes through a window into the boys' bedroom. Underneath a dresser he sees what appears to be a doll's hand.

He lifts the dresser and says, "Oh my God."

Firefighters find all three children dead, their bodies in a corner, touching.

23. April 11, 2013, 11:29 p.m. West Allis

Detective Thomas Kulinski turns on the tape recorder and waits for Angelica Belen. It's 11:29 p.m., about four hours after Belen learned of her daughter's and sons' deaths.

"How you doing? Doing OK?" he asks as she enters.

Kulinski interviewed Belen once already, earlier tonight. She'd told him that when she'd left for work today, she had left her kids at home with her sister Nicole. But police now know that's a lie. They've interviewed Nicole, and Nicole has detailed her day, and the police have corroborated her timeline.

Kulinski, a former marine with a graduate degree in theology, reads Belen her rights. Then he tells her: "Your sister wasn't there. I can prove beyond a shadow of a doubt that your sister wasn't there."

He asks Belen, "Who was with the kids when you left for work?"

For thirteen seconds, there is silence. Then Belen says, "No one, sir."

She tells him that she had no one to babysit, that she'd called around, with no luck, that she'd just started her job, she needed the job, and if she didn't show, she would have been fired.

"There was nobody in your life at all that could have watched your kids?"

"I have nobody."

"Why didn't you build a better support system for yourself?" Kulinski asks.

"What support system? These people were never there for me."

Belen tells the detective: "There's been nobody in my life. For twenty-four years I've been either beaten, abused, left alone to fend for myself. That's, that's what I've had."

24. April 12, 2013, 4:49 a.m. West Allis

"Don't make me look. Please don't make me."

Angelica Belen is being interviewed by Detective Nick Pye, who has brought photographs to the cellblock where she's now being held. Pye says the medical examiner is having trouble telling her sons apart, so they want her help. One boy died with his face away from the flames. Pye would like her to say if it is Alex or Adrian.

"No, no, no, no, no, no, please don't," she says.

She describes her sons, to help distinguish them. Adrian was taller, his hair curlier. He sucked his thumb, and his bottom teeth, the ones in the middle, were pushed in.

"You're not going to show me the pictures, please don't," she says. "Please, sir, please, I'm begging you, please. Please."

As Belen speaks, her breath is short. She sounds panicked, exhausted. But Pye expects tears. After eighteen minutes, he says, "How come you're not crying?" She tells him she has cried and screamed, horrified at what she's done, and now she's numb. She says she wants to remember her kids the way they were. She asks the detective if he'd want to see his kids this way.

After a half hour, Pye tells her, "I'm not going to force you to, I mean, OK?" When she starts to waver, he says: "I'll tell you what. Your choice. I'll slide it face down under the door, OK, and you can take as brief a glimpse . . ."

"No, no. I can't, I can't do that alone," she says.

So he stays. "You ready?" he says. She looks at the photo.

"Alex," she says, and he turns off the recorder as she gasps and wails.

25. April 12, 2013, 6:45 p.m. West Allis

Detectives Pye and Kulinski interview Belen for what is now the fifth time. This interview lasts more than two and a half hours.

Belen talks of leaving her children alone. She never wanted to do what her mother did, to hurt her kids. But "in the end," she says, "I did exactly what she did, only three times worse." She didn't want to lose her job, Belen says. She'd told her kids that with her first paycheck, she'd buy them toys. Naya wanted a Barbie Dreamhouse. The boys wanted action figures—for Adrian, Batman, for Alex, Captain America.

The detectives want Belen to admit locking the bedroom door. "I swear to you, I swear to you, on everything that is holy, I would never lock my kids in the room," she says. They offer her an out: By locking her kids in, she thought she was keeping them safe. The kids couldn't get to the kitchen and play with knives. They couldn't leave the house and wander into traffic. Belen refuses their offer.

Finally, after an hour, Pye screams at her, "How did they get locked in the room!"

"I don't know!" Belen screams back.

Soon after, she gives in. She admits turning the lock. "Because it kept them safe," she says. She tells the detectives that when she was a kid, she was left alone and nothing happened, "everything was fine."

Did her kids try to open a window? Belen asks, at one point.

"I think they did. Because there were some toys laying on the ground," Pye says.

"She tried," Belen says. "She tried, she did what I told her to do. She tried. My sweet baby girl, she tried."

Death certificates show the children died from inhalation of soot and products of combustion.

The detectives tell Belen that with the high level of carbon monoxide in the children's blood, the kids would have become numb. Euphoric, even. "You just close your eyes," Pye says. "You go to sleep," Kulinski says.

"The fire didn't get them first?" Belen asks.

"No," Kulinski says.

Pye tells Belen about electrical problems in the house. He describes the power hookup to one bathroom as "about the most careless thing I've ever seen in my life."

"The fire is not your fault," he says.

Kulinski talks about how old the house is and says, "What are the odds that it would burn down the three hours you're gone?"

There's no predicting how things will turn out, Kulinski tells Belen. Some jurors could understand why she did what she did. Some could sympathize with what she's endured. And some jurors, he says, "will look at you as the devil and want to take you out back and shoot you."

26. April 15, 2013. 7750 West Hicks Street, West Allis

A lieutenant from the West Allis Fire Department meets with an electrical engineer at the house in West Allis where the children had died four days before. They are among twelve people from four departments—federal, state and local—investigating the fire's cause.

They start outside, at a pole-mounted transformer. Then they follow the electricity, looking for evidence of arcing, where a current may have jumped off course. They examine the service panel in the basement, then trace the circuits running up, removing drywall and flooring to ensure they don't lose track of each current's path.

Ultimately, their investigation takes them to the kitchen and to a space, DATE \@ "M/d/yyyy" 5/23/2023 foot deep behind a wall, filled with plumbing, heat vents, and wiring. Here, they find their answer. The fire, they conclude, started with a failure in the circuit that powered the light above the kitchen sink.

The state classifies the fire's cause as "accidental."

No one is charged in connection with the fire's ignition. Only Belen is charged, for what came after. Prosecutors charge her with three counts of criminal neglect of a child, resulting in death.

27. June 27, 2013. Waukesha County Court Commissioner's Office

An employee with Badger Process Service Inc. goes to Brunner's home on May 31, 2013, to serve an order requiring Brunner to answer questions about money he owes the city of Milwaukee.

No one answers the door. She leaves a card. She returns on June 4 and finds the door open. But no one answers. On June 6 she returns at 10:10 a.m. and again at 8:30 p.m., and both times, "someone is home but won't answer," she later writes. On June 9 she sees Brunner's wife outside. "I'm not accepting anything," Brunner's wife says, to which the server says, "That's OK," and lays the papers at her feet, which does the job.

Brunner shows up on June 27 to answer questions from a lawyer. But Brunner becomes "argumentative," standing and swearing and asking why he has to be there, according to a court commissioner's affidavit. Sit down and stop swearing, the commissioner tells

Brunner. Brunner does neither; he shouts and waves his arms. The commissioner orders him out, but Brunner refuses, so the commissioner asks his secretary to notify the police, at which point Brunner leaves, "using profanity all the way out the door."

Brunner gets held in contempt, and a new hearing is scheduled, for which Brunner fails to appear, leading to another motion for contempt, for which Brunner must be served, leading another process server to his door, where, twice, the server hears a dog barking but gets no answer.

28. September 27, 2013. Milwaukee County Circuit Court

Twenty-one years after Angelica Belen's mother was sentenced in the death of Marisol, Belen appears for sentencing in the deaths of her three children. The prosecutor is the same. It's Mark Williams, an assistant DA with thick, gray hair, who, according to one newspaper story, has likely prosecuted more homicides than anyone in the country.

Colleagues call him a "machine." Williams, in another newspaper story, says that he works from morning to midnight and that prosecuting homicides is his "dream job." Before he's through, he will prosecute more than 700.

Belen has pleaded guilty to all three felony counts of child neglect resulting in death. Each count carries a maximum prison sentence of fifteen years.

The defense submits a memorandum from a sentencing mitigation specialist who writes, "Ms. Belen unfortunately experienced perhaps one of the most tragic developmental histories that this writer has come across in twenty years of working with indigent, criminal defendants." Belen's crime, he writes, "was an offense of omission rather than commission. . . . Additionally, there has never been any report of Ms. Belen abusing her children physically, emotionally, or verbally."

Members of Belen's family address the sentencing judge, some to condemn, others to defend.

Two of Belen's sisters describe the pain of losing their nephews and niece and blame Belen. "Time will not heal these wounds," one sister says. Belen "had so much help and support around her" but turned it away, this sister says.

Angelica's aunt—who was in court when Angelica's mother was sentenced, in the hospital when Angelica was born, and now in court as Angelica is sentenced—says: "She was ill-equipped and overwhelmed. And it's not true when people say they were falling all over themselves, offering to help her. That's not true."

This same aunt, in a letter to the judge, described her niece's history of being abused: "People wonder why Angie didn't reach out for help. But I have to ask, would you? The system and the important people in her life failed her over and over. She learned as a young girl not to trust anyone."

Williams, the prosecutor, laces into the Bureau of Child Welfare for leaving the children with Belen despite all the reports of her neglect. "And this house, we—everybody knew that this house was not exactly in good repair," he says. "It was possible that anything could have happened."

When Belen's mother was sentenced, Williams had said of her crime, "I don't understand it." Now, he says of Belen's crime, "It's beyond comprehension." He asks the judge to sentence Belen to a "period of substantial confinement" for each of the three counts. And he asks that the sentences run back-to-back, saying that's what each child deserves.

Belen, offered the chance to speak, tells the court: "I would like to say that I'm sorry to my children, my beautiful Adrian, Alexis, and Nayeli. I'm sorry they will never grow up. I'm sorry I will never see you graduate from high school and get married and have children of your own. I'm sorry that my decision that day took that from you."

Belen apologizes to her sisters, to her aunt, to the police and firefighters. She says of her children, "They were everything to me, and I loved them so much."

At the hearing's end, the judge, Jeffrey Wagner, tells Belen: "I don't think there's anybody in this courtroom that would disagree that you loved your children very much."

"I understand your—your terrible, terrible upbringing. I know that you've been victimized yourself growing up," he tells her. "But there shouldn't be this cycle."

He gives her six years in prison on each count—and orders the sentences to run back-to-back.

Belen, sentenced to eighteen years, gets sent to Taycheedah, the same prison where her mother was sent.

29. October 7, 2014. Pewaukee

A federal grand jury returns an eleven-page indictment against Todd Brunner and his son Shawn for financial misdeeds. To reach this point, the government has expended enormous resources. Here's the investigation and charges, by the numbers:

> Agencies involved in the investigation: 4 (FBI, IRS, U.S. Department of Housing and Urban Development, Milwaukee Police Department)
> Boxes of evidence collected in search of Todd Brunner's home: 22
> Documents collected: nearly 46,000
> Felony charges against Shawn Brunner: 4
> Maximum years he could face (all charges, combined): 95
> Felony charges against Todd Brunner: 15
> Maximum years he could face (all charges, combined): 350

The indictment accuses father and son of both bank fraud and bankruptcy fraud. Todd Brunner used invoices that were duplicated, forged, altered, or inflated to make draws on that $2 million construction loan for the senior center, the indictment alleges. With his son, he used three shell companies to hide cars, boats, and more than one hundred parcels of real estate, federal authorities say. The value of those hidden assets, according to the indictment, totals about $7 million.

Brunner also "fraudulently concealed" the engines from *El Diablo* and claimed to have no income when his rental properties were generating, on average, more than $30,000 a month, the indictment alleges.

In a press release, U.S. attorney James Santelle says Brunner's crimes undermine the operations of bankruptcy court and "compromise the strength of our financial institutions."

Rather than arrest the Brunners, federal agents try to serve a summons, instructing them to appear in court. Papers in hand, U.S. Marshals go to Todd Brunner's home in Pewaukee. The lights are on. A dog is barking. But no one answers.

After multiple failed attempts, government officials conclude they're being dodged. They get an arrest warrant. Early on a Monday morning, U.S. Marshals, heavily armed, backed up by three other police agencies, bang on Brunner's door, get no answer, then break the door down. They come out with father and son.

Accompanied by officers, Todd Brunner walks from the house to a sheriff's van. His steps are slow and labored. That afternoon, he gets arraigned. Then he's released, on condition he post $2,000 cash bail. Outside the courthouse he gets into a black pickup and drives away.

30. December 10, 2015. Madison, Wisconsin

Local governments see it as a threat to tenants.

A bill being debated by state lawmakers in Madison will gut the ability of cities to inspect rental properties. And, say local officials from across the state, it will prevent them from forcing owners to fix code violations before renters move in.

One state legislative sponsor says the bill "promotes regulatory fairness" by treating all properties alike, whether occupied by renters or owners.

But Milwaukee says the bill's prohibitions "strike at the heart of what a local government does—to protect the health, safety and welfare of its citizens." Its inspection program, in place since 2010, has allowed the city to target areas with higher-than-average building-code complaints, officials write. The city of

Beloit also opposes the bill. This year, in two months alone, its rental inspection program found thirty-three units unfit for inhabitation.

The bill passes the Republican-controlled Assembly along party lines, 60–31. The Senate gives its approval, and Gov. Scott Walker signs the bill into law.

The bill is one of five major, landlord-friendly laws passed between 2011 and 2019.

Among lawmakers voting on these measures, about one in five are themselves landlords or property managers.

31. June 30, 2017. Milwaukee

At times in a wheelchair, at times using two canes, Todd Brunner makes his way from the federal courthouse's entrance to the courtroom where he will be sentenced. It takes two hours. In the hallway, his screams of pain draw courthouse employees from their offices.

It's been nearly five years since the FBI searched his home and nearly three since he was indicted. There's been no trial—Brunner took a plea deal—but still the case has dragged, due in part to Brunner's obesity and poor health.

Brunner's lawyer argued, unsuccessfully, to let Brunner appear at one hearing by video, citing his lack of mobility. Transporting him to court would cost $3,000 to $4,000, the lawyer estimated. Then there was the matter of Brunner's mental fitness. Brunner suffered a stroke, but, following a psychiatric evaluation, both sides agreed he was competent to enter a guilty plea.

Brunner has pleaded guilty to three felonies: two for bank fraud and one for concealing assets from bankruptcy court. Fraud deemed sophisticated can yield a longer sentence. But Brunner's lawyer, a public defender, argues his client was, as a criminal, incompetent: "The sophistication level was bordering on the juvenile."

As his criminal case lingered, Brunner kept making news. In 2016, the *Journal Sentinel* revealed that Milwaukee Municipal

Court keeps a list, called "Egregious Defendants," of landlords with delinquent fines for code violations. Brunner was the list's No. 2, owing $161,019.

In the courtroom, awaiting sentencing, Brunner sobs. His lawyer says he has cried at the sight of Brunner's agony. "Mr. Brunner shouldn't be in court. He shouldn't have to endure that, that long walk," he tells the judge. "It hurts my soul to see someone like Mr. Brunner suffer this much." The lawyer argues against any prison time for Brunner, saying, "I don't believe Mr. Brunner is long for this world." Brunner's existence, he says, is now confined to "living in his bed."

Federal guidelines suggest a sentence of between 37 months and 46 months.

The prosecutor, who says of Brunner, "Every time he turned around, he did something that was intended to deceive someone," asks for a sentence of two years.

She says Brunner has "morbid obesity," which can be treated in a prison medical facility. She describes Brunner's various frauds: the falsified invoices, the hiding of money from bankruptcy court. Brunner hid so much cash, she says, that a bank employee had to help Brunner's son shove a stuffed safety deposit box back into place.

As the prosecutor makes her case, the judge, J. P. Stadtmueller, interrupts her. "You've got to put this case in context," he says. Brunner committed his crimes during a time of lax financial oversight, when "it was go, go, go, go, go, and we don't need to get verification for anything."

"Perhaps, but that doesn't excuse what he did," the prosecutor says.

"I'm not suggesting that he be excused. What I'm suggesting is, this case is the product of bent rules and blind eyes. Make no mistake about it!"

Before announcing the sentence, the judge asks Brunner if he'd like to say anything. "No, sir," Brunner says.

The judge says, "Obviously, the core facts of this case are not much more than a very simple fraud."

Brunner is "barely, barely ambulatory," the judge says. He now weighs more than 600 pounds. To put him in prison, the judge says, "borders on the unconscionable."

The judge sentences Brunner to probation—two years on each of the three felony convictions.

Rather than lasting six years, Brunner's probation will last two. The judge orders the probationary periods to run concurrently instead of back-to-back.

The judge says: "Obviously, there is no fine. He doesn't even begin to have the resources to pay."

After the sentencing, Milwaukee police Detective Elisabeth Wallich gets a phone call. A fellow detective gives her the news. Together, they investigated Brunner for more than six years. When she hears Brunner's getting no time, she's devastated. "All of this work went for nothing," she'll say later. "We often said, 'If I were a criminal, I'd be a white-collar criminal, because nothing ever happens to them.'"

(A reporter recently emailed questions to Stadtmueller, asking if he felt his sentence held Brunner accountable. The judge declined to be interviewed.)

32. February 12, 2018. Milwaukee

In pursuing felony fraud charges against Todd and Shawn Brunner, the federal government viewed the son as more sympathetic. Shawn did what he did, one prosecutor said, "because he loved his father."

Now, in early 2018, the government drops its charges against Shawn as part of a deferred prosecution agreement. By this point he is twenty-seven.

If there is a cycle in Angelica Belen's family, the same goes for Todd Brunner's.

On Facebook, Shawn calls his father "the wisest man I know."

In 2014, Todd Brunner transferred twenty-four properties to his son.

In 2015, one of those rental homes caught fire. The ignition sources included a floor lamp plugged into an outlet, according to Milwaukee Fire Department records.

In 2016, a sheriff's deputy arrested Shawn on a charge of drunk driving. Shawn told the deputy he was weaving because his glasses were dirty, according to police records. Shawn was convicted and ordered to pay $1,000.

In 2017, 2018, 2019, and 2020, judgments or tax warrants are filed in circuit court against Shawn for money owed. One, for delinquent state taxes, is for $456,079.12. (Shawn did not respond to requests for an interview for this story.)

In 2021, Shawn is found guilty of eighty counts of violating Milwaukee's municipal code for problems with his rental properties ranging from black mold to a missing stair handrail to noncompliance with the rules requiring smoke alarms. He is fined about $20,000—and as of this week, still owed more than half.

33. December 10, 2018. Delafield, Wisconsin

A little after midnight, deputies get dispatched to a call of a sixty-one-year-old man who has fallen in his home in Delafield, west of Milwaukee. It's Todd Brunner, in a bathrobe, on his living room floor.

As police and emergency responders try to help Brunner, he becomes "rowdy and boisterous," according to court records. "Fuck off," he says. He hits a firefighter on the arm and tells a deputy he is going to kill him, court records say. Brunner gets charged with two felonies: battery to an emergency rescue worker and threatening a law enforcement officer. In a plea deal, he's convicted of the first while the second is dismissed.

The battery conviction carries a maximum sentence of six years.

In November of 2020, Brunner appears for sentencing and tells the judge: "If this happened, which apparently it did, I fell and hit my head. I don't remember it. It's not like me." The judge, calling this a "serious offense," sentences Brunner to a year's probation and payment of $1,158.

In 2017, when sentenced on the federal fraud charges, Brunner received two years' probation. The judge attached seventeen conditions, one being, "The defendant shall not commit another federal, state, or local crime." Brunner committed this battery within those two years. But it took eight months for the authorities in Waukesha County to charge Brunner. By that time, his federal probation had ended.

34. March 31, 2020. Milwaukee

Angelica Belen sues Todd Brunner. Her lawsuit, filed in federal court on March 31, 2020, accuses Brunner of negligent upkeep of the rental home in West Allis, resulting in her children's deaths.

Unable to find a lawyer, she ends up representing herself.

Belen writes her seven-page complaint by hand, in block letters. She attaches exhibits: the notice of code violations sent to Brunner ("two outlets east side of house") and investigative reports that describe the basement's exposed wiring and conclude the fire's cause was electrical.

Belen also sues Guardian Investment, the real estate company put in charge of managing the house, and Tri City National Bank. After Tri City foreclosed on the house, a bank representative, accompanied by a Guardian employee, did a walk-through inspection, Belen writes. Neither "expressed any concerns" to Belen about the house's condition, her lawsuit says. This was in February 2013, two months before the fire.

When called recently by the *Journal Sentinel*, a Tri City spokesman said he would research this but then never got back. Rick Geis, of Guardian Investment, told a reporter that he couldn't recall what repairs, if any, his company may have ordered. "It was a while ago," Geis said. "And unfortunately it brings back bad memories and I don't want to talk about it."

"I did nothing wrong," he said.

In November of 2020, eight months after Belen's lawsuit was filed, her lawsuit is dismissed.

The federal court lacks jurisdiction, a judge determines. In tossing the suit, the judge—the same judge who earlier sentenced Brunner to probation on the federal fraud charges while imposing no fine—says Belen must pay a $350 filing fee. He orders the funds be collected from her prison trust account.

35. October 8, 2022. Wisconsin's state prison system

Sitting across from a reporter, the sun glittering off razor wire through the windows behind her, Angelica Belen says she feels the safest she's ever felt.

"Prison saved my life," she says.

It's been more than nine years since the fire, much of it spent in a cell with little more than memories and books. In comments still online, Belen is vilified, with people writing: "stupid, ignorant whorebag"; "selfish maggot"; "burn her at the stake."

Belen clings to her pastor's words after her children died. "The Lord is close to the brokenhearted," he told her, quoting Psalm 34. "He saves those who are crushed in spirit." It was what she needed to hear. Now, at thirty-four, halfway through her sentence, she credits God for getting her through.

Since the *Journal Sentinel* reached out to Belen in February, she's shared details of her life in emails, phone calls, and visits.

"I am to blame for my poor choices," she says. "I want to be able to atone."

Through counseling and a peer mentorship program, she's processed the hurt she's suffered and caused. She's forgiven her abusers. Now she's a mentor herself. In recent evaluations, staff called her an "excellent example" to others and "extremely engaging and positive." As a certified peer specialist, Belen was recently transferred to a prison that specializes in mental health services.

"This job has given meaning and purpose to every bad thing that has ever happened to me," she says.

Belen, preparing for her future, has saved up $4,000 in the years she's been locked up, she says.

In Wisconsin, Belen's sentence of eighteen years stands out. Reporters analyzed forty-plus cases statewide from 2007 to 2018 in which people were convicted of child neglect resulting in death. Belen's sentence is the longest, although she's the only person convicted in three deaths. Wagner, the judge who sentenced Belen, several years later sentenced another mother whose toddler died in a fire after she left her three young children alone. He gave her seventeen months.

Wagner recently told the *Journal Sentinel* he barely remembers Belen's case. As for the fire itself—and the problems with the house's wiring—Wagner said it was for others to decide whether to assign blame to any landlords or property managers. "I would think that some other law enforcement agency or entity would seek prosecution of that," he said. Williams, who prosecuted Belen and her mother, recently told a reporter, "The cops did not ask for those types of charges." Pye, the fire's lead investigator, said, "We never really went that direction."

After the deaths of Belen's children, the state investigated the Bureau of Milwaukee Child Welfare's handling of the case. The bureau violated state standards in a number of ways, including in how it assessed the dangers and provided support services to Belen, the state concluded.

After Belen's arrest, the bureau placed her surviving child with his dad.

Belen's son is now eleven.

Soon after Belen was sentenced, she requested that he be able to visit. A family therapist, in a court-ordered evaluation, interviewed Belen and her son separately. The therapist concluded that knowing his mom would be good for the child.

But it never happens. Belen still has parental rights, but once the courts grant her estranged husband custody, he moves with their son to another state.

The father doesn't want him in contact with Belen. "She walked out on us," he recently told a reporter before hanging up.

Belen says she misses her son beyond words. She remembers how he'd stare her in the eye and throw food from his highchair and giggle when she'd pick it up. How he carried around a Bob the Builder book shaped like a wrench, hoping to get his mom or sister to read it to him. And how he adored Naya, who he called Ya-Ya.

Now, she wonders how he's doing, what he's learning in school, who his friends are, what his favorite color is, what he wants to be when he grows up. Things a mom should know.

She wants him to know that she's always wanted to be part of his life. She wants to apologize.

She wants to be worthy of his forgiveness.

36. October 26, 2022. Delafield

This February, a *Journal Sentinel* reporter goes to Todd Brunner's home in Delafield. He declines to come to the door but calls her in her car, parked just outside. Since his stroke, Brunner tells her, "My memory's shot." She asks about the house on West Hicks Street in West Allis, and he says: "It's so long ago, I don't remember a lot. All I know is, you know, we never did any electrical work there."

He says of the house, "I don't even know what it looks like."

In late August, she returns, hoping to ask more questions. Two small lion statues sit at the end of the driveway. On the side of the house, near a wheelchair, there's a black Lincoln pickup. A sign above the garage says "Brunner Blvd." The house appears under construction, as it has for months. Porch planks are half laid, the siding half finished. In the driveway there's a car, covered by a tarp. Peeking out is a hood ornament so famous it has its own name. It's the Spirit of Ecstasy, the Rolls-Royce's crowning touch.

The reporter sees a lit candle in the window. When she knocks, a dog barks. Nobody answers the door.

Later, on October 26, Brunner picks up the phone. He says he didn't own the house when it caught fire. He won't answer questions and hangs up. Then he texts, asking for questions in writing. The reporter mails eleven pages of questions.

Brunner responds by fax. Some questions he addresses. Some he does not. "To the best of my knowledge," he writes, he never knew about Belen's lawsuit against him. Of his arrest on federal fraud charges, he says police broke down his door before his family could answer. Of his battery conviction, he says rescue workers strapped him down against his wishes: "They had no right to do that and in my opinion, they should have been charged."

Figuring out what Brunner owns, and how he's faring financially, has long been a challenge, even for law enforcement. Years ago, when creditors seized Brunner's possessions after he was denied bankruptcy protection, a police detective interviewed Brunner as part of the joint task force investigation.

Brunner told the detective he'd managed to borrow money from friends and secure a new bank loan, and with that infusion, he'd bought back "most of his property" that had been put up for auction, according to the detective's interview notes. That thirty-foot catamaran? Brunner tells the detective he bought it back for $26,000.

As for rental properties, Brunner may no longer be the owner of title, but that doesn't mean he's out of the real estate business.

In 2017, when Milwaukee receives a complaint of leaking pipes and loose wires at a house on North Thirty-Sixth Street owned by Shawn Brunner, an inspector for the Department of Neighborhood Services writes, "Talked with Todd Brunner." In 2019, when Milwaukee receives a complaint about no hot water at another house of Shawn Brunner's, an inspector writes, "Called owner Todd—said he drove down there today and they wouldn't let him in so he turned off gas because they said they smelled gas."

This year, Milwaukee gets a complaint of no heat at an apartment on West Sheridan Avenue owned by Shawn Brunner.

An inspector writes, "Called Todd Brunner, who identifies as the property manager."

How We Reported This Story

This story, a partnership between the *Milwaukee Journal Sentinel* and *ProPublica*, is the product of nine months of reporting.

We obtained records from at least eighteen local, state, and federal agencies and from eight different municipal, circuit, and federal courts. The records include notes of police detectives, code inspectors, and process servers; emails among Milwaukee police and federal agents; autopsies; deeds; fire reports from the West Allis, Brookfield, and Milwaukee fire departments, the Wisconsin Division of Criminal Investigation, the U.S. Fire Administration, and the U.S. Bureau of Alcohol, Tobacco, Firearms and Explosives; building-maintenance reports in Milwaukee and West Allis; Angelica Belen's state Department of Corrections file; and more than one hundred photographs of the fire scene in West Allis.

The story's dialogue comes mostly from audio records or transcripts. We obtained recordings of the 911 call on April 11, 2013; the police detectives' five interviews with Belen on April 11 and 12, 2013; and Todd Brunner's sentencing hearing in federal court in 2017. We gathered transcripts of Dawn Sosa's sentencing hearing in 1992; a neighbor testifying about Brunner threatening him in 2004; Brunner being questioned by a bank's lawyer in 2012; Belen's sentencing in 2013; and Brunner's sentencing in 2020 on a battery charge.

This article includes accounts of childhood abuse provided by Belen and her sister Rosalie Breckenridge. We spoke with both women, separately, in multiple interviews during which they recalled similar details about their time in foster and adoptive homes. We interviewed Belen in fifteen-minute phone conversations spanning more than three hours and in dozens of emails and visits to prison. We interviewed Breckenridge over the phone and at her home in Iowa.

To try to verify their accounts, we inspected a voluminous file in Milwaukee County Children's Court. (Getting access required permission from Belen and Breckenridge and approval by a Milwaukee Circuit Court judge.) These records provided details about the girls' biological parents, the girls' history and health, their movement through foster homes and schools, and assessments by social workers. The documents spelled out abuse the girls endured before being placed in foster care. The records did not include information about abuse by foster parents, saying only that the girls were removed abruptly from the home in Waukesha via an emergency order.

Details about the harm to Belen in the foster and adoptive homes came, in part, from another Children's Court file, regarding placement of Belen's son. (Getting access to this file also required a judge's approval.) In this file, social workers recapped Belen's history in foster care. Referring to the home in Waukesha, they wrote, "Angelica and her sibling wanted a father and were moved to a two-parent home pending adoption, but were physically abused."

Social workers also noted that when Angelica was a teenager, living with the mother-daughter duo, they received a referral about marks on her wrists from being grabbed.

In court, Belen's aunt spoke and wrote of Belen's abuse in foster care. In addition, a client services specialist in the Office of the State Public Defender wrote a memorandum saying Belen "was victimized sexually in several foster placements."

We received limited records from the Wisconsin Department of Children and Families confirming payments to the Waukesha foster parents during the time Belen was with them. The department did not have a complete file on the family as the record retention requirement was twenty years and had expired.

We did not name the foster parents as our investigation did not turn up any court records indicating they were charged with any crime. Records from the Department of Children and Families show payments to the couple ceased at the time the girls were removed from the home, indicating they did not have additional foster children placed with them.

We interviewed the foster father from the Waukesha home. He denied they abused the girls. (We also tried to reach the foster mother. The foster father sent a text in response that he said was on behalf of both of them. "We Love them Very Much," the text said of Angelica and Rosalie.)

The daughter and mother who twice took in the two girls— when Angelica was five and ten—are no longer alive. We found no records indicating either was charged with any crime relating to the girls' care.

We contacted Michael Guolee, the judge, now retired, who sentenced Dawn Sosa in 1992. (He's the judge who told Sosa, "You are weak.") He said he didn't remember the case.

We tried to reach Shawn Brunner, both through his family and his lawyer. We sent letters to the address he shares with his parents and to the PO box that he lists in court records as his official address. We received confirmation from the Postal Service that they were delivered. We also sent him a message through Facebook. (We also sent written questions to Todd Brunner's wife and did not get a response.)

In our reporting, we were sometimes unable to get records because they were so old they had been destroyed. For example, we were unable to get the records from when Brunner first filed for bankruptcy protection, in 1992. We also could not find records detailing the resolution of Dawn Sosa's arrest in 1985.

At times we drew on newspaper clips, including, most prominently, stories done by the *Journal Sentinel*'s Cary Spivak and an investigation published by the paper in 2021 about electrical fires.

Stat

"Death Sentence" is a package of stories—more appear on the Stat website—that encapsulates Nicholas Florko's sweeping two-year investigation into the refusal by state prisons to test and treat for hepatitis C. As a result, more than 1,000 incarcerated people have died from hepatitis C in the six years since a simple cure became available. *"States are effectively killing their prisoners by withholding treatment,"* explained the National Magazine Awards judges. *" 'Death Sentence' is an alarming and ultimately damning indictment of their inaction."* Florko joined Stat *in 2018 and now covers the impact of business decisions on public health. An online-only publication launched in 2015,* Stat *is dedicated to covering health care and the life sciences. This year* Stat *was nominated for the National Magazine Award for General Excellence as well as the award for Public Interest.*

Nicholas Florko

Death Sentence

T here is a simple, outright cure for hepatitis C. But state prisons across the country are failing to save hundreds of people who die each year from the virus and related complications.

A *Stat* investigation has found that more than 1,000 incarcerated people died from hepatitis C–related complications in the six years after a curative drug hit the market. The death rate in 2019 was double that of the broader U.S. population.

In the stories in this piece, reporter Nicholas Florko documents prisons' blatant refusal to test and treat people with the condition, even, in some cases, in the face of legal orders to do so. He introduces incarcerated people who watched their health deteriorate or lost their lives because of the rationing of hepatitis C drugs. Prisons say the medicine, even as its price drops, is too expensive for them to distribute widely. But incarcerated people are fighting back: some have fought for the treatment in the courts and won, forcing the system to care for them and, in some cases, other incarcerated hepatitis C patients.

Death, Despite a Cure

Falls City, Nebraska—John Ritchie shouldn't have died.

He knew he had hepatitis C. And he knew, too, about the simple, once-daily pills that could fully cure him of the potentially deadly viral infection in about twelve weeks.

But Ritchie was serving a twenty-year sentence for armed robbery, and the Missouri Department of Corrections refused to treat him.

Ritchie begged repeatedly for the medicine. He went through all the formal steps to request medical care. The prison system knew he was getting sicker and sicker—it documented his deteriorating condition in his health records. The prison's doctors wrote frequently he would benefit from hepatitis C treatment. But officials still denied him, in the same way a *Stat* investigation documented prisons around the country are still denying thousands of others the cure.

So the virus infecting Ritchie's blood continued to replicate, scarring his liver until it was so damaged that it could hardly function. Eventually he was diagnosed with liver cancer, a common complication of untreated hepatitis C. Now, the prison argued, he was too sick for the drugs to work. They refused him again.

"I don't have the energy to do nothing anymore," Ritchie told a court in 2019. "I try to talk too long, I can't breathe . . . I get out and get a little fresh air, but I can't do a lot of walking, and I can't get in the sun."

He died in June 2021 at the age of sixty-four, nearly five years after his first request for medication.

Stat's investigation found that 1,013 people died of hepatitis C–related complications in states' custody in the six years after the first cure, a Gilead antiviral drug called Sovaldi, hit the market in late 2013. This tally, based on an analysis of 27,674 highly restricted death records, has never before been reported.

Many of those 1,013 people were not serving life sentences; they would likely have had the chance to return home, reapply for jobs, and reconnect with parents, spouses, and children—or, in Ritchie's case, his one grandchild, Gabe.

Many should not have died. In fact, the treatment for hepatitis C is a modern medical marvel. The scientists who paved the way for its discovery won a Nobel Prize. Public health experts say it's possible to cut hepatitis C deaths to virtually zero and effectively eliminate the virus as we've done with smallpox or polio.

Francis Collins, the White House science adviser and former longtime director of the National Institutes of Health, called *Stat*'s findings "unacceptable."

"You have to wonder if this individual [Ritchie] had received [treatment] at the first opportunity, would he still be alive today?" Collins said.

Told of *Stat*'s findings, Chelsea Clinton, a global health advocate and vice chair of the Clinton Foundation, said the rationing of hepatitis C care by prisons and people dying as a result is "incredibly infuriating."

"It certainly is a gross injustice that we are continuing to punish people who are already incarcerated as a punishment," she said. "That sometimes there's a death sentence attached if there's untreated hepatitis C—that to me is morally indefensible."

Stat's investigation is based on interviews with nearly one hundred incarcerated people, grieving families, prison officials, and other experts; more than 225 public records requests; and reviews of over 150 lawsuits. The reporting underscores the harrowing and largely preventable toll of substandard hepatitis C care for prisoners.

It also reveals that state governments are failing to care for the people in their custody as they are required to do under U.S. and international law. In many cases, prison officials did not simply fail to act but actively erected barriers to hepatitis C testing and treatment with the curative pill. They are avoiding mass testing to ensure they wouldn't have to treat as many people, misleading incarcerated people about the effectiveness of available medicines and refusing to share death and treatment data that should be public.

Some states go even further to flout their obligations: in Illinois last year, for example, prison officials didn't treat anyone with the virus at a number of the state's prisons, despite orders from a federal judge to do so.

The hepatitis C–related death rate for people in prison was more than double the rate in the overall population in 2019, even without adjusting for the fact that the prison population is younger than the overall population.

"Most of those deaths due to hepatitis C—not all of them, but most of them—are preventable, and it's inexcusable that they died," said Jeff Keller, a board member and president-elect of the American College of Correctional Physicians, which represents clinicians who work in prisons, and the former chief medical officer of

Centurion, a major private prison health-care provider. "There's no reason for them to have died. . . . It's unconscionable."

Yet for those who run the prison systems, there is a reason: politicians and state corrections officials say the issue is money. Gilead drew extensive criticism for its initial decision to charge $84,000 for the medicine; even now, after an unprecedented price drop, treatments for hepatitis C cost roughly $24,000 per course of treatment. Missouri estimated in 2019, for example, that it would cost the prison system $90 million to treat every incarcerated person with hepatitis C—nearly 70 percent percent of its medical budget.

"In the end it all comes down to [the fact that] all prison systems are underfunded," Keller said.

Stat reached out to prisons nationwide to respond to the deaths. Most did not respond at all. In one case, Missouri, the prison forwarded *Stat* to its private contractor for medical care, Centurion. Centurion did not respond.

But some prisons are finding ways to make the math work. Death rates in prison from hepatitis C are starting to drop. Some two dozen state correctional systems have publicly pledged to ramp up their screening and treatment for hepatitis C.

Most of that progress has been driven by the extraordinary efforts of incarcerated people themselves, who have filed lawsuits challenging their state's policies, often without the help of a lawyer or even the internet, in hopes of saving their own lives or those of their friends.

"There are a lot of people that feel that just because I'm in prison I can't make a difference in the world—and that enrages me," said Mathiew Loisel, the lead plaintiff in a lawsuit that successfully forced Maine to ramp up treatment of hepatitis C in prisons. "I feel like . . . I have done something meaningful with my life."

• • •

For those who lose their lives to hepatitis C, it is a bitter irony: Few conditions that cause so much suffering are so easily curable.

The new treatments had especially raised hopes for prison doctors because they have seen the virus run rampant among the populations they treat. Hepatitis C primarily spreads through risky behaviors like IV drug use or unsanitary tattooing. It's estimated that between 12 percent and 35 percent of people in prison have hepatitis C, while less than 2 percent of the overall U.S. population carries the virus.

If untreated, the bloodborne infection can lead to scarring and permanent damage of the liver known as cirrhosis. The scarring can lead to life-threatening complications, including liver cancer or dangerously swollen blood vessels prone to hemorrhage; in some cases, hepatitis C destroys the liver entirely.

The outsized toll it has taken on the prison population is particularly distressing for public health experts because prisons should be the ideal setting for treatment. They provide health care to the very population at high risk for the virus and who often do not have regular contact with the medical system due to factors like unstable housing, lack of health insurance, or drug use.

"You know that this population has high rates [of infection], you have them there for a period of time where you can screen every single person that comes through," said Ranit Mishori, the senior medical adviser for Physicians for Human Rights. "It's a wonderful opportunity to start and complete the treatment."

Even modest increases in testing and treatment for the virus would have massive consequences not just for incarcerated people but for the broader community, too. Roughly 95 percent of people in prison will be released into the community at some point—and if untreated, so will their infection.

"Preventing and treating hepatitis C protects families, friends, and communities after they reenter society," said Tom Frieden, the former director of the Centers for Disease Control and Prevention. "Ensuring quality care in correctional facilities and good linkage to care as individuals go back into the community results in fewer infections, healthier lives, and lower health-care costs."

Gregg Gonsalves, an associate professor of epidemiology at Yale, who has written about the rationing of hepatitis C care in prisons, put it even more bluntly: "Prison walls aren't as concrete as you think. Things go in and out of prisons—and so does infectious disease."

One peer-reviewed study found that universal testing of people in prison coupled with treatment for just a subset of hepatitis C–positive prisoners would prevent 4,200 to 11,700 liver-related deaths over 30 years, 80 percent of which would have occurred in the community.

And unlike many other medical issues that plague the prison system, such as complex mental health problems and substance use disorders, hepatitis C is easy both to diagnose and to treat with a once-daily pill.

Yet prisons haven't capitalized on the new medicines. The hepatitis C–related death rate in prisons in 2019 was 10.0 per 100,000 people, compared to a rate of 4.3 per 100,000 in the general population, even before adjusting for age in either population.

That discrepancy represents a glaring inequity between the care afforded to the broader U.S. population and that provided to incarcerated people across the country, Clinton said.

"It's a health equity issue because of the structural vulnerability of people who are incarcerated," she said. "It's a health equity issue because of who we disproportionately incarcerate in this country, particularly men of color. It's a health equity issue because we are not taking a whole-of-community approach to really eliminating hep C."

It's hard to grasp just how much death the 1,013 figure represents. The count is more than quadruple the number of people who died from AIDS-related complications in the same time period in state and federal prisons combined. It is more, too, than either the number who died of homicide behind bars or who died of drug and alcohol intoxication. In fact, it's nearly the same number of people currently housed in Vermont prisons.

"These statistics are simply awful," said Charles Rice, one of the three scientists awarded the Nobel Prize for their work on hepatitis C. "We need to find better ways to get those infected into treatment."

Stat's analysis focuses on 2014 to 2019 because the federal government extensively changed the way it collects data on deaths in custody in 2019. But data from individual states that publicly report deaths in their facilities suggest that incarcerated people continue to die from hepatitis C complications. In Texas, which publicly reports the cause of death for every incarcerated person who dies, more than sixty people have died of hepatitis C–related complications since 2020.

The investigation focused exclusively on state prisons, which house roughly 85 percent of the incarcerated people in this country. (The far smaller federal prison system has also generally done a better job at testing and treating for hepatitis C than state prisons.)

Public health experts said the death rates seen in prison are far higher than they'd expect. Carolyn Wester, the director of the Division of Viral Hepatitis at the Centers for Disease Control and Prevention, called the rate "very concerning."

"I'd like to see those related death rates much, much lower," Wester said. "With highly effective curative treatments, everybody should be treated for hep C—we should be tackling these [cases] well before disease progression, liver cancer, death are on the table."

The aggregate statistics obscure particularly striking inequalities in hepatitis C care in certain states.

In Oklahoma, for example, the prison death rate for hepatitis C–related deaths was more than five times the overall state rate in 2019: 71.9 per 100,000 for people behind bars compared with 13.5 per 100,000 statewide.

Some of the outsized death rates in prison from hepatitis C are likely due to the fact that prisons have a higher prevalence of hepatitis C than the average population—and some people likely come into prison with hepatitis C that is so advanced that they're already at a much higher risk of dying. But experts *Stat* spoke to said that unequal care plays a large role.

John Ward, former head of the CDC's hepatitis work, told *Stat* that prisons should be able to lower their death rates from hepatitis C to at least those seen in the outside community.

"This is a real problem, we have a real solution, and it's not being delivered to the people who need it the most," said Ward, who is now director of the Coalition for Global Hepatitis Elimination at the Task Force for Global Health.

•   •   •

Incarcerated people like John Ritchie are dying of hepatitis C because prisons are gambling with their lives to save money.

The drugs that cure hepatitis C were astronomically expensive when they first hit the market. The first such drug, Gilead's Sovaldi, cost $84,000 per course of treatment, and prison systems argued that limiting treatment to only the sickest individuals was the most realistic way to control costs.

Now, the drugs cost $24,000 per course of treatment, and prisons can often cut better deals to bring it closer to $15,000 per course of treatment.

That still represents a massive sum of money for prisons, which often have to operate with extremely tight budgets set by state legislatures.

"It's still a high price when you have so many patients," said Josh Sharfstein, a vice dean at Johns Hopkins University who has helped correctional departments figure out how to pay for these drugs.

Prisons say that limiting care to the sickest patients is a sensible policy, given those constraints, because hepatitis C damages the liver gradually—over years or decades—allowing correctional systems to prioritize who gets treatment based on their budget needs.

Prison systems have also argued that prisoners' pleas for the drugs constitute, as Missouri officials put it, a "mere difference of opinion concerning appropriate medical care," and are attempts by prisoners to direct their own medical treatment. In one legal filing, Missouri called the broader medical community's recommendations to treat people as soon as they're diagnosed with hepatitis C "aspirational public health proposals."

Missouri officials did agree in October 2020 to modestly ramp up the correctional system's testing and treatment for hepatitis C in response to a lawsuit brought by Ritchie and a number of other incarcerated people infected with the virus.

However, the department is still treating just a fraction of its hepatitis C–positive population. Though the state knows of more than 900 hepatitis C–positive people in custody, just 13 percent of them received the curative pills last year, according to public records obtained by *Stat*.

Even now, a number of other states still rely on policies like Missouri's first one. Prisoners in South Dakota and Ohio, for example, aren't eligible for treatment until they are on the cusp of cirrhosis.

Many policies *Stat* reviewed were too vague to confirm whether people without advanced liver disease are ever eligible for treatment. Nebraska's policy, for example, says that patients with cirrhosis are the "highest priority" for treatment, but that policy does not concretely say how the department would handle people with less severe illness.

As a result, just a fraction of the people who have hepatitis C in these states are getting access to treatment.

In 2021, at least a dozen states were treating less than 20 percent of their hepatitis C–positive population. A number of states, including Indiana, Iowa, Nebraska, and West Virginia, were treating less than 10 percent. South Dakota, which housed at least 382 people with hepatitis C in 2021, treated just seven people.

Additional states may have similarly low treatment rates, but several declined to share how many people were getting hepatitis C medicine. And some provided incomplete data that made it impossible to discern their rates.

Roughly 30 percent of people with hepatitis C clear the virus without treatment, so it is possible some portion of prisoners with the condition didn't need the medicine. But prison records were not detailed enough to determine what proportion of those with hepatitis C were newly infected, and therefore able to clear the virus, or were chronically infected and needed medication.

Some states, moreover, are still not doing the bare minimum to address the virus in their facilities: testing everyone.

Hepatitis C is referred to as the "silent epidemic" because it often does not cause symptoms until a person is very sick. Universal testing for the virus should catch most cases, but prisons in Texas—the largest correctional system in the country—don't proactively test everyone in their care for hepatitis C, a spokesperson told *Stat* in June.

Georgia tests only a tiny fraction of its incarcerated population. In 2021 the state reported that just 2,286 prisoners had a hepatitis

C test on record. Another 44,250 incarcerated people were listed as "not reported."

This lack of testing almost certainly means doctors only catch hepatitis C when an individual is very sick and has developed a complicating illness, such as cancer.

Asked why prisons wouldn't test everyone in their care for hepatitis C, Keller, the official from the American College of Correctional Physicians, was blunt: "They don't want to find every inmate that has hepatitis C, because if they find them then they're on the hook."

•   •   •

For every incarcerated person who dies of hepatitis C, there are countless more individuals who will live the rest of their life with the collateral damage of an irreversibly wrecked liver, including an outsized risk of liver cancer.

"If we wait until they already have cirrhosis, we are condemning them to this lifetime of cancer risk," said Jordan Feld, a hepatitis C expert at Toronto General Hospital. "That liver is never a normal functioning liver again."

As of January 2021, more than 1,100 men and women in Florida's prison system alone have cirrhosis.

"In what world do we . . . think it makes sense to turn them out worse than what they were when they went in?" asked Gregory Belzley, an attorney that represented people in prison with hepatitis C.

It's not just the people infected with the virus who suffer. Families have to push to get their loved ones into treatment or to get them home before they die behind bars.

Charlene Hill, Ritchie's longtime partner, spent hours on the phone with Missouri's Department of Corrections each week, begging for him to get treated.

Hill lives in a subsidized, 600-square-foot one-bedroom apartment on the Kansas-Nebraska border, in Falls City. Her "hooptie," an old grey Ford Taurus, could hardly even make the drive to visit Ritchie, 260 miles to the southeast in Jefferson City, Mo.

The two, married as teenagers, had been together on and off for nearly four decades. After a divorce, they reconnected in their late fifties, thanks to online sleuthing by their daughter, who found Ritchie's location online. Hill and Ritchie hadn't spoken in a decade, but they quickly realized how little had changed since they met in the 1970s, when Hill asked Ritchie for some spare change at a nightclub and he handed her a twenty instead.

Hill called everyone she could think of in her quest to get him treatment. Once, she tracked down the number of a local representative and tried to convince him to intervene. She even tried to pay for the treatment herself and have it brought into the prison.

"He just wanted help before he died, and we couldn't get him no help—nobody wanted to help," Hill said through tears. "They just let him die. . . . I begged and I pleaded and I cried and I hollered and I cursed—and it didn't matter."

Missouri officials argued they had spent the better part of the year before Ritchie's cancer diagnosis preparing to treat him for hepatitis C. Once he had cancer, though, their hands were tied. *Stat* was unable to obtain Ritchie's medical records, and Ritchie's personal attorney declined to comment for this story. Ritchie's personal lawsuit was settled in August 2020, according to public records.

Ritchie's case pains Hill all the more because she herself is proof of what the drugs can do, if they're taken at the right time. Hill was prescribed Gilead's Harvoni for her hepatitis C in 2018, and just as Ritchie was formally requesting the therapy, she started taking hers.

Her treatment was quick and simple. Within a few weeks, she was cured.

Though she was never able to get him the pills she knew would save his life, Hill was able to get Ritchie medically paroled when his cancer was in its final stages. She hoped they could have a few good months together.

At one point, the couple had hoped to remarry once he made it out of prison. Ritchie had bought Hill an engagement ring and a new wedding ring, a gift to replace the one he bought her at Woolworths back when they first got married, when she was sixteen and he was seventeen.

In the end, Ritchie lived just five days out of prison. He was comatose the entire time, confined to a hospital bed. Hill stayed by his side the entire time, whispering in his ear, reassuring him that it was OK for him to let go.

"I think about him every day and all the struggles that we went through," Hill said. "And how close we were to being able to be together."

"We were so close," Hill said. "We were so close."

The Worst States

In 2022, whether an incarcerated person gets cured of hepatitis C is largely determined by where they're locked up.

If you're sentenced for breaking a state law in most of middle America, you're likely out of luck. Iowa treated less than 4 percent of its hepatitis C–positive prison population last year with the new class of curative antiviral pills. South Dakota has a policy on the books that blocks treatment for anyone who doesn't have serious liver damage. And Nebraska even forces people to sign forms acknowledging these drugs might not work—when they almost always do.

If you're incarcerated in New England and have hepatitis C, you don't want to be in New Hampshire, which treated just 22 people in 2021, despite housing an estimated 250 people with hepatitis C in its prisons. The state declined to share its exact figures.

If you're in Georgia or Texas, you might not even know you have hepatitis C. Those states don't actively check everyone in their custody for the virus. But if you're locked up in Utah or Virginia, prison officials will more aggressively seek out your infection. The former stood up a massive testing effort in 2021 that identified roughly 800 previously unknown cases of the virus.

The patchwork of hepatitis C policies and treatment rates is a testament to the advocacy of incarcerated people, who have managed to secure treatment and change restrictive policies in quite a few places. But it also underscores how much still is broken about hepatitis C treatment in prisons, nearly a decade after curative drugs hit the market.

"Progress is uneven," said Carolyn Wester, the head of the Centers for Disease Control and Prevention's hepatitis C work. "Some are already implementing best practices, and there are others that have not."

As part of its examination into the U.S. prison system's failures to prevent deaths in prisons from hepatitis C, *Stat* is highlighting eight states that are doing the worst job taking care of incarcerated people with the virus.

We chose some states, like Nebraska and Illinois, because they are actively discouraging incarcerated people from getting the care they need or defying lawsuits that require them to treat prisoners with the virus. We chose others, like Texas and Florida, because they have some of the highest numbers of deaths from hepatitis C, though each has pledged to change that in the months and years ahead.

Nebraska

Nebraska tops this list because its officials mislead people about the effectiveness of hepatitis C drugs, in a seeming effort to dissuade them from getting hepatitis C treatment.

The state makes incarcerated people sign a consent form before initiating treatment that claims there is "a diversity of medical opinion as to what constitutes the best way to manage HCV infection."

That's not true. "There isn't debate," said Raymond Chung, the director of hepatology at Massachusetts General Hospital, who previously led the American Association for the Study of Liver Disease. "This is the standard of care."

The form also claims there's "no guarantee this treatment will make you feel any better or live any longer." But it makes no mention that more than 95 percent of people who take the drugs are completely cured of the virus.

The form is not only incorrect, it's unethical, said Arthur Caplan, the founding head of the Division of Medical Ethics at NYU Grossman School of Medicine. If that consent form was presented to a patient at a wealthy hospital, he added, the hospital would be sued.

"Any doctor who administered that consent form should be thinking hard about whether that's consistent with professional ethics," said Caplan, who called the form "utterly deceptive."

Laura Strimple, the chief of staff for the Nebraska Department of Correctional Services, said that the state "does not actively discourage anyone from receiving Hep C treatment" and that the consent form, which *Stat* obtained through a record request in March, "is currently undergoing review and update."

Beyond its form, the state's treatment rates are among the worst in the country. In 2021, Nebraska only treated 9 of the 286 people in its custody that are known to have hepatitis C. Strimple noted that the treatment number increased to 22 in 2022.

Arizona

Arizona agreed to overhaul its prison health care system back in 2014, but at least 112 people in the state died from hepatitis C–related complications in the six years after, according to *Stat*'s tally.

Incarcerated people have filed more than a dozen lawsuits against the state in recent years after they've been denied access to the curative drugs, according to *Stat*'s analysis of legal filings.

One such lawsuit, filed by Brian Dann in 2017, alleged that the state had delayed providing him hepatitis C drugs though he had severe liver damage. By the time Dann was able to access the medications, his liver was too damaged to recover. He died in March 2018 during a procedure meant to temporarily repair his liver, the *Arizona Republic* reported.

The state's own confidential reviews of in-custody deaths appear to confirm that several incarcerated individuals died unnecessarily from hepatitis C, including a patient who had the virus for twenty years but wasn't considered for treatment until "months before his death from complications of hepatitis C and liver cancer," according to a recent lawsuit filed by the American Civil Liberties Union, which references portions of the death reviews.

Progress has been so meager that a federal judge in June held the state in contempt for its failure to improve its health-care system. "Defendants have failed to provide, and continue to refuse to provide, a constitutionally adequate medical care . . . system for all prisoners," wrote federal Judge Roslyn O. Silver. "Defendants have been aware of their failures for years and Defendants have refused to take necessary actions to remedy the failures."

The Arizona Department of Corrections declined to provide *Stat* with up-to-date treatment data, despite its obligation to do so under the state's public record law. Records released as part of the ongoing ACLU lawsuit indicate that as of October 2021, upward of 8,000 people were known to have hep C in the state's prisons; the state has lately been treating roughly fifty people per month for the virus.

A spokesperson for the DOC said the state "has taken a proactive approach to the treatment of chronic Hepatitis C in our patient population and will continue to treat patients consistent with evidence-based practices," and that it is working to "optimize" the number of people being treated for the virus.

South Dakota

South Dakota treated just seven people in 2021 with hepatitis C medications—the smallest number of people treated by any of the correctional systems that shared their data with *Stat.*

South Dakota houses roughly 3,500 people, making it one of the smaller correctional systems in the country, but even so, seven people represents less than 2 percent of its hepatitis C–positive population. The state knows of 382 people in its custody in 2021 with the infection, it said.

The state's policy requires people to have severe liver scarring, known as F3 fibrosis, or another serious risk factor, like an HIV diagnosis, to even be considered for treatment. There are a number of ways patients can be kicked off the state's treatment wait-list, too. If they've recently taken part in high-risk behaviors like tattooing or used drugs or alcohol in the past twelve months, they can be removed from the list for a year. Even refusing a medical appointment disqualifies people from being considered for treatment for a year.

The most surprising part of South Dakota's restrictive policy is that up until recently, it was actually administered by the state's public health department, rather than by the prison itself or a private medical contractor. That unusual agreement means that the same department in charge of combating infectious diseases in South Dakota is the one erecting barriers to care for the state's prison system.

A Department of Corrections spokesperson told *Stat*, however, that the medical care for incarcerated people was transferred back to the Department of Corrections in October. "We are in the process of reviewing, revising, and developing policies that follow national best practices, including enhancing our policy for the treatment of hepatitis in a way that is consistent with community standards of care," the spokesperson said.

Illinois

Illinois agreed in 2019 to revamp its entire prison medical program, as part of a civil rights settlement. But it's still falling woefully short—and the Department of Corrections' own documents indicate that people are still unnecessarily dying of hepatitis C.

An independent review of one such death found that a fifty-six-year-old man had been referred for hepatitis C treatment in 2017 but was never formally considered for the treatment until a few months before his death in November 2021.

That same report found that the agency wasn't recording the recommended regular liver cancer tests for people with advanced liver disease. Instead, the report found that "only two of [the] 30 correctional facilities provided data in their Chronic Care Rosters indicating that liver ultrasonography screening is being performed on small numbers of patients with hepatitis C."

As of December 2021, Illinois knew of more than 800 people in its custody with Hepatitis C, but six prisons didn't treat a single patient that year. Stateville, a maximum security prison that houses more than 2,000, treated just one.

Illinois did not respond to requests for comment.

Kentucky

Kentucky is actively fighting against improving its hepatitis C policies. In 2016, a group of incarcerated people sued the state on behalf of more than 1,200 people with the virus in custody. The state fought the case in court and won. A federal judge found that a modest 2018 effort to revise the state's treatment protocols was enough.

Kentucky treated just over 100 people in 2021, when it knew that at least 1,841 people in its custody had the virus.

Kentucky did not respond to requests for comment.

Oklahoma

Oklahoma prisons have a massive hepatitis C problem for a state its size. In 2021, prison officials estimated that 2,119 people had the virus.

State officials acknowledge that hepatitis C played a role in the deaths of more than eighty-four incarcerated people from 2014 to 2019—the third-largest total of the fifty states. The mortality rate for prisoners in Oklahoma was 71 per 100,000 people in 2019, more than five times higher than in the outside community.

The state, however, does appear to be trying to improve its response to the virus. The corrections department requested nearly $100 million to increase hepatitis C treatment in the state, though legislators have appropriated only a fraction of that. Oklahoma treated 589 people for the infection in 2021, roughly 27 percent of those it knew to have the virus.

Oklahoma did not respond to request for comment.

Florida

Hepatitis C was a cause of death for at least 130 people in the Florida's custody from 2014 to 2019.

The state's high death count is likely due partly to the sheer size of the state's correctional system, which is the third-largest in the nation. But the state also has a long history of denying people access to hepatitis C cures. A federal judge chastised the state in 2019 for a "long and sordid history of neglect" for people with the virus.

But there is reason to be hopeful: The state was ordered, thanks to a prisoner-led lawsuit, to expand its treatment and testing for the virus.

Already, between January 2018 and January 2021, Florida treated more than 3,000 people for the virus. But in January of last year, Florida prisons still housed roughly 7,000 people with hepatitis C who hadn't been treated for it. The state initially declined a record request seeking updated treatment data from the state, but just ahead of publication, the state responded that it "has treated 9,128 patients for Hepatitis C," total, through November 22.

"[Florida Department of Corrections] takes the health and safety of every inmate very seriously," the spokesperson added.

Florida, more than other states, will also be watched in the coming years for how well it cares for those who are already dangerously ill with the virus. As of January 2021, more than 1,100 men and women in Florida's prison system were known to have permanent liver damage, known as cirrhosis. At least twenty-eight were on the verge of liver failure, meaning they will likely need intensive monitoring and care to stay alive. Under the court order, it is required to refer anyone with the most advanced form of cirrhosis to a liver-transplant specialist within thirty days.

Texas

More than sixty people have died of hepatitis C–related complications in Texas prisons since 2020, and hepatitis C has played a role in more than 200 deaths since curative therapies hit the market, according to Texas's own data, which is more detailed than the data it submits to the federal government.

The state, which operates the largest correctional system in the country, does not test everyone in its care for the virus, despite experts' recommendations. As of June, only half of the system's intake facilities have stood up opt-out testing programs, according to a department spokesperson.

In fiscal year 2020, Texas treated 970 people for hepatitis C. The number of incarcerated people infected fluctuated that year from 11,301 to 15,563. Officials refused to provide 2021 treatment data.

There are signs, however, that the situation in Texas may improve in the coming years. The state agreed to settle a prisoner-led lawsuit last year. Under its terms, Texas will give the antiviral drugs to at least 1,200 prisoners per year until it's treated at least everyone diagnosed with hepatitis C in Texas custody as of September 2020.

A spokesperson for the Texas prison system said in a statement after this article was published that since the state settled the 2020 lawsuit, it has treated 3,000 of the 8,000 prisoners it knows to have hepatitis C.

An $84,000 Cure

State prison systems say they can't afford to cure everyone with hepatitis C. The drug, even after a dramatic price drop, is still expensive.

But several states have recently figured out how to make the math work.

When Gilead launched Sovaldi, the first-ever cure for hepatitis C, in late 2013, it charged $84,000 for a course of treatment. Today, a version of Gilead's most popular hepatitis C drug, Epclusa, retails for $24,000, less than a third of that price.

Now, prisons in states including Washington, Michigan, and Virginia are cutting deals with Gilead and makers of competing drugs to further reduce how much they spend on the medicines. Louisiana, which has one of the lowest corrections budgets per capita, has treated more than 1,600 people for the virus since signing a deal with Gilead in 2019. Other prisons have forged creative partnerships with hospitals and health departments to bring the costs down, too.

The recent progress demonstrates that the future of hepatitis C care in prisons doesn't have to look like the early years after these drugs first launched, when more than 1,000 incarcerated people died from hepatitis C–related complications.

There's no denying it: the drugs remain pricey, and treating everyone infected with the virus would eat up a big chunk of the prison medical budget in some states. In Oklahoma, for example, there were 2,119 people with hepatitis C in 2021. At $24,000 per course of treatment, the medicine would cost the state $50.9 million. That year, Oklahoma's entire correctional health care budget was $85.7 million.

In Maine, the state with the third-smallest prison population in the country, the Department of Corrections needed the legislature to greenlight an infusion of $5.5 million when it had to expand its hepatitis C treatment program after settling a prisoner-led lawsuit.

"Although funding is difficult to come by, it was very difficult for anybody to argue for a better use of money," said Ryan Thornell, the deputy commissioner of Maine's department of corrections.

Further headway will depend on prison doctors, administrators, legislatures, and governors agreeing that it's worth investing millions of dollars into hepatitis C treatment for incarcerated people and looking for deals and appropriations to help make it happen.

"These correctional facilities and their administrators . . . they need to see value in the public health intervention," said Erin Fratto, a consultant who helps states craft hep C pricing deals. "They need to see value in the incarcerated individuals' lives."

· · ·

In many ways, state prisons must contend with the same high drug prices that eight in ten Americans deem "unreasonable." Though they have some power to negotiate a discount, they are excluded from the lower rates that federal agencies, like the Bureau of Prisons, command. Same as everywhere else in the U.S, drugmakers themselves set the price for their products.

Gilead, the company behind most of the successful hepatitis C treatments, has made billions off of these pills—pulling in $2.27 billion from Sovaldi in the first three months after it launched alone. Epclusa has garnered Gilead more than $12.5 billion in global sales since the drug launched in 2016.

The company has defended its prices as "fair and reasonable," and "in line with the previous standards of care." A statement to *Stat* highlighted that 95 percent of patients who get the drugs are cured.

"We are committed to helping make these medicines accessible to those who need them, including incarcerated individuals, and exploring innovative approaches that address access gaps in today's healthcare system," the company said. "Ensuring all patients have access to this highly effective and valuable treatment is a priority."

Still, most states have set up systems to ration access to hepatitis C medicines because they say they're too costly to give to everyone with the condition.

There is some truth to their argument, that not everyone needs immediate treatment with the medicines. About 30 percent of cases clear up on their own. And the disease is often very slow-moving; it's estimated that roughly 15 percent to 30 percent of those with long-term infections will develop severe liver damage, known as cirrhosis, in twenty years.

Treatment for the virus also doesn't prevent people from getting infected again, if they go back to risky behaviors like prison tattooing. That means prisons could be on the hook for multiple courses of treatment for a single person.

But public health experts say prisons' focus on the sticker shock of these drugs is shortsighted. The top organization that addresses liver disease in the United States recommends that prisons treat people for the virus as soon as they're diagnosed. That's because getting cured of hepatitis C early not only prevents cirrhosis, it reduces the risk of other illnesses like liver cancer. Those with hepatitis C are also at higher risk for a number of other conditions that can seem totally unrelated to liver disease, like type 2 diabetes and coronary artery disease.

Ramping up treatment for hepatitis C also would dramatically reduce the prevalence of the disease in prisons over time, because those who are cured are no longer infectious and cannot spread the virus to other incarcerated people.

Jagpreet Chhatwal, an expert on the cost effectiveness of hepatitis C drugs and a Harvard professor, argues that the medicine's price is now at the point that the health-care system overall would save money over the long term to pay for these treatments now.

"We are preventing all those future complications of hepatitis C that are expensive," he said, estimating that a national effort to eliminate the disease—inside and outside of prisons—would cost between $8 billion and $10 billion, but would save the health-care system $26 billion.

· · ·

So how does an underfunded prison make the math work to get these drugs?

A number of prison systems have turned to a federal drug discount program known as 340B to buy hepatitis C medicines. To do this, corrections departments partner with a public health department or another player in the health-care supply chain, such as a hospital, that is eligible to receive the discounts, which are only available to certain entities that treat the poor. Texas, Alaska, and Utah have all used this approach.

Other correctional systems have hammered out deals directly with drugmakers. States including Louisiana and Washington have devised so-called subscription deals that give the states access to an unlimited supply of these drugs for a set overall price. Others, like Virginia, have negotiated discounts with Gilead in exchange for preferring their drugs over their competitors.

"It really was a very, very easy process," said Jamie Smith, the chief pharmacist for the Virginia prison system, regarding the state's contract with the drugmaker.

Even so, Virginia spent a total of $29.3 million on hepatitis C drugs in fiscal years 2019, 2020, and 2021, according to Trey Fuller, assistant director of health services at the Virginia Department of Corrections. It treated nearly 2,300 incarcerated people during that time, according to records obtained by *Stat*.

· · ·

For every state that's cutting a deal, there's another that isn't.

In 2020, Florida's Republican governor Ron DeSantis vetoed a $28 million funding increase for hepatitis C treatment in the state's prisons. In Oklahoma, legislators have repeatedly rejected the state's requests for significant spending increases for this population. Wyoming's Republican governor Mark Gordon lobbied the state legislature to reject a modest $4 million bump requested by his own corrections department. DeSantis and Oklahoma's top appropriator didn't respond to requests for comment. A spokesperson for Gordon said that the governor believed that the department of corrections could cover the cost of hepatitis C medicines with their existing budget.

"Not everybody agrees that the corrections population should be treated medically in the same manner, for all the same issues, that the general population in the community is," said Thornell, the Maine corrections official.

Jeff Keller, the president-elect of the American College of Correctional Physicians, put it even more starkly: "We physicians in the system are trying to do the best we can. The issue is that the legislators in the states [that don't treat hepatitis C] don't care . . . it doesn't play well politically."

A Crisis Kept Hidden

It's virtually impossible to get information from states and correctional facilities about why people die in prison.

For more than two years, *Stat* endeavored to document the number of incarcerated people who died due to complications from hepatitis C, part of a broad investigation into prisons' failures to prevent avoidable death and suffering related to the condition.

Prison systems fought our attempts at every turn.

This undertaking underscores how easy it is for prisons to hide the true reason why people die behind bars and how useless the existing data are for determining whether people in prison are dying from preventable conditions. The overwhelming difficulty of the task raises questions about whether and how family members or community advocates could ever use the information to sound the alarm about especially dangerous facilities, help families and friends figure out if a death was preventable, or pinpoint inadequate care for certain diseases.

By law, states are supposed to record the details of every death that occurs in prison. The Death in Custody Reporting Act, a federal law on the books for more than twenty years, requires states to fill out a four-page form that lays out basic information about every incarcerated person's death, including the name, age, and ethnicity of each person who died and their cause of death.

The Department of Justice uses those data to compile high-level reports about deaths in prison, but the data are often reported at such a macro level that it's not useful. Those reports, for example, only provide a tally of how many people die of "liver disease," which could have been caused by everything from hepatitis A, B, and C to liver damage from alcohol use.

When *Stat* filed public record requests seeking the information, states gave multiple reasons for hiding it. Arizona, for example, said it didn't maintain death data in the format *Stat* requested. When *Stat* sent a follow-up request demanding the exact forms the state already submits to the federal government, the state then said it couldn't provide those documents because they were owned by the Department of Justice. (Other states provided the exact same forms.)

Arkansas is one of several states that declined to provide *Stat* with any data at all because the state's records law doesn't require it to provide data to out-of-state residents. (Arkansas governor Asa Hutchinson wrote the Death in Custody Reporting Act when he was in the U.S. House of Representatives.)

Other states, like Texas and Alaska, told *Stat* the forms they are required to submit to the federal government simply don't exist. Texas added that it doesn't have access to the forms because they're submitted via a "data upload."

Iowa said the information was confidential. Others, like Connecticut and Georgia, simply ignored *Stat*'s request altogether, in clear violation of public records laws.

Some states, like Indiana, shared data that were largely useless: The state only categorizes deaths as "homicide," "use of force," "suicide," "accident," or "natural causes," making it nearly impossible to assess the adequacy of the prison medical system there.

In fact, *Stat* was only able to document the number of people who died of hepatitis C after crafting an agreement with the federal government to analyze the death data submitted by state prisons pursuant to the federal Death In Custody Reporting Act. That data is housed at the University of Michigan and is typically only available to Ph.D. researchers who are approved by the Department of Justice—an option unavailable to the average American. For our research, the DOJ withheld names and other demographic information.

Even those data were highly imperfect. Often, they were not detailed enough to discern whether someone died of hepatitis C. We excluded any such death from our tally, meaning it is likely an undercount of the actual death toll from this disease.

Prisons are only required to submit one cause of death to the federal government. What that means in practice is that a person who died of a hemorrhage due to hepatitis C–induced bleeding is often listed as dying of a hemorrhage, making it impossible to know if that bleeding was caused by something like hepatitis C or a homicide.

The problem is especially acute when it comes to hepatitis C–induced liver cancer. The Centers for Disease Control and Prevention estimates that nearly 50 percent of liver cancer cases are attributable to hepatitis C, but prisons across the country only report when people die of liver cancer, not what actually caused the cancer. *Stat* counted 416 deaths since 2014 that listed liver cancer as the cause of death with no additional causes; those are not included in our count of 1,013 hepatitis C–related deaths in prison.

Stat's tallies also only include deaths from 2014 to 2019 because responsibility for collecting these data was transferred in 2019 to another office in the federal Justice Department, which is known as the Bureau of Justice Assistance.

There are growing signs that the reporting of prison deaths has worsened under the new office. The Government Accountability

Office, the federal government's oversight arm, found earlier this year that 70 percent of the records submitted to that office in 2021 were incomplete. The Department of Justice itself also issued a lengthy report this year acknowledging it had limited "capacity to collect accurate and complete information."

The Bureau of Justice Assistance declined to share more recent data.

"We know now that the Department has received underreporting of deaths in custody since late 2019," a spokesperson said. "The Department is not releasing [death] data from this period as it is taking steps to improve the quality and completeness of state reporting."

The reporting of deaths in custody is so shoddy that academics and advocacy groups have launched their own projects to cobble together information on how people die in custody.

"The way that we have to do it is frankly unacceptable," said Lauren Brinkley-Rubinstein, an associate professor of population health sciences at Duke University who heads the Third City Project. "It shouldn't fall on curious citizens to go dig and find what they can."

Andrea Armstrong, who compiles and releases data on deaths in Louisiana jails and prisons, noted a number of shortcomings with the federal data, including that they typically are released years after deaths actually occurred and that the data do not specify the facility or even region of the state where the person died. That, she said, makes it impossible to pinpoint problematic prisons in the state.

Armstrong's project, which also memorializes people who die by name, also couldn't be compiled using the federal data because the federal government doesn't release identifiable information about those who died in custody. Her team relies on media reports, litigation, and public-record requests to get this more detailed information.

"We made that commitment to say the names out loud, and therefore some of the other datasets [wouldn't work]," Armstrong, a distinguished professor of law at Loyola University New Orleans, explained.

Some of the privacy around deaths in custody is supposed to protect people's personal health information. Under the federal privacy law, known as the Health Insurance Portability and Accountability Act, information about a person's health is confidential for fifty years following their death. States like Texas, which report the cause of all prison deaths, are able to disclose this information because their state legislatures have passed specific laws allowing them to do so.

Privacy lawyers say it's reasonable, generally, for states without clear-cut laws to be cautious about disclosing anything that could be considered protected health information because they could be dragged to court for an invasion of privacy.

"You can't unring the bell if [private information] leaves and you shouldn't have let it go," said Barry Herrin, a health privacy lawyer, who noted officials usually won't give up potentially protected information unless someone sues for it.

But there are ways to disclose why a person died without divulging identifying information. States like California, for example, release a yearly report outlining how many people die of specific medical conditions in the state, including hepatitis C. That sort of disclosure, HIPAA experts told *Stat*, would not violate privacy rules.

"You Want to Give Life"

Warren, Maine—For the prisoners who receive it, hepatitis C treatment is more than a cure. It offers a second chance, an opportunity to live long enough to get out of prison and become a productive member of the community.

Take Mathiew Loisel, thirty-seven, who was cured of the hepatitis C virus at the Maine State Prison in the spring of 2021. Just a few years ago, Loisel was cycling in and out of solitary confinement, much in the way he cycled in and out of foster homes and then psychiatric facilities. Then, jail and prison, on and off, for trespassing, criminal mischief, parole violations. Now he is serving thirty years for murder after he shot a man during a robbery.

But he earned a college degree in prison and is eyeing online business and law degrees he could put to use when he's out, in 2034. He already has some legal experience—he's actually the reason why Maine is treating hundreds of incarcerated people for the virus. He successfully sued the state in 2019 to challenge its policy of treating only the sickest individuals in its care.

"I have taken a life," Loisel told *Stat* in the summer of 2021, sitting in the visiting room at the Maine State Prison. "At some point, you want to give life."

Treating people with hepatitis C while they're in prison makes sense from a public health perspective. It is perhaps the most opportune time to reach an often transient and uninsured population and ensure they take every dose of the daily medication. But it also presents a chance to help people reenter the outside community healthier than when they entered prison.

"These are all human beings who deserve the best we can find to help them stay healthy and resume—hopefully—a normal and productive life once they're released," said Francis Collins, the White House science advisor. "That's what public health is all about."

· · ·

In 2018, Loisel was one of just a handful of men incarcerated in Maine to earn his associate's degree. Soon after came his bachelor's degree, which he finished with a 4.0 grade point average.

He's a self-proclaimed autodidact and an eclectic reader. When he spoke with *Stat*, he brought along books by Karl Marx and Princeton psychologist Daniel Kahneman. He's an avid writer, of treatises on the prison system and the values of dog training, of love poems, and of essays on his struggles with ADHD.

"What I once was is not the same as the person I now am today," Loisel wrote in one poem.

"I now am a resilient, determined and unstoppable force to be reckoned with."

At six-foot-four, with a voice that can match the pitch and power of a boat horn, Loisel is an unmistakably positive presence in the 900-person maximum security prison, the largest in the state.

"He's actively engaged in good work inside the facility," said Ryan Thornell, deputy commissioner for the Maine Department of Corrections.

Loisel says it was the grace he felt at Riverview Psychiatric Center that helped him turn his life around. Maine State Prison officials sent him there soon after he was charged with murder.

Riverview was more focused on rehabilitation than punishment, unlike the jails and prisons Loisel had come to know. There, a bad day was just a bad day. It didn't mean another trip to the segregation wing, where cells were the size of a walk-in closet. Where protests and self harm often led to blood, urine, and toilet water seeping into the hallway from the cells around him.

"I know now how important it is to have that help, and that nurturing, and that care," Loisel said. "I want to be a person who can use that experience . . . to use that to create some sort of reform or change to help others."

When he returned to the Maine State Prison, Loisel began taking college courses, training therapy dogs, and teaching English and math to other incarcerated people.

He'd work in the Maine State infirmary, a quiet sanctuary tucked into a corner of the prisons' medical wing. There, the prison bunks are replaced with hospital beds, and the walls are painted to resemble the log cabins in the woods of Acadia National Park, eighty-five miles north. The experience, he insists, strengthened his resolve to fight for better health care services in prison.

"When you watch men die because of a lack of services . . . it strengthens your convictions," Loisel said.

Loisel came across a copy of *Prison Legal News*, a monthly publication by the criminal justice reform nonprofit Human Rights Defense Center that is circulated in many prisons. One article described how incarcerated people in Florida and Tennessee had successfully sued to challenge their state's rationing of hepatitis C care.

He decided to follow their lead.

Like many in prison, he filed his first lawsuit without the help of an attorney. He finally found one, Miriam Johnson, by literally going through the phone book. Johnson had never represented an incarcerated person in a civil rights case, but Loisel's encyclopedic knowledge of the law convinced her to help him.

"I got off the phone with Mathiew, and I think I said to my colleague, 'I just talked to someone at the Maine State Prison and he knows more about this particular issue than when I typically deal with a forwarding attorney, and I'm looking at this and I think he might be right,'" Johnson told *Stat*.

The Maine Department of Corrections ignored Loisel's lawsuit for three months. Once lawyers were involved, the case settled relatively quickly.

The quick resolution was influenced by the political climate in the state: Maine had just elected Democratic governor Janet Mills, replacing Republican governor Paul LePage, who just a year earlier had pledged to go to prison himself before expanding health care to the state's poor.

"Governor Mills came in with a very aggressive and forward-thinking public health approach," said Thornell, the DOC official, who was appointed during the LePage administration. "That's what made it possible here—in her administration—where it may not have been as possible in other administrations."

After the settlement in February 2021, the prison system began testing every person booked into custody for the virus, unless they refuse, and nearly everyone with hepatitis C is eligible for treatment.

Maine treated 205 men for hepatitis C drugs in 2021—including Loisel.

For him, the treatment was simple: he took a daily walk from his cell to the pill line in the main building. He'd get a cup of water from the fountain, retrieve a yellow tablet from the pill officer behind the plexiglass window, and swallow it. He'd open his mouth to prove he'd taken it and then go back to his daily routine. Within six weeks, he was cured.

•   •   •

Even now, Loisel isn't quiet about his frustrations with prison life.

Sitting in a multipurpose room one afternoon, not more than a few yards away from the warden, he sounded off to *Stat* about the injustices of the criminal justice system and his negative experience with a prison clinician who's related to Maine's corrections chief.

He only paused when his attorney arrived; he couldn't wait to speak to her about a document he was being asked to sign that would have released the prison's health-care provider of any liability as part of his settlement.

"I'm not quite satisfied," Loisel said. "It's hard for me to enter into any agreements or settlements that may further restrict people from pursuing justice."

That zeal explains how Loisel has become a vocal and engaged member of his own legal team, even without a law degree. His lawyers regularly send him legal filings to review before they file them with the court. In 2019, a judge even agreed to bus him to the federal courthouse in Bangor, seventy miles to the northeast, to take part in the formal settlement negotiations for his case.

It explains, too, his plans to go to law school. He's now applying to MBA programs, but after that, he's eyeing a legal career.

Maine allows certain convicted felons to practice law—and he already won his first case.

Glamour

WINNER—PUBLIC INTEREST

"The Time to Pass Paid Leave Is Now" explains what the failure to enact a national paid-leave policy means for millions of Americans. Included here are two "as told to" stories that portray the struggles of new mothers. Readers are also urged to seek out "28 Days" at https://www.glamour.com/. Part of the online package with "The Time to Pass Paid Leave Is Now," "28 Days" follows the lives of eight women in the four weeks after they gave birth—four weeks that nearly everywhere else in the world is covered by family leave. The National Magazine Award judges lauded Glamour for championing the cause of paid leave and noted the impact this package had on policy makers. Natasha Pearlman is the executive editor of Glamour. Ruhama Wolle, who cowrote parts of the package with Pearlman, is the special projects editor at Glamour.

Natasha Pearlman

The Time to Pass
Paid Leave Is Now

3 31 million people live in the United States.
167.6 million of them are women.
Of those, at least 71.75 million women are employed.
And on average, there are over 3.5 million births a year.

Yet despite these statistics, despite the millions of children being born in the country each year, despite the millions of parents who struggle through those early weeks of sleepless nights and sheer exhaustion, despite the many women and birthing people who have often gone through intense physical and emotional trauma during pregnancy and childbirth—tears or cuts around their vagina and in the perineum, long labors, C-sections, bleeding for weeks afterward, infections, their children needing medical treatment, and more—there is no national paid-leave policy.

Whether you give birth or have a child through adoption, surrogacy, sperm or egg donation, IVF, or more, if you work, you are afforded no federally supported paid time off.

Yes, if you are employed by an organization with fifty or more employees, the Family and Medical Leave Act of 1993 allows you to take twelve weeks off without losing your job to recover from serious illness or to care for a newborn, an adoptive child, or a family member with serious health conditions—but it is *unpaid*.

And that's it. You have to get lucky, with an employer who happens to have a good company-based paid-leave policy. Or you're not lucky. And either you earn enough to put aside money to live off during your maternity leave, or you don't, and for each day that you are not at work, each day that you are physically recovering from childbirth, or exhausted from raising a newborn, or simply wanting to be at home and bonding with your child, you and your family fall into debt or eat away at savings.

This is a problem that threatens the entire construct of the family in this country. But also, make no mistake, it impacts women—and disproportionately women of color, women in low-income jobs, and women in service and domestic industries—the most. In 2019 only 19 percent of workers in the United States had access to paid family leave via their employers. For the lowest quarter of wage earners, most of whom are women, this fell to 9 percent.

It is as depressing as it is unsurprising that one in four women living in the United States returns to work within two weeks of giving birth. She will often be bleeding, swollen, sleep deprived, barely functioning—but in order to provide for her family, she will be working.

And yet if you had a child in almost any other country in the world, including in the most oppressed, you would have access to paid leave. The United States is one of only six countries in the *entire* world, and the only high-income one of those six, that has no paid-leave policy. The others? The Marshall Islands, Micronesia, Tonga, Nauru, and Papua New Guinea.

This might seem a lot to digest, but it matters. Because in a world where 189 other nations support women and parents in the toughest weeks postpartum, America's lack of paid leave should be a point of shame. And yet, somehow, it isn't.

More than one hundred years on from when the International Labor Organization called for twelve weeks of paid maternity leave, free medical care during and after pregnancy, job guarantees upon return to work, and periodic breaks to nurse infant children—and after an influx of women globally to the workforce during World War I—the United States is still no closer to a federal policy. And surprisingly few politicians, on either side of the political divide, seem troubled by this deep social inequity.

Globally, the average paid maternity leave is twenty-nine weeks, and the average paid paternity leave is sixteen weeks, according to

2019 data from the World Policy Analysis Center. Yet after the U.S. House of Representatives passed the Build Back Better Bill in November 2021 that contained a barely adequate four-week paid family leave provision, the Senate failed to pass it. The man who blocked its passage? West Virginia Democratic senator Joe Manchin—proof if it was needed that passing laws that support women lacks support across both parties.

When components of this bill were reintroduced in 2022 as the part of the Inflation Reduction Act, it came without the childcare and leave benefits from Build Back Better and passed without incident in August of this year. It's hard to look at the course of events and draw any other conclusion than that women don't matter.

Frustrating though it may be that we need to do so, it's important to lay out the argument for paid leave. And making this case is exactly why *Glamour* has followed eight women through the first twenty-eight days postpartum. In the article, the physical, financial, and emotional experiences of women with varying access to paid leave are laid bare—as we call for a national conversation on the passing of paid leave to be reignited.

One of staunchest political advocates of paid leave is New York senator Kirsten Gillibrand, who in February 2021 introduced the Family and Medical Insurance Leave Act (FAMILY)—a program that would provide up to twelve weeks of national paid family leave, covering childbirth, family illness, and more, for—in her words— "about the cost of a cup of coffee a week." This is, depressingly, the fourth time it's been introduced (it failed in 2013, 2015, 2017, and 2019), but Gillibrand—who has never given up—and the lobbying organization Paid Leave for All speak in hushed but hopeful whispers of a growing momentum across the political divide to get something done.

Gillibrand names senators Susan Collins, Deb Fischer, Joni Ernst, Mitt Romney, and Bill Cassidy as the Republicans "most interested in paid leave." But she notes that the road to success is long, because as yet, there is no agreement on a financial model to get it through.

"Senator Manchin has said he only wants to do [paid leave] on a bipartisan basis," Gillibrand explains. "But the truth is there are no Republicans who want to support the FAMILY Act as written, and so by saying it has to be bipartisan, he's killing it."

In the meantime, she is exasperated at the impact of the country's lack of paid leave on the economy: "Every time a family member needs to stop working because they've had a new baby or an ill parent or a sick child—for many people they either have to quit their job and meet that need. Or they have to suffer through not meeting that need and continue to work because they have to put food on the table. That's a choice people shouldn't have to make. It's devastating for many families and many individuals. It's essential that families have that time together."

Dawn Huckelbridge, the founding director of Paid Leave for All, is equally passionate: "I'd studied paid leave, and I knew about it at this abstract or intellectual level. But it was when I became pregnant and gave birth that it just became so core to me. It felt like this is one of the root problems that leads to so many other inequities. I was shocked at how badly I felt treated, as a woman with a lot of privilege, with health care, with a supportive family, with a little bit of paid leave, but not enough.

"My son had really bad colic, and he screamed every day, all the time. He wouldn't sleep; he wouldn't let me sleep. So for the better part of a year, I barely sat down. I didn't eat. I barely slept. I nursed around the clock, just trying to keep him from blowing up. And by the end of it, I remember saying, 'I get why some mothers in this country just snap.' I was so tired. I was ready to give up, and I felt trapped. And I just kept thinking, If it's this hard for me, how is it possible that one in four people in this country go back to work within two weeks? It blew my mind. And I felt like this was this whole world of injustice that, until I lived it, I didn't understand how urgent it was. Now I plan to do whatever I can to achieve paid leave for everyone who works."

Here's the thing: The issue of paid leave is deeply and inextricably personal. It is personal to Dawn Huckelbridge, who as a highly successful policy advocate only truly understood its importance when she became a mother.

It is personal to Meghan Markle, the duchess of Sussex, who has been an outspoken supporter of paid leave. It is personal to former supermodel Christy Turlington, founder of Every Mother Counts.

It is personal to actor Freida Pinto, who recently had her first child and tells *Glamour*, "I feel very fortunate that I was empowered to take as much time as I needed, both by my family and my team. I understand that is not the case for most women, which is why we need to discuss this more. It's time to empower changes to the systems and standards in place."

It's personal to Hillary Clinton, who tells *Glamour*, "When I had Chelsea I literally had to create the maternity leave policy at my law firm. Even unpaid leave was not a guaranteed right. Four decades later, we've made progress, but we still have much to do."

It is personal to me because after the birth of my first daughter, I was so physically impacted by a challenging vaginal delivery that it hurt to walk or sit for two months. Whatever my complicated emotional feelings were about becoming a mother, physically I needed every single day of the six months I took off—three months fully paid, three months at half pay. (I had both my children in the UK, and had I taken off longer with my first, I would have transitioned to the country's standard weekly maternity pay.)

It's personal to Gillibrand, whose own two births and postpartum experiences, no matter that they were nineteen and fourteen years ago, were full of such deep challenges that it shapes her policy today. "I had preeclampsia. I had gestational diabetes. I was really sick after I delivered Theo [her eldest] with an emergency C-section, and I was in the hospital for a whole week. My body shut down. If I didn't have a husband—which a lot of women don't have, and are birthing children on their own—the baby wouldn't have eaten. We had to do formula feeding that first week.

"And my law firm didn't have a paid-leave program. So I was like, 'I'm going to write you one, because this is a liability for you.' And I was able to take three months' paid leave, and it worked for me, and it got me on my feet again. It got me time to learn how to nurse. It got me time to learn how to be a mom."

And it's personal to many millions of families and working women and men in this country who have likely been through the complex swirl of joy and confusion and exhaustion and financial stress that new parenthood brings with it.

But it raises the question: When something can mean so much and can impact women's lives so detrimentally and has been an issue for successive governments, why for over one hundred years has it been so impossible to pass into law?

Huckelbridge and Gillibrand don't hold back: Sexism.

Huckelbridge says, "We are not a partisan organization. But what we've seen in Washington recently, which is disheartening, is it's become about which side is getting a win. The opposition [to paid leave] has been pretty irrational, and it is bearing out as clear sexism. It is bearing out as total devaluing of women's work and women's lives."

When asked if the reason we can't get paid leave into law is that there are so many men in Congress, Gillibrand answers without hesitation: "Yes. There's not enough caregivers in Congress, which tend to be women. We only have 25 percent women in Congress."

Their goals are clear: to urgently change the minds of the men blocking paid leave or find a way to work around it—in Gillibrand's case, a compromise bipartisan deal. "I think this year the only thing we can get done is a minimal bipartisan optional paid-leave program, unless Joe Manchin changes his mind, which I don't think he will." And to activate voters—all voters—to demand paid leave and to only cast their vote for candidates who back it. Candidates across the political spectrum should take note—according to a new survey, four in every five Americans support paid family leave.

Chelsea Clinton, vice chair of the Clinton Foundation and Clinton Health Access Initiative, is deeply frustrated by the increasingly partisan nature of this topic: "Supporting children and families should be a nonpolitical issue that has sadly, and wrongly, been politicized. This is not an issue of party or politics. We need policies that ensure all parents are afforded the time to be the parents they hope to be, starting with paid parental leave throughout the country."

Some critics might argue that it is not for the federal government to provide this leave and that it's on individual states to create their own paid-leave programs. But Lauren Smith-Brody, author of the seminal working-parents handbook *The Fifth Trimester* and cofounder of the advocacy organization Chamber of Mothers, argues: "The challenge with that is that the policies vary so widely state by state that there's no consistency. [Only eight states have policies enacted right now, with four more becoming effective in the coming years.] Particularly now that people are working remotely, your business may be domiciled in a different state than you're living, and the insurance that your business has that you're covered by may be domiciled in a different state. So are you covered by that state? Or by the state you're living in?"

This confusion is, in fact, precisely what faced Tiffany Mrotek, one of the women *Glamour* followed for twenty-eight days. Only after giving birth did she discover she was ineligible for the state paid leave she had been counting on—because while she worked for a Washington, DC, company, she lives and now works remotely just across the border in Virginia.

Had she had access to federal paid leave, the pay she had been counting on would have been guaranteed, rather than—as it turned out—inaccessible.

•   •   •

The irony is that for all the difficulty facing lobbyists and policy makers in passing a national paid-leave policy funded by employers and employees, in 2019, during Trump's presidency, one of the most significant breakthroughs was actually made with the passing of the Federal Employee Paid Leave Act. This granted certain federal employees twelve weeks of parental leave to care for a newborn or adopted child and is fully funded by the government. Transportation Secretary Pete Buttigieg was able to use this when he took four weeks off after the birth of his twins in August 2021.

This likely contributed to the momentum that got paid leave into the Build Back Better bill, despite its ultimate failure. And now with the overturning of *Roe v. Wade*, rather than cast paid leave aside for another day in the fight to protect abortion, the most powerful women's organizations have taken up the battle once more.

Reshma Saujani, activist and founder of Marshall Plan for Moms, says, "With the Supreme Court's decision this summer overturning *Roe*, it feels like every day we are fighting for our right to live freely and thrive.

"We have to meet this urgent moment by fighting for paid leave. This policy is critical for families, especially for working mothers, who for too long have been expected to return to work too soon after giving birth, without adequate time to recover or bond with their newborns. Paid leave is incredibly popular across partisan lines, as a study that we did at Marshall Plan for Moms in 2021 demonstrated that over three quarters of all female voters supported policies like paid leave."

Similarly, a new poll for Paid Leave for All found that more than eight in ten voters in battleground states support a paid-leave policy ahead of midterm elections.

There is a huge amount of vital work being done to encourage individual businesses to take greater responsibility for, be transparent about, and provide their own competitive company paid-leave policies for employees—TheSkimm's viral #showusyourleave initiative has resulted in the launch of database of paid-leave policies for over 480 companies.

But the question at the heart of it all is this: How can we finally get a federal paid-leave bill passed that benefits *all* workers in the country? Without question, politicians need to take note that this is a vote winner, as well as simply just good policy.

As is often the case, politicians need to be reminded of the popularity and importance of paid leave. And this is where you come in. *Glamour* urges you to call or write to your senators and demand that they take up the fight for all of our futures.

But that alone may not be enough. Your lives and your stories matter. We are asking you to join the women in our piece by sharing your own unique experiences or your hopes for change with those you know and in your communities. Let's use this moment to ignite a national conversation and a demand that those elected to power cannot ignore. It's time. It's way past time—one hundred years is too long of a wait. #Passpaidleave—now.

"I Started Working Six Days After Having My Daughter"

Karina Garcia, twenty-nine, is a chef from Harlem in New York City. She lives with her husband, Eduardo Rodriguez, and their daughter, Yohualli, now four months. She had no paid leave and went back to work within a week of giving birth. As told to Natasha Pearlman.

My husband and I saved for a year and a half in order to have a baby. I am a chef, and my husband is a music teacher. We also run a supper club from our home on weekends, and I bake doughnuts for a café in Brooklyn four nights a week.

We put enough money aside so that we could take eight weeks off running our supper club. But there is no option to stop completely, so I always planned to keep doing the doughnuts without taking any break. I have to work. I worked until two days before I gave birth to our daughter, Yohualli, in May this year, and started up work again six days after she was born.

There is a part of me that always needs to feel productive, and creatively I'm in my element in the kitchen. It's my happy place. But when I think about having another child, I don't know if I could do what I've just done again—working so soon after the baby was born and being so incredibly tired while also juggling two businesses that are both run from our home. It makes me think we really have to get a brick-and-mortar location so someone else could take it on while I break or somehow figure out how to live without my income for a period of time.

Having Yohualli has been incredible, but it's been a journey. My labor was long. It started on a Sunday night, and I didn't sleep all of that night. I slept a little on the Monday, a little more on the Tuesday, but then on the Wednesday, I was managing only seven minutes of sleep in between contractions. I was ready to give up. I wanted this natural birth, no painkillers, no nothing, and to do it at home, in a pool. But I had no energy and I didn't know if I was going to be able to take the pain, but that day she finally came. I can't remember a lot, but I didn't tear, and it was so beautiful to finally meet her.

Eduardo, my husband, had to go back to work immediately at the schools he works at. So I was on my own at home from day one. It was so hard for him, being away from our daughter for a lot of the days. He would say to me: "Every time I go out, I want to be back home. I want to see her." When the summer holidays started, it was so much better.

Originally I had planned to start working on maybe day two postpartum, but we were just too tired. We make the doughnuts between midnight and eight a.m., and we have to be up and down in the night because we have to make the dough, let it rise twice, then shape the doughnuts, fry them, let them cool, and then fill them. I called the café we supply the doughnuts for, and the owner was completely understanding. But we didn't want to stop for long, so within a week of Yohualli being born, we were working again. We make twenty doughnuts a day for the café, and every Thursday I make an extra forty doughnuts for local Harlem moms. I started selling to them through a Facebook group. Moneywise, I make $400 a week from the café doughnuts and $400 from selling direct locally.

I'm happy, but I'm also tired. Yohualli is perfect, but sleeping is tough, especially being up so many nights a week working. The other day I was so exhausted, I lay down next to her on the floor and fell asleep. But I thought I would find it harder. I thought I would be in a less joyful mood to be changing diapers and to hear her cry. But it doesn't bother me. Yes, sometimes I would like to be able to take a shower when all she wants to do is be on the boob, but it's a beautiful time. Financially, however, I don't know if I'd want to do it this way again.

Life is fair. It's also unfair. But hopefully something will change. I knew going into the situation that I would have to take care of myself, that I wouldn't have access to paid leave, so it wasn't a surprise. But should I have had to go back to work straight after having a baby, just to make sure we would be able to keep our apartment, to pay our bills? No. I hope things will change.

"In the First Days After Giving Birth, All I Could Think About Was Money"

Shukura Wells, twenty-eight, was a mortgage credit underwriter and is launching a business supporting Black-owned cosmetics brands. She lives in Detroit with her daughter, Zendaya, age four; her boyfriend, Dazz; and their son, Dakari Gold, three months. She had no paid leave. As told to Natasha Pearlman and Ruhama Wolle.

I had my son on June 25 this year. And a few weeks before I gave birth, I took severance from my job. I was working for a mortgage company in Detroit, but the housing market has been slow and our department was really affected.

I thought it would be okay because the money I was being paid in severance would take me through to November, my health care was still covered for six months, and I thought it would give me time to put into the beauty business I started recently. But I think I thought I was superwoman and that even while heavily pregnant and in the early days postpartum, I would be able to do what I needed to with my website: reaching out to businesses, pitching to carry their products on my site, promoting everything. But I didn't, and in the first few days after giving birth, all I could think about was money—stressing about what we did and didn't have and the fact that the severance money I had was coming to depletion. I didn't mean to cry, but when I said it out loud, it felt real.

On day four I knew I would have to start back working pretty quickly doing something—at the very least part-time just so that we would have enough money with my and my boyfriend's income. So it was the two of us working, so we weren't struggling. This isn't what I wanted. I would have loved to take a proper maternity leave. I wasn't able to do it with my first child, as I had no paid leave from my previous job and only about $500 in paid time off.

The irony is that I feel if I wasn't so stressed about money, I would be really happy. When I had my daughter, Zendaya, who's now four, I was so sad and depressed. It just wasn't a good post-partum experience, and it was really tough learning how to parent for the first time. But with Dakari, he's such a chill baby. He's had some trouble latching, but he does feed well. I gave birth naturally and it went pretty fast, and I should have felt so good, and in many ways I do. It's definitely money that's become the greatest stressor.

Stability is so important to me because we didn't have a lot of money when I was growing up. We lived in a lot of houses, and at one point we didn't have a home. Two of the houses that I grew up in aren't even standing anymore. So I always knew I wanted to own a home of my own, so I could always give that to my children. I never want them to think, "Oh, where am I going? And where am I going to live?"

When I came back to Detroit after graduating from college—I went to Grand Valley State—I started working and saving. In fact, until now, there hasn't really been a day where I haven't worked. And then last year I'd saved enough to buy the house we live in now. I wanted to do it on my own, that meant a lot to me. I'm so proud of what I've achieved, but that's why I care so much about keeping everything I've worked so hard for. About two weeks after giving birth to Dakari, I started working from home, doing hair a few times a week. It's enough to take a bit of the financial pressure off, but it's tiring, and I have the baby with me all the time too.

Luckily, Dakari is great. His name, like mine and my boy-friend's, has an African origin. The "Kar" means happiness. And his second name, Gold, is because I don't just love the color; I love that it's a natural element and has a connection to the earth. And he really is brilliant. He has his own little schedule. He feeds around eleven a.m., one p.m., three p.m., six p.m., nine p.m., and then usu-ally midnight. And he sleeps in between, but I also have to work, look after my daughter, and then pump as well. So when I do get to sleep, it's like for a second only, and then I'm up again. The incre-ments are so close. And I've just had to be like, "Let's push through."

Along with the tiredness, I wish more people would talk about the physical aspects of postpartum recovery. I thought I was doing okay at first, but if you want to get real personal, my butt really hurts. I think I've got hemorrhoids, and honestly, for the entire twenty-eight days, I found it quite terrifying to go to the bathroom.

I bled for nearly four weeks. After two weeks I was still getting cramps in my stomach, and I sweat in my sleep now. I feel like my body is so different, as far as everyday things go. My doctors told me that everything can take a while to get back to normal, but it's really tough. And people don't really tell you about this, about how hard it will be. I don't know if enough women know about this. You definitely don't want to be intimate with a partner with all this going on. Then the other day my daughter was like, "Hey, Mommy, let's race." I was like, "No, I'll just cheer you on."

My daughter has been amazing. She wants to help all the time, and I love to have her. I just want to make sure that I give my chil-dren the best life I can. I'm already applying for full-time jobs to hopefully start in October. My business is my dream, but I don't know if now is the right time.

New Yorker

WINNER—COLUMNS AND ESSAYS

In this series of articles, Jia Tolentino briskly summarizes the impact of the Supreme Court's decision to abandon Roe v. Wade: "We have entered an era not of unsafe abortion but of widespread state surveillance and criminalization—of pregnant women, certainly, but also of doctors and pharmacists and clinic staffers and volunteers and friends and family members." The judges who chose these articles as the winner of the National Magazine Award for Columns and Essays described them as "searing and beautifully articulated." A staff writer at the New Yorker, Tolentino was also nominated for the National Magazine Award for Columns and Commentary in 2020. Her first book, Trick Mirror: Reflections on Self-Delusion, was published in 2019. The New Yorker received seven National Magazine Award nominations this year in categories ranging from Video and Photography to Reporting and Public Interest.

Jia Tolentino

A Post-*Roe* Threat
and The Post-
Roe Era *and* Is
Abortion Sacred?

A Post-*Roe* Threat

January 22, 2022, marked the forty-ninth anniversary of *Roe v. Wade*—and, likely, the last year that its protections will remain standing. In December, during oral arguments, the Supreme Court's six conservative justices signaled their intention to uphold a Mississippi law that, in banning almost all abortions after fifteen weeks of pregnancy, defies *Roe*'s protections. Most of those Justices seemed prepared to overturn *Roe* entirely. Without *Roe*, which prohibits states from banning abortion before fetal viability—at twenty-eight weeks when the law was decided, and closer to twenty-two weeks now—abortion could become mostly inaccessible and illegal in at least twenty states.

Some of the potential ramifications are obvious. The majority of people who get abortions are already mothers, and 75 percent live near or below the federal poverty line. It is the least advantaged of this disadvantaged group who will be unable to cobble together the time, money, and child care required to travel across state lines to determine their own reproductive futures. Some will be able to self-administer abortions through telemedicine and mail-order pills—a safe and increasingly common method for early pregnancies. But for those who can't, the long-term consequences could be severe. The Turnaway Study, a research project that tracked a thousand women seeking abortions in the United States in the course of five years, found that women denied an abortion have an almost four times greater chance of living below the federal poverty line than women who were not denied one, as well as an increased risk of serious health problems, and their children are more likely to grow up in an abusive environment.

But there are other severe, metastasizing consequences that could follow *Roe*'s repeal. *Roe* rejects the idea of fetal personhood, which is a pillar of the antiabortion movement. It also repudiates the argument that the Fourteenth Amendment grants equal protection and consequently equal legal standing to fetuses. (That claim was used as early as 1971, when a lawyer filed suit against the state of New York over its liberalized abortion law, and it has been resuscitated by organizations such as the March for Life, whose 2022 theme is "Equality Begins in the Womb.") The Supreme Court remains a distance away from this extremist position—even Justice Antonin Scalia said that the Constitution applies only to "walking-around persons." Still, antiabortion groups have been pushing fetal personhood on state legislatures, which have introduced more than two hundred pieces of legislation supporting it in the past decade. Most of the bills have failed; they are unpopular as well as unconstitutional. But, in 2019, Georgia passed a near-total abortion ban that allows a fetus to be claimed as a dependent on one's taxes. (The same year, a judge in Alabama allowed a man to sue an abortion clinic on behalf of an aborted embryo's estate.) The Georgia law is currently before the Eleventh Circuit Court of Appeals, awaiting the Supreme Court's Mississippi ruling. If such laws can no longer be challenged at the federal level, they will surely begin to proliferate in earnest.

Recent events in Oklahoma provide an example of what might follow. Though the state's Supreme Court struck down a fetal-personhood amendment to the state constitution in 2012, the idea has been affirmed in other ways. In 2015, state law was amended to require that any fetal death past twelve weeks be reported as a stillbirth. The Humanity of the Unborn Child Act, passed in 2016, requires that the state department of health "clearly and consistently teach that abortion kills a living human being." Since

2017, according to a report by the *Frontier,* an Oklahoma journalism nonprofit, at least forty-five women in that state have been charged with child abuse, child neglect, or manslaughter because of drug use during pregnancy. In 2020, according to the *Frontier,* the district attorney for Kay and Noble Counties charged seven women with felony child neglect for using marijuana during pregnancy, even though some of them had medical-marijuana licenses. The charge does not require the state to demonstrate actual harm.

The same year, the district attorney for Comanche and Cotton Counties charged three women—Brittney Poolaw, Ashley Traister, and Emily Akers—with manslaughter after they miscarried at seventeen weeks, twenty-one weeks, and twenty weeks pregnant, respectively. The fetuses were autopsied, as necessitated by the 2015 change in the law, and each tested positive for methamphetamine. As thirteen physicians and researchers recently affirmed in an amicus brief in support of Akers, studies have shown that meth use is associated with issues connected to low birth weight but not with miscarriage or stillbirth. Traister pleaded guilty and is awaiting sentencing. Akers's case was dismissed due to lack of evidence, but Comanche County has appealed. Poolaw was incarcerated for eighteen months before being convicted by a jury that deliberated for less than three hours; she was sentenced, at age nineteen, to the minimum sentence of four years.

These cases are not anomalous—they're part of an intensifying pattern. In the late eighties and early nineties, at least 160 women who used drugs while pregnant were charged with child neglect and distribution of drugs to minors. Between 2006 and 2016, according to *ProPublica,* some 500 Alabama women were charged with felony chemical endangerment for using drugs during pregnancy, even in cases in which the drugs were prescribed by doctors. One woman, Katie Darovitz, was arrested when her son was two weeks old and healthy; she had controlled a seizure disorder with marijuana after her doctors advised her that her normal medication could be unsafe for pregnancy. (The case was eventually dismissed.)

Every year, there are about a million miscarriages in the United States. Under the doctrine of fetal personhood, these common, complicated, and profoundly intimate losses could become legally subject to surveillance and criminalization. The blame, as always, would fall on individual behavior, not on the chromosomal or placental abnormalities that often cause miscarriage or the social factors that have been proven to increase a person's risk of losing a pregnancy: poor nutrition, limited health-care access, night shifts and long hours, exposure to environmental toxins. Poverty and racism pose an unequivocal threat to fetal life and child well-being. In a post-*Roe* world, poor and minority women would find themselves not protected but targeted for further suffering.

The Post-*Roe* Era

In the weeks since a draft of the Supreme Court's decision in *Dobbs v. Jackson Women's Health Organization*—a case about a Mississippi law that bans abortion after fifteen weeks, with some health-related exceptions but none for rape or incest—was leaked, a slogan has been revived: "We won't go back." It has been chanted at marches, defiantly but also somewhat awkwardly, given that this is plainly an era of repression and regression, in which abortion rights are not the only rights disappearing. Now that the Supreme Court has issued its final decision, overturning *Roe v. Wade* and removing the constitutional right to abortion, insuring that abortion will become illegal or highly restricted in twenty states, the slogan sounds almost divorced from reality—an indication, perhaps, of how difficult it has become to comprehend the power and the right-wing extremism of the current Supreme Court.

Support for abortion has never been higher, with more than two-thirds of Americans in favor of retaining *Roe*, and 57 percent affirming a woman's right to abortion for any reason. Even so, there are Republican officials who have made it clear that they will attempt to pass a federal ban on abortion if and when they control both chambers of Congress and the presidency. Anyone who can get pregnant must now face the reality that half of the country is in the hands of legislators who believe that your personhood and autonomy are conditional—who believe that, if you are impregnated by another person, under any circumstance, you have a legal and moral duty to undergo pregnancy, delivery, and, in all likelihood, two decades or more of caregiving, no matter the permanent and potentially devastating consequences for your body, your heart, your mind, your family, your ability to put food on the table, your plans, your aspirations, your life.

"We won't go back"—it's an inadequate rallying cry, prompted only by events that belie its message. But it is true in at least one sense. The future that we now inhabit will not resemble the past before *Roe*, when women sought out illegal abortions and not infrequently found death. The principal danger now lies elsewhere and arguably reaches further. We have entered an era not of unsafe abortion but of widespread state surveillance and criminalization—of pregnant women, certainly, but also of doctors and pharmacists and clinic staffers and volunteers and friends and family members, of anyone who comes into meaningful contact with a pregnancy that does not end in a healthy birth. Those who argue that this decision won't actually change things much—an instinct you'll find on both sides of the political divide—are blind to the ways in which state-level antiabortion crusades have already turned pregnancy into punishment, and the ways in which the situation is poised to become much worse.

.　　　.　　　.

In the states where abortion has been or will soon be banned, any pregnancy loss past an early cutoff can now potentially be investigated as a crime. Search histories, browsing histories, text messages, location data, payment data, information from period-tracking apps—prosecutors can examine all of it if they believe that the loss of a pregnancy may have been deliberate. Even if prosecutors fail to prove that an abortion took place, those who are investigated will be punished by the process, liable for whatever might be found.

Five years ago, Latice Fisher, a Black mother of three from Mississippi who made eleven dollars an hour as a police-radio operator, experienced a stillbirth, at roughly thirty-six weeks, at home. When questioned, she acknowledged that she didn't want more kids and couldn't afford to take care of more kids. She surrendered her phone to investigators, who scraped it for search data and found search terms regarding mifepristone and misoprostol, i.e., abortion pills.

These pills are among the reasons that we are not going back to the era of coat hangers. They can be prescribed via telemedicine and delivered via mail; allowing for the prescription of an extra dose, they are 95 to 98 percent effective in cases of pregnancy up to eleven weeks, which account for almost 90 percent of all abortions in the United States. Already, more than half of all abortions in the country are medication abortions. In nineteen states, doctors are prohibited from providing abortions via telemedicine, but women can seek help from clinicians in other states and abroad, such as Rebecca Gomperts, who leads Aid Access, an organization based in Austria that is openly providing abortion pills to women in prohibition states and has been safely mailing abortion pills to pregnant people all over the world since 2005 with the organization Women on Web. In advance of the U.S. bans, Gomperts has been promoting advance prescription: sympathetic doctors might prescribe abortion pills for any menstruating person, removing some of the fears—and, possibly, the traceability—that would come with attempting to get the pills after pregnancy. Misoprostol can be prescribed for other issues, such as stomach ulcers, and Gomperts argues that there is no reasonable medical argument against advance prescription. "If you buy bleach in the supermarket, that's more dangerous," she has said.

There was no evidence that Latice Fisher took an abortion pill. She maintained that she had experienced a stillbirth—an occurrence in one out of every hundred and sixty pregnancies in the United States. Nonetheless, she was charged with second-degree murder and held for several weeks on a hundred-thousand-dollar bond. The district attorney, Scott Colom, had campaigned as a progressive reformer; advocates pushed him to drop the murder charge and to provide a new grand jury with information about an antiquated, unreliable "float test" that had been used as a basis for the allegation that Fisher's baby was born alive. The grand jury declined to indict Fisher again; the ordeal took more than three years.

Even if it remains possible in prohibition states to order abortion pills, doing so will be unlawful. (Missouri recently proposed classifying the delivery or shipment of these pills as drug trafficking. Louisiana just passed a law that makes mailing abortion pills to a resident of the state a criminal offense, punishable by six months' imprisonment.) In many states, to avoid breaking the law, a woman would have to drive to a state where abortion is legal, have a telemedicine consultation there, and then receive the pills in that state. Many women in Texas have opted for a riskier but easier option: to drive across the border, to Mexico, and get abortion pills from unregulated pharmacies, where pharmacists may issue incorrect advice for usage. Some women who lack the freedom and money to travel out of state, and who might fear the consequences of seeking a clinical confirmation of their gestational stage, will order abortion pills without a clear understanding of how far along they are in pregnancy. Abortion pills are safe and effective, but patients need access to clinical guidance and follow-up care. Women in prohibition states who want to seek medical attention after a self-managed abortion will, as a rule, have to choose between risking their freedom and risking their health.

· · ·

Both abortion and miscarriage currently occur more than a million times each year in America, and the two events are often clinically indistinguishable. Because of this, prohibition states will have a profoundly invasive interest in differentiating between them. Some have already laid the groundwork for establishing government databases of pregnant women likely to seek abortions. Last year, Arkansas passed a law called the Every Mom Matters Act, which requires women considering abortion to call a state hotline and requires abortion providers to register all patients in a database with a unique ID. Since then, six other states have implemented or proposed similar laws. The hotlines are provided by crisis pregnancy centers: typically Christian organizations, many of which masquerade as abortion clinics, provide no health care, and passionately counsel women against abortion. Crisis pregnancy centers are already three times as numerous as abortion clinics in the United States, and, unlike hospitals, they are not required to protect the privacy of those who come to them. For years, conservative states have been redirecting money, often from funds earmarked for poor women and children, toward these organizations. The data that crisis pregnancy centers are capable of collecting—names, locations, family details, sexual and medical histories, nondiagnostic ultrasound images—can now be deployed against those who seek their help.

If you become pregnant, your phone generally knows before many of your friends do. The entire internet economy is built on meticulous user tracking of purchases and search terms. Laws modeled on Texas's S.B. 8, which encourages private citizens to file lawsuits against anyone who facilitates an abortion, will proliferate, giving self-appointed vigilantes no shortage of tools to track and identify suspects. (The National Right to Life Committee recently published policy recommendations for antiabortion states that included criminal penalties for anyone who provides information about self-managed abortion "over the telephone, the internet, or any other medium of communication.") A reporter for *Vice* recently spent a mere $160 to purchase a data set on visits to more than 600 Planned Parenthood clinics. Brokers sell data that make it possible to track journeys to and from any location—say, an abortion clinic in another state. In Missouri this year, a lawmaker proposed a measure that would allow private citizens to sue anyone who helps a resident of the state get an abortion elsewhere; as with S.B. 8, the law would reward successful plaintiffs with $10,000. The closest analogue to this kind of legislation is the Fugitive Slave Act of 1793.

For now, the targets of S.B. 8–type bounty laws are those who provide abortions, not those who seek them. But that seems likely to change. Connecticut, a progressive state on the matter of abortion, recently passed a law that prevents local agencies from cooperating with out-of-state abortion prosecutions and protects the medical records of out-of-state clients. Other progressive states will follow suit. If prohibition states can't sue out-of-state doctors, and, if abortion pills sent by mail remain largely undetectable, the only people left to target will be abortion advocates and those trying to get abortions. *The Stream,* a conservative Christian publication, recently advocated mandatory psychiatric custody for women who get abortions. In May, Louisiana advanced a bill that would allow abortion patients to be charged with murder. The proposal was withdrawn, but the threat had been made.

●　　　●　　　●

The theological concept of fetal personhood—the idea that, from the moment of conception, an embryo or fetus is a full human being, deserving of equal (or, more accurately, superior) rights—is a foundational doctrine of the antiabortion movement. The legal ramifications of this idea—including the possible classification of IVF, IUDs, and the morning-after pill as instruments of murder—are unhinged and much harsher than what even the average antiabortion American is currently willing to embrace. Nonetheless, the antiabortion movement is now openly pushing for fetal personhood to become the foundation of U.S. abortion law.

If a fetus is a person, then a legal framework can be invented to require someone who has one living inside her to do everything in her power to protect it, including—as happened to Savita Halappanavar, in Ireland, which operated under a fetal-personhood doctrine until 2018, and to Izabela Sajbor, in Poland, where all abortion is effectively illegal—to die. No other such obligation exists anywhere in our society, which grants cops the freedom to stand by as children are murdered behind an unlocked door. In Poland, pregnant women with cancer have been routinely denied chemotherapy because of clinicians' fears of harming the fetus.

Fetal-personhood laws have passed in Georgia and Alabama, and they are no longer likely to be found unconstitutional. Such laws justify a full-scale criminalization of pregnancy, whereby women can be arrested, detained, and otherwise placed under state intervention for taking actions perceived to be potentially harmful to a fetus. This approach has been steadily tested, on low-income minorities in particular, for the past four decades. National Advocates for Pregnant Women—the organization that has provided legal defense for most of the cases mentioned in this article—has documented almost 1,800 cases from 1973 to 2020 of prosecutions or forced interventions related to pregnancy; this is likely a substantial undercount. Even in states such as California, where the law explicitly prohibits charging women with murder after a pregnancy loss, conservative prosecutors are doing so anyway.

Most pregnancy-related prosecutions, so far, have revolved around drug use. Women who used drugs while pregnant or sought treatment for drug use during pregnancy have been charged with child abuse, child neglect, distribution of drugs to a minor, assault with a deadly weapon, manslaughter, and homicide. In 2020, law enforcement in Alabama investigated a woman named Kim Blalock for chemical endangerment of a child after she told delivery-room staff that she had been taking prescribed hydrocodone for pain management. (The district attorney charged her with prescription fraud—a felony—before eventually dropping the prosecution altogether.) There has been a string of shocking recent prosecutions in Oklahoma, in which women who used drugs have been charged with manslaughter for miscarrying well before the point of viability. In Wisconsin, state law already allows juvenile courts to take a fetus—meaning a pregnant woman—into custody for the fetus's protection, resulting in the detention and forced treatment of more than 400 pregnant women every year on the suspicion that they may be consuming controlled substances. A proposed law in Wyoming would create a specific category of felony child endangerment for drug use while pregnant, a law that resembles Tennessee's former Fetal Assault Law. The Tennessee law was discontinued after two years because treating women as adversaries to the fetuses they carry has a chilling effect on prenatal medicine and inevitably results in an increase in maternal and infant death.

The mainstream prochoice movement has largely ignored the growing criminalization of pregnancy, just as it has generally ignored the inadequacy of *Roe*. (It took Joe Biden, who campaigned on making *Roe* the "law of the land," more than a year to say the word "abortion" on the record after he became president; the Democrats, given the chance to override the filibuster and codify *Roe* in May, predictably failed to do so.) Many of those who support the right to abortion have tacitly accepted that poor and minority women in conservative states lost access to abortion long before this Supreme Court decision and have quietly hoped that the thousands of women facing arrest after pregnancy, miscarriage, stillbirth, or even healthy deliveries were unfortunate outliers. They were not outliers, and, as the columnist Rebecca Traister noted last month, the chasm between the impervious class and everyone else is growing every day.

.   .   .

Pregnancy is more than thirty times more dangerous than abortion. One study estimates that a nationwide ban would lead to a 21 percent rise in pregnancy-related deaths. Some of the women who will die from abortion bans are pregnant right now. Their deaths will come not from back-alley procedures but from a silent denial of care: interventions delayed, desires disregarded. They will die of infections, of preeclampsia, of hemorrhage, as they are forced to submit their bodies to pregnancies that they never wanted to carry, and it will not be hard for the antiabortion movement to accept these deaths as a tragic, even noble consequence of womanhood itself.

In the meantime, abortion bans will hurt, disable, and endanger many people who want to carry their pregnancies to term but who encounter medical difficulties. Physicians in prohibition states have already begun declining to treat women who are in the midst of miscarriages, for fear that the treatment could be classified as abortion. One woman in Texas was told that she had to drive fifteen hours to New Mexico to have her ectopic pregnancy—which is nonviable, by definition, and always dangerous to the mother—removed. Misoprostol, one of the abortion pills, is routinely prescribed for miscarriage management because it causes the uterus to expel any remaining tissue. Pharmacists in Texas, fearing legal liability, have already refused to prescribe it. If a miscarriage is not managed to a safe completion, women risk—among other things, and taking the emotional damage for granted—uterine perforation, organ failure, infection, infertility, and death.

Most miscarriages are caused by factors beyond a pregnant person's control: illnesses, placental or uterine irregularities, genetic abnormalities. But the treatment of pregnant people in this country already makes many of them feel directly and solely responsible for the survival of their fetus. They are told to absolutely avoid alcohol, coffee, retinol, deli turkey, unpasteurized cheese, hot baths, vigorous exercise, drugs that are not prescribed to them, drugs that they have been prescribed for years—often without any explanation of the frequently shoddy reasoning behind these prohibitions. Structural factors that clearly increase the likelihood of miscarriage—poverty, environmental-chemical exposure, working night shifts—are less likely to come up. As fetal personhood becomes law in more of the land, pregnant people, as Lynn Paltrow, the director of National Advocates for Pregnant Women, has pointed out, "could be sued, or prevented from engaging in travel, work, or any activity that is believed to create a risk to the life of the unborn."

•   •   •

Half a century ago, the antiabortion movement was dominated by progressive, antiwar, pro-welfare Catholics. Today, the movement is conservative, evangelical, and absolutely single-minded, populated overwhelmingly by people who, although they may embrace foster care, adoption, and various forms of private ministry, show no interest in pushing for public, structural support for human life once it's left the womb. The scholar Mary Ziegler recently noted that today's antiabortion advocates see the "strategies of earlier decades as apologetic, cowardly, and counterproductive." During the past four years, eleven states have passed abortion bans that contain no exceptions for rape or incest, a previously unthinkable extreme.

In Texas, already, children aged nine, ten, and eleven, who don't yet understand what sex and abuse are, face forced pregnancy and childbirth after being raped. Women sitting in emergency rooms in the midst of miscarriages are being denied treatment for sepsis because their fetuses' hearts haven't yet stopped. People you'll never hear of will spend the rest of their lives trying and failing, agonizingly, in this punitive country, to provide stability for a first or fifth child they knew they weren't equipped to care for.

In the face of all this, there has been so much squeamishness, even in the prochoice camp: a tone that casts abortion as an unfortunate necessity, an approach to messaging that values choice but devalues abortion care itself, that emphasizes reproductive rights rather than reproductive justice. That approach has landed us here. We are not going back to the pre-*Roe* era, and we should not want to go back to the era that succeeded it, which was less bitter than the present but was never good enough. We should demand more, and we will have to. We will need to be full-throated and unconditional about abortion as a necessary precondition to justice and equal rights if we want even a chance of someday getting somewhere better.

Is Abortion Sacred?

Twenty years ago, when I was thirteen, I wrote an entry in my journal about abortion, which began, "I have this huge thing weighing on me." That morning, in Bible class, which I'd attended every day since the first grade at an evangelical school in Houston, my teacher had led us in an exercise called Agree/Disagree. He presented us with moral propositions, and we stood up and physically chose sides. "Abortion is always wrong," he offered, and there was no disagreement. We all walked to the wall that meant "agree."

Then I raised my hand and, according to my journal, said, "I think it is always morally wrong and absolutely murder, but if a woman is raped, I respect her right to get an abortion." Also, I said, if a woman knew the child would face a terrible life, the child might be better off. "Dead?" the teacher asked. My classmates said I needed to go to the other side, and I did. "I felt guilty and guilty and guilty," I wrote in my journal. "I didn't feel like a Christian when I was on that side of the room. I felt terrible, actually. . . . But I still have that thought that if a woman was raped, she has her right. But that's so strange—she has a right to kill what would one day be her child? That issue is irresolved in my mind and it will eat at me until I sort it out."

I had always thought of abortion as it had been taught to me in school: it was a sin that irresponsible women committed to cover up another sin, having sex in a non-Christian manner. The moral universe was a stark battle of virtue and depravity, in which the only meaningful question about any possible action was whether or not it would be sanctioned in the eyes of God. Men were sinful, and the goodness of women was the essential bulwark against the corruption of the world. There was suffering built into this framework, but suffering was noble; justice would prevail in the end because God always provided for the faithful. It was these last tenets, prosperity-gospel principles that neatly erase the material causes of suffering in our history and our social policies—not only regarding abortion but so much else—that toppled for me first. By the time I went to college, I understood that I was prochoice.

America is, in many ways, a deeply religious country—the only wealthy Western democracy in which more than half of the population claims to pray every day. (In Europe, the figure is 22 percent.) Although seven out of ten American women who get abortions identify as Christian, the fight to make the procedure illegal is an almost entirely Christian phenomenon. Two-thirds of the

national population and nearly 90 percent of Congress affirm a tradition in which a teenage girl continuing an unplanned pregnancy allowed for the salvation of the world, in which a corrupt
government leader who demanded a Massacre of the Innocents
almost killed the baby Jesus and damned us all in the process, and
in which the Son of God entered the world as what the godless
dare to call a "clump of cells."

For centuries, most Christians believed that human personhood
began months into the long course of pregnancy. It was only in the
twentieth century that a dogmatic narrative, in which every pregnancy is an iteration of the same static story of creation, began both
to shape American public policy and to occlude the reality of pregnancy as volatile and ambiguous—as a process in which creation
and destruction run in tandem. This newer narrative helped to
erase an instinctive, long-held understanding that pregnancy does
not begin with the presence of a child and only sometimes ends
with one. Even within the course of the same pregnancy, a person
and the fetus she carries can shift between the roles of lover and
beloved, host and parasite, vessel and divinity, victim and murderer; each body is capable of extinguishing the other, although
one cannot survive alone. There is no human relationship more
complex, more morally unstable than this.

●   ●   ●

The idea that a fetus is not just a full human but a superior and
kinglike one—a being whose survival is so paramount that another
person can be legally compelled to accept harm, ruin, or death to
insure it—is a recent invention. For most of history, women ended
unwanted pregnancies as they needed to, taking herbal or plant-
derived preparations on their own or with the help of female healers and midwives, who presided over all forms of treatment and
care connected with pregnancy. They were likely enough to think
that they were simply restoring their menstruation, treating a
blockage of blood. Pregnancy was not confirmed until "quicken-
ing," the point at which the pregnant person could feel fetal

movement, a measurement that relied on her testimony. Then as now, there was often nothing that distinguished the result of an abortion—the body expelling fetal tissue—from a miscarriage.

Ancient records of abortifacient medicine are plentiful; ancient attempts to regulate abortion are rare. What regulations existed reflect concern with women's behavior and marital propriety, not with fetal life. The Code of the Assura, from the eleventh century BCE, mandated death for married women who got abortions without consulting their husbands; when husbands beat their wives hard enough to make them miscarry, the punishment was a fine. The first known Roman prohibition on abortion dates to the second century and prescribes exile for a woman who ends her pregnancy because "it might appear scandalous that she should be able to deny her husband of children without being punished." Likewise, the early Christian Church opposed abortion not as an act of murder but because of its association with sexual sin. (The Bible offers ambiguous guidance on the question of when life begins: Genesis 2:7 arguably implies that it begins at first breath; Exodus 21:22–24 suggests that, in Old Testament law, a fetus was not considered a person; Jeremiah 1:5 describes God's hand in creation even "before I formed you in the womb." Nowhere does the Bible clearly and directly address abortion.) Augustine, in the fourth century, favored the idea that God endowed a fetus with a soul only after its body was formed—a point that Augustine placed, in line with Aristotelian tradition, somewhere between forty and eighty days into its development. "There cannot yet be a live soul in a body that lacks sensation when it is not formed in flesh, and so not yet endowed with sense," he wrote. This was more or less the Church's official position; it was affirmed eight centuries later by Thomas Aquinas.

In the early modern era, European attitudes began to change. The Black Death had dramatically lowered the continent's population and dealt a blow to most forms of economic activity; the Reformation had weakened the Church's position as the essential intermediary between the layman and God. The social scientist Silvia Federici has argued, in her book *Caliban and the Witch*, that church and state waged deliberate campaigns to force women to give birth, in service of the emerging capitalist economy. "Starting in the mid-16th century, while Portuguese ships were returning from Africa with their first human cargoes, all the European governments began to impose the severest penalties against contraception, abortion, and infanticide," Federici notes. Midwives and "wise women" were prosecuted for witchcraft, a catchall crime for deviancy from procreative sex. For the first time, male doctors began to control labor and delivery, and, Federici writes, "in the case of a medical emergency" they "prioritized the life of the fetus over that of the mother." She goes on: "While in the Middle Ages women had been able to use various forms of contraceptives, and had exercised an undisputed control over the birthing process, from now on their wombs became public territory, controlled by men and the state."

Martin Luther and John Calvin, the most influential figures of the Reformation, did not address abortion at any length. But Catholic doctrine started to shift, albeit slowly. In 1588, Pope Sixtus V labeled both abortion and contraception as homicide. This pronouncement was reversed three years later, by Pope Gregory XIV, who declared that abortion was only homicide if it took place after ensoulment, which he identified as occurring around twenty-four weeks into a pregnancy. Still, theologians continued to push the idea of embryonic humanity; in 1621, the physician Paolo Zacchia, an adviser to the Vatican, proclaimed that the soul was present from the moment of conception. Still, it was not until 1869 that Pope Pius IX affirmed this doctrine, proclaiming abortion at any point in pregnancy to be a sin punishable by excommunication.

•   •   •

When I found out I was pregnant, at the beginning of 2020, I wondered how the experience would change my understanding of life, of fetal personhood, of the morality of reproduction. It's been years since I traded the echo chamber of evangelical Texas for the echo chamber of progressive Brooklyn, but I can still sometimes feel the old worldview flickering, a photographic negative underneath my vision. I have come to believe that abortion should be universally accessible, regulated only by medical codes and ethics, and not by the criminal-justice system. Still, in passing moments, I can imagine upholding the idea that our sole task when it comes to protecting life is to end the practice of abortion; I can imagine that seeming profoundly moral and unbelievably urgent. I would only need to think of the fetus in total isolation—to imagine that it were not formed and contained by another body, and that body not formed and contained by a family, or a society, or a world.

As happens to many women, though, I became, if possible, more militant about the right to an abortion in the process of pregnancy, childbirth, and caregiving. It wasn't just the difficult things that had this effect—the paralyzing back spasms, the ragged desperation of sleeplessness, the thundering doom that pervaded every cell in my body when I weaned my child. And it wasn't just my newly visceral understanding of the anguish embedded in the facts of American family life. (A third of parents in one of the richest countries in the world struggle to afford diapers; in the first few months of the pandemic, as Jeff Bezos's net worth rose by 48 billion dollars, 16 percent of households with children did not have enough to eat.) What multiplied my commitment to abortion were the beautiful things about motherhood: in particular, the way I felt able to love my baby fully and singularly because I had chosen to give my body and life over to her. I had not been forced by law to make another person with my flesh or to tear that flesh open to bring her into the world; I hadn't been driven by need to give that new person away to a stranger in the hope that she would never go to bed hungry. I had been able to choose this permanent rearrangement of my existence. That volition felt sacred.

Abortion is often talked about as a grave act that requires justification, but bringing a new life into the world felt, to me, like the decision that more clearly risked being a moral mistake. The debate about abortion in America is "rooted in the largely unacknowledged premise that continuing a pregnancy is a prima facie moral good," the pro-choice Presbyterian minister Rebecca Todd

Peters writes. But childbearing, Peters notes, is a morally weighted act, one that takes place in a world of limited and unequally distributed resources. Many people who get abortions—the majority of whom are poor women who already have children—understand this perfectly well. "We ought to take the decision to continue a pregnancy far more seriously than we do," Peters writes.

I gave birth in the middle of a pandemic that previewed a future of cross-species viral transmission exacerbated by global warming, and during a summer when ten million acres on the West Coast burned. I knew that my child would not only live in this degrading world but contribute to that degradation. ("Every year, the average American emits enough carbon to melt ten thousand tons of ice in the Antarctic ice sheets," David Wallace-Wells writes in his book *The Uninhabitable Earth*.) Just before COVID arrived, the science writer Meehan Crist published an essay in the *London Review of Books* titled "Is It OK to Have a Child?" (The title alludes to a question that Alexandria Ocasio-Cortez once asked in a live stream, on Instagram.) Crist details the environmental damage that we are doing and the costs for the planet and for us and for those who will come after. Then she turns the question on its head. The idea of choosing whether or not to have a child, she writes, is predicated on a fantasy of control that "quickly begins to dissipate when we acknowledge that the conditions for human flourishing are distributed so unevenly, and that, in an age of ecological catastrophe, we face a range of possible futures in which these conditions no longer reliably exist."

In late 2021, as Omicron brought New York to another COVID peak, a Gen Z boy in a hoodie uploaded a TikTok, captioned "yall better delete them baby names out ya notes its 60 degrees in december." By then, my baby had become a toddler. Every night, as I set her in the crib, she chirped good night to the elephants, koalas, and tigers on the wall, and I tried not to think about extinction. My decision to have her risked—or guaranteed—additional human suffering; it opened up new chances for joy and meaning. There is unknowability in every reproductive choice.

As the German historian Barbara Duden writes in her book *Disembodying Women*, the early Christians believed that both the bodies that created life and the world that sustained it were proof of the "continual creative activity of God." Women and nature were aligned, in this view, as the material sources of God's plan. "The word nature is derived from *nascitura*, which means 'birthing,' and nature is imagined and felt to be like a pregnant womb, a matrix, a mother," Duden writes. But in recent decades, she notes, the natural world has begun to show its irreparable damage. The fetus has been left as a singular totem of life and divinity, to be protected, no matter the costs, even if everything else might fall.

The scholar Katie Gentile argues that in times of cultural crisis and upheaval, the fetus functions as a "site of projected and displaced anxieties," a "fantasy of wholeness in the face of overwhelming anxiety and an inability to have faith in a progressive, better future." The more degraded actual life becomes on earth, the more fervently conservatives will fight to protect potential life in utero. We are locked into the destruction of the world that birthed all of us; we turn our attention, now, to the worlds—the wombs—we think we can still control.

• • •

By the time that the Catholic Church decided that abortion at any point, for any reason, was a sin, scientists had identified the biological mechanism behind human reproduction, in which a fetus develops from an embryo that develops from a zygote, the single-celled organism created by the union of egg and sperm. With this discovery, in the mid-nineteenth century, women lost the most crucial point of authority over the stories of their pregnancies. Other people would be the ones to tell us, from then on, when life began.

At the time, abortion was largely unregulated in the United States, a country founded and largely populated by Protestants. But American physicians, through the then newly formed American Medical Association, mounted a campaign to criminalize it, led by a gynecologist named Horatio Storer, who once described the typical abortion patient as a "wretch whose account with the Almighty is heaviest with guilt." (Storer was raised Unitarian but later converted to Catholicism.) The scholars Paul Saurette and Kelly Gordon have argued that these doctors, whose profession was not as widely respected as it would later become, used abortion "as a wedge issue," one that helped them portray their work "as morally and professionally superior to the practice of midwifery." By 1910, abortion was illegal in every state, with exceptions only to save the life of "the mother." (The wording of such provisions referred to all pregnant people as mothers, whether or not they had children, thus quietly inserting a presumption of fetal personhood.) A series of acts known as the Comstock laws had rendered contraception, abortifacient medicine, and information about reproductive control widely inaccessible, by criminalizing their distribution via the U.S. Postal Service. People still sought abortions, of course: in the early years of the Great Depression, there were as many as 700,000 abortions annually. These underground procedures were dangerous; several thousand women died from abortions every year.

This is when the contemporary movements for and against the right to abortion took shape. Those who favored legal abortion did not, in these years, emphasize "choice," Daniel K. Williams notes in his book *Defenders of the Unborn*. They emphasized protecting the health of women, protecting doctors, and preventing the births of unwanted children. Antiabortion activists, meanwhile, argued, as their successors do, that they were defending human life and human rights. The horrors of the Second World War gave the movement a lasting analogy: "Logic would lead us from abortion to the gas chamber," a Catholic clergyman wrote, in October 1962.

Ultrasound imaging, invented in the 1950s, completed the transformation of pregnancy into a story that, by default, was narrated to women by other people—doctors, politicians, activists. In 1965, *Life* magazine published a photo essay by Lennart Nilsson called "Drama of Life Before Birth," and put the image of a fetus at eighteen weeks on its cover. The photos produced an indelible, deceptive image of the fetus as an isolated being—a "spaceman," as Nilsson wrote, floating in a void, entirely independent from the person whose body creates it. They became totems of the anti-abortion movement; *Life* had not disclosed that all but one had been taken of aborted fetuses and that Nilsson had lit and posed their bodies to give the impression that they were alive.

In 1967, Colorado became the first state to allow abortion for reasons other than rape, incest, or medical emergency. A group of Protestant ministers and Jewish rabbis began operating an abortion-referral service led by the pastor of Judson Memorial Church, in Manhattan; the resulting network of prochoice clerics eventually spanned the country, and referred an estimated 450,000 women to safe abortions. The evangelical magazine *Christianity Today* held a symposium of prominent theologians in 1968, which resulted in a striking statement: "Whether or not the performance of an induced abortion is sinful we are not agreed, but about the necessity and permissibility for it under certain circumstances we are in accord." Meanwhile, the priest James McHugh became the director of the National Right to Life Committee and equated fetuses to the other vulnerable people whom faithful Christians were commanded to protect: the old, the sick, the poor. As states began to liberalize their abortion laws, the anti-abortion movement attracted followers—many of them antiwar, pro-welfare Catholics—using the language of civil rights, and adopted the label "prolife."

W. A. Criswell, a Dallas pastor who served as president of the Southern Baptist Convention from 1968 to 1970, said, shortly after the Supreme Court issued its decision in *Roe v. Wade*, that "it was only after a child was born and had life separate from his mother that it became an individual person," and that "it has always, therefore, seemed to me that what is best for the mother and the future should be allowed." But the court's decision accelerated a political and theological transformation that was already under way: by 1979, Criswell, like the SBC, had endorsed a hard-line antiabortion stance. Evangelical leadership, represented by such groups as Jerry Falwell's Moral Majority, joined with Catholics to oppose the secularization of popular culture, becoming firmly conservative—and a powerful force in Republican politics. Bible verses that express the idea of divine creation, such as Psalm 139 ("For you created my innermost being; you knit me together in my mother's womb," in the New International Version's translation), became policy explanations for prohibiting abortion.

In 1984, scientists used ultrasound to detect fetal cardiac activity at around six weeks' gestation—a discovery that has been termed a "fetal heartbeat" by the antiabortion movement, though a six-week-old fetus hasn't yet formed a heart and the electrical pulses are coming from cell clusters that can be replicated in a petri dish. At six weeks, in fact, medical associations still call the fetus an embryo; as I found out in 2020, you generally can't even schedule a doctor's visit to confirm your condition until you're eight weeks along.

• • •

So many things that now shape the cultural experience of pregnancy in America accept and reinforce the terms of the antiabortion movement, often with the implicit goal of making pregnant women feel special or encouraging them to buy things. "Your baby," every app and article whispered to me sweetly, wrongly, many months before I intuited personhood in the being inside me or felt that the life I was forming had moved out of a liminal realm.

I tried to learn from that liminality. Hope was always predicated on uncertainty; there would be no guarantees of safety in this or any other part of life. Pregnancy did not feel like soft blankets and stuffed bunnies—it felt cosmic and elemental, like volcanic rocks grinding or a wild plant straining toward the sun. It was violent even as I loved it. "Even with the help of modern medicine, pregnancy still kills about 800 women every day worldwide," the evolutionary biologist Suzanne Sadedin points out in an essay titled "War in the Womb." Many of the genes that activate during embryonic development also activate when a body has been invaded by cancer, Sadedin notes; in ectopic pregnancies, which are unviable by definition and make up 1 to 2 percent of all pregnancies, embryos become implanted in the fallopian tube rather than the uterus and "tunnel ferociously toward the richest nutrient source they can find." The result, Sadedin writes, "is often a bloodbath."

The Book of Genesis tells us that the pain of childbearing is part of the punishment women have inherited from Eve. The other part is subjugation to men: "Your desire will be for your husband and he will rule over you," God tells Eve. Tertullian, a second-century theologian, told women, "You are the devil's gateway: you are the unsealer of the (forbidden) tree: you are the first deserter of the divine law: you are she who persuaded him whom the devil was not valiant enough to attack." The idea that guilt inheres in female identity persists in antiabortion logic: anything a woman or a girl does with her body can justify the punishment of undesired pregnancy, including simply existing.

If I had become pregnant when I was a thirteen-year-old Texan, I would have believed that abortion was wrong, but I am sure that I would have got an abortion. For one thing, my Christian school did not allow students to be pregnant. I was aware of this and had, even then, a faint sense that the people around me grasped, in some way, the necessity of abortion—that, even if they believed that abortion meant taking a life, they understood that it could preserve a life, too.

One need not reject the idea that life in the womb exists or that fetal life has meaning in order to favor the right to abortion; one must simply allow that everything, not just abortion, has a moral dimension and that each pregnancy occurs in such an intricate web of systemic and individual circumstances that only the person who is pregnant could hope to evaluate the situation and make a moral decision among the options at hand. A recent survey found that one-third of Americans believe life begins at conception but also that abortion should be legal. This is the position overwhelmingly held by American Buddhists, whose religious tradition casts abortion as the taking of a human life and regards all forms of life as sacred but also warns adherents against absolutism and urges them to consider the complexity of decreasing suffering, compelling them toward compassion and respect.

There is a Buddhist ritual practiced primarily in Japan, where it is called *mizuko kuyo*: a ceremony of mourning for miscarriages, stillbirths, and aborted fetuses. The ritual is possibly ersatz; critics say that it fosters and preys upon women's feelings of guilt. But the scholar William LaFleur argues in his book *Liquid Life* that it is rooted in a medieval Japanese understanding of the way the unseen world interfaces with the world of humans—in which being born and dying are both "processes rather than fixed points." An infant was believed to have entered the human world from the realm of the gods and move clockwise around a wheel as she grew older, eventually passing back into the spirit realm on the other side. But some infants were *mizuko*, or water babies: floating in fluids, ontologically unstable. These were the babies who were never born. A *mizuko*, whether miscarried or aborted—and the two words were similar: *kaeru*, to go back, and *kaesu*, to cause to go back—slipped back, counterclockwise, across the border to the realm of the gods.

There is a loss, I think, entailed in abortion—as there is in miscarriage, whether it occurs at eight or twelve or twenty-nine weeks. I locate this loss in the irreducible complexity of life itself, in the terrible violence and magnificence of reproduction, in the death that shimmered at the edges of my consciousness in the shattering moment that my daughter was born. This understanding might be rooted in my religious upbringing—I am sure that it is. But I wonder, now, how I would square this: that fetuses were the most precious lives in existence, and that God, in His vision, already chooses to end a quarter of them. The fact that a quarter of women, regardless of their beliefs, also decide to end pregnancies at some point in their lifetimes: are they not acting in accordance with God's plan for them, too?

The Atlantic

FINALIST—PUBLIC INTEREST

"Caitlin Dickerson's painstaking investigation of the Trump administration's shambolic, deliberately cruel family-separation policy—in which the United States systematically took thousands of children away from their parents—is breathtaking in its scope and detail," said the National Magazine Award judges of "We Need to Take Away Children." "One of journalism's most vital tasks is to remember," they continued. "With the 2024 elections looming, Dickerson's careful, accurate record of the Trump administration's misdeeds is, and will remain, extraordinarily valuable." Now a staff writer at The Atlantic and formerly a reporter at the New York Times, Dickerson received the Pulitzer Prize for Explanatory Reporting for "We Need to Take Away Children." This was the third consecutive year in which The Atlantic was nominated for the National Magazine Award for Public Interest, having won the award on five previous occasions.

Caitlin Dickerson

We Need to Take Away Children

As a therapist for children who are being processed through the American immigration system, Cynthia Quintana has a routine that she repeats each time she meets a new patient in her office in Grand Rapids, Michigan: she calls the parents or closest relatives to let them know the child is safe and well cared for and provides twenty-four-hour contact information.

This process usually plays out within hours of when the children arrive. Most are teens who have memorized or written down their relatives' phone numbers in notebooks they carried with them across the border. By the time of that initial call, their families are typically worried, waiting anxiously for news after having—in an act of desperation—sent their children into another country alone in pursuit of safety and the hope of a future.

But in the summer of 2017, Quintana encountered a curious case. A three-year-old Guatemalan boy with a toothy smile and bowl-cut black hair sat down at her desk. He was far too little to have made the journey on his own. He had no phone numbers with him, and when she asked where he was headed or whom he'd been with, the boy stared back blankly. Quintana scoured his file for more information but found nothing. She asked for help from an Immigration and Customs Enforcement officer, who came back several days later with something unusual: information indicating that the boy's father was in federal custody.

At their next session, the boy squirmed in his chair as Quintana dialed the detention center, getting his father on the line. At first the dad was quiet, she told me. "Finally we said, 'Your child is here. He can hear you. You can speak now.' And you could just tell that his voice was breaking—he couldn't."

The boy cried out for his father. Suddenly, both of them were screaming and sobbing so loudly that several of Quintana's colleagues ran to her office.

Eventually, the man calmed down enough to address Quintana directly. "I'm so sorry, who are you? Where is my child? They came in the middle of the night and took him," he said. "What do I tell his mother?"

That same summer, Quintana was also assigned to work with a three-year-old Honduran girl who gave no indication of how she'd gotten to the United States or where she was supposed to be going. During their first several sessions, the girl refused to speak at all. The muscles on her face were slack and expressionless. Quintana surmised that the girl had severe detachment disorder, often the result of a sudden and recent trauma.

Across her organization—Bethany Christian Services, one of several companies contracted by the American government to care for newly arrived immigrant children—Quintana's colleagues were having similar experiences. Jennifer Leon, a teacher at Bethany, was at the office one day when the private company that transports children from the border delivered a baby girl "like an Amazon package." The baby was wearing a dirty diaper; her face was crusted with mucus. "They gave the baby to the case manager with a diaper bag, we signed, that was it," Leon recalled. (Leon rushed the baby to the hospital for an evaluation.)

Mateo Salazar, a Bethany therapist, went to his office in the middle of the night to meet a newly arrived five-year-old Honduran girl. At first, the girl was stoic, but when the transportation-company employees started to leave, the girl ran after them, banging on the glass doors and crying as she fell to the ground. Salazar sat with her for two hours until she was calm enough to explain that her mother had made her promise—as Border Patrol agents were pulling them apart—to stay with the adults who took her no matter what because they would keep her safe.

For more than a year, Quintana and her colleagues encountered cases like this repeatedly. To track down the parents of children in their care, they would scour American prisons and immigration detention centers, using clues from social media or tips from friends inside the government. They would struggle to explain to parents why their kids had been taken away or how to get them back. The therapists, teachers, and caseworkers would try to maintain their composure at work, but they would later break down in their cars and in front of their families. Many debated quitting their job. Though they were experts in caring for severely traumatized children, this was a challenge to which they did not know how to respond.

"I started questioning myself," Quintana said. "Am I doing the correct thing by serving these kids, or am I contributing to the harm that's being done?"

"It just seemed unreal to me," she said of the moment she understood that these were not one-off cases. "Something that was not humane."

•　　•　　•

During the year and a half in which the U.S. government separated thousands of children from their parents, the Trump administration's explanations for what was happening were deeply confusing, and on many occasions—it was clear even then—patently untrue. I'm one of the many reporters who covered this story in real time. Despite the flurry of work that we produced to fill the void of information, we knew that the full truth about how our government had reached this point still eluded us.

Trump-administration officials insisted for a whole year that family separations weren't happening. Finally, in the spring of 2018, they announced the implementation of a separation policy with great fanfare—as if one had not already been under way for months. Then they declared that separating families was not the goal of the policy but an unfortunate result of prosecuting parents who crossed the border illegally with their children. Yet a mountain of evidence shows that this is explicitly false: separating children was not just a side effect but the intent. Instead of working to reunify families after parents were prosecuted, officials worked to keep them apart for longer.

Over the past year and a half, I have conducted more than 150 interviews and reviewed thousands of pages of internal government documents, some of which were turned over to me only after a multiyear lawsuit. These records show that as officials were developing the policy that would ultimately tear thousands of families apart, they minimized its implications so as to obscure what they were doing. Many of these officials now insist that there had been no way to foresee all that would go wrong. But this is not true. The policy's worst outcomes were all anticipated, and repeated internal and external warnings were ignored. Indeed, the records show that almost no logistical planning took place before the policy was initiated.

It's been said of other Trump-era projects that the administration's incompetence mitigated its malevolence; here, the opposite happened. A flagrant failure to prepare meant that courts, detention centers, and children's shelters became dangerously overwhelmed; that parents and children were lost to each other, sometimes many states apart; that four years later, some families are still separated—and that even many of those who have been reunited have suffered irreparable harm.

It is easy to pin culpability for family separations on the anti-immigration officials for which the Trump administration is known. But these separations were also endorsed and enabled by dozens of members of the government's middle and upper management: cabinet secretaries, commissioners, chiefs, and deputies who, for various reasons, didn't voice concern even when they should have seen catastrophe looming; who trusted "the system" to stop the worst from happening; who reasoned that it would not be strategic to speak up in an administration where being labeled a RINO or a "squish"—nicknames for those deemed insufficiently conservative—could end their career; who assumed that someone else, in some other department, must be on top of the problem; who were so many layers of abstraction away from the reality of screaming children being pulled out of their parent's arms that they could hide from the human consequences of what they were doing.

Congress, too, deserves blame because it failed for decades to fill a legislative vacuum that anti-immigration officials moved to exploit. For too long, an overworked and underequipped border-police force has been left to determine crucial social, economic, and humanitarian policy. It should be no surprise that this police force reached for the most ready tool at its disposal: harsher punishments.

What happened in the months that led up to the implementation of Zero Tolerance—the Trump administration's initiative that separated thousands of families—should be studied by future generations of organizational psychologists and moral philosophers. It raises questions that have resonance far beyond this one policy: What happens when personal ambition and moral qualm clash in the gray anonymity of a bureaucracy? When rationalizations become denial or outright delusion? When one's understanding of the line between right and wrong gets overridden by a boss's screaming insistence?

In reporting this story, I talked with scores of Trump-administration officials whose work was in some way connected to the policy. Very few were willing to speak on the record, for fear that it would affect their employment prospects. A number of them told me they were particularly nervous because they had children to think about and college tuitions to pay. During interviews, they asked to call me back so that they could run and pick their children up from school; they sat their children down in front of homework or toys so that we could speak privately in their homes. "Can you hold on? My daughter is about to get in her car to leave and I need to kiss her goodbye," one government official said as she was in the middle of describing a spreadsheet of hundreds of complaints from parents searching for their children. I listened as the mother and daughter said "I love you" back and forth to each other at least five times before the official returned and our conversation continued.

Recently, I called Nazario Jacinto-Carrillo, a thirty-six-year-old farmer from the western highlands of Guatemala whom I first wrote about in 2018. Back then, with his field barren and the price of crops stagnant, his family had been straining to survive on the four dollars a week he brought home during harvest season. Most days, he and his wife went hungry; some days, his two young children did too. They were destitute and felt unsafe in their community. So that spring, he and his five-year-old daughter, Filomena, set off for the United States. A "coyote" guided them to the American border near San Diego. All they had to do was walk across.

Things didn't go as planned. As six Border Patrol agents surrounded them, Filomena grabbed onto one of Nazario's legs, as did another girl her age with whom they were traveling. The girls screamed as the agents pulled the three apart, one of them holding Nazario by the neck. Nazario eventually agreed to be deported back to Guatemala because, he said, a federal agent told him that if he did so, Filomena would be returned to him within two weeks. This false promise was made to many separated parents, who were later portrayed by the administration as having heartlessly chosen to leave their children alone in the United States. "I would never abandon my daughter," Nazario told me when we first spoke. More than a month had passed since Nazario's deportation, and Filomena still wasn't home.

Nazario's voice cracked as he interrupted my questions with his own. When will Filomena be returned to Guatemala? How many weeks? What number of days? When is the United States government going to give back the children it kidnapped? What does it want with them? *They're children.*

It would take nearly three months, a team of lawyers, the sustained attention of journalists, and a federal court order for Filomena to be reunited with her family. By then she was six; she'd celebrated a birthday in U.S. government custody.

When I called Nazario again recently, his children were still hungry, and his family still felt unsafe. I told him that four years later, some parents still don't have their children back. "I honestly don't know what to say," he said. When I asked him if Filomena, now nine years old, thinks back on what she experienced in the United States, he handed her the phone so she could answer herself. She eked out a few words that I couldn't understand and then went silent and handed the phone back to her father.

"Sorry," he told me. "She's crying."

Chapter 1: The Dawn of Zero Tolerance

To understand how the American government took children away from their parents with no plan to return them, you have to go back to 9/11. Following the deadliest attack in U.S. history, the Bush administration created a new federal department. Comprising twenty-two offices and agencies, the Department of Homeland Security became the largest federal law-enforcement agency in the country. Its hundreds of thousands of employees were charged with vetting foreigners as they entered the United States, any of whom could be carrying out the next plot to take American lives.

Among the agencies folded into DHS was the Border Patrol. A federal police force established in 1924, the Border Patrol resembled something out of an old western. The agency drew thousands of young men and women who wanted to fight crime and carry weapons—and because for decades it did not require a high-school degree, it attracted many who might not have qualified to work for their local police department. For every one person the Border Patrol caught, chasing after them on foot, horseback, or ATV, one hundred others seemed to slip through. Even the agents themselves knew that their work was mostly ineffectual.

But after 9/11, the agency took on a national-security mission, and the way that it viewed border crossers evolved. Though a denigrating posture toward migrants was nothing new—agents referred to people they apprehended as "bodies" and categorized them with terms like *guats* and *hondus*—suddenly the agency's leadership began describing these day laborers as hardened criminals and grave threats to the homeland. The Border Patrol Academy transformed from a classroom-like setting, with courses on immigration law and Spanish, into a paramilitary-style boot camp.

No longer content to police the national boundary by focusing on the highest-priority offenses, the Border Patrol now sought to secure it completely. A single illegal border crossing was one too many. The new goal was zero tolerance.

•　　　•　　　•

In 2005, during George W. Bush's second term, an enterprising Border Patrol chief in Del Rio, Texas, named Randy Hill came up with an idea for how to eliminate unauthorized border crossings for good: he would make the process so unpleasant that no one would want to do it. He looked to a legal provision added into federal immigration law in the 1950s that had only rarely been enforced; it made any unauthorized border crossing a misdemeanor crime and any repeat offense a felony. Before 2005, federal judges and prosecutors had tacitly agreed to leave migrants alone, except in high-profile cases. People picking crops for under-the-table wages were not a principal concern for most Americans; overworked U.S. attorneys preoccupied with major drug- and weapons-smuggling cases viewed border crossing as a minor infraction not worth their time. (Hill could not be reached for comment.)

But the Del Rio chief persuaded his counterparts in local law enforcement to participate in an experiment in which every adult who was caught crossing the border illegally, no matter the reason, would be prosecuted. This would subject the migrants to formal deportation proceedings and trigger even harsher penalties if they were caught trying to cross again in the future, all but cutting off their route to citizenship.

This initiative, named Operation Streamline, would form the basis of a school of thought that has made "prevention by deterrence" a centerpiece of the United States' immigration enforcement today. Parents traveling with children were generally exempt from prosecution under Operation Streamline, but this approach to securing the border would eventually culminate in family separation.

The experiment started out promisingly enough. Within four years, apprehensions at the border in Del Rio dropped by 75 percent, and in Yuma, Arizona, by 95 percent. Border Patrol headquarters was so impressed that it moved to implement the plan nationwide. But the effort may have been less successful than those numbers suggested.

In regions that didn't adopt Streamline, border crossings increased, indicating that the program was pushing people to cross in different areas. "I call it 'squeezing the balloon,'" Anthony

Porvaznik, who served as the Border Patrol chief in Yuma during the Obama and Trump administrations, told me. While the first half decade of Streamline coincided with an overall decline in nationwide crossings, academic research indicates that this was largely attributable to economics. (Declining births in Mexico had resulted in far fewer adults who needed work while demand for labor in the United States plummeted in 2008, during the recession.) Those who did appear to be deterred by Streamline were migrant workers who had never been to jail before, Porvaznik said. People carrying drugs or weapons across the border didn't seem to care.

In many ways, the implementation of Streamline was a mess. Courthouses along the border became so overwhelmed that they had to close to the public. Judges began holding mass hearings, with groups of up to one hundred shackled defendants being tried at the same time. Arizona declared a judicial emergency in early 2011, temporarily suspending the right to a speedy trial for all federal defendants, including American citizens. Law-enforcement officers argued that the onslaught of misdemeanor prosecutions required by Streamline took resources away from serious felony cases.

Yet criminal prosecutions against border crossers became more and more politically popular. Under the Bush and Obama administrations, DHS officials who were eager to show that they were keeping the nation safe testified before Congress that Operation Streamline was an industry "best practice." Border Patrol agents embraced the model too, finally feeling empowered after decades of impotence.

By the mid-2010s, deepening poverty and an explosion of gang and domestic violence in Guatemala, Honduras, and El Salvador were driving children and families to the border in larger numbers. (Today, the State Department discourages Americans from traveling to those countries, because of rampant kidnapping and murder.) Jonathan White, a longtime Health and Human Services social worker, was sent to assess the situation. He saw children crammed into tiny, concrete Border Patrol holding cells or sleeping under bridges while they waited to be processed into the United States. In one facility, "the fire-marshal sign over the door said max occupancy thirty-five people," White told me. More than eighty teenage boys were passing around water in paper cups and climbing over one another to access a single toilet. He saw a baby lying alone on a flattened cardboard box. "We were horrified from a public-health, child-health perspective."

In 2014, Jeh Johnson, President Barack Obama's secretary of Homeland Security, called John Kelly, a Marine Corps general who was serving as the highest-ranking U.S.-military official in Central and South America, for advice. "I said, 'Come down here,'" Kelly recalled telling Johnson at the time. "'You have to come down here and look north and see what the other side of the problem is all about.'"

During Johnson's July 2014 visit to Guatemala City, Kelly explained that the mass migration of children and families seeking asylum in the United States was not a threat to national security but said that the crush at the border would continue to build unless jobs became more plentiful and violence less rife across Central America. No amount of "deterrence," Kelly told Johnson, would outweigh all of the factors driving Central Americans to the United States. Johnson left Guatemala City with a better understanding of the dynamics he faced but no solution for his overwhelmed agents or his boss, President Obama.

So Johnson convened a meeting in Washington with his top border-enforcement officials to discuss ideas. Among those present were Kevin McAleenan, who was then the deputy commissioner of Customs and Border Protection; Ron Vitiello, the deputy chief of the Border Patrol; and Tom Homan, the executive associate director of enforcement and removal for Immigration and Customs Enforcement. All three would subsequently be promoted and become integral to implementing family separations four years later.

Of those in the room, Homan was the most strident. He had spent decades in immigration enforcement, beginning in his early twenties as a Border Patrol agent. Homan said he wanted to apply the perceived lessons of Operation Streamline to migrant families, by prosecuting parents who crossed the border illegally with their children. Though many of these families came to the United States seeking asylum, under this new model they would be treated as criminals. Homan explained that the parents would be taken into federal criminal custody, just like with Operation Streamline—only this time the process would trigger an automatic family separation.

This is the earliest instance I've discovered of family separation being proposed as a way to deter migration to the United States. This makes Tom Homan the father of what might be the Trump administration's most controversial policy. "Most parents don't want to be separated," Homan told me recently. "I'd be lying to you if I didn't think that would have an effect."

Homan acknowledged that many people would think him evil for proposing the idea, but he said it was intended to help families, not hurt them. He explained himself by way of an experience that, he said, still troubles him today. One day in the spring of 2003, he said, he got a call from ICE headquarters asking him to rush to a crime scene near Victoria, a city in southeast Texas. He flew to the border, where more than seventy migrants had been discovered packed into the back of an overheated semitruck. When the authorities found them, seventeen of the passengers were already dead; two more died soon after. Lifeless bodies spilled out of the truck. Most of the passengers had stripped down to their underwear for relief from the heat.

As Homan surveyed the trailer, he noticed a boy who turned out to be five years old—the same age as Homan's youngest son—lying in his father's lap, both of them dead. "I got down on my knees, put my hand on the child's head, and said a prayer because I could only imagine what his last hour of life must have been like, how scared he must have been. Couldn't breathe, pitch black, begging his father to help him. His father couldn't help. What was his father thinking? He'd put him in that position, right? His father was probably saying, 'I can't believe I did this.'" He said the experience had driven him to therapy. "That one instance made me who I am today, because it's preventable. We could stop this."

Homan said he had families like this in mind when he pitched Secretary Johnson on the idea of prosecuting parents and taking their children away. Yes, the separated families would suffer, he acknowledged, but at least "they're not dead."

"The goal wasn't to traumatize," he added. "The goal was to stop the madness, stop the death, stop the rape, stop the children dying, stop the cartels doing what they're doing."

When the official Zero Tolerance policy went into effect, in the spring of 2018, the Trump administration made frequent use of this defense. I heard it again and again while I was conducting interviews for this story: families were separated not to harm them but to keep others like them safe. What I never heard anyone acknowledge was that "deterrence" methods such as family separation have been shown to increase the likelihood of these terrible outcomes—because harsher enforcement induces children and families to try to sneak across the border using more dangerous methods, such as hiding in the back of a tractor trailer.

Johnson eventually rejected Homan's proposal. Though he professed belief in the value of deterrence, he said that, as a father, he couldn't stomach separating children from their parents.

"Family separation was raised and rejected for two reasons," Johnson told me recently. First, "I already had in my mind the vivid visual image of a mother clinging to a child in a Border Patrol holding station—and I was not going to ask somebody from the Border Patrol or ICE to take that child away." Second, "it would have overrun" government shelters for children. "So it was heartless *and* impractical."

Chapter 2: The C-Team Assembles (November 2016–January 2017)

In the executive branch of the American government, policy ideas are traditionally vetted first by subject-matter experts—lower-level staffers whose knowledge is specific and deep. The ideas that pass muster are elevated to managers who are familiar with multiple areas of study and, therefore, a potential policy's broader implications. Finally, proposals are handed to political appointees who ensure that they meet the objectives of the administration. Only those policies that survive these layers of vetting are presented to principals—the cabinet secretaries or agency heads who decide, based on exhaustive briefings, whether or not to authorize them.

The system serves multiple purposes: It protects those at the top from getting so entangled in the specifics of one part of their portfolio that they neglect another. And given the little firsthand knowledge they have, it's supposed to prevent those in authority from making uninformed decisions. "It's a very poorly kept secret in Washington that principals never have any idea what they are talking about," one Trump White House official told me. Keep that in mind as we move forward in this timeline.

As Donald Trump prepared to fill the political positions that sit atop the bureaucracy in January 2017, he had a thin bench from which to draw. During Trump's campaign, many prominent Republicans had sworn publicly never to support him. The list shrank further when Chris Christie, Trump's transition head, was fired. When Christie left, so did many establishment Republicans he'd lined up. It was time to bring in the C-team.

The political appointees who came to work on immigration issues in the new administration can be sorted into two groups.

In the first group were establishment Republicans—I'll refer to them as the Careerists—who were compelled not by the president but by the call to serve their country, as well as by personal ambition: with so few qualified candidates eager to work for Trump, those willing to do so got installed a few rungs higher in the bureaucracy than they likely would have in a traditional administration. Like other moderate Republicans, they still hoped that Trump would be less erratic and extreme as president than he had been as a candidate. And if not, they told themselves, the bureaucracy would save them: Trump's most outlandish ideas would never survive the layers of expert review.

Some members of this group came from a tight-knit community of national-security wonks who had occupied the lower rungs of leadership in the Department of Homeland Security when it was first established. Now midcareer and entering middle age, they had stayed in close touch; at Bush-alumni events, they could usually be found huddling about cybersecurity or antiterrorism issues. They were not particularly hawkish on immigration by the standards of Trump's GOP. Among this group was Kirstjen Nielsen, a senior policy director at the Transportation Security

Administration upon its founding, who was selected to "sherpa" John Kelly, the president's nominee for DHS secretary, through his confirmation process. She would later become the face of family separations.

For the second group—I'll refer to them as the Hawks—Trump was a vehicle for the implementation of ideas they had been honing for years. He doubled down on their plans to slash immigration after seeing how popular they were at campaign rallies. Credit for that success went to Stephen Miller, the Hawks' leader, who had already achieved minor infamy while working as the communications director for Senator Jeff Sessions of Alabama. He signed on as chief speechwriter and senior adviser to the president. Sessions, who had previously been ostracized by his own party for his almost fundamentalist stance on immigration, became Trump's first attorney general.

Lesser known than Miller was Gene Hamilton, a lawyer who had worked for ICE in Atlanta before going to Capitol Hill as then-senator Sessions's general counsel. He became senior counselor to Secretary Kelly. Hamilton's reputation is complex; he stood out to colleagues as exceptionally kind and, indeed, family oriented and frequently asked colleagues about their children and personal lives. But he believed that immigration laws should be applied with draconian rigor. Though Atlanta had the country's harshest immigration courts, where more than 90 percent of immigrant defendants lost their cases, he had left that job angry, according to a longtime colleague, because he felt that too many undocumented immigrants were given a "free pass." (Miller declined to comment for this story. Hamilton did not respond to requests for comment.)

To staff his team in the White House, Stephen Miller hired a variety of people from the anti-immigrant fringes of official Washington. Many had personally helped thwart bipartisan reform efforts in the past. Now they planned to bypass Congress altogether, using every possible presidential authority to shape the nation's immigration policies without any input from legislators.

The Hawks knew that their plans were going to be controversial, but they didn't care. New colleagues were viewed as closeted liberals until proved otherwise. "There's this worship of process," John Zadrozny, who joined Miller's team as a member of the White House Domestic Policy Council, told me. "Process, process, process. *Process* is code for 'We can slow down the quick impulses of a fiery political administration with no experts.' Well, that's not what was voted for."

"Our posture was 'If you don't want to make these tough decisions, go,'" Zadrozny said. "'There are plenty of us here who will do these things and sleep at night. . . . We know we'll take a few arrows. That's okay. That's why we're here.'"

Prone to paranoia and insularity, the Hawks signed nondisclosure agreements and met during the transition in secret war-room sessions, unencumbered by general-counsel staff who might say their ideas were illegal or by bureaucrats who might call them unrealistic. They composed a raft of executive orders, many of which read more like press releases, though Miller would later use them to strong-arm cabinet secretaries into fulfilling his wishes.

In any other presidential administration, Miller's disregard for the chain of command would have been grounds for his dismissal. But he possessed a kind of mystique that insulated him from consequences. Almost no one, including cabinet secretaries, dared challenge him, even as he drove them to distraction. (At least one cabinet secretary negotiated an effective ban on ever having to deal directly with Miller, and another demanded that Miller never speak to his subordinates without permission—an order that Miller did not heed.)

Miller was better than other advisers at managing his relationship with the president. He avoided the limelight and never pushed back, as others did, against the president's more ill-considered ideas. But when I asked his colleagues why he was afforded such protection, they reminded me that this was an administration plagued by insecurity and imposter syndrome: the president and his family had not expected to win the 2016 election. When they did, a narrative formed that gave Miller and his immigration speeches the credit. Miller's messaging came to be seen as crucial to securing a second term.

At meetings about immigration policy during the transition, Miller and Gene Hamilton displayed how little they understood about border enforcement. According to people who attended the meetings, they proposed ideas that were outlandishly impractical—such as sending National Guard troops to the border to block migrants from setting foot on American soil, or building barriers across private land, including through waterways where such structures would not be able to withstand seasonal weather patterns. "They were talking like people who'd never been down on the border," one official said.

But instead of pushing back against bad ideas in those early meetings, the Careerists just rolled their eyes and commiserated afterward. I asked a number of them why they hadn't explained the obvious reasons such policies should not be pursued. These were "speak when spoken to" environments, they told me. And precisely because the proposals being batted around were so terrifically bad, they felt confident that the bureaucracy would neutralize them. In the end, these officials assumed—incorrectly—that the only harm done by those meetings would be the time they wasted.

One idea that surfaced multiple times in early 2017 was Tom Homan's Obama-era proposal to prosecute parents coming across the border with their children and separate them. John Kelly, who did not hide his distaste for the Hawks, told me that Stephen Miller pitched the idea to him directly, with support from Hamilton. Kelly came into his position at a disadvantage, as did Kirstjen Nielsen, whom he'd appointed as his chief of staff. Though they understood, at a high level, the push-and-pull factors influencing immigration trends, they had little knowledge of the actual federal immigration code or the mechanisms through which it was enforced. This made Kelly reliant on Hamilton's knowledge of the system, despite his disdain for Hamilton's politics. "There would be this unusual dynamic where Kelly would kind of rib Gene," a senior DHS official told me about the daily morning staff meetings. "He would say, 'Oh, Gene-O, has your buddy Stephen been calling you up lately?' That was Kelly's way of saying, 'I know that you've got friends in all these places and there's this right-wingy immigration network here, but I'm the boss, so make sure everything comes through me.'"

Kelly told me he immediately opposed separating families, not just on moral grounds but also for pragmatic reasons: based on his own experiences in Central America, he didn't think it would work. Kelly knew the moral argument wouldn't sway Trump, so he focused on the logistical challenges. He asked for a cursory review of the policy, after which he came to the same conclusion as Jeh Johnson: though the idea was likely legal, it was wildly impractical—executing it successfully would require hundreds of millions of dollars to build new detention facilities and months to train staff within both Homeland Security and Health and Human Services, the latter of which would be charged with caring for the separated children. (In March 2017, Kelly told CNN that the idea was under consideration, fueling rumors and confusion that would linger for the next year.)

Based on this review, Kelly told me, he decided definitively not to authorize a separation program. He shared his decision publicly, first in a meeting with Senate Democrats on March 29, 2017, and subsequently with the press.

After that, Kelly told me, every time the idea was proposed in a cabinet or other meeting, he would refer back to the results of the review, as if reading from a script: separating families was simply impossible. He told Trump that the president would have to ask Congress for the funds for it, knowing that he would never agree to do that, "because that then links him to the policy, and he loses deniability," Kelly said.

But the idea to separate families was proceeding anyway, on numerous tracks at once, including some that were out of Kelly's sight. On Valentine's Day 2017, Kevin McAleenan, now the acting head of Customs and Border Protection, hosted a large meeting with representatives of CBP, ICE, HHS, and a smattering of White House Hawks.

On the other side of the table from the Hawks, both literally and figuratively, was Jonathan White, the social worker. A former academic, White had become a commander in the U.S. Public Health Service Commissioned Corps and risen quickly within HHS: weeks before Trump was elected president, White had been tapped to head the program that houses immigrant children in

U.S.-government custody, a division of the Office of Refugee Resettlement (ORR). Along with most of that office's employees, he is an expert in childhood trauma. He views the children in the office's care as the most vulnerable in the Western Hemisphere, not merely because they are alone in a foreign country but because they are "off the charts when it comes to ACEs," or adverse childhood experiences, such as exposure to violence, food insecurity, and the feeling that their life is at risk. Even before Trump took office, ORR had often been left out of meetings because it was viewed as an impediment to border enforcement.

White says the environment was like a pep rally, with two deputies of Tom Homan's—Matt Albence and Tim Robbins—announcing their plans for securing the border, which included separating migrant families. (Robbins did not respond to requests for comment.) As the initiative was described, White says, he turned pale and began strategizing about how to stop it. He requested a white paper articulating the idea, knowing that having such documentation would allow him to lobby against family separation directly to the Health and Human Services secretary, Tom Price, and to share it with other parts of the HHS bureaucracy that could begin to outline its many ethical and logistical flaws. (Documents show that White would continue to request the white paper from CBP and ICE officials, who promised it was coming, though it never materialized.)

Meanwhile, Kelly learned that Miller was contacting various DHS officials to push forward the idea of separating families, and he was furious. Kelly stormed into one of his daily morning staff meetings and declared that anyone contacted by Miller needed to refer him directly to Kelly—and that, in any case, DHS would not be moving forward with the idea, no matter how many times it was raised. He told Reince Priebus, Trump's chief of staff, to keep Miller away from his subordinates at DHS.

By the time Kelly replaced Priebus as Trump's chief of staff, he thought he had shut down the discussion of separating families for good. But a local initiative was already under way that would soon be used to justify separations on a nationwide scale.

Chapter 3: The Pilot (March–November 2017)

In the spring of 2017, as illegal border crossings were undergoing their typical seasonal spike, Jeff Self, the Border Patrol chief in El Paso, Texas, acted on a general message that he and other sector chiefs had received after Trump's election—to work with their local counterparts at the Department of Justice to crack down on border crossings in service of the new president's agenda. Self decided that the best way to do that would be for his agents to start referring parents traveling with children for prosecution. Though he likely didn't realize it at the time, Self was laying the groundwork for a national policy that called for separating families. Federal officials would later call his local initiative a "pilot" and use it as a model for expanding the practice nationwide. (Self declined to comment for this story.)

A Border Patrol agent working under Self emailed an assistant U.S. attorney for the Western District of Texas about the departure from prior practice. Though phrased in such a way as to suggest an insignificant administrative change, the email was in fact describing a revival of the idea Tom Homan had proposed to Jeh Johnson in 2014—using prosecution and family separations as a means of deterring would-be migrants.

At the time, the Western District of Texas was being run by Richard Durbin, who was keeping the U.S. attorney's seat warm until a Trump appointee could be nominated and confirmed. Durbin, who had been with the office for decades, responded to the policy change with skepticism. "History would not judge that kindly," he wrote to his colleagues. Though Durbin agreed that exempting *all* parents from prosecution seemed unwise, he said he had "no confidence" in the Border Patrol's ability to determine which ones deserved to face prosecution. "We don't want small children separated from parents and placed into some bureaucratic child services or foster agency in limbo."

Durbin eventually consented to prosecuting some parents, but he wanted to focus on those who were also being accused of much more serious crimes. "If culpability is very low and they have their own children we don't need to prosecute," he wrote in an email. "If they are a *sicario* [cartel hit man] we should prosecute and figure out how to deal humanely with children."

But the instructions sent to Border Patrol agents, which I obtained through a Freedom of Information Act request, contain none of the limitations Durbin requested, instead emphasizing that "the US Attorney's office will be contacted to seek prosecution for the adults of *every* family unit arrested." The document is dedicated mostly to warning agents against contacting assistant U.S. attorneys about the cases late at night or on weekends. It does not contain any guidance on how to separate parents and children or what each should be told about what was happening.

A person familiar with Durbin's thinking told me he was incensed when he discovered that the Border Patrol's change in policy was not intended to punish hard-core criminals who might have been using children to gain entry to the United States but was instead a strategy to deter families seeking asylum. "I was bamboozled," Durbin reportedly said. "They didn't care about our prosecutions. They wanted a reason for separating children from parents."

Wesley Farris, a Border Patrol agent in El Paso, was asked to handle some of the separation cases. In one instance, a boy who was about two years old grabbed onto him in confusion, refusing to let go. "The world was upside down to that kid," Farris told PBS's *Frontline*. "That one got me." Farris told his supervisor afterward not to assign him to separation cases anymore. "That was the most horrible thing I've ever done," he recalled. "You can't help but see your own kids."

Meanwhile, the El Paso Border Patrol immediately started looking to expand Jeff Self's initiative to New Mexico. "Although it is always a difficult decision to separate these families," an agent wrote to the acting U.S. attorney there, "it is the hope that this separation will act as a deterrent to parents bringing their children into the harsh circumstances that are present when trying to enter the United States illegally." Some separations also occurred in Yuma, Arizona, under a separate initiative.

In the spring of 2017, Nora Núñez, a public defender in Yuma, noticed that the cellblocks at the federal courthouse were overflowing with detainees, many of them hysterical parents. The system was already under strain from other prosecutions, so Núñez had to move briskly to keep it from breaking down. "Having to get really firm with someone who was crying and upset because they didn't know where their kid was was heartbreaking," she told me.

Though Núñez had never seen misdemeanor charges filed against parents migrating with their children, she assumed that the families would be reunited as soon as their cases were completed, so she rushed them through the process even quicker than usual. Núñez only realized months later that by the time her clients were returned to immigration custody, many of their children had been sent to shelters in different states.

Alma Acevedo, who was then working at Bethany Christian Services in Michigan, said the organization was inundated with children so inconsolable that teaching them was impossible. "It wasn't just tears," Acevedo told me, as I reported at the time. "It was screams."

When Acevedo managed to reach separated parents by phone, they asked for her advice about whether they should sign paperwork that immigration officers had given them. Acevedo feared that the parents were being asked to consent to their own deportations. "Parents are saying, 'The immigration officer told me if I signed this document, they would give me my child back,'" she said. "The parents would sign in desperation and then, the next thing you know, they would call me from their home country and say, 'I'm here, where's my child? Give me my child back.' It was really sad and really depressing hearing the parents cry all the time."

Explaining the situation to separated children was even harder. "The therapists and I would do a meeting with the child and use pictures or puppets. We would say, 'Your daddy is really far,' and kind of show them—'this is Guatemala and this is the U.S., and you guys are far away.'" She learned not to give separated children any specific timeline for when they might see their parent again because the children would latch on to those promises, however vague, and then ask about them constantly. "We would have to say, 'In many, many days you will be reunited with your parent, but we have to do a lot of paperwork.'"

Supervisors at Bethany and other organizations that operate shelters repeatedly called Health and Human Services headquarters in Washington, pressing for details about what was going on, but they were given none. Don't speak with the media, some were told.

Chapter 4: Ignoring the Warnings (July–December 2017)

When John Kelly left the Department of Homeland Security to become President Trump's chief of staff in July 2017, Stephen Miller and Gene Hamilton moved in tandem to fill the power vacuum that Kelly's departure created. They appeared determined to institute family separations nationwide.

Elaine Duke, Kelly's deputy, became the acting Homeland Security secretary. Duke had only joined the Trump administration after being coaxed out of retirement by former colleagues desperate to fill the open positions at DHS. Within weeks of her taking over the department, she confronted two natural disasters—Hurricane Harvey and Hurricane Maria—and Miller and Hamilton saw an opportunity in her distraction.

Miller phoned DHS staff day and night, barraging them with demands and bullying career bureaucrats into a putative consensus on his ideas. At a meeting that fall, Hamilton distributed a document listing more than a dozen immigration policies that he said the White House wanted implemented, according to several people who were present. At the top were two proposed methods of achieving family separations: either administratively—by placing children and parents in separate detention centers—or via criminal prosecutions, which would place parents in the Department of Justice's custody instead of the Department of Homeland Security's. In both cases, the children would be given to a division of the Department of Health and Human Services. (The El Paso pilot was still under way, unbeknownst to most people at DHS headquarters, including Duke.)

Duke declined to move forward with administrative separations, and sought advice about the prosecution initiative from John Kelly, who assured her that if the president wanted her to do something, he would have told her himself. Duke agreed and proceeded accordingly. "There was a disconnect between those that had strong feelings about the issues and those that could sign things," Duke told me. "And I was the one with the authority to sign things."

The majority of Duke's staff were moderates. At this point, many of them told me, they still believed that Hamilton's idea for separating families nationally was so outlandish that they didn't take it seriously. "What I remember saying is 'This is the most ridiculous proposal, so this doesn't even require all that much work,'" a senior DHS official said. But Miller, recognizing Duke's resistance, started going around her, to her chief of staff, Chad Wolf, who asked that the DHS policy office produce documentation supporting Hamilton's proposals. Soon after, this official said, he "started getting phone calls from Chad Wolf, and you could tell he was under tremendous pressure, saying, 'I gotta have that paperwork—where are we on the paperwork?' And I said, 'Chad, you know and I know this isn't how government works. We've gotta get a lot of eyeballs on it. We have to find out if this is legal, moral, ethical, good policy, geared toward success, etc.'

"What followed was a lot of bad government," the senior official continued. "Bad draft memos were put together. They went up the chain but were bad because they weren't fully vetted policies."

Several of the DHS officials who were present at the meeting with Hamilton told me that after a few weeks, talk about separating families petered out, so they assumed the idea had been abandoned or at least put on hold. It hadn't been—those who were perceived to be doubters were just excluded from subsequent meetings. "I think what I recall most is that I wasn't in the discussions," Duke said, adding that perhaps because she was viewed as a moderate, "I wasn't in the inner circle."

Inside and outside the government, people were beginning to notice that separations were already under way. Immigration lawyers who practiced in Texas and Arizona started reporting individual separation cases to national networks of advocates, who began drafting an official complaint to file with the DHS inspector general. Those advocates also began to share cases with reporters, who prepared stories about them. But the DHS press office insisted that no policies had changed.

Throughout the summer and fall, problems cropped up in the pilot regions. Under the guidelines imposed by Richard Durbin, who was still the acting U.S. attorney in El Paso, DOJ lawyers in the sector rejected two-thirds of the cases referred to them by Border Patrol. Despite that, some of the worst outcomes Durbin had anticipated and tried to prevent were indeed happening. "We have now heard of us taking breast feeding defendant moms away from their infants, I did not believe this until I looked at the duty log and saw the fact we had accepted prosecution on moms with one and two year olds," Durbin's deputy criminal chief wrote to him in August. "The next issue is that these parents are asking for the whereabouts of their children and they can't get a response."

FOIA records show that in the summer of 2017, the DHS's Office for Civil Rights and Civil Liberties, which serves as an internal watchdog for civil-rights violations by the agency, noted a dramatic uptick in complaints involving separations but remained in the dark about what was driving them. The increase in separations was also being tracked by HHS. Shortly after the meeting on Valentine's Day 2017 when the idea to separate families was presented, Jonathan White and several colleagues had begun an internal campaign to try to stop separations from happening.

Documents I obtained show that White took his concerns about the family-separation proposal to his superiors dozens of times and asked them to inquire about it with DHS. He underscored that the HHS shelter system was not prepared to take a large number of separated children, who tend to be younger than those who cross the border alone and require specialized housing that was in short supply. Hoping to catch the attention of others in the bureaucracy who might mobilize against the policy, White repeatedly inserted subtle references to looming family separations in internal and external reports that he wrote, even ones mostly unrelated to the subject. Meanwhile, his colleague James De La Cruz, an HHS administrator, began an effort to track every possible instance of separation and to strategize about how to help reunite as many families as possible.

But White's concerns were intercepted by his politically appointed boss, Scott Lloyd, who was not inclined to help him. Lloyd told me he has many relatives in policing and corrections; he was predisposed to support the views of law enforcement over those of his own department. "I had an affinity for DHS and just tended to take them at their word and got annoyed when people didn't," he said.

Finally, in mid-November 2017, White managed to get Lloyd's attention with an alarming email. "We had a shortage last night of beds for babies," White wrote. "Overall, infant placements seem to be climbing over recent weeks, and we think that's due to more separations from mothers by CBP." Lloyd requested a phone call with Kevin McAleenan, so that White could ask the acting Customs and Border Protection commissioner directly about what he was seeing. During the call, on November 16, McAleenan repeated Kelly's statement that a separation policy had been considered but ultimately rejected. Lloyd would cling to this assurance for months—even when evidence seemed to call for action on his part. (Today, Lloyd says he believes the facts show that he acted appropriately.)

White's warning prompted McAleenan to ask his acting chief of the U.S. Border Patrol, Carla Provost, what was happening. Provost learned about the El Paso initiative from Gloria Chavez, one of her deputies, and immediately shut the program down. "It has not blown up in the media as of yet but of course has the potential to," Provost wrote to McAleenan. After this clear indication that the pilot could be controversial, McAleenan and others at CBP did not disclose the fact that it had ever existed, even to other government agencies that were dealing with its consequences.

At the end of November, a Border Patrol employee emailed several colleagues, including Chavez, asking how to respond to questions from a reporter from the *Houston Chronicle*, Lomi Kriel, who had been tipped off about the initiative. By this point, Chavez not only knew about the pilot; she had been chastised for not alerting her superiors about it earlier. Yet the Border Patrol spokesperson who ultimately responded to Kriel cited an old policy manual stating that agency protocol required maintaining family unity "to the greatest extent operationally feasible." (Provost and Chavez both declined to comment for this story.)

Kriel's article foreshadowed what would go wrong under a nationwide program the following year—problems that DHS officials who served under Trump now claim they never could have anticipated. "There aren't mechanisms in place to systematically allow a parent or child to locate one another once they have been separated," an NGO told Kriel. "Family members lose track of each other."

In December, immigration advocates filed their complaint with the DHS inspector general's office detailing the experiences of more than a dozen separated families, which prompted CBP officials to meet with the agency's chief counsel, according to records obtained through a FOIA request. The complaint, which was shared with Congress and the media, noted that separated children were ending up in shelters in different states, as far away as New York.

For months afterward, in response to questions from reporters, representatives of DHS would continue to say that there had been no change in the agency's treatment of parents traveling with children, not acknowledging that the pilot program had already separated hundreds of children from their parents.

In January 2018, warning of potential "permanent family separation" and "new populations of U.S. Orphans," documents I obtained show that the DHS Office for Civil Rights and Civil Liberties recommended that criteria be established to prevent the separation of very young or especially vulnerable children. They also recommended that an online database be created that family members could use to find one another in the detention system. This tool, if it had been created, would have proved immeasurably valuable the following year, when thousands of parents were searching for their children.

The Border Patrol's internal summary of the pilot program, which has not been reported on until now, also highlights potential issues such as children getting lost or ending up in long-term foster care. The document repeats versions of the phrase *family separation* more than ten times. Despite that, CBP leaders said they were not made aware of any problems that came up during the program.

Chapter 5: Ambient Ignorance (December 2017–May 2018)

By the end of 2017, DHS and White House officials say, Stephen Miller appeared to be losing patience with Elaine Duke, who had refused to sign off on any of his major plans. Rather than continue to argue with the acting DHS secretary, the White House Hawks started looking for a replacement.

Discussion centered on Kansas secretary of state Kris Kobach, who had made a career out of pushing controversial anti-immigrant policies. John Kelly worried about someone like Kobach overseeing DHS. So he floated Kirstjen Nielsen, who had worked with him at the agency and come with him to the White House as his no. 2. Trump accepted Kelly's recommendation, perhaps thinking that Nielsen would be pliable. According to colleagues, Gene Hamilton was so upset when the president chose a moderate to run DHS that he went to work for his former boss Jeff Sessions at the Justice Department, thinking he could have more of an impact on aggressive immigration restrictions from there.

It is somewhat ironic that the person most associated with the Trump administration's harshest immigration policy turned out to be Nielsen. She signed the memo allowing Border Patrol agents to take children away from their parents so that the adults could be prosecuted. But Nielsen had not wanted to sign off on Zero

Tolerance; for months, she refused to do so. In fact, throughout her tenure as secretary, Nielsen would be accused by administration colleagues of being a "squish" over and over again. Each time, she would go a little further in order to appease her critics. Eventually, she followed them off a cliff.

Compared with many of her hard-line colleagues at DHS, Nielsen was technocratic and restrained. After graduating from Georgetown and the University of Virginia School of Law, she had worked at a private law firm in Texas, until September 11 motivated her to take a position with the newly established Transportation Security Administration (soon to become part of DHS); she also worked in the Bush White House and over time became one of the country's foremost experts on cybersecurity policy.

Nielsen's own employees noted that she had considerably less leadership experience than any previous DHS secretary, and some took issue with that. Before joining the Trump administration, she had run a consulting company that had a handful of employees. Now she was leading an agency that employed a quarter of a million people. She was exceptionally hardworking but in a way that didn't always endear her to colleagues. "She read eighty-page briefs for breakfast, lunch, and dinner," one high-ranking DHS official told me, adding that in meetings, Nielsen "asked questions that embarrassed you because she knew more than you did about what you were supposed to be doing."

Nielsen was defensive about any criticism of the department. Unlike Kelly, who had let staffers sift through the pile of news clips published about DHS and only share with him the ones they deemed important, Nielsen devoured them on her way to work each morning, pillorying staff because she hadn't been alerted beforehand about negative stories. But in the eyes of key advisers and staff, anything the press wrote was inherently suspect—likely liberal hysteria. Because of this, they viewed Nielsen's demands for inquiries into allegations of wrongdoing by DHS staff as an annoying waste of time. By the time family separations were being described in the national media, much of her staff didn't believe what was being reported, even when clear evidence supported it.

The DHS that Nielsen took control of was virtually unrecognizable compared with the one that she had worked for when it was started under President Bush. Its energy was now directed toward the southwestern border, with much less attention focused on other matters, including the issue that had sparked its creation: global terrorism. Nielsen was being summoned to the White House so often to talk about immigration that she started working out of a makeshift office at the nearby CBP headquarters on Pennsylvania Avenue, which put her in close proximity with her immigration-enforcement chiefs, Tom Homan and Kevin McAleenan.

From the moment she was confirmed, Nielsen fielded a barrage of immigration-policy proposals from Stephen Miller, which he conveyed through incessant phone calls, day and night. When John Kelly was secretary, he would ignore Miller's late-night calls. But Nielsen frequently found herself listening to him rant after midnight.

Nielsen would hear Miller out, knowing that his approval was crucial to her success in the job. "I would say, 'Okay, Stephen, we'll have a meeting on it; we'll get the lawyers and we'll figure out what's possible and we'll talk it through,'" she told me. "Or I'd say to him, 'Have you talked to anyone at CBP? Did you talk to anybody at HHS? Did you talk to the lawyers? What does [White House Counsel] Don McGahn say?' It would just be him saying stuff and me being like, 'Okay, Stephen, let's find a process here. I don't just make policy on phone calls with you. We have a whole department that I run.'"

By this point, Miller had insinuated himself deep into DHS, identifying allies at its lower rungs who either agreed with him or were open to persuasion. Under the traditional chain of command, only a department's senior leadership has direct contact with the White House, to prevent miscommunications and decisions being made by people lacking authority. Now random employees throughout DHS were speaking directly with Miller and his team, who would then claim to have buy-in for their ideas "from DHS."

Miller's incursions extended to the communications department. For example, he requested photos of detained immigrants with tattoos, presumably to suggest that most of those crossing the border were hardened criminals. When he faced pushback, Lauren Tomlinson, a senior DHS communications aide, told me, "a phone call would go to someone else further down the chain, and the next thing you know, they've got the photos. They would just keep calling until they got to yeses."

Miller blocked numerous candidates to replace Gene Hamilton as senior counselor to the DHS secretary, apparently intent on assuming the role informally himself. Nielsen's staff learned not to bring Miller any job candidates who had served in the Bush administration because they would be automatically rejected. A handful of people cycled through the position over the next several months, but none lasted long because "no one could pass the Miller smell test," a senior DHS official recalled.

Soon after Nielsen's confirmation in December, colleagues of Kevin McAleenan say that he began to agitate for a meeting about rising border crossings, which the White House was pressuring him to contain. Like Nielsen, he'd pursued work in Homeland Security after 9/11, leaving behind a career in corporate law. In the Trump era, he was also under pressure to prove that he wasn't a squish. He had leapfrogged over those in CBP leadership who'd worked their way up from the front lines of the Border Patrol and who tended to view leadership recruits with posh résumés as "street hires." Brandon Judd, the head of the Border Patrol union, may have been McAleenan's most influential skeptic. Judd maintained close access to Trump after winning his affection with an early endorsement in 2016 and occasionally attended private Oval Office meetings where he lobbied for McAleenan to be fired for being too weak on enforcement.

But McAleenan navigated this terrain deftly. He could pass as a Hawk, professing an adherence to the gospel of deterrence, but moderates and progressives on Capitol Hill appreciated that he was more polished than his brasher colleagues during congressional briefings. He made abundant use of Latin phrases (*sui generis, ex ante, ex post facto*) and words like *confirmatory*, even during small talk. In meetings, he rattled off facts and statistics with such facility that people were reluctant to challenge him. During his frequent media appearances, he outlined harsh enforcement policies, coming off not as someone who felt strongly about them one way or the other but as the coolheaded adult in the room who was making sure they were implemented smoothly. Over time, more than fifteen of McAleenan's colleagues told me, he became one of the most vocal advocates for Zero Tolerance.

Chad Wolf, who was now Nielsen's acting chief of staff, told McAleenan that if he wanted a meeting with Nielsen about the rising number of border crossings, he first needed to put together a proposal with possible solutions for her to study. Nielsen liked to be well prepared ahead of meetings, to avoid being put on the spot about issues she hadn't fully considered. This ended up being a primary way that extreme immigration policies were delayed under Nielsen: she would ask questions in meetings that her staff was not prepared to answer then send them off to look for more information.

"There was a joke we all had because everything needed sign-off from the secretary," John Zadrozny, of the White House Domestic Policy Council, told me. "So we'd get something up to the secretary's desk, and weeks would go by where we hadn't gotten something back, and we're like, 'Where is this?' 'Oh, it's on the secretary's desk, hahaha.' Meaning it sat there because she didn't want to deal with it. . . . We were basically always pushing Jell-O up a hill."

When McAleenan and Homan ultimately presented a set of ideas to Nielsen, she and others who were there say, they started by proposing separating families administratively. (Homan says he doesn't recall this.) This would have allowed the agency to separate not only families that crossed the border illegally but also those who presented themselves at legal ports of entry, requesting asylum. Nielsen rejected the idea out of hand, invoking John Kelly's prior decision, which she told the men she viewed as standing DHS policy. Homan and McAleenan shot back that border crossings had increased since Kelly's tenure as secretary and that other strategies to quell them weren't working. "My response was more or less 'I agree we need to do something big,'" Nielsen told me. "'Let's talk about realistic options.'"

McAleenan and Homan then began to describe an initiative to prosecute all adults—including those traveling with children—who crossed the border illegally, telling Nielsen that a pilot program along these lines had already been successfully implemented in El Paso and that the prosecutions could serve as a deterrent on a larger scale.

Nielsen was upset that a pilot had been implemented, seemingly in defiance of Kelly's orders. She asked how the border-enforcement apparatus would absorb the burden of so many additional prosecutions. McAleenan and Homan, who was now the head of ICE, testily assured her that the agencies involved "had a process"—without specifying what it was. Unsatisfied with their responses, Nielsen ended the meeting by telling them to run down answers to her questions and report back.

Elizabeth Neumann, Nielsen's deputy chief of staff, told me she was shaken by the nonchalance with which McAleenan and Homan had proposed taking vast numbers of children away from their parents. "They were not grasping the humanity of the situation; they were just all about 'I need Stephen [Miller] off my back. I need the president off my back,'" she said. (McAleenan denies this account.)

After the meeting, Neumann, who had spent more than a decade working with Nielsen in and out of government, said she approached another top adviser to ask whether taking children from their parents was truly being considered. If the answer was yes, she was planning to lobby against it. The colleague told Neumann that Nielsen was holding firm against separating families. "I was really relieved because I didn't feel I had to have the next conversation," Neumann said.

What she didn't realize was that the second proposal—to refer for prosecution every adult coming across the border illegally—would have the same result and was still on the table.

Across Washington, a new immigration-prosecution initiative that was being considered by the White House came up in various meetings. But the blandness with which it was described—as a way to crack down on lawbreakers—served as a sleight of hand. Because fluency on immigration policy is so rare in Washington, few people grasped the full implications of what was being suggested until it was already happening.

As Nielsen debated these proposals, my sources at DHS alerted me to their existence. Once I'd confirmed the details, the *New York Times* published my report in December 2017, which included the story of a father and his one-year-old son who had already been separated. The *Washington Post* published a story about the proposals the same day. The response both papers got from the DHS press office not only failed to acknowledge that separations were already taking place; it also characterized families seeking asylum in the United States as abusive to their own children: "It's cruel for parents to place the lives of their children in the hands of transnational criminal organizations and smugglers who have zero respect for human life and often abuse or abandon children. The dangerous illegal journey north is no place for young children and we need to explore all possible measures to protect them." The statement alluded to "procedural, policy, regulatory and legislative changes" that would be implemented "in the near future."

. . .

Unlike Kirstjen Nielsen, Jeff Sessions is exactly the sort of person one might expect to be responsible for a policy that would result in widespread family separations. Throughout his career, his approach to both criminal justice and immigration enforcement could be defined by the phrase *zero tolerance*, a law-enforcement term of art that is almost always used euphemistically because snuffing out all crime is impossible. But for Sessions, the phrase is literal. He supported enforcing all laws—or at least the ones that he deemed important—to the fullest extent possible, with no room for nuance or humanitarian exception.

In interviews, DHS officials blamed Sessions for ordering the separation of thousands of families. Some of Sessions's own staff at the Justice Department blamed him as well. Gene Hamilton and Rod Rosenstein, the deputy attorney general, who are revealed to have pushed persistently for Zero Tolerance in a report published by the DOJ inspector general, told the IG's office that they did so solely at the behest of Sessions. (Sessions says that the report appeared to be politically biased, pointing to the fact that it had been leaked prior to the 2020 election. He says President Trump had clearly ordered the executive branch "to reduce the immigration lawlessness at the border." Rosenstein declined to comment for this article.)

Though it is true that Sessions pushed hard for aggressive immigration-enforcement policies, including Zero Tolerance, nothing I found in my reporting suggests that prosecuting parents traveling with children was his idea, and nothing that he did as attorney general, from a legal perspective, caused the policy to come into being.

Exactly how much Sessions even understood about Zero Tolerance is unclear. He is not, former colleagues say, one to get entangled in details or to let facts get in the way of what he thinks is a good idea. Sessions was distracted during his tenure as attorney general, battling constant rumors that he had had untoward interactions with Russian operatives. He was also trying to salvage his relationship with President Trump, who never forgave Sessions for recusing himself from the congressional inquiry into Trump's own ties to Russia.

In a functioning bureaucracy, none of this should have presented any great impediment to Sessions's understanding of Zero Tolerance: a cabinet secretary generally makes decisions based on the recommendations presented by advisers, which in turn are based on expert analysis. But Sessions's principal immigration adviser was Gene Hamilton. As one of the only DOJ staff members fully dedicated to the subject, Hamilton worked in relative isolation, with few colleagues to challenge his positions. And Hamilton showed an unwillingness to take seriously any of the policy's pitfalls that he was alerted to before and during its execution.

As Hamilton prepared to formally propose Zero Tolerance to Sessions, Rosenstein's office asked John Bash, the newly confirmed U.S. attorney in El Paso, for a briefing on the separation pilot program there. Bash had previously served as a White House legal adviser and was considered a trusted Trump ally. Bash asked his new colleagues in El Paso to bring him up to speed on the pilot, according to email excerpts that were published by the DOJ inspector general. He then briefed Hamilton and others at DOJ. His notes indicate that the initiative had faced "significant 'pushback'" from local stakeholders; they also reference pending litigation in the Western District of Texas filed on behalf of five people whose children (and in one case a grandchild) had been taken away from them. The magistrate judge in that case complained that the defendants before him were "completely incommunicado" with their children "while being prosecuted for a very minor offense" and that parents and children had no apparent way to find each other after being separated.

Hamilton later told the inspector general that he didn't remember the meeting. This is the first of many documented instances—all of which he would later tell the inspector general he could not recall—when Hamilton was warned directly about the problems that would take place if the pilot was expanded nationwide. He forged ahead anyway.

A few weeks later, Bash received a memo from his colleagues explaining in even greater detail problems that had arisen during the prosecution pilot. But headquarters hadn't followed up with him about expanding it, so he didn't share the memo with anyone, and he later told the inspector general that he'd assumed the idea had died. No one at headquarters ever contacted Richard Durbin—the acting U.S. attorney in El Paso during the pilot program who had been told that infants were being separated from their mothers—for his input.

Meanwhile, immigration advocates were still learning of families that had been separated during the pilot but had not yet been reunited. They were also hearing reports of families that had been separated after presenting themselves at a port, where it is perfectly legal to request entry to the United States. The advocates prepared to file a lawsuit, which they hoped would result in a nationwide injunction against separations and a court order to reunify the families that had already been torn apart. Lee Gelernt, a lawyer with the ACLU's Immigrants' Rights Project, would lead the case. "It's not just that the parents and children are separated for months and months," Gelernt told me at the time. "It's that the parents have no idea where their children are, what's happening to their children, or whether they are even going to see their children again."

Gelernt was gathering tips from advocates with connections to shelter workers in the Department of Health and Human Services, who defied orders not to speak publicly about what was happening, out of concern over what they were seeing. The shelter workers "don't even know where the kids are coming from, who the parent is, where the parent is," Gelernt told me. "They are two, three, four, five years old."

During this period, each time I asked Trump-administration officials about a specific case, they would say that the separation had taken place only because the child was thought to be caught in a trafficking scheme or otherwise in danger, which would have been in keeping with past policies. But in many of these cases, lawyers representing the families said none of those circumstances held true.

In February 2018, Gelernt met a woman from the Democratic Republic of Congo who had been separated from her six-year-old daughter. The girl had spent several months in an HHS shelter in Chicago; her mother was being held in an immigration detention center in the desert on the outskirts of San Diego. When she walked into a cinder-block room to meet Gelernt, she appeared gaunt and confused—"almost catatonic from what had happened to her," Gelernt told me. The woman explained that when she and her daughter had crossed the border, agents had taken them to a motel for questioning—a common practice when border facilities run out of space—and put them in adjacent rooms. Because the mother and daughter, who became known in court as Ms. L and S.S., respectively, had been living in South America before requesting asylum in the United States, S.S. had picked up Spanish. When the agents began to discuss separating the girl from her mother, perhaps thinking that they were being discreet by speaking in Spanish, Ms. L heard her daughter's screams through the wall between them.

Though Gelernt had been planning to build a case for a class-action suit, he was so disturbed by the meeting that he began drafting a complaint on Ms. L's behalf as soon as he returned from the detention center. "Her child's been gone for nearly four months," he told me at the time, "and I just could not justify delaying going into court any longer to get her and her child reunited. Hearing her talk about her child screaming 'Don't take me away from my mommy.'"

While they waited for a ruling on the Ms. L case, Gelernt and his colleagues scrambled to prepare filings for other plaintiffs, quickly adding another mother, known as Ms. C, who had been separated from her fourteen-year-old son during the El Paso pilot six months earlier. (Ms. C had ended up in West Texas; her son had landed in a shelter in Chicago.) At this point, the ACLU asked the judge to certify the case as a class action, estimating, based on accounts it had collected—some from concerned government sources—that at least 400 to 500 separations had occurred by then.

The government responded to Gelernt's suit in a legal briefing with the same message that reporters kept hearing—that the Department of Homeland Security did not have a separation policy and that nothing had changed in its treatment of migrant families. The response did not acknowledge the existence of any pilot program. "Such a policy," the government's brief stated, "would be antithetical to the child welfare values of the Office of Refugee Resettlement."

The government argued that agents had separated Ms. L from her daughter because they were skeptical that the pair were truly related; Ms. L had not provided documents proving she was the child's mother. Gelernt thought this was merely a pretense to justify the separation. "She spent three months walking here,"

Gelernt told me. "She was robbed. So of course she didn't have documents." A judge called for a DNA test, which proved that Ms. L was in fact S.S.'s mother. Soon after, the government released Ms. L onto the street outside the desert detention center. Several days later, with the help of lawyers, Ms. L was reunited with her daughter.

•   •   •

In the spring of 2018, I learned about the list of separated children that James De La Cruz, Jonathan White's colleague at the Office of Refugee Resettlement, was compiling. De La Cruz and a handful of others at ORR were using the list to seek help from ICE in tracking down the parents of those children and trying to reunify them, or at least connect them by phone—many of the separated parents were still detained or had been deported. De La Cruz and the small group of his colleagues who had access to the list were keeping its existence quiet, knowing that the document would be controversial because the administration was still publicly denying that children were being separated from their parents at the border with any greater frequency than under previous administrations.

Most of those with access to the list initially told me they worried that a news article about it could be traced back to them—or worse, that it might somehow jeopardize what, at the time, was the only known effort to track family-separation cases. But by early April, the list grew to include more than 700 names—enough that my sources began to conclude that the situation was too dire to go unreported any longer. And they knew that the total number of separations was even higher: the list contained only the names of children whose cases had been reported to HHS headquarters by shelter staff.

At that point, I contacted the HHS and DHS public-affairs offices at the same time, letting them know that I was preparing to publish a story about the list of separated children, and asking them to confirm its authenticity. Mark Weber, an HHS spokesperson, says he called Katie Waldman, a DHS spokesperson who later married Stephen Miller. Waldman yelled at him, telling him that DHS was not separating children from their parents. (Waldman told me the same, saying that I would be misleading the American public if I published my story as planned.) But Weber's own colleagues at HHS eventually acknowledged, according to emails that were made public later as part of a congressional inquiry, that De La Cruz was keeping track of separations. When Weber went back to Waldman, telling her that he planned to corroborate my story, he says that Waldman and her boss, Tyler Houlton, insisted that he officially deny that DHS was separating families any more than in the past. "They made me lie," Weber told me recently. (Waldman said Weber's memory of the conversation is not accurate; Houlton did not respond to a request for comment.) Waldman and Houlton provided a statement for my *Times* story, insisting that families were not being separated for the purposes of prosecution and deterrence. All the while, separations were still increasing. By April 23, three days after the story was published, documents show that De La Cruz had tracked 856 separations, more than a quarter of which involved children younger than five.

When my *Times* story came out, Scott Lloyd, De La Cruz's boss, was distressed. "I was just like, 'Why do we have a list?'" Lloyd told me recently. "It looked like ORR keeping tabs on DHS. And possibly leaking it to the *New York Times*." Lloyd asked ORR staff to stop adding to the list because the document made "it look like something that isn't happening is happening because I didn't know there to be any sort of a zero-tolerance policy." But De La Cruz told Lloyd he felt the list was necessary to ensure that the children would be reunited with their families. He continued adding to it.

•   •   •

Through the early spring of 2018, border crossings continued to rise. Fox News commentators took note of the trend and blamed Kirstjen Nielsen. Stephen Miller prompted the president to chastise her. Knowing that Trump did not like to read official reports, Miller would instead print out articles by a few choice immigration reporters at right-wing outlets and leave them on the president's desk, saying they were evidence that Nielsen was a bad leader. Soon, Nielsen was being summoned to the West Wing for even more frequent—sometimes daily—meetings about what to do. The discussions consisted mostly of Miller ranting about how the ideas he'd been pitching for months had needlessly stalled. Jeff Sessions would sometimes pile on, telling the president that Nielsen was being gutless, allowing him—if only temporarily—to escape Trump's ire himself. Once, Sessions told Trump that Nielsen could simply choose not to let people cross the border, but was refusing to do so. Trump screamed at Nielsen, making her cabinet colleagues deeply uncomfortable. Kelly stepped in and tried to adjourn the meeting, but he stayed quiet about the specific policies.

Indeed, the limitation of Kelly's approach to opposing Zero Tolerance may have been that, in front of the Hawks, he focused on his logistical concerns. Kelly felt that approach was the most likely to stop the policy from being implemented, but the Hawks now say they didn't register Kelly's general opposition to it, only that he thought it would require additional resources. (Kelly says his opposition to separating families was plainly clear throughout his tenure in the administration.)

According to colleagues, Tom Homan and Kevin McAleenan continued to minimize the significance of Zero Tolerance, saying that they merely wanted to increase enforcement of laws already on the books. "Under what authority do you tell the police 'Don't enforce law'?" Nielsen told me McAleenan said to her. "He was basically like, 'Look, you're not allowing me to do my job. We need to stop having the conversation and just move forward and do this.'" (McAleenan says he never suggested that the policy was uncontroversial and that he raised logistical concerns with Nielsen repeatedly. Homan says he never pressured Nielsen.)

Nielsen still didn't feel she had enough information to make a decision: Did Border Patrol stations have the capacity to house additional migrants waiting to be sent to court? Did the Justice

Department have enough lawyers to take on extra cases? Did the U.S. Marshals have enough vehicles to transport separated parents? What would happen to the children while the prosecutions were carried out? Nielsen and her colleagues say that McAleenan and Homan were dismissive, the implication being that it was not her job as secretary to get mired in enforcement details; she was micromanaging.

Every key member of the Trump administration's DHS leadership team whom I interviewed told me that separations were never meant to play out as they did. But when I asked them to explain how separations, prosecutions, and reunifications were supposed to have worked, every one of them gave me a different version of the plan. Some said they thought that parents and children were going to be reunited on an airport tarmac and deported together. Others said they thought that after being prosecuted, parents would go back to Border Patrol stations, where their children would be waiting. Others thought that kids would be sent to HHS facilities for only a few days. But it doesn't really matter which plan was supposed to have prevailed: None of them was feasible or had any precedent. This points to how little knowledge of the system most of these people had and how unclear communication was throughout what passed for the planning process.

In early April 2018, Stephen Miller, Gene Hamilton, and Kevin McAleenan (who had recently been confirmed as the CBP commissioner) began citing various documents to insist that Nielsen was violating a lawful order by delaying the implementation of Zero Tolerance, according to colleagues. One was an executive order, "Enhancing Public Safety in the Interior of the United States," crafted by Miller and his faction during the transition and issued in January 2017. It was clearly directed toward ICE, which operates in the interior of the country, unlike the Border Patrol. But by refusing to command Border Patrol agents to refer parents for prosecution, the Hawks said, Nielsen was violating a clause in the order that stated, "We cannot faithfully execute the immigration laws of the United States if we exempt classes or categories of removable aliens from potential enforcement."

Two new documents were issued on the same day, April 6, 2018, perhaps to increase the pressure on Nielsen. In one, Jeff Sessions officially announced a new "zero-tolerance policy," under which U.S. attorneys would, "to the extent practicable," accept 100 percent of the illegal-entry cases referred to them by the Border Patrol. (Sessions had also issued a similar memo the year before.) The second, a presidential memorandum, called generally for the end of "catch and release" immigration enforcement. Materially, the documents did not mean much for the Border Patrol, which Nielsen, a lawyer, theoretically should have known: Sessions had no authority over that agency, including over which cases its agents referred for prosecution. And Trump's memo didn't contain any specific directives regarding parents traveling with children.

The Border Patrol could have continued processing families the same way it always had without violating any law or order. Records show that Border Patrol sectors even received guidance indicating that Sessions's initiative applied only to adults traveling without children. But colleagues say that McAleenan, Hamilton, and Miller again told Nielsen that by declining to refer parents traveling with children for prosecution, she was defying orders.

As the Zero Tolerance announcement was hyped to Nielsen for its alleged importance, it was played down to the U.S. attorneys whom it would ultimately affect. Originally, they were told that Sessions's memo was no big deal. According to the DOJ inspector general's report, Sessions had asked Hamilton to "ensure it was workable, and there were no red flags," before writing it. But Hamilton didn't do that. Instead DOJ asked for feedback on the document from the five U.S. attorneys stationed along the southwestern border—without making clear to them that it would change the department's treatment of migrant families. The attorneys later told the inspector general that they assumed parents would continue to be exempt from prosecutions for illegal entry, as they had been for the entirety of DHS's history. Ryan Patrick, the U.S. attorney in South Texas, told me that each time "zero tolerance" messaging came up, DOJ officials told him explicitly that his district was already doing plenty to combat illegal immigration and that he could disregard the initiative.

Again and again, Gene Hamilton ignored or rejected anything suggesting that the execution of a policy that separated children from their parents would create moral, legal, or logistical problems. When I asked a close colleague of Hamilton's at the Justice Department why Hamilton was so persistent about moving the policy forward, she took a guess based on her own experience: "Stephen Miller told him to." She added, "Stephen Miller often told people that if they tried to work through the system that they would get pushback . . . so it was really important for that person to just go around the system and do it themselves and circumvent the chain."

"For Stephen and Gene," she told me, "anything that got stalled was evidence of the failure of the system," not of any weakness in their policy ideas.

Beyond actual experts, official Washington has very little knowledge of how the immigration system works. (Immigration "is a career killer," Lauren Tomlinson, the senior DHS communications aide, told me. "You can't solve it. All you're gonna do is piss everyone off.") Still, in retrospect, it is astonishing how many people throughout the federal government were engaged in conversations about a policy that would result in prolonged family separations apparently without realizing it.

This ambient ignorance enabled the Hawks to hoodwink the Careerists and to make certain facts appear more benign than they were. Kirstjen Nielsen and members of her inner circle all told me they recalled constantly hearing the line "We've done this before" in reference to prosecuting parents and separating them from their children; Kevin McAleenan and Tom Homan and their respective staffs repeated that line incessantly. Nielsen, Scott Lloyd, and others said they understood this to mean that Border Patrol agents under previous administrations had done the same thing.

When I first heard this argument from one of Nielsen's advisers, I assumed that he had misspoken or that I had misheard. It seemed preposterous that he didn't know separating children from their parents was not something that had been done on any significant scale. But then I heard it again from Nielsen and her senior staff. Some of them told me they remembered hearing certain statistics—that 10 or 15 percent of parents had been referred for prosecution in the past. Others said that the details were never clear or that the White House or Justice Department would claim it didn't keep data on that. These officials said they believed that the idea Nielsen was debating was nothing new. "It just seemed like a nonissue that I shouldn't spend any time on," May Davis, who held various roles in the Trump White House, recalled.

When I would tell these officials, including Nielsen, that parents traveling with a child had rarely been prosecuted in the past, they sounded shocked. Those who reportedly gave these assurances about the policy, including Homan, McAleenan, and Ron Vitiello, the acting deputy commissioner of CBP, all denied doing so; some suggested that the DHS secretary and her advisers must simply be confused.

●   ●   ●

The relentless pressure from the White House Hawks seemed to be wearing on Kevin McAleenan. Caravans of asylum seekers from Central America had formed, headed for the United States, and twenty-four-hour coverage of them incited a new level of panic in the administration about border crossings. After debating the idea for months, McAleenan took his most direct step to push for prosecuting parents, knowing that they would be separated from their children by the Border Patrol. In an email dated April 19, 2018, to Tom Homan and Francis Cissna, the director of U.S. Citizenship and Immigration Services, he stated his intent to formally recommend the idea to Nielsen.

"Please see a draft decision memorandum proposing increased prosecution (toward 100%) of all adults who cross illegally, whether they present as single adults or in family units," McAleenan wrote. "I do believe that this approach would have the greatest impact on the rising numbers, which continue to be of great concern." He said he planned to send the memo to Nielsen by close of business the next day, adding that even without their support, "I am prepared to submit solo."

Homan and Cissna decided to sign on. McAleenan now says the email was only a "small snapshot" of a larger bureaucratic process in which he was just following directions.

Nielsen received the memo with annoyance, feeling squeezed by her own subordinates. Attached was a legal analysis by John Mitnick, the top lawyer at DHS, who found that "although it would be legally permissible to separate adults and minors as outlined above, any such decisions will face legal challenges." He warned that a court could find family separations on a large scale, without any proven mechanism for swift reunification after prosecutions, in violation of "various laws or the Fifth Amendment due process clause." (Though Mitnick's analysis is written with lawyerly detachment, a White House staffer who attended a meeting about Zero Tolerance with him in April said that he was "freaking out" about the litigation risks associated with the policy.)

Nielsen told me she supported the idea of prosecuting all those who crossed the border illegally, including parents traveling with their children, but she feared that DHS was not logistically prepared to implement the policy without causing chaos in courts and detention centers and losing track of parents and children. She asked the White House to allow her to defer her decision on the program for six months so she could travel to Central America herself and announce that the policy was imminent, in hopes that doing so would encourage families that needed to seek asylum to use legal ports of entry. Stephen Miller was unwilling to wait. Nielsen told me he claimed to be in contact with Border Patrol officials who were eager to get started. With him, Nielsen said, "the tone is always frantic. 'The sky is falling, the world is ending, it's going to be all your fault. The president promised this, and we have to deliver on the promise.'"

"The White House was growing frustrated" with the delays, an adviser to Nielsen told me. "They basically said, 'Look, the attorney general gave you a lawful order. You need to execute it.'" This was not true. "And we kept pushing back. Eventually the pressure got to be just overwhelming." McAleenan and Homan were saying, "We're ready to go. We're ready to go. We're ready to go. We've got it in place. We've got a good battle rhythm with DOJ. We can do this."

None of the other agencies that would be affected by Zero Tolerance had been alerted to what was looming. That included the Department of Health and Human Services. "I don't know how to say this delicately, so I'll just say it: It's really not like HHS's opinion mattered here," John Zadrozny told me, explaining that because HHS did not have any authority over immigration policy, it was not uncommon for the department to be left out of such discussions. Zadrozny said that although he did not recall a specific decision to keep the Zero Tolerance policy secret from HHS, it wouldn't surprise him if there was one. "There were times when we were having meetings where we would specifically say, 'Keep HHS out of it; they're just going to babble and cause problems. They're not actually going to be helpful.'"

Astonishing as this sounds, it seems that no one at the department that would be charged with taking care of thousands of separated children was given any official warning that the Zero Tolerance program was in the offing. "We did not find evidence that DOJ leadership had discussions about the zero tolerance policy or family separations with HHS prior to the announcement," the inspector general's report later concluded.

At the end of April, several developments took place almost at once. Gene Hamilton's office asked the five U.S. attorneys who were stationed in southwestern border districts if their staffs had seen an increase in prosecution referrals for parents traveling with children based on Sessions's April memo, and if not, when they expected to. The email was written as if the attorneys should have known that a change was coming, but their response made clear that this was, in fact, the first notice they had received that the treatment of families would change. The attorneys issued a joint response stating that none of the five districts had the resources to handle the increased volume of cases that prosecuting parents would create. "This change in policy would result in new referrals of 20 to 400 cases per day, depending on the district," the U.S. attorneys wrote. Furthermore, Homeland Security and Border Patrol would not be able to process these cases fast enough. "The medical screening for TB, chicken pox, measles; much less the processing of these individuals in establishing identity, alienage, criminal and/or immigration history, etc. would be practically impossible to accomplish within the constitutionally mandated time constraints." Hamilton would later tell the inspector general that he'd "missed" the response from the U.S. attorneys—which was one he'd requested—and that he was not aware that the U.S. attorneys had raised these specific concerns about prosecuting parents.

Rich Hunter, the second-highest-ranking official in the U.S. Marshals Service in south Texas, heard about what was coming from a colleague who had been tipped off by a friend at the Justice Department. The marshals are responsible for housing pretrial detainees facing federal criminal charges, including border cross-ers, and transporting them to court for their hearings. Even in nor-mal circumstances, their facilities along the border are constantly at capacity. Under the influx of new detainees that a zero-tolerance policy would bring, Hunter anticipated that the system would break down.

"The more and more information we got, it just painted a bleaker and bleaker picture for us," Hunter told me. "I could see the impact headed down the tracks straight at us, and no one had talked to us. No one had prepared us for this. No one had asked us, 'Do you have space for this? Do you have resources, man-power?'" Hunter helped produce a report that was delivered to the Justice Department on April 27. It stated that the marshals—like the U.S. attorneys—did not have the resources to implement Zero Tolerance. The marshals sent copies of the report to Jeff Ses-sions's office and to Rod Rosenstein, who would later push DOJ attorneys to apply the policy as aggressively as possible. Both Hamilton and Rosenstein would tell the DOJ inspector general that they were unaware of any problems with Zero Tolerance raised by the marshals—yet another warning they claim to have missed.

That same week, McAleenan's memo pressing Nielsen to activate Zero Tolerance was leaked to the *Washington Post*, which published an article about it on April 26. To this day, it is not clear whether the memo was leaked by those who supported Zero Tolerance or those who opposed it. Many speculated that opponents of the program had leaked it in order to generate popular blowback and make the policy's implementation less likely. But if that's the case, the scheme backfired. After the *Post* article appeared, the pressure on Nielsen to authorize Zero Tolerance only increased. "It seemed like Kirstjen was sitting on all these memos and wouldn't do anything," Lauren Tomlinson recalled.

In early May, Miller convened yet another meeting about Zero Tolerance, in the Situation Room. Nielsen says she started listing all the reasons the department was not ready to move forward. "First Stephen said, 'We've had this meeting a million times—who thinks despite all of that we need more time?'" Nielsen told me. She raised her hand—the only person in the room to do so. "The follow-up from Stephen was 'Okay, who thinks we just need to go forward? We're done talking about this.' And at that point, I remember what felt like a sea of hands."

According to notes that he prepared, Hamilton acknowledged that separated children would be sent to HHS. To anyone familiar with HHS's operations, this would have immediately indicated that the government would face significant barriers in trying to bring parents and children back together—among them, children and parents would be separated by hundreds of miles because of the way HHS placements typically work, and many parents would not qualify to regain custody of their own children under the requirements for sponsoring a child officially deemed an unaccompanied minor. But no one with such knowledge was in the room.

On May 1, McAleenan emailed Hamilton, saying, "Looking at next week, likely," for the Border Patrol to begin referring parents for prosecution. Three days later, McAleenan went to see Nielsen, his draft memorandum in hand for her to sign. A heated conversation ensued, according to Nielsen and several people who overheard it.

Nielsen told me that McAleenan made the usual arguments—you can't tell Customs and Border Protection not to enforce the law; you can't exempt parents from prosecution; the president wants this. "But I had been telling Kevin, 'You cannot implement Zero Tolerance until I'm convinced that we have the resources.'" Nielsen said she thought that "in Kevin's mind, I was holding up what they had been told to do, basically under law. And I'm sure Stephen was calling all of them five times a day, like, 'Why aren't you doing this?' And the [Border Patrol and ICE] unions were freaking out because they wanted it to happen."

Nielsen told me she wanted to be "the type of leader who deferred to the experts and the careers," using shorthand to refer to those, like McAleenan and Homan, who had spent years working at their agencies and insisted that they had the resources necessary to implement the policy smoothly. She also could not afford to be seen as the sole moderate who was stalling for time. "DHS is a department of 250,000 people, so for me to pretend that I know better than everyone else, to me, seemed to be the opposite of the type of leader that I wanted to be," Nielsen told me. "So, yeah, ultimately, I took Kevin at his word," she said, adding that McAleenan demanded, "Why don't you believe me and why don't you believe the careers? They know what they're doing!" (McAleenan denied ever pressuring Nielsen on his own behalf. He said he did convey directives that he was receiving from the White House and others.)

The argument would have continued but, Nielsen told me, she had to leave for another meeting. "I was like, 'Okay, I believe you.'" She signed Zero Tolerance into being. "Frankly," she told me, "I wish I hadn't."

· · ·

On the afternoon of May 7, standing at the border in San Diego, overlooking the Pacific, Jeff Sessions held a press conference. With Tom Homan standing at his side, he announced that Zero Tolerance was going into effect as a national policy. Kirstjen Nielsen and other DHS staff say they weren't informed about the press conference until a few hours beforehand, when a Justice Department spokesperson shared a draft of Sessions's remarks. When they read it, Nielsen's staff asked for the removal of one line, hoping that they could ask Border Patrol to hold off on applying the policy to families until they could prepare: "If you are smuggling a child, then we will prosecute you and that child will be separated from you as required by law." Sessions's staff declined; that's our "money line," they said, according to *Border Wars*, a book by Julie Hirschfeld Davis and Michael D. Shear.

John Kelly told me that during the televised press conference, Nielsen burst into his office in the West Wing, incensed. She was worried that a sudden and dramatic increase in prosecutions was going to cause chaos at the border. "Nielsen was saying, 'We're not ready to do this. We don't have any facilities. We don't have any training.'"

She was right, Kelly told me. "It was a disaster as predicted."

After months of unheeded warnings and unread reports, the mass separation of families was about to begin. Though many have argued that the policy was born out of malice, those who watched it unfold up close say they saw something subtler but no less insidious among Homan and McAleenan and others who pushed the policy forward.

"They were trying to do their jobs," Elizabeth Neumann, Nielsen's deputy chief of staff, told me. "And they were absolutely flummoxed about how to stem the tide" of migrants flowing across the border. "And I think they lacked a really important filter to say 'There is a line that we can't cross.'"

She paused, then put this another way: "If the president suggested, 'We should have moats with alligators in them, and maybe shoot people from the border, and that would be a deterrent,' I think most every Border Patrol agent would be like, 'Hey, that's a red line we will never cross.' We all know the bright-red lines.

"They just were up against this wall, and they couldn't see the red line anymore."

Chapter 6: Implementation (May–June 2018)

The implementation of Zero Tolerance was a disaster. For forty-eight days, catastrophes cascaded. After two and a half weeks, the Border Patrol leadership finally told agents to write down which children belonged to which parents. Internal emails show that when a magistrate judge in south Texas demanded that the Border Patrol there provide the court with weekly lists of separated children and their locations, threatening to hold the agency in contempt for failing to do so, agents panicked at their inability to fulfill such a basic request. "I might be spending some time in the slammer," one supervisor wrote to a colleague, who replied, "I ain't going to jail!!!!!!!!!!!!!!"

Some of those dealing with the fallout of Zero Tolerance—the bureaucrats, judges, social workers, U.S. attorneys, and law-enforcement officials—registered warnings or complaints with their supervisors. They received different versions of the same response: push harder.

After Jeff Sessions's announcement, the five U.S. attorneys stationed on the southwestern border requested a meeting with Gene Hamilton. Four days later, on May 11, as the attorneys sat on the line waiting for a conference call to begin, they received an email informing them that Hamilton would no longer be able to attend. The attorneys decided to talk among themselves, while a liaison from the Justice Department listened in and took notes. Afterward, the liaison wrote a summary of the call that concluded, "BIG CONCERN: What is happening with these children when they are being separated from the parent? It appears that once DHS turns the child over to HHS, DHS is out of the picture and cannot give information. What are the safeguards to the children?"

His attention apparently piqued, Sessions agreed to speak with the attorneys by phone later that day. His responses seemed out of touch with reality. He had promised to assign thirty-five additional attorneys to southwestern border districts to help with the implementation, but they wouldn't be able to start those jobs for months.

Several of the attorneys' notes about the call record that Sessions articulated a central goal: "We need to take away children."

Soon after, the U.S. attorneys were assured that parents and children would be swiftly reunified after prosecution. With that, they forged ahead.

Internal emails show that some assistant U.S. attorneys who resisted prosecuting parents under Zero Tolerance faced reassignment—and the parents whose cases they declined were separated from their children anyway. In early May, for example, DHS officials heard that attorneys in Yuma, Arizona, were declining to prosecute Zero Tolerance cases except in those instances where children had crossed the border with both parents, so that at least one parent could remain with them. As Border Patrol officials scrambled to confirm that this "problem" was not occurring elsewhere, one warned that "there will be repercussions" for prosecutors who turned down cases. Another added that "the AG's office"—presumably a reference to Hamilton—had assured them that any attorneys refusing to break up family units "will find themselves working in another district, away from the Southwest Border."

Hamilton made several attempts in early May, after Zero Tolerance began, to convene meetings between the Departments of Health and Human Services, Justice, and Homeland Security, in hopes of getting all three agencies, with their tens of thousands of employees, on the same page—but it was far too late. His emails betray such naivete about the system that it's unclear if they were sincere or feigned. For example, in one email, he proposed that perhaps the U.S. Marshals could use abandoned jails to house separated parents—an idea that went nowhere because it would have taken millions of dollars and months of contract negotiations to bring such facilities up to federal code. At the same time, Hamilton was bragging internally about how much prosecutions had increased, writing to a colleague on May 21 that, although 2,700 monthly prosecutions had been typical in the months before Zero Tolerance, "we're now on track to do at least that many each *week*."

The brutality of Zero Tolerance was immediately evident. The father of a three-year-old "lost his shit," one Border Patrol agent told the *Washington Post*. "They had to use physical force to take the child out of his hands." The man was so upset that he was taken to a local jail; he "yelled and kicked at the windows on the ride," the agent said. The next morning, the father was found dead in his cell; he'd strangled himself with his own clothing.

The influx of anguished parents into government detention centers across the country turned the facilities into pressure cookers, where detainees and correctional workers alike were on edge. Even during the busiest season at the border, an individual U.S. Marshals facility would typically deal with only a few dozen daily intakes. Now the facilities were suddenly being asked to find housing for hundreds of new detainees every day.

Marshal supervisors ordered that temporary, stackable overflow beds be crammed into dorms so that the separated parents had a place to sleep. "Our manpower has been completely depleted," a marshal in the Southern District of California wrote in an email to staff in mid-May. "We are in 'crisis mode,' 'critical mass' 'DEF-CON 1' or however you want to phrase it."

On top of this, the marshals were fielding urgent calls from shelter staff working under the Office of Refugee Resettlement who were improvising any method they could to track down the parents of separated children, to satisfy requirements that children in federal custody be given the chance to speak with their family members or sponsors twice a week. According to the DOJ's inspector general, some of the marshals had never heard of ORR and had to research it on the internet. Many marshals declined to make parents available for the calls because the marshals were too busy or said they were not required to do so.

Rich Hunter, the high-ranking marshals official in Texas who had anticipated such chaos, traveled from his office in Houston to the federal court in McAllen to try to troubleshoot problems. He arrived to find the street outside the courthouse lined with charter buses that had been procured at the last minute to transport the surge of separated parents to court. Because the court didn't have enough cellblocks, parents had to sit for hours inside the parked buses until it was their turn to be called before the judge. The courtroom itself resembled a packed concert venue; the court reporter "was crammed in the corner," Hunter told me. "The prosecutors are standing up over by the jury box that had additional defendants in it. It was just not a picture of a federal courtroom that I had ever seen before."

As a thirty-year veteran of the agency, Hunter said his first concern was safety. But he also found the scene emotionally disturbing. "I remember their faces," Hunter said. "You deal with this issue long enough, you realize that the overwhelming majority of people are not cartel members. . . . You would hear them asking their defense attorneys, asking anybody, for information [about their kids]. As a dad, as a person, it would take a toll on you because you can imagine what that was like."

He recalled parents struggling to use the court's interpretation headphones. "A lot of them had not seen technology like that before ever in their life, so they're put on wrong," he said. "And then the look on their faces of *What am I going through?*"

Neris González, a Salvadoran consular employee charged with protecting the rights of migrants from her country in U.S. custody, was stationed at a CBP processing center in McAllen when she read about Zero Tolerance. "In my little mind," she told me, "I thought they were going to separate the families" by putting parents in one cell and children in another. "I never thought they would actually take away the children."

But when she walked into the processing center for the first time after Zero Tolerance was implemented, she saw a sea of children and parents, screaming, reaching for each other, and fighting the Border Patrol agents who were pulling them apart. Children were clinging to whatever part of their parents they could hold on to— arms, shirts, pant legs. "Finally the agent would pull hard and take away the child," she said. "It was horrible. These weren't some little animals that they were wrestling over; they were human children."

Other than Wesley Farris, the Border Patrol officer who spoke to *Frontline*, González appears to be the only official to have gone on the record to describe the separations themselves. (I asked members of the Biden administration to provide Border Patrol officials who'd participated in Zero Tolerance for an interview. I was told that no one would agree to speak with me.) González said the facility was effectively locked down during Zero Tolerance; almost no one outside Border Patrol and ICE was allowed in, whereas in the past, journalists, representatives from faith-based organizations, and human-rights lawyers had sometimes been given access. "It wasn't right," she said. "They didn't want anyone to expose what they were doing."

González asked a Border Patrol agent what was going on. "He said that ICE and BP were under orders from Trump, and he said to separate the kids from their parents—as in, completely separate." Desperate scenes played out everywhere. Border Patrol agents who were yanking children away asked González to help them prevent fights. In several instances, she placed herself between parents and agents, trying to calm the families down. González said that at the height of Zero Tolerance, about 300 children were separated each day at her facility and crammed into caged enclosures. She spent most of her time inside the enclosures, helping children call their relatives. Sometimes the younger children didn't seem to fully understand what was going on.

González says the sound in the facility was chilling—the children's cries formed an ear-piercing, whistling wind. The sound worsened when it came time for her to leave at the end of the day. "They grabbed me, squeezed me, hugged me so that I couldn't leave."

For her, the scene triggered flashbacks to the war in El Salvador, where thousands of children were disappeared and the sound of their wailing mothers was hard to escape.

•   •   •

While zero tolerance was in effect, Kirstjen Nielsen defended it before Congress and in the media using the same clinical language that had been deployed to convince her that the policy was reasonable. She and her team argued that some of the separated families were actually part of trafficking schemes in which children were either kidnapped or paired with random adults in order to give both parties free passage into the United States. (Several Trump-administration officials stipulated that they would talk to me for this article only if I agreed to mention "false families" in my story. Instances of such false families do exist, but subsequent investigations into family separation have not yielded many examples. In the federal class-action lawsuit over family separation, the government indicated that it suspected only a small number of false families existed, and Michelle Brané, who is heading up the Biden administration's Family Reunification Task Force, recently told me the group had not found a single false-family trafficking case.)

Another argument Nielsen made is still popular today among veterans of the Trump administration: that separating migrant children from their parents for the purposes of prosecution was no different from what happens in American criminal proceedings every day. "If an American parent is pulled over for a DUI and their child is in the back seat," this argument goes, "the child doesn't go to jail with them."

But as U.S. attorneys—who are arguably the highest authorities on this subject—came to understand what was happening to families after separated parents left the courtroom, they wholly disagreed with this assessment. American parents who are arrested in the United States typically have access to a system for getting their children back when they are released from custody. According to a source, John Bash, the Trump-appointed U.S. attorney in El Paso, recently testified in federal court that he was horrified to discover in June 2018 that in the few days it took his office to finish prosecuting parents, their children were already being shipped as far away as New York, with no system in place for reuniting them. "It was like, 'You're telling me the kid is nowhere to be found and they're in some other state?!'" Bash reportedly said.

Bash and other U.S. attorneys were flabbergasted by the ineptitude of those who had created the policy. "I remember thinking, *Why doesn't someone just have an Excel file?*" Bash reportedly said. "I mean, it's a large population in human cost and human terms, but it's not a large population in terms of data management. We're talking about a few thousand families. You can have all that on one spreadsheet with the names of the people, where the kid's going. It was just insane. I remember being told that there was going to be a phone number parents could call and know where their kids were. And I told a public defender that and she was like, 'This phone number doesn't work, one. And two, most parents don't have access to phones where they're being held, or they have to pay for the use of the pay phone. So that doesn't work.'"

Bash asked the Justice Department to launch an investigation into why parents and children were not being reunited expeditiously, still not fully understanding his agency's role in the scheme. He created a list of questions that he wanted answered, which were shared with Gene Hamilton, Rod Rosenstein, and others at DOJ: "What technology could be used to ensure that parents don't lose track of children?"; "Is it true that they are often pulled apart physically?"; "Why doesn't HHS return the child to the parent as soon as the parent is out of the criminal-justice system, on the view that at that point the child is no longer an 'unaccompanied minor'?" Rosenstein responded that the U.S. attorneys should try to find out what was going on themselves. The attorneys sent the questions to their Border Patrol counterparts, but their inquiries were ignored. "DHS just sort of shut down their communication channels to us," Ryan Patrick, the U.S. attorney in South Texas, told me. "Emails would go either unanswered, calls would go unreturned, or 'We're not answering that question right now.'"

Recently disclosed internal emails from that time help explain what Bash, Patrick, and the other U.S. attorneys couldn't figure out—why the plan for reunifying families was faulty to the point of negligence. Inside DHS, officials were working to *prevent* reunifications from happening.

Within days of the start of Zero Tolerance, Matt Albence, one of Tom Homan's deputies at ICE, expressed concern that if the parents' prosecutions happened too swiftly, their children would still be waiting to be picked up by HHS in Border Patrol stations, making family reunification possible. He saw this as a bad thing. When Albence received reports that reunifications had occurred in several Border Patrol sectors, he immediately sought to block the practice from continuing, contacting at least one sector directly while also asking his superiors—Tom Homan, Ron Vitiello, and Kevin McAleenan—for help. "We can't have this," he wrote to colleagues, underscoring in a second note that reunification "obviously undermines the entire effort" behind Zero Tolerance and would make DHS "look completely ridiculous." Albence and others proposed "solutions" such as placing parents whose prosecutions were especially speedy into ICE custody or in "an alternate temporary holding facility" other than the Border Patrol station where their children were being held. This appears to have happened in some cases.

Albence also suggested that the Border Patrol deliver separated children to HHS "at an accelerated pace," instead of waiting for federal contractors to pick them up, to minimize the chance that they would be returned to their parents. "Confirm that the expectation is that we are NOT to reunite the families and release" them, Albence wrote. (Albence declined to comment for this article.)

DHS headquarters sent out an email on May 25 saying that—when it was possible—the agency had no choice but to reunify children with parents whose criminal sentences were complete. The responses made clear that this was new information and not part of the original plan. Mere prosecution was "not exactly a consequence we had in mind," wrote Sandi Goldhamer, a longtime agent and the partner of Carla Provost, the head of the Border Patrol at the time.

Still unaware that DHS officials were working to keep parents and children apart, both Bash and Patrick started to devise strategies wherein parents could be prosecuted on misdemeanor charges, satisfying their orders from Sessions, but still get their children back quickly: Patrick developed a plan to transfer some detainees to less burdened courts in his district, farther away from the border, so that they could be prosecuted faster. Bash hashed out another plan to conduct prosecutions via video teleconference, so families would not have to be separated in the first place. Neither idea ever got off the ground.

Bash recently reviewed the exchanges between Albence and others at DHS, which were made public this past June as part of the court case for which Bash was deposed. He was outraged. In no place in the American criminal-justice system, he reportedly testified, would it be considered either ethically or legally permissible to keep children from their parents for punitive purposes after their legal process is completed. "We wouldn't do that to a murderer," much less a parent facing misdemeanor charges as a result of their attempt to claim asylum, Bash reportedly said.

In federal court cases, several parents whose children were taken away allege being taunted by agents who said "Happy Mother's Day!" And parents say they were told that their children would be put up for adoption or that they would never see them again. Others recount being threatened or ignored when they asked where their children were. Perhaps to avoid physical altercations, some agents began deceiving families in order to lure them apart or pulling children out of holding cells while they and their parents were asleep. Bash reported to DOJ headquarters that two plaintiffs in his district said they had been told their children were being taken to have baths and then never saw them again.

HHS child-care facilities evolved rapidly to meet the new demands of their work. Bethany Christian Services, which had previously cared mostly for children twelve and older, had to open a makeshift preschool to accommodate the influx of separated children who were not yet potty-trained and who needed to take naps. Bethany's teachers stopped trying to give traditional lessons, resorting instead to playing soothing movies throughout the day, in hopes of preventing a domino effect where one child's emotional outburst could quickly lead to an entire wailing classroom.

"What it demonstrated was that we do not, in fact, want your tired and poor and huddled masses," Hannah Orozco, a supervisor at Bethany, told me. "We want to deter you from coming here, and we were the face to the children of that message."

When the entire HHS shelter system reached capacity, Bethany resisted pleas to expand its program, which consists mostly of foster homes and a few small shelters housing only up to thirty-six kids at a time, to ensure that each child still received individualized care. But other companies eagerly accepted multi-million-dollar government contracts, housing children in huge facilities such as a former Walmart, which was at one point used to detain more than 1,000 children.

Large-scale institutions had long since been eliminated from the domestic child-welfare system because they were found to be traumatizing and unsafe. Indeed, many such facilities for immigrant children have faced significant allegations of physical and sexual abuse, and some have bypassed federal background-check requirements to weed out predators. But they are where most separated children ended up, in part because the lack of advance planning left no other option.

Some of the social workers under contract with HHS wrestled with the ethical dilemma presented by Zero Tolerance, unsure if they were helping separated children by continuing to go to work each day or if they were enabling the system that had taken them away from their parents in the first place. In mid-June, Antar Davidson quit his job at a large shelter in Arizona, calling himself a "conscientious objector" to Zero Tolerance. Children at the shelter had been "running up and down the halls, screaming, crying for their mom, throwing chairs," he told MSNBC, which led to a "harder, more authoritarian approach by the staff in attempting to deal with it."

The public did not know what to make of HHS's role in the situation either. Reporters and protesters showed up outside HHS child-care facilities, whose addresses are typically tightly guarded because of the vulnerability of their clients. Staff put Halloween masks on the children or shielded their faces when they were outside to protect them from being photographed. A Bethany caseworker in Michigan was spit on at a gas station and accused of kidnapping.

Even high-ranking Trump-administration officials were deeply confused. For weeks, the White House communications team asked the Justice Department to put forward lawyers who could explain the policy to the media, but no one at DOJ headquarters wanted to do it. May Davis, then the deputy White House policy coordinator, tried to explain the situation to a group of senior staff, including Sarah Huckabee Sanders, the press secretary, who was being questioned by reporters about the policy. But Davis inadvertently added confusion by suggesting that parents and children were being swiftly reunited. "I did a few diagrams of what I thought was happening," Davis told me. "Of course, what I thought was happening was 'separate for two to three days while they go get time served from a judge and then come back.'"

At one point, Claire Grady, Nielsen's deputy, emailed Rod Rosenstein at the Justice Department to ask for help: HHS had run out of space, so more than one hundred young children had been stuck for several days in Border Patrol holding cells. Rosenstein, who had previously admonished John Bash's office for declining to prosecute parents of very young children (a charge Rosenstein disputed to the DOJ inspector general, though it was explicitly documented), responded by asking if the seventy-two-hour time limit on when children must be transferred over to HHS for their safety could simply be changed. Grady and Gene Hamilton had to explain to Rosenstein that the limit was nonnegotiable; it had long been enshrined in law. The email chain eventually made it to Jeff Sessions, who replied unhelpfully: "If things are not moving at any DOJ agency don't hesitate to report it to me, and Rod or I may need to call them. We are in post 9/11 mode. All is asap."

Meanwhile, the DHS Office for Civil Rights and Civil Liberties was being overrun with pleas for help from separated parents looking for their children. The requests tended to be fielded by entry-level contract employees. Each time an employee started processing a new complaint, a mug shot of the child taken by the Border Patrol appeared on their computer screen. In some photos, a very young child appeared unaware of what was about to happen—smiling as if on school-picture day. Photographs of older children, who seemed to have a better understanding of what was going on, showed some in tears or still screaming. Young staffers in the office started breaking down at their desks.

Government records indicate that, just like with Operation Streamline, Zero Tolerance began preventing Border Patrol agents and federal prosecutors from focusing on higher-stakes work. The Border Patrol "is missing actual worthy felony defendants, including sex offenders," the DOJ liaison for the U.S. attorneys wrote in an email to colleagues in Washington.

Ron Vitiello told me the main goal at CBP during Zero Tolerance was to encourage agents, whose morale was eroding. "This was supposed to be short-term pain for long-term gain," Vitiello said. "I was trying to communicate with the workforce, telling them, 'Hopefully we'll see a dip in the numbers. This is going to work.'"

But as individual parts of the immigration enforcement system each wrestled with their own logistical crises, a gruesome larger picture began to come into view. The policy was so broken—perhaps intentionally—that it could not be fixed.

Vitiello and others at CBP and DHS headquarters said they were not aware of the wrenching separations being reported by the media. "I would feel bad if someone went to the shower and their kid was gone when they got back. I'm a human being," Vitiello told me. He and others said they did recall the mood beginning to sour when it seemed as if the department had "lost the narrative" on Zero Tolerance in the press. McAleenan has since said that he felt the policy needed to end because CBP was losing the public's trust—though he and others have also expressed a belief that journalists exaggerated their reporting on separations to make them seem more egregious than they were.

Some at DHS, however, did believe the well-documented reports that they were reading in the press—many of which involved leaks by government workers. Elizabeth Neumann, Nielsen's deputy chief of staff, recalls a career civil servant walking into her office around this time and saying, "I can't believe they're doing it. This is evil."

•   •   •

On June 18, the fog of denial abruptly dissipated when *ProPublica* published leaked audio of separated children crying for their parents inside a government facility. It called into question the official assurances that separations were happening smoothly and humanely. More than that, it made clear that the targets of the Zero Tolerance policy were not criminals but children.

Throughout the seven-minute recording, a little boy speaking through a low, wobbly sob repeats "Papá, papá," over and over. "I want to go with my aunt," one little girl tells agents. Over their cries, a detention official can be heard joking with the children. "*Tenemos una orquesta*," he said. "We have an orchestra—what we're missing is a conductor."

By that point, the U.S. government had separated from their parents more than 4,000 children under Zero Tolerance and the preceding local initiatives.

The audio clip was picked up by news outlets around the world. Comments posted on the YouTube version of the *ProPublica* audio show the news of family separation finally penetrating the public's consciousness.

As I listened to this I cried till my stomach hurt so much.

My heart breaks hearing these innocent children crying. I hope that they will be reunited soon. God help us.

Never have I ever been more ashamed with America.

•   •   •

Facing an overwhelming outcry, even the staunchest Republican allies of Trump's immigration agenda began condemning Zero Tolerance, some of them sincere and others motivated by politics. "All of us who are seeing images of these children being pulled away from moms and dads in tears are horrified," Senator Ted Cruz told reporters. "We should keep children with their parents. Kids need their moms. They need their dads."

One high-level HHS official told me it took weeks for her to accept what she was reading in the news, including that immigration officers were pressuring parents to agree to be deported without their children. "It was something so horrible that it wouldn't occur to any normal person that this was happening," the official said.

When denial was no longer viable, the administration wasted no time looking for someone to scapegoat.

"It was very apparent that they wanted a fall guy," Lauren Tomlinson, the senior DHS communications aide, told me. When *ProPublica* published the recording, Kirstjen Nielsen was in Louisiana for a speech. At that point, she had already declined several requests from Sarah Huckabee Sanders to address the press from the White House podium.

While still on the plane back to Washington, Nielsen was summoned to the White House by Sanders, who told her when she arrived that she was the administration's best person to address the policy and that Jeff Sessions's attempts to do so had only made things worse. (Days earlier, the attorney general had invoked scripture to justify the separation of families.) Nielsen and her inner circle huddled in the West Wing with John Kelly, who strongly urged her against doing the press conference. "I said, 'Look, whoever goes out there is going to own this,'" Kelly told me. Nielsen told me she felt she had no choice. Her agents were being attacked, and it was her job to defend them.

Nielsen sat down in the makeup chair off the White House pressroom while an aide, Jonathan Hoffman, peppered her with mock questions. Minutes later, she walked to the podium. Kevin

McAleenan, who had urged Nielsen to approve the policy and was officially responsible for the actions of the Border Patrol, stood off to the side, outside of most of the news cameras' frames, silent and unnoticed.

At DHS headquarters, staff huddled around televisions. "I think in that moment it became very clear to everyone just how bad everything was," a senior DHS official told me. "For some people, that was their first time really understanding how much of a crisis this was."

At the podium, Nielsen was defensive, causing reporters to bear down. She tried to distinguish between separating families and prosecuting parents—ignoring the fact that in practice this had amounted to the same thing. She emphasized that the parents being separated were committing the crime of crossing the border illegally, even if to exercise their legal right to claim asylum. She did not acknowledge that DHS had been limiting access to official ports of entry through a process called "metering," effectively blocking people from requesting asylum without breaking the law to do it. Nor did she acknowledge that substantial numbers of families that had been able to cross at official ports of entry, or who had crossed elsewhere but were not being prosecuted, had also been separated. And she repeatedly blamed Congress for Zero Tolerance, suggesting that she'd had no choice but to enforce the statutes that made unauthorized border crossing a crime, which was a lie—outside Operation Streamline, few people were prosecuted in the decades prior to Donald Trump taking office.

To viewers watching the press conference, for whom the pleading cries of separated children were still fresh in mind, Nielsen's focus on technical details seemed astonishingly tone-deaf.

Nielsen told me that at the time of the press conference, she was unfamiliar with news reports indicating that babies had been taken from their parents or that family members were getting lost in the maze of federal detention or that parents had been deported without their children, which happened more than 1,000 times, according to federal records. This is almost impossible to believe given her reputation as someone who was obsessively well prepared and consumed with following media coverage of her department's operations.

"The last thing I would ever support or defend is some sort of tragic scene where someone is grabbing a baby out of someone's arms," Nielsen told me. "That's just so the opposite of every bone, every cell in my body."

After the press conference, Nielsen made her way out of the White House. As she left, people patted her on the shoulder as if they were touching a casket at a funeral one last time.

Chapter 7: Reunification

Across the federal government, futile attempts at damage control began the next morning. It was "a minute-to-minute disaster," a Justice Department official told me, recalling a meeting that day. "We were taking on water from all sides." DOJ's congressional-affairs team reported being inundated with official requests for information from Capitol Hill while Rod Rosenstein finally conceded that he did not see any way of solving Zero Tolerance's logistical problems. In the meeting, Sarah Isgur, the chief spokesperson for DOJ, said that the narrative around the policy had become so bad, there was no way to recover from it. As district-level reports—initially tightly controlled—circulated more widely at headquarters, it became clear that "there were some unfair stories out there," the official told me, "but even the fairest ones were bad. And with some of the ones that the reporter had gotten wrong, the facts were actually worse than the reporter realized."

Congressional Republicans began asking not only for an end to family separations, but for a bill outlawing them in the future. Paul Ryan, the speaker of the House, told John Kelly at a breakfast meeting that if Congress didn't outlaw family separations, "we will lose the House [in the 2018 midterms]. It will kill the Republican Party." Kelly recounted the meeting in a discussion with Stephen Miller and some DHS officials, according to the contemporaneous notes of a Nielsen staffer who was present. Miller argued that the program should continue.

The White House scrambled to issue an executive order—one that is among the most confusing and nonsensical of all those produced by the Trump administration. It called for the Justice Department to continue exercising "zero tolerance" toward illegal border crossings—but at the same time for the Department of Homeland Security to maintain the family unity of those who were prosecuted. This was executive order as oxymoron: Zero Tolerance had meant separating families.

"It didn't make a damn bit of sense," May Davis recalled.

Nevertheless, the next day, June 20, Trump signed it. "He just kind of caved," one Hawk told me. The administration indicated that families that crossed the border would be detained together in DHS's family-detention centers for the duration of their criminal and immigration cases. This also made no sense. For one thing, DHS had about 3,000 family-detention beds. Based on the number of people crossing the border, those beds would have filled in less than two weeks. For another, asylum cases take more than a year to complete, on average, and a long-standing federal consent decree held that families could be detained for a maximum of only twenty days because of the harm that long-term detention does to children.

During a conference call that same day, Gene Hamilton told reporters that the administration planned to challenge the consent decree and that if the judge did not agree to lift it, family separations would begin again. "It's on Judge [Dolly] Gee," he said, referring to the Central District of California judge who would rule on their challenge. "Are we going to be able to detain alien families together or are we not?" The consent decree, Hamilton said, "put this executive branch into an untenable position"—as if the twenty-day limit had not already been in place for several years and as if it were the judge, not the Trump administration, that had changed things with Zero Tolerance.

•   •   •

By late June, new separations had stopped. But it was still not at all clear what would happen to the estimated 3,000 separated children who remained in government custody, not to mention those who had been released to a sponsor in the United States but still had not been reunited with their parents. Soon after the executive order came down, an HHS spokesperson told reporters that the separated families would not immediately be reunited because their parents were being detained on criminal or immigration charges. A second HHS spokesperson from the same agency followed up later in the day to say that the first one had misspoken, explaining that "it is still very early, and we are awaiting further guidance on the matter," but that "reunification is always the ultimate goal."

Only at the height of Zero Tolerance did Alex Azar, who was the secretary of Health and Human Services and therefore the overseer of the system tasked with sheltering the separated children, begin to understand his agency's role in what was happening, according to his staff. (Azar declined to comment for this story.) A former corporate lawyer and pharmaceutical executive, Azar was appointed after the administration's first HHS secretary, Tom Price, was ousted in scandal. He was given a mission of overhauling federal regulations on prescription-drug pricing, and he had pursued his target with exacting focus. Azar was so obsessed with efficiency that HHS employees were not allowed to contact him directly, lest he be distracted; his email address was a tightly kept secret. Azar's chief of staff and deputy chief of staff fielded all internal inquiries to his office; anything that was not of utmost importance to Azar, they delegated. This included all matters related to immigration.

Azar didn't know or care much about immigration policy when he joined the administration. He didn't view this as a problem, because it seemed to him to be a fraction of HHS's work. The entire immigration portfolio was given to Azar's deputy secretary, Eric Hargan. Colleagues say that Hargan was not taken seriously—that he was frequently out of the office, appeared less than fully engaged in meetings, and lacked mastery of the policy details for his areas of responsibility, including immigration. Hargan declined to comment, so I was not able to confirm whether he had any knowledge of Zero Tolerance prior to it being announced, but Azar and others close to him insisted repeatedly that they had been wholly blindsided. Although Nielsen and others at DHS said that Azar was warned that the policy was coming, they conceded that perhaps no one "shook him by the shoulders" to explain exactly what it meant. Those close to Azar say that if he had been involved in any discussion of an innocuous-sounding prosecution policy, it would have flown over his head. He would have had no idea that prosecution would entail taking the parents' children away, much less making them his responsibility as part of the larger pool of unaccompanied minors in the United States whom HHS was tasked with caring for.

Once he fully understood Zero Tolerance, some of his employees told me, Azar was furious. But at no time, it appears, did he or other Health and Human Services officials argue against separating children before the policy was implemented nationwide. Yes, HHS officials had been cut out of the conversation by the Hawks in the White House—but they hadn't noticed, they freely admit, because they hadn't been paying attention. This is especially noteworthy in Azar's case. He had a close relationship with Ivanka Trump and Jared Kushner, which Azar leveraged to keep Miller from ever contacting him directly. If Azar had been attuned to what Zero Tolerance would mean, he may have been able to head it off or reshape it.

News coverage now made his agency's connection to the crisis undeniable. Azar's office heard from Rachel Maddow's producers that her MSNBC show was getting ready to report that during Zero Tolerance—while his agency was erecting a tent city in the Texas desert to house the overflow of separated children in its custody—Azar had attended his Dartmouth College reunion. Azar demanded that Scott Lloyd, at the Office of Refugee Resettlement, immediately locate the parents of the separated children whom HHS was sheltering. When Lloyd went to Azar's office the next morning to say that the parents were in ICE custody, Azar started yelling: He wanted precise locations for all of the parents. He didn't yet understand that such information did not exist.

Casting Lloyd aside as useless, Azar deputized Bob Kadlec, the agency's assistant secretary of preparedness and response, to take over the effort to put parents and children back in touch with each other. Kadlec, a physician, had spent two decades in Air Force Special Operations and the CIA, serving five deployments, before moving over to HHS. Though he had done stints advising Republicans in Congress and the George W. Bush White House, he identifies as an independent.

Recognizing immediately that he knew next to nothing about immigration law or the shelter system that HHS oversaw, he did something that those in charge of Zero Tolerance had yet to do: he turned to the bureaucracy for help. He asked his staff to identify experts in the agency who could brief him. Soon after that, Jonathan White was in his office. (White had eventually become so infuriated with Scott Lloyd that he'd left ORR and moved to a different department in HHS. In addition to rebuffing White's pleas for an intervention on family separation, Lloyd had also been trying to stop unaccompanied girls in ORR care from getting abortions, using a spreadsheet with data including their last menstrual cycle. "We were in a human-rights free fall," White recalled.) After a half-hour conversation, Kadlec announced that White would take charge of the entire operation.

For White, the appointment felt like an opportunity to redeem himself from his failure to stop family separations from happening. A week later, Lloyd still had not satisfied another one of Azar's requests—to produce a list of potentially separated children. Azar told his staff to brew coffee and order pizzas; no one was going home. About a dozen members of Azar's inner circle sat down in the secretary's command center in front of computers, while Jallyn Sualog, a longtime civil servant at HHS who had been working with White to oppose separating families, taught them how to use an online portal to review every available detail about every child in their care.

At the time, Health and Human Services was housing roughly 12,000 children, the majority of whom had come to the United

States alone—the population the HHS shelter system was created to serve. They would have to sift through those records in order to figure out which children—nearly a quarter of the total—had arrived at the border with a parent and then been separated.

Photos taken at the ORR shelters, similar to the mug shots that had brought employees in the DHS Office for Civil Rights and Civil Liberties to tears at their desks, now filled the computer screens of Kadlec and his colleagues. When I met with Kadlec recently, he teared up when he told me that the pictures he saw that night still haunt him. "The first one was a little girl kind of smiling. Another was a little boy crying. Another was a teenage girl who looked fearful," he said. "You could just see that what was happening was devastating to these kids. . . . Some of the children were infants. Some were one and two years old, five years old, ten years old."

He recalled the "stupefying silence" that came over the room where he and the rest of the task force were working. "People afterwards had a hard time. I had to put some on extended leaves of absence because of emotional trauma."

That night was the first time officials running HHS had to confront the faces of separated children—something many of those responsible for the policy have never had to do.

●　　　●　　　●

Internal emails reveal that officials at Immigration and Customs Enforcement, which was assuming custody of separated parents after the completion of their criminal proceedings, were still determined to block the HHS task force from reuniting any families unless it was for the purposes of deportation. "They will want to know what can be done to facilitate immediate reunification," Matt Albence, who was soon to become the deputy director of ICE, told colleagues in an email. "I told them that wasn't going to happen unless we are directed by the Dept to do so."

Sensing that reunification was nowhere in sight, the ACLU's Lee Gelernt asked the judge in his case against the government to intervene. Most of the separated children, except for those who had been released to other relatives in the United States, were still in

HHS custody. For the most part, separated parents who had not yet been deported were either serving time for their illegal-entry convictions in the custody of the Bureau of Prisons or being detained by ICE. Many parents still didn't know where their children were, and vice versa. (One woman, Cindy Madrid, only located her six-year-old daughter, Ximena, after recognizing Ximena's voice in the audio released by *ProPublica*, which was played during a news broadcast shown in the South Texas detention center where Madrid was being detained.)

On June 26, Judge Dana Sabraw of the Southern District of California responded to Gelernt's request, ordering that the government return children younger than five to their parents within two weeks and that the rest of the separated children be reunited with their families within thirty days. Alex Azar's general counsel warned him that he could be held in contempt of court if the government did not successfully comply, which theoretically meant that Azar could be put in jail.

Kadlec and White, who were leading the HHS task force, sought out a few select representatives of ICE and CBP to help with their efforts. "We had to pick those people carefully so that they would be willing to share," Kadlec told me, anticipating that not everyone at the law-enforcement agencies would try to be helpful.

"The ICE leadership didn't want us to succeed," White said. "They wanted to sabotage the reunification effort." According to White, Tom Homan's initial position as the head of ICE was that families should be reunified only "at the flight line in Phoenix"— meaning he didn't want to return any children to their parents unless their immediate deportation was guaranteed. But there was no way to adjudicate everyone's asylum claims (many of which were eventually successful) before Judge Sabraw's deadline, so White requested that four DHS processing facilities be designated to serve as reunification sites. Even then, White says, ICE leaders started coming up with excuses for why they needed more time. Emails show that some children were told that they were going to be reunited with their parents and then were driven or flown to reunification sites hours away, only to learn upon arrival that ICE still wanted to interview their parents before they could be released or that their parents were not even there yet. (Homan denies trying to delay family reunifications.)

"They were trying to run out the clock," White said. He addressed HHS staff: "If we miss the judge's deadline, there is nothing that we can use to hold the administration's feet to the fire to make this happen. Do you understand? Then those kids will wait, their parents will be deported, and they will be separated potentially for the rest of their lives."

White told his colleagues to marshal vehicles and flights they needed to move thousands of children across the country in a matter of days. "Here's what we are going to do: You push those kids, once they're green-lighted, to ICE's door. You park them outside the door. We will move the kids to them and force them to do the reunifications, or the whole world will see kids surrounding them. . . . Take snacks, take blankets. I am besieging ICE with children until they reunify them as they're required to do."

As officials in the Departments of Homeland Security, Justice, and Health and Human Services prepped for congressional hearings, the DHS communications aides Jonathan Hoffman and Katie Waldman showed up at HHS for a "murder board" session to prepare Jonathan White and others to answer questions. Quickly, arguments broke out, as White and Judy Stecker, a public-affairs official at HHS, felt that White was being pressured to suggest, inaccurately, on the witness stand that HHS had been given advance notice of Zero Tolerance. Stecker asked Brian Stimson, the lead HHS lawyer working on litigation over family separations, to provide backup. According to those present, Stimson told Hoffman to "fuck off" and called him a "moron." (Hoffman disputes this.)

Afterward, Waldman pulled White aside and called him a bleeding-heart liberal. White unloaded on her, shaking and turning red. "It is difficult to maintain my emotional equilibrium where family separation is concerned," he told me. "I do not accept that any immigration outcome, however important it might be to people, can be bought at the price" of separating families. "Like, you do understand these aren't theoretical children? They're all real children. . . . They're as real as my kids."

The Aftermath

On August 1, a week after the court deadline, more than 500 separated children remained in federal custody; many others had been released to sponsors in the United States but still had not been reunited with the parent with whom they'd crossed the border. The government still had made no effort to contact parents who had been deported without their children. Judge Sabraw called the government's progress "just unacceptable," adding that "for every parent who is not located there will be a permanently orphaned child. And that is 100 percent the responsibility of the administration."

Additional separated children were later added to Lee Gelernt's class-action lawsuit; as of now, the total number of known separations between January 2017 and June 2018 is more than 4,000. After entering the White House, President Joe Biden signed an executive order forming the Family Reunification Task Force, headed by Michelle Brané, to continue tracking down and reuniting the 1,500 families that remained separated when his administration took office. At least 360 parents have been reunited with their children. Those who had been deported after they were separated were allowed to return to the United States and given a three-year temporary-parole status. But approximately 700 families still have not been officially reunited, according to the task force's most recent estimate. Some families are presumed to have found each other independently without reporting it, fearing any further interactions with the U.S. government.

Though prominent child-welfare organizations have labeled the family separations carried out by the Trump administration "child abuse" and "torture," Gelernt avoids such language because he believes it risks causing people to tune out even more. But he struggles with the reality that so many people seem to have moved on. "The average American parent, when they leave their child the first time for one night with a babysitter, is worried every minute of it, or when they drop their kid off for the first time in preschool and worry what the child is going through or the first time a teacher treats them unfairly," he said. "Do they really not think these families suffer the same way they would from losing their child?"

His main goal at this point is to push for the separated families to receive permanent legal status in the United States—"something Congress could do tomorrow," he said. Others are still advocating for the law that Paul Ryan requested, making it illegal to separate children from their parents for the purposes of deterrence. Both efforts have stalled.

The lasting effect of family separation is undeniable. Cheryl Aguilar, a therapist in Washington, D.C., who has treated more than 40 formerly separated families, said the children are still experiencing regressive behaviors such as bed-wetting and pronounced immaturity, as well as nightmares, flashbacks, and severe withdrawal and detachment from loved ones. Healing "takes a very long time when that kind of trauma takes place at such an important developmental stage," she told me. "It impacted the wiring of their brain so that they have been primed to expect scary experiences like that in the future. They are hyperaware and hypervigilant of dangers—some of which are real and some perceived." Aguilar hosts a support group for separated parents, who also struggle with severe depression and anxiety; some feel rejected by their children, many of whom believe their parents abandoned them or gave them up willingly. "We're trying to give children and families basic tools to reconnect and start processing," she said.

Various studies have looked at the effect of separation on migrant families. In April, Physicians for Human Rights published a report based on clinical evaluations of thirteen separated parents. All of them had some form of mental illness linked to the separation; eleven had PTSD. Anne Elizabeth Sidamon-Eristoff, now a medical student at Yale, who led another study, pointed out that in animal research used to assess risk for mental illness, separation of mice from their mothers is used as a kind of gold-standard strategy for modeling stress in humans. "My first thought was, *That's what our government is doing to children*," she told me.

"These studies reaffirm what science has been saying all along" about what the impact of a program like Zero Tolerance would be,

Sidamon-Eristoff told me. "And it's honestly quite frustrating to me that we even have to collect this data to try to prove a point that we've always known: family separation is bad for children."

The frontline workers who were pulled into Zero Tolerance against their will have also struggled. Last summer, I visited Nora Núñez, who no longer works as a public defender. She invited me into her living room, where the lights were off. She was in low spirits. A *Washington Post* reporter had recently contacted her for a story about a separated mother whom Núñez had represented in court. He'd shown Núñez a picture of the mother and daughter being reunified four years after they were separated. The girl's arms were limp at her sides while her mother embraced her through tears. "You could tell that little girl was traumatized. Her mother was hugging her, and you could see her face and her eyes looked kind of vacant," she told me, her mouth quivering. "You didn't see any normal emotion of happiness of being reunited."

Núñez said she felt sick as she recalled rushing parents through their prosecutions because she thought that it would get them back to their children more quickly—not realizing that the government had other plans.

"I'm not sure if I can do this much more right now," she said after a while, eventually asking me to leave.

. . .

As the Trump administration sought to defuse the anger over Zero Tolerance, White House officials proposed blaming separated families for what had happened to them. A damage-control working group developed fact sheets suggesting, without evidence, that most of the separated children were trafficking victims, according to two people who were present. At one meeting, one of these officials told me, "they were like, 'Why don't we just show these women throwing their children over the wall, and then people will think, *How could they do this?*'"

Throughout the remainder of his presidency, Trump pushed to relaunch family separations. "The conversation never died," Kirstjen Nielsen told me, recalling a series of discussions that took place at the White House and on Marine One. "I started saying, 'Sir, we really can't reinstate it. Nothing has changed. We still do not have the resources. It will result the same way. The system didn't get fixed.'" She says she threatened to resign and appealed for support to the first lady, Melania Trump, who would place a discouraging hand on her husband's shoulder when Trump ranted about "turning it back on," generally while watching Fox News.

Nielsen had been persuaded to sign off on Zero Tolerance by people who either minimized its implications or cloaked its goals, but the president himself didn't bother speaking in euphemism. Trump would "literally say 'family separation,'" a senior DHS official recalled. "Stephen Miller was always very cautious and would frame it as 'reinstituting Zero Tolerance.' But Trump himself just blurted it out." (Trump could not be reached for comment.)

The official continued, "The level of visceral description that the president gave would freak Nielsen out because she was like, 'I'm out here trying to explain that this isn't what the administration intended to do,' and the president's talking like it totally was."

Nielsen said she tried framing separation as something that would harm the president's reelection prospects, but the strategy didn't work, because Miller would counter that he believed the opposite was true. She told Trump he would have to write yet another executive order to reinstate Zero Tolerance, knowing he would never agree to backtracking publicly, because it would make him look weak. A few times, Nielsen called Alex Azar to ask him to back her up. Azar also indicated that he would resign if the policy were to be reinstated.

As time went on, Trump became further incensed about the number of people crossing the border, proposing more and more outlandish ideas to stop it from happening, many of them preserved in the senior DHS official's notes: The president once "ordered Kelly to tell Nielsen to, 'Round them all up and push them back into Mexico. Who cares about the law,'" one entry says. "Silence followed."

·　　·　　·

Nielsen's relationship with the president never recovered; she was asked to resign in the spring of 2019. Trump elevated Kevin McAleenan to replace her temporarily. During his tenure, DHS and its subagencies pursued other controversial tactics targeting families, such as conducting raids in homes with children and detaining them along with their parents for the purposes of deporting them, something ICE had historically tried hard to avoid. Trump refused to officially nominate him for the position. He eventually resigned as well.

"To me, the person who did not get enough scrutiny or enough blame or enough attention was Kevin McAleenan," a lawyer working for one of the congressional committees that investigated family separations told me. This idea was repeated by many of those closest to Zero Tolerance, who criticized McAleenan for insisting—publicly and privately—that he was merely a bystander. In an interview with MSNBC's Chuck Todd at the height of the policy, when asked who had ordered Zero Tolerance, McAleenan invoked Sessions's Zero Tolerance memo, not mentioning that his own memo had been the catalyst that activated the policy or that he had repeatedly urged Nielsen to sign off on it. "Kevin knew everything that was going on, he pushed it, he supported it, and he was the key to implementing it," the lawyer said. After Zero Tolerance ended, McAleenan said publicly that he felt it was a mistake. "The policy was wrong, period, from the outset," he told me. "It should never have been undertaken by a law-enforcement department, even while facing the stark challenges we faced at the border."

Ron Vitiello, who became the acting director of ICE in June 2018, also owned up to the policy's shortcomings, becoming emotional in some of our interviews. "We could have done the logistics better," Vitiello told me. "It wasn't messaged right. We rushed into this failure, basically. . . . It's definitely one you wish you could get back, but it wasn't cruel and heartless to be cruel and heartless. We surmised it was a way to get us out from under this crush at the border, but we sort of lost it."

Nielsen said she decided to speak to me for this story "because the border and immigration situation in this country is heartbreaking and is only getting worse." She said that it is up to Congress to reform our immigration laws in a way that allows people who need to come to the United States to do so legally, and for the laws to be fully enforced in a way that is humane. With regard to Zero Tolerance, Nielsen said she wouldn't apologize for enforcing the policy. She echoed an argument I heard frequently from people I interviewed for this story: that they or their agency had been unfairly blamed. "HHS had the children, DOJ had the parent, we had neither," Nielsen told me.

But she wished she hadn't approved the policy because of its deep flaws. "I made the decision based on what turned out to be faulty information," she told me. She insisted that she had prevented the worst from happening because she never signed off on the administrative-separation proposal, which could have led to thousands more children being taken from their parents.

People who know Miller say he believes that Zero Tolerance saved lives and that immigration enforcement was Trump's most popular accomplishment among his base. Miller has told them that the administration laid the groundwork necessary for a future president to implement harsh enforcement even more quickly and with greater reach than under Trump.

In my interviews, the Hawks argued that Zero Tolerance had been effective—or that it would have been, if only it had been left in place a little longer—suggesting that if Trump or someone who shares his views on immigration were to be elected in 2024, family separations would almost definitely recommence.

•   •   •

Recently, I spoke with Alejandro Mayorkas, President Biden's Homeland Security secretary, who has been dealing with yet another influx of border crossers, most of whom are now coming from places outside Latin America. Biden campaigned on a promise to tackle the root causes of migration to the United States from Central America—poverty and violence—but little progress has been made on that front. In June, fifty-three migrants died trying to sneak into the interior of the country in the back of a tractor trailer, a deadlier incident than the one Tom Homan witnessed in 2003.

Despite the fact that such incidents tend to result from harsh enforcement at the border, Mayorkas has faced criticism from Republicans for being too soft on immigration, in particular for the Biden administration's move to scale back Title 42, a Trump-era policy linked to the coronavirus pandemic that effectively sealed the border. In response, Mayorkas has started reaching for the same solutions that led to Zero Tolerance—using the Border Patrol to ramp up prosecutions and generate other forms of "consequence delivery," though he says those tools should be deployed only "in concert with ample humanitarian protections for people seeking asylum." Congressional action on border issues continues to stall, leaving immigration policy squarely in the hands of the executive branch.

Mayorkas said he hoped the media would help hold those responsible for family separation to account. While some deterrent strategies "arguably fall within the parameters of our value system," Mayorkas said, family separation was "way outside the bounds of what we as a civilized and humane country would ever countenance."

When I asked Mayorkas about any official government accountability for those who were responsible for separating families, he said that was outside his purview at DHS and was up to the Justice Department. But DOJ has been defending Zero Tolerance—and the individuals responsible for it—in court, insisting in a recent hearing that a family-separation policy "never really existed. What existed was the Zero Tolerance policy which started in April of 2018. . . . We have testimony from the CBP and ICE witnesses and from Hamilton, who was at DHS at the time, that these separation policies, as plaintiffs put it, never existed, and they were never enacted."

But the judge was unconvinced. "This is a continuing argument that the government's been making," she said, pointing out that the plaintiffs in that particular case, migrants who were all separated from their children, were never even prosecuted. (The Justice Department declined to comment for this story but has said previously that it is devoted to "bringing justice to victims of this abhorrent policy.")

A comprehensive accounting of what happened during Zero Tolerance would require the government to look not only ahead toward reunifying families but backwards as well—to be fully transparent about the past. This seems unlikely to happen. "DHS was lying to us and not giving us documents," the lawyer who investigated Zero Tolerance for a congressional committee while Trump was still in office told me. "They very much withheld stuff from us, and I would catch them red-handed and flag it for them, and they're like, 'Oh well, we'll go back and look,' and it was a constant BS battle."

Many of those who were involved in the development of Zero Tolerance are still working at DHS or its subagencies. But Mayorkas said it would be too hard for him to determine "what they knew, what they didn't know, what they understood, what they didn't understand." That lack of accountability for those who participated in separating families has some in the government worried that the practice could restart under another administration. "There is no cautionary tale to prevent this from happening again," Jonathan White said. Without that, he told me, "I fear that it will."

If anyone is likely to lead another push for the American government to separate families, it's Stephen Miller. For a year and a half, I tried to reach him so that I could ask him directly, among other things, why he had lobbied so forcefully for this to occur in the first place and whether he would do so again in the future. A close friend of Miller and his wife explained that ever since the couple became parents, they had been consumed by child care and were hard to reach.

As my deadline approached, Miller repeatedly ducked or delayed speaking with me. Once, when I got Miller on the phone, he quickly told me that he had to go, and hung up. He soon sent a follow-up text to explain why he had been so abrupt. "With the extended family." he said. "And our little one."

Esquire

FINALIST—FEATURE WRITING

The Feature Writing judges described "The Militiamen, the Governor, and the Kidnapping That Wasn't"—about the six men accused of planning to abduct Michigan governor Gretchen Whitmer—as "a colossally entertaining story, distinguished by Chris Heath's trademark wit and expansive reporting, which makes you think deeply about radicalism, one of the most pressing issues of our moment, and its intersection with government overreach." Heath is a longtime magazine writer who began his career writing for the British magazine Smash Hits *and later worked for* Details, Rolling Stone, *and* GQ *in the United States. His story "18 Tigers, 17 Lions, 8 Bears, 3 Cougars, 2 Wolves, 1 Baboon, 1 Macaque, and 1 Man Dead in Ohio" won the National Magazine Award for Reporting in 2013.* Esquire *is a four-time winner of the National Magazine Award for Feature Writing.*

Chris Heath

The Militiamen, the Governor, and the Kidnapping That Wasn't

I n these fragile and fractured times, terrible people seek to do terrible things. We reel from one assault to the next, facing down a relentless barrage of devilry and depravity. But—give thanks—sometimes, just in time, the forces of good catch a break. Sometimes those we rely upon to protect us do manage to intervene. Sometimes the terrible people's most terrible deeds are prevented from ever happening.

That, in general terms, was pretty much the story unveiled on October 8, 2020. As Andrew Birge, U.S. attorney for the Western District of Michigan, declared at that day's press conference: "All of us standing here today, we want the public to know that federal and state law enforcement are committed to working together to make sure violent extremists never succeed with their plans, particularly when they target our duly elected leaders." The specifics of the plot in question, recounted in the accompanying criminal complaint and related court filings, were intricate and horrifying, laying out a conspiracy to "unlawfully seize, confine, kidnap, abduct and carry away, and hold for ransom and reward, or otherwise, the Governor of the State of Michigan." ("Or otherwise"—what awful and chilling chasms of possibility lay left unsaid there?) Copious documents described how, in the spring and summer of 2020, a dark design coalesced among a group of men aligned with various militias and laid out some of the steps subsequently taken as these men prepared for action: conducting daytime and nighttime surveillance on Michigan governor Gretchen Whitmer's vacation home; undergoing focused military training to rehearse for their mission, including drills run through a "shoot house" that served as a mock-up of the governor's home; testing explosive devices that could be used as antipersonnel devices during the kidnapping; seeking high explosives to bring down a bridge they'd reconnoitered near Whitmer's home to hinder the expected police response; and so on. When not plotting face-to-face, they would practice meticulous OPSEC (operational security), methodically cloaking their ugly schemings by using code words and encrypted chat apps.

But, mercifully, they were being watched. That's how, just under a month before the presidential election in a country still reeling from the ideological divides exposed by COVID, on that October day six men came to be charged with the main conspiracy-to-kidnap charge—a potential life sentence—and subsequently with various explosives and weapons charges. "The latest example," summarized the *New York Times*, "of anti-government domestic terrorism among far-right extremists."

Further corroboration, if even required, that these men were just who they seemed to be came when two of the six (Ty Garbin and Kaleb Franks) struck plea bargains, agreeing to plead guilty and testify against their accomplices in hopes of receiving a reduced sentence. Need more? Among the property confiscated from those arrested were at least seventy guns, along with sundry magazines, suppressors, scopes, and silencers; abundant ammunition; and various explosives. Even more? Well, perhaps it's easiest to get a clear flavor of who the remaining four men (Adam Fox, Barry Croft, Daniel Harris, and Brandon Caserta) were, and of how they thought, and of their intentions, by listening to their own words, recorded while under surveillance.

Fox: "Snatch and grab, man. Grab the fuckin' governor. Just grab the bitch. Because at that point, we do that, dude—it's over."

Caserta: "When the time comes, there will be no need to try and strike fear through presence. The fear will be manifested through bullets."

Croft: "*Wham!* A quick, precise grab on that fucking governor. And all you're going to end up having to possibly take out is her armed guard."

Harris: "Have one person go to her house. Knock on the door, and when she answers it just cap her . . . at this point. Fuck it."

Fox: "I want to have the governor hog-tied, laid out on a table, while we all pose around like we just made the world's biggest goddamn drug bust, bro."

Caserta: "And I'm telling you what, right now, man, I'm going to make this shit 100 percent clear, dude, if this shit goes down. Okay? If this whole thing starts to happen. I'm telling you what, dude, I'm taking out as many of those motherfuckers as I can. Every single one, dude. Every single one."

Reading all this, maybe you're thinking that the only other words you really want to hear are a succinct confirmation that the speakers will all be in prison for a very long time.

That from these particular terrible men, at least, we're all safe.

•   •   •

May 2022

Brandon Caserta messages me to say that he can't speak just now. "I'm helping my mom clean behind these shutters of wasp nests right now so I can txt but can't talk on the phone just yet." He promises to call soon.

•   •   •

When I initially started digging into the story of these four men a few weeks before their long-delayed trial this past March, my agenda was straightforward. First, I hoped to piece together, in as much detail as possible, the narrative of what they had actually done and said as they careened down such a toxic and alarming path. Second, I wanted to discover all I could about each individual who had somehow ended up in this place. The basic facts of what they had planned appeared well established, but it still seemed that if I could burrow deep enough into the visceral mess of it all, there would be something worthwhile to learn here. There always is. Whether as warning or wisdom or inoculation, we can never understand too much about all the ways in which lives can go wrong.

I found no shortage of material to look at. Even aside from the collected media coverage from the seventeen months between the men's arrest and the trial, there were an implausible number of court filings—530 of them by the time the trial started, nearly all available to read. In a large number of these, the prosecution and defense lawyers were effectively bickering about what evidence would be allowed to be presented to a jury. There was a staggering volume of material that had been collected by the FBI—one document refers to more than a thousand hours of recordings and "what appears to be over 400,000 direct electronic messages." While the bulk of this material was inaccessible to the public, protected by court order, one quirk of the legal system is that as the lawyers argued back and forth—typically quoting from the recordings and texts they respectively found most incriminating or most exculpatory—more and more of this material was, incrementally, made public. And so, even though the judge would often rule to exclude from the forthcoming trial what had been quoted, by reading through hundreds of these documents I could submerge myself in the morass.

As I did so, I found myself somewhat taken aback to be contemplating thoughts I hadn't expected to entertain. For instance, it became increasingly apparent to me that, despite all the surveillance and recording over many months before these men were arrested, the connective tissue of the purported conspiracy seemed perplexingly elusive. By cherry-picking and stitching together disparate statements, incidents, and circumstances, you could certainly fashion an argument that such a conspiracy may have existed—just as the prosecution maintained—but it did seem surprising that the kinds of sustained conversation you might have assumed would be there, in which the principal participants sat around and discussed both the broad scope and the practical minutiae of what they intended to do, didn't appear to exist.

It was also perplexing to see how much of the connective tissue that did exist involved people who were acting on behalf of the FBI. Take, for instance, what seemed, at first glance, to be one of the more damning events in the alleged narrative of this conspiracy. It is one thing to be told that, on the night of September 12, 2020, Adam Fox and Barry Croft, who according to the prosecutors were the plot's de facto ringleaders, conducted a nighttime reconnaissance of Whitmer's Elk Rapids vacation home, driving around the area after first stopping to inspect the underside of the bridge on Highway 31, where they might plant explosives. But it is perhaps another to piece together that the truck in question, a Chevy Silverado, had five people in it. And that Fox and Croft were in the backseat, Croft in the middle, next to a man who turned out to be an FBI informant. And that the truck was being driven by its owner, Dan Chappel, who had been at the center of everything that had or hadn't been happening for several months. And that he was also an FBI informant. And that next to him up front was another man, whom Chappel had introduced to the group as an explosives expert. And that this man was not an FBI informant. He was an FBI *agent*.

Not that this strange circumstance—three of the five people in a car at such a crucial moment being affiliated with the FBI—itself absolves the accused men of criminality. The law offers extraordinary leeway for undercover operatives to interpose themselves in such situations in order to expose wrongdoing. But as I learned more about this, and similar scenarios—one defense filing claimed to have identified *twelve* government informants contributing to this case in one way or another, "assisted by FBI agents working undercover"—it felt as though it cast a more complex and problematic gloss over what was taking place and what it might have meant.

Also, there were times when these different kinds of problems—the curiously prominent role of informants and the strangely disjointed and unexpected nature and tone of the allegedly incriminatory material—seemed to compound each other. Here's just one example: The prosecution drew attention in the indictment to the fact that the demolish-a-bridge plan apparently emerged shortly after the first daytime reconnaissance trip to the area of Whitmer's vacation home. "In an encrypted message on or about August 30, 2020, Ty Gerard Garbin suggested taking down a highway bridge near the Governor's vacation home would hinder a law enforcement response." So does it make any difference to know that the relevant text exchange between Garbin and the FBI informant Chappel included nine emojis, two Borat GIFs, multiple movie references (one to *Monty Python and the Holy Grail*), and an "LOL"? Agreed, there is no particular qualifying degree of gravitas required to make evil plans. Flippancy and playfulness are not reliable indications of innocence. But it certainly wasn't how I'd expected methodical, hate-spewing terrorist extremists hell-bent on destruction would be strategizing, and it made me even more curious to know more.

• • •

Daniel Harris was a twenty-four-year-old ex-marine—ages are as of the March 2022 trial—who had been honorably discharged and received disability benefits. Back in Michigan, he moved into the basement of his parents' house. He was working locally as a security guard and was looking for a similar job in Afghanistan. In June 2020, Harris had been interviewed by a Michigan news outlet as he took part in a Black Lives Matter protest in the aftermath of George Floyd's killing, telling a reporter, "Everyone's voice should be heard, no matter the color on your skin. . . . Protesting is important to me because it gives us all a voice to be heard."

Adam Fox, thirty-eight, lived in the basement of a Grand Rapids vacuum-cleaner business, the Vac Shack, where he sometimes worked behind the counter. To descend into his improvised living space, visitors went through the door with the "Building the Best Vacuums of Yesterday, Today, and Tomorrow" poster on it. He reportedly had two dogs, a black Labrador named Bruno and a white pit-bull mix. Fox liked to get high and had a Twitter feed that, since 2016, had called out perceived foes: Bernie Sanders ("fucking idiot," "you're commy ass is a traitor to this country"), Nancy Pelosi ("shut up hag"), Chuck Schumer ("you little bitch"), Barack Obama ("everything you represent is weakness," "go fuck yourself"), Jimmy Kimmel ("freedom hating commie"), Hillary Clinton ("Shut up traitor"), and, um, Twitter itself ("fuck you Twitter"). Many of the most inflammatory statements netted by the government were Fox's and, as already noted, painted him as one of the plot's leaders.

Barry Croft, forty-six, was a long-distance truck driver from Delaware raising three girls from an earlier relationship with his partner, Chastity Knight. An avid constitutionalist, Croft had a wild graying beard and liked to wear a tricorn hat—"because," he would explain, "I feel like we've forgotten our past and our history." On the back of Croft's left hand is a large tattoo depicting a Roman numeral III inside a circle of thirteen stars, the symbol of the militia movement the Three Percenters, whose name pays tribute to the highly dubious claim that only 3 percent of people in the thirteen original colonies rose up against the British. According to the prosecutors, Croft "held himself out as a national leader of the Three Percenters group." My search for any clear corroboration or visible traces of this role came up cold, though finding disturbing things Croft has said was not hard. Take, say, this Facebook video message from May 2020: "I don't play part in that stupid-ass political mafia shit that you dumbasses wash your heads in. I don't do any of that. That's gay to me. I want to hang all them motherfuckers, all of them. There is not one motherfucker serving in this bullshit government that I don't want to take, stick to a motherfucking tree, and dangle until they ass tongue hang out their mouth."

That certainly made him sound like a monstrous, tightly wound ball of hatred, though not everything did. Croft gave an interview for a YouTube channel, *The Bradley Bennett Show*, in July 2020, before he was incarcerated—when, according to the prosecution, Croft was neck-deep in a secretive and extreme kidnapping conspiracy. In this forum, you find a much politer Croft. "One of the things I do," he tells Bennett, "is educate people on constitutional awareness, sir." He also has a peculiar understanding of the etiquette of doing a video interview. Early on—the video lasts an uninterrupted forty-nine minutes—Croft starts moving around his home in Bear, Delaware. Then, without explaining—and never breaking his flow—he leaves the house (wearing his tricorn hat), gets into his car, starts driving, arrives at a local store, orders "two packs of Marlboro Red, box" (giving out his phone number, presumably for some kind of discount program—where's the OPSEC here?), gets back into his car, and arrives home, carrying on talking all this time.

During this conversation, Croft makes a range of cultural references that I hadn't anticipated. Laying out his principles of living, he says this: "Don't just demand that somebody be a good person. You take the initiative to be that good person, and I guarantee you it'll rub off on other people—they'll rise to be around you. They'll bring themselves up to be around you. You know, I took that from Biggie Smalls, the rapper. He said, 'Excellence is my presence, never tense, never hesitant.' And I thought, well, that's an awesome place to be. How do you attain that? Superior knowledge, wisdom, experience, a culmination of intelligence. Pour it together: never tense, never hesitant. And guess what—I'm a truck driver, but excellence is my presence. Sir."

I'm not callow enough to suggest that knowing the lyrics to a nineties rap song absolves anyone of any kind of bigotry or of anything else. Or that Croft's genial affect here precludes a wide variety of other beliefs and actions. But if we care to understand him, maybe we'll need to understand this, too.

• • •

The last of the four men facing trial, Brandon Caserta, thirty-three, lived alone in an apartment in the Detroit suburb of Canton and worked as a CNC machinist at a factory called Master Automatic. He was an avowed anarchist—the reflex assumption that these men were all hardcore MAGA cheerleaders and that this could all be neatly linked to the country's wider political ructions took a hit sometime after the arrest when an old clip circulated of Caserta speaking about Trump: "You know, Trump is not your friend, dude. And it amazes me that people actually, like, believe that. When he's shown over and over and over again that he's a tyrant. Every single person that works for government is your enemy, dude."

I found myself particularly intrigued by Caserta. At first glance, he seemed to ooze all the right kinds of guilt. He spouted violent rhetoric about potential vaccine mandates and forced quarantines—"A possibility should be on the table to eliminate some contact tracers. . . . We're going to create a dynamic where no one wants to be a contact tracer 'cause they might fucking die"—and a video released by the prosecution that had been filmed by Caserta in the early hours of October 7, the day of his arrest, was certainly scary enough. Caserta had just been waylaid by the police for not using his blinker, his second traffic stop in recent weeks. After the first stop, he had been plenty angry, venting immoderately in one of the online encrypted chats: "The end times are approaching for these piece of shit cops. I mean that with every cell in my body." In this new video, speaking into the camera back in his apartment, the fury overflows further. He explains that he is sick of being robbed and enslaved by the state and that if they come across any of these "gang fucking criminal-ass government thugs" during a recon who don't leave immediately, "they are going to die . . . because they are the fucking enemy. Period."

If that didn't give a clear enough indication of who he was, well, maybe you just needed to look at him. When the *Detroit Free Press* published a story topped by Caserta's mug shot—a photo in which he stares into the camera, the tattoos snaking up his neck just visible on either side of his orange beard, his long earlobes hanging distended, their inserted tunnels removed by law enforcement—the comment section took it from there: "Are his eyes too close together?" "The eyes are looking at each other." "Yep, probably inbred." "Evil little white dudes . . ." "Someone in prison is going to have sex with those ear holes." "These people always look genetically . . . off." "Dead eyes." "Small brain." "Does anyone else hear banjo music?"

Perhaps the most savage measure of the minuscule level of sympathy or of even the vaguest open-mindedness to other possibilities in the air in the days after the arrests is what happened when Caserta's mother started a "Help Brandon fight for his freedom" GoFundMe page. She declared that "Brandon is one of the most kind, honest and generous people you will meet" and requested the wider world's support. But why sully yourself by touching the untouchable? Why waste time or money trying to save the unsavable? Where is the kindness in enabling the delusions of a mother who won't accept the obvious truth of what her terrible son has done? The world responded with $120.

•   •   •

Brandon Caserta calls me from the road, telling me about what it is to no longer be where he has been.

"Like, eating good food and then having silence. Having peace. Being able to be comfortable. In jail, you could never get in a comfortable position. Everything is designed for you to be uncomfortable, mentally and physically. And they keep you uncomfortable mentally by keeping you uncomfortable physically. So having physical comfort. Taking a real shower with real soap. Just really simple stuff like that. Enjoying seeing the sky. And clouds is what was really mesmerizing for me."

Caserta is driving to Grand Rapids. An errand, you might say. Today he will pick up the guns and other property that the government confiscated when he was arrested.

•   •   •

In a dusty corner of the internet that seemed to have eluded those writing about the case sits a cache of Brandon Caserta's YouTube videos, videos someone had archived before they were deleted. There were hours and hours of footage, filmed in the two years before his arrest, and though he looked like the same man in his mug shot and his post-traffic-stop rant, he sounded quite different. Mostly these videos consisted of Caserta talking to the camera, patiently expounding and debating his anarchist beliefs, talking about books he'd read, dilemmas he was thinking through, ideas he was mulling over. In one, arguing against the fetish for imagining that constitutionalism might solve all ills, he bolstered his argument by calling up web pages on a screen behind him of all the countries with a constitution. I didn't find myself agreeing with too many of his conclusions, but there was often something sincere, open, thoughtful, and curious about the way he talked that took me by surprise. And there was one video—on the face of it, the least relevant one of all—that I couldn't stop thinking about.

I was already finding plenty of reasons to question my initial prejudices about these men and this case: the lacunae in the legal evidence; the disconcertingly heavy-handed role the FBI seemed to have played; the dissonant signals communicated by the accused men's actual speech, writing, and actions. But the odd truth is that, for some reason, it was this one Caserta video that most jarred me, that forced me to think again. In it, as Caserta speaks, he circles and backtracks through his apartment, in constant motion, so that you can see some of the markers of his life: an anarchy flag on one wall, the Bill of Rights on the wall opposite, a Gadsden-flag coiled snake with the slogans "Don't Tread on Me" and "Liberty or Death," the Second Amendment Since 1789 banner. There's no indication that he's high or acting out in any way for an audience. He just seems genuinely, sincerely interested in exploring the philosophical paradoxes and recursive loops of logic of the topic suggested by the video's title, that title being "Contemplating on whether or not I friggen suck."

This, in full, is what Caserta says:

You know, I'm kind of just walking around my apartment . . . and I was thinking, how do you really know if you suck? You know what I mean? I mean, I don't know, like, I got a decent place here. How do I really know, though, if I suck or not? Know what I mean? Like, maybe I do. 'Cause you already know there's a bunch of people out there who think they're really sweet, but they actually fucking suck. And you know that. You know that's true. I guess I could maybe, like, believe that I don't suck, but what if I actually do? You know? What if I actually suck real fucking hard and I just, like, can't see it? I just don't know it, you know? [*Laughs.*] You ever think about that? Like, what if that's true, man? Like, what if you're just a big, fat, sucky loser? You know? How do you really know? How do you really, actually know? You can believe that you don't fucking suck ass, but what if you do? What if you'll always suck? You know? How do you really know? What, are you going to ask someone else? "Hey, do you think I suck?" Maybe you're asking another sucky-assed person if you suck. And they say, "Nah, you don't suck." Even though in reality they fucking suck. How do you know? There's people that think they fucking suck, and they actually don't suck. At all! Who decides who sucks? [*Laughs.*] How do you know? I'm trying to figure it out, dude. I think it's possible that I fucking suck. At least a little bit. You know? I kind of think I suck a little bit. I think it's gotten better. I don't know, man. I'm kind of just looking around. I think it's possible that I might fucking suck a little bit. I think I need to do something about that. Later, guys.

I'm aware that far meeker, geekier, more likable, and more thoughtful people have proved capable of the most heinous acts. But—and I don't quite know how to put this without it sounding like some kind of weird and oblique personal confession—in these moments, I somehow felt like I recognized something fundamental about who this guy was. As with his other videos, it wasn't that I agreed with a lot of what he said, but I did understand the way that he thought. And that threw me. I couldn't work out how to square the person I believed I saw in this video with the person who appeared in the government narrative of this plot. Maybe that was my failing.

•　　•　　•

In Brandon Caserta's memory, it happened like this: One day in October 2020, he went to work and never came home.

Caserta worked the midshift, 2:30 p.m. to 12:30 a.m., five days a week. Fifty hours a week, a little more than twenty dollars an hour, making steering columns for Ford trucks. Around 6:20 p.m., he ordered his usual sandwich from Bode's Corned Beef, a combination of his own devising, "a double bacon cheeseburger with jalapeño, onion, and avocado" that they'd named the Spicy Brando. That Wednesday, just as he was about to go out for his regular Spicy Brando, he was told that the plant manager wanted a quick word. Walking into the room where he expected the manager to be, Caserta was surprised to discover that the lights were out. Then they flipped on and about fifteen plainclothes law-enforcement agents, their faces covered by balaclavas, jumped on him.

"Stop resisting!" they kept yelling. "Stop resisting!"

"I'm not resisting at all," he pointed out.

At first, he hadn't a clue who was doing this and was a little relieved—funny, he would wryly observe, in retrospect—when he realized that his captors were working for the government. "I had no idea what was going on," he says. It was maybe two hours later that he began to understand that he was accused of being part of a conspiracy, one that involved Adam Fox and Barry Croft.

"Are you serious?" he asked.

•　　•　　•

In the buildup to the trial, there were other developments that seemed more screenplay than reality. In July 2021, Richard Trask, the FBI agent whose account had formed the central narrative of the initial complaint, was arrested, having viciously assaulted his wife after they returned home from a swingers' party, and subsequently fired. The following month, *BuzzFeed*'s Ken Bensinger and Jessica Garrison broke the news that a Twitter account describing itself as run by the CEO of a cyber-intelligence firm called Exeintel had, ahead of the Whitmer kidnapping arrests, tweeted coded celebratory tweets about this impending law-enforcement triumph. According to the story, one of the firm's listed owners was another FBI agent, Jayson Chambers, a man so integral to the investigation that, according to one defense attorney, between March and October 2020 he had allegedly exchanged 3,236 messages with the embedded informant Dan Chappel. These potential FBI misdeeds would be adjudged inadmissible in court, but even if you weren't minded to believe the most extreme conspiracy theories—that the whole kidnapping plot had been fabricated by people within the FBI, say, to draw attention and business to this private company—it all felt very untoward and disconcerting.

Even so, I found it difficult to imagine that the defendants wouldn't be found guilty. For one thing, even if the FBI's immersive role might offend an everyday sense of fairness, I knew that, legally, the bar to using entrapment as a successful defense was generally a high one. Likewise, what was required to establish guilt on the main charge of conspiracy to kidnapping was slighter than you might assume. Whether the plan was confused or impractical or in all likelihood would never have been carried out was irrelevant. What was required was that two or more people conspired or agreed to commit the crime of kidnapping, that anyone involved joined knowingly and voluntarily, and that at least one member of the conspiracy committed a single overt act to advance or help the conspiracy. That's it. The indictment detailed nineteen such acts, and the jury need only be convinced of one.

·　　　·　　　·

To prepare for their defense, defendants were provided access in jail to all of the FBI's surveillance material on laptops. Caserta spent months, up to ten hours a day, listening and reading, trying to understand the case against him. "I wanted to know what was really going on," he says, "because it didn't make any sense to me why I got in charged with this." He knew there was plenty of stuff said in private that sounded bad. "All this rhetoric from us," he says. "It's pretty gruesome, I'm not going to lie." But he maintained that that was all. "I didn't do anything. I just said mean stuff." He and his legal team scoured the material nonetheless, searching for any moment when it might seem like he had agreed to be part of this plot. "Looking for this thing, right?" he says. "And it was just never there, dude. It was never there."

As he thought back, even when he'd been aware of some component of what was now considered this grand plot, it just hadn't been like that. He remembers, for instance, a moment during a September training weekend in Luther, Michigan, when Adam Fox referred to the idea of a trip to the governor's house.

"It seemed like a joke to me," Caserta says. "Like, Oh yeah, you're going to go look at her house? What, are you going to go and TP her house or something like that? Are you going to go poop in a brown bag and put it on her porch and set it on fire and be like, 'Screw you, dumb bitch,' you know what I mean? That's literally what it seemed like to me."

•   •   •

In the second week of March 2022, the four defendants were brought to Grand Rapids for the trial. As it began, the two sides started to lay out their positions. The government's tale was of a terrifying, focused plan: "The Defendants agreed, planned, trained, and were ready to break into a woman's home where she slept with her family in the middle of the night, and with violence and at gunpoint they would tie her up and take her from that home, and to accomplish that they would shoot, blow up, and kill anybody who got in their way, in their own words, creating a war zone here in Michigan." Statement after statement and action after action over a period of months was portrayed as articulating, propelling, and fulfilling this plan.

The defense's counterargument reiterated a series of themes. First, that while the accused may have said terrible things, it was all talk. Second, that much of the worst talk that the government presented as relating to this purported conspiracy was often about other things altogether. Third, that despite some of the things said and done, there was never a clear and sustained plan to do what was alleged. Fourth, that insomuch as there was ever even the vaguest semblance of a plan, it was one that was pushed forward at crucial moments by the FBI and its informants.

I don't want to belittle the substance of some of what the government presented. The worst of the defendants' statements—some of those I've already quoted, as well as very many others—were abominably nasty and callous and threatening and often gave good reason to wonder and worry whether these words reflected actions that the speaker might take. To actually hear the sound of the words spoken, as the recordings were played out loud in the courtroom, was deeply disturbing.

Aside from anything else, it was clear that the defense would need to undermine the prosecution's implication that these statements were practical declarations of intent. An early, memorable preview of one way in which this might be done was given in the opening statement of Barry Croft's attorney, Joshua Blanchard. Croft's statements were probably, at face value, the most damaging in their full, untrammeled unpleasantness. Proclamations like this: "I'm going to hurt people. I'm going to hurt people real fucking bad. I'm going to burn motherfucking houses down and blow shit up. I'm going to do some of the most nasty, disgusting things that you have ever read about in the history of your life." If the jury believed that these outbursts bore any definite relation to actual plans, only one verdict seemed likely.

Given that there was no disavowing what Croft had actually said, Blanchard instead argued that his client's speech should be considered not as a practical road map to future real-world action but as a subset of a rich and wide seam of Barry Croft crazy talk—talk that generally erupted when Croft was, in Blanchard's vivid nonlegalistic phrasing, "absolutely bonkers, out-of-your-mind stoned."

And then Blanchard offered a colorful list of other outbursts that he knew the authorities had listened to:

"When they heard Mr. Croft was talking about diverting rivers into underground caverns in the Shenandoah Valley so he could grow food by redirecting light using mirrors, they should have known this was stoned crazy talk and not a plan. When their snitch reported back that Mr. Croft was telling him about how the Egyptian pyramids create a counter magnetic flow that would allow a celestial chariot to enter the atmosphere at three times the speed of light without crashing into the earth's crust, they knew it was crazy stoned talk, not a plan. . . . When the snitches heard that Mr. Croft said, well, what we should do is we should cut down all the trees along the Indiana/Ohio/Michigan border to protect the state . . . because, I don't know, people can't step over trees? They knew it was stoned crazy talk and not a plan. . . . When they heard talk about shooting down airships. . . ." And so on—there was quite a bit more of this.

A good argument, maybe. But there was far more to the government's case than that.

•   •   •

June 2022

I drive to Michigan to meet with Caserta. He has been strangely evasive about where exactly he is staying and texts to suggest that we meet in a tiny park off a road near a lake in the northern outskirts of Detroit. I sit at the single picnic table and wait. There's no one else around.

According to what I've heard in court, I should be worried. Dan Chappel—an army vet and firearms instructor with an impressive Iraq service record—testified that when he visited Caserta at his apartment, he hadn't felt safe alone in Caserta's presence. In fact, Chappel explained how he'd been sufficiently concerned that he always made sure that the door was behind him as they talked, so that, if need be, he could escape. "He just had violence in him," Chappel said.

Today, Caserta arrives on a bicycle. "Hey," he says. "What's up?" When we start talking, the sun is bright. Before we stop, it's dark. There's still no one here but us and the evening mosquitoes. At one point he mentions how it's good to be able to "show people that I'm not this crazy, psychopathic terrorist that they kept saying I was, you know what I mean? I'm just a regular guy, works at a machine shop in Detroit, Michigan. That likes shooting guns, that likes freedom. And yeah, my philosophical beliefs may not be in agreeance with everyone else's, and I may have opinions that offend people, but, you know, I'm not a bad guy, you know what I mean?"

After a while, I discover what he hadn't explained about where he was staying. He's still piecing his life back together, and a few days ago he was invited to move in for a while at the nearby home of a friend's parents. As the night's conversation winds toward an end, the dark is broken by the headlights of a car pulling up, and the driver—the person Caserta is staying with—walks over.

"Nice to meet you," says Caserta's friend, his fellow defendant Daniel Harris.

⚬ ⚬ ⚬

The government's case wasn't, on the surface, a flimsy one—it was built up over twelve days and featured thirty witnesses. The key points of dispute were often less about what had happened than about what each event meant, and this was never more apparent than in talking about the various militia-training sessions that had taken place. Even though the prosecution tacitly acknowledged that non-incriminatory versions of such events do exist—after all, the ostensible reason informant-to-be Chappel gave for having joined the Michigan militia group known as the Wolverine Watchmen was to keep up with his firearms training—they relentlessly portrayed a series of such training events in the summer of 2020 as specific preparation for this kidnapping plot. In this context, some of what took place—practicing maneuvers in a "shoot house" or "kill house," say—at first glance sounded pretty bad, especially if, like me, you know next to nothing about gun-training routines. But on closer scrutiny, moments like these often felt less conclusive. For one thing, this kind of training maneuver turns out to be a fairly generic and commonplace one. The testimony suggested that everyone participating at training events took part in these exercises, including participants not implicated in this plot. And there was no persuasive evidence that the defendants had ever obtained details of the layout of any Gretchen Whitmer residence, let alone specifically styled what happened in these shoot houses on such information. It might still be true that the defendants had privately agreed to be practicing particular skills for a particular goal, but from what was presented in court, that seemed far from proven.

At times, so different were the narratives being presented that it felt as though the same evidence seemed equally satisfactory to both prosecution and defense. One example was what might be called the Dorito recording, an audio clip the prosecution considered damning enough to visit twice. Along with the conspiracy-to-kidnap charge, Croft and Harris were charged with possession of an unregistered destructive device, related to their attempts at blowing up improvised explosive devices at two training events, the first time unsuccessfully, the second successfully. The defense view seemed to be that these were nothing but glorified fireworks, being blown up for the reasons anyone blows up fireworks. The prosecution asserted something very different and far more sinister:

"These IEDs were meant to use to kill police or security who may be with the governor when they attacked."

The audio in question had been recorded at a weekend-long training event in Cambria, Wisconsin, in July 2020. As it begins, Croft can be heard being approached by his twelve-year-old daughter, Amber.

> AMBER: "Daddy!"
> CROFT: "What, honey?"
> AMBER: "Do you want a Dorito?"
> CROFT: "Honey, I'm making explosives. Can you get away from me, please?"
> AMBER: "Oh, okay."
> CROFT: "Yeah, thank you. I love you. Get out of here."

It felt as though the prosecution imagined that the casual brutality and inhumanity of the whole despicable affair was laid bare right here, in these few naked seconds, for all to hear. And you might see it like that. But maybe you could see it another way. Those at this weekend event emphasized that it was a family occasion. Other people had kids there, too. There was a swimming pool, a barbecue. This might not be everyone's idea of a great weekend out—it's certainly not mine—but if you're unaware that there are people who see great appeal in a family get-together with food, swimming, running around with guns, and maybe a bit of extra fun blowing shit up, without there necessarily being any actively seditious or felonious agenda, then you may wish to consider whose ignorance that reflects.

Hearing this clip, I also wondered whether listening to Croft here might influence the jury in a more intuitive way, one the prosecution didn't anticipate. The jury had effectively been told that this man was a monster, and they had already been played a series of other recordings in which Croft did a fair job of living up to that billing. But here, if the presence of explosives didn't make you disregard everything else, as presumably the prosecution hoped or assumed it must, you could hear someone who sounded far less like a monster than like a parent, one who seemed to have a sweet, respectful, and gentle rapport with his daughter, one it wasn't easy to imagine he was preparing to throw away.

•   •   •

Caserta and I talk at some length about his journey to become the man who would be arrested on October 7, 2020. After what he describes as "a pretty normal childhood"—skateboarding, shooting his BB gun, learning guitar, fantasizing about being a rock star, mountain biking—in his midtwenties he found himself feeling adrift. His life wasn't going the way that he wanted it to go. "I felt like kind of like Morpheus says in *The Matrix*, it was 'like a splinter in your mind.' It's bugging you. You know there's something wrong with the world and you know something's going on, but you don't know what it is. And that's kind of what I felt. So I started reading a lot more books about philosophy and freedom."

When Caserta reels off a list of the people whom he subsequently discovered and found useful or influential—David Icke, Alex Jones, Lloyd Pye, Jordan Peterson, Mark Passio, G. Edward Griffin, Ron Paul, Larken Rose, and Lysander Spooner—I flinch more than once. Even so, when Caserta explains what he took from them, it's hard to see how it differs from a standard liberal we'd-like-the-young-to-think-for-themselves screed. "Things weren't going my way, and I realized, You know what?" he says. "The problem isn't the world. The problem isn't outside. The problem is me. The reason why I'm not getting what I want and what I desire is because of me. So I need to change myself, and then the external world will change for me. If I enact good behaviors into the world, the consequences that I'll receive will be better, especially if I work hard at it. So I developed that mentality to where the taking on of personal responsibility will generate happiness. I kind of learned that from Jordan Peterson. And I said, You know what? I'm going to try this. And it worked."

Guns became important to him after the March 2019 mass shooting in Christchurch, New Zealand. To him, the New Zealand government's subsequent moves to restrict gun ownership made no sense. "I thought to myself, We have a lot of those mass shootings in America, and there's a lot of people that are in fear," he says. "So the best thing I can do for myself and for people I care about is to actually get a firearm and really, really learn how to use it in case something like that happened." He bought a Smith & Wesson SD40 VE, then a Bushmaster XM15-E2S, then a Glock 29. The Glock 29 is what he's carrying right now—he has a concealed-pistol license. He notes that he's never shot, or even drawn, a gun in anger.

He had also begun to identify as an anarchist, again inspired by his latest reading, specifically Larken Rose's *The Most Dangerous Superstition* and Lysander Spooner's *No Treason: The Constitution of No Authority.* "When they were explaining the concepts of authority, that is something that really helped me wake up," he says. "I realized that the state is an institution of violence and that everything that it does is predicated on the initiation of force. And that's in violation of the anarchist principle, which is the nonaggression principle. And that's a huge problem that we have going on today is that everyone thinks that anarchy means chaos and mayhem. So when you say you're identifying as anarchist, they think that you want people to die."

In 2020, as the COVID weeks turned into months, Caserta decided he wanted to find people to train with. "Prior to that, I've been training on my own, like in my apartment and stuff." He started researching militias and was soon invited to Wolverine Watchmen training events, though as far as he's concerned he was never a formal member. "The way I would explain to someone is just like: a group of guys getting together and going out in the woods and shooting guns and just having fun. And that's how it was the whole time. It was never like this secretive, in-depth, conspiratorial, like, 'Let's figure out how we can attack the government.' It was never like that. They took random conversations out of context, applied their own context to it, and then tried to leave the context out of court and make it to where the defense couldn't actually put the context into the statements so that the government's narrative would hold water, essentially. But yeah, it was always like just a friendly camaraderie type of environment where people just had fun and being American and shooting guns in the woods, man."

Caserta had been prepping for some time before that. "Spending money on storage-able food, water, filtration, ammunition, knives, saws, fire-starting kits, stuff like that. I already had everything pretty much ready in case something bad happened." One bit of common ground among people he would meet in this world was a sense that you have to prepare for WTSHTF. When the shit hits the fan. Many of the statements that, in court, were taken as references to "when we kidnap the governor" were, says Caserta, references to this more general sense of a coming upheaval. "They think we're this apocalyptic white-supremacist group of just gun-toting violent extremists that just absolutely hate the government and they want war to happen," he says. "I've never met anyone that legitimately wanted war to happen." The way Caserta paints it, what they're readying for is what other people might do. "Pretty much everyone thought, Okay, well, if shit hits the fan, we're going to defend ourselves."

According to the government, as 2020 progressed, Caserta's life was descending into darkness. It didn't seem that way to him. "I mean, honestly, man, that was one of the best summers I had. I was doing so good. I was getting raises and excelling at my job even more. I mean, I got my car fixed to where I didn't even have to worry about anything anymore about it. I just signed a new lease on my apartment. I was still hungry for knowledge, still hungry for life. I had multiple dates set up with a couple of different girls, getting back into the dating world again after taking a break for, like, six months. Things were great, man. . . . I mean, I had a blast, and I got to shoot guns and use my gear. And I learned so much skills. Life was going so good."

•　　　•　　　•

Whatever stumbles the prosecution may have made, over these twelve days they were able to show the jury plenty that didn't sound good. And even though two accused men who had pleaded guilty before the trial, Ty Garbin and Kaleb Franks, were far from perfect prosecution witnesses—they seemed to contradict each other on some details and got others demonstrably wrong—there was a forbidding power to having two men declare that this conspiracy had been real and that they had been part of it, along with the four defendants.

Then it was the defense's turn. With it, a big surprise. The conventional wisdom was that it would be too risky for defendants in a case like this to testify. But against expectations, Daniel Harris, the youngest of the accused, took the stand.

To begin with, as his attorney, Julia Kelly, led him through a series of questions, it couldn't have gone much better. Harris came across as kind of quiet and goofy, a politely spoken military kid who carefully explained all the many occasions on which he most definitely did not agree to kidnap the governor of Michigan. But this part isn't why criminal-case defendants tend not to testify. It's what comes next.

Harris was cross-examined by one of the prosecutors, Jonathan Roth. For about seven minutes, it went okay. Then Roth referred to the episode that supposedly triggered this whole investigation:

the instance when Dan Chappel, having signed up with the Wolverine Watchmen to do some weapons training, was so horrified by what he saw in the group's private chats that he called a friend in law enforcement, who put him in touch with the FBI.

"You heard testimony," said Roth, "that Dan Chappel, he is so bothered by the things that are going on in the chats that he immediately calls the police, correct?"

Harris's reply—it seemed to slip out. It was like he just couldn't help himself.

"Well, he's a bitch," Harris said.

And in that moment, you could feel the air freeze, as though maybe more had changed in the past three seconds than had changed in the previous thirteen days.

You could sense Roth's *got him!* excitement, like he knew this was the *A Few Good Men* moment he'd been dreaming of.

"I'm sorry, what was that?" Roth asked.

"He's a bitch," said Harris, quickly, as though if he said the same words fast enough they might somehow cancel out the first time.

"Tell me about that, sir," demanded Roth.

Seconds ticked by before Harris answered, "Next question." As if he'd be allowed out of a hole like that so easily.

"Nope," snapped Roth, the swagger of triumph in his voice. "Tell me about it. Why is Dan Chappel a bitch?"

"I was like, Oh, shit, that's not good," Caserta remembers thinking as he watched this unfold. To Harris, on the witness stand, it felt much worse. "It just came out," Harris tells me. "I'm like, Yeah, there's two life sentences right there. I'm going away. That is it." Harris could see how excited Roth was and that the defense lawyers were each clutching their head in their own way, just like, as he saw it, "the see-no-evil, hear-no-evil, speak-no-evil monkeys." Later, he heard that one of the defense attorneys had received a two-word text from his wife, who had been listening to the trial's live phone feed: "Oh fuck."

On the stand, Harris still needed to answer Roth's question. Again and again, he tried backing away from it, but Roth wasn't going to let that happen. "Sir, you just told me that he is a bitch for being scared of these memes," Roth pressed. "Tell me what was going on with these memes that he shouldn't be afraid of them."

Dan Chappel was someone Harris had trusted. Someone he had looked up to. Chappel had more military experience than anyone else around, had helped lead the Wolverine Watchmen's weapons training, had shown Harris and others a video one of his buddies had filmed of operations in Iraq, had seen combat and been injured there, and had talked about being part of a quick-reaction force that had once saved Chris "American Sniper" Kyle. At times, Harris had called Chappel "Dad." (Sometimes, because they were both Daniels but Chappel was both more senior and larger, Harris would also call him "Big Dan.") But whatever admiration Harris once had for Chappel was long gone. And now he found himself standing here, fighting for his future, trying to explain why he had just blurted out that Chappel was a bitch. He realized that he might as well just tell the truth. He might as well explain to the jury—and he would look right at them as he finally gave his answer—exactly why he had just said what he said.

"You are scared by words," Harris began, "but yet you say that you saved Chris Kyle? You went to Iraq, came out, right, hurt—but *words* hurt you? Words scare you? You are a bitch. Words are words."

The jury began its deliberations; days passed. The defendants, who had been mostly kept apart for the previous seventeen months but were sharing a cell during the trial, sweated it out together, coping as they could. Caserta and Croft preferred to talk things through, trying to keep positive. Harris would read the Bible or the self-help books that his legal team had given him. Fox would just lie there, day and night, his eyes closed. On the fifth day—Caserta's thirty-fourth birthday—word came that a verdict had been reached.

No one was found guilty. The jury couldn't agree on the charges against Croft and Fox—a mistrial was declared and the government swiftly announced that it would try the two men again. Harris and Caserta were acquitted of all charges. Both slipped out of the courthouse undetected. Harris went straight home to play with his puppy, Ollie. Caserta ate Popeye's chicken in a Grand

Rapids hotel room, and those around him fetched what he most needed: toothpaste, deodorant, and a change of clothes.

* * *

That first time I meet Daniel Harris, after dark in a Michigan park, he is wearing a gray sweatshirt, a gift from his attorney's brother-in-law the day after the verdict came through.

"I wear this everywhere," he tells me.

On the front of the sweatshirt are five words, fourteen letters, in block capitals:

BIG DAN IS A BITCH

* * *

As much as the trial troubled me, so did the reaction to these verdicts. Out in the world, much of what was being said seemed to fall into two different camps of thoughtlessness, mirroring an all too familiar modern-day ideological divide. On one side—to give the most cartoonish version—the jurors were Trumpian fools who had been hoodwinked into allowing dangerous psychopaths to go unpunished. On the other, it was confidently proclaimed that a jury had stated unequivocally that the FBI had framed four innocent men in a fictitious plot. Neither presumption seemed justified—if the jury had fully embraced the entrapment defense, for instance, there could have been no mistrial—but few people seemed to bother to look at the very real, specific, and messy reasons why the jury could have sensibly come to the verdict it did.

Anyway, a jury's verdict is a judgment on what can or cannot be proved, not a definitive pronouncement on what actually happened. So what did? Might it be that at least some of these men really did intend to do precisely what they were accused of doing, even if, despite the FBI's labors, the assembled evidence remained frustratingly scattershot and tenuous? I suppose so.

Or, conversely, could it really be true that the FBI did, in fact, plan all this, fashioning what some commentators enjoyed calling a "fednapping" conspiracy out of thin air for its own purposes? We live in an era when people often seem only too eager to believe in such duplicitous machinations, but for what it's worth, my own prejudices run against that. My default belief when faced with a choice between dastardly master plan and accidental shit show is that the latter is far more likely. What if the FBI truly believed it saw the seeds of something scary and dangerous and this belief then became—as beliefs sometimes may—a runaway train? Even setting aside my resistance to accepting that those who are supposed to work for us routinely work against us, one persuasive argument against the FBI having consciously engineered any of this is that, if it did, it made a pretty poor job of it. If it had really agreed to cross that moral line, surely it would have been simple enough to have concocted much clearer and much better evidence—evidence that would have been undeniable.

And there's another possibility, one that sits in a messier middle ground—the stuff that we don't much talk about and that the legal system is perhaps ill-equipped to judge, one that hovers in a real world where people think and say all kinds of immoderate blabber to each other without ever being sure how much of it they mean or what exactly is meant or understood by those they are talking to. In actual lives, how thin and ill-defined is the line that separates bluff, playacting, verbal entertainment, and braggadocio from those things that, if the right circumstances fell into place and the wrong kind of momentum gathered pace, someone could easily enough find themselves doing?

Does the truth of what was or wasn't exist somewhere in that murky in-between?

Whatever the precise reality, it disturbs me how readily those who consider themselves in the mainstream presumed to know exactly what this was. We're living through an epidemic of certainty, one not confined to the extremes. Sometimes, hearing what happened during both the investigation and the prosecution, it felt as though men who looked like this and spoke like this, who expressed fierce disaffection with the government, who believed in military training and advocated for gun rights, who talked about preparing for some future time when the shit hits the fan, were considered, by definition, already almost, say, 80 percent guilty of some serious crime. It's one thing to be baffled or affronted or alienated or appalled by the beliefs or choices or lifestyles of others. But, as ever, anytime a society starts acting as though a subset of the population who acts or thinks differently in a way that might puzzle or unsettle others is, de facto, guilty of something, that sounds to me like a society in trouble. Sometimes it's those who most fear a confrontation who create it.

•   •   •

Brandon Caserta and I sit talking, back at the same picnic table. I think one could have these kinds of measured, thoughtful conversations with Caserta for days, ones in which he'll debate and acknowledge all manner of nuance—he'll detail the parts of government that he considers valuable, for instance, and acknowledges the irony that the same legal system that he feels framed him also, in the end, set him free. But he's not some kind of cuddly, sensitive savant. What I see on his social media I often find deeply troubling, and while he has a very carefully thought-out moral universe that doesn't seek conflict, he's ardently clear that there are possible scenarios in which, if sufficiently provoked by authorities he considers illegitimate, he would feel duty bound to respond with force.

Today, as we talk, the sun overhead is blazing. I fashion a shade from a cardboard folder because I know that otherwise my phone, recording our conversation, will soon overheat and switch off. But the wind keeps blowing the folder away. I need something heavier to hold it down. Helpfully, Caserta produces the extra magazine for his Glock 29, which he carefully lays over one edge of the cardboard, keeping everything in place.

• • •

In August, the second Barry Croft and Adam Fox trial took place in the same Grand Rapids courtroom. Neither Caserta nor Harris had really gotten to know Croft before they shared a cell for the earlier trial. "Barry is definitely a character, man," says Caserta. "He gets riled up and he likes to talk a lot. But he's not a terrorist. He's not a dangerous person." They knew Fox a little better and didn't much like him—"that guy aggravated the crap out of me," Caserta says—but having listened to and read all the interactions between Fox, Chappel, and other informants and FBI agents, they considered him a victim. "All those people were in his head," says Caserta, "just pouring gasoline on the fire and getting him riled up and manipulating him and confusing him and making him feel that bad ideas are good ideas. You know, they propped him up to make him feel like he was actually a leader, like he was in control."

For this second trial, both sides, predictably, had honed their cases. The defense relentlessly highlighted the logical gaps in the prosecution's evidence and narrative and hammered away at all the ways in which those associated with the FBI had played a role. The prosecution repeatedly argued that the earliest inflammatory statements from the defendants showed that a plot to kidnap Whitmer predated any FBI involvement; the defense maintained that these statements meant no such thing.

This time, by all accounts, the jury deliberated for just eight hours over two days: Croft and Fox guilty on all charges.

Caserta saw it as the system reasserting itself. "If you say anything wrong about the government or criticize the government in any way, they will spend millions of dollars to come after you and put you in a cage. And if they can't get a conviction, they'll retry you again and again and again until they get your body and your soul in a cage." Outside the court, asked about appeals and other options, Fox's attorney Christopher Gibbons declared, "We will be pursuing all avenues . . . vigorously"; they subsequently moved for a new trial. Meanwhile, the Department of Justice put out a press release in which Andrew Birge said, in words that seemed to balance triumph and relief, "Today's verdict confirms this plot was very real and very dangerous." The tone of much of the media coverage suggested that sanity and stability had belatedly prevailed.

That's not how I felt. I can't tell you with any confidence that none of these men would ever have done anything terrible. I can't tell you with any confidence that, allowed the chance, none of them ever would. But neither can I tell you that I'm comfortable with any sense that an authentic and terrible threat has been satisfactorily and appropriately dealt with, its damage finally contained. What I can tell you is that, as our world evolves in ways that unnerve us, we might thank ourselves to be as careful as we can, every one of us, not to act as though we know for sure what we may not know in the least. And I can tell you this: if everything you knew about these men is what you heard on October 8, 2020, you knew almost nothing at all.

New York

WINNER—LIFESTYLE
JOURNALISM

Labeled "sharp and fizzy" by the National Magazine Award judges, this piece was the introductory essay for "The Year of the Nepo Baby," a multipage package on nepotism in the entertainment business. "New York," continued the judges, "snatched the phrase 'nepo baby' from the digital zeitgeist and bottled it into a master class in magazine making, supercharging a conversation that was already bubbling." The result was "a pitch-perfect mix of absurd maximalism, faux outrage, and unbridled delight." Nate Jones is a senior writer at New York *and its online arts and entertainment channel,* Vulture. New York *topped the list of National Magazine Awards finalists this year with ten nominations, winning two awards, for Lifestyle Journalism for "The Year of the Nepo Baby" and for Single-Topic Issue for "Ten Years Since Trayvon," a special issue on Black Lives Matter.*

Nate Jones

How a Nepo
Baby Is Born

In 2022, the internet uncovered a vast conspiracy: Hollywood was run on an invisible network of family ties—*and everybody was in on it!* Everyone is someone's kid, but it was as if everybody were *somebody's* kid. *Euphoria*, the buzziest show on television, was created by the son of a major director and costarred the daughter of another. Actress Maya Hawke was not only born to two famous parents but looked like them, too. Half of Brooklyn's indie artists had dads with IMDb pages. Even *Succession*'s Cousin Greg turned out to be the son of one of the guys who designed the Rolling Stones' lips logo. Aghast, content creators got to work. An unwieldy phrase—"the child of a celebrity"—was reduced to a catchy buzzword: *nepo baby.* TikTokers produced multipart series about nepo babies who resembled their famous parents, exposés on people you didn't know were nepo babies (everyone knew), and PSAs urging celebrity parents to roast their nepo babies "to keep them humble."

Like psoriasis, the label was something you were born with, and those who had it found it equally irritating. Maude Apatow (daughter of Judd Apatow and Leslie Mann) told *Porter* magazine the term made her "sad." It filled Zoë Kravitz (daughter of Lenny Kravitz and Lisa Bonet) with "deep insecurity." Gwyneth Paltrow (daughter of Blythe Danner and Bruce Paltrow) commiserated about it with Hailey Bieber (daughter of Stephen Baldwin and niece of Alec) on the latter's YouTube channel: "People are ready to pull you down and say, 'You don't belong there.'" Scratching the itch could only make it worse. At sixteen, the model and actress Lily-Rose Depp landed her first campaign with Chanel, the same house her mother, Vanessa Paradis, worked with; the year before, she'd made her film debut alongside her father, Johnny Depp. In a November *Elle* profile, she brushed off suggestions that her path had been cleared for her: "It just doesn't make any sense." The response was swift. On TikTok, floating heads begged Depp to "shut up and stop being delusional." Her fellow models castigated her on Instagram. "i have many nepo baby friends whom i respect," the top model Vittoria Ceretti wrote in an Instagram Story, "but i can't stand listening to you compare yourself to me. i was not born on a comfy sexy pillow with a view."

The intensity of the backlash may suggest we live in a world where bands of sansculottes are roaming Pacific Palisades rounding up anyone whose parents' names are blue on Wikipedia. In truth, nepo babies have always been a fact of Hollywood. Today, they're not only abundant—they're thriving. In an industry built on reboots, a famous last name can be valuable intellectual property. A celebrity child brings an easy marketing hook as well as millions of TikTok followers who, the theory goes, will slide seamlessly from watching their wardrobe reveals to watching their war-drama reels. Ang Lee tapped his son, Mason, for the starring role in his Bruce Lee biopic, and 2021 saw two sons of actors, Michael Gandolfini and Cooper Hoffman, follow in their dearly departed fathers' footsteps. Streaming series such as *Stranger Things*, *Never Have I Ever*, and *The Sex Lives of College Girls* may well be federally funded make-work projects for well-connected private-school graduates. This year, small films such as *I Am Ruth* and *Sam & Kate* seemingly exist solely to pair famous actors with their less famous offspring (Kate Winslet and Mia Threapleton in the former; Dustin Hoffman, Jake Hoffman, Sissy Spacek, and Schuyler Fisk in the latter). And that's just the working actors. Elsewhere, the celebrity-media complex allows Brooklyn Beckham (son of David and Victoria Beckham) to headline *Variety*'s "Young Hollywood" issue without ever approaching anything you or I would recognize as a normal job.

Nepo baby: How could two little words cause so much conflict? A baby is a bundle of joy; a nepo baby is physical proof that meritocracy is a lie. We love them, we hate them, we disrespect them, we're obsessed with them.

•   •   •

In a single tweet in February, a Canadian tech-support worker named Meriem Derradji brought the idea of nepo babies into the public conversation. The twenty-five-year-old was born in Montreal, but when she was nine, she and her family moved to Algeria, where her parents had been born. She spent three years there with no internet, cut off from pop culture. When she returned to Canada as a tween, plugging back in was like taking a starving man to a Cheesecake Factory. In 2013, she joined Twitter and enlisted on the side of the Barbz, Nicki Minaj's obsessive, protective stan army. There, she learned how to speak fluent internet, crafting tweets that would push people's buttons.

The stir over Hollywood nepotism had begun to percolate at the start of the pandemic, which both supercharged the backlash against celebrities and heightened the salience of their dynastic ties. (Since many famous families were quarantining together, even the most exalted stars felt *a little bit D-list*, ripe for the plucking.) It didn't take much to set off a round of discourse: A *Deadline* article about a short film called *The Rightway*—directed by Steven Spielberg's daughter, starring Sean Penn's son, and written by Stephen King's son—spurred days of online controversy. As Derradji caught up with the conversation, a lot of things started to make sense. She often passed time watching catwalk videos. "You would see models walk super-well and then there's Kendall Jenner walking, and you're like, *Oh my gosh. It's really bad*," she says. How bad? "She walks like a normal person." Like many zoomers, Derradji watched *Euphoria* and absorbed everything about it online. She wasn't a particular fan of Maude Apatow's character ("Her acting wasn't bad, but it wasn't anything special"), and when she discovered both of the actress's parents had Wikipedia entries of their own, she fired off a tweet: "Wait I just found out that the actress that plays Lexi is a nepotism baby omg 🙋 her mom is Leslie Mann and her dad is a movie director lol."

Her tweet received more than 4,000 likes, but the more important figure was the 2,500-plus quote tweets, mostly from millennials and Gen-Xers incredulous that someone had gotten to Judd Apatow *through* Maude Apatow. Prompted by the hubbub, major publications wrote explainers on the subject of nepo babies, and soon no celebrity child could do press without getting grilled on their parentage. To Derradji's critics, few of whom were aware that she had been a child living in North Africa during Apatow's heyday, she was emblematic of Gen Z's naïveté. (In turn, the anger her tweet stirred up was partly attributable to older generations' discomfort with their own cultural irrelevance.) The pot stirrer in her couldn't help but be a little proud. If you called out a nepo baby online, they might be forced to respond. "Whatever you say could get the attention of those nepotism kids, get a reaction out of them," she says.

You can trace the origins of the modern backlash to two pivotal events. First, the *Girls* wars of 2012, in which nepotism allegations became tangled up in discourses around race, misogyny, and privilege, prompting unanswerable questions like "Aren't they actually *satirizing* people with zero Black friends?" Second, the Operation Varsity Blues scandal of 2019, which revealed the underhanded methods by which celebrities like Lori Loughlin and Felicity Huffman sought to get their children into high-ranking universities. By exposing the inner workings of the process in humiliating detail, down to staged photos of the applicants posing on rowing machines, it stripped them of their mystique. Nepotism became *funny*. Nobody exemplified this better than Loughlin's daughter Olivia Jade Giannulli, a YouTube personality seemingly uninterested in the expensive education her mother had risked prison to help her obtain. One of the earliest instances of *nepotism baby* being shortened to *nepo baby* appears in a 2020 post from the blog *Pop Culture Died in 2009*, which describes Olivia Jade as our era's answer to Bling Ring icon Alexis Haines. While Haines embodied the aughts' unsightly hybrid of sleaze and luxe, Olivia Jade exposed the lie at the heart of relatable social-media fame: "The stars pretending to be just like you and me whilst shacked in a palace in Beverly Hills."

It makes sense that zoomers, a generation steeped in pop analyses of structural oppression, would hit on the nepo baby as their particular celebrity obsession. Though as anyone who followed the journeys of *mansplain* and *gaslight* could tell you, a word that goes viral can shed its nuances. Hollywood is built on minute gradations of status, which the online conversation has a tendency to elide. At times, it seems any young star whose parents did anything more interesting than accounting is liable to be named and shamed as a nepo baby—and even accountants' children aren't safe, as Jonah Hill and Beanie Feldstein, whose father was the tour accountant for Guns N' Roses, can attest.

Better to imagine nepo babies on a spectrum. At the top are the classic nepo babies, inheritors of famous names and famous features: Dakota Johnson, Maya Hawke, Jack Quaid. The next tier down are people who got a leg up from family connections even if they were not famous per se. These include figures like Lena Dunham, whose artist parents supplied the necessary cultural capital, as well as "industry babies" like Billie Eilish, daughter of a voice actress, and Kristen Stewart, whose mother was the script supervisor on *The Flintstones in Viva Rock Vegas*. The Hadid sisters are a tricky case: as with that other famous Palestinian, Jesus Christ, the benefits of the filial relationship clearly flowed both ways. And we can probably draw a line when it comes to figures like Paris Hilton, for whom the term *rich people* is already sufficient.

· · ·

The nepo baby's path to stardom begins when they're a literal baby. A celebrity child takes center stage in a series of highly visible tabloid rituals: "We're expecting" photos, birthday parties, holidays. As they age into adolescence, the mere fact that they physically resemble their famous parents is a news event on par with a closely fought primary. (In the past five years, People.com has written no fewer than seventeen articles about how Ava Phillippe looks like her mother, Reese Witherspoon.) There can be delicious schadenfreude in the realization that, far more than most of us, a nepo baby's destiny is determined by a spin on the genetic roulette wheel. The model Kaia Gerber has profited handsomely from looking exactly like her mother, Cindy Crawford, while Bruce Willis and Demi Moore's daughters were undoubtedly hampered by inheriting their father's most famous feature, his chin.

Once children receive their own Instagram handles, they become tabloid protagonists in their own right. (From "7 Reasons to Follow Reese Witherspoon's Daughter on Insta": "No. 2: She Takes Perfect Selfies with Mom Reese.") Gwyneth Paltrow's daughter, Apple, went from an object, most notable for her unusual name, to a subject by issuing sassy clapbacks on her mother's posts. Kate Beckinsale's daughter, Lily Mo Sheen, made headlines for posting selfies with her boyfriend, who fans thought resembled her father, Michael Sheen. But if they want to stick around into adulthood, an ambitious nepo baby must soon justify their place in the Hollywood firmament.

How can they begin to prove themselves? Traditionally, Mom and Dad have helped out. Apatow is the latest in a long line of directors' children who got big breaks in their parent's projects, one that stretches at least as far back as 1969, when a teenage Anjelica Huston made her debut in her father's film *A Walk with Love and Death*. The disgraced screenwriter Max Landis got his first credit alongside his father on an episode of *Masters of Horror*. Jake Kasdan cowrote the behind-the-scenes book for his father's film *Wyatt Earp*. Hawke was one of many actresses who auditioned for a small part in *Once Upon a Time in Hollywood*, but she was the only one whose self-tape costarred Ethan Hawke and hopefully the only one who received "an extra-tight hug and a wink from Quentin" after her callback. When Witherspoon told her friend Mindy Kaling that her son Deacon Phillippe was interested in acting, Kaling cast him as a prep-school cutie in two episodes of *Never Have I Ever*, in which he did an impressive job of not staring directly into the camera. "He's obviously so talented, and he's great-looking, and we just thought he would be great," Kaling told *Variety*.

In a rough study, approximately 100 percent of celebrities' children were hailed by their collaborators as talented, humble, and ready to put in the work. Noah Baumbach recalled going "through audition after audition and all the callbacks" to find actors who could play Adam Driver's children in *White Noise*, only to land upon "these two Nivola kids"—Sam and May, whose parents are Emily Mortimer and Alessandro Nivola. ("They were just so wonderful.") Donald Glover praised Malia Obama's work ethic in the writers' room for his upcoming Amazon series, telling *Vanity Fair*, "Her writing style is great." Such quotes often appear in the nepo baby's traditional coming-out party: a profile in a glossy magazine. (The Nivolas recently got one in the *New Yorker*.) The hottest trend in media right now is the intergenerational team-up, which *GQ* has made a specialty, running spreads of John C. Reilly posing with his "model-musician son," LoveLeo, and Pierce Brosnan alongside his "model-musician-filmmaker sons," Dylan and Paris.

· · ·

Like Obama, a few brave nepo babies step outside their parents' chosen field. (The bravest don't try to become famous at all. Bruce Springsteen's son is a firefighter while Willem Dafoe's is a law clerk.) Cazzie David made her name through funny Instagram captions, which prompted 2017-era headlines like "I Wish I Was Larry David's Cool Daughter" and landed her a book deal. Gordon Ramsay's daughter Holly started a podcast about young people's mental health, which helped get her signed to CAA (presumably, the 300,000-plus TikTok followers didn't hurt either). Sometimes, capturing the internet's attention for a moment is enough. After Kamala Harris's stepdaughter, Ella Emhoff, showed up at the inauguration looking like a goth Margot Tenenbaum, she landed a modeling deal, which led to her walking New York Fashion Week and being named an "icon" by *Harper's Bazaar*.

For those not ready to commit to one profession, the industry can provide a buffet of opportunities. In August 2020, Ísadóra "Doa" Bjarkardóttir Barney, the then-seventeen-year-old daughter of Björk and Matthew Barney, was cast alongside her mother in Robert Eggers's *The Northman* on the plausible basis that the role called for a specific type of medieval Norse singing that only someone related to Björk could pull off. In February, Doa received her first magazine profile in the British quarterly *The Face*, which highlighted the avant-garde video diary she shot in lockdown (current views: 8,100) and the Joanna Newsom cover she recorded to benefit refugees. In April, *The Northman* flopped, but never mind; in July, Doa signed a modeling contract with Miu Miu.

This is the nepo baby's credo: Try, and if at first you don't succeed, remember you're still a celebrity's child, so try, try again. No one exemplifies this maxim better than Brooklyn Beckham—in the words of *The Guardian*'s Marina Hyde, a celebrity scion incapable of having "what other mortals might regard as amateur hobbies without considering them nascent professional empires." At twenty-three, Beckham has already cycled through aborted attempts to follow in his parents' footsteps in the worlds of football and modeling. He next tried to become a professional photographer, releasing a coffee-table book full of out-of-focus pictures of elephants. Then he was a chef, a career he embarked upon despite possessing a level of culinary talent most commonly seen in *BuzzFeed* videos. While these endeavors have not been successful in the traditional sense, they have enabled him to amass 14.6 million followers on Instagram, where the only important metric is the one thing a nepo baby is assured of on the basis of their name: attention.

We have all heard the anti-anti-nepotism argument: Sure, children of the famous may have an advantage at the beginning, but eventually talent will win out. Those who can't hack it will fade away while the truly gifted nobodies will be discovered if they only keep at it.

"This is ludicrous," Fran Lebowitz wrote in a 1997 issue of *Vanity Fair*. "Getting in the door is pretty much the entire game, especially in movie acting, which is, after all, hardly a profession notable for its rigor." Lebowitz brought this up in service of a metaphor about structural racism: just as the children of celebrities got a leg up from the fact that they physically resembled people who were already famous, so too did America's whites benefit from fitting the nation's mental image of who should be in charge. In this context, being a nepo baby is the Cadillac of privilege. Nobody's got it better.

Those in a position to know often agree with Lebowitz's assessment. "They don't realize how lucky they are because this is their world," says one talent manager who has worked with multiple celebrity offspring. "I am very transparent with my clients that there are steps they need to take to be able to be relevant past the fifteen-second mark. It's not just about your clout. Where is your résumé? A lot of them are working toward their own thing, but at times they're trying to bypass the steps a person coming from nowhere would have to do." Having been spared the seasoning of everyday hardship, a nepo baby can often seem guppyish, unformed. Pauline Kael once wrote of Peter Fonda, "He doesn't have a core of tension; something in him is still asleep, and perhaps always will be."

It's no surprise so many nepo babies get their start as models, the manager says: the child doesn't have to open their mouth. "I've learned that once they start speaking, the public doesn't go along for the ride," they say. "The more they talk, the more unrelatable they become." The most self-aware among them have the savviness to play against type, but that creates its own problems. "On Instagram, a lot of them are not necessarily showcasing their life as a socialite. They're like, 'Oh my God, look at me at this dive bar.' *Girl, weren't you just on a yacht last night?*"

Within the industry, there is little use in being subtle about the familial strings. "Someone once said to me, 'We should hire so-and-so because their parents will come to the opening night,'" says a veteran casting director. The need to maintain relationships can ease a famous child's path through the door. "A big agency will write and say, 'This is so-and-so's kid,' and you understand that to mean 'So you have to see this kid.'" If the nepo baby is obviously untalented, it usually ends there. "I have learned to simply say, 'Not right for the role. But lovely.' There are a number of veiled responses rather than saying, 'Are you guys kidding me?'"

The casting director puts it bluntly: "A lot of the children of famous people are not good." How often are they meeting with them? "God, there have been so many over the course of my life." They once met with an aspiring actress who was the daughter of two movie stars. "There was something else that walked in the room with her," they say. "Like, 'My parents are famous, and I'm here because somebody told me to meet you.' A lovely person but definitely a sense of entitlement. She left, and I was like, *That person doesn't excite me. The struggle isn't there.*" This is not always a deal breaker. Afterward, the daughter booked the role that made her a household name.

Despite suspicions, you don't always know someone's background. A while back, a young actress with a famous family but a common last name came in to read for her first lead role. "I had no idea who she was," says the casting director. "I don't know why I didn't get the memo. From my vantage point, she won that job fair and square." (The actress's performance was widely acclaimed, and she became a major star.)

The casting director laments changes in the industry that have perhaps enabled the nepo babies' rise. "I don't think people know or understand what acting is anymore," they say. With the advent of streaming and social media, the big screen no longer rules. "A lot of these people watch this crap, and they think that what they're watching is good acting, and they mimic what that is," the casting director says. "And it's not good." That devolution explains why it may feel as though there are so many more well-born mediocrities than ever before: the medium's standards are merely lower.

We need not sign on to the fiction that nepo babies actually have it worse to acknowledge that there are elements of their lives we wouldn't trade for our own. "Nobody treats you seriously," filmmaker Owen Kline (son of Kevin Kline and Phoebe Cates) told *The Guardian* in September. "No one wants to read someone's kid's 'thing.'" Others taking you seriously doesn't necessarily cure the anxiety. "For a long time, I wondered whether my career had come to me because of my own talents or because of some kind of genteel nepotism," a thirty-something Jeff Bridges told the authors of *Hollywood Dynasties*. "The guilt caused big problems for me."

The casting director can empathize: "How do you know if somebody really likes you?" Some nepo babies take this vulnerability and use it—the struggle is the spice that finally makes them interesting. "And others, it's the thing that gets in their way."

· · ·

The industry's original nepo baby was Douglas Fairbanks Jr., son of Douglas Sr. and stepson of Mary Pickford, who in the 1920s were arguably the most famous couple on the planet. Sensing the power of a good name, Paramount's Jesse L. Lasky handed the thirteen-year-old a $1,000-a-week contract and set about trying to make him a star. Like many who followed in his footsteps, Fairbanks Jr. never came close to equaling his father's legacy, but he had a long career, was briefly married to Joan Crawford, and seemed entirely at ease with his station in life. "I have, since maturity, known full well the limits of my capabilities," he wrote in his memoir. The younger Fairbanks, who was mobbed by adoring throngs upon his arrival in Los Angeles, likely escaped the backlash that hits today's nepo babies, though presumably there were a few bitchy telegrams sent about him.

Those who came after were often treated as tragic figures. Take Frank Sinatra Jr.: While Frank hung out with criminals in a cool way, Junior did it in an extremely uncool way. (He got kidnapped.) It wasn't until the late sixties, when second-gen stars like Liza Minnelli and Jane Fonda came onto the scene, that the first celebrity kids were able to climb out of Hollywood's primordial soup and carve identities apart from their lineage. Each was aided by a natural divide separating them from their famous parent: Fonda by working in Europe, an ocean away from America, Minnelli by the somewhat more dramatic distance between the living and the dead.

Long before TikTok got ahold of these descendants, scholars had been studying our obsession with multigenerational stars. Austrian academic Eva Maria Schörgenhuber argues that celebrity children function as living links to a shared pop-culture history, connecting us to a nostalgic vision of the past. You can see this keenly in the types of nepo babies the culture does not have a problem with. Stars like Minnelli, Mariska Hargitay, or Freddie Prinze Jr., who all had a parent die in tragic circumstances, garner respect, not scorn, for following in their footsteps. The same way the Kennedys went from nouveau-riche bootleggers to inhabitants of a fairy-tale castle, so does the passage of time transform a nepo baby into someone "from a famous family." Few today care that Michael Douglas, Laura Dern, or Tracee Ellis Ross had celebrity parents. The same principle holds true for someone like Dakota Johnson, who reps multiple generations of Hollywood legends and is thus exempt from the tasteless striving that defines celebrity children of a more recent vintage. Paradoxically, the nepo babies we like best are often the ones who are *most* privileged.

The director Luca Guadagnino, who cast Johnson in two of his films, once told me, "I can see Tippi Hedren" in her. He glimpsed flickers of her grandmother, the great Hitchcock blonde. We often talk about the "It" factor, the otherworldly charisma that stars like Clara Bow exhibited in front of a camera. As the career of Chet Hanks makes abundantly clear, this quality is not guaranteed to be passed down through the generations. But it can be off-putting to discover that "It" may indeed be hereditary, to see a Zoë Kravitz or Kate Hudson display that same intangible sparkle you saw in their parents. "They walk in the room, and they have this *thing,*" says the casting director. "They just know. They literally know. You're drawn to that, and you're a little bit afraid of it. Because it's bigger than you."

New York

Allison P. Davis writes that nearly ten years after she first downloaded Tinder, "the longest-term relationship I've had from Tinder is with Tinder itself." "In this smart, sweeping essay, Davis captures the confusion of a generation shaped by dating apps," said the National Magazine Award judges. "In frank, humorous detail, she examines her search for intimacy (and sex). But it's not just about her. 'Tinder Hearted' is about the many young adults whose lives are defined by disconnection." Davis writes feature stories for New York and The Cut. Her work for New York was previously nominated for the National Magazine Award for Personal Service in 2015. New York is a regular National Magazine Awards finalist. This year the magazine was nominated for the eighth consecutive year for the most prestigious National Magazine Award, General Excellence.

Allison P. Davis

Tinder Hearted

I first downloaded Tinder in the spring of 2013, seven months after it launched. I'd heard about it as a concept (Grindr for straights) but felt exempt from needing it until one evening at the tail end of a drawn-out breakup with someone I'd told myself I would marry. We were at a restaurant in San Francisco, having one of too many brutal good-bye dinners that led to this-is-the-last-time-I-swear sex, and I put the app on my phone in front of him. He stoically chugged his negroni while I marveled at the hundreds, presumably thousands of men who were waiting for me on the other end, should he decide to go through with the breakup. "Look!" I said, waving my iPhone 5 in his face. (I didn't mention that at this early point in the app's history, it was mostly populated by twenty-year-old college students and S.F. tech bros who exclusively wore free T-shirts from start-ups.) By June, my boyfriend had gone through with the breakup and moved on—quickly and not via app—to a woman he'd met through mutual friends. I wanted to die. But instead of the sweet relief of death: Tinder.

That July, after several swipes and false starts and conversations about "logistics" with friends who, like me, had downloaded the app but never gone out with a match, I had my first actual Tinder date: Jameson. Either his bio had a joke about "taking a shot of Jameson" or my opening message did. I'd chosen a pale-blue mini-dress that showed some tit but not too much tit because I was meeting him straight after work. And he'd chosen happy hour at an Irish pub in Alphabet City that was dive-y but not too dive-y. I'd chosen him because he had hair like *Felicity*-era Scott Speedman, and while nothing he said was that impressive, it also wasn't boring or offensive, which I'd already recognized as hallmarks of most Tinder conversations.

Jameson worked for a carpet-importing business and paid for everything (nice!) from a thick roll of cash (uh, okay!). I had too many whiskey gingers on an empty stomach and was drunk ninety minutes in. To his credit, he waited until around 120 minutes before suggesting we move to his place for another drink, which was coincidentally less than a block away. Even though everything about Tinder was new, I still understood he meant it was Time for Sex. I thought to myself, *This is ahead of schedule.* We'd been hanging out for only two hours, and it was still light out. And I needed to eat, I told him. He waited patiently while I ate two slices of pizza at a tourist trap. Then he tried again, abruptly kissing me with grease all over my chin and pepperoni on my breath. As his tongue worked its way around my mouth with such agility I considered asking him to unearth some pepperoni stuck between my molars, I felt my body flood with the possibility of a great romance. Instead, I went home alone and felt sad he wasn't my ex.

It wasn't a good date or a bad date, but I liked how easy and fun it had been, and I felt certain that it would continue to be easy and fun to do again and again with other people until I settled down with someone and deleted the app.

Tinder turns ten in September, and I'm still "againing and againing with other people." Around Tinder's fifth anniversary, essayists and academics set out to chart the specific, permanent ways we had been reshaped and reformed by every swipe, as if we were our own sculptor's hands. It's now clear Tinder has become the dating air, or maybe the pollution, we all breathe. Every straight couple (Tinder will never lose its original heteronormative gloss) who admit they met on the app in their *New York Times* wedding announcement make Tinder seem like a legitimate path toward a happy ending. And yet as part of the first group of people to naïvely sign up for the app, I am surprised at how unobtainable a committed long-term relationship feels. Even those who have never downloaded Tinder aren't immune to its societal effects, the kinds that make smug couples sigh with relief when they say, "I'm glad I met my partner before there were apps." But it's easy to overestimate the way technology shapes us and to discount the way technology bends to our needs and wills and desires. It's possible Tinder didn't do anything but promise us connection and we're the ones who decided how we wanted to connect.

•   •   •

There are factors that may make my time on the apps different from yours—I am thirty-six, Black, a woman, a resident of one of Tinder's densest dating markets (New York), and I mostly date men. At this age, I often feel old—and frankly a little embarrassed—to still be using Tinder. I'm not in the most common age group of users (more than 50 percent are eighteen to twenty-five). I represent something like 20 percent of people who are swiping, and even Tinder seems to sense some desperation—or at least a business opportunity—in my age. Until recently, people over thirty had to pay $29.99 a month for Tinder Platinum, 50 percent more than the price for a younger user.

You may be a different user, perhaps closer to the standard (75 percent are male, according to outside sources, though Tinder was unwilling to confirm), but if you signed up near the beginning as I did, I'm sure the broad strokes of our time there aren't so different. It started with drinks over small-batch cocktails at too-precious speakeasies and lasted through picklebacks at ironic dives and is still going through natural orange wines at intimate wine bars. In between the drinks, there have been dinner dates, comedy-show dates, concert dates, nondates that were just hanging out for sex. There's been bad sex, meh sex, do-it-for-the-story sex, occasionally good sex, and sometimes sex that's made me need to take a break from sex. We might even have matched, met, and fucked the same person, an overlap I discovered with two different people I spoke to while writing this. (Remarkably, one guy was an art handler from Chicago who was only in town for a weekend, and yet somehow . . .)

I've rejected people for bad grammar, racial slurs, boring first questions, aggressive and immediate sexual overtures, overly earnest chat, GIF usage, delay of IRL meeting, or an inexplicable ick, often involving their choice in footwear. I've forgotten I dated and slept with someone and rematched with renewed interest. I've been lightly catfished and probably almost scammed. I've received dick pics without warning, solicited dick pics, sent nudes. It never occurred to me some specifics would turn me on: a snaggletooth, a bad tattoo in a good location, clean fingernails. I've ghosted and been ghosted and taken all the rejection like a champ but then been so randomly, disproportionately felled by one single rejection I'm surprised at the intensity of my rage and despair. I've been lucky that I've never had anything truly bad happen to me.

I've deleted the app and redownloaded the app, deleted and done it again. I've had so many long-term text-only encounters that for a moment I wondered if I was a digisexual. I've strayed and used Hinge (why don't I get any matches?) and Bumble (just because I can message first doesn't mean you'll message back) and Raya (C-LIST CELEB WITH ACCESS TO A PI, CAN YOU PLEASE?), and I once downloaded something called Headero, but I've always come back to Tinder. I've had a lot of fun. I've run out of matches on more than one occasion. I've never made it to a fifth date, which means the longest-term relationship I've had from Tinder is with Tinder itself.

As a teenager, I had some early and potent sexual awakenings in Napster chat rooms. Those X-rated online conversations with strangers taught me how to be both intimate and distant at once. In my twenties, I dated people I met on OkCupid and match.com, even though I'd lie about how we met. So I was not prone to moral panic over dating apps; it seemed obvious that technology could provide a dating assist. Plus I'd seen *Sex and the City*. The "simpler times" of clumsy come-ons in coffee shops had their own heartaches and missed connections and misread signals. For those reasons, I was willing to trust the app with my romantic hopes and ignore the douchebaggery lurking in its DNA.

Tinder's launch party was a sorority-sister filled rager at the home of cofounder Justin Mateen's parents. Less than two years later, Mateen's behavior around the office led to a sexual-harassment lawsuit. The next year, another cofounder, Sean Rad, bragged about resisting bagging a supermodel who had propositioned him on his app and misused the word *sodomy* ("Apparently there's a term for someone who gets turned on by intellectual stuff. You know, just talking. What's the word? I want to say 'sodomy'?") in what was meant to be his redemption press interview.

At the time, you may recall, Silicon Valley venture capitalists threw money and adoration at hotheaded unicorn kings, and the only accepted ethos in tech was "move fast and break stuff" and "disrupt": be it laundry or the taxicab industry or helicopters to the Hamptons. Tinder wanted to disrupt sites like match.com and eHarmony and OkCupid, which favored long profiles or "scientifically" backed quizzes to pair you with your ideal date, winnowing the meat market to just a handful of possible romantic partners. Tinder would dump all that, as well as the vague aura of "only desperate people online-date."

"It was just like . . . apparently, this is what people are doing now," Jane (who, like the other Tinder users I interviewed, requested anonymity) explains about her reasoning for signing up in 2013. "I'd tried to do OkCupid. I was on it for a day. I was very overwhelmed by the amount of information you had to give out." She liked that on Tinder she could be "as oblique" as she wanted. "You could put out weird signals and see who fit." On her first profile, she wanted to project a version of herself that was "adventurous and smart and cool." She selected a photo from a Halloween party of herself dressed up as Molly Ringwald. Her bio was short: "Annie Oakley slash Annie Hall," which she thought both revealed her native Californian pride and made her sound like she had sophisticated taste. (At least that's how it read in 2013. She jokes that now the guns and Woody Allen combination would be better suited for Parler.)

She had success in her first years on the app, winding up in more than one long-term-for-Tinder relationship (three or four months) with people who left toothbrushes and met her friends. "But I was also totally manic. I used it obsessively," she says. "I remember a really bad episode where I heard an ex of mine was on it and I would check for hours to try to find him."

That impulse was familiar to me. All the buzzwords that wound up making Tinder seem impersonal and gross later—gamification and geolocation, behavioral science, game theory—were also its greatest advantage in those early days. Suddenly, I had all of the people I would ever want to want on my phone, in my hand. I could now see the entirety of the marketplace of possible partners available to me. I could optimize. I could find an ex and make him realize I was still out there, available, and maybe he'd try to restart things. I could, if I swiped fanatically enough while sitting at the bar around the corner from my crush's apartment, find his profile, swipe right, match, make him realize we were harboring secret feelings for each other. With one weeknight binge, I could shave years off the search for long-term companionship. "It's a numbers game," I learned to say.

Each date proved me to be both incredibly brave and the biggest wimp. Even as I tried to be a game theorist, it was hard not to read genuine possibility into every encounter. "I think I just found the love of my life," I dramatically Gchatted my friend Liz one afternoon during work (did I even work during these years, or did I just use Tinder?). We hadn't exchanged numbers yet, but I was certain he'd be mine, I told her. "Oh, really, how do you know?" Liz, who was not on Tinder, challenged. Well, Liz, because each time I swiped on someone I had decided I liked—really liked—based on some arbitrary mention or photo no. 4 on their profile, and we matched, and they messaged, I'd get a psychic flash of our entire relationship as if it were a rom-com, from the first kiss to dancing together at a friend's wedding. I didn't say that; instead, I told Liz the specifics of him: He was a documentarian and liked pizza. In one photo, he was holding a puppy; in another, he was sitting in a heart-shaped hot tub in a sleazy motel room. He had a lot of chest hair. Love, thy name was Jay.

According to the rest of the chat history, Jay and I did agree to meet. Liz joked she couldn't wait for the wedding so she could print out these Gchats and read them out loud during a speech at the reception. Before the date, I had a preexisting appointment with my usual tarot-card reader. Naturally, I asked where things would go with Jay. "Nowhere. It will go nowhere," she divined.

Over the years, there were so many Jays I cannot count them all. I learned to be buoyant in the face of disappointment. So many of these dates were just people plucked out of a random void and returned to that void after. The memory of their rejection couldn't last if they didn't. Plus there was always another message, another hit, another Jay to distract me. If there were long-term effects from this creeping sensation of disposability, I didn't pay any attention.

Instead, I was like a laboratory: both scientist and experiment, learning what parts of my personality worked on another person. I learned to dress as someone who dated but wasn't obviously on a date: no dresses, minimal makeup, casual shoes, "accidental" cleavage. I could intuit when the conversation had landed on the right frisson point to offer my number and on the inside joke that would carry us from text to in-person meeting. I had a handful of bars I could rely on for lighting that suited me, music that made me seem knowledgeable, and a repartee with the bartender in case the date was bad. I kept mental notes about what worked. I threw out the Madewell jeans I was wearing when the dude excused himself, talked on the phone for an hour, and came back with a halfhearted excuse about an elevator emergency in the building he managed. It was certainly the jeans' fault he was setting up his next date while on our date. Every nonstarter was a chance for self-improvement.

Even as I got used to inventive new ways of rejecting and being rejected (ghosting, pigging, breadcrumbing, slow fading, relationshopping, weaponization of attachment theory), swimming in the murky waters was still fun. This was before profiles showed the scars of too much time on dating apps ("No, I will not follow you on Instagram," "serious relationships only," "please don't catfish me") or boasted "necessary" virtue signaling ("If you voted for Trump swipe on, BLM, ACAB, Anti-capitalist only") or became ads for people's open relationships ("ENM, happily partnered but we play separately").

I began to think about my dates in terms of a cast of characters on a TV show, with cameos by DAN TINDER, SETH HINGE, SAM DECENT DICK, CON-AIR (an annual cross-country connection), and the people who are in my phone only as DO NOT ANSER, DO NOT ANSWER, and DO NOT TEXT, though I can barely remember why they're blacklisted now. There was "That's *sick!*" Guy, who yelled "That's *sick!*" when he came. He had only a one-episode appearance. There was the Tall Teacher, who had enough steam for a multiepisode arc but was too nice and boring to carry a season. The only multiseason story line was Adrian, who, for one year, would message me every few months. In December, he asked, "can I lick your [*redacted*] for breakfast lunch and dinner?" In March, he reached out to let me know we could "[*redacted*] and then we can taste you together." In June, a man of consistency, he returned to declare "I wanna [*bleeped out*] let you [*redacted*] on my [*redacted*] can I try that?" This past fall, I rematched with him and carried out a whole conversation before I realized his requests to perform cunnilingus had an eerily familiar linguistic signature.

Of the dozens of people I've spoken to about their early experiences on Tinder, the ones who successfully found a partner seem to fall into two camps: They're either the annoying people who met their partner on their "first-ever Tinder date" during the first year, or they determinedly and doggedly dated with clinical precision, making dating a second job. A woman named Hannah, who popped into my DMs to share her experience, explained how she developed a "date zero" tactic, meeting for a single drink for one hour to suss out the vibe. After that, she'd take a moment to consider if she actually wanted a real first date. Some apps seem to promise specific outcomes, forcing users to understand what they want out of connections. (Hinge you download if you want to date seriously; Feeld you download if you want to hump respectfully.) Tinder has always promised and attracted chaos. For some, the chaos magically produced a great match, while for others, the chaos was something to manage and tame, dating by quota and Excel spreadsheet or automated bot. The less meticulous or lucky are simply at the mercy of the chaos.

.   .   .

By 2015, studies were regularly popping up about Tinder's effects on brains and hearts and societal well-being—how it was lowering our self-esteem and making us lonelier, how the snap-judgment swiping was enabling racial bias, and how the apps' lack of safety features let people get away with harassment in messages and in person.

At the time, I knew it was doing something to me, but I didn't see the impending dating apocalypse that Nancy Jo Sales wrote about in *Vanity Fair*. The article suggested, for the first time, that Tinder was irrevocably fucking up our ability to date normally. To prove it, she followed a handful of insufferable (weren't we all) twenty-somethings in New York as they navigated Tinder, chronicling how "Fuckboys" and "Tinderellas" (I promise we didn't call anyone that) dated one another and slept with one another. Sales reported how Tinder normalized the psychologically and socially damaging behaviors of hookup culture, where young people devalued sex and themselves in their relentless pursuit of short-term flings. I remember being struck in particular by a guy in the story who was so sick of fucking women, yet off he went, begrudgingly, to fuck another woman he didn't care about just because they'd matched on the app.

TINDER IS TEARING SOCIETY APART, the New York *Post* summarized after the article went viral.

I read it and thought, *If it was really all that dramatic, wouldn't we have stopped using the damn app?* I also worried I'd been confused about sexual capital and sexual freedom. Did I like sex this way, or was I just told to like sex this way? Then I read the story again and realized it was sort of an instruction manual. The reason Tinder wasn't working for me had nothing to do with me, I theorized with friends, and everything to do with the fact that I thought I was using it to find a boyfriend when I should have been using it to fuck, as everyone else was, apparently. And off I went, giving myself full permission to abandon the pursuit of love.

I changed my photo from a smiley me on a baby-pink bike, laughing, to a sullen-faced me, throwing fuck eyes, alone on vacation in Argentina. I changed my bio to "Yeah. Sure. Why not." Should I have worried? Seen this as an indication that I no longer saw love and partnership as a realistic goal? Maybe, but I didn't.

It felt like a natural progression of something that had become an increasingly unnatural feeling. There were people I saw one day a week for weeks in a row whose roommates' names I never learned; that would have been an overassertion of intimacy not matching our actual knowledge of or attachment to each other—everything was built to be disposable and short term. I didn't like it like this. I didn't want intimacy lite, so I decided I might as well cut intimacy out of my diet altogether.

Tinder was now just Seamless for sex. I swiped while traveling. In L.A. for work, I made use of company-subsidized hotel rooms. On vacation, using Tinder's new Passport feature, I had flings with interesting people who also gave me restaurant recommendations. ("Here for a good time, not a long time," my bio said.) I took more chances. I didn't dismiss people for showing up as a green bubble. It didn't matter if they were truly bizarre humans (often better) or if they said ridiculous things to impress me like "Yeah, I rap sometimes"—they weren't people to me anyway. Sometimes the meetups and exchanges ended in sex, and sometimes they didn't, but I felt more in control than I had when I was trying to date for something more.

Sometimes, though, I wondered if my desire was being manufactured. In 2016, then-CEO Rad explained in an interview with *Fast Company* that Tinder matched members based on "desirability" using the same scoring system that ranks chess players: When you've played an advanced player with a high score, you gain more points than if you've played someone with a lower score. On Tinder, then, if you matched with someone hot, you got hotter matches. The marketplace wasn't wide open. Instead, you were given your aesthetically compatible matches and told of the rest, "Don't even bother." In 2019, a post on the company's blog said it had abandoned that algorithm (presumably for something even more exacting). Still, it's impossible not to see myself on an attractiveness scale determined by Tinder and to wonder if what I find attractive is modulated by the matches I am "good enough" for. Do I even like men with mustaches, really, or has this weird social experiment just conditioned me to want to sit on the face of a man who has one?

One night at home in 2015, I sat on my couch, picking a playlist, waiting for a Thor-looking dude who worked in book publishing to arrive. I'd showered, hidden my piles, let my friends know someone was coming over, and sent them a name and a photo just in case I got disappeared. The doorbell rang around ten p.m. He was shorter than I expected, par for the course, but more muscular. If there were things about me that fell short of his expectations, he didn't show it. I turned and led him inside. "I knew you'd have a nice butt," he commented.

I poured us some whiskey because I'd said I was a whiskey girl, even though I am whiskey ambivalent. We made nice small talk. I didn't move him to the bedroom—that was too personal—instead, we had sex on the couch. After, while sitting naked next to each other making more uncertain small talk, he started crying. About a girlfriend he'd broken up with, how they were still living together, about the torture of trying to figure out a modification for the stick and poke she'd given him. I felt resentful that he had brought his emotional needs into my carefree fuckpad. As his tears dried up, so did my horn. "You look sexy in that robe," he sniffled, and began to loosen it, looking for solace in a second round.

I assumed if the apocalypse Nancy Jo Sales predicted ever did arrive, it would feel catastrophic and abrupt and destructive. Instead, I was just weary. Soon after Crying Guy, I deleted the app.

•   •   •

The urge to delete and redownload and delete for me never really feels instigated by one horrible incident. Something can go wrong and I'll double down on swiping, trying to update photos or tweak my bio for better results. Another time, one little snag, a dropped conversation or a match with someone who unmatched me as soon as I messaged "hello ✌️" or getting excited for a date and finding the real-life version smelled overwhelmingly like corn, and I'll groan in disgust and delete my account. Sometimes, after a pleasant run of conversation or a good date that goes nowhere, I am too tired to start again with new banter and new rhythms and new reveals and a new, enticing self.

Amanda also got on the app ten years ago when she first moved to New York. She figures she has been on almost 1,000 dates by now. "I'm a hopeless romantic and also a practical optimist," she explains, almost the ideal psychological profile (other than a sociopath) for someone who remains on Tinder after all these years. When she deleted it at the end of 2015, it wasn't because of one bad date—like, for example, the time she went out with a guy who told her she had "shark Jew eyes." Instead, she had started thinking of Tinder as "derogatory and crass." At thirty-two, she was beginning to ask herself why she hadn't yet had a serious relationship. She wanted to know she could get into one without an app. She met someone, a coworker she'd always felt an attraction for, but wasn't sure she could date until, ironically, she saw him on Tinder. When that relationship ended, she realized she'd missed being able to go out on adventures with new people. Also, she says, "I think I've been so accustomed to meeting people and dating from apps that on the rare occasion when I have been hit on IRL, I get thrown for a loop and end up feeling blindsided and unprepared." She recalls an outing with friends on a loose acquaintance kept hinting they should hang out. "I told him, 'We're hanging out right now?'" She couldn't recognize, in this context of real life, that he was pursuing her. She got back on Tinder.

That was in 2017, the same year I returned, in my case because Tinder seemed like a way to wean myself off an expensive Candy Crush habit; after all, it lit up the same pleasure centers of my brain. Also, a relationship I'd wanted to work out hadn't, and it felt like there was nowhere else to turn. When you come back to the app, it's like saging the room. Everyone you swiped right on and didn't match with and everyone you swiped left on and everyone that unmatched you must consider you again.

Almost immediately, that winter, I started dating (for three weeks! Which was only four dates) a Norwegian artist. He was a ginger and vegan, kind and alert. He had a strong nose and had once been arrested in Oslo for tagging a building. He told me about the prison sauna, and we had a whole debacle with a clam pie at Speedy Romeo that could have mortified me, but instead we laughed hysterically about it. I was in. But when I sent him a photo of me and a friend enjoying one-dollar Long Island iced teas and a mountain of mozz sticks at Applebee's, he ended things by simply never responding. I was bothered, but it's still my reference point for "using the app correctly": meeting someone interesting I never would have met; having good conversation and fun sex with them; walking away with fond feelings, a few good stories, and most of my sanity intact.

The years since then are a blur of swiping and matching and talking and stopping and then deleting and downloading and seeing Jared, forty, on Tinder every time I do and feeling sad that he's probably stuck on the same emotional roller coaster I am, but I won't swipe right because he likes Crossfit. In the liminal spaces between people of interest, I do wonder if the app has exacerbated certain aspects of my personality, made it easier to be nasty or avoidant or careless or clingy or overstimulated and flaky. If I had never downloaded the app, would I still be single?

.   .   .

Early in the pandemic, I would take walks in Fort Greene Park. Usually, if I was walking up to the monument at the center of the park, I would skip the path Frederick Law Olmstead had designed a century ago and instead walk up a grassy hill where dogs play during off-leash hours because it was faster and less difficult. Many people did the same thing, so many that the grass was trampled and refused to grow back. Urban planners call these "desire paths," well-worn ribbons of foot traffic in the terrain that are "a consequence of the usage of the shortest route to a destination." In the pandemic, though, there was time to reengage with things we had been rushing through. I stopped taking the shortcut.

In the face of acute loneliness becoming a terminal condition, my dating-app ennui miraculously lifted. On March 29, about two weeks after New York shut down, there were 3 billion swipes on Tinder. People were willing to treat people like, well, people, because all of a sudden we were without them. Our assessments of matches changed. We could go slower, be more selective. We had to. We reverted to what was rebranded by *Time* as "intentional dating." A different kind of intimacy emerged. There were stories of phone conversations and video dates before meeting in person and chaste meetings in the park and slow courtship and rapid moving in together and soul mates. There was a realization that we didn't have to use Tinder the way we had been using it. We could improve it.

April 2020: I was staying in my mother's house, surrounded by personal artifacts of "simpler times" (a flip-phone graveyard, an empty Magic Wand box) in my childhood bedroom, when I got a message from PJ, thirty-nine, back in Brooklyn. There was a red flag: He didn't have a bio (mine was "Can someone tell me what day it is? To which he responded, "Wednesday." It was Friday). He had just emerged from a ten-year relationship and was brand new to the apps, but he was chatty and quick-witted, and we talked every day for months before we met. I learned his taste in music (Gen-X white-guy rock), and he watched movies I recommended. He hated pop culture but liked when I talked about it. He could make plants grow, and I lamented the fact that I killed every plant I purchased. For the first time in a long time, I wanted someone in a way that felt organic and not calculated and Tinder-y. Because I'd taken the slow loop, it felt like I really got to know him, so by the time we did have sex, one afternoon, when he showed up at my door holding the thoughtful gift of a murderproof plant, it was next-level spiritual soul-mate shit.

Given the outcome of most pandemic pastimes (did anybody keep up those sourdough-baking and Lego-building hobbies?), it should not surprise anyone when I say PJ was less next-level spiritual soul mate and more shit. In fact, he was married with two children and using Tinder to cheat. And that November, when it all came to a head, in my devastation, I reverted to using Tinder the way I knew how. Seamlessing a man: a librarian with a big dick who Rollerbladed to my house just when I needed the emotional distraction and left exactly when I needed him to.

"I don't think it's Tinder's fault that I'm still single," Amanda said over the phone, suddenly making me aware of the fact that I do. Amanda was getting ready for a date as we spoke. She was hopeful, excited even, but realistic. She has a lot of great first dates, she says, then she's disappointed on the second one, and she knows it really takes her about five dates to determine if she likes someone.

I wonder, listening to Amanda, if perhaps I'm again defining success and failure on Tinder incorrectly. I had been using Tinder for things that occur only sporadically and chaotically—relationships, good sex, adventure. What Tinder is good at, what it seems designed to do, is make me much better at being single.

If I find myself alone on a Saturday when I don't want to be, Tinder's marketplace offers an ambient comfort that I can find a way out of specific loneliness and into a drink. And because the people I meet are strangers with very little connection to my actual life, I can compartmentalize my dating instead of letting it pervade parts of my life that bring me the most satisfaction: if I go to a party, I'm not overly concerned whether there will be a single person there (so annoying); I travel alone; I'm not always badgering people for setups. Friends never see even a screenshot of someone I'm going on a date with anymore. I live my life; I go on dates. One doesn't really affect the other. If I think about Tinder in these terms, I've conquered it, even if it's not in the way I expected.

Not to say I can't still be thrown off course when it goes awry, like last summer, when I was temporarily living in the Catskills. I went on a date with a British actor named Alex. The date was great;

he saved me from a skunk. And after we parted ways, he immediately messaged me to say he regretted not asking me to come have a beer back at his house. By the time I got home, there were several messages asking for a second date. We confirmed a day, the day came, and surprise! He canceled. "Maybe COVID," he said and left me to wonder if he was lying and why. The highs, I suppose, have gotten flatter, but it's harder to sustain the lows. For days, I Googled "Skunk good omen bad omen," again looking for some sort of supernatural explanation for this very earthly rejection.

Even my therapist was confused by this one. She made me tell the story again. I went through it all woefully, a thorough autopsy of a dead hope. And then she suggested, "He was an actor, right? Maybe he was rehearsing? For a part? Of a person in love?"

I was haunted by that, but I am guilty of it too. According to a study called "Swiping for Love," it's maybe a necessary tactic, not just one man's psychopathy. The study investigated whether it was possible to incorporate traditional ideas of love into modern modes of dating, specifically Tinder. Subject after subject reported that they were on Tinder to find someone to love and to love them back and defined love in the most traditional of terms: something that took work, a container in which sex was sacred and where intimacy built over time. They acknowledged that their encounters on Tinder didn't offer that, yet they went to Tinder to find it. The contradiction was confusing: They wanted sex to be meaningful but felt that Tinder removed the sacredness. They wanted bonds to be lasting but acknowledged they were easily broken. To make sense of the contradictions that disturbed them, the subjects insisted upon a bifurcation of the self. There was the person who was seeking love and the person who was on Tinder. To protect the part of ourselves that feels enough hope to keep us on Tinder forever, we've split in two.

Recently, I went on an early-evening date, and after two beers, I decided, *You'll do.* We made plans to meet again, and I continued on with my night and met friends at a bar where people actually danced with one another. I reported to everyone: "The date was good! He spoke five languages and had a great beard and seemed to like me!" All of my friends, who are married or in serious relationships, looked relieved. "Oh, good," they said. "You normally don't sound this excited about a person." Then I got caught talking to a friend of a friend—this scumbaggy guy with a tiny little mullet and a tiny little earring. Unfortunately, against reason, I realized I wanted to fuck him so badly I let him explain the nuances of American Sign Language to me (he does not know ASL). It was worth it for the moment he leaned in so close to my ear he bonked his nose on my temple and I had a full body reaction.

I talked about it for days, the nose bonk. This, I told my friend, was what was missing from Tinder dates. Tinder was robbing me of pheromone, it was messing with my ability to feel my horniness and follow it wherever. Yes, steady, tidy, prearranged encounters were helpful, but this was attraction, so feral and potentially life-ruining I didn't know what to do with it anymore, so I did nothing at all. Instead, the next day, I reached out to You'll Do guy, who ghosted me before date two.

Stranger's Guide

FINALIST—COLUMNS
AND ESSAYS

"*The average New Orleans reveler may never have an experience like the one Courtney Desiree Morris had at 'Acid Church,'*" reads the judges' citation for this article from Stranger's Guide. "*Through the lens of a single drug-filled night, 'Acid Church' explores the unique alchemy of the Crescent City. Morris's prose takes the reader on a deeply emotional journey through a 'wild, wounded, fucked-up, magical place.'*" Morris is an associate professor of gender and women's studies at the University of California, Berkeley; her book To Defend This Sunrise: Black Women's Activism and the Authoritarian Turn in Nicaragua *was published this year by Rutgers University Press. She is also a visual and conceptual artist. Founded in 2018,* Stranger's Guide *received three National Magazine Award nominations this year and won the award for General Excellence in both 2021 and 2022.*

Courtney Desiree Morris

Acid Church

I t is really easy to fall in love with New Orleans. Especially when you are on drugs.

Ask me how I know.

"I wouldn't be alive if it weren't for acid. Acid saved my life."

Alli Logout is a bona fide rockstar. A café con leche, butterscotch woman—down South, we'd call them a yellow bone—with a blonde Afro that floats around their head like a golden cloud. They are the ferocious frontperson of a rock group called Special Interest. The first time I saw them perform at the WITCHES party during Mardi Gras weekend, they roared through the crowd on a motorcycle wearing nothing but combat boots, a black thong, fishnets, a black bikini top and topped with a black feather cape and a Pocahontas wig. Then they climbed onstage and roared into the microphone, "Sodomy and LSD!"

That's how you start a night in New Orleans off right.

·   ·   ·

We are standing in a backyard smoking cigarettes at a house party somewhere between the Seventh Ward and Bayou St. John. The party is winding down. The early morning air feels cool and good on my skin. Emotionally, I feel empty.

It's been a hard night. It's been a hard day. A day that started 200 miles away from New Orleans in Lake Charles, Louisiana, at my grandmother's house.

When I come into her bedroom that morning, she is already awake, propped up on a bunch of pillows watching some evangelical preacher on the Trinity Broadcasting Network and humming gospel songs to herself. I walk over to her bed, plant a kiss on her forehead and pull up a chair next to her.

"Good morning, Miss Bobbie. How you feeling?"

"Pretty good, baby. My arm's a little bit sore this morning, but you know I'm feeling pretty good."

Now that I am closer, I catch the faint odor of urine wafting up from the sheets, and I wince. I don't like the idea of my grandmother stuck in bed sitting in her own piss.

"Hey Mamma, you ready to take a shower?"

"Yeah baby, that sounds good."

"Alright then, honey, let's get you out of these dirty clothes."

I get up and slide my right arm behind her back; once she is upright, I slide her gently to the edge of the bed until her tiny feet are grazing the floor. Then I slide my arm behind her once more as she leans back so I can pull off the adult diaper she wears to bed each night. It is soaked with urine.

"This thing ain't chafing you, Mamma?"

"No, baby, I'm fine."

She's being polite, but she's lying. Nothing chafes the skin worse than piss. I used to get annoyed at these omissions, but I know that she doesn't like us to worry or to seem needier than she actually is. Even now as she is dying, she is terrible at asking for help. I sigh. We are alike in so many ways.

I prop her back up, then turn around to grab the metal walker tucked away next to her dresser. As I do this, I catch a glimpse of her in the mirror. She looks vulnerable and awkward sitting naked on the bed. I hurry back and place the walker in front of her. She grabs the handles and pulls herself forward. As she shifts her weight from the bed to the walker, she begins to pant as she struggles to find her balance.

"You good, Mamma?"

"Yeah, baby. I'm good."

She leans forward and begins to waddle towards her bedroom door. I position myself behind her just in case she begins to look too wobbly. I can feel her shivering as we walk the short distance down the hall to the bathroom. My uncle has already turned on the portable heater in the bathroom. I begin to sweat immediately when we step inside, but my grandmother continues to shiver. She complains about being cold all the time since she started the chemotherapy treatments.

She parks the walker up against the side of the sink while I turn on the hot water in the tub. Then we begin the awkward dance of maneuvering her into the bathtub. The narrow bathroom is not designed to accommodate an elderly, overweight, ill woman and an adult granddaughter trying to bathe her. I pull the detachable showerhead from its cradle. As the warm water pours out of the shower head I move it over my grandmother's body, watching the water stream down over her shoulders, her wide breasts, sliding into the folds of her back and stomach, down her thighs and calves. Her body reminds me of the Venus of Willendorf. I linger over her neck, shoulders, and back 'cause I know she likes that, and she sighs quietly.

"Girl, that hot water feels good."

"Yeah, I bet it does, Miss Bobbie," I say and we both laugh.

In the beginning, she is still strong enough to soap up her own washcloth and scrub her upper body. By the end, when she is too weak to lift her arms, I take the rag and scrub her down like a baby, pulling the soapy rag around her neck, washing her armpits. The easy part finished, I turn my attention to her genitalia.

"Alright, Mamma. I gotta get in there and clean out your pocketbook." At this, her face breaks into a toothless cackle.

In the beginning, I knew she was embarrassed having her grown granddaughter wiping her ass and soaping up her private privates. But I learned that if I breezed through it like it was no different from cleaning her armpits, then she would feel less embarrassed— and honestly, after the first two or three times, it really started to feel just like that. She leans back and spreads her legs, and I go to work, wiping between the folds and making sure she smells clean and fresh. After I rinse her off, she rolls her body to the side, exposing her bottom. She holds one cheek up while I scrub her behind vigorously until I am satisfied that she is clean.

"Alright, sugar. We done with that."

I towel her off, help her out of the tub and get her back to her room. I powder her down, put on a fresh diaper, slide a pair of stretchy cotton sweatpants onto her and help her push her arms through a soft gray sweatshirt.

When she is dressed, she takes her walker and slowly makes her way to the living room. I follow her with a jar of Miracle Gro hair grease, a comb and a brush. Once she is settled, I slide myself between the recliner and the wall and gently begin parting her thick, gray hair with the comb. Even with the chemo, Bobbie got a full head of beautiful wavy hair. I cut pathways through her hair with the widetooth comb and then grease each row. She doesn't need much product—her hair lies down with just a little bit of grease and water. After I wet her hair, I take that brush and pull it through and over her hair until it shines like polished silver. Once it's smooth to the touch, I take her hair and twist it into a simple bun on top of her head and then secure it with a few bobby pins. I reach into my pocket and fish out some gray pearl earrings I bought at Wal-Mart for her. I place these in her ears and step back to admire my handiwork. She looks so good I can't keep it to myself.

"Damn, Bobbie, you still got it."

She laughs, smiles at me, blushes and then waves me away like she's shooing away a foolish young suitor.

"Go on now, girl!"

•   •   •

Ostensibly, I am in Louisiana to do research on environmental racism and my family's displacement from Mossville, a small, historic freedmen's community just north of Lake Charles. At least, that is what I told the Ford Foundation when they awarded me a fellowship to pursue the project. I spend entire days poring over old documents in the Frazar Archives at McNeese University, flipping through ancient, dusty ledgers of property records in the Calcasieu Parish Clerk of Court tracking the history of black land ownership and dispossession and interviewing my relatives and the small diaspora of former Mossville residents scattered across east Texas and southwest Louisiana. Southwest Louisiana is a forgotten pit stop on Cancer Alley, a marshy petrochemical landscape of oil refineries and natural gas processing plants.

As a kid, I always knew we had arrived when I saw the clusters of pine trees along I-10 and could taste the metallic, toxic air. Now, nearly thirty years later, I drive through the region and try to imagine what Black social life might have been like in this place before the arrival of the refineries more than eighty years ago. Or 200 years ago, when indigenous Atakapa peoples maintained their small, migratory settlements along the shores of Prien Lake before first the Spanish and then the French and then the British and white American settlers arrived and decimated their communities with disease, Christianity, and alcohol. I go to Mossville to remember a history I do not fully know.

Mossville is a small place: an unincorporated town located just north of the industrial Port of Lake Charles in southwest Louisiana. Varying accounts of the town's early formation suggest it was founded as early as the 1790s, potentially making it one of the oldest free Black communities in the South. The town flourished during Reconstruction as a safe haven for recently freed Blacks looking to escape the racial terror of the emergent Jim Crow social order. But since the 1930s, the community has been home to a cluster of petrochemical plants whose operations have irreversibly contaminated its air, soil, and water. Fourteen petrochemical companies currently surround Mossville, including an oil refinery, a coal-fired power plant, several vinyl manufacturers, and a chemical plant in a town that is approximately five square miles in area. In the 1940s, southwest Louisiana became a critical site in the international petrochemical industry. Today, its proximity to natural gas and oil fields in Texas and northern Louisiana as well as the Port of Lake Charles and the Gulf of Mexico, about thirty miles away, make the region a strategic location for the industry. The petrochemical industry drives the state's economy; in 2019, it generated $73 billion of the state GDP and supported 249,800 associated jobs. But that wealth has come at a high cost, one that has been disproportionately borne by the people of Mossville.

In 2011, then-governor Bobby Jindal announced that Sasol, a South African multinational petrochemical corporation, would begin construction of an ethane cracker complex that extended farther into the town than any of the plants in the area—actually, right across the street from the cemetery where my grandmother is now buried along with all her people. The ethane cracker facility breaks down natural gas into smaller molecules that are used to make ethylene, a chemical product used in a variety of everyday consumer products including cosmetics, detergents, adhesives, packaging materials and plastics used in laptops, cell phones, IV drip bags, and faux leather vehicle interiors. Following the announcement of the expansion, Sasol launched a voluntary buyout program that left only sixty-two residents in the community.

But aside from the research, the truth is that I am really in Lake Charles to see my grandmother. Barbara Jean Freeman has a lot of names. Her husband and her sisters called her Bobbie. Her neighbors called her Mrs. Freeman. Her children called her Madear. Her grandchildren and great-grandchildren called her Mamma, in a slight Anglicization of the French, maman. She was born in 1933 in the town of Westlake, just east of Mossville. Her father was from Westlake but her mother's people, the Williams family, lived in Mossville and were among the founding families. She was a small child when the first plant, the Cities Services Corporation oil refinery, opened. She died in 2019, three years after the Sasol buyout.

In the summer of 2014, I was driving with my husband as we made a cross-country move from Houston, Texas, to State College, Pennsylvania, when my grandmother called. The news was not good. She had been diagnosed with colon cancer, which quickly spread to first one lung and then the other. The cancer was tough, but Bobbie was tougher. When I saw her a few months later and asked her how she was feeling, she was defiant and unequivocal: "I'm gonna kick this cancer in the ass." She proceeded to do just that. But by the time her cancer came back a few years later, things were different. It didn't take long to notice how tired she was, how slowly she moved. I began to understand. This time, the cancer was going to kick her ass, and it wasn't going to be pretty.

So I began going home to my grandmother and Lake Charles and Mossville as often as I could. Each time I came, I sat with my grandmother and asked her about her life: about growing up in Mossville, the arrival of the plants, her memories of life under Jim Crow, stories about her ancestors. At first, she was self-conscious about the camera recording her every word. But then she became used to it and started dropping dimes.

So I was not altogether surprised when I arrived in Lake Charles in October 2018 and she told me that her doctor had delivered more bad news: the latest round of chemotherapy had not yielded any results. Her cancer was terminal. When he asked her if she wanted to try another round of chemotherapy, she was as resolved as she had been four years earlier. "Why spend money when it's not doing any good? So let's just sit this out and do nothing."

As she speaks, I listen quietly, hearing everything she isn't saying. My people are deeply religious. My grandmother reads her Bible every morning, talks to God every day. She reminds me that Hebrews 9:27 says, "It is appointed unto men once to die, but after this the judgment." My grandmother is dying. Her speech is deliberate and certain. There is no fear. She is at peace and ready to face her Maker. My heart sits like a brick in my chest, and as she speaks, I feel a small knot tighten in my throat. The weight of her pending death feels like more than I can bear. I had planned to go to New Orleans the following day. Now, I am unsure if I should leave her. She is nonplussed. "No, baby. Go and see your friend. Have a good time. I'm not leaving yet." She smiles. "I will see you when you get back."

• • •

I make the drive from Lake Charles to New Orleans in a daze. I keep thinking about Mamma and the cancer tearing through her body. On the radio, a journalist on NPR is reporting that a lone gunman entered the Tree of Life synagogue in Pittsburgh, killing eleven people and wounding six others. They report several Holocaust survivors among the victims. My jaw clenches with rage and grief. Those folks survived Hitler but couldn't survive America.

The bad news continues to pour in. Ntozake Shange, the Black feminist writer and author of *for colored girls who have considered suicide when the rainbow is enuf*, is dead.

By the time I reach New Orleans, I am exhausted with grief. I don't know what to do with myself. So I check my phone and text my friend, Alix.

"Just made it to NO. What we doing tonight?" He writes back fifteen minutes later, "Anything we want!"

I'm down.

There's a house party happening, he says. It's going to be a queer POC vibe, should be cute. Dancing sounds like a godsend right now. He sends me the address, and we make plans to meet up. I don't know exactly what kind of evening I'm getting into, but with Alix—my black Adonis, good looking in the kind of way that makes people stop and stare at him on the street—in the mix, it will most certainly involve any number of mind-altering substances.

I arrive in front of a nondescript, white, double shotgun house. Before I step out of the car, I can hear the music pulsing from inside. I make my way along the side of the house to the backyard and find Alix there. "You made it," he shouts before scooping me up in his arms and covering me in kisses.

"I just got some molly. Want some?"

Without blinking, I say, "Yes." He gives me a tiny capsule and a beer to wash it down with. After I swallow everything, he claps, takes my hand, and we walk into the house like Hansel and Gretel.

The living room has been cleared out for a makeshift dance floor. I got a thing for DJs and musicians, and this one—a cute, extra thick, genderqueer, indigenous Hawaiian covered in tattoos—is working the turntable like a licensed massage therapist. The molly starts to hit, and I feel my body open up and begin to vibrate with the bass pulsating through the speakers. Suddenly, the

DJ drops the beat, and the strains of Fleetwood Mac's "Everywhere" fill the dance floor. *Can you hear me calling / Out your name? / You know I'm falling / And I don't know what to say / I'll speak a little louder / I'll even shout / You know that I am proud / And I can't get the words out.*

My heart is beating in time with the song, and before I know it, I am rocking and bouncing on the balls of my feet and singing, "Oh I, I want to be with you everywhere." I spin and see Alix dancing alongside me out of the corner of my eye. People flock to the dance floor, and soon, I am enveloped in a crush of vibrating flesh. The molly is pulsing through me in waves, and I can feel the heat of the high spreading from my scalp down my back through my arms and into my feet. I realize the feeling is joy.

Suddenly, I feel sick. I rush to the bathroom. I barely have the door closed before I feel my stomach heave, and suddenly, I am on my knees retching into the toilet. I vomit over and over. I feel as though I am hacking up all the sorrow living in my body. As I puke, I wonder if I am dying. I am sad for a moment. Alix will have to tell my husband; I know it will hurt him to learn that I am dead. But I am not dying. Instead, I vomit until I am exhausted and sitting breathless on the floor. I have no idea how long I sat there. Eventually, I pull myself up to the sink, rinse out my mouth, and stare at myself for a long time in the mirror.

When I finally stumble out of the bathroom, I look around and then plop down onto the nearest couch I can find. My body feels empty and clean. I am out of my head entirely, descending into myself as the molly reverberates in my body. It takes me a minute to come back up for air. When I do, I realize that two women are fucking next to me. I hadn't noticed them, and they don't seem to mind that I am there. I feel strangely better. Like now the molly can finally do its work.

I return to the dance floor and dance for the DJ for what feels like hours. I roll my hips like the Mississippi, joints loose and easy, feeling light and free. I cannot remember the last time I felt this way. That makes me sad. I accept this insight and let it go as quickly as it comes. I am here in my body right now, and I am dancing like a bad bitch. The beat drops into a smooth bassline as I sweat the grief out. I dance for my grandmother. I dance for the elders in the synagogue. I dance for Ntozake. I dance for all the Black women I know dying from cancer and strokes and stress and sadness. I dance and dance and dance and laugh and celebrate and feel my aliveness.

Later when I give the DJ, whose name—appropriately—is Heavy Pleasure, my gratitude for their set, they say, "I know. I was spinning for you."

This isn't my first time in New Orleans. I've come to New Orleans a handful of times over the past decade, usually for academic or activist conferences. Even though I am an anthropologist and I know better, I have moved through the city like a fucking tourist. I eat the beignets at Café du Monde and delicious fried chicken at Dooky Chase's, admire the art at the Sydney and Walda Besthoff Sculpture Garden in City Park, spend a few nights bar hopping on Frenchman Street. I do the things you are expected to do in New Orleans. But I haven't really connected to the soul of the city. Tonight, however, feels different.

It's late, and the party is winding down. Alix and I head out to the backyard. Most of the revelers have already left, and we are down to the party faithful. Alix introduces his friends: Juicebox, a stunning Black femme who reminds me a bit of Grace Jones and is elegantly dressed in a full length ball gown and bridal veil; Choux, a sweet and quietly hilarious day laborer, who shyly welcomes me to the group; and his partner, Pi, a stunning mixed-race Chamoru sex worker wearing an enormous curly wig and holding court like a bored monarch. I finally meet the DJ who saved my life: Kahelelani, AKA DJ Heavy Pleasure. And then there is Alli. They remind me of my beautiful, silver grandmother who is dying, and suddenly, I feel homesick and sad.

Alix comes and snuggles next to me. We can feel each other's pain from miles away, and in the moment, I feel more grateful for him than I ever have before.

Someone announces that they've got acid. Alix turns to me and says, "You want to take acid with me?" The molly is wearing off in a clean, steady burn, and I am feeling relaxed and safe. Also, I am not quite ready for the night to end and am dreading going home to be alone with my feelings. We smile at each other as we swallow our tabs.

I am not sure when the acid starts to kick in, but I am suddenly having three conversations at once, not including the one that I am simultaneously having with myself. I am holding Kahelelani's tiny dog, Maka, in my arms, and he licks my nose and sniffs at my hair. Alix is whispering something in my ear as Choux lights my cigarette, and I smoke and listen and laugh at everything and feel myself quietly expand.

I find that I am telling Alli about my grandmother. I don't mean to—it just comes pouring out. They are quiet and listen thoughtfully. When they respond, they are gentle and sympathetic.

"When I'm sad, acid helps a lot." I lift an eyebrow. "I'm serious! Acid is the best thing that has ever happened to me." They'd been in a bad relationship that left them feeling raw and stripped. "I didn't want to live," they say. "The acid pulled me back from the edge and made me want to hold onto life. That's when I knew that acid is medicine. That's why they don't want anyone to have it." Everyone chimes in, sharing their own acid deliverance stories. They all agree: acid, like a good DJ, can save your life.

Pi says, "That's why everyone needs to make a trip to Acid Church at least once in their lives."

Alix turns to me and asks: You wanna come to Acid Church?

I don't know what that means at all, but I love it, and without blinking, I say, "Yes, I do."

And then the night really begins.

In a stroke of serendipity, Pi has a car that she borrowed from a friend. When she pulls up in front of the house, we pile into the SUV like the Brady Bunch. And we are off.

I feel warm and safe in the back seat, snuggled between Alix and Kahelelani and Maka. Alix puts a bounce track on, and the whole car feels as though it is rocking as we dance inside. When Pi stops at a traffic light, Alix jumps out and begins twerking on the hood of the car, in the crosswalk, in the lane next to us. He jumps back in the car just as the light turns green—this ain't his first time stopping traffic like this.

We careen through the streets, flying down the city's wide boulevards, the truck soaring like a spaceship. Suddenly, we hit a massive pothole that sends the truck's nose up into the air before crashing back on the surface so hard that it blows out the headlights. Pi slams on the brakes, and the group swings into action. Every single last one of us is riding dirty, and driving through New Orleans at four in the morning with no headlights is a no-go. Pi pops the hood, and she and Alli begin inspecting the engine to see what is going on. Minutes pass in tense silence. It might be the end of the evening if we can't get these fucking lights back on.

Alix: "Maybe try turning the car off and then on again?"

It works on computers, we reason. Why not? Pi shuts off the car and then cranks it back up. Miraculously, it works. Alix shouts, "CTRL + Alt + Delete!" We roar our approval, and the trip to the Acid Church continues.

Choux is fiddling with his phone and asks everyone and no one in particular, "What ya'll want to listen to?" I don't remember who recommends Fiona Apple, but it's the perfect choice because she's a funky white girl like Joni Mitchell, and I like that bitch. We settle on "Criminal," and suddenly everyone is singing along:

I done wrong
And I wanna suffer for my sins
I come to you
Cause I need guidance to be true
And I just don't know
Where I should begin

The entire group pauses dramatically along with Fiona before launching into the chorus:

What I need
Is a good defense
'cause I'm feeling

Like a criminal
And I need to redeemed
To the one I sinned against
Because he's all
I ever knew of love.

The city feels empty and peaceful as we barrel down St. Claude's
Avenue past the Bywater towards Pi's house. When we cross over
the canal into the Lower Ninth Ward, the sun comes up, breaking
through the clouds with a brightness that I have never seen in my
life and expect never to experience again. The clouds are fat and
lush, tinged with a pink and orange glow that looks so warm that
my cheeks feel hot. The acid is hitting me hard now, and I feel like
weeping and laughing and dancing and fucking and kissing and
twirling, and I feel a happiness that I have never known before. I've
never seen a sunrise so bright. I've never felt this much joy rushing through every cell in my body. I feel as though my whole life
before this moment has been muted shades of gray, and suddenly,
my heart, my ears, my soul is flooded with technicolor. Acid is saving my life. I want to scream this epiphany at the top of my lungs.
But instead I just sing.

I am falling in love with this queer tribe of brilliant freaks. I
know it in real time. Singing in the warmth of the car, driving
into the sunrise, they feel like the family I have always longed for,
full of wounded, beautiful survivors who wear their scars proudly
like the city. Smart and tough like New Orleans, they alchemize
their trauma into art, music, and dance parties, those sacred safe
spaces big enough to hold all kinds of folks in their arms, including a lost little colored girl like me. That night, I felt held in a way
that is hard to explain—it is like the old folks say: "Better felt
than telt."

· · ·

Pi is an elegant hostess. She offers us tea, coffee, a light breakfast,
cuts neat lines of coke onto a mirror on a rickety coffee table. When

she says make yourself comfortable, I know that she means it. This is the Acid Church.

I walk outside and sit in the garden. The grass is an otherworldly shade of green so vibrant it glows.

I hold this feeling of aliveness in my chest, look at my skin as it vibrates. It occurs to me that there is a lesson here. My grandmother is dying; in fact, one day, everyone I love will die. So will I. But today I am alive. She is dying, but I must live. I close my eyes and think of Mamma's tired body, which I know almost as well as I know my own body. When she is gone, I will hold the feeling of her flesh in my hands forever. In accompanying her to the end, she is teaching me how to live—and how to die. I do not try to wipe away my tears as they fall to the ground. I am alive.

The rest of the group finds me there. Pi brings me a cup of coffee. We spend the rest of the morning lounging on Pi's trampoline in her backyard. When Alix strips down to his underwear to enjoy the warmth of the rising sun, it suddenly strikes me as a brilliant idea, and I take off my top. The sun feels good on my skin. I snuggle with Maka, who is wrapped up with Kahelelani in a warm quilt. Pi takes a drag of a cigarette, offers it to me. I thank her, take a quick puff, hand it back. Already I feel that we are sisters and will be for a long time. We talk about everything and nothing. We talk about our families, where we grew up, where we come from. We debate the merits and mechanics of trying to have sex on a trampoline. We inquire about each other's astrological signs. Pi, obviously, is a Pisces, but with her sexy ass, you'd swear she's a Scorpio. We talk about music. We talk about art. We talk about drugs. When the conversation stops, it feels natural, as though we are all collectively exhaling while the sun works on our bodies. We all breathe quietly, slowly. Watch the sun climb into the sky. There is nowhere else to be. We hold the moment in silence and gratitude. It feels good to be alive this morning.

The day slowly resumes its natural pace. Pi and Choux climb off the trampoline and migrate inside to finally go to bed. Housemates are waking up. Alix needs to catch a flight, and Kahelelani needs to get Maka home and get ready for work.

On the ride home, I glide down Esplanade Avenue up to the I-10 and take the on-ramp. I rise above the city as downtown comes into view. The disk of the Superdome shines in the sunlight. Behind it sits the old Charity Hospital, abandoned in the triumph of post-Katrina disaster capitalism. On either side of the freeway, I can look down and see the city streets lined with oak trees draped in Spanish moss and edged by stately old wood frame houses that resemble cakes with their pastel shades, intricate latticework, and ornate embellishments. I look at the city, place my hand over my mouth, and feel something like wonder swelling and aching in my chest.

I look over the city from the highway, see the Mississippi snaking along its shoreline and I realize that I love this wild, wounded, fucked-up, magical city.

I have never felt as free as I do when I am in New Orleans. I think it's the freest city in the United States of America. And my people know something about freedom. What it means to make your own freedom, to lay claim to the land, and to try to make a place for yourself that you can call your own. Watching Mossville die taught me that not all freedom dreams survive. Sometimes, the powerful show up and crush them. But freedom is not found in buildings or monuments but in the love that we share for each other, for the land. Freedom is found in the insistence that we live and live and live, even when everything around us feels as though it is dying. But we cannot live until we grieve and honor what we have lost. I went to Louisiana to mourn the death of everything that I love in Mossville. My tears led me to New Orleans, and the city and her wild children have held me ever since.

They say that if you love New Orleans, she will love you back. NOLA drives me crazy. When I am away, she is all I think about, and when I'm there, I spend all my time just rolling in her hair.

New York Review of Books

In this article, Namwali Serpell examines the figure of the Whore, from the Old Testament to the latest movies. But don't worry—" 'She's Capital!' " won't remind you of the last time you took a course in world literature. Instead, as the National Magazine Award judges said, "Serpell's essay leaps from literature to social media, exploring the busy interplay of sex, money, gender, and race while celebrating the Twitterverse phenomenon of A'Ziah 'Zola' King." Serpell is a Zambian writer and professor of English at Harvard University. Her books include Seven Modes of Uncertainty *and* Stranger Faces *and two novels,* The Old Drift *and* The Furrows. *Founded in 1963, the* New York Review of Books *is widely regarded as one of the most important literary magazines in the United States. The National Magazine Award for " 'She's Capital!' " was the magazine's first.*

Namwali Serpell

"She's Capital!"

When we meet her in Revelations 17, "the great whore" whose name is "Mystery, Babylon the Great, the Mother of Harlots and Abominations of the Earth," she's dressed to kill. "Arrayed in purple and scarlet color, and decked with gold and precious stones and pearls," she holds "a golden cup in her hand full of . . . the filthiness of her fornication," and rides "a scarlet-colored beast" with "seven heads and ten horns." She is "that great city, which reigneth over the kings of the earth"; the waters on which she sits are "peoples, and multitudes, and nations, and tongues."

Here is one of our earliest icons of whoredom: draped in luxury, crusted with opulence, drunk on the filth brimming from her cup, balanced uneasily upon those whom she's conquered—those who, we are told, will in turn hate, abandon, consume, and set her ablaze. Though she is described and named at elaborate length, the Whore of Babylon is silent.

The figure of the Whore teeters between a position of power and a condition of abjection. We find this ambivalence in her etymology: the word *whore* may come from a root meaning "one who desires" or another meaning "sin, filth"; there's still uncertainty in our diction today about whether a *ho* has sex for pleasure, for money, or for the pleasure of money. There also lurks a suspicion that the Whore *likes* her job, making her a rare example of the unalienated worker.

Perhaps for this reason, her relationship to capital remains murky. Is she a canny producer or a rapacious consumer? A thing to be used or an experience to be exchanged? A fetishized commodity or a figure for capitalism itself? "Prostitution is only the *specific* expression of the *general* prostitution of the labourer," Marx writes. Elsewhere, with a nod to Shakespeare, he describes money as "the common whore, the common pimp of peoples and nations." *Is* she common? What is the Whore's class position? She is traditionally the lowest in society but can be catapulted to the top in an instant. She still magnetizes resentment and desire from everyone.

Yes, feminist analysis has had a lot to say about the endless whorification of women, the relentless misogyny that reduces us to objects, instruments, things to be used. And we've seen political movements over the centuries to abolish prostitution, make it safer, decriminalize it, unionize it, obviate it. But the Whore herself is still neglected as a political actor. Wherever she appears, she's pressed into service as a rhetorical or symbolic conceit.

It is this insistent mediation of whoredom that interests me, the way she seems always to be a medium *between* things or *for* something else. The historian Herodotus, in the fifth century BCE, claimed that the first prostitutes lived in "houses of heaven" along the Tigris and Euphrates, where they sold their bodies as a fertility rite, a holy marriage, or a sex ritual—whatever the case, as a channel to the divine. In the secular imagination, too, she's the means through which others attain ecstasy, apostasy, luxury, sublimity, infamy, reality.

The Whore is betwixt: an intermediary in intercourse, within the madding crowd, among worldly goods. She's capital ("She's capital!"), the golden idol, mammon's gal, the classic blonde with a heart of gold, the golden mean—the proportional ideal, the perfect fuck, the "means" meaning the money.

And curiously enough, we find that the Whore reappears as a pivotal figure (or a figural pivot) when it comes to the medium of art, too: the painting, the play, the novel, the movies, the internet.

·　　　·　　　·

Consider, for instance, this entrance onto the stage of the heroine of Émile Zola's *Nana*. It feels apocalyptic:

> A shiver went round the house. Nana was naked, flaunting her nakedness with a cool audacity, sure of the sovereign power of her flesh. She was wearing nothing but a veil of gauze; and her round shoulders, her Amazon breasts, the rosy points of which stood up as stiff and straight as spears, her broad hips, which swayed to and fro voluptuously, her thighs—the thighs of a buxom blonde—her whole body, in fact, could be divined, indeed clearly discerned, in all its foamlike whiteness, beneath the filmy fabric. This was Venus rising from the waves. . . . All of a sudden, in the good-natured child the woman stood revealed, a disturbing woman with all the impulsive madness of her sex, opening the gates of the unknown world of desire. Nana was still smiling, but with the deadly smile of a man-eater.

Zola first introduced Nana in an earlier novel in his twenty-volume Rougon-Macquart cycle, *L'Assommoir* (1877), as the daughter of an alcoholic couple; she runs off with an older businessman then becomes a prostitute. *Nana*, published three years later, is the account of her zigzagging and ruinous ascent from streetwalker to courtesan during the last three years of the Second Empire. At the start of the novel she is eighteen, has had a child out of wedlock, and has just been cast in a production of *La Blonde Vénus*. When she transforms into her true (nude) form as the goddess of love, her true (blue) art becomes clear: the drama is merely an occasion to expose her body.

The Whore oscillates between fleshly person and work of art. Critics have noted that Zola's descriptions of Nana mimic the erotic painting, the pornographic broadsheet, and the pin-up photograph. Even as a celebrated figure, the Whore circulates in a recursive loop among men. Zola wrote an essay in praise of Édouard Manet's famous 1863 painting *Olympia*, which features a nude white woman gazing at the viewer, accompanied by a clothed black maid whose mere presence signals sensuality; Manet, inspired by Nana's brief appearance in *L'Assommoir*, painted a hypothetical portrait of Zola's character in 1877; this painting then inspired Zola's later description of her body in *Nana*, in particular its association with a "primitive" sexuality.

Onstage, Nana's heat, "the madness of her sex," as if from a "rutting beast," infects the theater:

> The whole house seemed to be swaying, seized by a fit of giddiness in its fatigue and excitement, and possessed by those drowsy midnight urges which fumble between the sheets. And Nana, in front of this fascinated audience, these fifteen hundred human beings crowded together . . ., remained victorious by virtue of her marble flesh, and that sex of hers which was powerful enough to destroy this whole assembly and remain unaffected in return.

The scene plays on the legendary indifference of the Whore—who reputedly does not discriminate between acts, between body parts, between men—while raising the vexing and thrilling proposition of one woman having sex with thousands, at once.

Zola is the master of the crowd: its psychology, its shape, its intensities of sensation, the way it sounds like "the twittering of a host of talkative sparrows at the close of day." The crowd morphs like a murmuration across his work: frenzied shoppers in *Au bonheur des dames* (1883), manic brokers in *L'Argent* (1891), rioting miners in *Germinal* (1885)—swarms, throngs, motley arrays throughout.

Nana, like the locomotive or the market in other novels, is an engine of multiplication. After her performance, suitors line up in an endless queue outside her door: "a whole mob of men, jabbing at the ivory button, one after another." The rapturous crowd later reappears at a climactic scene where Nana holds court after a chestnut horse named for her ("Who's riding Nana?" . . . "It's Price") wins a race. There is always a violent, hateful edge to this vertiginous attention; Nana incites in peoples and multitudes and eventually nations the "dread of Woman, of the Beast of the Scriptures, a lewd creature of the jungle."

.   .   .

Beyond the Old Testament, Zola relied for his portrayal of Nana on a long literary tradition from Chaucer's Wyf of Bathe to eighteenth-century novels like Daniel Defoe's *Roxana* and Pierre Choderlos de Laclos's *Les Liaisons dangereuses*. Zola also borrowed curse words and slang from his encounters on the streets of Paris, scandals from the gossip rags, and colorful details—like an ornate gold "throne" of a bed—from the life of the courtesan Valtesse de la Bigne, the author of a thinly veiled autobiographical novel, *Isola* (1876). (Valtesse found the fictional character that Zola based on her to be "a vulgar whore, stupid, rude!")

To wit, *Nana* is far from the original Whore story. But Zola's novel crystallizes its archetypal characters, displays them like jewels on velvet. There's Nana the Whore, young, buxom, and blonde; the fellow whore / best friend / queer lover (Satin); the facilitating maidservant ("Zoé, a brunette who wore her hair in little plaits, had a long thin face . . . livid and blemished, with a flat nose, thick lips, and black eyes"); the matronly Madam Tricon, in competition with the pimp-like figures who seduce and brutalize the Whore, like the actor Fontan. There's a range of johns: the man of the arts who pulls strings for her (Bordenave); the writer who documents her (Fauchery); the scorned lover driven to suicide (Georges); the self-debasing zealot (Comte Muffat, a religious devotee as intoxicated by a chorus girl's "forgotten chamber pot" as by Nana's beauty). And we find a fine-grained parsing of sex workers that turns on the explicitness of either the sex or the money involved: *grisette, cocotte, courtisane, maîtresse, demimondaine*.

As Nana moves from patron to patron, we move through a series of houses that map onto her social ascent. She fills them with bric-a-brac, indulging in the "vulgar splendour" of

> a stained glass window, whose pink and yellow panes suggested
> the warm pallor of human flesh . . . at the foot of which a Negro
> in carved wood held out a silver tray full of visiting cards, and
> four white marble women with bare breasts raised lamps in
> their uplifted hands.

In her homes, the foreign and the familiar, the haute and the gauche
intermingle freely.

Her basest and finest commodity is, of course, her body:

> One of Nana's pleasures consisted of undressing in front of the
> mirror on her wardrobe door, which reflected her from head
> to foot. She used to take off all her clothes and then stand
> stark naked, gazing at her reflection and oblivious of every-
> thing else.

Nana squeezes her breasts, rubs her cheeks over her shoulders,
kisses the skin near her armpit, "laughing at the other Nana who
was likewise kissing herself in the mirror." This narcissistic self-
consumption before the looking glass is the self-fulfillment of
Nana's aspirations as a young flower girl who "used to dream in
front of shop-windows in the arcades."

One night, the Comte Muffat, delirious with jealousy that Nana
has chosen an abusive actor over him, wanders these arcades. He
pauses before a "window full of knick-knacks, where he [gazes] . . .
at an array of notebooks and cigar-cases, all of which had the same
blue swallow stamped on one corner," then fixes on a "line of little
round windows above the shops." This hints at the *hirondelles*, the
women who work the windows in the arcades' upper stories, which
Walter Benjamin likens to "choir lofts in which the angels that men
call 'swallows' are nesting." In *The Arcades Project*, Benjamin
argues that "love for the prostitute is the apotheosis of empathy
with the commodity" and that prostitution reveals "the dialecti-
cal function of money": it "buys pleasure and, at the same time,
becomes the expression of shame."

Eventually, Nana brings shame and ruin to nearly all of France:

She alone was left standing, amid the accumulated riches of her mansion, while a host of men lay stricken at her feet. Like those monsters of ancient times whose fearful domains were covered with skeletons, she rested her feet on human skulls and was surrounded by catastrophes.

This doom is wrought by the corruption that runs in her family's blood but also by capitalism, which Nana both enacts and becomes: she is compared to an "aqueduct . . . which had cost millions of francs and ten years of struggle"; to a "port under construction, with hundreds of men sweating in the sun, . . . building a wall on which workmen were occasionally crushed into a bloody pulp"; and to a "palatial edifice of royal splendour which had been paid for by a single material—sugar."

This insinuation of colonialism trails Nana even when she leaves town in disgrace. Rumor has it that either she has "conquered the heart of the Viceroy, and was reigning, in the innermost precincts of a palace, over two hundred slaves," or she has "ruined herself with a huge Negro, satisfying a filthy passion which had left her without a penny to her name, wallowing in the crapulous debauchery of Cairo."

She returns to Paris only to die in a hotel of a "pox" caught from her son. Outside, crowds take to the streets at the news that France has declared war on Prussia, a harbinger of the Second Empire's collapse, symbolized by Nana's decadent decay:

What lay on the pillow was a charnel-house, a heap of pus and blood, a shovelful of putrid flesh. The pustules had invaded the whole face, so that one pock touched the next. . . . And around this grotesque and horrible mask of death, the hair, the beautiful hair, still blazed like sunlight and flowed in a stream of gold. Venus was decomposing.

Even as a heap of rot, Nana is Venus, a stream of gold, a myth.

Nana could never conjure such a myth herself. She's a lousy actress, a worse singer, a hapless decorator; it goes without saying that, unlike Valtesse de la Bigne, Nana could not write (and would not read) Zola's *Nana*. The figure of the Whore is never a creator; she can only be the medium with which one creates.

●　　　●　　　●

Janicza Bravo's 2021 film *Zola* begins with a voiceover: "You wanna hear a story about why me and this bitch fell out? It's kinda long but it's full of suspense." We are watching two young women, one black, one white, standing in a mirrored room, gazing at their reflections as they apply their makeup, which, like the skimpy clothes and jewelry they wear, is shiny and bright. This could be the arcades, where beauties gaze at beauties in glass, where the body's pleasures are for sale. The mirrors also stand in for the big screen we're watching and the handheld ones we're probably scrolling through at the same time. The film is based on a series of tweets posted by A'Ziah "Zola" King on October 27, 2015, about a disastrous trip she took to Florida with another stripper.

The opening presents these young women as doubles: friends, foes, foils. We flash back to how they first met: at a Hooters-esque restaurant, where Zola, a Black eighteen-year-old waitress played by a laconic Taylour Paige, is serving Stefani, a white twenty-one-year-old customer played by a campy Riley Keough. Stefani compliments Zola's "perfect titties," and they suss each other out:

"You dance?"

"It's been a minute."

"I dance."

"Okay, bitch. Me too."

They go out together—a giggly, jiggly sequence that clarifies that "dance" means "strip" and that "bitch" is meant affectionately—which prompts Stefani to invite Zola to go to Florida. Zola replies, "Damn—bitch—we just met and you already tryin' to take ho trips together?" but agrees, only to discover that they will be accompanied by Stefani's white "boyfriend" Derrek (a mealy-mouthed, measly Nicholas Braun) and her Black "roommate," who is initially called X and who turns out to be her pimp (a pattern-clad, swaggering Colman Domingo).

The effect of *Olympia*'s maid lives on. Stefani, the white sex worker, is thin and blonde and all-American, but her voice and manner—she combs her baby hairs, twerks her ass, raps along to hip-hop—are infused with Blackness. This is meant to reverse some stereotypes. At one point on the road trip, Stefani exaggeratedly mocks a Black stripper for being "nasty" and "dirty," when we've just seen Stefani herself being exactly that during a pit stop. In the gas station bathroom, the camera floats above the stalls (the chamber pot again), dividing the screen between Stefani's stall (she sits; she doesn't wipe; her urine is an unhealthy egg-yolk yellow) and Zola's (she hovers; she asks for some toilet paper; her urine barely tinges the water). The white woman, not the black one, is the "dirty ho."

By the end of the film, Stefani has had sex with dozens of men, and we're led to believe that this includes X, her Black pimp. Under his smooth American charm rumbles a sinister fierceness marked as "African," which is to say, "savage." His Nigerian accent first erupts when he threatens Zola, booming, "Get your ass back in this car! I know where you live. I know where you work." He clears his throat wetly as he pisses—the stream loud, the door open. He shouts at Stefani, he kisses her head. The imagery is unmistakable and centuries old: the brute and the maiden.

·　　·　　·

Indeed, the film could be set to the old beats of the Whore story we saw in *Nana*: Stefani is the classic blonde Whore, airheaded and two-faced, monstrous and beautiful, associated with the lower classes but eventually barred from true solidarity with them. In Derrek, she has an overwrought lover whose jealousy drives him to attempt suicide; in Zola, a bestie/madam/maid who brokers and authorizes sex work; in X, a brooding pimp whom she both fears and clings to. As in *Nana*, the action rises as Stefani's fees do. This is staged through architecture: the road-trippers move from a seedy motel to a decent hotel to a fancy five-star one and finally end up at X's immense glass-and-marble Tampa Bay condo, which overlooks a turquoise pool and the ocean beyond.

Zola is at its best when it lets this archetypal plot lie and plays with its filmic form instead. Its aesthetic, like other films produced by A24, has an air of gentrified graffiti, a palette like a neon bruise. But Bravo beautifully contains the sun-shot pastels of Florida in the manner of a David Hockney painting, and the film deftly references its origins on social media. With a camera-shutter sound, the screen freezes into a snapshot that shrinks into a corner, like on an iPhone; with a *cha-ching* of change, hearts flash or rise up the screen, like in an Instagram Live; with clickety-clicks and emoji bursts, texts are typed into being; the date and time appear at the top of the screen in a thin white font, then vanish—both with a click; and we occasionally hear the Twitter whistle, as the screenplay explains, "to pay homage when a line in the script is identical to one of @_zolarmoon's tweets."

The centerpiece of *Zola*—its climax, so to speak—is an extended sequence in the second hotel. Stefani changes into an innocent-schoolgirl outfit straight out of Britney Spears's "... Baby One More Time" video. A bearded middle-aged white man arrives. As soon as Zola opens the door, he complains: "I ordered a white chick." Zola rolls her eyes, negotiates the transaction, then turns away from the bed as her voiceover deadpans, "They start fucking, it was gross." When the sex is over and Zola hears how little money he has paid, she's aghast: "Pussy is worth thousands, bitch." She takes a new picture of Stefani to advertise her services on BackPage and raises the prices. Soon, as in *Nana*, the men are practically lined up at the door. For some reason (aren't we in Florida?), they're all white.

The film highlights the johns' interchangeability in their turns with Stefani: they take off their clothes; they manipulate her body; they climax. These shots appear in horizontal rows so we see a sliding blazon of male chests, stomachs, crotches. We seem to be scrolling through them as if we're on Tinder or Instagram, bestowing exploding heart emojis over pecs and dicks. The grotesquerie of the images is meant to interrupt what pleasure the scene might otherwise prompt. It's, again, a reversal—men rather than women divided into parts, turned into a series.

X, having noted and recompensed Zola for leaning in as a madam, forces her to accompany Stefani on a house call. In the words of the screenplay: "The door opens. At it a Latino man in boxers, we'll call him JUAN. Further in and somewhat obscured another Latino man, we'll call him ALSO JUAN." The interior has the trappings of "Latinidad": "Old black and white photos of mostly women and farm life. Presumably their Abuela in the old country." More brown men come out of the woodwork. They request a gang-bang. "We savages, Miss," one says. The others utter in unison, "We ain't proper." Zola panics but Stefani kneels in a pile of crumpled dollar bills and puts her finger in her mouth. The men surround her, stand over her: an unmistakable tableau from hardcore porn.

Just then, as if the film is balking at what it's gotten itself into, Stefani breaks the fourth wall. We shift into her account of the road trip, based on a rant the original Stefani (a woman named Jessica) published on Reddit after King's tweets went viral. Keough, as Stefani, narrates a stilted account of the events, painting herself as respectable and Zola in hyperbolic caricature as "very ratchet, very black." In the dramatization, Zola wears a trash bag, her uncombed afro sprinkled with hay. This excursion to the other side of the story is meant to highlight by contrast the film's counterintuitive depiction of Zola as "elegant"—"proper," you might say—and of Stefani as "gross."

·　　·　　·

But zoom out and another racial pattern comes into focus. The white men in the film are sometimes racist but mostly pitiable or laughable; the brown men, the undifferentiated "Juans," are dangerous and deviant; the Black men aren't johns but pimps, and they're the ones we see committing assault. With the help of (per the screenplay) "A BIG BLACK DUDE," a rival pimp with dark skin and a gold grill kidnaps Stefani and beats her unconscious then holds a gun to Zola's head while he puts his fingers inside her. The only Black women other than Zola are her knucklehead coworker and a gaggle of thicc strippers played by extras, who parody a preshow prayer circle, asking God to "send us niggas with culture, good credit, and a big dick." It's almost uncanny how the film's effortful reversal of stereotypes always seems to intensify them.

Audience expectations about race can be manipulated to cutting, hilarious effect—ideally when artists press on the promiscuity and contradictions of stereotypes about everyone, rather than recapitulating only white people's misconceptions of nonwhite people as dirty, savage, poor, violent, lewd, etc. This focus on the pathologies of whiteness is a theme in Bravo's short films; it's also not surprising to see such fetishism in a film cowritten with Jeremy O. Harris, who gained notoriety for his ostentatiously "edgy" drama *Slave Play* (2018) and is presumably responsible for cues like "a black thigh meets a white torso." Bravo's camera sometimes dwells moodily, giving us ominous pans through the car window: an American flag, a big white cross, and—Bravo's jarring insertion—a distantly viewed scene of police brutality. Maybe it's foolish to ask that an A24 movie's politics go beyond stricken pointing.

It's a shame that *Zola* shrinks from giving us the real Zola, though. The film infantilizes this woman, victimizes her, tames her with a sulky respectability that feels frankly incongruous with the lines it borrows from King's tweets. Zola says she's a "full nude typa bitch," but we see her mostly covered up, her dancing more Alvin Ailey than *P-Valley*. Zola knows that "pussy is worth thousands," and yet the film strongly implies that she doesn't turn tricks or "trap," as she puts it. King's ribald story only makes sense if you know that she has done sex work, as she freely and proudly admits.

By being coy about this, the film ends up inadvertently making Stefani the more intriguing of the two women. Even King agrees. "She's probably my favorite character in the film," she has said. Bravo circles the blonde's body with a heady, disavowed mix of desire and disgust, pity and disdain. Meanwhile, the titular Black heroine seems merely ornamental—beautiful but extraneous—instrumental only in the sense that she makes herself useful, the Black sidekick/savior/server, not the star. Stefani is the center of the action, while Zola is merely the frame.

This may be a difference between media forms. King's tweets use what literary critics call "dual narration": Zola in the present describes and comments on Zola in the past. But in the film, we mostly have access to the character as a player in the moment, not as a narrator; some of her best lines are dampened into reactive dialogue. In a sense, adaptation mutes her. Bravo recounts how she explained the role to Paige: "It is sort of a more silent film character, you are a watcher." It's true. It's hard to imagine the Zola of the film telling this raunchy, rambling tale in the form of 148 tweets.

·　　·　　·

Or more: A'Ziah "Zola" King actually wrote four versions of the series of tweets that came to be known widely as "#TheStory." The filmmakers who adapted them tend to use another name:

> It was called #TheThotessy, and what we really liked about that was that it put it in conversation with like, the beginnings of Western literature, it put it in conversation with Homer. . . . We didn't want to be above our source material, we wanted to look at it as though it was above us. . . . We took all of the imagination and care and heart that we would put into a beloved piece of literature that you read in school into this beloved piece of literature we all read on our phones.

Creating this genre of "Twitterature," so to speak, requires that Bravo and Harris harp on a far less common and rather precious portmanteau of Homer's *The Odyssey* and the slang word *thot* (an acronym for "that ho over there"). The filmmakers even got A24 to publish a print book of the tweets, with hipstery fonts and a shimmery purple cover, to "legitimiz[e] things for people," as King puts it.

But Twitter, its digital medium, is crucial to #TheStory—and vice versa. It is said that the popularity of her 148 tweets prompted the social media network to develop the "threading" function that has transformed the grammar of the platform. (King's Twitter bio still says, "I invented threads.")

King doesn't come across as a noble or superhuman hero in her tweets, and she doesn't really have a quest. #TheStory resonates less with the epic than with the folktale, in particular the *One Thousand and One Nights*, whose heroine Scheherazade, with her sister Dunyazad, must duck rape and murder through wit and storytelling skills. Their art is to convert the erotic potential of their bodies into narrative promise. King's opening tactic is as old as the folktale itself—or the world's oldest profession. You ask a question: "Y'all wanna hear a story about how me & this bitch here fell out????????" Then you drag out the answer: "It's kind of long but full of suspense."

The folktale happily incorporates other genres: romance tragedy, comedy, poetry, satire, the picaresque, even erotica (as in the subtly titled "Ali with the Large Member" from the *One Thousand and One Nights*). These are sometimes nested, the thread connecting them not one hero but the tellers themselves, who masterfully choreograph narrative techniques—cliffhangers, innuendo, unreliability—to enthrall the reader. Or rather, the *readers*. The frame and the codex are just an excuse to gather together some tales that folks have long been telling together. It's a fundamentally communal form.

This is also how I would describe Twitter. As Roxane Gay puts it in her foreword to the published version of #TheStory, "The platform is a cacophonous bazaar. . . . It is endless pageantry." King describes discovering "that live interaction, that essence of storytelling," when she was sending her tweets, some of which went viral on their own, and attributes it to "this moment in time" on Twitter: "I don't know how that could ever be captured again . . . that essence of a live theater moment."

•   •   •

This essence of a sociality is why Twitter appeals to Black people, so much so that there's a subset of the platform with its own proper noun (Black Twitter). It is a striking fact, one that most analyses of the internet willfully ignore, that Black people disproportionately use social media. The artist Aria Dean cites a 2015 Pew survey finding that "nearly half of black internet users use Instagram, as opposed to less than a quarter of white users. Twitter is more evenly distributed but still mostly minority-driven." Memes, the critic Lauren Michele Jackson argues, "gravitate towards a Black way of speaking . . . latch onto Black cultural modes of improvisation."

Zola's tweets themselves are unquestionably strung through with Blackness. Some of this is simply Black English, which the book of #TheStory displays for us in all its glory: eye dialect (*wanna, wit, ima, cus, naw, dis, dawg, aiight*); dropped verbs (*this story long, we all talking, this fool gone*); distinctive tense aspect modality (*I had went, he done promoted me*); postpositive intensifiers (*old ass big ass, nice ass, dead ass, sorry ass*); rhythmic repetition (*I feel it I feel it, ok ok ok*); and nominal slurs (*bitch, nigga, ho*). Most delightful to me are King's idiomatic words (*raggedy, bae*) and phrases, some classic (*who's all going, dont even trip*), others blessed with her own blinguistic inventiveness (*vibing over our hoism, Im in the back on mute*). While she doesn't hesitate to use a high register (*verbatim, bipolar, livid*), internet vernacular, acronyms, and punctuation crackle through her tweets, dragging #TheStory to the very edge of phonic recognition (*oooommmmgggggg*). And from the tweets' opening question to "Bear with me. It's almost over" to "(PAY ATTENTION HERE)," we find directive asides to the audience.

Toni Morrison traces these elements of Black aesthetics in her 1984 essay "Rootedness: The Ancestor as Foundation": "The affective and participatory relationship between the artist or the speaker and the audience . . . is of primary importance. To make the story appear oral, meandering, effortless, spoken." #TheStory also has a particular tone. After the pimp fucks the white girl in front of everybody, her boyfriend says, "i wanna go home," and Zola tweets: "😂📱😂💀 📱😂 I laughed out loud. I couldn't help it." This small series of emojis for laughing, weeping, and "dead" (i.e., "I died laughing") encapsulates the irony Ralph Ellison finds in the "near-tragic, near-comic" tone of the blues, which he defines as "an autobiographical chronicle of personal catastrophe expressed lyrically." King's tweet-chronicle is a new techno-strain of this tragicomic black lyricism.

This kind of irony is built into the position of the Black writer, a paradox inaugurated by the slave narrative, which is conditioned on a seeming impossibility: *I am writing a story about a condition that forcibly prohibits literacy.* From the start, people questioned King's authority and authorship. She shrugs off those who doubt or diminish her story: "People . . . just don't wanna believe black women."

Like Nana, King shamelessly bodies forth her sexuality onstage; unlike Nana, she puts it into words—online. This "Zola" is literally self-made. While Émile got the name from his Italian father (it means "mound of earth"), A'Ziah King chose it for herself—not for any high-minded literary reason but, as she explained when I asked her on Twitter, "Bcus I needed a stage name & bcus I liked it. I made it up. I wrote it & it was pretty."

·   ·   ·

With the internet, the Whore has found her medium at last. The Whore of Babylon's "peoples, and multitudes, and nations, and tongues"; the crowds in *Nana* that sound like "the twittering of a host of talkative sparrows"; the arcade windows filled with knick-knacks, "all stamped with the same blue swallow," like the *hirondelles* in their eaves—these persons and things that so love to swarm around the Whore are online now. Text, image, video, and GIF gather in a hybrid space quite like the theater, an everyday carnival that juggles hierarchies and norms, and whose manifold ephemerality—virality, interactivity, im-provisation, transience, relativity—allows the Whore to keep dancing.

If the Whore has always been a medium, #TheStory is radical enough to give us an actual whore's meditation on that medium.

Zola's Nana and Bravo and Harris's Zola gaze upon a body mirrored in the glass. But King turns her mind upon that body, specifically upon its material conditions. It's telling how often she talks about sex work *as work* in tweets and interviews:

> It's a job, it's hard work. We don't all come from the same type of background, we are not all from the hood, or looking to be rescued or saved from something. Some of us, like myself, just are confident in our sexuality and expressing it that way and we like to make money.

At the same time, she stresses that the film shows a "much darker reality," one "much more dramatic and violent" than her own experience: "I was never assaulted or touched or, you know, preyed upon in that way." She emphasizes that "sex work and sex trafficking are two completely different conversations. . . . People mesh the two together. There's one huge difference and that's consent." King isn't interested in judging or idealizing whoredom. She is interested in being protected and getting paid as a sex worker, alongside other sex workers.

She wants the same thing for artists, too:

> When it comes to black writers and black creatives and black women, I just want them . . . to share their stories . . . and claim agency over their voice. So many people will come to me, like . . . I can't believe you got compensated for your story, and it's like, why is that so rare?

Last January, King called out the Independent Spirit Awards on Twitter for neither nominating her as a writer nor inviting her to their ceremony. But when you go to @_zolarmoon's Twitter page these days, you'll mostly find her advertising her OnlyFans page, sometimes with the tagline "Watch my porn so I can pay my rent. Thanks 👄👀."

New York Times Magazine

WINNER—PROFILE WRITING

This was one of the two stories that won Jazmine Hughes the National Magazine Award for Profile Writing. The second was a profile of Whoopi Goldberg. "In a single year, Jazmine Hughes profiled two of our most acclaimed actresses," said the National Magazine Award judges. "In 'Viola Davis, Inside Out,' Hughes illuminates the sources of Davis's range as a performer. Hughes's thoughtfulness and curiosity yields an intellectual and emotional depth increasingly rare in celebrity profiles." Hughes is a staff writer for the New York Times Magazine. She won the ASME NEXT Award for Journalists Under 30 in 2020. The Times Magazine received six National Magazine Award nominations this year and won two awards, for Profile Writing for Hughes's work and for Reporting for Rozina Ali's story "The Battle for Baby L.," which is also included in this anthology.

Jazmine Hughes

Viola Davis, Inside Out

For a month, Viola Davis had been stuck. In the spring of 2020, in the late nights of lockdown, she set out to write her memoir. She had her routine: get out of bed in the middle of the night, make herself a cup of tea, start writing in her movie room, fall asleep in one of its leather recliners, wake up, write some more, nod off again. But for weeks, she couldn't figure out exactly where to begin. Should she start with her life as a celebrity or the beauty contest she lost when she was a child or the fact that people always wanted to hug her when they ran into her in public? Nothing worked.

Then one night, a conversation she had years ago with Will Smith on the set of *Suicide Squad* came floating back into her consciousness. He asked her who she *really* was, if she had been honest enough with herself to know the answer. She was fifty at the time and replied confidently, indignantly, that yes, she knew. He tried again, saying: "Look, I'm always going to be that fifteen-year-old boy whose girlfriend broke up with him. That's always going to be me. So, who are you?"

A memory returned to her. When she was in third grade, a group of eight or nine boys made a game out of chasing her home at the end of the school day. They would taunt her, yelling insults and slurs, throwing stones and bricks at her, while she ducked and dodged and wept.

One day, the boys caught her. Her shoes were worn through to the bottom, which slowed her down. (Usually she would run barefoot, her shoes in her hands, but it was winter in Central Falls, RI, where she grew up.) The boys pinned her arms back and took her to their ringleader, who would decide what to do with her next. They were all white, except for the ringleader. He was a Cape Verdean boy who identified as Portuguese to differentiate himself from African Americans, despite being nearly the same shade as Davis. Unlike her, he could use his foreign birth to distance himself from the town's racism: he wasn't like *those* Black people.

"She's ugly!" he said. "Black fucking nigger."

"I don't know why you're saying that to me," she said. "You're Black, too!"

Time slowed down. The ringleader howled in fury, screaming that he wasn't Black at all, that she should never let him hear her call him that again. He punched her, and the rest of the boys threw her onto the ground and kicked snow on her.

By the time Davis and Smith had that conversation in 2015, she was a bona fide star: she had been nominated for two Oscars, won two Tonys, and was playing the lead role in a network television show, *How to Get Away with Murder.* ("Hell, Oprah knew who I was," she writes.) But in that conversation, she realized that not only had she remained that terrified little girl, tormented for the color of her skin, but that she also defined herself by that fear. All these years later, she was still running, trying to dodge the myriad tribulations—anti-Blackness, colorism, racism, classism, misogyny—that she had faced, other people's problems with her. Davis's early life is dark and unnerving, full of blood, bruises, loss, grief, death, trauma. But that day after school was perhaps her most wounding memory: it was the first time her spirit and heart were broken. She had her beginning.

To watch Davis act is to witness a deep-sea plunge into a feeling: even when her characters are opaque, you can sense her under the surface, empathetic and searching. This skill has been on display since the beginning of her film career, when she garnered award nominations for performances that were fewer than fifteen minutes long. There's an industry achievement called the Triple

Crown of Acting: an actor winning an Oscar, an Emmy, and a Tony. Only twenty-four actors hold the title, and Davis is the only African American.

Davis is also, then, a member of the small troupe of former theater actors who have made the jump to movie stardom, and you can recognize that gravitas, that same finesse that makes me sit up straighter whenever I see James Earl Jones onscreen. But there is also vulnerability alongside her poise. The more time I spent with her, the more I wondered if, by embodying someone else's tragedies, she was able to wrench her own to the surface. Reading her memoir, *Finding Me*, which is being published on April 26, you understand where her ability comes from: only someone who has already been dragged into the depths of emotion readily knows how to get back there.

Davis told me that there's so much vanity in Hollywood that she thinks people are afraid to take the nonpretty roles. "It's more important for me to see the mess and the imperfection along with the beauty and all of that, for me to feel validated," she said. "If it's not there, then I feel, once again, the same way I felt when I was keeping secrets as a kid. But the only reason to keep secrets is because of shame. I don't want to do that anymore."

.   .   .

In one of our first conversations, Davis described the difference between method acting, which requires a performer to completely subsume herself into the life of her character, and a more technical approach that might, say, rely on breathing techniques to be able to readily cry. "I believe in the marriage of both, because I want to go home at the end of the day," she said. She thinks that actors need to study life itself. Feelings are never simple; the mind wanders off track. "I always use this example of when my dad died, and we were devastated," she told me. But at the wake, when people streamed through the doors to pay their respects, "it became this big reunion of laughing and remembering—real laughter to real joy, then tears. But I was observing my thoughts, and I went from being devastated one moment to thinking about what I was going to eat." It's like a Chekhov play: you can't tell the story of the joy without telling the story of the pain alongside it.

"Your thoughts go every which way," she said. "They run the gamut. There's a wide berth of life. It's like, as soon as you think your life is falling apart, then you're laughing hysterically. That's how life works."

Davis was born in 1965 on a plantation in South Carolina. Her grandparents were sharecroppers who raised eleven children in a single-room house. Mae Alice and Dan Davis, her parents, moved Viola and two of her older siblings to Rhode Island soon after Davis's birth so that her father could find a better job. Dan was a well-regarded but underpaid horse groomer. He also regularly abused his wife after drinking binges, stabbing her in the neck with a pencil or thrashing her with a wood plank. Sometimes Davis would arrive home and see droplets of blood leading to the front door; at least once, Dan asked his daughters to help him look for their mother, who had run away in the middle of a beating, so he could kill her.

The family rarely had heat, hot water, gas, soap, a working phone, or a toilet that flushed. Rats overtook their home, so ravenous that they ate the faces off Davis's dolls. She and sisters would tie bedsheets around their necks before they went to sleep to stave off rat bites. Her father often beat her mother at night, and Davis started wetting the bed, a habit she didn't break until she was a teenager. The conditions of her home meant that she often couldn't wash up or change into another set of clean clothes. A teacher shamed her about her hygiene but never asked the root cause. Other teachers just ignored her: one day, Davis raised her hand to go to the bathroom, but the teacher never called on her, so she peed in the seat. The teacher sent her home, and the next day, when she arrived back at her desk, the urine was still pooled in her chair. Davis surmised that she was so disgusting that even the janitor didn't want to clean her mess. She was six years old.

Her sisters were her anchor. The eldest, Dianne, had recently reunited with her siblings, moving from their grandparents' home in the South, and Viola was obsessed with her. She had a new coat and pocket change, and she smelled nice. It was the first time Dianne saw how the rest of her family lived, and she decided that her baby sister needed to get out. She whispered to Viola: "You need to have a really clear idea of how you're going to make it out if you don't want to be poor for the rest of your life. You have to decide what you want to be. Then you have to work really hard."

One evening, Davis sat watching TV, the working set sitting atop a broken one, connected to an extension cord from one of the few functioning outlets in her home. *The Autobiography of Miss Jane Pittman* came on, and for the first time, Davis saw a dark-skinned woman, with full lips and a short Afro, on the screen. She thought the woman was beautiful; she thought the woman looked just like her mother. "My heart stopped beating," she writes. "It was like a hand reached for mine, and I finally saw my way out." Dianne had made clear that Viola could be somebody. Cicely Tyson was somebody Viola could be.

·   ·   ·

When she was fourteen, Davis intervened in one of her parents' fights for the first time. Her father stood opposite his wife, screaming and carrying on, a drinking glass in his hand like a dare. "'Tell me I won't bust yo' head open, Mae Alice? Tell me I won't?'" she writes. Davis tried to cut in, her eighteen-month-old sister in her arms, calmly pleading for him to stop.

Dan lifted his arm and smashed the glass onto Mae Alice's face. A shard sliced her temple. As he moved to swing again, Davis yelled. Dan froze, still gripping the glass. "I screamed, 'Give it to me!'" she writes. "Screaming as if the louder I became the more my fear would be released." It worked. Her father handed Viola the glass, and she stashed it away.

Davis grew up to be the sort of actor whose range feels best measured by her steady command of pressure: maintaining it, raising it, letting it go. She sets the tone of every scene, the eyes of her cast-mates flicking toward her as soon as she appears, as if reacting to her is a crucial part of the job. She often plays characters who cry only in the moments she's inhabiting, weeping as if it were a rare, almost undignified departure from their norm. Her name has become internet shorthand for dramatic crying: after an episode of HBO's *Euphoria*" this winter in which Zendaya sobbed and snotted her way through a scene, she drew enthusiastic comparisons to Davis. Davis doesn't cry so much as she leaks, her eyes and nose like faucets. During her performance as Mrs. Miller in the 2008 movie *Doubt*, she cries one drop at a time. Her tears hang over the edges of her lashes; a single teardrop stays on its precipice for fifteen seconds. Mucus runs down her face undisturbed for two minutes, an eternity, its very presence signaling something terribly wrong. In the 2016 film adaptation of *Fences*, when her character unloads her stymied dreams onto her husband, her curled upper lip is no match for the snot dripping down her face.

In real life, Davis doesn't cry that much. "As a matter of fact, if someone confronted me with something, I would probably come at them with more unbridled anger than tears," she said one March afternoon at her home in Los Angeles. When I arrived, her dog, Bailey, greeted me with an enthusiastic familiarity; Davis laughed and wondered aloud whether he thought I was her sister. Eventually, we made our way to the movie room, where she sat curled up under a plush blanket. She wore a dark head wrap knotted in the front and a key-lime linen jumpsuit. Davis is goofy and surprisingly coarse (her favorite swear words, she said, are basically unchanged from when she was eight), and looking at her, it was difficult to imagine that anyone had ever doubted her beauty.

In order for Davis to descend into a new character, she told me, she first has to become a "human whisperer," inviting the person into her life and making space for her revelations. She's the vessel, not the creator. From a script, an actor may learn only the broad strokes of her character, and the rest is up to her to intuit. "You begin to ask your questions based on those facts," Davis said. Say your character is 300 pounds. "'Why are you so big?' 'Oh, I eat too much.' 'Well, why do you eat too much?' 'Because it comforts me.' 'Well, why does it comfort you?' 'Because I have a lot of anxiety.'

'Why do you have a lot of anxiety?' 'Because I was sexually abused when I was five. And every time I go to bed at night, I think about that sexual abuse, and I can't go to sleep, so I eat.'" She punched the air. "Bam. You have a character. Keep asking why." This has sometimes led her to doing intensive preparation, even for minor roles. After three weeks of rehearsals for *Doubt*, for example, she still wasn't able to figure out Mrs. Miller. She went home and wrote a hundred-page biography of the character, finally cracking her open after a discussion with a college professor, who explained why a mother would turn a blind eye to a priest abusing her son: She had no other choice. The bigger threat to her son's well-being was his homophobic father, who might kill him if he found out he was gay. She was protecting her son the only way she knew how.

Denzel Washington directed Davis as an absent mother in the 2002 film *Antwone Fisher* and in *Fences*, in which he also costarred, and he spoke of her work with deep respect. "Acting is investigative journalism, and we interpret the world differently," he said. "The beginning work is similar: you circle the subject, your character." Washington studied journalism at Fordham University, but he learned this strategy, he said, from Carl Bernstein and Bob Woodward, whom he met while researching a role. "She, as an actress, will circle. I don't know if she goes inside out or outside in, but you circle it, for lack of a better word, and she makes it her own, and you can't take it from her, and you better keep up with her."

Talking to Davis about herself feels both analytical and spiritual, as if a flower child went to therapy. When she described how she emotes, she kept likening herself to a prehistoric man, standing at the edge of an ocean, slowly gaining sentience: "'Who the hell am I?'" she said. "'Who made me? Is there someone out there who I can talk to? Who loves me? Why do I have feet? Can I speak?'" Davis told me that too often the artistic representations of Black people are flattened into pure devices, who, say, inspire the white heroine or comfort the white heroine or support the white heroine's decision to get a divorce and fly to Bali. Early in her career, she was relegated to those sorts of parts, so she tried to sneak a bit of humanity into her scenes, giving unmemorable stereotypes some life.

The author Zora Neale Hurston argued that Black life in fiction should be so realistic that it feels like eavesdropping; true authenticity would encapsulate a feeling of discovery. Davis embodies this in her acting: it can seem so truthful that it feels almost uncomfortable, as if you've barged in on something you weren't supposed to see. By going slightly too far, letting her tears drip uninterrupted, she lets you in on a secret no one else will tell.

．　　．　　．

Soon after she saw Cicely Tyson on television, Davis and her three older sisters entered a local contest with a skit they based on the game show *Let's Make a Deal.* They won—gift certificates and a softball set, including a bat that they used to kill rats in their home. But for Davis, the real prize was recognition—not just of her talent but of her personhood. She writes: "We weren't interested in the softball set. We just wanted to win. We wanted to be somebody. We wanted to be SOMEBODY."

When she was fourteen, she participated in an Upward Bound program for low-income high school students, where an acting coach encouraged her to pursue acting professionally. Later, a teacher recommended she apply to a national performing-arts competition. She auditioned with two pieces from *Everyman* and *Runaways,* which, she writes, "had a lot of great monologues about feeling abandoned." She was flown out to Miami for the contest, where she was named a promising young artist. Eventually, she studied theater at Rhode Island College. For money, she took multiple buses to her hometown, worked a few shifts at the local drugstore, slept on her parents' floor, and then headed back to school in the morning.

After graduation, Davis wanted more training, but she could afford to apply to only one conservatory. She chose the Juilliard School, squeezing in her afternoon audition in New York before performing in her first professional production that evening in

Rhode Island. "I just thought you should know, I've got forty-five minutes," she told the faculty. She didn't realize the audition process typically took three days. She explained the situation, the train she absolutely had to catch. "You have to tell me whether I'm in or out." She got in.

But after enrolling at Juilliard, she felt trapped, limited by its strictly Eurocentric approach. She spent her days squeezing herself into corsets or powdered wigs that never fit over her braids, listening to classmates ponder how good life would have been in the eighteenth century, an imaginative game enjoyable only for white people. Juilliard was about shaping a student into a "perfect white actor," she writes. "The absolute shameful objective of this training was clear—make every aspect of your Blackness disappear. How the hell do I do that? And more importantly, WHY??!!!"

She applied for a scholarship that would allow her to spend the summer in Gambia. In her application essay, Davis wrote about the burden of performing material that wasn't written for people like herself. There was no cultural connection or recognition—she felt lost and uninspired. That summer, she was on a flight to West Africa with a group of people who wanted to study the music, dance, and folklore of various tribes.

Immediately after landing, she fell in love: the ocean wind, the faint smell of incense, the oranges and purples of twilight. The people of the Mandinka tribe, with whom she visited, embraced her group like family. She went to a baby-naming ceremony, a wrestling match; she watched as women drummed and danced. Her fixation with "classical training" melted away. Finally, after years of acting, she was witnessing art, true genius. "I left Africa 15 pounds lighter, four shades darker and so shifted that I couldn't go back to what was," she writes.

Her time at Juilliard was ending, and she was eager to jump into a new chapter of her life, but all the roles she auditioned for—even in Black productions—were limiting: the only roles she was being seriously considered for were drug addicts. She tried out for other parts, but casting directors thought she was "too dark" and "not classically beautiful" enough to play a romantic lead.

A few plays came her way, but she barely made enough money to live on, let alone pay off her tens of thousands of dollars in student loans. She survived on white rice from a Chinese restaurant, with three-dollar wings if she could afford it; she slept on a futon on the floor of a shared room.

Her agent asked her to audition for the touring company of August Wilson's *Seven Guitars*, for the role of the strong-willed and guarded Vera, who must decide if she can trust her cheating ex-boyfriend again. She got the part, and after touring for a year, she made her Broadway debut. She received a Tony nomination for the role, but her life was hardly glamorous. A few of her siblings, she writes, were struggling with drugs or money issues, and her parents, still together, cared for some of their children. Davis sent home as much money as she could, racked with a sort of survivor's guilt. "If I saved anyone, I had found my purpose, and that was the way it was supposed to work," she said. "You make it out and go back to pull everyone else out."

After her success in *Seven Guitars*, theater parts came steadily, and she finally made enough money to afford premium health insurance. An operation to remove nine uterine fibroids gave her a small window of fertility. She was in her early thirties, and every child she passed on the street made her want her own, but she had been in only two relationships, neither of them any good, and there was no one on the horizon. One of her castmates in a production of *A Raisin in the Sun* encouraged her to ask God for a nice man. One night, she got down on her knees: "God, you have not heard from me in a long time. I know you're surprised. My name is Viola Davis." She went through her requests: a Black man, a former athlete, someone from the country, someone who already had children. A few weeks later, on the set of a television show, Julius Tennon—a handsome, divorced Black actor from Texas with two grown children—played opposite her in a scene.

Within four years, they were married. But the reproductive challenges kept coming: she had a myomectomy, this time to remove thirty-three fibroids. It felt as though the women in her family were cursed. Two of her sisters nearly bled to death after labor and had hysterectomies. Some years later, she had one, too—during an operation on an abscessed fallopian tube. (Before going under, she told the surgeon, "Let me tell you something, if I wake up and my uterus is still here, I'm going to kick your ass.") With Tennon, she eventually adopted a daughter, Genesis, inspired by the fellow actress Lorraine Toussaint, who adopted a child because she didn't want "series regular" to be the only words on her tombstone.

After years of therapy, Davis healed her relationship with her father, who had transformed into a docile, sweet older man trying to make amends for his past; he spent the last years of his life catering to the needs of his wife and family, as if every single one of his remaining days could be an apology. Some films floated her way, but none of the material was particularly meaty.

Then, in 2007, Davis beat out five other actresses—Audra McDonald, Sanaa Lathan, Taraji P. Henson, Sophie Okonedo, and Adriane Lenox—for the role of Mrs. Miller in *Doubt*. It was more than five-year-old Davis could've dreamed: acting opposite Meryl Streep, being directed by John Patrick Shanley, working on a prestige film. Davis had finally reached the summit desired by so many professional actors—awards bait. Of her performance, the film critic Roger Ebert wrote: "It lasts about 10 minutes, but it is the emotional heart and soul of 'Doubt,' and if Viola Davis isn't nominated by the Academy, an injustice will have been done. She goes face to face with the pre-eminent film actress of this generation, and it is a confrontation of two equals that generates terrifying power."

There was no injustice: Davis was nominated for best actress in a supporting role, though she lost. Then in 2010, she won her second Tony, for playing Rose Maxson in *Fences*. The next year, she starred in *The Help*. Davis played Aibileen Clark, a maid working for a white socialite in the 1960s in Jackson, MS, who shared her stories of racism and mistreatment with a young, progressive white female reporter. The film, one of the most successful endeavors of the white-savior genre, was nominated for four Oscars, including one for Davis for best actress. After *The Help*, Davis had two Tony

Awards, two Screen Actors Guild Awards, and two Oscar nominations—and no offers for leading roles. People would call with a few days of filming here, a few days there. Her life had changed, but Hollywood hadn't much. She still felt sidelined for her skin tone.

But then she got a call from Shonda Rhimes. She and Peter Nowalk were developing a sexy, soapy prime-time drama for ABC, *How to Get Away with Murder*, and they offered Davis the lead role as Annalise Keating. (In an email, Rhimes wrote that she was shocked when Davis, their dream choice, agreed to a meeting. "I remember saying we may as well ask and let her say no so at least we can say that we asked.") Before the series, Davis's biggest roles had been strong, tough, sharp, but sexually neutered women, as if the deepness of her skin tone and her sensuality were inversely correlated. A friend told her she overheard some male and female actors, all Black, saying she wasn't pretty enough to pull it off. For the first time in her professional career, Davis couldn't shake all the racial criticisms she had heard over her career. She was fortyseven and terrified. She took the job anyway.

Annalise is a hard-nosed, highly sought-after professor and lawyer; in the pilot, she's compared to Alan Dershowitz. She has a white academic husband and a Black cop boyfriend and a former female lover. She is also maybe a sociopath. The way Davis tried to make Annalise realistic was to have her become completely different in private than she was in public. Before accepting the role, Davis asked that they write a scene in which Annalise removed her wig and makeup, which became the most memorable scene in the series's run. "The TV and film business is saturated with people who think they're writing something human when it's really a gimmick," she writes. "But if I took the wig off in a brutal, private moment and took off the makeup, it would force them to write for THAT woman."

Davis won an Emmy and a Screen Actors Guild Award for her work that season and has since moved from success to success. There was finally an Oscar for her performance in the movie version of *Fences*. She was cast in a recurring role in the D.C. Comics

Suicide Squad franchise and continued to be able to play characters with the depth she craved, including the fearless Veronica Rawlings in *Widows* and the cantankerous diva Ma Rainey in *Ma Rainey's Black Bottom*, which earned her a fourth Oscar nomination last year. She and her husband used the production company they started, JuVee Productions, to work on their own projects, including *The Woman King*, a historical epic about the all-female army of the Dahomey Kingdom that has been pitched as a Black female *Braveheart*, which premieres in the fall. This month, Davis stars as Michelle Obama in the Showtime series *The First Lady*.

When I spoke with Denzel Washington, he described a conversation with his daughter before she auditioned for the acting program at New York University. She had performed a dry run of her monologue for him. He told her he had good news and bad. The good: she was talented. The bad: "It's going to be harder for you," he said. "Because you're not the skinny light-skinned chick." He told her that casting directors wouldn't want to see her in substantial roles, that they would want to cast her as a friend or a sidekick. His advice? "Just follow Viola Davis," he said. "Look at what she's doing, and know that, on the other side of it, even if it takes longer, you can be where she is."

·   ·   ·

Early in her career, after a performance of Wilson's *Seven Guitars*—"absolutely an Everyman tragedy story," Davis said—she and the rest of her cast, all Black, hosted a talk-back. A white audience member, she recalls, asked why he should have to care about the lead character: "It's not like he's James Brown or anyone famous." (Davis would later go on to play Brown's mother, Susie, in a 2014 biopic of the singer.) "I don't think I'll ever forget that," she told me. "I don't think that people see the value in a lot of Black people unless you made it into a history book. I don't think they think your life matters. I don't think they feel like you're interesting if you're ordinary. And that is, absolutely, without question, not the case with white people."

Zora Neale Hurston might've called this a confinement "to the spectacular," or focusing so much on uplifting the race from its oppressive shackles that you start to mythologize it. Sure, race is always relevant, and stories that use it as a prism are largely edifying, giving dimension to the figures in our history books. "I think our response as Black people—and I get it, from so many years of oppression and dehumanization—has been about putting images out there that are positive and likable and beautiful," Davis said. But it's an overcorrection, she cautioned, a glossing over: "That image and message shouldn't be more important than the truth."

The challenge for the Black artist, she says, is that "the audience they're trying to usually reach are not people who look like us and not people who get us and not people who know who we are." Acting, as Davis repeatedly told me, is about portraying people living life. Contemporary Black dramas often posit that Black lives are either secondary (best friends, drug dealers, therapists) or extraordinary (healers, fighters, heroes), when life is rarely one or the other. Davis fills in the in-between, rescuing stories from the restrictive imagination of whiteness: she plays the truth, and we see it reflected back at us in our shade.

Over her career, she has become the sort of celebrity you want to claim as distant family; maybe whatever greatness runs through her veins also runs through your own. Without exaggeration, every single Black person I told about this article asked me to tell Davis hello—not that they loved her work or that they were a fan, just to pass along a greeting, as if they were extending a conversation they had long been having. The beauty of Blackness is the myth that across diasporic differences, we're all part of the same extensive, sprawling, complicated family, accountable to and for one another. It's impossible, of course, but in the face of entrenched dehumanization, it feels necessary, the relief in the knowledge of a "we." It's easy to root for her when her wins feel like your own.

For years, I watched *How to Get Away with Murder* every single week, for no discernible reason. In 2014, when it premiered, I had only a passing familiarity with Davis, had never seen any of Rhimes's other work, and hadn't watched much network television since the finale of *30 Rock*. (I also hadn't seen the article in this newspaper that called Davis "less classically beautiful" than Kerry Washington.) But something compelled me to keep with it. It wasn't as simple as being drawn to Davis because we slightly resemble each other, but I liked that the character kept surprising me, twisting away from what I expected. A product of Shondaland, Annalise had an absurd inner life, and everyone around her couldn't stop getting murdered, but she had an inner life! She had flaws and no eyebrows and real, traumatic issues with her family and sometimes bad wigs. Annalise wasn't an inspiration; she was neither a stereotype nor a gimmick, neither a white writers' room's stab at a Black person nor a tortured Black person's idea of what dark-skinned women are like. She was a *person*.

Davis's ascent feels like delicious revenge, an "I'll show you," pushing past obstacles like a rose through concrete. She fought her way to a position where she could demand the same respect denied to her in her childhood. It's the same respect denied to her mother, repeatedly beaten; to her grandparents, who had to stuff all their dreams into a one-room house on a white man's land. It's the same respect long denied to Black women, especially dark-skinned ones.

Each time I finished an interview with Davis, she escorted me outside and waited with me until my car arrived. In Los Angeles, we hugged goodbye. Out the window, I could see she had taken a familiar stance—legs spread wide, hips jutting forward, one hand on her back, the other waving—as she watched the car drive off, waiting until it passed her house before she went back inside. The Uber driver, a Black man, turned and asked me, "Is that your mom?" I laughed and said no, but admitted that we do sort of look alike, so I could see why he asked. It wasn't just that, he said: as soon as he pulled up, she was watching him closely, as if she were wondering if she could trust him enough to keep me safe.

•　　　•　　　•

One day last February, I joined Davis on location about an hour outside Cape Town as she wrapped up filming *The Woman King*. Dozens of extras, all brown- and dark-skinned, congregated in the set's main square. They were dressed in thick fabrics of tropical colors, marking their steps. Davis plays Nanisca, the army's general, and she was filming a victory dance with her warriors. She wore a bandeau, a cape and a printed skirt in an aristocratic purple, with thin golden cuffs on her upper arms and a necklace of shark teeth. Her hair was in a blown-out Afro, with a golden rope securing a small section at the top of her head. While her makeup artist rubbed cream into her back, careful not to disturb a spatter of painted-on scars, she watched the dancers, marking moves along with them using only her forearms and her feet. She rose from her chair and started dancing on her way toward the camera, grinding her hips in precise circles and smirking, eliciting a shower of "AYYYEEE"s from crew members.

The scene they were working on began with a tight shot of Davis watching the dance wistfully from a perch. Her face continuously transformed: in one second, she looked as if she were trying not to smile, then immediately as though she were fighting back tears. She had been filming close shots all day, and her range of emotions was vast but unambiguous: resigned, fearful, disturbed, flummoxed, each change descending onto her face as smoothly as a blind.

Davis cupped the face of the actor playing opposite her, touching their foreheads together, a feud between them finally settled. In one take, she smiled tightly, and for a moment she was washed by disappointment; in another, she clasped her costar's face with great intention and smiled wide and sweet. She then turned to face her warriors, already celebrating the end of the battle, and joined the fray. Drummers kept them in a polyrhythm. Her back to the camera, she rolled her hips, her hands thrown to the air. She hiked her knees to her stomach, her feet two-stepping, all her movements light but still rooted to the ground. The dancers circled her, cheering her on. When the director, Gina Prince-Bythewood, yelled "cut," everyone burst into applause.

For most of the cast, it was the last scene they would film. Davis joined the principals in a group hug, and the dancers, mostly hired locals, began gleefully singing in Xhosa while they danced and embraced one another. When I asked Phumzile Manana, the film's publicist, if the singing had any significance, she said they were "just keeping vibes alive, I suppose."

It took Davis six years to get *The Woman King* made because the studios were reluctant to back a film that featured so many Black women. That they were all dark-skinned—the production cast women from across the diaspora, Black Americans and South Africans and Brits and Jamaicans and West Africans—might have made it even harder. "All praise to *Black Panther* and its success because that absolutely paved the way for people to see the possibility of this movie," Prince-Bythewood told me. "*The Woman King*," Davis said, "reflected all of the things that the world told me were limiting: Black women with crinkly, curly hair who were darker than a paper bag, who were warriors."

Seconds after she wrapped her final scene, Davis was in a black robe and Crocs, milling around for pictures and goodbyes before she gave a short speech. "The thing about what we do is that you can be transported back in time," she said. "You can be whoever you want to be. And, you know, for Black people, sometimes the only thing we've had to rely on is our imaginations."

As she talked about how powerful it was to watch these Black women transform into warriors, a sea of dark faces, crested with braids and fades and Bantu knots, reflected back at her. "What the caterpillar calls the end of the world, the master calls the butterfly," she told them. "We've been so misunderstood. Limited, invisible for so long. And now, people are going to see us be butterflies."

New Yorker

Here Raffi Khatchadourian profiles the artist Matthew Wong, whose paintings stunned the art world before he took his own life at the age of thirty-five. "The judges," reads the citation for "Light and Shadow," "were impressed by the unsentimental intimacy of this profile, in which Khatchadourian carefully reconstructs a complex life without romanticizing it, as well as by the stylishness of his writing about art history and the art market." Khatchadourian has been a staff writer at the New Yorker *for fifteen years. His first piece for the magazine, "Azzam the American"— another subject Khatchadourian never met—was nominated for the National Magazine Award for Profile Writing in 2008. The* New Yorker *won the Profile Writing award the last two years, for "Past Imperfect," by Rachel Aviv, in 2022 and "Survival Story," by Jennifer Gonnerman, in 2021.*

Raffi Khatchadourian

Light and Shadow

Matthew Wong, the gifted Canadian painter who died by suicide at the age of thirty-five, just before the pandemic, worked from a studio in Edmonton, on the east side of the North Saskatchewan River. The neighborhood is industrial, but not in an arty way. It is industrial in an industrial way. The squat building that houses Wong's workspace—which remains as he left it, with barely a brush moved—has more loading docks than doors and stands before a parking strip that can accommodate eighteen-wheelers. One part of the facility is devoted to a manufacturer of industrial lubricants, another to a food-processing company.

Wong's studio, protected by a metal door and an alarm, is tucked into a corner office on the second floor. For years, unknown to the other tenants, he came to paint—producing, in a furious outpouring, works of astonishing lyricism, melancholy, whimsy, intelligence, and, perhaps most important, sincerity. He played with a dizzying array of artistic references, but he shared the early modernists' conviction that oil on canvas could yield intimate and novel forms of expression.

In Wong's lifetime, his work was heralded—remarkably so, given that he was largely self-taught and spent no more than seven years with a brush in hand. "One of the most impressive solo New York debuts I've seen in a while," the critic Jerry Saltz wrote in 2018. After Wong took his life, the *Times* proclaimed him "one of the most talented painters of his generation." Museums began assembling his art into major exhibitions, with one currently at the Art Gallery of Ontario and a retrospective opening this year at the Dallas Museum of Art. Wong's paintings have been acquired by MOMA and the Met.

This institutional recognition has been accompanied by a crasser kind of interest. Wong, who was diagnosed as having depression, Tourette's syndrome, and autism, conducted most of his relationships through social media, and even some of his closest contacts found him hard to know. In the three years since his death, the art market has been in a frenzy over his work, with prices escalating to multiple millions, and the rabid auctioneering has helped to shape his story into the caricature of a brilliant but tortured outsider: another Basquiat, another van Gogh.

I arrived at Wong's studio with his mother, Monita: tall, rail thin, elegant, her hair tightly pulled back. Since her son died, she has sought to protect his legacy and, still grieving, has barely given interviews. Monita was Matthew's business manager, confidante, and omnipresent companion, and she still speaks about him in the present tense. "My son is half of myself," she told me. She drove him to the studio every day that he went there and has kept paying rent on the space in the hope of reconstituting it, object for object, in a building in Edmonton that will house the Matthew Wong Foundation, which she firmly controls.

We climbed the stairs to the second floor, and I waited at the studio door while Monita deactivated the alarm. It felt as though a safe containing a cherished memory was being unlocked. For Matthew, the studio was a sanctuary. After moving in, he texted a friend, Peter Shear, a painter in Indiana, that he would spend sixteen hours a day there if he knew how to drive. "It's a great space," he said. "No artists, as technically this is an office building." He sent a photo, taken through venetian blinds, of the vast, empty lot outside. "As you can see this area is pretty dead," he said approvingly.

Monita and I entered an antechamber, where some canvases were stacked, and she paused. She had warned me that she could tolerate only a brief time inside. Wong's paintings—mostly imagined landscapes—are portals to luminous, vibrant, moody places. Though not surreal, they are the product of reverie: poetic concoctions inspired by memory, stray ideas, or the paint itself as he compulsively worked it. Midnight forests glow, somehow, without light, by a painterly magic. A milky tundra extends across a horizon, looking soft, opulent, ominous. Spectral icebergs—vulnerable, tentative, lost—drift in glasslike seas.

Wong bent perspectival space to fit his own emotional coordinates, and he allowed discrete categories to dissolve into dream dialectics: what is inside might be outside or the other way around. Trees take on the shape of leaves; forests take on the appearance of folkloric embroidery. But it is also possible to ignore the representational elements and receive the images as pure abstraction. He applied paint urgently, in divergent gestures—thick impasto beside mesmerizing pattern work or even areas with no paint at all—that cohered in an unsteady harmony.

The physicality of Wong's process was evident around us. He often painted with the canvas propped against a wall, scooping pigment from paper-towel palettes or applying it directly from the tube. Drop cloths were stained with explosions of spent color and covered in supplies: half-squished tubes of oil paint, cardboard boxes, a five-gallon Home Depot bucket filled with brushes.

Walking through his space, Monita hardly spoke, except to ask me not to touch anything. I stepped carefully around a pair of paint-splattered sneakers and past a large piece that had been shipped from southern China, where Wong made his earliest oils. An easel held a black-and-white painting of two figures.

After a few minutes, we rushed out. The studio, frozen in time, spoke of a life interrupted. It was a fitting memorial. At the start of his career, Wong had written of his interest in "the residue and traces of human activity." Fascinated by voided surfaces, he hoped to conjure "in various states the mysterious ghosts of what-has-just-been."

•　　•　　•

Many of Wong's paintings feature solitary figures, set adrift. They are overwhelmed by nature—riding in a car at dusk, or traversing a ribbon of paint that becomes its own end. Sometimes they are hard to see or are present only in the form of an empty chair or an object left behind. Their footprints tell us where they are going.

Wong knew what it meant to feel uprooted. He spent much of his life shuttling between continents, and even before he was born his family wrestled with displacement. When Monita was a young girl, on the eve of the Cultural Revolution, her family fled mainland China for Hong Kong, and her father, formerly a rich man, found work in the marble industry. He rebounded well enough to send Monita to boarding school in Toronto. As an adult, back in Hong Kong, Monita married Matthew's father, Raymond, and together they ran a company that distributed fabrics. In 1983, she became pregnant. Mistrusting the local health-care system, she flew to Toronto to give birth to Matthew then returned with her son. "It was very simple," she told me.

Raising Matthew was far from simple, though. He was curious and intelligent, but from a young age he found social interactions overwhelming. He later told a friend that on his first day of kindergarten he was "crying in a corner not wanting to let go of Mom's hand." Bullied and ridiculed, he came to hate school. "To this day, I shrink a little when I pass a group of adolescent friends," he said. "There is a distinct kind of laugh that exists in the world that makes me jump out of my soul every time I hear it."

Wong was aware that he was wired differently from others; he once told Monita, "Mom, why do people take cocaine? So that their brain will function fast—but for me that's natural." He had a near-photographic memory, able to absorb vast amounts of information about whatever he was interested in. In time, he developed a striking conversational style—disorienting or charismatic, depending on his interlocutor's view—because he was often several steps ahead, making associations across topics.

By the age of thirteen, struggling with his racing intellect, Wong began to express suicidal thoughts, and he was diagnosed as having depression. Given a prescription for Prozac, he discovered that art, too, could be fortifying. An American friend had introduced him to Puff Daddy's *No Way Out*, and the music was a revelation. Wong started reading hip-hop magazines, memorizing lyrics, sometimes spontaneously breaking into raps. "At school, I was powerless and the biggest loser, but afterwards back home with my headphones on I was somebody different," he once wrote. In his imagination, he was a guest on *Lifestyles of the Rich and Famous* or partying with beautiful people at the Tunnel, the famed hip-hop nightclub. Like Jay-Z, he was telling anyone who didn't know the difference between a 4.0 Range Rover and a 4.6 to "beat it."

When Matthew reached high-school age, Monita decided to return to Toronto. She worried about navigating the complexities of Hong Kong's educational system, and she was convinced that her son would receive better medical attention in Canada. Recognizing that she and Raymond would have to shut down their business, she pitched the move as an adventure. "It's a good time to travel," she told her husband.

In Toronto, they enrolled Matthew in a private school. By then, doctors had explained that he also had Tourette's syndrome, and Monita urged him to embrace the new diagnosis. "Nobody can look down on you unless you are doing it, too," she told him. With her encouragement, he took to announcing his Tourette's at the start of conversations.

Wong began to thrive in his new school, exhibiting a teenager's enthusiasm for high and low culture. On trips to New York, he went to IMAX screenings of professional wrestling. "I would actually walk around town alone, in my head imagining I was in some WWF scenarios," he later recalled. He also got heavily into free jazz. "Coltrane's *Meditations* was playing around the clock in the house," he once told Peter Shear. "Ornette Coleman was my idea of easy listening, no joke."

Later, Wong attended the University of Michigan, in Ann Arbor, moving into an apartment off campus with his father, who helped care for him, while Monita returned to Hong Kong. He hoped to become an investment banker—believing that the profession was a gateway to a glamorous life—until he took Econ 101 and realized that he was disastrous at math. Instead, he majored in cultural anthropology, and he excelled; he was a sharp observer, an avid reader, a connoisseur of culture. Socially, too, he was doing well.

Then, in his junior year, he fell into a suicidal depression. Monita, in Hong Kong, arranged for him to return to Toronto, and his doctors there helped him navigate the episode. From afar, she tried not to worry about her son's future.

· · ·

Wong was nearly six and a half feet tall, handsome, thin, with high cheekbones and eyebrows that ramped toward the bridge of his nose, intensifying his gaze. He disliked having his photo taken except in carefully executed selfies, and even those he often deleted soon after posting them online. A photo that Monita took of him on graduation day at Michigan, in 2007, shows him in a slim-cut suit, with his back to her. Aware that he is being photographed, he gives an awkward victory sign as he hurries to avoid the lens.

After college, Wong returned to Hong Kong, and the family settled in Discovery Bay, a resort town on an island accessible by ferry. He found work as a corporate headhunter, impressing the company's CEO with his erudition, but the job required smooth talking, and he didn't stay long. "He hated it," Monita told me. "You have to lie. That was not his mentality." Through a golf acquaintance of Monita's, Wong got an internship at Pricewaterhouse-Coopers. Between the long hours and the commute, he was getting home close to dawn, napping, then returning to work, but he was determined to succeed. Hyper-keen on fashion, he bought some fancy suits. "He looked like a prince," Monita recalled, though his conspicuous style did him no favors with the other interns. "He didn't really behave that well, either," a friend added. After nine months, he was unemployed again.

Wong was trying to find his way in a city that offered him no clear berth: he was neither a native—his Cantonese was just passable—nor an expat. In his midtwenties, he had no friends and no way to support himself. Searching for something to hold on to, he began attending open-mic poetry readings, and soon he was writing and sharing poems, improving fast. "He spoke honestly, bluntly—and this made communication uncomfortable sometimes," John Wall Barger, an American poet who was living in Hong Kong, wrote in an unpublished reflection. "If he hated a poem of mine, no matter how excitedly I presented it, he'd say so. He was very tall, but quiet: hovering at the edge of the group. You forgot he was there, but then he would cut in a conversation with a snippet of hip hop or a joke that didn't always make sense."

At the readings, held in bars, there were internecine squabbles and dramas, and some of the poets treated Wong unkindly. He looked down on them, too. "He masked his sadness with a scowl," Barger noted. One evening, drunk and frustrated, Wong burned some of his poems outside a bar. Then he began insulting people's families. One poet attacked him, and a fight ensued, with the poet swinging at Wong while others tried to pull the men apart. Police became involved, and Wong was suspended from the readings, but he eventually returned. "This is practically the only social interaction I have," he told an acquaintance, Nicolette Wong.

Although he never felt that he truly belonged, Wong befriended a few poets who, like him, were on the group's margins. At one of the readings, he met a woman who worked at a gallery, and they began dating. Often, Wong and Barger sat on a bench outside Barger's home, where they smoked, talked about art, and read their poems. Wong was in awe of the surrealists John Ashbery and James Tate. In his own poems, he was interested in "expressing an indeterminate space where names, places and situations don't really matter—just a faint glimpse of a gut feeling, something in the air." He was drawn to Freud's theory of the uncanny and to Lorca's notion of *duende:* a creative force—emergent from flesh, touched by death—that is indifferent to refinement and intellect.

"Seeking the *duende*, there is neither map nor discipline," Lorca wrote, in an essay that Barger and Wong discussed. "We only know it burns the blood like powdered glass, that it exhausts, rejects all the sweet geometry we understand, that it shatters styles and makes Goya, master of the grays, silvers and pinks of the finest English art, paint with his knees and fists in terrible bitumen blacks."

·　　·　　·

One day in 2009, shortly before Wong began writing poetry, he was in his grandfather's bedroom in Hong Kong. "Something in me was pushed by an urge to visually reproduce the uncalculated, almost accidental slice of poetry in front of me," he later recalled. Using an old Nokia phone, he took a photo of his grandfather's belongings. "It was the first thing I remember doing out of my own creative volition."

Wong continued taking pictures—"street signs and found geometric arrangements out in the urban environment"—and his girlfriend suggested that he get a master's in photography at the City University of Hong Kong. He enrolled, even though the program was for "creative media" professionals, not artists. In a report to his adviser, he described his work as if it were going in an exhibition. He documented mementos that Monita's mother had saved from her home in mainland China. ("Domestic surfaces of my maternal grandmother's storied apartment on the eve of its permanent evacuation.") He shot night skies in which the ground was a lightless mass. ("Again, there is the insistence on perception of a void.")

Wong had an eye for lone, vulnerable figures, and he loved the photographer William Eggleston, who exalted the mundane. But he despised formal techniques, like bracketing, and compositional guidelines, like the rule of thirds. There was no *duende* in any of that: such fussiness, he thought, made photos lifeless and stiff. Eventually, he started to take pictures without even looking through the viewfinder; he was interested in how the process made *him* feel. "To take photographs is a way of confirming that I exist, which is something I question all the time," he told Dena Rash Guzman, a poet who interviewed him in 2012. "When I can make an image I'm satisfied with, then that question goes away for a little while."

Perhaps inevitably, Wong developed a deep skepticism of photography, which he came to think of as "an incredibly unnatural art form." Bothered that photos could often be "immediately grasped," he instead pursued a loose, poetic ideal. For a student exhibition in the fall of 2011, he pressed tree branches between paper and glass: stark, spindly shapes that offered no easy interpretation. He also included digitally manipulated images of a photo that he had painted over, creating swirling abstractions. Wong reassured his adviser that his work was "derived from a technique whose arc is similar to photography." He titled the show *Fidelity*.

After the exhibit, Wong flew to Italy to serve as a docent for the Hong Kong pavilion at the Venice Biennale. During off hours, he encountered a Julian Schnabel retrospective and some large Rorschach-blot-style paintings by Christopher Wool; these works, he later noted, caused a "radical shift" in his thinking. He began to draw obsessively and made several abstract works with ink, acrylics, Wite-Out, and spray paint. He told his adviser that these "quizzical reflections" had arisen "out of a clash between material and chance."

By summer, Wong was drawing with charcoal on paper, smearing it in wild gestures, as if releasing anxieties, or in sedate fields of gray. He also conducted experiments inspired by Wool's Rorschach paintings and by traditional Chinese works. As he later wrote, "I just bought a cheap sketch pad, along with a bottle of ink, and made a mess every day in my bathroom randomly pouring ink onto pages—smashing them together—hoping something interesting was going to come out of it." He was painting watercolors, too. Pretty soon, most of his attention was focused on making marks on paper, "a last resort, with no prior skill." That December, he told Barger that he thought *duende* had never touched his poems, but "I think it may have struck me one or two times in my paintings."

·   ·   ·

On a recent afternoon, I met Monita for lunch at Joss Cuisine, on Santa Monica Boulevard, in Beverly Hills. Every winter, she and her husband flee the cold and darkness of western Canada. Often, they go to Los Angeles, where they have friends, and where they can play golf in the California sun. These trips also offer a respite from the loss that hangs over them in Edmonton.

When I arrived, Monita was at a sidewalk table, conducting business on her phone. Plans were under way for the building that will house the Matthew Wong Foundation, and she was in negotiations with the engineering firm that built the Sydney Opera House. Special care would be needed, she said, to create a repository for Wong's work which can withstand harsh weather. "It will be like a vault," she said.

To launch the foundation, Monita had to create a full catalogue of her son's work, a task that proved challenging. Wong at one point was making multiple paintings a day, some of which he documented but later destroyed. His art also became harder to track as it rushed into the secondary market. A few of Wong's earliest supporters had sold pieces that they had acquired, and for Monita that stung—though she softened, a little, when it became clear that some of the sellers were artists who needed the money. Fakes and opportunists also surfaced. One painter showed me a complimentary note that Wong had sent him, and said, "If you promise to include his quotes about me, it might help my career."

In managing the estate, Monita has surrounded herself with a small, trusted circle. At the table, we were joined by an old family friend, Cecile Tang—a glamorous émigré from Hong Kong, who had come to California in the 1960s to study film then returned home, where she wrote and directed movies, one of which found its way to Cannes. For years, she has been running Joss Cuisine.

Cecile had known Matthew. "When he first was exploring what his medium of expression was—that was so touching," she said. "He didn't use photos or a pencil so when he picked up his paintbrush he was almost like a child." (Wong had told Guzman, "I can't draw at all—if you told me to draw an apple or your face, what would result would likely be a disaster.")

As Wong devoted himself to painting, he wanted to work with oils, but studio space in Hong Kong was impossibly expensive. Then Monita learned that Cecile's brother, who lived in Zhongshan—a city just across the water, in mainland China—had been painting in the studios at a cultural compound called Cuiheng Village. Rent was negotiable, even free.

"Do you want it?" Monita asked Matthew. "I can organize it." He said yes. He and his girlfriend had grown apart, and he told Monita that he wanted to focus on art. "I'm too inward to really give in a relationship," he confessed to a friend. Still, the separation tore at him; he was sure that she was his only love. "I have a hope," he added. "I will succeed, and we will have earned the right to be together." Wong said later that this was the moment when he began to paint and draw in earnest: "It was basically that or suicide."

The Wongs had a condo near a golf course in Zhongshan, and they relocated there. "They were so concerned with Matthew," Cecile said. "He was in their mind all the time—to help him find his way of expressing himself. And how will he support himself after they're gone?"

At Cuiheng Village, Monita had one of the studios renovated; she added air-conditioning and racks for paintings and put together furnishings. (When I asked if Matthew had worked with her, she said, "My son? Ask him to assemble something? Forget it! My son is scared of sharp objects.")

After weeks of preparation, Monita dropped Matthew off to paint. When she returned that evening, she found the studio in disarray. "Paint was *everywhere*," she told me. "I looked at him and said, 'Oh, my God. What are we going to do?' The entire floor was covered in oils. I tried to clean it up, so that he could work a second time."

•　　•　　•

In those first weeks in the studio, Monita sometimes joked that her son was like a gorilla wielding a paintbrush. But Matthew was pursuing a deliberate goal. After his epiphany in Venice, he had begun to read about art voraciously, and he kept at it in Zhongshan. Wong later recalled that when he went to visit Monita's mother, who lived near a row of park benches, "I would often borrow painting books from the library and sit on one of these immersed and obsessed."

Wong absorbed art across history and geography, China and the West. In these early years, he was fascinated by the work of Bill Jensen, the American abstract expressionist. "It comes from some place outside talk, somewhere deeper and ineffable," he told Peter Shear. Jensen sometimes began his process with arbitrary marks and allowed the paint itself to guide him toward order. In Zhongshan, Wong attempted a similar approach: "I may just pick a few colors at hand and squeeze them onto the surface, blindly making marks, but at a certain point I will inexplicably get a very fleeting glimpse of what the image I may finally arrive at will be, sort of like a hallucination."

Wong bought his paints with no particular image in mind, and he used cheap brushes. "Throw 'em away after one use," he recalled. "Or, rather, they fall apart after one use." His work was shaped by intense movement, at close proximity to the canvas. He did not have technical virtuosity, but he had good instincts. He hoped to create work that reflected his devotion to "living a day-to-day life in paint."

Every night, after achieving a "painting buzz," he ate dinner and watched a movie with Monita. Then he typically read—poetry, novels, essays—or texted with artists he met online or painted on paper. He went to bed contemplating art. ("Can't sleep in such a state thinkin bout paintin.") He woke up in the same state.

"Man, I'm so far gone off the painting deep end," Wong told Shear after months of working this way. "I register virtually everything I see outside in terms of a painterly effect. Now it is really scary. I have internalized it, so it is kinda normal to me and not panic inducing, but I can imagine if a stranger were to walk these shoes for like a block they'd be terrified of how they were experiencing the world." He added, "Faces jump out at me everywhere . . . shadows of branches on a night street, selectively lit by lamps, eyes, mouths, patina on walls. I don't think hallucinatory is the word for it. . . . I wish I knew if there was a word."

"Pareidolia," Shear suggested.

While painting, Wong would allow glimmers of a landscape or figuration to emerge—mirages in pigment. The result, he hoped, would be something akin to Coltrane's *Meditations*. As he told Shear, "After about the fifth consecutive listen you get numb to it and only then do your ears open up and it sounds like 'music.'"

The canvases quickly piled up. When the piles overwhelmed his space, he moved paintings into the director's studio—or *he* moved, to work in someone else's space. In 2015, he noted, "There must be over a thousand works of mine in both Hong Kong and Zhongshan combined." He knew that painting had become a compulsion. "Is there something wrong with working as much as I am?" he asked Shear. "Sometimes, I feel guilty. But I can't stop."

Every morning, Wong would roll out of bed and, on the family's terrace, make a quick ink painting on Chinese paper, while his parents slept. When it rained too hard to paint outside, he felt "immobilized, neutered." If he finished before his mother was ready to bring him to the studio, he tried to manage his anticipation. "I'm waiting for a ride to the duty hole," he told Shear one morning. "In the meantime just firin' off Facebook messages like blank bullets to anywhere and anything that will listen."

• • •

Goethe wrote that "talent is nurtured in solitude," but good art often blossoms out of human connection. Basquiat maintained a creative symbiosis with Warhol, as Robert Rauschenberg did with Jasper Johns. Van Gogh believed that his brother Theo was essential to his paintings—"as much their creator as I."

Wong was a solitary presence at Cuiheng Village, but he was not a loner. On trips to Hong Kong, he met with a friend or two to paint, watch movies, smoke weed, conduct stoner debates: could a painting evoke John Bonham's drumming? "When Matthew made a good joke, it was clever and required you to move into some mental space with him," one of his friends recalled. "He would be grinning like a horse, and it would be funny as hell."

Online, Wong became enmeshed in a much larger community. He had discovered painting at a time when Facebook was hosting a vibrant, wide-ranging artistic conversation. "There was this glorious moment when artists from all over were connecting in an authentic, meaningful way, without 'branding' or ugly competition," Mark Dutcher, a painter in Los Angeles, told me. Dutcher himself opened his process to hundreds of followers. "It was sincere and special," he said.

Wong was ideally suited to the medium. Communicating from behind a keypad, he was vulnerable, opinionated, witty, able to talk about anything. In a milieu known for polish and snobbery, he had no filter. From China, Wong sought guidance on questions like what the optimal brand of paint was, or if it was possible to mix acrylics with oils. (Not recommended.) He gave his friends the feeling that together they were preparing to storm the citadels of the art world.

"He was one of those people who made you want to go into your studio," Spencer Carmona, a painter in California, told me. Another artist recalled, "He had an intense, wild depth of curiosity." Wong shared thoughts on Freud and Rilke and on contemporary fiction, such as Lisa Halliday's *Asymmetry*. Opinions on movies spilled out of him fully formed. *As Good as It Gets* was "a perfect romantic comedy in the way it constantly deflates sentimentality." *Inherent Vice* was "occasionally brilliant but quite scattered, which I guess is the point."

With Shear, Wong texted mostly about the painting life. Almost daily, he would ping him with a playful permutation of his name: "Whodashear" or "Shear Volume" or "Overnight Sheardom." On one occasion, Wong opened with "The Shear drama of the scale shifts."

"Sorry what??" Shear replied.

"Just a sentence," Wong explained.

"I've been sentenced," Shear said. "Sentenced to confusion."

"Gonna go do an ink," Wong said.

The two men acted as though they were walking in and out of each other's studio. Wong frequently showed that he was attentive to Shear's art. "Sometimes I'm painting for a while along the road and at a certain point I realize I've gone down a Shearesque mode of painterly inquiry," he once told him. He was quick to praise and

delicate with criticism. When Shear mentioned that he was working as a janitor, Wong said, "It's a fine job if you're an artist." He
made it clear that he had no such obligations himself. "The only
person I have any contact with outside of Facebook is pretty much
my mom," he said. "If you are ever wondering how all these paintings are getting painted . . . well, imagine life with nothing and
nobody to answer to and there you go."

•　　•　　•

After just a week in his Zhongshan studio, Wong was speaking
about his work with the confidence of a rapper gone platinum. He
told Nicolette Wong that his paintings were "sheer, genuine acts
of will." He wondered aloud if he was a genius. "I've already decided
the title for the film that will be loosely based on the beginnings
of my artistic life—a film which will win the Palme d'Or and Best
Actor awards at Cannes," he said. "The film will be titled *The
Master.*"

But along with the bravado Wong had crushing doubts. "Do you
ever look at the stuff around you then get hit with a paralyzing grip
of insecurity?" he once asked Shear. "I feel like that now." A month
before his first solo exhibition at Cuiheng Village, Wong talked
down the show: "Nothing too glamorous, but at least it's not a vanity exhibition LOL." As the date approached, he grew more pessi-
mistic. "I dunno, man," he told Shear. "The whole scenario right
now just looks fucking bleak."

Only two friends came. They found Wong stylishly dressed—
striped shirt, black pants—but anxious. He gave a tour, discussing
each canvas in detail, down to the brushstrokes, as if the works
were made by someone else. Then he retreated. "Mostly we were
standing in a corner as if it were not his exhibition," one friend
recalled. Then Wong cryptically said, "You want to check this out?"
He left the hall and led his friends to his studio. He put some rice
paper on the floor. Silently, he made an ink painting.

Wong had been nursing a growing apprehension about his work.
He knew that his abstractions were good, but also that they were

not especially distinguishable from abstractions by countless other artists. He regarded the praise he received online as "a comforting mirage." For an untrained painter hopelessly far from New York, Facebook was essential, but he feared that it was also an invitation to mediocrity, a "love fest in a dead end kinda way."

The alternating currents of insecurity and confidence became a propulsive force in Wong's creative life. After the exhibition in Zhongshan, he pinged Shear. "How does one hop onboard with any of the various factions of ascendant thirty somethings in the global art scene today?" he asked. "It seems like they're all ascending together. Nobody ascends alone anymore."

From southern China, though, Wong's only way forward was alone. He told Shear that he was going to change his approach to painting. The problem with abstract expressionism, he said, was that few people could tell whether it was good or bad. He wanted to make use of symbolic imagery, to play with figuration. He reworked some old pieces; in one, he scratched the outline of two people. "Ugliness executed with finesse seems to go over well," he told Shear. "Late Picasso is always good to go back to for that."

Wong's paintings became stranger, cruder. Uncanny forms—semiorganic shapes, with stray kinks and curves hammered flat—assumed an unlikely congruity. They appeared first in his morning ink exercises, which began to mature into consequential works in their own right. (After his death, they became the subject of a show in New York.)

Wong lost some followers who were committed to his earlier work. But important fans remained. When he posted a painting in this new vein on Facebook, he got a complimentary response from John Cheim, whose gallery, Cheim & Read, represented several accomplished artists. In the painting, called *Memento*, a dark, twisted mass stood against a yellow background, resembling cracked soil. There was angst and fury in the central form, with some features that were legible—a face partly obstructed by wild hair, some prisonlike netting—and others that weren't. It wasn't necessarily a museum piece, but it was good, and people on Facebook affirmed it.

He wondered how to further advance his work. "Painting a good piece doesn't alleviate anything," he wrote to Shear. "First thought: 'Ken I doo eet agen?'"

"Hehe I struggle, too," Shear wrote.

"Everyone is crying best piece ever," Wong said. "That's actually the worst feeling in the world lol. I believe not in God, but I believe in signs from the ether. Stuff like this is sobering. It tells one, 'Now imagine if you were a blue chip artist—this feeling is magnified and intensified a thousand times over every time you pick up a brush.'"

Wong was learning in public, creating and posting images at tremendous speed. "It was shocking how every day he just kept making leaps in his work," Dutcher, the painter in L.A., told me. But Wong sometimes posted pieces even before they were finished, and the quality varied. When a well-known artist suggested that he slow down, he was irked. Terrified that painters in Brooklyn might mock him, he obsessively deleted images of paintings that he had reworked, telling Shear, "I feel like I'm pretty exposed to the winds right now, just a weird shiver down the spine."

In October 2015, Monita helped Wong secure a three-day show at a government-run art center in Hong Kong. He filled the space with forty pieces, and this time with many more friends. One threw him an after-party. It was Wong's first genuine exhibition. The venue was not prominent, but he sold his paintings, which provided him a little money to make more art.

Afterward, Monita told me, Matthew fell into another deep depression. It is not entirely clear why. Around this time, according to a friend, he had learned that his ex-girlfriend was engaged. In response, he painted that whole night. He once confessed to another artist that Monita had chided him, "You're never going to have a girlfriend. Nobody will be able to please you. You're a prince." Monita says that she maintained a pragmatic attitude—she told him that, given his struggles, he should never have children—but that she hoped he would find a woman.

For months, the depression did not abate. "It's pretty pervasive in my overall life right now," Wong told Shear in January. "I don't even really feel like fighting or resisting it, this darkness. The weird perverse part is I'm painting in the midst of it all. Even as my attitude is only one of futility, the game plays on."

Monita took Matthew to America for a months-long stay—an escape, a quest for momentum. Shear had arranged a joint show for them, titled *Good Bad Brush*, in Washington State. Matthew and Monita also visited Michigan, Los Angeles, and New York. While traveling, Wong made art every day. But even as his environment changed, his melancholy remained. He was barely earning money, and his oil paints and canvases remained in China. "I'm feeling really terrible, shaking and shit," he told Shear. "Walk two steps then I get nauseous and dizzy."

Visiting a friend in Edmonton, Monita decided that they would stay, reasoning that Matthew would benefit from the Canadian health-care system. Put on a waiting list to see a therapist, he continued to seek relief through ink drawings, watercolors, gouaches on paper. A few weeks later, Shear shared a painting from his studio. "Very nice," Wong said. "In the middle of an anxiety attack." Twenty minutes later, Shear checked in on him. "I'm fine," Wong assured him. "Just did a painting."

· · ·

Two years after Wong was inspired by the paintings at the Venice Biennale, the exhibition's curator showcased a curious artifact, called *The Encyclopedic Palace*. It was an eleven-foot-tall architectural model, built in the 1950s by an auto mechanic in Kennett Square, Pennsylvania ("The Mushroom Capital of the World"). The structure had taken years of obsessive work to construct—out of wood, brass, celluloid, hair combs—with the hope that it would inspire a museum on the National Mall which housed all human knowledge. Instead, it languished for twenty-two years in a storage locker in Delaware until it was transferred to the American Folk Art Museum. The exhibition at the Biennale caused a stir, and the art world responded. "Outsider" artists began to appear with increasing frequency in galleries and museums.

The term "outsider art" is almost impossible to define, but its origins can be traced to a trip that Jean Dubuffet took to Switzerland in 1945 to visit psychiatric hospitals, seeking art made by patients. He called what he found "*art brut*": "raw art," which was "created from solitude and from pure and authentic creative impulses—where the worries of competition, acclaim, and social promotion do not interfere."

In that sense, Wong both was and was not an outsider artist. He had an MFA, but he had taught himself to paint. He worked out of compulsion, but he also cultivated an audience and a community of peers. He was caught between East and West: he had once noted, "I'm trying to see where I can fit into the Chinese painting equation," but he was primarily seeking entry to the New York art world.

From Zhongshan, Wong wrote to Shear, "I'm technically an outsider artist. Are you?"

"I never got my test results," Shear wrote.

"Just not very brut," Wong responded. "lol."

While looking for a way to show in New York, Wong learned about White Columns, a nonprofit space specializing in artists who are not formally represented. On John Cheim's recommendation, he submitted images of six paintings by e-mail, with a request to stage an exhibition. Two hours later, the director, Matthew Higgs, responded. He explained that White Columns was booked through the next year, but that he was curating a group show in September 2016, for an East Village gallery called Karma. Focused on landscapes, the show was titled "Outside"—"as in 'the outdoors,' but also to allude to an 'outsider' aesthetic/attitude/spirit." He invited Wong to include two of his paintings. One featured a naked man, possibly Narcissus, gazing into a pond; the other portrayed a man on a rock masturbating to a woman. Rendered in acrylic, they had the raw but honest figuration of an untrained painter.

Wong was running errands with his mother when Higgs's offer arrived on his phone. Monita, who turned sixty that year, recalled, "It was the best birthday present." Thrilled, they asked Cheim how to price his paintings. He suggested an ambitious figure—three thousand dollars apiece—but noted, "It's about the opportunity, not about the money." Monita told her son, "We should go to New York!"

At the opening, in Amagansett, Long Island, the two showed up early and found Higgs in the gallery. "Hi, Matthew—I'm Matthew," Wong said. Higgs was confused. He told me, "Very few artists travel that kind of distance to go to a forty-person group show." Monita and Matthew had brought more paintings in the trunk of their car, and they were eager to show them. "If you went to art school, they would have told you, 'Do not do that,'" Higgs added. "But there was an extraordinary un-self-consciousness about it, and that was quite disarming."

Karma's founder, Brendan Dugan, was similarly intrigued; in the run-up to the show, people who knew Wong from social media registered enthusiasm about his work. "They were talking as if I should know who he was," he told me. At the show, Dugan heard about a crowd in the parking lot. Walking out to investigate, he found Monita and Matthew trying to sell pieces from their car. Struck by their sense of urgency, he offered to meet the following week in New York.

In the meantime, Wong visited painters he had befriended online. One of them, Nicole Wittenberg, invited him to a gathering at her Chinatown studio. He arrived, again with his paintings, and they propped them up on windowsills and radiators—an impromptu exhibit. Wittenberg thought that they were good but encouraged Wong to be bolder. As her friends chatted, Wong smoked intently and talked very little. After the others left, he opened up and asked questions. "He wanted to know how his work would get into the public eye," she recalled.

A few days later, Matthew and Monita went to Karma, with paintings and drawings, to make the case to Dugan that the gallery should represent him. It was an awkward meeting. Dugan struggled with their forwardness, and they struggled with his polite reserve. Afterward, Monita and Matthew left to have lunch.

"What do you think?" Matthew asked.

"It's good he did not say anything negative," Monita said.

After their meal, they returned to Karma to pick up their paintings, and they ran into Dugan again. This time, Monita recalled, "he was so warm." She guessed what had happened. Earlier, Wong had mentioned selling two paintings to Andrea Schwan, an influential art-world publicist. Monita figured that Dugan must have been in touch with her while they were at lunch: "He said, 'Andrea is like a sister to me.' He walked us out onto the street, and he was so talkative, and he said, 'Why don't you send me some more images? We'll see what we can do.'" The next day, Dugan offered to take a few of Wong's paintings to an art fair in France, the Paris Internationale.

Dugan's offer was a kind of audition, but Monita and Matthew strove to treat the relationship as formal representation. During an extended visit to Hong Kong, Wong tracked Karma's Instagram feed, hoping to see his work hanging in the show. He wrote to Dugan asking for updates. "It was so intense," Dugan recalled. "Imagine you have someone you haven't even really met, and he's calling you, like, twenty-four hours a day, while you are trying to make it all happen." Dugan eventually sent a photo from the show and then stopped responding.

For Wong, the wait was excruciating. "That was one of the worst weeks of my life," he later recalled. He worried that Dugan's silence indicated that the work was not selling (which turned out to be true) and, perhaps worse, that it reflected a deeper lack of acceptance. Dugan, for his part, told me that he was uncertain how to manage Wong's expectations. "He was desperate to make this happen quickly," he said. "He *needed* it."

•　　•　　•

As Wong waited anxiously for news from Paris, he was changing his approach again. With the prospect of backing from a New York gallery, he became tougher on himself: he was no longer painting for the internet. Ruthlessly, he destroyed pieces that he did not think were promising. He switched to smaller brushes. He slowed down. Rather than teasing out images from the pigment as he worked—or "simply painting every day aimlessly," as he put it—he sought to begin with a vision. His output dropped to a painting a day, though this, he noted wryly, "still isn't really slow by any rational standards."

Wong's travels in North America had given him new ideas. He had visited artists' studios, and gone to museums where he could study masterworks with his nose inches from the canvas. The pieces that he made on paper had become more lyrical, with his old gestural fury giving way to subtler, more obsessive mark-making. He was allowing overt beauty to creep in. In January, 2017, he and Monita returned to Edmonton, where he resumed working with oils on large canvases—something that he hadn't done in about a year. He had studied the use of light in works by Eleanor Ray and Chen Beixin, and absorbed lessons from such masters as Gustav Klimt and Yayoi Kusama. He told Shear, "I finally figured out how to paint."

Confused about where things stood with Karma, Matthew and Monita traveled to New York, and met Dugan at a diner on the Lower East Side. Wong struggled to suppress his sense of hurt. He didn't want to hear that he was *developing;* he wanted to be fully represented. Dugan regretted his lack of communication from Paris. "When you are a gallery, you want to deliver for your artist," he told me. He offered Matthew and Monita an optimistic update: since the Paris fair, Karma had been able to sell two of his works.

Dugan had not seen any of the new paintings that Wong was making in Edmonton, but, at the table, Wong pulled out his phone and showed him a piece titled *The Other Side of the Moon.* Dugan was stunned. "It was a huge breakthrough," he told me. The painting—which portrayed a lone figure in a sublime, lush landscape—had a refinement rarely evident in Wong's earlier pieces. It transmitted the glowing magic of a Persian illuminated manuscript, the charge of an impressionist masterpiece, the strangeness of a sixties sci-fi book cover. Karma took the canvas, and three other new paintings, to an art fair in Texas. This time,

Wong's work sold. The Dallas Museum of Art even purchased a piece.

A few weeks later, Karma exhibited more of Wong's paintings at Frieze New York. Jerry Saltz, the senior art critic for *New York* magazine, told me that he was wandering among the booths when his wife, Roberta Smith, an art critic at the *Times*, called him. "Get over to Karma right away," she said. "You have to see this."

Smith told me that she had called Saltz partly out of excitement and partly out of professional competitiveness—to establish that she had discovered the work first. "I had walked into Karma's booth and there was this amazing landscape," she recalled. "You looked at it quickly, then looked again and realized its intensity, the technique, all these small brushstrokes. You understood that it was made in this obsessive way, but also with a certain amount of wit."

Saltz rushed over. "It was like the top of my head caught on fire," he recalled. "I saw a kind of visionary. I just saw something that seemed to be informed by a thousand sources, like this incredible cyclotron of possible influences. Yet unlike most artists who are influenced by early-twentieth-century styles, and never quite escape those influences, here I felt like I was seeing right through them to his own vision."

Self-consciously, Wong was allowing all that he had gathered in his head to emerge on canvas. Describing one of his works to Frank Elbaz, a Parisian gallerist, he explained, "There's that oblique seeming referentiality to historical precedents like Vuillard and Hockney but filtered through something more personal." Occasionally, the references were overt. He painted an homage to Klimt's *The Park*, adding a man reading. He rendered a version of Hokusai's *The Great Wave* in a manner that recalled van Gogh. The water was angular, daggerlike, with the sky an electric orange and the negative space around the wave resembling a bird gazing out beyond the edge of the canvas.

Wong's paintings were melancholy but playful, growing in size and ambition. It's easy to imagine how they might have failed: with the slightest aesthetic nudge tilting them into cliché or illustration or banal earnestness. That he had kept them teetering made them only more alluring. Elbaz told Wong that he was like an early modernist, shuttled to the twenty-first century in a time machine built out of a DeLorean. "*Back to the Nineteenth* could be a good title for your biopic," he said.

•   •   •

Just six years after Wong had picked up a paintbrush in Hong Kong, Karma staged his first New York solo show, in 2018. He had been tremendously eager to have it, but the more successful he became the more he felt the need to outdo himself. "Something can become a mannerism so quickly, especially with artists who have established themselves," he told Shear in 2014. "The things they do that were at some point, even recently, a breakthrough have long worn out their welcome."

Wong told Dugan that for his second solo exhibition he envisioned paintings united by a single color; the title, he said, would be *Blue*. The idea—with its nod to Picasso—spoke of Wong's ambition and state of mind and also his interest in a register that was "neither ironic nor wholly sincere" but, instead, something like Kanye West's video for "Bound 2," an elusive blend of kitsch, fame, and earnestness.

He worked furiously on *Blue*, telling Nikil Inaya, a friend in Hong Kong, "If I continue at this pace, I will be dead in a few months." The paintings were full of otherworldly longing. *Blue View* portrays a window in a haze of cyan, its gradations so subtle that reproductions fail to capture its sorrowful glow. In *Autumn Nocturne*, a moon becomes entangled in an azure forest, the brushwork intricate and deft. In *Unknown Pleasures*, named for an album by Joy Division, a road approaches a mountain but never reaches it.

By the end of 2018, Wong was telling Inaya, "I am deep in a cave of nihilism." He said that part of him hoped for a more conventional life. "He would speak about the idea of finding a final painting, and then, at last, retiring," Inaya told me. "But the counter-argument for Matthew was 'I don't know what else I could do.'"

In January, Monita took Matthew to Los Angeles to escape Edmonton's winter weather and isolation. "When we are there,

Cecile spoils him," she told me. Though thin, Wong had a relentless appetite; it was not beyond him to eat a second entrée while others got dessert. Cecile fed him lavishly.

Wong had developed friendships with some well-known artists: Nicolas Party, Jennifer Guidi, Jonas Wood. On a visit to Wood's studio, he asked about technique and scrutinized his paintings. Later, he returned to join a poker game. Wong fell in with a Hong Kong fashion designer and impresario, Kevin Poon, who took him partying late into the night. "He was having fun," Poon recalled. "People were taking photos of him, and he wasn't even that wary."

That spring, Wong's work was included in a book on landscape painting by the critic Barry Schwabsky, and he flew to New York for a panel discussion about it at the Whitney. At a dinner afterward, "Matthew had the magnetic personality at the table," Schwabsky told me. "He was the one everyone wanted to talk to. But the striking irony was that it was clear that Matthew considered himself to be socially awkward and ill at ease, even though this was not visible at all. My wife was basically ready to adopt Matthew. She was trying to convince him to move to New York. She was going to find girlfriends for him."

Wong still yearned to be with a woman, and though he was able to build friendships online, he was never fully comfortable in person. One female friend, meeting him in New York, ran up and hugged him; he tensed and said, "I don't hug people." Another told me, "I felt like I loved him. He was so intimate but in the least creepy way." A Canadian painter who had a crush on him begged him to meet at an artists' retreat. He declined. In 2017, he had been given a diagnosis of autism, and he suspected that he also had borderline personality disorder or something like it. Schwabsky told me, "He felt he was incapable of being in a relationship."

•　　　•　　　•

Wong rarely depicted himself in his art. Just after his first real breakthrough, in 2017, he painted *The Reader*, offering a view of himself, from his grandmother's window in Hong Kong, immersed in art history on a park bench. On the windowsill, he painted a knife in a glass of water, to mark his metamorphosis; the detail, he later noted, signified the "implied violence fundamental to any change."

In 2019, Wong revisited the symbol. In an oil on canvas, he painted the same knife in a glass, up close, as if it were a towering monument. The liquid appears to be blood. The sky is an apocalyptic orange. There is no artist, just his icon of change.

By that summer, Wong seemed to be hinting at an intention to disappear, in ways that now haunt his friends. He had finished the work for *Blue*, but he was still feverishly making art: "Not painting is pain," he had once told Peter Shear. On June 30, Wong sent Dugan an image of an ambitious new canvas that, he said, would be his sole contribution to Karma's booth at Frieze London that fall. The work depicted a solitary figure gazing at an inviting home, across a white expanse that looks like a frozen lake. If you stand close enough, you can see that the expanse is unpainted canvas—an artistic void. Flying across it is a bird, perhaps a phoenix, rendered almost in calligraphy. Wong titled the painting *See You on the Other Side*.

Wong's student preoccupation with voids seemed to be returning. That May, he told Claire Colette, a painter in Los Angeles, that he had written a poem for the first time in three or four years. Titled "The Shape of Silence," it contained these lines:

Imagine reading a novel
Where instead of looking at the words
Your gaze was fixed on the spaces
Between them. When you get to the end,
What would you say of what you saw and felt?

On a trip to Hong Kong earlier in the year, Wong had told Inaya, "This is the last time I'm in this town." He began saying that he would no longer go to art events, not even his own. "Enough of that," he told a painter that August. "I never have a good time."

From Edmonton, Wong focused on friends he had made online. When Shear posted a photo of his window on Instagram, Wong asked if he could paint a version of it. He produced dozens of paintings like this for others, in some cases including friends' names in the titles: *Sunset, Trees, Telephone Wires, for Claire.* Together, the paintings mapped a web of relationships, with the artist in the empty space between them.

In mid-September, Wong and his mother returned to New York. *Blue* would open on November 8 and was poised to be a tremendous success. Wong was already earning tens of thousands of dollars from his paintings, and buyers were lining up. At Karma, Wong expressed a specific idea of where every painting should hang but also told Dugan that he was extricating himself, personally, from his work. He explained that he would not attend the opening and that he wanted the cover of the catalogue to contain no title, no name, no images. Instead, the frontispiece would feature a line from Beyoncé's "Party." Dugan agreed to Wong's vision for the catalogue but tried to convince him that his presence was also important. On September 19, the two met for a parting breakfast. Dugan was flying to London for Frieze. Wong was preparing to return to Edmonton. As they said goodbye on the sidewalk, Wong told him, "I'll see you on the other side."

That afternoon, Wong had lunch with his mother and Scott Kahn, an elderly painter whom he had befriended. During the meal, the talk was upbeat, but when Monita left the table Wong's sadness poured out. "He said, 'I go into these deep, dark places that I wouldn't wish anyone to go to,'" Kahn recalled. "And he said it in such a way that it shook me to my core, nearly bringing tears to my eyes."

By evening, Wong had become engulfed in darkness. "Felt really close to death," he told Colette, "even if just mentally/spiritually." He said that he sensed malevolent energies coursing through the city. Unsure if they were psychotic figments, he still worried that the energies were endangering him and his friends: "It's like a wind or a shudder. Evil."

The following morning, Wong stopped by Karma, where the artist Alex Da Corte had recently finished installing a show. Titled *Marigolds*, it was inspired by Eugenia Collier's story about a young

Black girl struggling with the vagaries of race, poverty, and adolescence—as Collier wrote, "Joy and rage and wild animal gladness and shame become tangled together." In a fit of resentment, the girl tears up her neighbor's marigolds but later recognizes the moment as a turning point from blind innocence to maturity and compassion.

At a gathering at Karma, Da Corte spoke about the story. "It's about reconciling moments when one feels grief or rage," he told me. "Living in the world can be so fraught, and you have to navigate it the best you can with humility and grace."

Listening to Da Corte speak, Wong felt thunderstruck. "He said some things that sent a crack right down my soul for a direction of good and light," he told Colette that evening. Weeping, he ran from the gallery. For a while, his anxieties ebbed: convinced that he had attained clarity, he spoke about healing and transformation. But he remained in the grip of his illness. "There is so much darkness everywhere right now, and yet I feel very tender and vulnerable, empathetic and no longer resentful of many things," he went on. "Perhaps it's an empathetic tendency, but walking around New York despite being in the midst of circumstantial bliss both physically and mentally I feel a pull of death walking these streets."

•   •   •

In 1908, Pablo Picasso was in Paris, browsing in a shop that specialized in secondhand goods, when he noticed a painting jutting out of a pile. It was selling for five francs—basically the value of the canvas—but Picasso was enthralled by the image, of a woman leaning on a branch. It was both striking and naïve: the woman's left hand was hard to distinguish from her right. The painter was a retired customs officer named Henri Rousseau. Later that year, Picasso held a banquet for him, a gesture of respect and also of light mockery. Painters like Picasso were interested in untrained artists for their authenticity, but to fully embrace them risked slighting their own sophistication.

Monita told me that her son could never shake the feeling that members of the art establishment viewed him with condescension even as they celebrated his work. He was terrified of being a rube, like Rousseau, celebrated and dismissed all at once.

As if to demonstrate his sophistication, Wong unleashed a storm of images on Instagram as he left New York. From LaGuardia Airport, he used his phone to take screenshots of juxtaposed art works and posted scores of them in rapid-fire sequence. The work spanned the well known and the obscure, and the connections between them ranged from obvious to unfathomable. He brought together a painting by Dike Blair, of vending machines under a pagoda-like structure, and a Korean poem, "Ear," by Ko Un. He posted a floral Louis Vuitton jacket alongside Matisse's seminal *Le Bonheur de Vivre*. He paired his friends' paintings with masterworks.

The images piled up more rapidly than anyone could take in. Some artists were intrigued, some baffled, some worried. It's not clear that Wong understood what he was trying to achieve. "He reached out and said, 'I hope it isn't strange that I am doing this,'" the painter Louis Fratino recalled. Wong told Colette, "It all happened so quickly, on a subconscious level."

Eventually, Wong decided that his posts represented a stripping away of artifice. "I am aware of the intensity of this spectacle, but this kind of flow, rhythm, speed is the default natural state of my mind and senses 24/7," he told his Instagram followers. "It is how I have managed to teach myself some things about painting, relying on the Internet and the library. Being diagnosed as autistic, this is how I connect the dots."

Wong was suffering, but he still projected generosity. He reached out to a young painter, Benjamin Styer, whom he had once unsentimentally critiqued. "I have incredible respect for you," he said. "Keep going." He bought friends' work. Cody Tumblin, a painter who knew Wong well, told me, "He was looking to support people in these hyper-specific ways. It seemed like this desperation, like he really wanted to do something good." Wong posted a video demonstrating how he made his gouaches. He invited his followers to watch *Pineapple Express* with him. He was entering a manic state.

. . .

On the morning of September 30, Wong started texting Spencer Carmona, the painter in California, in long, frantic passages. "A lot of what he was saying didn't make a whole lot of sense," Carmona told me. "He was saying that he was being, like, gang-stalked through targeted ads online—from Instagram posts, from the Karma gallery, from Brendan. He was convinced that they had subliminal messages." Wong feared that the music he loved was being secretly altered. "I immediately knew something wasn't right."

Wong reached out to Colette, asking if she was free for a call, but she was sick with the stomach flu and didn't respond. He texted Tumblin. "Can we FaceTime?" he asked. "We don't ever see each other to talk, and I'd like to have that kind of relationship with my friends." He appeared on Tumblin's phone in a black T-shirt, unshaven, his hair all pushed forward. "He was talking ninety miles an hour," Tumblin told me. Wong spoke of his juxtapositions and of his anxieties, and he described conspiracies that extended from Kanye to members of his family. At one point, he wept. "He said, 'It's important that you know, so that you can talk about these things,' and that's when it started to get scary."

The following morning, October 2, *See You on the Other Side* was unveiled at Frieze. Wong texted Brendan Dugan, who was at the Karma booth, standing beside the painting. "Drinking coffee," Wong wrote. "About to do a little drawing." He asked Dugan to call whenever he could. "Nothing urgent," he added, "but, yeah."

As Dugan tended to the booth, Wong's texts grew troubling. One included an image of a piece that Alex Da Corte had posted on Instagram, titled *True Love Will Always Find You in the End*. It featured a cartoon skeleton emerging from a candy-colored staircase. "Now I'm genuinely frightened," Wong wrote.

Dugan called. It was clear that Wong was not well. Dugan and Monita spoke, too. Calls went back and forth. Eventually, Wong sent three texts indicating that they would see each other soon for the opening of *Blue*. At some point, he climbed to the roof of the building where his family lived, and stood in the cool air under a big Western sky, with clouds adrift ten thousand feet above.

Suicide was rarely far from Wong's mind—he often referred to it—and the lightness of flight had long preoccupied him. When he began his life as an artist, he was taken by Yves Klein's iconic *Leap Into the Void*, which uses photomontage to portray a man in a suit swan-diving off a building: he is going to either escape gravity or crash to his death. As a student, Wong took a photo in homage to it, and he had returned to Klein's photo in his juxtapositions. Birds and wings and wind were themes that recurred in his art—right up to *See You on the Other Side*, with its calligraphic phoenix crossing a void toward home, leaving the artist stranded.

Just a few days before Wong climbed to the rooftop, he had sent a fellow-painter a poem by A. R. Ammons. It was about yellow daisies. They are "half-wild with loss." Then they

> turn
> any way the wind does
> and lift their
> petals up
> to float
> off their stems
> and go.

.   .   .

During my trip to Edmonton, Monita offered to take me to Matthew's resting place. It was a short drive over the North Saskatchewan River: a few turns and we were at a nondenominational cemetery on the edges of a golf course. We passed a tiny chapel, its gray modernist steeple pricking the sky, and pulled up to a cluster of mausoleums. Monita was wearing a gray puffer and a white surgical mask. As she parked, she said, "I will take off my mask." I did, too.

A suffocating loss surrounds her. All the work that she does for the foundation—all the respectful attention showered on her son by museums, artists, auctioneers, and critics—is a reminder of this loss. "I am in so much pain, no one will understand," she told me. From afar, some of Matthew's friends also struggle with his death—"I miss having him in my studio," Shear told me. They weigh nagging questions. Was there any way they could have intervened? Were his vulnerabilities somehow overlooked? "You kind of saw the machine of the art world devour him a little bit," one painter told me.

Monita and I followed a cobblestoned path among the mausoleums. Matthew's was made of polished Canadian red granite and stood five or six feet tall, with space for two people. It was unclear why she chose a structure for two. At some point, she filled the second chamber with books by writers Matthew loved: David Foster Wallace, Donna Tartt, Ocean Vuong.

Matthew's funeral was held two weeks after he died. A few people from the art world made the trip to Canada. Some locals also came: a contractor who had worked on the Wongs' apartment, a therapist. Online, artists who knew him paid tribute. Some made pieces in his honor. Shear painted a haunting gray oil titled *Edmonton*. Matthew Higgs, the curator who first showed Wong in New York, told me he expects that, after the market noise around Wong fades, a deeper understanding of his work will emerge. "I think it stands for something more than itself," he said. "We'll have a clearer idea of what Matthew was trying to say to us."

Since Matthew was put to rest, Monita has been visiting his grave site weekly. At the mausoleum, she poured water from plastic bottles into two plants. At Christmastime, she told me, she adds a small tree.

Two Chinese inscriptions are chiseled into the granite. One is a quote from a Cantonese pop song, about crossing a landscape of obstacles—"high mountains and deep seas"—with grace, detachment, and love. The other is a statement from Raymond about the joys and worries that Matthew had brought him and Monita, their commitment to remaining strong for him, and their undying affection.

The mausoleum also features a poem, "June," that Matthew wrote in 2013, shortly after he separated from his girlfriend and immersed himself in painting. Its narrator has pulled away from his love and dissolved into fragments. But he coheres, somehow, and trails her, like a ghost or a dream. Imagining that she is waiting for him—"perhaps expecting me to turn up around the corner in the rain"—he tries to close the gap between them by shutting his eyes and kissing her.

I asked Monita why she chose this poem. "I felt that it was speaking to me," she said. "June is my birthday month."

We were standing in the crisp air, with a remote northern sun lightly warming us, when a huge white-tailed jackrabbit emerged from a shrub. It sat in some mulch by Matthew's mausoleum, a few feet from us, and fixed its gaze on the polished granite, as if paying respects—like a surrealist detail in a poem by James Tate. Monita and I stopped talking and watched. Some birds took off from a nearby tree. In the distance, there was a murmur of suburban traffic. We waited for the hare to run off, but it seemed content to just sit there and wait. At last, Monita whispered, "Maybe it's keeping Matthew company."

Paris Review

The ASME Award for Fiction was established in 2018 to honor the historic link between literary fiction and magazine journalism. "Winter Term," by Michelle de Kretser, was one of three short stories that won the Paris Review *the award this year. The other stories were "Trial Run," by Zach Williams, and "A Good Samaritan," by Addie E. Citchens. The Fiction judges praised these stories as "arresting, electric with tension, and unfailingly alive" and said they "remind us that short fiction should leave readers discomfited and alert to new possibilities." De Kretser is an Australian writer born in Sri Lanka. Her most recent novel is* Scary Monsters, *published in 2021. Founded in 1953, the* Paris Review *also won the ASME Award for Fiction in 2020 and was nominated this year for the National Magazine Award for General Excellence.*

Michelle de Kretser

Winter Term

S
he walked to school along streets named for English poets, but the one thing everyone in Melbourne knew about her suburb was its nameless canal. It was held to be behind headaches, sore throats, and babies who wouldn't settle, and was considered little better than an open drain. The reek of it sprawled in summer. Halfway along, the towpath relaxed into an open, grassy patch where, all year round, fights took place after school.

She'd been called Anny since arriving in Australia two years earlier. Her best friend was Lou. Lou lived minutes from school, but the morning bell often found her racing, and she would burst into classrooms with hair that looked as if it contained twigs. Mr. Cullen (history) didn't mind, nor did Mrs. Dobek (maths), but on Wednesdays (English), Anny waited tensely at her desk beside Lou's empty place. The third time Lou was late, Miss Kelso sent her to the deputy principal. Heaps of boys had crushes on Miss Kelso, who had cleavage and ringlets. The girls noticed that she had lipstick on her teeth.

Miss Kelso left no bruises that showed, but calculated the bestowing and withholding of smiles. She was the year-ten co-ordinator, and Anny had a form that required her signature. She rehearsed saying, Sorry, miss, I know you're very busy. At the end of English she went up to Miss Kelso and blurted, Sorry, miss, I know you're very boring.

.   .   .

Lou's brother had dropped out of school to go traveling in Asia, but his friend Sandor lived at her place. Her mother, Maeve, had got together with Sandor the previous year, when she was the school receptionist. When Sandor's parents found out, his mother paused on her way into the principal's office to call Maeve a filthy Jew. Maeve was confused—who was this beehived woman shouting at? Later that day, Anny was at Lou's place when Sandor explained that "Jew" was merely the worst insult his mother knew. The girls were eating ice cream, drinking Irish coffee, and listening to *Nilsson Schmilsson*, celebrating with Maeve and Sandor because he'd moved in. The school was powerless to prevent it, and so were the cops— he was almost seventeen.

•   •   •

On winter evenings, Anny added to a list in her notebook. Monday: green-flowered corduroy midi skirt, navy polo jumper, maroon boots, long camel-colored coat. Tuesday: brown corduroy midi skirt, beige polo jumper, boots, coat. Wednesday: denim midi skirt, black polo jumper, boots, blue velvet blazer . . . The notebook also contained poems on the theme of lasting love, poems like "When You Are Old" and "John Anderson my jo, John." In autumn, a season that now seemed as remote as a different century, she'd copied out those poems and learned them by heart.

The list recorded the clothes worn by Rahel, whose family had immigrated from Israel in February, at the start of the school year. Around that time, Anny had started lying to her parents. Every Saturday, having said that she was going to Lou's place to have dinner and study, she would put on her best top, blue with long, puffed sleeves, and meet Dave at the tram stop. They'd go to the city, where they would see a film or eat hamburgers in a diner. Dave always put five cents into the jukebox for "Smoke on the Water." Afterward, they'd lie kissing in parks where the grass was covered in fallen leaves.

One recess just before the May holidays, Anny and Dave were sitting at the top of the rear stairs in the science block. He'd taken her there to tell her that his grandmother, lifting a slat in a blind, had seen them kiss at his gate the previous day. When Dave went in, a scene had begun that continued all evening, accruing intensity as each of his parents came home to be informed in turn that their son was carrying on with a Black shiksa. Anny began twisting her love beads, and Dave said she was not to worry about him. He'd explained that the kiss was nothing serious, just a bit of fooling around, because he was actually seeing an Israeli girl. He'd called Rahel straightaway, and she'd agreed to have lunch with his family on Sunday and go to the cinema afterward. Dave had started off speaking in a rush, but by the time he got to Rahel he sounded calm and expectant. Days later, it dawned on Anny that he'd been waiting for applause. He was the school star at maths and had once again demonstrated smart problem-solving. Reliving their conversation, she started fiddling with her necklace. It snapped, shooting tiny blue beads across her lap.

•   •   •

The winter term began before she could bring herself to tell Lou what had happened, omitting the word *Black*. Anny knew two things about Dave's grandmother. The old woman had a tremor in her hand that caused her to grasp her table knife tightly and saw at the meat on her plate; the screech that resulted caused Dave's teeth to tingle unpleasantly. His grandmother also had a line of numbers on her arm. Anny told Lou that a concentration camp survivor had moral authority—no one could defy that, which was why Dave had to break up with her. Lou replied that the old bitch held the purse strings for sure. When Anny objected, Lou asked why anyone would pay attention to an old woman who wasn't rich.

The girls were heading for the gate after school when Miss Kelso's louse-colored Holden went past. Lou gave it the finger at the moment when Miss Kelso looked in her rearview mirror. The next day Lou was no longer class president. Lou couldn't care less, she said, because she was no longer comfortable with privileges designed to elevate her above the masses. Then she said that Kelso was a stupid bitch. She closed her lips around her forefinger and withdrew the finger smartly and said that was all you had to do.

*   *   *

Mr. Cullen, their favorite teacher, was American. At the thought of America, Anny felt weary in advance. America was modern life, the no-nonsense future, a glass cliff she'd have to clamber up one day. At the top of the cliff lay a broad expanse, like the grassy widening of the towpath: a place of wonder and punishment.

But Mr. Cullen pointed out that still today, in 1974, the People's Republic of China, established twenty-five years earlier, was a featureless space on American maps. His class also learned that the notorious Christmas bombing of Hanoi, just one year before Kissinger got the Peace Prize, had been America's largest air strike since World War II. By contrast, Australia had declared an end to its war in Vietnam and set up an embassy in Peking. The country's progressive politics were the reason Mr. Cullen had chosen to live there. He explained that under communism China had done away with poverty, famine, and flies, while the Cultural Revolution was currently sweeping away the last traces of bourgeois thinking. His copy of Chairman Mao's Little Red Book was passed from desk to desk. Anny read, "Recently there has been a falling off in ideological and political work among students and intellectuals, and some unhealthy tendencies have appeared."

When Mr. Cullen's glasses slipped down, he would wrinkle his nose to raise them. While Anny's eyes remained on him, she was far away on a long march through mountains, a red banner triumphant overhead. Not that everyone in the class was marching in step. Ivan raised his hand and his croaky-squeaky voice to ask what happened to homosexuals in China. Mr. Cullen said there were no homosexuals in China.

Ivan's sleepy gray eyes and lanky body had caused volcanic disturbances in Anny in her first term at the school. Then some boys bashed him and chucked him into the canal, and in the fallout she finally understood the meaning of the word she'd imagined was spelled *p-o-u-f-f-e*. Lou hadn't been her best friend then. That happened the following year, when they discovered that they both liked to scratch out the faces in their class photo.

.   .   .

The school library yielded *Away with All Pests*, an English surgeon's account of living in China in the fifties and the pioneering medical work done there. Among other feats, the Chinese had synthesized insulin for the first time. The book moved and sickened Anny—the descriptions of reattaching severed limbs! She was guilty of unhealthy tendencies, preferring *The Good Earth* and *Man's Estate*, weeping over each in turn. It was becoming clear to her that it was Lou who was cut out for ideological and political work.

Boys used to fight one another over Lou, an indiscriminate kisser. Then her gas-blue eyes and thrilling breasts drew the attention of Joe, who was in year twelve and the editor of the school magazine. For some time now, she'd been accompanying him to the weekly meetings of Hashomer Hatzair, a Jewish youth group with socialist-Zionist aims. Hashy was secular, Lou reported, so no one objected to the presence of a gentile. Anny associated *gentile* and *Jew* with the Bible. Before Australia she'd thought of them as dusty designations, like *Hittite* or *Assyrian*.

Lou was writing an essay for the magazine called "Socialism Is the Grammar of Justice," and reading *QB VII*, *Lord of the Rings*, and *Manifesto of the Communist Party*. She advertised her contempt for democracy by wearing jeans and desert boots. Her khaki canvas shoulder bag, sourced from Aussie Disposals, signaled total opposition to war. Revolution, on the other hand, was necessary and inevitable, according to Lou.

Anny was keen on justice and also on grammar, and it was the parsing of justice that alarmed her. Events in the country of her birth had caused her to dread violence, despite Lou's lucid account of why Trotsky had to die. She wrote an anti-war poem that contained birds, soldiers, and the line "Strange green jungles in a harsh green land." She slipped it into the manila envelope taped to the door of the room where Joe's editorial committee met once a week.

•   •   •

Dave and Rahel were in year twelve and therefore easily avoided, but Rahel always ate her lunch in the art room, where the year twelves were allowed to smoke. As she headed there from the science block, her creamy oval face, wavy hair, and fabulous clothes could be observed from a distance. Every evening, when Anny wrote down what Rahel had been wearing, she was transferring a fraction of the power and beauty of those clothes to herself. A long coat and tall, shining boots would rescue even a Black shiksa from humiliation and lovelessness. Anny believed and didn't believe this. It was an analgesic, an intermittently effective one.

The school had abandoned uniforms at the start of the year, so there went the money invested in tunics, school jumpers, motto-and-crest blazers. For winter Anny had jeans, a good jumper, a pilled one, a parka, and sneakers. She couldn't ask her parents for new clothes. For a long time now her mother had spent the greater part of her days in bed. At night she might cook, or walk about the house taking things out of certain drawers and putting them in others. She no longer showered every day. Anny knew when her mother had visited her room from the trailing smell.

Her father worked alongside clerks half his age in the public service. He bought one giant sliced loaf a week, and took ham paste sandwiches to work and to the evening classes that would bring him the Australian qualifications he needed to practice law. He was saving for a deposit on a house. Rent was money out of the window, but a stronger motivation was his belief, confided in Anny, that a new house on an estate would mean a fresh start for her mother. Now and then, when Anny remembered, she still prayed. She prayed that the move wouldn't happen until she was safe at uni, when Lou and she intended to share a Victorian terrace house with seagrass matting on the floor. It was vital to think "before" and "when" and "after," to arrange herself along a taut line where one thing led logically to the next. In the absence of that line, her life might go straggly and directionless like her mother's.

.   .   .

Lou spent the night of her sixteenth birthday with Joe. She described how Maeve had prepared her bedroom with incense, candles, and marigold petals scattered on sheets that showed crease lines from the packaging. Three months earlier, Maeve had got Lou on the pill, saying that she'd been pregnant at seventeen and no way was Lou going the same route. Lou made Anny swear never to tell Maeve that she'd been fucking Joe in his car for weeks. Anny had already sworn never to tell Maeve that back when Lou was in year eight, she used to fantasize about Sandor while masturbating.

.   .   .

An ankle-length velvet coat hung in the window of a secondhand clothing shop on Carlisle Street. It was dusky pink, lined in silver satin that had darkened at the armholes and was ripped near the hem. The shopkeeper said it had belonged to a white Russian who fled to Australia from Harbin when China turned to shit. He stroked the coat, smiling at Anny, and introduced himself as Travis. When she told him her name, he said he'd been hoping for something exotic but Anny would have to do. He encouraged her to try on the coat. In his cheval glass she beheld herself transformed, charged with the glamour of famous events.

The coat cost eighteen dollars fifty. She returned to the shop with the seven dollars she'd saved from babysitting as a down payment. After that there was only the dollar she received once a week to buy lunch. A cheese-and-tomato roll from the canteen cost nineteen cents, so by Friday she had enough for a five-cent packet of chips as well. But now she started shoveling in cornflakes at breakfast and skipping lunch. In the girls' locker room, deserted at recess, she peered under the rows of lockers, where sometimes she found a coin. She always held a pen, and was scrabbling under a locker to retrieve it if anyone came in.

Every Saturday she handed Travis another dollar note. He would urge her to slip into the coat, coming up close and lifting her hair free of the collar. Sometimes she gave him five or ten cents less, which meant she'd caved in and bought chips.

. . .

Once a week the girls patted their faces with cotton wool soaked in egg white that they left on for ten minutes. Maeve said if there was only one thing you did for your complexion, that should be it.

. . .

Anny's mother joined the family for dinner one evening. She used funny old expressions like *yeoman service*, trying to make her daughter laugh. Halfway through the meal, she laid down her cutlery and told her plate, very softly, Help me help me help me. Then she went on chatting in an upbeat tone.

. . .

Phys ed switched from hockey to ice skating at St. Moritz. When the girls left the rink, the afternoon was already fainting along the horizon. They called in to see Maeve and be fed hot chocolate and *kugelhupf* in the cake shop where she now worked.

Lou described Anny's hair as "anarchic." She envied it, Lou said. She was trying to radicalize her own fine, pale hair by sleeping in damp plaits and never brushing the result.

. . .

Miss Kelso, wearing jeans tucked into boots, required her class to write an essay on *The Permissive Society*. Anny would have preferred to write about poetry, but Miss Kelso always set boring subjects picked over by journalists and advised everyone to read *Time*— that mouthpiece for the capitalist-imperial machine.

Anny researched the overthrowing of the Chatterley ban, but she was really thinking about Maeve: her flares, her dolly haircut, the way she held her cigarette with her palm up, the lounge room she had furnished with cushions, large speakers, and hanging plants.

·   ·   ·

A roadie friend slipped Maeve a couple of freebies for Sherbet at St. Kilda Town Hall. When Maeve's horn sounded, Anny's father left his textbooks open on the kitchen table and came downstairs with his daughter. He greeted Lou and was introduced to Sandor, and Maeve told him no worries, Anny would be quite safe. It was plain to Anny that her father thought Sandor was Lou's brother and that Maeve was going to the concert, too. She could remember him, when she was small, demonstrating how to strike a match safely, angling it down against the side of the box. She felt a scornful sort of pity for him now, so readily trusting and duped.

Sandor and Maeve dropped the girls off and headed to a club, because he was teaching her about jazz. When the concert ended, Anny and Lou set out to walk home with ringing ears. It was misty and very cold, and cars slurred past, men hanging out of them and yelling stuff that always meant, Fuck us, yer fucken molls! Lou shouted back, Hear me roar! All evening there'd been a loud, false vividness to Lou. She'd botted smokes off boys and laughed flirt- ily with them between the support band and Sherbet. Anny could tell that this was because Joe had refused to go to the concert, say- ing Sherbet sucked. Marching along Brighton Road in her oversize ex-army jacket, Lou said that years ago, Joe's father, who was a den- tist and had just cleaned Lou's teeth, waited until the nurse left the room and told Lou she had a nice bum. She linked arms with Anny, who pictured their two tiny figures on the long march to knowl- edge, Lou's far in advance.

At Broadway, where they hugged goodnight, she warned Lou to stay off the towpath, and Lou said she planned to. But she was giving off those flaky vibes, so Anny stayed watching until Lou was safely past the shortcut beside the canal.

. . .

Anny's essay was suspiciously good, said Miss Kelso, and asked whether it was all her own work. Lou got top marks for writing about women's lib and the pill.

. . .

Anny lay in bed, thinking that what she missed was not so much Dave as putting on her pale blue blouse and going out to meet her boyfriend on Saturday evening. It was a relief not to have to like Deep Purple, but she wished she were lying on leaves with Dave's hand inside her knickers, the moon round and white as a Valium overhead. Beneath her longing was an awareness that having a boyfriend was an experience that would come again, maybe even before she left school. Perhaps her mother, too, would reappear one day, just as she used to be, funny and fierce.

. . .

Joe had decided to work on a kibbutz in Israel after finishing school. Lou was considering doing the same, she said. What about us, Anny asked, and Lou's face went vague. Just an idea, she said, closing a door with three words.

. . .

Thursday: green velvet midi skirt, black jumper, boots, coat. The green skirt was a dream possession, one to set beside the entrancing, unavailable objects yearned for in childhood. The weighty swing of it, the color, plunged long spikes of pure, cold wanting into Anny's heart.

With only two weeks of the winter term left, she still owed Travis five dollars. On Saturday she went to the shop just before it closed. She took the coat into the corner rigged up as a fitting room, and Travis continued carrying in racks of shoes from the street. When all her clothes were lying on the floor, Anny put her head around the curtain and called. Travis came over, and she told him that he could look for as long as he wanted, but he wasn't to touch. Travis went away and locked the shop door, and ten minutes later he unlocked it. Anny left, wearing the coat.

·   ·   ·

On Monday morning, as they queued up outside their classroom, Ivan looked Anny over and said, Nice. As well as the coat, she was wearing golden leather shoes, creased across the instep, with a chunky heel. Travis had given them to her, warning her that they were character shoes, not intended for outdoor use. He also told her not to come back again.

Rahel wasn't to be seen at lunchtime, nor when school ended, nor the following day. Word got around that she had glandular fever and wouldn't be back before the spring.

·   ·   ·

Everyone had tickets to a university production of *The Crucible*, which year ten was doing in English. Joe wanted to see the play, too, so Lou, Anny, and Ivan gathered at his place after school for a lift to the campus. Ivan had changed into his best outfit: wide blue-and-brown tartan trousers with cuffs, a caramel body shirt, and platform shoes.

Joe had the benign yet impersonal manner of a medical professional, borrowed, Anny imagined, from his father, the dentist. Sitting behind him as he drove, she pictured his red-gold Afro bent over her poem and considered jumping out of the car.

Miss Kelso and Mr. Cullen were among the teachers in the packed auditorium. The atmosphere was rowdy and joyful, as if the holidays had already begun. It lingered after the performance, with a bunch of people from their school hanging about outside the theater, loudly discussing the play. Joe and Mr. Cullen got on to McCarthyism, and ignored Ivan when he said that Chinese Red Guards denouncing their parents was witch hunting.

Abigail and Tituba emerged from the theater. It took a minute to identify Tituba, now wrapped in a sheepskin jacket and no longer Black. Miss Kelso called, Bravo! as the actors went past. She waggled her car keys and told Mr. Cullen that if he wanted a lift home, she was pushing off. Mr. Cullen and Joe were on to Watergate, and Joe said he could easily fit one more in his bomb. Mr. Cullen thanked Miss Kelso, and said he didn't want to take her out of her way twice in an evening. She went in one direction, and the five of them set off in another across the campus, Mr. Cullen still deep in conversation with Joe.

Lou offered Mr. Cullen her seat, but he said he was just fine in the back. Joe's demister didn't work, so everyone had to keep their coats and scarves on, and their windows open at the top. Mr. Cullen, sitting next to Anny with his knees wide, draped his arm along the back of the seat. Ivan, half turned away on her other side, was looking out at the sky. He sang "Starry, starry night," just that line over and over, a croaky counterpoint to Mr. Cullen's account of revolutionary praxis as enacted by Chinese peasants. After a while Joe stopped replying and picked up Ivan's tune, whistling between his teeth. When he took a corner too fast, Anny clutched the seat with both hands, and Mr. Cullen slid up against her. He stayed that way, pressed warm and close, as excitement tinged with unease bristled inside Anny. Then his hand burrowed through her hair. One finger set about tracing tiny circles at the base of her skull, and she turned shimmery with lust. Eager to convey expertise, she slipped her hand under Mr. Cullen's jacket and began stroking him through his jeans. He continued to caress her, now and then lightly twisting her hair to adjust her pace.

By the time they got to St. Kilda Junction, the racket of the engine was the only sound in the car. Ivan's head had slumped forward, but jerked upright when Joe hit the brakes. Work to widen the intersection was being carried out at night, and the car had to creep past barriers, jackhammering men in hard hats, and flashing orange lights. The Victorian buildings that lined the road lacked roofs and facades, or were already rubble. Lou remarked that Hanoi must look like that. Hanoi on a good day, said Anny, dreamily taking in the devastation and the din, and was surprised when the others laughed.

Having ascertained addresses, Joe stopped at Mr. Cullen's place first. Mr. Cullen said it had been a fun night and he hoped they could get together again soon. He gave Anny's hand a quick, firm squeeze as he spoke, and she understood that he was talking to her.

. . .

She left the canteen with her roll, saliva starting up in anticipation of salty tomato and cheese. Dave appeared and began to walk with her. Recalling Dave, middle-aged Anny would think, His bones looked older than he was. He usually went home for lunch, but was saying that he'd waited to see her. He felt bad, he went on, about the way things had turned out. Dave's eyes were small, slanted, and very blue. He had a face Anny had seen in old films. It showed up whenever men were herded together and given orders in black-and-white Europe. She looked away at the steep sky and bit into her roll.

. . .

The last day of winter, a Saturday, was the first day of the holidays. That evening Anny was minding a baby she'd minded before. He was a tremendous sleeper, but she left the door to his room open and didn't watch TV in case he cried. The lounge was snug from the kerosene heater, there were snacks on the coffee table, and she knew to help herself to hot drinks. For a while she ate Cheezels and went on with *The Mayor of Casterbridge*, pausing now and then to blow cheesy orange dust off a page. She hadn't had a class with Mr. Cullen in the two days of term left after *The Crucible*, but she'd observed him down corridors and across the yard. She saw a star-man, fallen from the sky. It wasn't only America he'd shed but every other country.

The cabinet in the lounge had stained-glass lozenges in the doors and a delicate brass key in the lock. The baby's parents kept the flat bottle there, hidden inside a china tureen. When they went out for an evening they always carried a bottle of wine; there was beer in their fridge and a cask of red on a kitchen shelf. It seemed obvious to Anny that the gin was an unwanted present. The bottle had been opened; she'd done that, risking a few swigs when she was last here. She had another gulp now, twisted on the cap, and tucked the bottle into her bag. The candle she'd used the previous time was still in its candlestick. She lifted it out, lay on the carpet, and wriggled her jeans and knickers below her knees.

When the baby's parents returned, the man offered to walk her home. She declined as usual, saying she lived only five minutes away. Fifteen minutes later she was across the street from Mr. Cullen's place: a blond-brick block, two flats downstairs and two up, with an external stair. A light showed in one window, TV was leaking through the venetians in another, and the parking lot was lit up like a stage. The only empty car space had a big white number 4 painted on the concrete. It told Anny which flat belonged to Mr. Cullen, who didn't drive. She loitered for a while, summoning authority from her coat, readying herself to knock on his door.

A car arrived from nowhere and swung into the vacant parking spot. The street was dark, and in any case the people who got out of the Holden were involved only with each other. Crossing that concrete stage, Mr. Cullen delivered a lesson in what it meant to be a starman: someone with no memories and no past. He put his arm around Miss Kelso, and she leaned into him as her boots went tok-tok-tok up the stairs.

·　　·　　·

Anny moved through the night, drinking gin. When she turned south, the wind was a wolf. There was something hard under her right foot, and she realized it was the pavement; her shoe had worn through.

The lights along Broadway had been placed there solely to expose stupidity and shame. But she had to go that way, past the plane trees that would give her hay fever in November, to get to Lou's. The first time she went to Lou's house, they'd dabbed scotch behind their ears like perfume. Through the bare vaults of the trees a toothy fragment of moon could be seen. A solid, awkward shape like that started working its way up through Anny's thoughts. Eventually it informed her that it was Joe's father's fiftieth and that Lou had gone to the party.

She wavered for an instant. But there was still Maeve—Maeve, who'd looked at her in the pink coat and said, Your face should be on money. Maeve would be warm and uninquisitive, she'd offer Irish coffee in a tall white mug with a shamrock and invite her to curl up on the cushions on her floor—at the thought of those big, soft cushions, Anny couldn't wait to lie down. A car slowed, its headlights assessing, before accelerating away. She saw the short-cut by the canal, its protective dark.

·   ·   ·

Stones poked up through her shoe and hurt her foot as she made her way past backyards with overhanging trees. When the path finally opened out, she stepped gratefully onto the grass. She sat down, removed her shoes, and rubbed her sore foot. It was another starry, starry night. Learning of the American bombs that fell over Hanoi for twelve days and nights, she'd pictured death-dealing Christmas stars. Was poetry a kind of ideological work, or just an unhealthy tendency? She was mostly aware of a subdued, greeny-brown smell, not altogether unpleasant, rising from the water. When the gin was gone, she unbuttoned her coat and spread it beneath her legs. Before lying down, she hurled the empty bottle into the canal, following it with her shoes, one by one.

Perhaps they heard the splashes and anticipated trouble, because they approached without a sound. She was still there, the cold just starting to enter her, when they arrived. They found her with her feet bare and her eyes closed, arranged on shining satin as if set out for their delight.

. . .

Time passed. Anny was strolling beside the river in Shanghai. In 1949, as Mao's army advanced, the Nationalist leader Chiang Kai-shek made off with all the gold in China. Laborers transferred the bullion from a bank on the Bund to a freighter waiting to take it to Taiwan. There was also the end of *Man's Estate*, when the revolutionary Katow sacrificed his cyanide to two young comrades in a Shanghai prison and went to his death by fire. These scenes flickered through her mind, illuminated fish, before sinking back into the weedy dark.

The drive home after *The Crucible* was present as well. She remembered shadowy companions, and a road that skirted a grassy field and ran between trees. The moon was out, there was a blaze of stars, and she saw everything distinctly, the leaning trees, the field. But there was nowhere like that on the way back after the play. It was like her poem about a harsh green place, something made from memories and dreams. But *Hanoi on a good day* was real, she knew that because she could hear them laughing. She couldn't understand why they laughed.

ESPN Digital

FINALIST—REPORTING

"Untold" is the story of Todd Hodne, "perhaps," as Tom Junod and Paula Lavigne write, "the most dangerous predator ever to play college football." The National Magazine Award judges described this piece as "riveting" and said it "gave voice to Hodne's victims while raising questions about the powerful institutions that may have protected him." Junod is one of the most honored writers in the history of the National Magazine Awards. Writing for ESPN, Esquire, GQ, and Atlanta, he has been nominated twelve different times in five different categories. His stories "The Abortionist" and "The Rapist Says He's Sorry" won the National Magazine Award for Feature Writing in 1995 and 1996, respectively. An award-winning investigative reporter at ESPN, Lavigne is the coauthor of Violated: Exposing Rape at Baylor University Amid College Football's Sexual Assault Crisis, published in 2017.

Tom Junod and
Paula Lavigne

Untold

K aren was alone in her apartment when the phone rang. She didn't like being alone. It had been weeks since she had been attacked there, but the apartment still felt to her like a crime scene, a place that had been turned over and rummaged through. She had called the police on the night of the attack, when she finally convinced herself that she might be safe. She had gone to the local hospital and submitted to an examination. She had opened the Yellow Pages and called a resource new to the town where she had gone to school and now lived, something called a rape crisis center.

But the police seemed to want more from her, even after she had told them everything she could remember. The hospital had run out of rape kits, and the nurse who examined her was rude, she thought, "mocking." The rape crisis center had no therapists to recommend, only women around her age who offered more sympathy than expertise.

Karen felt as though she were being pushed aside and forgotten. The attack she had endured was inescapably real, but in its aftermath she faced a sense of unreality so powerful that she kept in her pocket the scant newspaper clipping about her assault to remind herself that it really happened. The apartment provided no refuge. When she discovered that photos she kept of herself were missing, she knew they had been taken but couldn't be sure by whom. Nothing had gone untouched. When the phone rang, the call came through a line that a few weeks before had been cut by the blade of a knife.

She had heard from the police that there were others who had been attacked recently. She had heard some of the other women had received phone calls after their assault, possibly from the assailant. But when she picked up, she did not hear the voice she feared. This was someone familiar but not someone she knew. It was a man *everyone* knew. And when she realized who it was, she wondered immediately how he knew her name:

"Karen, this is Joe Paterno," the man said. "Are you OK?"

Act 1: Crime

Forty-three years ago, Penn State University played for its first national championship in a football season that began against Temple on September 1, 1978, and ended against second-ranked Alabama, on January 1, 1979. It was the season in which Penn State football became Penn State Football, a season that saw head coach Joe Paterno become an American icon. It was also a season that saw a serial sexual predator attack multiple Penn State students.

If you are any kind of sports fan, you probably know the first story, all the way through its shocking denouement ten years ago— the story of the football coach whose black shoes and white socks were seen as his moral underpinnings until they weren't . . . until his career ended when the sexual abuse committed by an assistant coach named Jerry Sandusky came to light. You almost certainly don't know the second. It is not just a story that hasn't been told; it's a story that doesn't exist, even in obscure corners of the internet. It's the story of a Penn State football player who, as his team ascended to the pinnacle of the sport, was ransacking the lives of women in the dark.

His name was Todd Hodne, and he was perhaps the most dangerous predator ever to play college football. "I have been a prosecutor for nearly thirty years," wrote John B. Collins, who prosecuted one of Hodne's crimes, in a letter to a parole board. "I have prosecuted serial killers and capital cases. Todd Hodne, to this day, remains among the three most dangerous, physically imposing and ruthless excuses for a human being I have ever faced in court."

Hodne arrived in State College in 1977 as a prized recruit from New York's Long Island, and in 1978, he was the Penn State Rapist. There were other rapes and rapists; Penn State, in the mid- and late seventies, was enduring an epidemic of sexual assault that female students of the day still talk about. But even against that backdrop, Hodne's rapes and attacks stand out because he was a football player who, according to one family member, "had no control over his dark impulses." He was big and strong, entitled and enabled. He was driven and determined and a little desperate. He was also cruel, the most predatory of predators, a hunter who liked to linger. He attacked with a knife to the throat, and when he attacked women, he made sure they couldn't see him, but he also liked to suggest they knew him. "Do you recognize my voice?" he'd asked Karen.

In October 1978, Hodne was finally caught on the strength of three fingerprints and a traced phone call. Five months later—two months after Penn State and Paterno lost the national championship game to Alabama and Bear Bryant—Hodne was found guilty of criminal sexual assault after one of his victims testified against him. But that was not the end of Hodne's string of attacks. It was, tragically, just the beginning of a series of crimes of such escalating violence that they have become generational, wreaking havoc on the lives of his victims and their descendants.

Todd Hodne died of cancer on April 29, 2020, six days after his sixty-first birthday, comatose but still under guard in the prison ward of a hospital in New York state. The story you are reading started with three questions about Hodne and his criminal career: What did he do, why wasn't he stopped, and why doesn't anyone know about him? We have examined hundreds of pages of surviving, often heavily redacted documents and have done hundreds of interviews with Hodne's friends, girlfriends, family members, teammates, and coaches, as well as those who investigated and prosecuted his crimes. We have contended with the obstacles of indifference and obstruction but also of time itself; after forty-three years, people grow old, people forget, and people die. But of course, they also remember, and the most consequential witness is offered by the women who survived the ravages not just of time but of Hodne himself—who survived their hours in the dark with a 240-pound Division I football player with a knife in his hand and no particular interest in their survival. Of the twelve women he is known to have attacked, four are dead. We spoke to six of the other eight and to the husband of a seventh. One did not respond. We asked them about the violent attacks they endured in 1978 and 1979—and forty-three years later, they remembered those crimes in unflinching detail. They shared the stories they'd had to bear in private. And out of that, out of the sheer scope of lives changed and ruined, emerged a portrait of a time and a place, a portrait of a football program and its coach, and a portrait of a terrifying predator who called himself "the All-American kid."

·   ·   ·

They were a bunch of kids, fourteen years old, but also strangers to one another. They were at freshman football camp, on a new team for a new school, St. Dominic in Oyster Bay, Long Island. They were just yakking before mealtime, in their bunks. You know boys like these: someone had to prove himself, someone had to dominate. So one of them, John Poggioli, started messing with the kid playing linebacker, the kid with the long face and the long hair combed to the side and the serious real estate at the jawline. Nobody even remembers what was said. But anyone who was there remembers what happened next. One second, Poggioli is talking, teasing the kid. Next second, the kid takes out a knife and throws it at him. He misses, but not by much—the knife sticks in the wall, vibrating like a tuning fork, a few inches from Poggioli's head. The linebacker, Hodne is his name, gets up and without a word pulls the knife from the wall. He slides it back in its leather sheath and heads for chow. The rest follow, wondering if they should tell one of the coaches what they just saw. They never do.

Hodne could hit. Even before he put on all that muscle, even when he was all shoulders and long legs and arms, he could ring bells, he could make the guy on the other side of the line quit or at least reconsider being a hero. "It was just different, getting hit by

Todd," Poggioli says. It's human instinct to slow down when you make a tackle—to pull up, just a little bit, right before contact. Hodne didn't have that instinct. He accelerated through the tackle. He accelerated through the ball carrier and liked to luxuriate in the aftermath, standing over the guy he laid out. There were rumors he stuck rolls of quarters in his arm pads.

His ferocity was what brought him to St. Dominic. It was a small school, with around 150 kids in each class, and not a traditional power. But the football coach, Tom Capozzoli, had been at St. Dom's for about a dozen years, and now he had a star player—his son Tony, who had won the national Punt, Pass, and Kick championship two years in a row. The athletic department decided to bring in players who would help the Capozzolis win a championship before Tom retired. Hodne was one of them, along with a teammate from the Levittown Red Devils travel team, Dave Smith. Hodne wasn't even Catholic. He was just rangy and violent, an intimidator.

He was even intimidating at the freshman dance in the fall of 1973. It was held at the Knights of Columbus Hall; the football players hung around a big round table, showing off for each other. Hodne wound up doing something they talk about even now. He pulled a girl at the dance under the table while his teammates stayed in their chairs—an act that made his reputation in some quarters and in some quarters undid hers. "To be very honest with you, we all pointed the finger at her," says Marge Galtieri, a St. Dominic cheerleader and one of Hodne's classmates. "We judged her. But maybe we judged her wrong, looking at the events of the following years."

Hodne was from Wantagh, a comfortably middle-class town between the little boxes of Levittown and the fulfillment of Robert Moses's vision in the boardwalk of Jones Beach. He had a hardworking father, a charming and stylish mother, and siblings with whom he was close. He became an All-Long Island linebacker whose very name rattled opponents. But even in ninth grade, Todd Hodne was a polarizing figure at St. Dominic because even in ninth grade, Todd Hodne was talking about breaking the law. He brought his knife to school and, according to Poggioli, "definitely" kept the quarters in his fists when he, as a freshman, battered a senior who challenged him. He also bragged about stealing car stereos and doing burglaries. His teammates listened, and they had to decide whether to believe him and what to do if they did. Dave Smith was the son of a Nassau County police officer, and when they were all sophomores, he told his father that Hodne was breaking into people's houses. Smith's father contacted Hodne's local precinct, which investigated. The result, says retired officer Don Smith, was that Hodne, at fifteen, was "custodialized" by the juvenile justice department of Nassau County and compelled to return the stereo equipment he had stolen. The intervention made enduring enemies of Hodne and Smith, the two inside linebackers for the St. Dominic Bayhawks. But it neither deterred Hodne nor threatened his status on the team.

Many of Hodne's teammates remember Tom Capozzoli repeatedly taking up for him with school administrators. One remembers a coach being fired after he tried to warn Hodne's parents about their son. Ralph Willard, who was the athletic director at the time and went on to coach basketball with Rick Pitino at Louisville, says, "I don't remember there being any problems with Todd, to be honest. I just remember how he hit."

St. Dominic won the state Catholic High School Football League championship in 1975, in Tom Capozzoli's final season as head coach. His son Tony, a senior, was named first-team Parade All-American, and he committed to Penn State as a quarterback and a kicker. Todd Hodne, Dave Smith, and John Poggioli had one more season together, and though Hodne and Smith once had a fistfight on the school stairs, Hodne and Poggioli were thought to be best friends. In truth, Poggioli said he remained in the friendship because he didn't know how to get out. He was drawn to Todd Hodne and he was afraid of Todd Hodne in equal measure, and Hodne made him pay every time Poggioli tried to emerge from under his sway. When Poggioli was a junior, he told Hodne that he might try out for the school play; Hodne responded by sneering, "You're no actor," and dumping a pail of water on his head. When Poggioli had a crush on a girl named Janet, he wouldn't dare ask her out because Hodne, though not her boyfriend, had claimed her. "In my four years at St. Dominic, nobody asked me out because they were so afraid of Todd," Janet Shalley remembers now. "I could only date boys from other schools. And back then, I had it going *on*."

Hodne followed Tony Capozzoli to Penn State. The coach who recruited both of them remembers Hodne as a good kid: "If he wasn't a good kid, we wouldn't have brought him to Penn State." But even with Hodne in Pennsylvania, Poggioli remained under his influence. After Hodne completed his freshman year as a Nittany Lion, he invited Poggioli and a friend from Wantagh to spend a weekend with him in State College. School had ended. But Hodne was living with some other athletes in a house off campus. He had made plans with his friends from home to drive to Philly for a Rolling Stones concert. They were going to have a cookout in the backyard, and so they went to the supermarket. "We went to get supplies for the barbecue and got a bunch of steaks," remembers his Wantagh friend. "He goes, 'I know this trick: You just turn the steaks over in the cart and walk on out.' So we robbed all these big steaks and had a feast."

The next morning, June 18, 1978, there was something else Hodne wanted. They went to a store on College Avenue, the main drag for Penn State students. It was called the Record Ranch, and Hodne, sometimes in the company of other athletes, had been stealing LPs from there since he'd come to school, hiding them under his coat. The store was closed on a Sunday morning, but Hodne wanted to go in. Poggioli thought it was a bad idea, he says now; the problem was telling his friend. "I didn't stop Todd because I couldn't stop Todd. If you tried to stop Todd, he would hurt you. You couldn't say no to him, and he could convince you to do things you wouldn't normally do." According to a police report, they kicked in a window of the Record Ranch and were in the process of stealing $30 in quarters and another $800 in merchandise—a Yamaha stereo amplifier; a Rolling Stones mirror; some T-shirts and Harley Davidson belt buckles; and record albums by Donald Fagen, David Gilmour, Little Feat, and Rick Wakeman, among others—when two employees from an adjacent store saw a door open and peeked inside. They saw Hodne's Wantagh friend dangling from the broken window and called the police. He was arrested along with Poggioli, who had stayed outside. But Hodne easily shrugged off the police and ran right through them. "Todd got away because Todd at that point was a criminal," Poggioli says. "He knew how to get away."

The next day, Hodne showed up at the police station, saying he heard two of his friends were in some trouble and wanted to visit them in jail. According to a police report, he first said his name was "Tom Harris." Then he changed his mind and "stated that his name was Todd Hodne . . . that he was a Penn State football player and that he did not want his name out." He was leaving the station when an officer told him he matched the description of the man who fled the Record Ranch burglary. The officer asked for permission to take a photograph of him, and Hodne agreed. Hodne drove back to Wantagh and, in his absence, was identified in a photographic lineup. When he returned to State College, he was arrested, and on June 21, he, along with his friend from the neighborhood, were charged and later convicted with felonies. "He ruined my life," says Poggioli, who wound up pleading to a misdemeanor. "But he ruined so many lives. I feel lucky to have gotten out when I did. I feel lucky compared to the others."

It was not a violent crime. But it was a felony, and Joe Paterno was a coach who called players into his office even when he heard they were not participating in classroom discussions. He was a disciplinarian, and there would have to be discipline. On August 19, 1978, two months after the burglary, Penn State held a scrimmage, and afterward, Paterno told gathered reporters that Todd Hodne had been suspended for the season. But he did not like to give up on his players, and he did not give up on Hodne. In his announcement, Paterno said that Hodne will be able to return to the team "if he has a good academic year and if he proves to us that [the robbery] was a mistake." He also sought to provide Hodne a role model for his sophomore season, and to that end, one of his seniors, Fred Ragucci, was summoned into the football office. Ragucci went to a Catholic high school on Staten Island, and now he played defensive end for Paterno. When Ragucci was told he would have a new roommate in Hamilton Hall, he didn't blink, even though he was two years older than Hodne and was not part of his crowd. Ragucci could figure out easily enough why he wound up in this unlikely pairing: "I was a pretty good student. I was pretty straight, never in any trouble. Nobody specifically mentioned this to me, but I think they were trying to put people in with people who might be a good influence."

They did not spend a lot of time together at 279 Hamilton. Why would they? In 1978, there was nothing in most college dorm rooms outside a stereo and perhaps a hot plate. But later, Ragucci will always remember one thing about his new roommate: his knife. It was Hodne's prized possession, a gift his grandmother gave him after she returned from a trip to her ancestral Norway, the blade forged from fine Scandinavian steel. But what Ragucci remembers is how much time Hodne spent with it, his fascination with it. "He was always playing with it when he was in the room," Ragucci says now. "It had a leather sheath, and he would take the sheath on and off, on and off. All the time, even when you were having a conversation."

· · ·

On September 13, 1978, a Wednesday, Betsy Sailor's phone rang all day. Two days before, she had placed a classified ad in the Penn State student newspaper, the *Daily Collegian*. She was living in the basement apartment of a brick home not far from one of Penn State's golf courses, the White Course. Her intended roommate had not returned to school for the fall term, and she was looking for someone to share expenses. In her ad she wrote: "Female room-mate needed to share quiet apt. near golf course. Rent $87.50 plus phone. Non-smokers only. Call Betsy." It was the kind of thing people did back then, and Betsy's ad ran along with eight others.

She was twenty-one years old, a senior at what she proudly called "my state university," and one of the few women majoring in business administration. She had curly hair and smiled with resolute cheer. Though still a student, she led a settled life, with a fiancé seven years older than she was who lived a couple of hours away in Johnstown, Pennsylvania. She believed that "going to Penn State football games was the most exciting thing you could do" and that Joe Paterno was "a demigod." She lived with two Siamese kittens. She had never heard of anything bad happening in State College. She thought it was a safe place to be—"good times all the time."

Betsy liked taking the calls. She liked talking to the callers—interviewing them, really, so that she could make the right choice. She might have been, as one friend remembers, more mature than other students, "like an older person coming back to school," but she was open to new things, eager for fresh perspectives. A previous roommate, Lisa Yelverton, says of her time with Betsy: "We just clicked. I was from Philadelphia, and I was inner city. And she was country. I was Black, and she was white, and I guess we were so intrigued and wanted to learn about each other's cultures more than anything."

As Betsy answered the phone, she hoped she could find someone like Lisa again. Two men called, but one annoyed her, asking if she was absolutely sure she didn't want a male roommate. The other was calling for his girlfriend. She had registered late, he said, and she needed a place to live. He asked about her apartment and its location and if he could come by and take a look at it. She told him that she was going out for a while and wouldn't be home. Then she spoke to a caller who connected with her over common interests and made her decision. She studied for a while, relishing her time alone, and then, near ten p.m. went upstairs to tell her landlord she was going to the store for some cat food. She was not gone long, and when she returned, her landlord, a motherly woman with whom Betsy was close, told her that the kittens had gotten frisky in her absence. She had heard them knock something down in the apartment.

When Betsy went downstairs, she turned on the light in her bedroom. The only thing she found amiss was a telephone book open on the floor, and she wondered to herself how her landlord had been able to hear such a small disturbance. She had already left a message on the answering machine of the woman she selected as her roommate, and she was nothing if not polite, so she also began making plans to call back all the others who had expressed interest in the room, including the boyfriend of the late arrival who now had no place to live. But making a choice had given her a strong sense of freedom and relief, and she celebrated by "doing those silly things you do when you're living alone"—singing to herself and "dancing with the refrigerator door." After a while, she remembered that she had to study for a test and went into her bedroom to find her books. She hit the light switch, but the room remained dark, and in the moment of surprise between expectation and reality, it felt suddenly and consumingly black. "The next thing you know," Betsy says, "I had a hand around my mouth and a knife at my neck, and a voice said, 'I'll kill you if you say a word.'"

She did not say a word. She did not scream. She began making choices right away, and the first was that "there was nothing he could do, nothing he could steal, that was worth my life." The second was that she would go into "information-gathering mode," and try to remember the details of everything that happened, though her assailant did his best to prevent her from doing so. He had been hiding in her room for as long as she had been home and had used that time to make preparations. He used one of her scarves to blindfold her and the belt from the robe she kept in her closet to bind her hands behind her back. Then he picked her up and planted her face down on her bed, and from his lack of strain or even apparent effort, she understood that his outsize strength made him particularly dangerous. When he went to her bathroom and began rummaging around the medicine cabinet, she told herself, "Good, he's leaving prints." But when he asked for her razor, she told herself, "No way I'm giving this guy my razor," and decided to gamble. She kept her razor in the bathtub. But she knew that men don't view shaving in terms of the bath; they view it in terms of the mirror. She told him that her razor was where he would have kept it, the medicine cabinet, and when he gave up trying to find it—when he returned empty-handed—she was grateful that men know so little about women.

Though she decided not to fight him, her mind never stopped resisting. Even when he flipped her over and sat on her chest, with his knees straddling her shoulders, she kept trying to see around the margins of her blindfold and then the pillowcase he had put over her head, kept trying to glean information she could use later to identify him or use now to stay alive. She saw his thumb and knew he was white. She saw the soles of his sneakers and the stitching of his jeans and knew what he was wearing. And yet she was still telling herself that he was there to rob her. "You can take my jewelry," she said. "I'll tell you where it is."

"I'm not going to do that," he said.

"What are you going to do?" she asked.

"I'm going to rape you," he replied.

His voice shattered her. It was the voice from the phone, the voice of the boyfriend who had called about the apartment, but it was so matter-of-fact, so untroubled and decisive, as if her fate were no longer her own. When she heard it, she felt herself split in two, so that she also heard herself, her own voice saying, "Oh no."

What happened next was described in excruciating and graphic detail in the police report for what became case 678-09229: "Actor returned and he took off all his clothes and sat on her chest and put his penis to her mouth and told her to suck it, she said she couldn't do that, he became angry so she opened her mouth and he put it in. He then moved to her crotch and began licking. He said 'say you like it,' she said, 'no, because I don't.' Actor then began to rape complainant and she said, 'Please don't cum inside because I'm not using birth control and don't want to become pregnate [*sic*] over something like this.' He said OK but complainant does not know if he did or not. Actor then put his clothes on and went out of the room.

". . . she heard him open the back door (outside exit) and then he came back in. Actor told her to open her legs. She refused saying, 'What are you going to do? Don't put anything inside me.'" Actor then began moving around the room opening dresser drawers. She asked him what he was doing and he said, 'Waiting for a ride.'"

·   ·   ·

When the phone rang in Ann Sailor's house, she didn't automatically think the call was from one of her children. Although she had three in college, long-distance calls were punitively expensive in September 1978 and therefore rare. Betsy called every few weeks. She wrote Ann letters, telling her mother about her studies in business administration. The Sailors were a family of schoolteachers, and Betsy would have made a great one, calm and kind, cheerful and strong, given to striking up long conversations with strangers she encountered on campus.

"I'm OK," Betsy began. As Ann remembers now, "When your child says, 'I'm OK,' you know something has happened. But she just calmly told me, step by step, what had happened." The one thing Betsy didn't say, wouldn't say, was that she had been raped. "I wouldn't use that word," Betsy says. "I wanted to spare her that. I said, 'Mom, I've been sexually assaulted.' As if that would make it better."

Rape. It was not something most people talked about back then, even if—especially if—it had happened to them. It often went unreported because of the shame associated with the word and the shaming the legal system routinely inflicted on those who survived it. Rape was an ordeal that promised more ordeals to come, chief among them silence. *Things like that didn't happen back then in State College,* people still say. But they did. It was just rare that someone came out and said so.

Ann Sailor knew her daughter was "one heck of a woman," so stoic she insisted that her parents not drive the three hours from northwest Pennsylvania to State College—that she could handle this ordeal on her own. But she was still so very young, and Ann says she would often wonder: "When she puts her head down on her pillow at night, is she having bad dreams?" Betsy was prepared to say to anyone but her mother that she had been raped in State College. She was prepared to go to court and press charges against whoever had done this to her. She was not afraid, and she was not resigned to silence. And yet, just as there is a cost to keeping silence, there is cost to breaking it. Decades after Betsy called Ann to tell her what had happened on the night of September 13, they both remain reluctant to speak the word that names what Hodne did to her. The daughter is now sixty-four. The mother is eighty-four. They are close; they know most of what there is to know about each other. But they both remember that phone call and the weight of the word and how breaking the silence broke them. They can say it now; they can say that Betsy was *raped*. But they still grieve each time they do. And both of them, far away from one another, in separate phone calls, still weep.

•   •   •

Hodne's roommate freshman year (who asked that his name not be used) was from upstate New York, and so at first he thought that Hodne was different from him because Hodne came from Long Island and hung around with "the Long Island clique"—older, edgier guys like Tom Donovan and Tony Capozzoli and a basketball player named Frank Brickowski. Then he began to sense that Hodne was also different from everyone else. On the field, Hodne was the same, one of a scrum of players more distinguished by toughness than by talent. Off the field too, he was just another guy who liked to drink, smoke weed, go to parties, and bring women back to the room. The difference, the roommate realized soon enough, was a matter of degree.

The realization came when someone told Hodne, "No." At Hamilton Hall, they lived between the two "jock house" fraternities, Phi Delta Theta and Phi Gamma Delta, otherwise known as "Fiji House." One night early in freshman year, Hodne and his roommate headed for a party at Fiji House, only to be told at the door that freshmen weren't invited. They left, but on their way back to Hamilton, Hodne saw an opportunity. "At Fiji House, they kept the kegs of beer in the back, near the stairwell," the roommate remembers. "And Todd goes, 'We're going to take one.' And he picks up a keg and carries it to our dorm room. And then he goes downstairs and puts up a sign that says there's a party in our room. We have twenty-five people in there, and he's charging at the door for beer that he stole from Fiji House. And I'm like, 'I'm not going to make it through my freshman year.' After two weeks, I thought,

'Oh, I'm in the shit.' I considered going to Joe [Paterno] and asking him for a room change. But Joe's going to ask me why. And what do I tell him? So I just decided to suck it up. But I spent my entire freshman year praying I wouldn't be arrested."

It wasn't just that when Hodne drank, he "could drink a bottle of Jack Daniels in a half hour." It wasn't just that when he went to the Record Ranch, he couldn't leave without a few LPs under his coat. And it wasn't even that when they both went to Hodne's home in Wantagh, he once stopped on the way back to State College and picked up a pound of weed for the purpose of selling it. No, it was that "Todd just didn't have the same moral compass that other people did."

Hodne was extreme in everything, in particular the activity that so many football players took as a privilege of being on the roster. "He had some wild sexual appetites," the freshman roommate says. "We had bunk beds, and I'm on the bottom, he's on the top. And he'd be up there going at it for *hours* at a time. It just wasn't normal. I mean, I knew something was definitely different in that aspect."

Most of the players who remember Hodne minimize the significance of their memories of him, either discounting the time they spent with him or the time he spent on the team. But the freshman roommate still thinks about him. "Living with someone like that is certainly something you never forget," he says. "What it's taught me is that you can't really know people and what they're capable of. That's what I struggle with. How is somebody capable of [the crimes that Hodne committed]? I mean, to me, it's not even a matter of morals or morality. It's what deep inside humans are capable of doing. And that's what freaks me out."

•   •   •

There were a lot of bars in State College. Beer—sometimes sold to tables by the case—was so extraordinarily cheap that the players followed weekly specials that let them drink nearly for free. They drank at the Saloon, they drank at the Rathskeller, they drank at the Corner Room. After Tuesday practices, a bunch of them used to go to the Train Station, a downtown restaurant and bar with a caboose out front. They ordered hoagies and beer and went back to an off-campus house to watch the Three Stooges. That's how Hodne got his nickname: "Shemp."

It was not a flattering moniker. Shemp was the fourth Stooge. Hodne had endured the meat grinder anonymity of freshman football and then had been suspended. Kip Vernaglia, one of the players who hung out with him, remembers Hodne as a "happy-go-lucky knucklehead kind of guy." Years later, when we told him of the full extent of Hodne's crimes, Vernaglia said, "Are you serious? . . . he was Shemp!"

．　　●　　●

Adrienne Reissman was a student at Penn State and a waitress at the Train Station. She kept her car parked close by, in the alley behind the restaurant. One night after work in the fall of 1978, she was walking out to the alley in the dark. She remembers what she was wearing because she has asked herself so many times what she looked like that night, what he might have seen. "What woman doesn't ask what she looked like?" she asks now. "Was I a target? Was I trashy?" She was wearing "black slacks and a tan sweater with suede patches at the elbows." She was twenty-four years old. She was five feet tall. She was an artist and a self-described hippie. She didn't know the football players who came into the Train Station because she didn't particularly care about them: "I was not boom-boom rah-rah."

She was opening the door of her car when she felt someone behind her and heard him say, "Give me your wrists." He bound her wrists and then blindfolded her with athletic tape and pushed her inside. She was sprawled across the front seats of her car, and he had his knee in the door. She had heard of students being raped at the golf course, and she was sure that's what he wanted to do—drive her to the golf course and rape her there. But her car was small, a Mazda RX-3, and he was big. He couldn't fit into the front with her already inside, and this gave her a few moments. She tried to discourage him by telling him she was on her period, even though she wasn't. She managed to free her hands. She couldn't see, but she knew where the latch was on the passenger side door. She reached for it and scurried across the front seats as he fumbled behind her. She opened the door and began screaming. He ran. When the cops came, she saw a pair of scissors lying by the driver's side door. "I've asked myself a million times, if I had known he'd had a pair of scissors, what would I have done? What would I have done? Would I have acquiesced? Would I have fought? He had a weapon. Oh, God."

She had been attacked from behind and never saw the perpetrator's face. But when news came out about Hodne being arrested for the attack on Betsy, she read the details of his build and felt certain it was him. He had blindfolded her and bound her hands and had tried overwhelming her with his size and strength. He hadn't worn gloves, and she was sure he had left fingerprints on her car and on the scissors she saw on the street. She wanted to press charges. Police came to the scene of her attack, but they seemed "disappointed that I didn't see his face," she says, and didn't contact her after the initial investigation. We requested reports of her case but were told by State College Police that they no longer existed.

"It took a long, long time to feel safe again," Adrienne says. She was an arts education major. She was taking a weaving course, and when she returned to classes the next week, she found that's all she could do, all day long: weave. "The monotony of putting that shuttle back and forth in the loom, it was cathartic for me," she says. She remembers surviving the semester by "never going alone, ever, anywhere" from that point forward. She also was taking a course from Penn State's bowling coach, the esteemed Don Ferrell, who was the university's first Black head coach and a close friend of Joe Paterno. She had not shared the story of what had happened to her beyond telling the police, close friends, and her weaving teacher. Ferrell has no memory of her. But in Adrienne's recollection, "When I went back to the class, the coach came over and he looked at me and he said, 'You don't have to come here one more time. You're done. You're passed. Now go try and take care of yourself.'"

●　　　●　　　●

Like Betsy Sailor, Susan (who asked to be identified only by her first name) had placed an ad in the paper looking for a roommate. She told one caller that she'd talk to him later, that she was going over to her friend's house to watch *Dallas*. When she returned, she noticed some potted plants that had been on the windowsill were on the floor. She tried to turn on the bedroom light. It didn't go on. He was hiding in the closet. "When he confronted me, he threw one of my shirts, one of my favorite shirts, over my head, put me in a bathtub and shaved my pubic area. And then had his way. Put it that way," she says. "Oh, actually he had a knife to my neck. It was one of my kitchen knives. If I would've known it was that one, I would have said, 'Go ahead and slit my throat,' kind of thing, because it was very dull." Susan, who sounds brash and fearless telling the story now, wanted to move on: "Suck it up, put your big girl panties on, and just deal with it." But he kept calling, to gloat, to threaten a return. The calls pissed her off. She told her father. Her father worked for the phone company. He had the calls traced. They took the records to the police department. The calls were coming from 279 Hamilton Hall.

The State College Police had Hodne's fingerprints on file ever since the Record Ranch burglary, along with his photograph. Investigators also found his fingerprints at Betsy Sailor's apartment—on a tube of Clinique eye cream in the medicine cabinet; on the prized Norwegian knife he left behind; and on the lightbulb he loosened ever so slightly in its socket. But the fingerprint system was years from being computerized at State College. There were no instantaneous matches. Centre County District Attorney David Grine needed a name, and the phone trace gave him one, he says. Todd Hodne, in the greedy predation of his phone calls to Susan, had revealed himself.

State College PD sent the prints to the FBI. On October 13, 1978, an officer at headquarters wrote the following: "On this date at 1335 hours, this officer returned [FBI] Agent [Larry] Harper's phone call to Washington D.C. Agent Harper told me that he had lifted one latent print from a knife blade, one from a light bulb, and one from a tube of cleansing cream. Harper told me that all three prints belonged to one Todd Steven Hodne."

Until this point, Hodne had remained a Penn State student despite his suspension from the football team on August 19, had remained on scholarship and lived at 279 Hamilton Hall with Fred Ragucci. It took a few hours for the police to produce a warrant for his arrest. At the end of October 13, the lead investigator on the case, Duane Musser, wrote a report summarizing the efforts that he and his partner, Garry Kunes, had made to find Hodne:

"At 1920 hours Off. Kunes contacted Joe Paterno in an attempt to determine the location of Hodne since Hodne rooms with Fred Ragucci, a PSU football player. Paterno indicated that he would attempt to determine this by contacting Ragucci. Paterno asked to be recontacted on Sunday 10/15/78 at 1830 hours for further information."

There is no record of a second call to Paterno on that Sunday. Hodne remained free for the weekend, a bye week for the Nittany Lions. He turned himself into Penn State University Police on Monday, October 16, 1978, at 6:45 a.m. He was driven in a police cruiser to headquarters in downtown State College, where Musser began questioning him. Musser had just turned thirty, and it was his first case as an investigator. He asked Hodne about his whereabouts on a series of dates between early September and the middle of October. Some of the dates corresponded to reported State College attacks with a similar modus operandi.

Hodne had answers and alibis. Hodne said that on September 1, he was in Philadelphia with Frank Brickowski, watching Penn State play Temple in its opening game of the season. He said that on September 13, the night Betsy Sailor was raped, he was at a Phi Delt party with his girlfriend. On other days and at other times, he said he was hanging out with Tony Capozzoli in his room at Hamilton Hall.

These were lies. In the days before turning himself in, Hodne had tried to convince Brickowski to vouch for him regarding one of the nights Musser was interested in. "Todd tried to tell me, 'That's bullshit, because you and I know we were both at the library that night,' " remembers Brickowski, who went on to play thirteen years in the NBA and whose father had taught Hodne driver's ed in high school. "And I looked at him. I go, 'What?' He says, 'We were at the library that night. Study hall.' And I'm like, 'Todd, we never stayed in study hall.' We would go to study hall, sign in the front and slip out the back and have someone sign our names. And he goes, 'No, no, on this night, we *did*.' And I go, 'No, we fucking *didn't*. And that was the break between him and I."

Three days after Hodne gave himself up to Duane Musser at State College Police headquarters, Musser went to 279 Hamilton Hall on the campus of Penn State to talk to Hodne's roommate, Fred Ragucci. "I didn't want to do it, to be honest," Ragucci says. "I'm with a roommate I didn't pick, and he's having this kind of problem—why am I involved? 'No,' Joe said. 'You have to do this. You have to talk to them.'"

After the interview, Musser wrote a brief report, dated October 19, 1978. "[Ragucci] was asked if he knew or ever heard of Todd Hodne speak of any of the following victims," the report reads. Musser then names five women, including Elizabeth Sailor. "He was asked if he could recall at what times on the following dates that Hodne left or returned to his room," the report reads. Musser then names four dates in September and October. Ragucci did not recognize the women's names nor recall the dates. "The knife used in this incident was shown to Ragucci," the report reads. "He stated that Hodne had a knife similar in appearance."

There are no surviving transcripts from the criminal trial of Betsy Sailor's case in Centre County. The half-page report of Musser's interview with Ragucci is the only surviving document in the state of Pennsylvania archives that demonstrates the scope of the Hodne investigation between his arrest for the rape of Betsy Sailor and the trial.

We obtained a copy of Musser's report from the Centre County district attorney's office last fall. The names of Ragucci and of the women other than Betsy Sailor had been redacted, but the document raised the possibility that the Hodne investigation in State College included multiple sexual assaults in addition to the rape of Betsy Sailor.

There were now other women to find.

Several months later, in May 2021, we obtained an *unredacted* copy of Musser's report. It came from John B. Collins, who as chief prosecutor in New York's Suffolk County had received documents from Pennsylvania while investigating Todd Hodne for later crimes in Long Island. It was part of three large files Collins kept about Hodne's crimes. It gave us the names of the other women—Karen (who asked to be identified only by her first name), Susan, and Adrienne Reissman (as well as of another former Penn State student who did not respond to our calls)—and access to their stories and voices.

Collins's files also yielded a report written by Musser two days after Betsy Sailor was raped. That report identifies "a similarity between this case [Sailor's] and 678-08239 [Karen's case], invol. Deviate Sexual Intercourse" and indicates Musser "reinterviewed [Karen] and showed her the [artist composite] sketch. She said he looks familiar, but the nose didn't seem quite right." Also in those files is a report in which Musser questioned Hodne, and later his parents, on the day he was arrested in State College. They had come to State College to post bail. "Mr. Hodne was shown the knife used and he indicated that he had never seen it," the report stated. "He stated that his son was at home on August 20th, 1978," the day after Karen was attacked.

In all, the Collins files showed that in addition to naming five victims, Musser and the State College Police questioned Hodne, his parents, his girlfriend, and two of his teammates—Capozzoli and Ragucci—about his activities on nine dates between the middle of August and the middle of October 1978.

As in the Betsy Sailor case, Susan, Karen, and Adrienne Reissman had reported being sexually assaulted by a very large, very strong man who bound their hands and threatened them with a deadly sharp object. Further records from *their* investigations have since been lost or purged.

·   ·   ·

On October 25, 1978, Todd Hodne was arraigned at a preliminary hearing for the rape of Betsy Sailor. Later that afternoon, the phone rang at the State College police station. Duane Musser wrote at the time:

"At approx. 1700 hrs. this date someone called this Bureau from the Centre County Jail to inform us that Todd Hodne had posted bail and was released.

"His photo and the above information were placed on the Daily Bulletin for patrol alert. I also contacted [Susan] (678-10416) and informed her of Hodne's release."

Susan (678-10416) was the daughter of the phone company employee who had traced Hodne's phone calls. Musser was calling to warn her.

Act 2: Punishment

On the night of August 18, 1978, Karen—one of the five State College women—came home to an empty apartment. She lived with her roommate, Jean, in an apartment building on Beaver Avenue, and Jean had gone away for the weekend, something she never did. Karen won't go into detail about what happened that night when her attacker found a way in and found her alone. It's too traumatic. An article in the *Daily Collegian* describes the attack like this: "State College Police are still investigating an incident in which a woman was forced to commit a deviate sexual act at knifepoint Aug. 19. Police had said a man entered the woman's East Beaver Avenue apartment through a window between 3:30 a.m. and 4 a.m. and then forced her to commit the act." The August 19 crime is the first of a series of sexual assaults for which Todd Hodne would be investigated. And August 19 is also the afternoon Joe Paterno announced Hodne's suspension from the Penn State football team.

In Karen's mind, the horror of the attack would always coincide with fond memories of her last summer in State College. Jean was dating Penn State defensive end Clyde Corbin, and Karen often accompanied them when they went to downtown bars like the Saloon for pitchers of beer. Karen had a lot of friends and a job she liked at the *Centre Daily Times*, but that summer she also socialized with football players. It was part of what made the summer special. It also was part of what left her with a lifetime of questions: How did her attacker know she was home alone? How did a *football player* know she was home alone? Why did her attacker ask if she recognized his voice? Had she met him before? Did he have an accomplice?

There was an investigation of the attack. "The police came over," she says. "They were in my apartment for a long time." Karen remembers her attacker going through everything, and now the cops were doing the same. Jean remembers seeing smudges of black all throughout their apartment where police had tried to lift fingerprints. Jean also remembers that when Hodne was arrested, Clyde had reminded her that the three of them had run into him at the Saloon a few weeks before the attack. Karen remembers police finding a footprint outside her window. But forty-three years later, what Karen remembers most is the sense she had that the police were investigating her as much as they were investigating what happened to her: "And basically what came out of it was that they told me they didn't have enough information to go to court. And that's what I heard from everyone involved in this: not enough evidence. They had evidence."

⋅ ⋅ ⋅

When we first called Karen in the summer of 2021, she asked why anyone would be interested in the story of what happened to her. "Is this going to be some kind of exposé about Penn State?" she asked skeptically.

The next day, she called back, asking how we had gotten her name. We told her about the police report Duane Musser had written after his interview with Hodne's roommate Fred Ragucci, noting the names of other possible victims. "Yes," Karen said. "I would have been one of those people."

For decades, Karen had felt like what happened to her "didn't matter to anyone," she says. But to be asked about Hodne now—to receive a phone call about Hodne now—changed things. "It was just something that was ignored, and there was nothing much I could do about it," she says. "That [someone] wanted to do a story about it, and felt that it was significant, made me realize, 'Well, maybe this is more important.'"

She had told so few people over the years. And when she did, she often regretted it. Indeed, it was as if her experience of long ago had determined the course of the decades to follow—as she once felt investigators pushed her aside, she later heard those closest to her urging her to push aside her traumatic memories. She told her parents, and they suggested she must not have been careful enough. She told her brothers and the man she married, and they asked her to move on—to not think about it. And she tried; how she tried, even through her nightmares and unending insomnia. "It was buried," she says. "And it would come out at the most horrible times."

When she called back, she started to tell us what happened to her in the summer of 1978—an experience that "has affected me to a great extent my entire life." She remembered a woman named Betsy as "the only one who could actually pin [Hodne] down" at the time. And she told us something else: "I know Joe Paterno was involved, and I'm trying to remember all the details."

There were other memories. The attacker used a knife; she didn't want to talk about it. He stole money from her purse. Later, the police asked about his hands. We circled back to Paterno. What did she mean she knew he was involved? "He knew who I was. He knew the police were interviewing me. The trial itself I was discouraged from going to, and not necessarily by the police. And I'm trying to remember how all that went as well."

How did Paterno know her? Did he reach out? Did he call her? "I think he might have. I think he might have," she said. "And I'm trying to remember all those details, and I hesitate to blurt things out because I'm not totally certain about how that all went. Yeah. I think he did. I think he did. And from then on, he knew me. He would say hello to me on campus if he would see me." She went on. "I'm trying so hard to remember. It was a rather shallow conversation. It wasn't anything. But the impression I got was he knew it was that guy [Hodne], but he wanted to probe and see if I knew that it was him. I think that was kind of the gist of it. Which at the time I was really—I don't remember what I said. I don't remember too much about what I revealed or didn't reveal. I don't think I revealed much of anything." Why did she think he was asking her questions? "Oh, to protect his player," Karen said.

. . .

Our conversations with Karen have continued since the day she called back. She says it has been an awakening for her, and she has kept us informed as she has remembered more and more details.

Library archives contain none of Paterno's phone logs from those years. There is barely any information available in the police report about Karen at all. And she remembers Paterno's call the way she remembers everything else about the days and months after August 19, 1978—fitfully, fretfully.

But the basic narrative has not changed. When Todd Hodne was arrested for his assault on Betsy Sailor, the police had reason to believe that he had also attacked Karen, so closely aligned was the modus operandi. In the fall of 1978, as far as she knew, no one other than Jean, Clyde, Karen's boyfriend, and State College Police investigators knew Karen was one of the named victims in an ongoing string of sexual assaults. But then she learned she might hear from Joe Paterno. "I seem to recall that somebody told me that he was concerned about it and that he might reach out to me," she says.

Paterno, in those days, was famous for doing the right thing. When he called Karen after Todd Hodne had been arrested for the attack on Betsy Sailor, Karen hoped he was doing the right thing for her, especially after he asked, "Are you OK?"

But the call went differently than she expected. To Karen, Paterno's call "was kind of an admission that his football player did it, and he was expecting me to move forward." Karen wanted to move forward but didn't want to forget. She was, in fact, hoping to prosecute. "He was trying to ascertain if I was going to go to [the Betsy Sailor hearing] and if the police had discovered anything concrete. My recollection is that he came out and asked me if I was going to testify—if I was planning to go to court." When Paterno called, she had hoped that he was calling out of concern for her. Instead, Karen felt he was calling out of concern for his program. "He was kind of scaring me I think a little bit," she says.

•   •   •

Paterno was in charge of discipline on the Penn State football team. "Sometimes they felt that because they were football players, they'd be getting special treatment," Lee Upcraft, university assistant vice president for student affairs at the time, says of players who got in trouble. "But they were more worried about Joe Paterno than they were of me, let's put it that way. Joe could just do anything he wanted and nobody was going to question him."

Paterno kept his own counsel and maintained his own doghouse, which had a number of rooms. The main room was for players who drank, who fought, who put their fists through windows, who had done "something stupid" and embarrassed him. These he punished at practice by making them run the steps of Beaver Stadium or wear the dreaded white jersey of "the foreign team." "If you messed up, you'd find it in your locker," says Tony Capozzoli. The second room was for players who were flunking out. These he sent to academic advisers and, if they proved themselves immune to intervention, dropped from the team. The final room was for those who either never left the first two or had made the newspapers by breaking the law. These he suspended unilaterally. He was not in the habit of consulting with his coaches during his deliberations; he only informed them of their result. "He would say, 'All we have to do is pretend he sprained his ankle yesterday and go on,'" remembers Booker Brooks, one of his longtime assistant coaches. But the players, the press and everybody else in the sphere of Penn State football would know that beyond incurring Paterno's displeasure, the player had been deemed unworthy. He had been excommunicated. He had been, in a phrase repeated again and again in any discussion of Paterno's decisive discipline, "sent home."

Todd Hodne did not fit within Paterno's system of crime and punishment. Paterno liked to make an example of players who had gotten into trouble, lecturing the team even as the players did their penance. But he had nothing instructive to say about the predatory behavior of Hodne. "There was something fundamentally wrong with Todd," Ragucci says. "And that was not something that could be corrected by making an example of him."

On October 21, 1978, a little more than two months after Karen had been attacked, the Nittany Lions beat Syracuse 45–15 for their seventh straight win of the season. A week later, they beat West Virginia 49–21 and were ranked second in the national polls. In between those two games, on October 25, several players attended Hodne's preliminary hearing at the Centre County Courthouse. Offensive tackle Irv Pankey, who would later become an offensive captain of the team, remembers they were late for practice that Wednesday. Assistant coaches were displeased, but Pankey says Paterno had approved their attendance at the hearing: "It doesn't matter what the assistant coaches think when Joe Paterno tells you it's OK." Paterno liked Hodne, some of his teammates say, and made a habit of calling him out with the grumpy affection he reserved for wayward charges: "Hodne, get a haircut."

Hodne was still one of them, a teammate. "He was still our boy," as Pankey says. Hodne had worked with them, sweated with them, drank and partied with them. He might have been "Shemp" to some, but to defensive back Micky Urquhart he was "a free spirit," and to Bill Dugan, a sophomore lineman and resident of Hamilton Hall, he was "one of the leaders of our class." They were shocked by the reports of his arrest. They wanted to give him a show of support, and so they came in force, the undefeated Nittany Lions still recognizable in their suit jackets.

Betsy Sailor remembers Centre County District Attorney David Grine telling her that Hodne's teammates were coming to court if not to intimidate her then at least to make it more difficult for her to identify a football player seated among his kind. And that is exactly what Betsy saw when she looked at the courtroom in Bellefonte, Pennsylvania, on October 25, 1978. "There were a bunch of big, burly guys in the courtroom," she remembers. "It was front-loaded with football players." But Betsy was neither intimidated nor confused. She spoke of the rape as she always had, forthrightly and with nearly forensic precision. She was not easily embarrassed, and she did not shy away from describing anatomical details if they helped her case. And in her recounting of the crime, she described the blue suede Puma sneakers her blindfolded eyes had struggled to see as she was pinned to the bed—the sneakers Hodne was wearing in court.

A lot of Hodne's teammates didn't think he did it. They didn't think he did it because they didn't think he needed to do it—because he already had two girlfriends, one from home and one from the Penn State swim team, because he seemed to have his pick of any girl he wanted. "Frankly, we thought it was bullshit," Kip Vernaglia says. "We thought that a girl just got pissed off or whatever. Because it just didn't make any sense. I mean, it wasn't like Todd was some dreamy-looking handsome dude. But back then, that didn't matter. You're not destitute on a desert island. In those days, if you played football for Penn State, the last thing you needed was a date."

The blue suede "Clydes" were what started to change minds because they were part of what made Hodne so "Long Island," as much a fixture of his public life as his knife was of his private one. When Betsy mentioned them in her testimony, they glanced at each other as she spoke—in the words of one of them, " 'Like, holy shit.' "

It was not easy for her. Betsy was but one person, still very young, daring to bring criminal charges against a Penn State football player. She had never known the power of Penn State football until she felt it firsthand—until she understood that by accusing one of its players, she had taken it on. "I felt like I had thrown dirt at the queen," she says. "I felt bad. I felt bad that one of the things that I admired about this institution, the football team, had produced this individual. They weren't at fault, but I just felt bad. I was just . . . I guess I was kind of shocked that part of the university that I admired would do that."

Betsy remained one person because although Karen, Susan and Adrienne Reissman all wanted to bring charges against Hodne, none were deemed to have enough evidence to do so. Betsy never met them, and they never met her. And although by this time there was evidence of Hodne attacking multiple women, the preliminary hearing marked an ambiguous milestone: it was both the beginning of Betsy Sailor obtaining justice for her rape and the end of ongoing investigations of her rapist in Pennsylvania. There are no reports indicating that police investigated either Karen's case or Susan's beyond October 25, 1978, the day of the hearing and the day Duane Musser called Susan to tell her Hodne was free on bail. Fred Ragucci knew that Hodne was being investigated for other crimes because he had been asked about them. So did Tony Capozzoli, who had also been asked about them. So did Joe Paterno, who knew to reach out to Karen in the time leading up to the preliminary hearing of the attack on Betsy Sailor.

"It was a bit of a different time," Ragucci says. "Police were authoritative and, presumably, they were doing the right thing. There was no question in my mind they were doing the right thing. There was no question in my mind that Joe was doing the right thing. He talked, you listened, and to be honest with you, it would never have dawned on me to go to the newspaper. And for the people that I talked to—my parents, my girlfriend, my friends—it never came up. We just assumed that the school, the administration, the football folks, and the police were all doing the right thing. I tell them what I know. And then they do what they're supposed to."

•   •   •

Ragucci remembers returning one day to 279 Hamilton Hall and finding all traces of his roommate gone. But Hodne stayed in State College. Out on bail, he was crashing with friends or living in his car, a yellow Ford Torino with New York plates. One night at the end of November 1978, an officer from the Penn State University Police approached his car to deliver him written notice from student affairs that he had been "summarily suspended." Hodne tucked the letter under the windshield visor; then he read it, crumpled it into a ball and threw it on the street, a report from the

University Hearing Board says. A week later, the director of student conduct told him that a disciplinary hearing had been scheduled for December 7.

Betsy Sailor showed up for the hearing. Hodne did not. In the company of Duane Musser, she told the story of her rape to what she calls "a room full of men," led by the director of Conduct Standards for the Office of Student Affairs, Don Suit. The University Hearing Board listened and ruled Hodne guilty as charged. He was dismissed from Penn State, and State College Police noted he was living in his car.

Betsy had left school after the rape. She remembers someone from the university telling her to leave State College. After Hodne's arrest, she returned to Penn State and moved into university housing—a freshman dorm. She could no longer live in her apartment. She was too afraid. She was afraid of being alone. She was afraid of taking a shower without someone standing close by, and she jumped "six inches in the air" when someone surprised her. In the dormitory, she had no roommate, and she felt not only alone but singled out. Once, when she walked the campus, she heard a group of guys she recognized as football players making catcalls: "There would [be] no other reason to do it other than they knew I was the one." Another time, early in 1979, she had a chalkboard on her door and, according to a police report, found a scrawled message with the name of one of Hodne's teammates: "Hi, I'm a football player and I'm nice too."

One night, there came a knock on Betsy's door that changed everything for her. "And I went to my door, and I opened it," she remembers, "and there was a man that completely, seemingly, filled the entire door frame, like there was not a lot of space other than him. And he put out his hand and introduced himself. He said: 'Hello, my name is Irv Pankey, and I just wanted to let you know that I was in the courtroom today and I listened to what you had to say. And I believe every word that you said. And, you will never have to be afraid, or be alone again. I will be by your side.'"

Irv Pankey was a junior and a natural protector—a tight end who had been moved to left tackle. He was six-foot-five and 270 pounds, with a thirteen-year NFL career in front of him. He had a deep solemnity about him that belied his penchant for good times. He was the roommate of Hodne's friend Kip Vernaglia. Pankey was part of the crowd that went to the Train Station on Tuesday nights. He and Hodne had ridden in the back of a teammate's pickup truck on a trip to New York City, drinking beer and peeing over the tailgate. But he had heard Betsy Sailor describe Hodne's sneakers, and Pankey had seen her on the stand, and he knew bravery when he saw it. "She came forward," Pankey says. "And that brought things to light—what the situation really was. If she hadn't stepped up and he hadn't gone to trial, no one would ever have known. And she started putting cracks in stories. It used to be 'he said, she said,' so with him being a Penn State football player, he would have been believed first. Kudos to her for stepping up and sticking to her guns about it. Kudos to her for not being buffaloed."

They were so different from one another in so many ways. But Irv had seen that Betsy was alone in State College, and in that he saw part of himself: "When I started playing for Penn State, there were twelve African Americans on the team. So being African American, I think we understand the play. You know what I mean? We have a commonly white school, and we have all been through some of that stuff. We could all relate, so to speak." He did not want her to endure the isolation he had: "She did not deserve to be a pariah." But they also had something else in common. Betsy was not just alone; she was singular. She had taken on the institution of Penn State football and, alone among Hodne's victims, had brought her case to court. Now Irv, alone among his teammates, walked to her dormitory and knocked on her door. Betsy stood up for herself. Irv stood up for Betsy.

He promised to protect her and not only kept his word but made sure that a few of his teammates followed his example. She had been brutally raped by a football player, but she spent the second term of her senior year in the company of football players, mostly Black, who made her feel less alone and less afraid—and who made her feel once again part of the campus she loved. They did not have to say anything; they simply included her, so that if they went to a party so did she.

"It was huge for me," she says. "It was huge to me that someone from the football team crossed over the line and befriended me. He could have closed ranks, and said, 'We don't talk to her; she's done something against one of our brothers.' But he did the exact opposite. He believed in me, and I was a stranger. And I was white, and he was Black. And he was my guardian angel."

.   .   .

On the last day of 1978, *60 Minutes* profiled Joe Paterno. Hosted by silvery-haired eminence Harry Reasoner, the sixteen-minute segment aired the night before Penn State was set to play Alabama for the national championship. Its title was "We're Number One," and it offered Paterno as a rumpled antidote to a nation obsessed with winning at any cost—"a man who is maybe less neurotic about being number one than others in his profession." With wry wonderment, Reasoner listed a familiar compendium of Paterno's values and virtues, extolling the coach's revolutionary belief that "football should be fun" and that "college coaches should be educators" before concluding with the affirmation that Paterno is a "genuinely nice guy" who is the "best-loved college coach since Knute Rockne." The piece wraps up with the line: "If he's not number one, maybe he should be."

The piece captured Joe Paterno and Penn State football at their moment of arrival, finally deemed worthy of the national stage. It also happened to capture the program in the same week that Todd Hodne was arrested. Reasoner visited State College as the Nittany Lions prepared to play Syracuse on Oct.ober 21, and Paterno fretted that his players were having a hard time concentrating. Hodne was in jail at the time that Reasoner toured the locker room with a camera crew and noted with amazement that even there "you see players studying." He never mentions the Hodne case.

Penn State did not end up number one. The day after *60 Minutes* aired, the Nittany Lions lost to Bear Bryant in the Sugar Bowl.

With the national championship on the line midway through the fourth quarter, Paterno called a conservative run play on fourth-and-goal from inside the one-yard line. Alabama stopped Penn State tailback Mike Guman from going over the top into the end zone, and when Paterno wrote his autobiography ten years later, he still lamented the call.

"I have talked about getting angry with myself when I lose. Nothing of the kind ever compared to this loss," he wrote. "I beat up on myself, not only immediately but for months afterward, halfway into the next season. Much as I blamed myself, I couldn't tolerate all that self-blame. I let my anger turn against the staff and against the team, even though the decision was purely mine. I had to spill some of it off. Writers and fans said, for all to hear, that Paterno couldn't win the big one at the critical moment. Even former players said openly, for quotation, 'He should have won that one.'

"It got to me. It hammered at my ego. *When I stood toe-to-toe with Bear Bryant, he outcoached me.*"

•   •   •

Two months after the national championship game, three of Hodne's teammates were called to testify for the defense at his trial. Gary Ptak, Gary Wagner, and Tony Capozzoli met outside of Joe Paterno's office shortly before the trial. He had called them in, wanting to know what each of them was going to say on the stand. He had not addressed his team about Hodne in the usual prescriptive way. But according to a report detailing a conversation between Ptak and Duane Musser, Ptak responded to a request for an interview "by stating that Coach Paterno had made a statement to the football players that no one speak to anyone in regards to this case without his permission." Musser also tried to interview Capozzoli—who had been arraigned on theft charges in an unrelated case—before the Hodne trial. Capozzoli was "very evasive and indicated he would like to cooperate but stated that he was advised by Hodne's attorney not to discuss the matter."

Paterno had been asked about Hodne's whereabouts by State College Police three days before Hodne was arrested and had made contact with Hodne's roommate, Fred Ragucci. He had directed Ragucci to talk to Musser. Paterno had allowed his players to attend Hodne's pretrial hearing and then later had prohibited them from speaking to law enforcement without his permission. Now the coach was meeting with Ptak, Wagner, and Capozzoli in his office prior to their giving testimony in the Hodne trial. Ptak and Wagner had been subpoenaed to confirm a timeline. Capozzoli remembers testifying voluntarily, as someone who knew Hodne from their glory days at St. Dominic.

"It was short," Ptak says of his conversation with his coach. "It was, 'Joe, we got subpoenaed; what are we going to do?' He goes, 'Well, you got to tell the truth the best you can.' And that was it." Capozzoli's conversation was different, as was his relationship with Paterno. As the son of a coach himself, Capozzoli often bridled at Paterno's authority, and he says he "wasn't afraid of him." Paterno sometimes called him a "wise guy from Long Island." In his office that day, Capozzoli recalls that Paterno didn't mince words. "So right off the bat, he says, 'Todd Hodne is guilty, and if you testify for him, you're off the team,'" Capozzoli says. "So I said, 'Look, Joe'—I laughed at him. I said, 'The guy's got a million girlfriends. Maybe he dumped her and she got mad.' I said, 'I'm just going to tell the truth.' I never took what he said to heart. I testified and went home for a few days, and when I get back, my room key doesn't work. All my shit is gone; somebody moved it. I've been moved down to this place we called the barracks, in the basement of the gym. He goes, 'You still have your scholarship; you can go to school. But you're off the team.' Isn't that, like, jury tampering? Isn't that a criminal act? But there's no recourse. What are you gonna do?"

Paterno's longtime offensive line coach Dick Anderson remembers Capozzoli's dismissal differently, saying: "I think he's making excuses for the fact that he was never good enough to play at this level." Capozzoli counters, "Why would I lie?" and adds, "To a fault, [Paterno] put the program ahead of everything else."

.   .   .

Some players had gotten into a jam downtown. It wasn't anything bad—at least, it wasn't anything evil. It was just stupid stuff, circa 1979. One of them had put his fist through a window; the others had given the cop who arrested him a hard time. They all wound up getting arrested. They were given a citation and worried about the black mark on their records and what their coach would say or do.

The next day, a lawyer in State College gave them a call. Bob Mitinger was a fixture around Penn State's athletic department. He had been an All-America end for Paterno when Paterno was an assistant and had gone on to play for the San Diego Chargers in the AFL. Mitinger had returned to State College after he retired and helped players headed for the pros with their contracts. He worked out in the gym with the team, one of the few civilians with that privilege. He taught a business law class popular with athletes, one of whom remembers walking into his class for the first time and being told that all he would have to do was sign his name. Now Mitinger was telling Hodne's freshman roommate and a few other players that he was going to be their lawyer. When they asked how much it was going to cost, he said not to worry about that. A few days later, they met him in court and paid a fine, and the charges went away.

"Looking back, he was what I would now say was the fixer," the roommate says. "He did that on a regular basis. In State College, and with Joe Paterno, if stuff happened across the line from the standpoint of the law, to whatever degree it could be taken care of, it was taken care of. Based on knowing the judges, etc., they were able to control the narrative, so to speak."

Mitinger represented a lot of players he liked to call "knuckle-heads," according to his widow, Marilyn—players he told to "knock it off" after he helped them wipe their records clean. At Hodne's trial, which began on March 1, 1979, Mitinger, along with his associate John Miller Jr., from the law firm of Miller, Kistler & Campbell, represented a defendant whose crimes could not be written off as the result of youthful excess.

•　　•　　•

It was the voice again.

District Attorney David Grine had prepared Betsy Sailor for the trial, instructing her to dress conservatively and to refrain from being too emotional on the stand. "He wanted no smiling and no emotion from me whatsoever," she says. She had been raised "with Pendleton skirts and sweaters and that sort of stuff," and she had been able to speak matter-of-factly about her rape since it happened. But nothing prepared her for the experience of sitting in the courtroom when Todd Hodne spoke for the first time. She knew that he was linked to the crime by what, in 1978, constituted scientific evidence—fingerprints, semen. But she had not seen him during the attack because he covered her eyes with a scarf and then her head with a pillowcase. She didn't know for certain that he was her rapist until she heard him open his mouth. It was his voice that had shattered her during the attack, when he had said, "I'm going to rape you" in a way that had destroyed all doubt and all hope. And it was his voice—low and flatly declarative—that now caused her to gasp and brought her to tears and prompted Grine to ask her to step out of the room to collect herself.

Betsy had believed, she says, that the March trial was going to be like the October hearing, "that it was just a matter of working through the evidence and everything was going to be fine." But as surely as Hodne's voice confirmed that he was the man who had raped her, it reminded her that he might yet go free. "I realized at this one moment that this is not a matter of my knowing this is right. It's a matter of the jury thinking it's right. And that's when I realized this is, you know, a crapshoot. And that really kind of blew me away. Only then did I feel like I was in jeopardy. Nobody knows what the outcome is. It's a roll of the dice."

Betsy had heard what happened to women who accused men of raping them in open court—"the horror stories" of what awaited them when they took the stand. She expected John Miller Jr. to attack her character and her sexual history. But there was one question she had not anticipated. Miller asked whether she had opportunities to leave during the two hours Hodne was in her apartment. "I thought, 'All right, I have an answer in my mind.' And I thought it was a little dangerous. But yeah, I am taking this approach. I said, 'You're absolutely right. I did. And I thought about it. But after a knife was in my neck twice, I made a conscious decision not to try and escape. I made a decision that I was going to get through this. And I wasn't going to test it. I wasn't going to test *him*. The answer is, 'Yes.'

"And that shut him down," she says.

Betsy won. And yet she says that "the hardest thing that I went through was when they found him guilty. They had to poll each of the jurors, and hearing that, '*Guilty, guilty, guilty*,' gave me a very unsettling feeling. I knew what he did. But in my heart of hearts, I felt sorry for him. I felt that prison was not going to be the answer for him and was only going to make him harder. And I felt that this was the end . . . I felt that this was a person that's now lost to us."

Guilty, guilty, guilty: twelve times Betsy heard those words, and each time, she says, "felt like a piece of broken glass." It wasn't just the foreboding she experienced; it was the response of Hodne's family, especially the women in his life, his mother and his sister and his girlfriend from home. "There were shrieks of horror. There was just so much sadness and disbelief. Nobody pointed a finger at me or said anything that made me feel they thought it was my fault. But it was a kind of chaos that was happening, and I was like, 'Please, let me just get out of here.'" The police formed a phalanx around her. They escorted her out of the courtroom, and Betsy Sailor never saw Todd Hodne in person again.

•   •   •

Moments after the verdict was read, the judge, Richard Sharp, silenced the courtroom. He did not remand Hodne into custody nor revoke his bail but instead announced he would be released to return home with his family while awaiting sentencing.

David Grine had done something thought to be impossible in Centre County. A Penn State football player had raped a Penn State student, and Grine had won a conviction. He had every reason to expect the football player was headed to county jail and then to prison. But that was not the case. "Usually, you revoke bail right there on the spot," he says. "It's, 'Bail is revoked; see the sheriff, please.' We got [Hodne] convicted, felony one—and then [Sharp] let him out on bail pending appeal."

Others in the courtroom also were stunned, Gretchen Fincke, who worked at the rape crisis center, remembers. The Hodne family gathered around Todd. His girlfriend held his hand. They walked Hodne out of the courtroom "in a protective bubble."

And then, Todd got in his parents' car and left Centre County, Pennsylvania.

"I remember sitting there looking at the girlfriend and thinking, 'Oh sweetie, you have no idea what you are in for if you stay with this person,'" Fincke says.

That same day, March 3, 1979, Duane Musser returned from the courthouse in Bellefonte to police headquarters in State College and wrote the following report: "On this date, the defendant, Todd Hodne, was found guilty of Burglary, Rape and Involuntary Deviate Sexual Intercourse after completion of a jury trial before Judge [Richard] Sharp. He was found not guilty of Possessing Offensive Weapons. A pre-sentence investigation was ordered and the defendant remained free on $25,000 bail."

They thought they got him. Musser, the detective; Ron Smeal, one of Musser's supervisors; David Grine, the prosecutor; Betsy Sailor, the victim and witness; at least one of the jurors: they all thought they had done enough to put Todd Hodne away. Yes, there were other victims, at least three of whom say to this day that they wanted to prosecute. But Grine remembers them not wanting to cooperate. Smeal says that a detective touched the lightbulb that Hodne had loosened in Susan's apartment and thereby contaminated the fingerprint evidence. Musser remembers there not being enough evidence in Karen's case. Adrienne Reissman says the State College Police didn't follow up on her case once Hodne was arrested and they found out she hadn't seen his face. But justice had still been done. Hodne was convicted on three very serious charges, and the cops thought these convictions would be enough. "We had multiple rapes that met this MO," Smeal says. "We were very concerned about apprehending him and stopping this spree."

They are gone or resolutely silent now, the men who might be able to shed light on how Hodne could be apprehended without his spree being stopped. Bob Abernethy, another of Duane Musser's supervisors, calls Bob Mitinger "one of the good old boys at the courthouse" and John Miller Jr. one of "the big muckety-mucks in Centre County." Mitinger died in 2004 and Miller in 2007. Miller's son, John Miller III, still works at Miller, Kistler & Campbell. Despite having signed important petitions in Hodne's defense, he denies having anything to do with the case and told us that if there were any documents left behind, "I couldn't give them to you." As for Judge Richard Sharp: he died of cancer a year and a half after Hodne's conviction, and John Miller Jr. led a remembrance service at the courthouse.

Four decades later, Grine, who became Sharp's successor on the bench, is still baffled by Sharp's decision: "I've never had anybody else do that. I'd never had it happen to me before. I'd never heard of it happening. I don't know if they do it in Philadelphia or New York or not but, they sure don't do it here in the country. But [Sharp] did. There is no logic or reason to it."

"I thought he shouldn't be out," former juror Romaine Bratton says.

"The judge let him go, and we were appalled," Fincke says.

They got him, but they didn't stop him. The $25,000 bail set by the magistrate judge after the preliminary hearing in October was not revoked, and instead of going back into custody, Todd Hodne was sent home to Wantagh.

•   •   •

The trial had been held over spring break when the campus newspaper wasn't published. There were a few short wire-service updates that ran in a few Pennsylvania newspapers. But the only local print coverage of the conviction came in a story two days after the verdict in the *Centre Daily Times*, written by staff writer Molly Bliss and reporter Jane Musala. Todd Hodne, Tony Capozzoli, Gary Ptak, and Gary Wagner testified for the defense. The story describes Hodne as "a former University student" and goes on to describe Capozzoli as "a University junior and friend of the defendant" and Ptak and Wagner as "students." The only reference to football comes at the end of the story, when it mentions Hodne's testimony regarding the Record Ranch burglary: "As a result, he said, he was suspended from the football team for a year though his athletic scholarship continued."

The story of a Penn State football player convicted of the rape of a Penn State student did not include the words "Penn State football player." "Believe me, it wasn't my choice," Musala says. "If we're covering this because he's a football player, why aren't we reminding people that he's a football player?" Musala's editor, who would later become mayor of State College, resisted the use of the language because he "was aware that this was sensitive because it was the Nittany Lions," she recalls. And when she and Bliss contacted Penn State's head of communications, Art Ciervo, for comment from Paterno on the conviction, Hodne was described to them as "inconsequential." The editor, William Welch, and Ciervo are now deceased. "We tried to beat the director [Ciervo] into saying something," Musala says. "'Look, have [Joe] say something. Can you have him say something?' 'Well, he's an inconsequential player and Joe really doesn't want to talk about it.'"

The only surviving member of Penn State's public information department at the time is Dave Baker, who was assistant sports information director in 1978. He became the director a year later, and he still has a job as an associate athletic director at the university. Baker also has taught a media relations course at the Donald P. Bellisario College of Communications. When we called to ask what he remembers about the Hodne case, Baker said first that he didn't remember the case and then that Penn State did all it could do. "I never met him, and I don't remember if he ever played a game for Penn State," he said. "It was a long time ago . . . he got in trouble and then he was no longer on the team." Over the course of a half-hour conversation, Baker kept repeating that Hodne had been dismissed from the program. He went on to say that he has no idea what happened to Hodne or where he went and that Hodne's conviction "got substantial press," was "dealt with at the time," was "one incident forty-two years ago," and was "an anomaly at Penn State." Baker never used the word "rape." He said he had a "rough idea" of the nature of the criminal charge but didn't want to speculate, saying, "I don't think that's fair to [Hodne] in case my memory of that is different than what actually happened."

Todd Hodne was one of seven players in Paterno's recruiting class of nineteen who lettered his freshman year. He played in at least seven games in the 1977 season, including the Fiesta Bowl. One of the few photos that the *Daily Collegian* ran of spring practice in 1978 shows Joe Paterno giving Hodne the benefit of his personal tutelage, above the caption, "Do it like this." Beyond the announcement of Hodne's suspension from the team, neither the school nor the football program ever made a public statement of any kind about Hodne or the students he attacked. He was, after all, a player of no consequence, involved in an isolated incident. He would leave State College and never be heard from again.

But that was not the case.

Act 3: Carnage

There were five of them, a bunch of nineteen- and twenty-year-olds jammed into a car for spring break 1979. They had all met each other at secretarial school in New York, and now they were headed for Florida on I-95. They were a little wild, if you want to know the truth; they had a CB radio, and when they weren't singing along with eight-track tapes, they were flirting with truckers and joining their convoys. They were young, of course. But they also were wild for a reason—wild because one of them was Todd Hodne's girlfriend, and they were trying to set her free.

Ellen (who asked that we refer to her only by her middle name) had met Hodne in 1977, on her eighteenth birthday. She had gone to a bar on Long Island with her friends, drinking legally for the first time. She noticed him in part because of his sweater—it was long, with a belt and an extravagant Mexican pattern, more stylish than the kinds of getups Long Island boys usually wore. "I'm Todd Hodne," he said.

"I know who you are," she answered.

That night, he wound up driving her home from the bar. "We parked near my house until the sun came up, just talking and talking and talking and talking," she says. "And he didn't try anything. He didn't even try to kiss me goodbye. I went into the house and I was like, 'Holy crap, that was unbelievable.' He totally hypnotized me."

At first, she couldn't get over the excitement of being with him—he would get her into clubs in New York; he would get her into parties in the Hamptons. "Nothing was out of our realm," she says. It was even more exciting when he went to Penn State, and she drove with his parents to every home game in State College. He didn't always play, but she had never experienced anything like the atmosphere of big-time college football. Afterward, he took her to frat parties, and that's where she began to notice the change in him.

He used to leave her there all alone—abandon her. "I didn't know where I was, and couple of guys on the team would be like, 'We'll get you home,'" she says. But when she went back to Hodne's dorm room, he wouldn't be there, and when he was—well, one time she knocked on the door and his roommate came out and stopped her from going in: "No, no, no, you don't want to go in there." She tried to pull away from Hodne after that, but he wouldn't let her. He was "persuasive," she says. "He could talk his way out of a metal box with locks on it. He had a way of making people say yes." Wherever she was, he would show up. She tried to tell herself it was normal until, she says, he showed up at a club where she was dancing with friends, grabbed her by the ponytail and swung her into a steel post. Her father forbade him from coming into the house, so he used to park down the block and wait for her in his yellow Torino. After Joe Paterno suspended him from the football team, she didn't go to State College to visit. But after he was arrested for raping Betsy Sailor, she listened to his avowals of innocence and testified at his trial. "He cried like a baby. To me and his mother, he cried like a baby: 'I didn't do it, I didn't do it, I didn't do it, I didn't do it, I didn't do it,' " she says. "So Tony Capozzoli and I wind up character witnesses for him. I mean, who wants to believe that your boyfriend's a rapist?"

She cried along with Hodne's mother when the jury read the verdict. But the conviction was also something of a relief. He was going to prison, so she could get into a car with a bunch of girl-friends and go to Key West for spring break. But as soon as they checked into their room, the phone rang, and she picked it up. It was Hodne. "I'm out front," he said. He had followed them down on their I-95 frolic, a convicted rapist driving 2,000 miles on the open road. He came to their room and tried to convince all of them that he couldn't possibly be guilty. And when he left, they all hugged Ellen and wept. "The whole purpose of the trip was to get her away," Ellen's friend Kathy says. "And for him to show up was our first realization that the accusations could be true."

Ellen knew she was in danger once she returned to Long Island in the spring of 1979. Hodne had been convicted on March 3. Now it was the end of April and he, for all intents and purposes, remained a free man, coming and going as he pleased. Hodne, she says, was robbing delis, asking her to hide the money in her car, and reading the newspaper obsessively, as if to find articles about himself. But she didn't know everybody else was in danger until she looked behind the passenger seat of his car. "There was a face mask and a new knife. And I was like, 'What?' I was like, 'Jesus Christ.' My whole world was collapsing, and he was like, 'No, sit down.' And he pulled me to sit back down. And we were driving, and I was like, 'Where are you going?' He goes, 'I just have to make a stop. And we pulled over into a parking lot. And he went over to the dumpster and took his sweater, the sweater that he cherished so much, and threw it into the dumpster.

"And he says, 'If you ever tell anyone, I will kill your father.' "

•   •   •

On April 21, 1979, not quite seven weeks after Todd Hodne had been convicted in State College, Anne Wright was returning late from a night out on Long Island. She had gone to Rumbottom's, a rock-and-roll club, and now she was returning to Wantagh. She had grown up there but had moved away with her family; she had come back to work as a nurse's aide and was staying with some old friends. She was twenty-three. At about four a.m. she was walking west on Sandhill Road and started to cut across a small local park with a playground when she was hit twice on the head from behind with what she later figured was a pipe or a club or a tree branch. It knocked her senseless. She grabbed her can of Mace, but her assailant said, "I have a knife." He bound and then raped her at the edge of the woods, saying, "You love sex, don't you?" When he finally left, she tried to stand up but fell to the ground. "My head hurt and I was full of blood," she later told the police. Three girls driving by came upon her and began screaming: "My God."

On April 23, a young man in a short-sleeved sport shirt with decorative stitching, white pants, a straw hat, and sunglasses knocked on the door of a house in Oyster Bay Cove, a small village close to St. Dominic and a house that any student who lived on the South Shore of Long Island and attended St. Dominic would have to pass on the way to school. Georgette Pirkl answered. She was a fifty-two-year-old woman at home with her mother, Caroline, who lived with Georgette and her family. Georgette's two children were in school. The young man at the door said that he worked for the Police Boys Club and was soliciting local men to be volunteer coaches. When Georgette told him that her husband was not at home, he asked if he could leave his name. She let him in. He took her phone off the hook, locked Georgette's seventy-nine-year-old mother in a closet and then in the same room raped Georgette in her son's bed, her hands tied behind her back with a telephone cord.

On April 30, Barbara Johnson went out for a run near her family home in Bethpage, halfway between Wantagh and Oyster Bay. She was twenty years old and ran five times a week, always around ten p.m., always the same route. She heard someone coming up behind her and thought he was another jogger. He put his hand over her mouth and the point of his knife into her ribs. He said,

"If you say anything I'm going to use this—do you feel that?" He was wearing a wool sweater with a Mexican design. He ordered her to pull her sweatshirt over her head and pushed her into the shadows of the John F. Kennedy Middle School, dragging her into the woods where she had gone sleigh riding as a kid. "He was very big . . . I didn't know what to do at the time because he was so much bigger. I didn't stand a chance against him physically. So I dropped. And he hit me in the head and said, 'Get up, get up, get up,'" she recalls. He bound her hands with her shoelaces and later with the string from her sweatpants. "He beat the shit out of me, and he raped me two ways to Sunday. I was on my back at first. Then he flipped me over." Her face was mushed into the leaves and branches. When she began kicking at him, he hit her across the head with his fist or his forearm. He said, "I guess you don't value your life." She said she was willing to take the hits because she was trying to buy time. "After he got done, I'm like, 'I'm dead. He's just going to freaking kill me.'" She told him her dad was a police officer and would come out looking for her as soon as he realized she wasn't home on time. He told her, "Don't move," and she heard him run off. "I saw white lights that night. I thought I was dead."

On May 12, a twenty-one-year-old secretary from Freeport walked to her car in the parking lot of Long Island's biggest and most popular mall, Roosevelt Field. When she opened the door, a man pushed her inside and showed her his knife. He told her to drive around for a while, until he found a park to his liking. He bound her with cord he had brought for the purpose and told her to "go down" on him—"and if it's not the best I've ever had, I'll kill you." When he was done, he told her where she lived, reading the address off her license. He said, "If you tell the police, I'll kill you or someone you love. You will need a police escort wherever you go." She went straight to her boyfriend's apartment, and he had to convince her and her parents that she must go to the police. "She never saw his face. But she heard his voice. And when she went to the lineup, she was easily able to recognize his voice," said her now husband, who spoke on his wife's behalf because he said she isn't comfortable talking about the incident and doesn't want her name made public.

On May 22, Denise O'Brien left her apartment at ten-thirty p.m. to make a phone call. She had just turned twenty-two. She was living in Roslyn, on the North Shore, with no job and not enough money for a phone line of her own. She used a pay phone in the parking lot of a bank across the street. A man bumped into her on the way and then grabbed her from behind and put his hand around her waist. "I know he had a knife because I felt it against my skin several times," she later said in a statement to the police. She kept saying to her attacker, "Let's talk about this," and he said, "Shut up." He dragged her into a dark recess of the parking lot and tied her up. He removed her tampon and started raping her. She kept telling him to stop, but this only angered him. "Never use the words 'can't' or 'stop,'" he said, and then told her that he recognized her—and that she might know him "from long ago."

On May 31, a sixteen-year-old girl (who asked that her name not be used) answered the doorbell at her family's home in Baldwin, west of Wantagh along the train line. A man wearing a Sherwin-Williams hat and sunglasses introduced himself as Tom Harris and said that his company was testing a new product by offering free paint jobs to lucky homeowners. When she answered that her parents weren't home, Tom Harris asked for a glass of water and she let him inside. He grabbed her around the neck and held a knife against her. She reached back and grabbed the knife, but he threatened to cut her if she didn't let go. He told her that he only needed money, and though he had to tie her up, he would be gone quickly and she would never see him again. She told him she was fifteen, a year younger than she was, with the hope he'd be deterred by the stiff punishment for assaulting a minor. He tied her up, made her lie down on the floor, and held her down with his foot. He dragged her back to the porch and said, "Maybe I'll fuck you. Or would you rather die?"

"I'd rather die," she answered. "I broke away from him. I just kept screaming to him, 'My mother is going to be home. She just went to the store. She's going to be home any minute.' I kept screaming it, and he kept telling me not to scream. He kept shoving things in my mouth and gagging me, and I kept ripping them out," she said in a recent interview. "Finally, he tied me up and left."

The girl, still bound, followed him outside. He was running. She ran into the street screaming, as her neighbor, John Henkel, a New York City cop, was pulling up to his house. He gave chase and arrested Tom Harris at the duck pond where he had parked his yellow Torino. Todd Hodne had once again been caught.

Hodne was questioned for days and confessed in detail. He admitted to the last crime first and the first one last, since he raped Anne Wright in his Wantagh neighborhood, around the block from his home, and he didn't want to embarrass his parents. In his statements, he seemed almost relieved to have been caught, as if he understood he was unable to stop himself.

"A normal person shouldn't do this," Hodne says in the statement he gave to Nassau County police about his attack on the sixteen-year-old girl. "There seems to be two sides of myself lately. When I sit down and think about what I do, it drives me crazy. How could I do something like that? I think I need to see a psychiatrist. If you could arrange it, I think I do. It's not normal for someone to want to do this, and I want to try to straighten out, you know."

•   •   •

Hodne was indicted on four counts of first-degree rape, three counts of first-degree sodomy, three counts of first-degree robbery, two counts of second-degree burglary, and one count of first-degree attempted rape in Nassau County Criminal Court. He reportedly tried to kill himself in jail a few weeks after his arrest. His lawyer, Martin Silberg, notified the prosecution that he intended to file an insanity defense. He never did. On September 7, 1979, six months after his conviction for the rape of Betsy Sailor, Hodne pleaded guilty to two counts of rape, two counts of sexual abuse, and one count of attempted second-degree robbery.

"I only wish I could recapture what I lost," Hodne told Nassau County Judge Richard Delin, weeping as he described his crimes. Delin said he had been inclined to withdraw his sentencing offer after he read the accounts of Hodne's attacks but that the letters of support Hodne had received had changed his mind. Thirty-five people had written on Hodne's behalf. One of them was his former high school coach Tom Capozzoli. The Pirkl family remembers Capozzoli also calling Georgette Pirkl's husband to tell him that the player he coached couldn't have done what Georgette had accused him of doing. "You got the wrong guy," Capozzoli said of Hodne, even though a few months earlier his own son Tony had testified in Hodne's rape trial in Pennsylvania.

Hodne had lost everything but his powers of persuasion. Had he gone to trial, he could have been sentenced to a minimum of at least eight years up to twenty-five. Instead, Delin accepted his pleas and sentenced him to minimum of seven years and a maximum of twenty-one, his Pennsylvania and Nassau County sentences to be served concurrently. In November 1979, shortly after Hodne entered the Pennsylvania prison system, psychologist Ed Perry evaluated him and came to this conclusion:

> His remorse appears hollow as he tends to project the blame for his misfortunes onto others or simply bad breaks. He assumes little, if any, responsibility, for his actions. He has shallow feelings and loyalties and appears to owe no allegiance to any particular person, group or code . . . Frustration tolerance is low and when denied his own way, aggressive outbursts are likely. He will need to be closely supervised. . . . Todd is manipulative and will likely take advantage of those who are physically and emotionally weaker than himself.

But the most comprehensive attempt to explain Todd Hodne comes from Hodne himself. Later in life, as a prisoner in New York state, he went year after year before a parole board and had to answer questions about why he did what he did. His answers, as preserved in redacted transcripts, are by definition self-serving and are often dishonest regarding the extent of his crimes. He admits only what he pleaded to, raping one woman in Pennsylvania and two in New York. He explains the attempted rapes on his record by saying he stopped if they resisted. He lies. But he also has clearly been forced to grapple with himself as a consequence of his institutionalized life, and he seems to know this *is* his life—that he's never getting out. He cites both drugs and steroids as a cause of his crimes. And yet the story he tells most often starts with football.

"On the outside, I was the All-American kid," Hodne says in a 2019 parole hearing, the year before he died.

> I was given a full scholarship. I had colleges coming to see me in high school, offering to buy me cars to go to school, to give me money. I chose Penn State and did very well there the first semester . . . And to understand what happened from here, I actually have to go back to the decisions I made when I was twelve or thirteen or even younger. The football was everything, my self-worth. It was who I was. It was also where I expressed what you might deem negative emotions. I never dealt with anything in my life, and I stored it up and turned it into anger on the football field, and it made me a very good football player. When I first started playing, I wasn't very aggressive, and they taught me to channel my emotions and become where you don't have empathy for people. The other team is your enemy, and it is your job to destroy them. So I started to develop at a very young age my view of [being] a man was that you didn't show emotion. I had older brothers; if I cried in front of them, they made fun of you. So I really didn't have any other coping mechanism other than you just internalize it and bring it on to the football field.

Hodne says without naming her that he had a girlfriend at home when he went to Penn State but that soon he found another measure of self-worth: "This is where it really kind of developed to look at women as sexual objects. You go to different parties at night, and there were always women you could have sex with, especially being a football player." When he was suspended after "one of my friends kicked in the window of a store"—that's how he describes the Record Ranch burglary—he lost not just the game that allowed him to control his impulses but also the opportunities for sexual gratification that the game provided. His relationship with his long-term girlfriend "started to fall apart," and

> at that time I felt that it was because I was no longer playing football and I was unable to deal with that rejection. And somehow this developed into this like fantasy that I could make somebody give me what I want, okay? There are certain types of rapes, if you know a certain type of rape, I was what you would deem a control rapist. I would use the necessary force to make them have sex with me. If they resisted too much I would run away. But what I was after was each time I had sex with a woman it was like a reaffirmation of who I was of my self-worth.

"I think any sexual crime is first a fantasy but the fantasy ends in the way you want it to end," he says in another parole hearing. In Hodne's case, he fantasized "that I would capture this woman, I would have sex with her. And in having sex with them, I would either, the fantasy, OK, was, I would either please them so much that they would love me, that they would accept me, that they weren't being hurt by this, they weren't being terrified by this."

In hearing after hearing, Hodne tells the parole board that he did what he did—that he became what he became—because he wanted to feel the way he did when he played football. "Football was who I was. It was all my self-worth. I felt that it brought me friends and girlfriends," he says.

It is impossible now to establish a direct causality behind Hodne's crimes. However, in State College, Pennsylvania, two things happened on August 19, 1978: Karen was sexually assaulted at knifepoint in her apartment in the early morning hours, and that same afternoon, Joe Paterno told reporters after practice that Hodne's name had been deleted from the Nittany Lions' roster.

•   •   •

Kathleen Pirkl had to get a ride home from St. Dominic. She was eleven years old and had missed the bus, so the mother of a friend drove her. She lived close by in a house with a long driveway, but her ride had to drop her off at the bottom. The driveway was full of police cars and people in uniforms and the solemn confusion of spinning lights. Her father ran down to meet her—to meet her before she reached the house. He was crying. She had never seen Donald Pirkl cry. Her mother, Georgette, and her grandmother, Caroline O'Neill, were in the driveway next door. Kathleen thought her house had been robbed and worried about the stereo she had just received as a gift. "Daddy, did they take my stereo?" she asked.

Her father told her to go inside and find some clothes. When she did, she saw blood all over the hallway and storm clouds of black fingerprint dust on the walls. A sliding closet door tilted crookedly off the rails. She went back outside and was allowed to see her mother and grandmother for a minute before she went to stay with a neighbor. Her mother was bloody and bruised and on a gurney. Her grandmother was wearing a robe not her own. Kathleen stayed the next two nights with her friend, and years would pass before she found out exactly what happened . . . before she began to understand that although her mother and grandmother went to the hospital, her whole family would bear the scars.

"My parents were very hush-hush," Kathleen says. "We weren't supposed to talk about it. We weren't supposed to even think about it." She would hear about it in school, through whispers and rumors—what her mother had to do. Kathleen didn't understand. Her mother was prim and proper and very Catholic, a volunteer at the St. Dominic library. Kathleen had never even seen her wear jeans. But the kids at St. Dominic always knew more than she did. One day at school, a classmate told her, "They got him." When she saw Todd Hodne's photo in the local newspaper, she recognized him. He used to drive by in his yellow car and wave to her. She waved back. From that day on, she felt that he might have attacked her mother and her Nana. But he had come for her.

Of all the women Hodne confessed to raping or assaulting in the spring of 1979, at least five faced him in Nassau County Court that September, with one too traumatized to participate in the prosecution. Georgette Pirkl, as one of the five, made her daughter proud. She was a brave woman—they both were, she and Nana.

They saved one another. When Hodne was attacking Georgette, Caroline had to listen to it from the closet. She heard her daughter say, "Please don't hurt my mother." She heard Hodne cut off her daughter's pants, girdle and underwear with scissors. She heard him demand that her daughter curse and masturbate for him. She heard him rape and sodomize her. Somehow Caroline freed herself from the telephone cord binding her hands in the closet and made a run for it. Hodne saw the shadow and said, "Damn." He left Georgette and ran after the old woman. He tackled her on the brick sidewalk between the main house and the guest house where she lived—a 240-pound former Penn State football player expending his full force on a seventy-nine-year-old woman. He crushed her. Georgette fled to the bathroom, where there was a tiny porthole window. She climbed up on the toilet seat and squeezed her naked body through it, cutting and bruising herself from shoulders to knees. When Hodne realized she had escaped, he ran, dropping the safe deposit box he had stolen. He had chosen to attack the Pirkls on the day of his twentieth birthday. Now the money flew all over the lawn.

It was an assault on all of them. They wound up staying in the house in Oyster Bay Cove because Kathleen's father was a lawyer who had deep ties to the community and political ambitions. But Nana never physically recovered from Hodne's tackle. Kathleen's brother couldn't stand sleeping in the room where his mother had been raped, and Kathleen did everything she could to get kicked out of St. Dominic. And Georgette rarely left the house until at last she and Donald left the house for good and moved to Florida in 1997. "I have a picture of when she first got to Florida, and I've never seen her smile a smile like that," Kathleen says. "She was just so happy to get the hell out of Oyster Bay. She said, 'I could not live my life.' I don't think she ever enjoyed herself again until they got to Florida, and then they were like little kids. And then my father passed away within a year, and that was the end of her again. I had such a hard life with her. I couldn't help her."

It was when Kathleen moved to Sarasota, Florida, to be with her mother that she finally began to understand what happened on April 23, 1979.

"I watched her diminish because of what Todd did to her," Kathleen says. "She was the type of woman, my father was her first and her only. She didn't even date. I think she went on one date prior to my father, and I knew it wasn't a sexual thing back in the day with them. Todd took away a lot from her. And we had discussions where she felt like, 'I was with your father and only him, and then this happens.' That really hurts a Catholic woman her age in her upbringing.

"And she told me—and she was very reluctant—she said, 'He forced me to give him a blow job.' And I could not believe that word came out of my mother's mouth because she's such a sweet lady. It was horrific to hear out of her mouth. And that's when she told me, 'If I didn't do it, he was going to hurt you when you got home.' He threatened her with me. He told her that if she didn't do what he asked her to do, he would just wait for me to come home. . . . I was right about the yellow car."

Georgette Pirkl died in 2007, when she was eighty-one. Kathleen knew she had kept a book in her bottom dresser drawer—"an old school photo album that had everything in it"—but she had never dared to look through it "out of respect" for her mother. When she started preparing the house in Sarasota for sale, she found it, and a friend convinced her to read it. "And that's when I learned everything," Kathleen says. The book included court files and her mother's notes but also something that shocked her: "A letter from Hodne's mother apologizing, saying she didn't know where she went wrong with her son. I remember reading it and sobbing. I do believe my mother responded back to her. I do believe she wrote her a long letter."

Kathleen does not have the book anymore. Her brother told her to burn it—"that it was time to put Mommy's grief to an end. That we shouldn't live it anymore, now that she was peaceful and with our father again." When she moved to her new home, she had a fire pit in the backyard . . ."and I put it in there. A part of me wanted to grab it, but a part of me said, it's time. It was time to get rid of that book that ruined our lives. Burning it felt like voodoo."

•　　　•　　　•

Seven years after Todd Hodne went to prison—three years in Pennsylvania for the rape of Betsy Sailor and four in New York for the serial crimes on Long Island—Francis Quigley wrote a letter. He was the Nassau prosecutor who put Hodne away. He had heard with the arrival of the new year, 1986, that Hodne was under consideration for parole and so wrote to the senior parole officer of the Eastern New York Correctional Facility in Napanoch and said that "the Nassau County District Attorney strongly opposes any release of inmate Todd S. Hodne. I am convinced that to release Todd Hodne will be to subject the community to a severe risk that Hodne will again victimize innocent women with rape, assault and the possibility of serious injury and death."

Quigley wrote that while Hodne was out on bail and awaiting sentence for a burglary and rape charge in Pennsylvania, Hodne "engaged in a series of exceptionally vicious rapes in Nassau County. . . . The victims all reported that Hodne was sadistic and based on my investigation into the case and my interviews with the victims, I believe that the victims were lucky to live through their ordeal. In fact, it was not through any restraint on Hodne's part but rather the cool-headedness of the victims that Hodne did not kill any of these women. . . . The foregoing demonstrates that Hodne is an extremely dangerous, potentially homicidal criminal, who presents the gravest threat to society."

Four months later, on May 2, 1986, Hodne was released from prison after serving the minimum seven years of his twenty-one-year sentence, by unanimous vote of the parole board—or, as John B. Collins later put it, "for some unfathomable reason, the New York State Parole Board saw fit to unleash this monster on the unknowing public after serving only the bare minimum of the sentence imposed by the Nassau County Court." According to the New York State Department of Corrections and Community Supervision, records from that parole hearing are "no longer available due to how old they are. They have been destroyed."

Hodne did not look like the college football player who went away. He had lost most of his hair. He wore a thin mustache, and the heaviness of his brow and jaw had become more pronounced. What had not changed was his body. He had worked out in prison, and if anything, he was bigger and stronger than when he left. He weighed about 250 pounds.

The notes and logbook of his parole officer indicate he went to live with his parents in Wantagh and to work in the family home-improvement business. On a visit to a client's home, he met a woman, and they began dating. He was checking in with his parole officer each week and seeing a therapist about his drug use and sexual compulsions. In July, he was questioned about a rape that occurred on his block in Wantagh but was told he wasn't a suspect. He failed to inform his parole officer that he had been questioned by the police. He moved in with his girlfriend in Bethpage. On February 24, 1987, he told his therapist that he had started smoking crack. He had begun to violate his parole requirements and by the start of summer, he had not seen his therapist in months, and his uncle had fired him from his job with the family business. As Collins later wrote, "Hodne committed multiple violations of his conditions of parole while at liberty. He was, however, not punished or taken off the streets by those charged with his supervision and control." In Wantagh, he showed up at his home with bruises on his face and his mother called the parole office to tell them that her son had been mugged in the parking lot of the local 7-Eleven by a gang of teenagers who told him he should go back to jail. He was evicted from his girlfriend's home in Bethpage after the landlord found out who he was. He lived in a hotel for a while and then checked himself in to a detox center in Hempstead. After a week, he returned to his parents' home in Wantagh and began smoking crack again. On Tuesday night, August 11, 1987, he met his girlfriend at a TGI Friday's in Huntington and then asked a friend to drop him off at the White Castle. There, he called a cab.

The driver's name was Jeffrey Hirsch. He was young, in his early thirties, with reddish hair and a larky smile set in a long, deadpan face. Hirsch had been a successful salesman in Maryland and was about to start his own business when his mother contracted cancer and he came back home to Long Island to take care of her. He had a wife, Mary Beth, and four young children, ranging in age from six months to seven years. His father owned the cab. Hirsch was driving to make ends meet but also because he liked talking to people and hearing their stories. He answered the call at the White Castle, and Hodne gave him the address on a side street behind the Walt Whitman Mall. When Hirsch stopped on the dark street, Hodne threatened him with a knife. Hodne tried to rob him, but Hirsch struggled, and they fought, Hirsch in the front of the vehicle and Hodne in the back. Hirsch was tall and wiry, but Hodne overpowered him. Hodne dropped his knife and put Hirsch in a choke hold and broke the hyoid bone in his neck. Hodne opened the door and stepped outside with Hirsch slumped over in the front seat, his body facing one way and his head another. According to police reports, a man named Robert Gruber stood in front of Hodne on his lawn. He had seen the fight through the window of his home and stepped outside. "I think I might have killed him," Hodne said.

"I think you did," Gruber said.

"Call 911," Hodne said. "He tried to rob me."

Gruber went inside and brought the receiver of his phone outside and handed it to Hodne, who told the dispatcher his name was Steven Hodne, the twin brother of Todd Hodne. As he said later in a parole board hearing, he didn't want the police to judge him unfairly because of Todd Hodne's notoriety. When he gave the phone back, Gruber tried to console him. "Get away from me!" Hodne snapped. For the next thirty seconds, Hodne stood motionless, staring at the cab and at Hirsch. "I'm sick of this shit," he finally said. Then he got in the cab and drove away.

Hodne left the car—with Hirsch still inside, along with his knife and the thirty-seven dollars in blood-soaked bills he tried to rob—in the parking lot of the mall and then made a run for it. The police dispatched a K-9 unit as Hodne fled through the backyards of Huntington. As Collins wrote, "This former athlete ran *through*, not over, *through* two stockade fences, trying to avoid the K-9 and human officers in hot pursuit of him." The dogs finally found him hiding under a bush. He was taken to the Suffolk County precinct house nearby and started concocting his story. Hirsch had picked him up in his cab and together they went looking for crack, Hodne said. They scored some, and when they smoked it, Hirsch made a pass at him. Hodne fought him off, but Hirsch threatened him with a knife. They grappled over it, which accounted for the blood. By this time, Hirsch was in the hospital, where the admitting physician diagnosed him as the victim of an overdose rather than a strangulation. When the police at the precinct received word from the hospital, they accepted Hodne's story, writing in a preliminary report: "double overdose of two gays with one in the hospital and the other under arrest by uniform for unauthorized use of a taxi." They changed the charge to unauthorized use of a vehicle; then Hodne, on his own recognizance, went home to Wantagh.

He had always been, as his former girlfriend said, persuasive. It was one of the things besides his strength that made him so dangerous. Now, by Thursday morning, he had been free for two days. Now, as Jeffrey Hirsch lay brain dead in a hospital, Hodne was in his own bed in Wantagh and his parole officer, Lenny Smith, came by for a visit. His mother told him Todd was sleeping and wouldn't let him in. He walked past her and went to Hodne's room. He pulled the blanket off Hodne's bed. His face was bruised and cut. Hodne had not shown up for therapy in months. He had been failing drug tests. He had been unemployed. But he told Smith something of the same story he told at the precinct. Smith said he wouldn't write him up for unauthorized use of a vehicle but reminded him that he had to report all contact with law enforcement.

Smith was headed for the door when he saw one of Todd's brothers sitting in the living room. They looked at each other. The brother had already called Smith a number of times to report on Todd being in violation. Now Todd had been arrested and was free on what the brother calls "a twenty-five-dollar station house bond." He knew Todd better than anyone; knew, he says, that "Todd was *out there* by then. And I just couldn't. I saw the writing on the wall, and I didn't want any part of it. I *don't* want any part. You know, he destroyed our family once, and I was like, 'I'll be damned if you do it again.'"

"He's lying," Todd's brother told Smith.

Act 4: Aftermath

They were in their sixties now and each was heading to State College for a reunion of sorts—a reunion with someone neither had ever met. Betsy Sailor lived in New Hampshire. Karen lived near Pittsburgh. But they were both driving to State College to meet each other and to find out what they could about the experience they held in common. They were very different women who had led very different lives. But they both had to survive Todd Hodne. And until this day in the summer of 2021, they each had to do it alone.

They met in a hotel that hadn't been built when they went to school, in a part of town that hadn't been developed. Karen arrived first, her hair blonde, her eyes wary and sharp, her manner deliberate and careful. The work she had taken on—of remembering and processing what happened to her—was visible, as if it all took place right under her skin.

Betsy announced herself headfirst, peeking around the partially open door of the hotel conference room. She had kept her curls, the salt-and-pepper spirals that offset her scholarly eyeglasses. She wore a loose shift and sandals, and to hear her talk was to remember what she was doing before Hodne invaded her life: interviewing potential roommates. She'd had a long career in human resources and raised a strong-willed, independent daughter. She had just recently become a grandmother and evinced the cheerful equanimity of a person who had heard and seen it all. Indeed, when she was asked to account for her verve in the face of all she's had to endure, she said, "When you have enough bad shit happen to you, you get to check off the boxes. You don't have to be afraid anymore."

They were very different women, yes—but they also were the products of very different experiences regarding their worst experience. Betsy had faced Hodne in court. She had won. The legal system had recognized her and what was done to her. If anyone had tried to dissuade her from pressing charges, she said, "I would have told them, 'Yeah, you and the horse you came to town on.'"

And yet the fate Betsy refused was precisely the fate Karen had had to face. "I knew there were others that were raped," Betsy said. "But I was told that none of them were pressing charges. They weren't interested in pressing charges."

Karen now told Betsy that she had cooperated with investigators for months: "I should have been informed what legal ramifications were involved, what assistance the university could give me."

"It wasn't a situation where you didn't want to prosecute," Betsy said. "But perhaps you didn't know what to do next."

"I didn't know where to turn," Karen said.

Betsy and Karen had never known each other's names. They both had heard that were "others," but they were never told who they were or how many there might have been.

"We should have been together all along," Betsy said.

The next day, they met Duane Musser. He was retired at seventy-four years old but still very much a small-town cop. He had a shiny head under his ball cap and a white, horseshoe mustache and goatee. When he spoke, he took his time. He remembered Betsy Sailor and Susan and where they lived. He remembered that the case came down to three fingerprints lifted from Betsy's apartment and phone calls traced from Susan's phone. He remembered the "arrogance" of the Penn State lawyer, Bob Mitinger. He remembered that Joe Paterno told his players not to talk. But Musser did not remember the specifics of what he wrote in his police reports of the time. He did not remember going to Hamilton Hall and questioning Fred Ragucci about the five women Todd Hodne was suspected of assaulting. He did not remember questioning Hodne himself about other assaults that had taken place in State College. "I'm beginning to think I didn't do such a good job," Musser would say, especially when he was reminded of the outcome—of what happened when one conviction wasn't enough to keep Hodne in jail. He greeted Betsy Sailor and Karen at the Waffle Shop just outside of State College. He recognized Betsy immediately, and they embraced like old friends. Karen watched and waited, and when he said hello, she asked, "Do you remember me?"

He answered, "No, I'm sorry. I don't."

She did not flinch, except in her eyes. But the awful disappointment provided a preview of what was to come. She and Betsy had both come to town to find their files. They went together to visit the county clerk at the courthouse in Bellefonte. They made requests to the investigators who worked for the district attorney. They visited campus and met with an official from student affairs. At each stop, Betsy came away with documents that both validated her memories and gave her information about what happened to her. At each stop, Karen not only came away with nothing, she was told that her files didn't exist.

"I was just forgotten," Karen said.

•   •   •

On November 4, 1975, a Penn State student reported a rape at Fiji House—one of the "jock houses" or "football fraternities" on the Penn State campus. The alleged crime was a gang rape that was reported to have taken place a few weeks earlier at a party the night before a football game, the victim drugged and unconscious. The incident generated public protests. Joe Paterno discouraged his players from any involvement in them. According to wide receiver Jimmy Cefalo, who later wrote a series of articles for the *New York Times* detailing his experiences playing a big-time college sport, "Coach Paterno called the seven Fijis on the football team into his office on the afternoon of the protest and told us to stay away from the house during the demonstration."

The protests wound up on the front page of the *Philadelphia Inquirer*'s metro section and catalyzed investigations by the State College police, Penn State's student affairs department, and its interfraternity council. The police ultimately determined the evidence insufficient to bring charges, and the university ended up suspending one male student for three terms and putting another on three-term probation. "The interfraternity council decided that they wanted to [impose sanctions] because there was some press that was going on," says Greg Hanks, the president of Fiji House at the time. "Nothing happened," says Shelley Gottsagen, one of the organizers of the protests. "Nothing happened at all. There were no repercussions."

But the end of the Fiji House investigations marked the beginning of the movement toward a rape crisis center in State College. Rape kits were an innovation not yet widely in use at the time, and the term rape culture was just being coined in feminist academia. It was a historical moment in terms of rape awareness, in which advocates and institutions were often at cross-purposes.

"It was generally our policy not to make [rapes] well known," remembers Lee Upcraft, the assistant vice president for student affairs at Penn State. "If I recall, we would make sure that the people that lived around her and in her building knew that it happened and knew that we caught him. But we tried to keep it out of the paper when we could because once it got in the paper, then the woman's privacy was gone. Nothing you could do to protect her."

The impulse to keep women safe from shame contributed to a culture of silence that left them feeling unheard and unsafe. "I just felt we were ignored," Gottsagen says. "It was even hard for us to make appointments or get time [with university officials]. Nobody wanted to hear what we had to say." Gretchen Fincke, from the State College rape crisis center, remembers: "The university didn't want to know anything about [the extent of sexual assault]. Nope, nope, nope, nope, nope."

There was a discrepancy between how institutions and advocates at Penn State talked about rapes and sexual assaults and in how they counted them at the time. A former Penn State student who gave campus orientations remembers being discouraged from telling parents of incoming freshmen how many rapes were happening in State College. Ed Nolder, an officer with the Penn State University Police at the time, says, "Rape was not a big thing then; I don't think I heard of eight rapes in my entire eight years with the police force." The FBI's Uniform Crime Reporting program counted a total of twelve rapes and sexual assaults at Penn State University and the borough of State College in all of 1978. The student newspaper ran an editorial that year counting thirty-five rapes and sexual assaults in and around Penn State as of September.

Besides Hodne, there weren't just other rapes at Penn State, there were other rapists. One was a student who dressed up either as a female or as a police officer and fondled and battered women at gunpoint. Another was a twenty-one-year-old man who snuck into dormitories and assaulted women as they were taking showers or sleeping in their beds. "Happy Valley has a rape problem," the *Daily Collegian* declared in April 1979 in a three-part series on rape at Penn State. The series was published a little more than a month after Hodne's conviction but never mentioned Hodne. The reporter who wrote it admits now that she had never heard of him.

Lizette Olsen, who worked at the rape crisis center at the time, remembers the university broadly supporting rape prevention and awareness efforts but that "they were low-hanging fruit." It was different when dealing with specific cases, she says. "When there were instances of sexual violence where the perpetrator was someone of value, i.e., the football team, things did not go so well . . . I can't actually say to you that that was an institutional response as much as it was the response of individuals in leadership who were trying to assist the football team or the athletic department."

⬤   ⬤   ⬤

When Joe Paterno and Penn State told the story of 1978 and 1979, it went like this: in 1978, he lost his chance at the national championship through a failure of nerve, and then in 1979, he lost control of the team. There was the team captain who refused to finish a lap; the star cornerback who, along with two others, was ruled academically ineligible; the running back caught driving drunk; the linebacker arrested for fighting; and the lineman busted for drinking on campus, and, finally, at the Liberty Bowl, the substitute tight end who showed up in a suburban bedroom in the middle of the night and was lucky he didn't get shot. These incidents were widely covered in newspapers and magazines, first one at a time and then in an onslaught. "Suddenly, it seemed like we were a bunch of felons down here," Penn State Sports Information director Dave Baker said in 1980.

What ensued was a period of self-doubt unprecedented in Paterno's career—a simultaneous fall from grace and loss of faith that caused him not only to question his purpose but to consider quitting. In articles in the *Washington Post*, the *Philadelphia Daily News*, and particularly *Sports Illustrated*, he did a kind of public penance, admitting in *SI* that "the Great Experiment"—as he called his own program—"is suddenly in disrepute" and wondering aloud if the violence he encouraged on the field had followed his players off of it: "We're dealing with aggressive kids; we encourage this aggressiveness and then we get mad when we can't saddle them. Maybe the fault is with us." What he didn't do in any of the articles was mention Todd Hodne by name or acknowledge his crimes.

It had never been easy for Joe Paterno to talk about sex, his son Jay writes in his book *Paterno Legacy*. He was squeamish about it in the best of circumstances and doubly so in the worst, for he clearly viewed sexual violence in terms of sex rather than of violence, his usual righteousness giving way to awkward befuddlement. "The most awkward," Jay Paterno writes, "was a sexual assault allegation involving a female student and two of our players that was later dropped. Our two players had engaged in sex with her at the same time."

"When it came up in a staff meeting, Joe read the report and a puzzled look came across his face. He paused, leaned back in his chair, and thought for a minute. 'So about this incident . . .' Joe said in a confused tone. 'It says she had sex with two of them . . . at the same time? How is that even possible?'"

It was a paradox that turned out to be a tragic flaw. He insisted on innocence as well as power. He portrayed himself as naive as well as all-knowing. He saw everything—as Fred Ragucci said, "He would throw a fit if you didn't wear *socks*"—except what he didn't understand. In 2002, Penn State expelled defensive back Anwar Phillips for two semesters after investigating him for sexual assault, but Paterno insisted on playing him in the Capital One Bowl on New Year's Day, later speaking about his decision with something like resignation: "If down the line, out of 125 kids, once in a while something happens that none of us are glad about, it happens. If I could change that, I'd change it. But I'm not gonna be able to change it." Four years later, as Penn State prepared to play Florida State in the Orange Bowl, Paterno was asked at a news conference about an opposing player accused of sexual assault, and he answered in a way that caused the local chapter of the National Organization for Women to call at the time for his resignation: "There's so many people gravitating to these kids, he may not have even known what he was getting into. . . . They knock on the door, somebody may knock on the door, a cute girl knocks on the door, what do you do? . . . Thank god they don't knock on my door because I'd refer them to a couple of other rooms."

What else did Joe Paterno think, about Todd Hodne, about sexual misconduct? We reached out to his children to find out. His daughter Mary initially said she needed some time to think and then didn't respond when we followed up. His son Jay asked about what documents we had but did not agree to an on-the-record conversation for this story. His daughter Diana said she didn't recall a player named Hodne and cut the call short saying, "This sounds to me like another chance to blame my dad for something he had nothing to do with." And his son Scott answered an email by explaining, "I was six. I have no idea what you are talking about. But based on what you tell me, the guy was arrested and convicted—seems like that story has been written for about two generations."

·　　·　　·

Two things in the story of Todd Hodne are inexplicable: the mind of Todd Hodne and the decision by Richard Sharp to let him go. The behavior of Joe Paterno and his involvement in the case are straightforward by comparison. He was involved in the case, early and late. But then by temperament, Paterno was always involved. He was the man behind the desk. As a matter of policy, he let the justice system do its job, Lee Upcraft, assistant vice president for student affairs, says: "Whenever football players were involved in sexual assaults, Joe Paterno was wonderful. He and I talked, and he said, 'If there's a football player involved, I want to know about it.' He said, 'But I don't want him treated any differently than any other student,' and that was the agreement we had in those years. I never had any pressure whatsoever from Joe or from any of his staff to do anything different to a football player that had gotten in trouble. It just wasn't who he was."

In the Hodne case, the justice system failed. Of course, Joe Paterno could not have foreseen that Todd Hodne would go back to Long Island nor what he would do when he got there. And as Paterno saw it, his job was not to control the justice system but to control the narrative. "Whenever a player got in trouble, he didn't want anybody to know about it," Upcraft says. "It was bad for him and bad for the program if a player got in trouble and it became public that the player was in trouble. . . . I think one of the things he always hoped was that nothing would come out. I'd do my thing, and he'd do his thing, and nobody would know about it. That was the best outcome as far as he was concerned."

"It's a matter of image," Robert Scannell, the phys ed dean who worked closely with Paterno, told the *Washington Post* in 1979. "Because of the exposure we've had the last few years, a lot of people have come to think that Penn State football players never lose games and always make straight As. We love that image. But it creates added pressure. What used to be a local story is now a national story." And what might be a national story also stays local: multiple cases become a single case, a single case becomes a one-time incident, a one-time incident becomes an anomaly. Todd Hodne is seen as dismissed, inconsequential, sent home.

As Paterno put it in the 1980 *Sports Illustrated* profile, published one year and fourteen days after Hodne was convicted in Centre County Court for the rape of Betsy Sailor, "We have never covered up things around here. We just didn't have problems."

• • •

Six months after we called her for the first time, Karen had another memory about State College. It was about something that happened after she was attacked. She was driving in her car at night. Another car began following her, close, with two men up front. The car and its aggressive pursuit scared her so much that she drove to State

College Police headquarters and parked out front. She pressed on her horn until the car went away.

She wrote about the memory in an email. The car, she wrote, was not like the family sedan she drove. It was "a guy car, sporty but 1970s big," and she sent us a photo that corresponded to what she remembered—a photo of a 1971 fastback Pontiac GTO, light green. Hodne drove a fastback Ford Torino of roughly the same vintage, light yellow.

"I was reflecting on the story you are writing, keeping still and thinking of sights, smells and sounds associated with memories of that night," she wrote. "I was wearing 'White Linen' perfume that summer. I used Clinique moisturizer, Palmolive soap. My car smelled like gasoline, old leaves and coffee."

Once, Karen had pushed her memories aside. Now, she is learning to live with them. "I try to find some little thread that could make a difference. I mean, he [Hodne] is gone now, but it doesn't feel like it's finished," she says. "I don't think it'll ever be over."

.   .   .

The Rape, Abuse, and Incest National Network advises using the term *victim* when referring to a person recently affected by sexual violence or when speaking of a specific crime or criminal justice proceeding. It is an ancient word that has never lost its elemental and disturbing power, a word that says violence has been done and violence endures. The term *survivor* is often used to describe someone living with the long-term effects of sexual violence, someone experiencing the impact of violence over time. It is a word that encompasses who the women we interviewed were at the moment when Hodne's assault threatened to annihilate them, as well as who they became, who they *had* to become, over the course of their lifetimes.

This is not to say that all his victims have survived. Three of them are gone, and those who have survived *them*—their family members and friends—believe that Hodne hastened their end. Anne Wright was attacked in Wantagh on Long Island on the early morning of April 21, 1979, bludgeoned from behind with a heavy object and raped in the woods. She was staying with friends, one of whom, Edie Howell, still remembers the sight of Anne coming back from the hospital: "I was sitting on the porch when they dropped her off. She got out of the car, and her entire head was wrapped. They had her in a wheelchair, and she couldn't walk. It was a hole. It was a big indentation in her head. I don't know if that ever went away. Believe me, it was bad. There was a very large amount of stitches." For the rest of her life, Anne Wright had to endure the debilitating pain of spinal stenosis. In 2011, she died of an accidental overdose of morphine. She was fifty-five years old.

Denise O'Brien was already struggling when Hodne grabbed her while she was trying to use a pay phone in Roslyn on May 22, 1979. She was twenty-two years old, without a job and estranged from part of her family. Of the six women Hodne attacked on Long Island, she was the only one who didn't participate in his prosecution; she was too traumatized. Her family not only never really knew what happened to her that night, they couldn't quite bring themselves to believe what she told them about it, especially as Denise kept on her difficult and erratic course, swallowed up by substance abuse. She died of lung cancer at thirty-six in 1993, and it is only now—now that they are learning what happened to her— that they can see in retrospect the point in time when the dark forces that seemed out to get her grabbed her for good: 1979. "Obviously, this person destroyed a lot of lives," her brother Jeff says of Hodne.

Georgette Pirkl made it into her eighties after surviving Hodne's sustained brutalities on April 23, 1979, in Oyster Bay Cove—after surviving being raped and sodomized in the presence of her mother, Caroline O'Neill, and then watching the lingering aftermath of Hodne flattening Caroline against the sidewalk. No, he didn't kill them, Georgette's daughter Kathleen says, but he took their lives anyway, their remaining years. Both Georgette Pirkl and her mother died at eighty-one, Caroline two years after the attack. Kathleen was lucky to be at school when Hodne invaded their home, but the more she learns about what her mother and grandmother survived, the more she understands the generational obligation survivorship entails. Though Kathleen burned the album Georgette kept about the attack, she battled the Nassau County bureaucracy for months to obtain the case file. "When I read it in black and white," Kathleen says, "it explains a lot of things in my life, a lot of reasons I wasn't allowed to do certain things that I wanted to do, that other kids could do. And now I forgive them. I forgive my parents because I used to think that they were horrible. And now, as an adult her age, [I understand that] being raped by a young kid, it's humiliating. And what he said about my father [as he attacked Georgette], humiliating. And I now understand why they were the way they were in raising children. I mean, he was brutal on what he did."

Despite his best efforts, Todd Hodne did not destroy all of them. Just as they fought for their lives then, they fight for their lives now. They not only can't forget him, they don't want to, because that means some part of themselves would be forgotten. The twenty-one-year-old secretary who was ambushed in the parking lot of a bustling shopping mall in Garden City is sixty-four now; she doesn't want to talk about what she went through nor does she want her name used. But she wants her story told, so she has given her husband the task of telling it. He was her boyfriend in 1979, so he has lived with it too, and he remembers the aftermath of May 12, 1979, through the lens of nearly lifelong family attachment. It was her parents' wedding anniversary, he says. She had gone to Roosevelt Field to shop for a Mother's Day gift. For many years, she couldn't shop in stores because of the memories associated with that experience, and even now, her parents' anniversary is a bittersweet milestone. "I can tell you, it has had an effect on her through her life," her husband says. "A lot of times we forget about it and life is normal. But there have been years where I've said, 'What's the matter?' And she'll say, 'It's my parents' anniversary.'"

Surviving a predator like Hodne requires strength, of course—strength, resourcefulness, a clear-headed decision to live no matter what. In the case of the sixteen-year-old girl whose fight against Hodne in the kitchen of her parents' home in Baldwin led to his Long Island capture, the strength seems frankly superhuman. On

May 31, 1979, she was still a child. But she made Hodne run, and the people who knew her story were, she says, in awe of her. It has been part of her life *all* her life, the memory of her strength also proof of her strength. She became an artist, and she has had to live in rough neighborhoods, but as a survivor, she always had the confidence she would survive. "It may have been that I just trusted myself to get out of a bind," she says.

The inevitable distinctions between survivors make it difficult to write about survival. The hard work of living with what has happened encourages the sharing of individual stories and ends up underscoring the fact that not all stories are alike, as Barbara Johnson, now sixty-three-year-old Barbara Kuffner, understood even at age twenty. On April 30, 1979, she went out running in her Bethpage neighborhood; when she ran past the local middle school, she felt Hodne running behind her, and then felt his knife. She does not in any way minimize the extreme brutality of the attack; when it was over, she felt certain that he would kill her, and she saw "the white lights." But she didn't die, and when Hodne left in the "sweater with the Mexican design" he would later throw in a dumpster, she went home with bruises on her face and rope burns on her wrists. "I ran home barefoot," she says, "holding my sweatpants up because I didn't even take the time to do the string." She had told Hodne the truth when she told him her father was a cop. He was retired NYPD, and once she got home, he took her back to the scene of the crime in order to find evidence and get the story straight. "He said, 'You have to do this.' And I'm like, 'Fine.'" After Hodne was caught a month later, Barbara went to the jailhouse to pick him out of a lineup and then to court to testify against him. And it was there she saw the other women; it was there she realized the differences between them.

"They looked awful," Barbara says. "You could see they were just shattered by it. And it taught me a lot about myself, honestly, that I looked at these women who had been raped by the same man many months before and they were still suffering. I saw all of them. They all looked ruined. And it made me realize my strength in myself." She got over the attack, she says, "the day after it happened. I was over it. I was not going to let it bog me down. But you never forget it. You never forget it for the rest of your life. You just don't. It comes up. It comes up in conversations. It comes up in parenting." And decades later, it also came up in sex with her former partner: "I said to him, 'I've been raped.' And it's crazy. Because it was, what, forty-two years ago? And I said, 'You need to be gentle with me.' And he said, 'I've heard the story.' And I said, 'But you need to still be gentle with me.'"

There is no prescription for surviving the trauma of sexual assault. The women who speak here offer their stories rather than their advice; they testify as individuals rather than as representatives of any sort of category or class. There is, however, a prescription for how the survivors of sexual assault should—and should not—be treated. The only universal response to trauma is grief for what came before. The women Hodne attacked on Long Island each responded to the experience in different ways, but they were allowed to grieve in court for themselves and each other. It was not that way in State College, where only one of the women whom Hodne was suspected of attacking went to court and where the rest had to grieve privately for, among other things, their loss of faith in the place they were supposed to love the rest of their lives. They had to grieve for their loss of happiness in Happy Valley during a season of frenzied celebration for a team and a coach pursuing the national championship. The team that provided the magic also had provided Todd Hodne support, moral and otherwise; the coach who provided leadership had provided him his scholarship. Joe Paterno took pride in his role as moral exemplar and had led millions of Pennsylvanians and then tens of millions of Americans to believe he had something to say about *everything*. He was very nearly silent about Todd Hodne.

Adrienne Reissman believes that Hodne was the man who attacked her in the parking lot outside the Train Station in downtown State College: "He did a fucking number on me, and I'm a brave soul." But she also believed back then in Joe Paterno, and she expected something of him: "The decency and humanity to acknowledge the pain that the women [Hodne] hurt suffer. That's what I expected. That's what I expected from Joe Paterno. But nothing. Nothing. They washed it under the rug. 'Oh, my God—it's one of Joe Paterno's football players? Oh, please God—no.' They kept that quiet. They kept it quiet."

Paterno is gone now, deceased and disgraced. But Adrienne is reminded of him every time she receives a fundraising letter from her alma mater, which she throws away unopened. She knows Paterno kicked Hodne off the team. In her mind, that was not enough.

"You only partly did the right thing," she says, addressing Paterno forty-three years later. "The humanity is the other part. Really: Who the fuck are you? God? That you can't acknowledge that someone that you brought to this campus hurt five women that I know of? And you don't have the decency to at least write a note? Because this man who was hurting women all over campus went to school for nothing, nothing. He had everything. And you sought him out, Mr. Paterno. You brought that rapist on to this campus, and you gave him money to come. Excuse my language. Fuck you, Joe Paterno"

• • •

Irv Pankey was once the biggest man Betsy Sailor had ever seen. Now he is just too big for his rental car, especially after four hours behind the wheel. He has come a long way for this, flying across the country and then driving across the state of Pennsylvania. He climbs out of the car one long limb at a time. He moves with the unmistakable gait of a man who played football for a living, a sixty-three-year-old man in a Hawaiian shirt and a ball cap who doesn't hurry, even in the rain.

He knocks on the door.

She is not surprised this time, and when the door opens, she embraces him, then clings to him, as if steadying herself after losing her footing. He has the same big cheeks, with the small, winsome smile squeezed between them. "What up, dear child?" he asks. "Where's my cookies?"

They have not seen each other since a chance meeting outside Beaver Stadium a year or two after they graduated. But they've been in touch lately, more than four decades after they each did something remarkable. "When I think back on him doing what he did, I'm amazed that he even thought strongly about it. And that he took that risk," Betsy says. "Here's a [future] captain of the football team, in a championship year, looking at the NFL draft; well, a lot was on the line for Irv. To have him going against the powerhouse of Penn State football and what his leader, Joe Paterno, was telling him was absolutely amazing."

Irv did not feel that Paterno had prohibited him from standing up for Betsy, but he did know he was taking a risk by breaking ranks: "Penn State football—we were winning, we were nationally ranked, we were doing well. It was a close-knit brotherhood, so to speak, kind of like an army platoon." Few of his coaches or teammates remember what Irv did for Betsy, but to a man they say it sounds like something Irv would do. "Irv probably said, 'This is a bigger statement than just playing football here at Penn State,'" says former defensive back Micky Urquhart.

And now here they are, reunited in 2021 over something that happened in 1978, Irv eating snickerdoodle cookies in the kitchen of a State College rental and Betsy immediately angled against his shoulder. "I had forty-three years' knowledge of this person and his impact on my life," she will say a few weeks later. "And I was never able to really express that fully and say a long overdue thank you. But then there's that magic that happened. As soon as I saw him, it was the most heart-to-heart transfer of appreciation and love that went right through me, and then from him back to me. And just that smile and my smile and the eye contact. It was magical. It was a deep connection that was, I guess, ever-present but never realized. It was always there, but I couldn't, didn't, seek it out. I didn't make it happen. So it was the magic of the moment and just seeing him and being able to hug him. Which I don't recall doing much of when we first met. But now I could hug him and look at him and hug him again."

A question often arises about the revelations in this story, a retrospective question about the responsibility and culpability of the coaches, players, and university officials, as well as of the cops, lawyers and judges, who found out about Todd Hodne in real time, without the benefit of hindsight:

What would you have had them do?

The story of Todd Hodne is so full of pain that to recount it is also to hope that someone steps in and stops him. There are people who perhaps have the chance to and don't; there are people—Dave Smith and his father, Don, at St. Dom's; Francis Quigley in Nassau County; David Grine and Duane Musser in State College—who try to. These are good people doing their jobs to the best of their abilities. But Hodne was an unstoppable force and a rare evil. He forced some people to find a place in themselves that went beyond themselves. The women, whose death-defying feats of courage, strength, and resolve in the face of their attacker seem unimaginable, had to go beyond themselves. So did Robert Gruber, who came out of his house in Huntington when Hodne was strangling Jeffrey Hirsch and offered testimony that enabled John B. Collins in Suffolk County to put Hodne away for life. And so did Irv Pankey, whose heroism was such that it allows a glimpse of what might be possible in the face of evil. He did not stop Hodne. Nor did he take the stand and testify against him. But he did something no one else was able to do. He saw himself in another and he took up her pain as his own. He imagined what it must have been like for her and led her back into the world. And so he became . . . he *becomes* what everyone in this story needs and what only Betsy Sailor actually gets, embracing him now in the kitchen—"my guardian angel."

·   ·   ·

Jeffrey Hirsch, a cabdriver and father of four, died on August 16, 1987. He had been on life support for five days. He was brain dead. His wife, Mary Beth, was at his side. And thirty-one years after lying in court about strangling him and then arguing in appeals for more than a decade that he did it in self-defense, Hodne told the parole board he was sorry.

"I ended his life," Hodne said. "It's unforgivable; it's inexcusable. And then I tried to blame it on him at the trial, tried to make myself the victim. I'm sorry." Hodne's daughter was born when he was in jail awaiting trial, and he married her mother when the trial began. His daughter had made him feel more empathetic, he said: "I've never been out there for her . . . and maybe the first family visit she had she was asking me when I was coming home. She wanted me home, and she started crying. And that night, I could only think about, 'This is what I've done to [Hirsch's] children.' I believe it helped me understand a little bit better the damage that I caused."

Kristen Hirsch has never really had a father. She was a baby when Hodne killed her father. Her oldest sister was seven; her youngest sister was six months old. Sobbing, she wants people to know: "To grow up without a Dad really sucks. The love from your father is the first true love you know, and I don't have that. I've never had that, and I probably never will."

Her mother, Mary Beth Hirsch, who died in January 2022, didn't talk much about the murder: "She had a real bad time after my Dad died." But she kept a briefcase with all the clippings from the trial. It was not something the children were supposed to open. But they did. "I was about eight years old, and I remember getting into it. And I remember reading that Todd knew my Dad and my Dad was selling drugs and I didn't know what to make of it. I knew from a really young age that my father was killed but not the specifics."

A few years ago, Kristen says, she was contacted by the parole board. "They got hold of me and asked about him being let out on parole. I said I really didn't know—all I knew was the same story I had heard, that [Hodne] was addicted to drugs and was robbing my father for money. As someone who has dealt with drug addiction, I felt that maybe he should get another chance, you know? But I didn't know the things I'm finding out now."

She didn't know who Todd Hodne was; she didn't know how strong he was, how persuasive and how violent. She didn't know what he had done before he killed her father. She didn't know he lied to the police about what happened. She didn't know her father was no drug dealer but simply a man caught in the wrong place at the wrong time.

Kristen Hirsch is close in age to Hodne's daughter. They have had very different lives, in that Hodne's daughter, for all she had to endure in her life, had what Kristen didn't. She had a father, and he was a constant and sustaining presence in her life. She has stories to tell of him and of growing up as a little girl in the prison yard. She spoke to him nightly by phone. She believes he got off drugs for her, and she believes his remorse over his crimes was genuine and agonizing. When he got cancer, she became his medical advocate. When he was dying on a ventilator, in the early weeks of the COVID-19 lockdown, she was able to see him for the first time in her life in a room without guards, who waited outside and told her when her five minutes were up. She had to wear PPE gear, "basically a hazmat suit," she says. But she touched his wrist, and had the chance to say goodbye.

And yet the two daughters also have something in common. Kristen did not know about the crimes of the man who killed her father until she was contacted for this story. And Hodne's daughter did not know about them, either; she had been told by her family that her father had killed a drug dealer in a drug deal gone wrong. She did not know what her father had done until after he died, when the prison handed her the few bags containing his belongings and personal effects. In them were his legal papers. In them were many of his crimes.

Hodne's wife now lives in a nursing home, according to his daughter. We succeeded in reaching her once and never again. His daughter has spoken to us a number of times over the past year and a half; last summer, she asked us to tell her the worst Todd Hodne did and listened to the excruciating entirety of our answer. She asked not to be quoted on the subject of her father. Instead, she wrote a statement addressed directly to his victims:

There is nothing easy about this for any party involved. I'm sorry you haven't been able to tell your stories; I'm thankful you can now. I only recently learned the extent of my father's crimes in July of 2021. Having a daughter changed my father in more ways than I can express, but that doesn't change what he did before my birth. His crimes haunted him till the day he died. It's not easy to come to terms with what he did. I know there is nothing I can say to undo the damage and trauma you and your families have endured. I hope this gives you some peace and closure after all you have gone through. I give my deepest condolences to you all and your families.

.   .   .

In 1989, Joe Paterno wrote an autobiography titled *Paterno by the Book*. Chapter 20, "If a Coach Wants Love, He Also Gets Losing," addresses his loss to Alabama and what he calls "the terrible season" of 1979.

"In the summer preceding the 1979 season, the team was shocked by the kind of incident that's not supposed to happen in Penn State athletics," he wrote.

One of our young players was arrested on multiple charges of rape. Then, on opening day of fall practice I had to bounce three players off the squad for losing their playing eligibility for academic reasons. One of these was all-American Peter Harris, who led the nation in 1978 with ten interceptions. That was not only a loss in itself, but fans felt the pain of it even harder because he was the kid brother of Franco Harris, who had graduated six years earlier. People came down on me as though I had committed disrespect to Franco's memory. When people demanded I explain, I did so bluntly. Pete goofed off. When that's so, I said, I don't care whose brother he is.

The passage is the only on-the-record statement Joe Paterno ever made about Todd Hodne's string of sexual assaults. It does not name Hodne. It does not say he was convicted or sentenced. It does not say Hodne's crimes began during the 1978 season, when the team was contending for the national championship. It does not mention the women he attacked who were students at Penn State or the pain they suffered. And it does not refer to the crimes Hodne went on to commit in Long Island.

In November 2011, twenty-two years after publishing *Paterno by the Book*, Joe Paterno announced his intention to retire in the wake of revelations of sexual abuse committed by his former assistant coach and close associate Jerry Sandusky, who remained close to the program. Days earlier, Sandusky had been accused of sexually abusing young boys for more than a decade. In his statement, Paterno reflected on his own responsibility and inaction: "This is a tragedy. It is one of the great sorrows of my life. With the benefit of hindsight, I wish I had done more."

A few hours later, Penn State fired him.

• • •

Ann Sailor lived near Pittsburgh when Hodne raped her daughter, Betsy, and she was accustomed to regular front-page stories about Penn State football and even, occasionally, the off-the-field peccadilloes of its players. She does not remember any featured coverage of Hodne's crimes against Betsy or of Betsy's act of witness. But more troubling to her, she says, was the complete silence from Penn State: "I was just under the impression that they were keeping it quiet. I suppressed the urge of going to the university myself. The university never, ever got in touch with us about this. As parents, we never heard a word from the university or from the athletic department or from Joe Paterno. Never one word.

"Everybody would talk about how wonderful Joe Paterno was," Ann says. "But I thought, *why didn't he ever pick up the phone and call parents?* If nothing else, as a parent himself. That his football player had done this to our daughter. . . . I can't imagine what Betsy's days and nights were like after that because I wasn't there. I wasn't with her. And yet Joe Paterno went to sleep every night and

I don't think he gave a damn about what her nights and days were, nor anyone at the university."

•   •   •

The victims we spoke to wanted to hear more from the university. We contacted current Penn State president Eric Barron, requesting access to Hodne's student file and asking for a meeting to discuss Hodne's crimes and their impact on the lives of his fellow Penn State students, the university's alumna. Barron never responded directly. Two university spokespeople met with us in person and arranged a meeting with the current assistant vice president for student affairs to discuss present-day Title IX strategies. Ultimately, one of the spokespeople released the following statement:

"First, Todd Hodne committed horrific crimes, and we have the greatest sympathies for each of those he victimized. We recognize their lifelong struggle to cope with the pain Hodne inflicted through his crimes, and we hope they can find some solace in the fact that Hodne was caught, convicted, and spent the rest of his life in prison for what he did."

The statement continued:

"Regarding your request for Hodne's file. While FERPA [student privacy] rights extinguish upon a student's death, in the interest of safeguarding students' legitimate privacy interests in their education records, the University's longstanding practice is to not release the education records of any deceased student unless required by law."

•   •   •

It happened a long time ago, and the time when it happened was different from today. Today, forty-three years after Hodne was convicted of his rapes and sexual assaults, there are laws on the books and policies in place that help prevent such crimes from taking place. There are provisions under federal Title IX gender equity laws that require schools to investigate such reports and provide support, counseling, and protection to students who have been the victim of sexual violence. There is a requirement for campus law enforcement to issue timely warnings, which students receive on their cell phones when a suspected predator is on the loose.

And yet the story of Todd Hodne is not simply a reminder of how much has changed since 1978. It's a reminder of how slowly change has come. It's a reminder that change didn't come until it had to. It's a reminder that, in the matter of athletic departments and sexual violence, change came because the worst that could possibly happen so often did. It's a reminder that incremental progress has occurred at the cost of indelible pain and that every law protecting students today exists because of the absence of such laws a few decades ago—an absence that gave rise to the notorious stories and impossible outrages that led to institutions and athletic departments finally being called into account.

The story of Todd Hodne should have been one of those stories—one that prompted change or at the very least one for which people were held accountable. It should have been a story that elicited outrage, but it wasn't, because the story of the Penn State football player who preyed pitilessly on women even as his team and his coach were competing for the national championship was never told. Like Betsy Sailor, who even after she won in court had to find out that the man who victimized her went on to victimize so many others, the women who suffered at Todd Hodne's hands had to suffer in vain, their pain a missed opportunity cloaked in a secrecy and silence that reverberated decades later.

Ten years ago, when the revelations of the secrets kept by Penn State's athletic department resulted in the conviction of Jerry Sandusky on forty-five counts of child sexual abuse involving ten boys and caused the statue of Paterno at Beaver Stadium to come down, Shelley Gottsagen, who in 1975 had participated in the protests against gang rapes at "the football fraternity," read the coverage expecting a reckoning that never happened: "It stunned me. I really thought, I just made that comment so many times when Sandusky's trial was happening ... I can't believe nobody's dug up what happened in the seventies there. The protests and the rapes—it's gone from history. It stunned me. I really thought, 'Why are they not looking?'" When Karen Zelin, who was working alongside Gottsagen in the 1970s, heard about Sandusky, it almost made sense to her: "This is what was happening then. This was common knowledge among us that things were covered up or ignored." Those incidents with women were the prelude of what was to come, says Joanne Tosti-Vasey, the NOW chapter president who called for Paterno to resign in 2006: "That climate of indifference allowed it [Sandusky's crimes] to happen. It took child sexual assault for the public to become outraged."

At the time of the Sandusky revelations—at the time a 2012 report determined that Paterno failed to respond appropriately when made aware of the accusations against his assistant coach— the general public's understanding was that this was the first time this program had been faced with the prospect of a serial sexual predator in its midst. The belief was that the coaching staff and the administration at Penn State had been caught unawares, that something had happened that they never could have imagined or prepared for.

But that was not the case.

Before Jerry Sandusky, there was Todd Hodne. Before the serial sexual predator who ended Paterno's career, there was the serial sexual predator who left his career untouched.

"I remember being in a group for dinner and people were discussing this," Ann Sailor says. "Here, [where she lives in Pennsylvania], it's very pro–Penn State. You know, there are an awful lot of Penn State graduates. And I piped up and said, 'There were incidents that happened at Penn State where they kept it under the rug, and it was not talked about.' They just looked at me.' I know for sure. It was just to be kept quiet. And it was kept quiet.'"

Cliff "Clyde" Corbin, who played for Joe Paterno, and who knew Karen and what happened to her, remembers debating with his Nittany Lion teammates Paterno's response—or lack of response—to Sandusky's crimes. "When the whole thing happened, people were reacting like, 'he couldn't have known,'" he says. "I was like, 'Come on—*stop*.' I love the man. But the buck stopped with him for fifty years. The president of the university was the president in name only when it came to football. The man handled everything."

•   •   •

The story of Todd Hodne wouldn't have been told at all if John B. Collins, who prosecuted Hodne for killing Jeffrey Hirsch and became a judge in Suffolk County, hadn't kept tabs on the investigative file in the event that the parole system ever considered releasing Hodne from prison. From that file came Karen, Adrienne Reissman, Susan, Anne Wright, Barbara Johnson, Georgette and Kathleen Pirkl, Caroline O'Neill, the twenty-one-year-old Freeport woman, Denise O'Brien, and the teenage girl. From that file came their voices, asking to be heard.

Most everything else is gone, and what "routine housekeeping of records" and laws that privilege institutional "discretion" can't achieve, time will. Lenny Smith, the parole officer for Todd Hodne before he killed Jeffrey Hirsch, remembers Hodne as a "wrecker," and as a one-word epitaph, it will suffice. But time is the original wrecker and does its own kind of violence. It kills and robs and distorts and plunders and turns what is provisionally remembered into what is at risk of being lost forever. The players who remember Todd Hodne have grown old, and the coaches who worked for Joe Paterno in many cases say they have no memories of Hodne whatsoever. Booker Brooks, the receivers coach, doesn't. Neither does Dan Riley, the strength coach. Neither does Jerry Petercuskie, the graduate assistant. Line coach Dick Anderson remembers the name, remembers the "incident." So does the coach who went to St. Dominic and recruited Hodne to State College, though he adds the inevitable caveat: "That was a long time ago, and my memory is not what it used to be."

We initially contacted all of these coaches by phone. One coach, however, was contacted, as a matter of necessity, by a letter sent in the U.S. mail to inmate No. KT2386 in a prison in Pennsylvania.

"I received your letter and must say I feel bad about my lack of recollection. I only vaguely remember [Todd Hodne's] name," he replied in a handwritten note. "I may have been the contact person because of my founding of the Second Mile in '77. It's possible I made some attempt to help him. My guess is that I didn't become heavily involved for some reason. It sounds as though he had problems well beyond what I was capable of helping. Sorry!—Jerry."

Permissions

Contributors

ROZINA ALI is a contributing writer for the *New York Times Magazine*. She is a fellow at Type Media Center and the Dorothy and Lewis B. Cullman Center for Scholars and Writers, where she is working on a book about the history of Islamophobia in the United States

KEN ARMSTRONG, a reporter at *ProPublica* since 2017, has won Pulitzer Prizes for Explanatory Reporting (2016) and Investigative Reporting (2012) and has shared in two staff Pulitzers for Breaking News Reporting (2010, 2015). One of his stories, written with T. Christian Miller, became an eight-part Netflix series, *Unbelievable*, and a *This American Life* episode, both of which won Peabody Awards. With the *Milwaukee Journal Sentinel*'s Raquel Rutledge, Armstrong wrote "The Landlord and the Tenant," winner of the 2023 National Magazine Award for Feature Writing. Armstrong previously worked at the Marshall Project, the *Seattle Times*, and the *Chicago Tribune*, where his reporting with Steve Mills helped prompt the Illinois governor to suspend executions and empty death row. His book with Nick Perry, *Scoreboard, Baby: A Story of College Football, Crime, and Complicity*, won the 2011 Edgar Allan Poe Award for Best Fact Crime. Armstrong, a graduate of Purdue University, has been a Nieman Fellow at Harvard University and the McGraw Professor of Writing at Princeton University. In 2009 he received the John Chancellor Award for Excellence in Journalism from the Columbia University Graduate School of Journalism.

ALLISON P. DAVIS is a features writer for *New York* and *The Cut*. She writes profiles, long-form features, essays, and columns that explore culture in the broadest sense of the word.

MICHELLE DE KRETSER's most recent novel is *Scary Monsters*.

CAITLIN DICKERSON is a staff writer at *The Atlantic*. Previously, she was a national immigration reporter for the *New York Times*. She is the recipient of the 2023 Pulitzer Prize in Explanatory Reporting and the 2023 Livingston Award for "We Need to Take Away Children." She has also received Peabody and Edward R. Murrow awards for her investigative reporting.

NICHOLAS FLORKO is the commercial determinants of health reporter for *Stat*, where he investigates the ways business decisions impact public health. He has also covered health-care politics and policy for *Stat* in Washington, including how rationing of care in the carceral system exacerbates existing health disparities. His investigation into the human toll of substandard hepatitis C care in state prisons was a finalist for the National Magazine Award for Public Interest, the Livingston Award for National Reporting, and an Investigative Reporters and Editors Award.

CHRIS HEATH is a writer based in Brooklyn. He previously appeared in this anthology series in 2006 with "The Last Outlaw," about the country legend Merle Haggard, and in 2013 with "18 Tigers, 17 Lions, 8 Bears, 3 Cougars, 2 Wolves, 1 Baboon, 1 Macaque, and 1 Man Dead in Ohio," a tragic odyssey within the world of personal zoos.

JAZMINE HUGHES is a staff writer for the *New York Times Magazine*. She won the 2023 National Magazine Award for Profile Writing.

NATE JONES is a senior writer at *Vulture* and *New York*, where he has worked since 2014. He writes the weekly "Oscar Futures" column.

ESPN senior writer **TOM JUNOD** has written some of the most enduring and widely read longform journalism of the last thirty years. He joined ESPN in 2016 and has specialized in deeply reported stories on subjects ranging from Muhammad Ali's funeral to Tom Brady's desire to play forever. He has been nominated for an Emmy for his work on "The Hero of Goodall Park," an *E60* program on the ancient secrets that were revealed when a car drove on a baseball field in Maine during a Babe Ruth League game in 2018. In a

2022 piece, "Untold," he and ESPN investigative reporter Paula Lavigne spent nearly two years uncovering the horrific crimes of Todd Hodne, a Penn State football player who in the late 1970s terrorized State College, Pennsylvania, and Long Island, New York. Before coming to ESPN, Junod wrote for *GQ* and *Esquire*, where he won two National Magazine Awards. For *Esquire*'s seventy-fifth anniversary, the editors of the magazine selected his 9/11 story "The Falling Man" as one of the seven top stories in *Esquire*'s history. In 2019, his story on the beloved children's television host Fred Rogers, "Can You Say . . . Hero?," served as the basis for the movie *A Beautiful Day in the Neighborhood*, starring Tom Hanks and Matthew Rhys. He has also written for *The Atlantic*. Junod's work has been widely anthologized in collections including *The Best American Magazine Writing*, *The Best American Sports Writing*, *The Best American Political Writing*, *The Best American Crime Writing*, and *The Best American Food Writing*. Junod has won a James Beard Award for an essay about his mother's cooking and is working on a memoir about his father for Doubleday. Born and raised on Long Island, he lives in Marietta, Georgia, with his wife and daughter.

RAFFI KHATCHADOURIAN has been a staff writer at *the New Yorker* since 2008. He covers a wide range of topics, including science, art, politics, foreign affairs, and national security.

As part of ESPN's investigative unit since 2008, **PAULA LAVIGNE** has reported on a variety of stories in sports at all levels, from youth sports to college and professional teams to international competitions. Her work appears on multiple ESPN platforms for digital, audio, and television. Lavigne has investigated sexual assault, gender equity, and Title IX failures in college athletics programs. Her skills in acquiring and mining public records and data have led to deep dives into analyzing crimes among professional and college athletes, fan food safety at professional ballparks, fraudulent pro-athlete charities, imbalances in gender equity, compromised athlete medical care, and college sports finances. Lavigne received a Sports Emmy and was an Investigative Reporters and Editors Awards finalist for her work alongside reporter Tom Junod in investigating a Penn State football player who was a serial rapist and murderer, which led to the digital story "Untold" and the film *Betsy & Irv*. She received a Peabody Award for her work investigating sexual assaults within the Michigan State University athletics program and an Alfred I. duPont–Columbia University Award for an investigation into a youth football gambling ring. Lavigne is also the coauthor, with Mark Schlabach, of *Violated: Exposing Rape at Baylor University Amid College Football's Sexual Assault Crisis*. Before joining ESPN, Lavigne worked as a reporter and data analyst for the *Des Moines Register*, the *Dallas Morning News*, and the *News-Tribune* in Tacoma, Washington. She earned a bachelor's degree from the University of Nebraska–Lincoln and an MBA from Creighton University and is a frequent speaker at journalism symposiums and conferences.

SAMANTHA MICHAELS is the criminal-justice reporter for *Mother Jones*.

COURTNEY DESIREE MORRIS is a visual and conceptual artist and an associate professor of gender and women's studies at the University of California, Berkeley. She is a social anthropologist and the author of *To Defend This Sunrise: Black Women's Activism and the Authoritarian Turn in Nicaragua* (2023). Her work has been published in make/shift's *Feminisms in Motion: Voices for Justice, Liberation, and Transformation; The Best American Travel Writing 2020; Stranger's Guide*; and *Jacobin*.

NATASHA PEARLMAN is the executive editor of *Glamour*. She is the recipient of the National Magazine Award for Public Interest.

RAQUEL RUTLEDGE is the investigations editor for *The Examination*. She joined the nonprofit start-up in April after nineteen years as an investigative reporter and deputy editor at the *Milwaukee Journal Sentinel*, where she covered a variety of subjects, from health and science to crime and taxes. Her investigation into fraud in Wisconsin's day-care subsidy program won the 2010 Pulitzer Prize for Local Reporting. In 2011, Rutledge was a Nieman Fellow at Harvard University, studying food regulation. The following year she led an investigation into a Wisconsin company responsible for tainted alcohol wipes linked to the death of a two-year-old boy. The series, "Shattered Trust," won a Gerald Loeb Award and other national accolades. More recently, Rutledge uncovered how a chemical known to cause deadly lung disease is endangering coffee workers and those who use e-cigarettes. In addition, her investigations into deaths and injuries of tourists in Mexico and the dangers barrel-recycling plants pose to workers and nearby residents were honored with national awards. In 2020, Rutledge helped expose how hospitals fail to protect nurses and other staff from serious—sometimes deadly—workplace violence while instead focusing expenditures on building aesthetics and executive pay. That work, too, earned national recognition, including being named a finalist for a Gerald Loeb Award. In 2022, Rutledge led an investigation into electrical fires in Milwaukee, uncovering how they hit Black renters hardest and how lawmakers and regulators do little to address the problem. That series, "Wires and Fires," was named a finalist for the 2022 Pulitzer Prize for Public Service. Most recently, she partnered with Ken Armstrong of *Pro-Publica* to coauthor "The Landlord and the Tenant," which won a 2023 National Magazine Award.

NAMWALI SERPELL is a Zambian writer and professor of English at Harvard University. She is the author of *Seven Modes of Uncertainty* (2014), *The Old Drift: A Novel* (2019), *Stranger Faces* (2020), and *The Furrows: An Elegy* (2022).

CLINT SMITH is a staff writer at *The Atlantic* and the author of the new poetry collection *Above Ground*. He is also the author of the poetry collection *Counting Descent*, which won the 2017 Literary Award for Best Poetry Book from the Black Caucus of the American

Library Association, and of the *New York Times* number-one 1 best-selling book *How the Word Is Passed*. He is the host of the *Crash Course Black American History* YouTube series.

NATALIE SO is a writer, researcher, and story producer who works at the intersection of true stories and TV. Her past projects include research and development for *Little America*, *The OA*, *A League of Their Own*, and the forthcoming limited series *Retreat*. She lives in San Francisco.

JIA TOLENTINO is a staff writer at the *New Yorker*. Previously, she was the deputy editor of *Jezebel* and a contributing editor at *The Hairpin*. Her first book, the essay collection *Trick Mirror*, was published in 2019.

RUHAMA WOLLE is the special projects editor at *Glamour*.